German Literature at a Time of Change: 1989-1990

German Literature
at a Time of Change
1989-1990

German Unity and German Identity
in Literary Perspective

edited by
Arthur Williams, Stuart Parkes and Roland Smith

PETER LANG
Bern · Berlin · Frankfurt a.M. · New York · Paris · Wien

Die Deutsche Bibliothek – CIP-Einheitsaufnahme

German literature at a time of change : 1989 - 1990 ; German
unity and German identity in literary perspective / ed. by
Arthur Williams ... - Bern ; Berlin ; Frankfurt a. M. ; New York ;
Paris ; Wien : Lang, 1991
   ISBN 3-261-04443-8
   NE: Williams, Arthur [Hrsg.]

Published with the assistance of the University of Bradford

© Peter Lang, Inc., European Academic Publishers, Bern, 1991

Printed in the United States of America

CONTENTS

PREFACE

The majority of the papers in this volume were written originally for the Second International Colloquium on Contemporary German Literature: *Zwei Literaturen einer Nation?* held in the University of Bradford in April 1990. The colloquium was made possible by the support of the Goethe-Institut, Manchester, the German Academic Exchange Service, London, and the University of Bradford's Department of Modern Languages. We are deeply grateful to them.

Many of the contributions were subsequently revised for this volume. I want to thank the contributors and particularly my fellow editors for their constantly cheerful and constructive responses to my suggestions and interventions, irrespective of their quality. All of the work has been completed in a spirit of friendly cooperation and with a sense of purpose that have implications way beyond this finished product.

It is, of course, the case that the opinions expressed are those of the individual contributors and are not necessarily shared by either the editors or the institutions which supported the original colloquium.

Although this discussion of German Literature is an unequivocally academic contribution to the understanding of developments in the literature and in the country, we have felt it necessary where we have quoted poems in their entirety to obtain permission to include them here. I am grateful to those contributors who obtained such permissions, particularly Katrin Kohl, Karen Leeder and Ian Hilton. Remarkably, not all German poets and not all German publishers recognize the right of academics to substantiate their work with appropriate quotations, we are therefore particularly indebted to those whose response to our request was immediate and understanding. All specific acknowledgements are indicated in our notes; however, I wish to mention here the poets: Heinz Czechowski, Bert Papenfuß-Gorek and Jürgen Theobaldy; and the publishers: Mitteldeutscher-Verlag, Carl Hanser Verlag, Suhrkamp Verlag, Kinderbuchverlag, Rotbuch-Verlag, Luchterhand Verlag, Residenz Verlag and S. Fischer Verlag.

It would not have been possible to prepare this volume as camera-ready copy without the help of the University of Bradford's Computer Centre whose smiling willingness to share their expertise is second to none. In particular, I want to thank that problem-solver *extraordinaire*, Nigel Rudgewick-Brown.

Finally, but not least, heartfelt thanks to my wife, Elizabeth, without whose totally selfless sacrifice of time and energy the appearance of this volume would have been unacceptably delayed.

Arthur Williams
Bradford
5 April 1991

ABBREVIATIONS

CDU	—	Christlich-Demokratische Union (Christian Democratic Union)
CSCE	—	Conference on Security and Cooperation in Europe
CSU	—	Christlich-Soziale Union (Christian Social Union)
DKP	—	Deutsche Kommunistische Partei (German Communist Party)
FAZ	—	*Frankfurter Allgemeine Zeitung*
FDJ	—	Freie Deutsche Jugend (Free German Youth)
FDP	—	Freie Demokratische Partei (Free Democratic Party)
FR	—	*Frankfurter Rundschau*
KPD	—	Kommunistische Partei Deutschlands (Communist Party of Germany)
MIT	—	Massachusetts Institute of Technology
ND	—	*Neues Deutschland*
ndl	—	*neue deutsche literatur*
NDPD	—	National-Demokratische Partei Deutschlands (National-Democratic Party of Germany)
PDS	—	Partei des Demokratischen Sozialismus (Party of Democratic Socialism)
SED	—	Sozialistische Einheitspartei Deutschlands (Socialist Unity Party of Germany)
SPD	—	Sozialdemokratische Partei Deutschlands (Social-Democratic Party of Germany)
SZ	—	*Süddeutsche Zeitung*
taz	—	*die tageszeitung*
VEB	—	Volkseigener Betrieb (People's Own Enterprise)

INTRODUCTION

STUART PARKES

'May you live in interesting times' runs a much-quoted old Chinese curse. It goes without saying that the years 1989 and 1990 were extremely interesting times for Germanists, but hardly a curse, except for those unwilling to revise either their materials or their assumptions. It was indeed a time for revision, reappraisal and reflection, both for participants in and for observers of the unexpected events. It is the aim of this volume to show and contribute to these processes with specific reference to literature and literary life.

Its origins lie in a colloquium that took place in the University of Bradford in April 1990 attended by some fifty scholars from the (at the time) two German states, Austria and Great Britain. The original intention was to address the question of whether it had become necessary to speak of two separate German literatures, the starting point being the claim made by Christoph Hein to this effect.[1] This question runs through many of the papers that then became the basis of this collection of essays; however, by the time the conference was held, it was impossible (and undesirable) to ignore the historic changes that were taking place, not least when writers and intellectuals were playing so prominent a role in them, as the contributions by Theo Buck, Helmut Peitsch, Axel Schalk and Dieter Stolz show.

Indeed, 1989 and 1990 were years when writers and their work, if not exactly front-page news, were given massive critical attention as well as opportunities to present their own viewpoint, if they were saying anything that appeared at all relevant to the unfolding events. Inevitably, controversy ensued; but the controversy was not related solely to the political question of the future of Germany, it also involved literary matters, in particular the status of what had been written in the two German states over the previous forty years.

Now that some semblance of stability, at least in the realm of politics, appears to have been achieved, it might be possible to draw some conclusions on the basis of the variety of reflections in this volume, reflections that in the editors' view are both exciting and stimulating. This introduction will briefly attempt this task, firstly by considering the continuing debate over the social role of writers and intellectuals, secondly by looking at the achievements of literature in the two German states, and lastly by a more general consideration of what the essays in this volume show in relation to its overall theme.

I Disunity amid Unity

The relationship between writers and the society they live in, especially the question of how far they influence it and are influenced by it, is one of the great imponderables for the student of literature. Suffice it to say that the complexities of this relationship became particularly apparent as the two German states approached political unity in 1989-1990. During this period of transition, intellectual life was marked by rancour and re-criminations, as Helmut Peitsch chronicles in his exposition of events (whilst himself making a trenchant contribution to the debate). In the case of Heiner Müller, Axel Schalk sees a return to an unhealthy German tradition of making the intellectual a scapegoat, an instance of which was arguably the claim made at the time of the Baader-Meinhof terror-ism that its instigators were Heinrich Böll and other leftist intellectuals.[2] Since the controversies continued up to and beyond the achievement of unity in October 1990, it is only now becoming possible to draw together some of the threads.

Needless to say, it was the events themselves, in particular the disintegration of the GDR that provoked most of the controversies. In general terms, these can be broadly reduced to three questions. Firstly, is it reasonable to judge writers and intellectuals on the basis of whether they behave in an exemplary manner at all times? Secondly, is it justified for West German critics, reinforced by what is now known about the activities of the *Staatssicherheitsdienst* and the hypocrisy of the SED leadership, to damn all writers who identified with the GDR, unless they confess their past mistakes with a resounding *mea culpa, mea maxima culpa*? Thirdly, are those writers who are enthusiastic about a single German state guilty of the same kind of German nationalism that led to two world wars, or is the converse true: that those who are unimpressed by unity lack the required quality of patriotism?

Those who attack the conduct of GDR writers generally see them as having been an unscrupulous, or at least cowardly, bunch, intent principally on enjoying the privileges and status that were offered by a régime, whose search for international recognition extended beyond such obvious realms as that of sport to include cultural achievement, with the proclaimed 'sozialistische Nationalliteratur der DDR' being regarded as contributing to a distinct GDR identity. In this connection, Helmut Peitsch refers to the way the ownership of a 'dacha' was maligned as a symbol of the corruption of writers by the offer of privilege.

Even if it is accepted that GDR writers enjoyed privilege,[3] it is worth recalling a few historical examples, before damning them along with their political leaders for their private vices behind the façade of public virtues. Many celebrated authors would be immediately disqualified if they were to be judged by their personal behaviour and morality rather than by their literary creations. One could start with François Villon, the fifteenth-century French poet and singer who was no stranger to gaol and banishment, go on to the absinthe-swigging Rimbaud, and on the way, not forget Goethe's treatment of Lenz and Kleist and, for good measure, of several of the women in his life. Obviously, it is absurd as a general rule to judge writers on the basis of their personal morality.

Does the same apply to the writers of the GDR, where it is perhaps more a case of political morality? The example of Brecht, with his dubious public reaction to the events of 17 June 1953, would suggest that it does. In other words, in the GDR too, literary talent did not preclude moral impropriety. Most recently, the debate has centred on the case of Hermann Kant, for many years president of the GDR *Schriftstellerverband* and, on his own admission, an apologist of that state.[4] He was no doubt in the mind of Jürgen Fuchs, a writer who suffered at the hands of the GDR authorities, when he accused both state and *Schriftstellerverband* of employing 'Hetze, Verleumdung, Nötigung, Erpressung, Publikationsverbot im In- und Ausland, Geldstrafen, Verbot öffentlicher und privater Lesungen, willkürliche Einberufung zum Reservedienst, Ausschluß aus dem Verband'[5] against dissident writers. Similarly Günter Kunert, another émigré from the GDR, expressed his hope, when answering the questions posed by *Die Zeit* at the time of unification to a number of authors 'Was erwarten Sie von Deutschland, was wünschen Sie dem vereinten Land?', as follows: 'Also wünsche ich mir nicht, jemals mit gefeierten Berufslügnern als Schriftstellerverbandspräsidenten zu tun haben zu müssen.'[6] These statements, both based on personal experience, are easy to understand. One appreciates that victims of the system will wish to have nothing to do with those who willingly served the state or even, as is claimed in some cases, let themselves be used by the *Staatssicherheitsdienst*.[7] Fortunately, it would seem unlikely that Hermann Kant, whose resignation from office is welcomed in this volume by Theo Buck, will ever again hold a position of prominence.

There remains, of course, the question of Kant the writer, in which role he will ultimately have to be judged. Martin Kane speaks of a need to reappraise his most famous work, *Die Aula*, in the light of recent events. At this point, it is proposed to consider his more recent *Die Summe*, which can be regarded as revealing enough.[8] It is set at an international conference on European culture at which the GDR is represented by one Comrade Schleede, who would appear to share many traits with his creator. In its satirical portrayal of the world of conferences and the foibles of many of the participants, *Die Summe* is frequently extremely amusing. At the same time, the main character is so smug and sanctimonious in his judgements both on a personal and a political level that it is not difficult to realize that one is reading the work of a closed mind rather than exploring the complexities of reality. This is reflected in the way the book fizzles out. It is incapable of development because its author is restricted to self-satisfied observations. Once he has run out of these, he engineers a conclusion by having Schleede simply decide to leave the conference and return home to his family, a worthy enough act in normal existence but unlikely to be the stuff of great literature.

If the egregious Kant stands condemmed by both his actions and his writing, what of the others? For a balanced view, it is useful to look at an article by Jurek Becker, another writer who left the GDR in the wake of the Biermann affair, entitled 'Zum Bespitzeln gehören zwei'. His thesis is that the citizens of the GDR in general submitted without much resistance to the political control exercised by the state: 'Wenn die Ergebenheit, mit der die DDR-Bürger ihren Staat ertrugen, sich im nachhinein in unvermeidliche Ergebenheit verwandelt oder gar in heimlichen Widerstand, beginnt die neue Zeit mit Lügen. Nein, Mut und Aufrichtigkeit standen in diesen vierzig Jahren nicht in hoher Blüte.'[9] Becker illustrates this general point with reference to a writer who kept putting off any attempt to publish a critical work because he could always find a pretext. Becker's point is that writers were typical of the GDR's citizenry as a whole, something that should be borne in mind by those who single them out for criticism from the vantage point of the Federal Republic, where similar courage was rarely required and often only manifested itself in the actions of individuals like Heinrich Böll. In certain cases, the anti-GDR vitriol seems to stem from a desire to cover up past less hostile, and now therefore unwelcome, comments about that state.[10]

Such motives would seem to apply to some who are now highly critical of Christa Wolf. Besides the criticisms of *Was bleibt* referred to by Helmut Peitsch and Elizabeth Boa, there is the insinuation that she was a kind of poet laureate of the GDR. Reference is made to her having been a candidate for the Central Committee of the SED in the early 1960s, but not to her having been dropped by the Party from this position.[11] Equally, her protests against the expulsion of Biermann and her defence of Stefan Heym, mentioned by Joseph Pischel and Roland Smith respectively, are generally overlooked. Whatever different views there may have been on whether she should have published *Was bleibt* earlier rather than waiting for the end of the GDR's old régime, its subject, her surveillance by the *Stasi*, surely belies the claim that she was hand in glove with the authorities. Moreover, the date of publication of *Was bleibt* cannot be seen simply as a manifestation of moral cowardice. That it was bound to provoke a furore because it had not been published earlier was entirely predictable.[12] The easy and obvious way out would have been not to publish at all.

As in the case of Hermann Kant, it is most appropriate to apply literary criteria, not least because *Was bleibt* is a consciously literary reworking of the period of surveillance. There is much concern on the part of the narrator that she should be able to find a new language which would be suitable for describing her experiences. Moreover, these are not related in the linear style of a documentary report. The narrative starts after the surveillance has been going on for some time. That Wolf, as in most of her works, concentrates on her feelings and emotions will be seen by some as another example of what Ulrich Greiner calls 'Gesinnungskitsch'.[13] Yet such a view would be wrong, as it ignores the self-critical honesty of much of the book, which is also written in a direct, economical style. The sentence: 'Ich wärmte mir die Rindfleischsuppe vom Vortag und aß achtlos, dabei hörte ich die gleichen Nachrichten wie am Morgen'[14] could hardly be plainer, but in it one suspects a barbed criticism of GDR media policy. *Was bleibt* is not a work to be casually dismissed.

The case of Wolf, who identified with the GDR long enough to sign the petition 'Für unser Land' in the autumn of 1989, (cf. Joseph Pischel's comments on p. 125 below), bridges the first and second questions posed above. These are, in any case, linked in that detractors of GDR writers no doubt feel that any identification with the GDR must have been based on unsavory materialistic motives. Before any conclusions are drawn on that point, it is surely advisable to consider how far writers did identify with the GDR. That many voiced criticisms is shown by Theo Buck; nevertheless it is axiomatic that anything published in the GDR must have got past the censors and unless these are deemed to have been either incompetent or disloyal, one must assume that criticism was less than total. On this point, Monika Maron, in the essay in *Der Spiegel* referred to by both Buck and Peitsch,[15] argues that it was easy to gain popularity through the most minor criticisms; whatever the truth of this, is one to take the view that anything published in the GDR until late 1989 reeked of compromise and that writers should have avoided all contact with the publishing industry? If this absolutist stance is taken, then Maron herself would have to be criticized for attempting to have her novel *Flugasche* published. Moreover, if it is assumed that even those writers who voiced criticisms were largely intent on enjoying privileges, then one must ask why they did not take the direct path to the despised dacha, namely that of total identification with the régime, as others did. Not differentiating between different degrees of identification is to lump together Hermann Kant and Volker Braun, Christoph Hein and Max Walter Schultz.

If one accepts that there were different levels of identification and that total identification with the Ulbricht or Honecker régime (or both) was at the very least a bad case of political blindness, there still remains the problem of how far any degree of sympathy with the GDR can be justified. Two reasons at least can be advanced: firstly the kind of Utopian belief in socialism referred to by Joseph Pischel, and secondly a rejection of certain aspects of the other German state. Unless one views the whole ideal of socialism as the devil's work and is willing to overlook such phenomena as the failure to deal with the legacy of National Socialism in the Federal Republic,[16] then a belief in a radical alternative can be justified. The question is whether the GDR ever offered any kind of latent alternative, and when it should have been realized that it did not: 17 June 1953, 13 August 1961, 21 August 1968 or only in the autumn of 1989. It was not until December 1989 that Helga Königsdorf confessed: 'Ich sehe meine persönliche Schuld vor allem darin, daß ich mein Wissen um die mittelalterliche Struktur dieser Gesellschaft, die sich zu Unrecht Sozialismus nannte, verdrängt habe',[17] although at that time she still remained in the SED/PDS. To think solely in terms of dates is superficial, even if Rolf Schneider has put a date on his disillusionment with the GDR, namely November 1976.[18] Similarly, it is difficult to argue that all writers should have left the country as Monika Maron seems to suggest. It could be claimed that Helga Königsdorf's categorical rejection of this (she has said that writers should not have made use of an opportunity denied to others) is reminiscent of the arguments used by authors of the 'inner emigration' after the demise of Nazism, the overall argument remains less than clearcut.[19] It has to be remembered that the possibly most celebrated exile of all, Wolf Biermann, was turned out against his will (prison or an exit visa was also a 'choice' frequently offered to dissidents) and that as long as the existence of the GDR seemed permanent, the decision to fight to improve things from the inside was often presented as heroic by certain parts of the Western media.[20]

In any case, the comparisons that have been made between the GDR and the Third Reich (alluded to by Helmut Peitsch) should not be simply accepted at face value. Although one must agree with Hans Joachim Schädlich that for those Social Democrats who found themselves in Buchenwald under both Nazis and communists similarities must have been only too apparent,[21] it has to be pointed out that the GDR did not unleash a war of aggression, nor did it systematically murder specific racial groups. Equally, as Hans Mayer has pointed out, neither its writers nor its citizens adulated Ulbricht as a gift from 'providence'.[22] It is true that Rolf Schneider argues that the GDR, modelled as it was on the Soviet system, has to be linked with Stalin's atrocities: 'Die DDR war ein Annex der Sowjetunion. Die dort geschehenen Verbrechen betrafen uns immer mit.'[23] However, whilst it would be wrong to minimize these crimes or to deny that the GDR until 1989 maintained features that can be described as 'Stalinist', it must be pointed out that Schneider, even though he specifically rejects them, does come close to those in the *Historikerstreit* who equated Stalin with Hitler or even saw him as providing the model. Schneider's chronology is also simplistic. The worst crimes in the history of the Soviet Union occurred before the GDR existed; directly to implicate it in them is to adopt a chronology almost as bizarre as the one used by those who sought to absolve the GDR from the German past, an attitude ridiculed in satirical comments such as: 'The GDR defeated fascism alongside the Soviet Union.' None of this means that individuals should not think over their past actions in the manner of Helga Königsdorf; indeed, *Trauerarbeit* is required on this personal level, but it cannot be imposed in any real way from the outside any more than 'antifascism' could be in the Soviet Zone and the GDR after 1945.

These accusations against GDR writers have frequently come from the political Right. The accusation in the first half of my third question, that enthusiasm for unity is tantamount to crude nationalism, is more often associated with the Left, which can claim that German unity is undesirable at the very least on moral grounds, with any right to unity having been lost because of the horrors of Auschwitz. This kind of moral debate goes beyond the scope of this introduction, as does speculation about the political question of German unity. Here it is intended to consider only the extent of writers' supposed nationalism. If the case of Martin Walser is taken, then, despite all the unwise things he has said (referred to by Peitsch and Parkes), it is still questionable whether he should be classed as an unreconstructed traditional nationalist.[24] If this view were to be taken, all his criticisms of re-unification rhetoric would be at best delusion and at worst dishonesty, the delusion being that there is objectively a patriotic alternative to old-style German nationalism. The question of the possibility of a different kind of left-wing patriotism was much discussed in the 1980s; as Peitsch points out, it was generally dismissed as politically naive because of the apparent permanence of division. Must it now be seen as dangerously naive, as it only serves the Right rather than presenting a respectable alternative to nationalistic extremes? A simple answer is impossible; suffice it to say that before Walser many others, admittedly in different circumstances, put forward a positive view of Germany without being nationalists in the traditional sense. None other than the Communist poet and subsequent GDR minister, Johannes R. Becher, incorporated the nineteenth-century refrain 'Deutschland einig Vaterland' into the national anthem of the GDR, a cry that came to the surface again in the autumn of 1989 after its suppression in the Honecker era. The positive ideal of Germany is also discussed in my contribution to this volume (pp. 187—203 below).

Time alone will show whether renewed German nationalism is going to prove a political danger; as yet it does not appear to be a powerful political force, however distasteful such phenomena as hostility towards foreigners living in Germany, not least in the former GDR, may be. Such occurrences do, however, provide some kind of answer to the second part of my third question. They show that those who warn against nationalistic hubris do have a case. The campaign of Günter Grass, referred to by Peitsch and Stolz, which has continued in such essays as 'Was rede ich? Wer hört noch zu?' and 'Ein Schnäppchen namens "DDR"' is not to be dismissed.[25]

Finally, one might ask if there are any objective criteria by which to judge the often bitter debate, conducted primarily in the Western media, among and about intellectuals in connection with German unity. The most promising approach would be to relate it to the social role of intellectuals and to ask how far this role has been fulfilled. The trouble is that there is no consensus on this point, although it is possible to pick out contentious areas.[26] A major question in this volume (in the essays of Peitsch, Shaw, Pischel and Boa, for example) is how far writers and intellectuals should hold Utopian views or alternatively, in the manner of Enzensberger, scorn them in favour of 'realism'. A further relevant area relates to the duty of approval or criticism. In the case of German unity, some expect intellectuals to simply offer their blessing (for example, Brigitte Seebacher-Brandt — see p. 163 below), but it is an idea that can be scotched if the more prevalent view, enunciated here by Theo Buck and Joseph Pischel, is accepted: namely that it is the task of the intellectual to question and criticize.[27] As for the question of Utopias, a prudent answer would be to demand both realism and Utopianism from writers, not least since the two are often closely connected. Walser's Utopia of German unity is now reality, whilst the dream of a different kind of GDR is destined to remain a lost Utopia, now that the reality of that state has disappeared. That only leaves the question of which Utopias should be pursued. If there were an easy answer to that, there would be fewer 'interesting times'.

II A Farewell to Literature(s)

'Die DDR-Literatur ist tot, es lebe die DDR-Literatur' read the second part of a heading given to a review by Hajo Steinert in *Die Zeit* of four individual works and one collection of poems published in Berlin in 1990. As these works were all by young, generally less well-known authors whose writing could not be published under the old GDR régime, they vindicated the paradoxical heading in that they showed that GDR literature lives on as long as previously unknown works come to the surface. Nevertheless, Steinert somewhat over-eggs the pudding when he claims: 'Zählt man zur DDR-Literatur neben Büchern auch Rezensionen und Literaturzeitschriften, so ließe sich — zumindest aus der Sicht der jungen Autoren — durchaus über die Frage streiten, ob es mit der DDR-Literatur jetzt nicht erst richtig losginge.'[28] In addition to newly emerging works and their reception, there is still another sense in which the phenomenon of the GDR might live on in new writing: if writers from the former GDR continue to be concerned with their earlier experiences. Helga Königsdorf goes as far as to make this a requirement: 'Und es muß geschrieben werden, was offenbleibt. Es ist unsere Pflicht, Zeugnis abzulegen.'[29] Nevertheless, if the literature written in a country is viewed as the literature of that country, then with the disappearance of the GDR as a state, GDR literature is also dead, and it is appropriate and inevitable that its achievements and failings will be subject to scrutiny.

It is only to be expected that, in the obituaries and quasi-obituaries, there has been both praise and criticism for GDR literature. The major criticism is the one applied by Monika Maron and already referred to in connection with the social role of GDR writers: that fame was easily acquired on the basis of social criticism, however mild. In this connection, Dieter E. Zimmer speaks of the positive benefits for a GDR writer if he or she managed to appear on a West German television chat-show or was subject to an unfavourable review in *Neues Deutschland*.[30] Such criticisms have been added to by those in the West who believe that GDR authors, irrespective of their literary qualities, enjoyed a bonus in the Federal Republic because of their apparent dissidence. The poet Peter Rühmkorf, for instance, is particularly scathing on this point: 'Wem es gelang, einen Koffer mit literarischer Konterbande durch die Mauer zu schmuggeln oder wer in der DDR nur eben mit ein paar verkrumpelten Dissidentenphrasen angeeckt war, wurde gefeiert, belobigt, prämiert, als ob es die ganz große Grenzüberschreitung zu berücksichtigen gäbe.'[31] This argument, which in any case ignores the discrimination in the West of certain GDR authors of literary merit because of Cold War attitudes, illustrated by Dennis Tate in his piece on Franz Fühmann, must be viewed sceptically, as it replicates the one used by Hermann Kant at the gathering of the *Schriftstellerverband* in 1979 which preceded the expulsion of nine members of the Berlin branch. The verbatim record of this procedure reveals all too clearly that the spirit of Stalinist show trials lived on long after the dictator's death: Chairman Kant, in his role as prosecutor or grand inquisitor, spoke scornfully of the way that 'ein Manuskript auf dem Wege von Ost nach West Veredelung erfährt.'[32] The mere mention of the names of some of those expelled in this sorry affair, Stefan Heym, Klaus Schlesinger and Karl-Heinz Jakobs, belies Kant's cynical contention.

A more reputable point about GDR literature and its relationship to society is that too much energy was devoted to fulfilling the role occupied in a pluralist society by the media or at least parts of them. In other words, literature took over the function of the public sphere to the detriment of the aesthetic dimension. This criticism, now often coupled with the expression of relief that this role will not now be needed in the new democratic state, raises again the fundamental questions about literature mentioned at the beginning of this introduction, questions that cannot be answered here. Nevertheless, if Thomas Beckermann's point that literature occupies a discrete position separate from the realm of direct political activity is accepted, this criticism would have to be taken most seriously, provided that it could be shown that all GDR literature had been largely social reportage.

Fortunately this volume, not least Beckermann's own contribution, pp. 97—115 below, invalidates any such fear. Whilst both Joseph Pischel and Theo Buck, from their different standpoints, are able to speak in general terms about the achievements of GDR literature, it is hoped that the numerous contributions on specific writers and themes within GDR literature will show its variety, which, if not infinite, goes far beyond what might have been hoped for given the attempts of the state to direct artistic expression in both form and content.[33] One can only endorse what Volker Hage says about writing in the GDR: 'Die Literatur, die in ihr geschrieben wurde und auf die wir was geben, ist nicht wegen der staatlichen Umarmung gelungen, sondern gegen sie.'[34] The essays in this volume can speak for themselves in reinforcing the claim in the title of Hage's article: 'Da war was, da bleibt was.'

How far is it correct to say the same thing about the literature of the Federal Republic? The merger of the two German states, or possibly more accurately the extension of the Federal Republic by the incorporation of five new *Länder*, has been used to signal the end of an era as far as West German literature is concerned and to ask critical questions. This has been done especially by Frank Schirrmacher in the *Frankfurter Allgemeine Zeitung* and Ulrich Greiner in *Die Zeit*. Schirrmacher's contention is that the literature of the Federal Republic stagnated after 1960, that the leading figures of that era (for instance Grass, Böll, Walser and Lenz) continue to dominate public perception of it so that it is possible to equate it with the *Gruppe 47*, whose leading figures were assigned major status in society. Schirrmacher's thesis in connection with West German literature is that far from inviting a radical confrontation with the past, it provided the country's citizens with a view of it as a monstrous distortion of history, something that could be accepted with a grateful *frisson*. Commenting on how many novels are written from a child's perceptive, Schirrmacher writes:

> Mit ungläubigen Augen, bejaht mit der klaren Moral des Naiven und Unschuldigen, zeigte man sich als Zeuge der monströsen Katastrophe. Und dankbar — keineswegs wie es die Legende will, reaktionär erzürnt — machte die Gesellschaft diesen Blick auf die Vergangenheit zu ihrem eigenen. Nicht nur die Literatur der DDR sollte diese Gesellschaft legitimieren und ihr neue Traditionen zuweisen; auch die Literatur der Bundesrepublik empfand diesen Auftrag und führte ihn aus.[35]

Even if one leaves aside the massive assumption in this statement about how people are directly influenced by literature, it remains open to challenge on a number of counts. Firstly, there is its accuracy as a piece of literary criticism. The most famous child's perspective on Nazism is Günter Grass's *Die Blechtrommel*. To describe Oskar Matzerath as either naive or innocent or even moral is breathtaking, to say the least. Nor does Grass present a monstrous catastrophe. In reporting the Eichmann trial, Hannah Arendt spoke of the 'Banality of Evil'[36] and this is what interests Grass, what Michael Hamburger calls 'de-demonization',[37] which is the opposite of what Schirrmacher is claiming. Secondly, one must question his comments on West German society. In as far as he assumes a homogeneous society in the Federal Republic and equates the literatures of the two German states by implying that West German literature was allotted a specific role (by whom?), they have to be dismissed. Moreover, 'reactionary' protest at the activities of writers was all too real. One needs only recall the epithets 'Pinscher' and 'Ratten und Schmeißfliegen' used by Ludwig Erhard and Franz Josef Strauß respectively about certain writers, as well as the comparison in CDU circles of the *Gruppe 47* with the Nazi *Reichsschrifttumskammer*. As for wider public hostility, the responses to Böll's comments on the Baader-Meinhof group and to Rolf Hochhuth's revelations about the activities of the prime minister of Baden-Württemberg, Hans Filbinger, in his previous incarnation as a Nazi military judge cannot be overlooked.[38] As for Schirrmacher's equation of West German literature with a single generation, even if one accepts his grouping together of Böll and Johnson (who were born in 1917 and 1934 and are normally seen as West and East German writers respectively) or that writers of the same generation are always similar (there are only three years between Böll and the experimental Arno Schmidt, whilst Grass and Walser with the common date of birth of 1927 are not entirely alike), it can only be maintained by the postulation of exceptions (Schirrmacher mentions Enzensberger, Handke and Celan) and by omissions. There is, for instance, no mention of Botho Strauß, whilst all women writers are ignored. It is as if the *Gruppe 47* had not collapsed under its own contradictions and the 'new subjectivity' of the 1970s had never occurred. Schirrmacher misses the point that West German literature is now less dominated by a few individuals and has become more diffuse.[39]

Ulrich Greiner builds on Schirrmacher's criticisms, as his title 'Die deutsche Gesinnungsästhetik' in itself shows. It was Max Weber who differentiated between the *Gesinnungsethik* of the intellectual and the more practical *Verantwortungsethik* of the politician; what Greiner is claiming is that West German writing has concentrated on 'Gesinnung' at the expense of aesthetics. He too sees similarities between the writing in the two German states. Citing Christa Wolf as his prime example, Greiner maintains: 'Es bestand die Übereinkunft, daß die deutschen Schriftsteller (die linken, die engagierten, die kritischen) das Gute gewollt, gesagt und geschrieben haben. Und die Literaturkritik ist dieser Übereinkunft gefolgt, indem sie nicht ästhetisch geurteilt hat, sondern moralisch und politisch.'[40] Here too a kind of conspiracy is being constructed by the use of the word 'Übereinkunft', whilst one must infer that unlike Goethe's Mephisto who created Good by wanting Evil, literary criticism has supported, if not evil, then at least aesthetically bad writing by wanting 'good' politics and morality. Once again, the argument revolves around the nature of literature. Greiner expresses shock that nobody seemed to worry too much when it was suggested that Günter Wallraff had not written every word of *Ganz unten* himself;[41] for him, this underlines the neglect of the aesthetic dimension. It is true that the living and working conditions of foreign workers exposed by Wallraff have remained the major point of discussion (although there has also been much argument about how he treated his Turkish sources), but this is surely correct. It is inappropriate to apply the same criteria to a social report as to a novel or poetry. As long as other media neglect certain contentious issues, then writing like that of Wallraff is a legitimate form of literature. Even if one accepts that literature cannot and should not replace the public sphere, as it was obliged to do in the GDR, it nevertheless remains part of it and not only because the public sphere operates imperfectly.[42] It is as well to remember the failure of those authors who, like the French Symbolists, wished to reduce literature to mere form.

Although this volume does not attempt a comprehensive treatment of West German literature, there is enough analysis of individual writers and themes to disprove Schirrmacher's and Greiner's assertions. Equally, as with the GDR writers, the West German writers treated are shown to possess literary qualities. Moreover, if West German literature has been nothing more than a soothing balm applied to national wounds, it is strange that it should have achieved such fame in other lands. One needs only to think of the award of the Nobel Prize to Böll, the world-wide succes of Grass and, more recently, the various productions of Strauß's plays in Great Britain.

III Connections and Leads

As stated at the beginning of this introduction, the starting point for this volume was the question whether, with the division of Germany, two separate German literatures developed. It is also possible to broaden the issue by asking whether there are distinct literatures within a single state. During a conference at the University of Nottingham in October 1990,[43] Hans Joachim Schädlich spoke of four possible literatures in the GDR: one that was entirely loyal to the SED (in addition to Hermann Kant, Dieter Noll comes to mind, the author of obsequious open letters and of the excruciatingly boring novel *Kippenberg*, which was much praised as an example of socialist realism and foisted as a gift on unwitting visitors to the GDR[44]), a second whose representatives had abandoned, possibly without being aware of it, any critical impulses, a third consisting of those writers who viewed the GDR from a Utopian Marxist standpoint (Volker Braun would be an obvious example) and a fourth made up of those writers who totally rejected the GDR (the poets discussed by Karen Leeder, in particular Sascha Anderson).

No doubt comparable divisions could be enunciated in relation to West German literature — what, for instance, do Ernst Jünger and the non-professional writers of the *Werkkreis Literatur der Arbeitswelt* have in common? In the face of such difficulties, it is as well to capitulate before the question of how many German literatures there might be, not least because there are two other countries where German is spoken and written that would have to be considered in any calculation. In any case, how is one to arbitrate between Christoph Hein and Günter Grass, protagonists of two and one literatures respectively, not to mention the contributors to this volume? A more promising approach is to put the numbers question to one side by accepting with relief Volker Hage's contention that the subject has been discussed enough[45] and concentrating on connections and comparisons between what was written in the two German states, as revealed in this book.

Many of the contributors set themselves this task of comparison: Ricarda Schmidt and Julian Preece being just two examples. Moreover, it is the editors' contention that there are also many links between the essays collected here that could provide the basis for useful comparisons. This was emphasized for them when they attempted to put the contributions in a particular order — a problem that had to be solved, however imperfectly. It is hoped, however, that the various references and cross-references will minimize the problem.

In addition to the individual themes, not least that of Germany itself, one other link cannot be overlooked: the way that literature and literary life in one German state was of interest in the other. Hella Ehlers, as a GDR Germanist, writes with passion about West German writers, whilst Jochen Wittmann's essay on the reception of Günter Grass in the GDR shows that however much it was claimed that he was an anticommunist with nothing to say to the GDR, he was never entirely ignored. Equally GDR literature was of interest in the Federal Republic, with great efforts being made by, for example, Thomas Beckermann to bring unknown authors to prominence. As mentioned above, unflattering reasons have been advanced for the success of GDR literature in the West, and it may be that non-aesthetic considerations played a part, with books possibly being published because they provided information that was not available elsewhere[46] or because they provided the reader with less of an intellectual challenge of the type Arthur Williams refers to in connection with Botho Strauß. Nevertheless, the fact of publication remains. None of this means that literary differences in attitude and perception can be overcome as a result of formal political unity. Many of the essays collected here underline such differences, whilst the strains revealed by Andrea Reiter in the correspondence between Monika Maron and Joseph von Westphalen appear in many ways paradigmatic of the divergence between East and West. The quotation from *Der Mauerspringer* where Schneider's narrator contends that he and his GDR counterpart cannot escape the influence of their respective states is important here and it is no surprise that Martin Kane should quote it in his essay on Thorsten Becker's whimsical attempt to write about division (see p. 361 below). Something else that comes to light in this volume is the specifically Utopian element in GDR writing, be it in connection with the theme of women (Ricarda Schmidt, Elizabeth Boa) or nature (Peter Graves). The importance of the idea of a political Utopia in the GDR has already been discussed in this introduction, so that one is left wondering if this was the key difference between the two German states in the realm of literature. This would reflect the difference between an ideological state and a more pragmatic one where many leading politicians and writers, Helmut Schmidt and Hans Magnus Enzensberger are just two examples, scarred by the experience of National Socialism, have epitomized what the sociologist Helmut Schelsky called 'the sceptical generation'.[47] This leads to the question whether, as Joseph Pischel hopes with reference to Christa Wolf, a Utopian element will be possible in a united Germany.

In the final essay in this book Arthur Williams looks into a literary future, one of whose many uncertainties is emerging as the place of the writer. This is not a new subject of debate, at least not for the Federal Republic where in the late 1960s and early 1970s it became a major point of debate. Whereas some saw themselves in the role of peripheral workers in the wood-processing industry, Heinrich Böll demanded an end to modesty and pointed to the importance of writers for the reputation of the Federal Republic.[48] The new debate also embraces a variety of views. In the essay by Martin Walser referred to by Williams (p. 458 below), Walser, in his condemnation of *Meinungen* (combined incidentally with a forceful expression of his own), comes close to the re-instatement of the traditional 'Dichter' in his praise for Strauß and Handke. Günter Kunert also speaks of the end of the writer's political role, although he sees it as a loss of the status that was enjoyed in the special circumstances of the Cold War. He considers this to be an advantage, a sign of normality 'wie sie in Deutschland so lange vermißt worden ist'.[49] German writers will now be no different from their European counterparts, according to Kunert; one might wonder, however, if in the case of Britain (Kunert refers to English writers) it is correct to speak of normality in the light of the Rushdie affair. By contrast, his fellow former GDR writer Jurek Becker thinks that the situation is far from satisfactory; he demands that writers find new themes appropriate to the age, demanding a concern for social issues.[50]

Irrespective of their different standpoints, Walser, Kunert and Becker all see a role for literature. This is a good point to conclude with. German literature and literary life seem set to continue to provide 'interesting times' for their devotees, whose numbers it is the aim of this book to increase.

NOTES

1   The theme of the colloquium: 'Zwei Literaturen einer Nation?' drew on both Willy Brandt's 'zwei Staaten einer Nation' and Christoph Hein's comments in an interview in *Sinn und Form* (vol. 40, no. 2, 1988). Dennis Tate, p. 286 below, refers specifically to the latter.

2   The controversy can be followed in Frank Grützbach (ed.): *Freies Geleit für Ulrike Meinhof: Ein Artikel und seine Folgen*, Cologne, 1972.

3   This simplistic assumption is challenged by Dieter E. Zimmer in his article 'Eine privilegierte Kaste?', *Die Zeit*, 7 December 1990, pp. 59—60.

4   See Kant's interview with *Der Spiegel*: 'Ich war ein Aktivist der DDR', *Der Spiegel*, 6 August 1990, pp. 156—60.

5   Jürgen Fuchs: *Einmischung in eigene Angelegenheiten*, Reinbek, 1984, p. 157.

6   *Die Zeit*, 5 October 1990, p. 52.

7   One victim, Erich Loest, has described his experiences in his book *Der Zorn des Schafes. Aus meinem Tagewerk*, Künzelsau and Leipzig, 1990. An article about Loest in *Der Spiegel* (17 September 1990), which mentioned among others Klaus Höpke (the former minister) and Hermann Kant, provoked a denial from the latter (*Der Spiegel*, 29 October 1990, p. 284). Reiner Kunze has also spoken of his experiences: 'Sofort unter operative Kontrolle nehmen!', *Die Zeit*, 26 October 1990, pp. 67—8.

8   Hermann Kant: *Die Summe*, 3rd edn, Berlin, 1989.

9 Jurek Becker: 'Zum Bespitzeln gehören zwei', *Die Zeit*, 3 August 1990, p. 36.

10 This was pointed out by Jürgen Busche, who asks whether West German critics are not equally open to the accusation of reacting too late to Christa Wolf as she is of reacting too late to the iniquities of the GDR. See *Fachdienst Germanistik*, vol. 8, no. 10, October 1990, p. 2.

11 Günter Grass defends Christa Wolf against such accusations in his interview: 'Nötige Kritik oder Hinrichtung', *Der Spiegel*, 13 July 1990, pp. 133—43. See also Helmut Peitsch pp. 173—4 below.

12 Beatrice von Matt has commented: 'Wäre die Autorin jene kalte Opportunistin als die sie jetzt gebrandmarkt wird, sie hätte *Was bleibt* wohl kaum gerade in diesem Halbjahr veröffentlicht.' Quoted in *Fachdienst Germanistik*, vol. 8, no. 10, October 1990, p. 2.

13 Ulrich Greiner: 'Die deutsche Gesinnungsästhetik', *Die Zeit*, 2 November 1990, p. 60.

14 Christa Wolf: *Was bleibt*, Frankfurt/Main, 1990, p. 65.

15 Monika Maron: 'Die Schriftsteller und das Volk', *Der Spiegel*, 12 February 1990, pp. 68—70.

16 For a full treatment of this theme the following book can be recommended: Ralf Giordano: *Die zweite Schuld oder Von der Last Deutscher zu sein*, Munich, 1990.

17 Helga Königsdorf: *1989 oder Ein Moment Schönheit*, Berlin, 1990, p. 107.

18 Rolf Schneider: 'Volk ohne Trauer', *Der Spiegel*, 29 October 1990, pp. 264—70.

19 Helga Königsdorf: 'Deutschland, wo der Pfeffer wächst', *Die Zeit*, 20 July 1990, p. 40.

20 This was, for example, the reaction to the return of Bärbel Bohley to the GDR after her period in Britain in 1988.

21 Hans Joachim Schädlich: 'Das Fähnlein der treu Enttäuschten', *Die Zeit*, 26 October 1990, p. 68.

22 Mayer is quoted as saying: 'Das Volk der DDR hat weder Synagogen angezündet, noch den totalen Krieg gewollt, noch Walter Ulbricht als Geschenk der Vorsehung verehrt.' His conclusion is that writers were in no way supporting a system comparable to the Third Reich. Mayer is quoted by Volker Hage: 'Da war was, da bleibt was', *Die Zeit*, 5 October 1990, Literature Supplement, p. 1.

23 Schneider: 'Volk ohne Trauer', p. 265.

24 Walser's active participation, alongside members of the Greens, in discussions that took place in the late 1980s about how former terrorists might be re-integrated into society suggests he is not averse to supporting some left-liberal causes.

25 The essays are collected in one volume: Günter Grass: *Ein Schnäppchen namens "DDR"*, Darmstadt, 1990.

26 For an introduction to the debate see K. Stuart Parkes: *Writers and Politics in West Germany*, Beckenham, 1986, pp. 1—8.

27 This is, for instance, the view also of Ortega y Gasset (see Parkes: *Writers and Politics...*, p. 4).

28 Hajo Steinert: 'Die neuen Nix-Künstler', *Die Zeit*, 7 December 1990, Literature Supplement, p. 5.

29 Helga Königsdorf: 'Der Schmerz über das eigene Versagen', *Kultur Chronik. Nachrichten und Berichte aus der Bundesrepublik Deutschland*, no. 6, 1990, p. 7.

30 Zimmer: 'Eine privilegierte Kaste', p. 59.

31 Quoted by Hage: 'Da war was, da bleibt was', p. 1.

32 Hermann Kant: 'Buch um Buch, Zeile für Zeile', *Der Spiegel*, 17 December 1990, p. 111.

33 For a review of GDR cultural policy see Manfred Jäger: *Kultur und Politik in der DDR*, Cologne, 1982.

34 Hage: 'Da war was, da bleibt was', p. 2.

35 Frank Schirrmacher: 'Abschied von der Literatur der Bundesrepublik', *FAZ*, 2 October 1990, Literature Supplement, p. 2.

36 Hannah Arendt: *Eichmann in Jerusalem. Report on the Banality of Evil*, London, 1963.

37 Michael Hamburger: *From Prophecy to Exorcism*, London, 1965, pp. 140ff. Page 141 refers to Hannah Arendt's reaction to the Eichmann trial.

38 Grützbach: *Freies Geleit...* offers a full discussion of the reaction to Böll. For background information on the controversies surrounding Hochhuth, Erhard and Strauß, see Parkes: *Writers and Politics...*, pp. 38, 60f., 108. It was the then prominent CDU politician Josef-

Hermann Dufhues who, in the 1960s, compared the *Gruppe 47* to a 'geheime Reichs-schrifttumskammer'.

39 A useful survey of this change is found in David Roberts's introduction to Keith Bullivant (ed.): *After the 'Death of Literature'. West German Writing of the 1970s*, Oxford, 1989.

40 Greiner: 'Die deutsche Gesinnungsästhetik', p. 60.

41 Günter Wallraff: *Ganz unten*, Cologne, 1985.

42 The best-known critique of the operation of the public sphere is: Jürgen Habermas: *Strukturwandel der Öffentlichkeit*, Darmstadt, 1962.

43 With the general theme of the Future of the United Germany, the conference was organized by the Institute of German, Austrian and Swiss Affairs of the University of Nottingham.

44 In an open letter published by *Neues Deutschland* (22 May 1979), Noll spoke of writers cooperating 'mit dem Klassenfeind [...] weil sie offenbar unfähig sind, auf konstruktive Weise Resonanz und Echo bei unseren arbeitenden Menschen zu finden.' The present writer was presented with two copies of *Kippenberg* (Berlin, 1979). A sixth edition appeared in 1983, perhaps indicating something of the number of copies in existence.

45 Hage: 'Da war was, da bleibt was', p. 1.

46 This was suggested as a reason why so much GDR literature was published in the West by Sybille Knauss at a conference organized by the Institute of German, Austrian and Swiss Affairs of the University of Nottingham in January 1991. The conference addressed the theme of Women in the German-Speaking States.

47 Helmut Schelsky: *Die skeptische Generation*, Düsseldorf, 1957.

48 See Heinrich Böll: 'Ende der Bescheidenheit. Zur Situation der Schriftsteller in der Bundesrepublik' in Wolfgang Kuttenkeuler (ed.): *Poesie und Politik*, Stuttgart, 1973, pp. 347—57. Böll's statement: 'Wir verdanken diesem Staat nichts, er verdankt uns eine Menge' (p. 356), which referred to the restoration of the German reputation through literature, provoked considerable controversy. (The essay first appeared in *FR*, 5 July 1969, and was used as the title of the fourth volume of his collected essays and speeches: *Ende der Bescheidenheit. Schriften und Reden 1969—1972*, ed. by Bernd Balzer, Munich, 1985; pp. 54—66, here p. 65) The phrase 'Randarbeiter der holzverarbeitenden Industrie' stems from the founding of the writers' union (VS) in 1970 (see Parkes: *Writers and Politics...*, pp. 86—9).

49 Günter Kunert: 'Der Sturz vom Sockel', *Kultur Chronik. Nachrichten und Berichte aus der Bundesrepublik Deutschland*, no. 6, 1990, p. 9.

50 After referring to the status of Brecht, Arno Schmidt and Böll, Becker adds: 'Ihre Nachfolger lösen den Laden allmählich auf [...] Sie bringen eine Literatur hervor, die von Einverständnis überquillt und in ihrer Freundlichkeit an Privatfernsehen erinnert.' Quoted in Georg Eyring: 'Von Füstenhäusern und Currywürsten', *Die Zeit*, 5 October 1990, Literature Supplement, p. 2.

THE GERMAN *OCTOBER REVOLUTION* IN THE GDR AND THE WRITERS

THEO BUCK

> *Stell dir vor, die DDR wäre sozialistisch, und keiner würde mehr*
> *weggehen.*
> (Christoph Hein, 24 October 1989)

> *Es wird keine DDR mehr geben. Sie wird nichts sein als eine*
> *Fußnote in der Weltgeschichte.*
> (Stefan Heym, 18 March 1990)

I A 'Peaceful Revolution' and its Classification

Who would have thought it? A revolution in Germany! Even during the celebrations in early October 1989 to mark the GDR's fortieth anniversary, nobody could have suspected how rapidly and completely the totalitarian state socialism ensconced between the Elbe and the Oder was to collapse in the weeks to follow. Of course the SED monopolists of power, impervious to any idea of change, did not quit the field willingly. The transformation had to be wrung from these blinkered neo-Stalinists by a very un-German means, namely rebellion. Entrenched as they were in their miserable roles in an authoritarian and dictatorial bureaucracy, full of their own importance and that of their mission, those in power failed to see the profound truth in a warning remark made by Mikhail Gorbachev during the anniversary celebrations that 'life punishes the procrastinator'.[1] However, the privileged citizens from the exclusive ghetto in Wandlitz were not given to reflection on such matters. Scarcely five weeks before his fall, Erich Honecker concocted the pathetic rhyme: 'Den Sozialismus in seinem Lauf/ hält weder Ochs noch Esel auf.' Hardly the kind of message in verse that people want to hear during an obvious crisis of legitimation. The ironic rejoinder came from Stefan Heym, quite rightly in a disarmingly grotesque couplet: 'An der Spitze steht ein Greis,/ der sich nicht zu helfen weiß.'[2] Soon afterwards things in the land of 'real existing socialism' ceased to be the way they had been for forty years. The enforced structures were forced out of joint. The political, economic and above all, moral bankruptcy of the putative 'Arbeiter- und Bauernmacht', which was demonstrated to all the world

by the way the population were voting with their feet, could only be resolved in one way: by the removal of the communists from the levers of
power. For a while, political structures were marked by vacancies. Politics was no longer a matter for the Party alone. The seeds of grass-roots
democracy had been sown.

This state of democratic action from below must be attributed
primarily to those people who were determined no longer to be fobbed
off with empty phrases. What was in train here on a broad basis was
neatly summed up by the writer Christoph Hein: 'das Volk [hat sich]
unter den Schlägen der Staatssicherheit und der Polizei uner-
warteterweise zum aufrechten Gang erhoben.'3 The muted emotionalism
was perfectly justified, for the non-violent mass demonstrations did indeed represent a departure without historical parallel in Germany. As
the uprising showed signs of success it became a signal for the democratization of a society which had lived under dictatorship for over five
decades. It was the opposition of the victimized, the insulted, the de-
graded. First in Leipzig, Dresden and Berlin and then in the rest of the
country, an ever swelling tide of peaceful opponents succeeded in con-
verting their battle-cry of 'Wir sind das Volk' so convincingly into reality
that it became impossible, short of serious bloodshed, to contain the
dynamic forces being released. From this point, history began to gallop.

It then became apparent that we were witnessing a 'peaceful
revolution' of the people in the GDR. Even Heiner Müller, who spoke
initially of a 'Straßenaufstand', rectified this with the observation: 'Es
handelt sich tatsächlich um eine Revolution.' For, so he reasoned, 'eine
Revolution ist vorerst, wenn eine Masse von Leuten das Gefühl hat, daß
sie etwas entscheiden kann und mit dem Risiko auf die Straße geht, daß
die Armee eingreift'. Müller ultimately concluded by classifying the
whole process of resistance as 'eine bürgerliche Revolution'.4 Although
subsequent developments have proved him right in this respect, it is
nevertheless appropriate to see the first successful revolution in Germany as a decisive stage in the the process of liberating the countries of
central and eastern Europe from communism.

It is with good reason, therefore, that one documentary account of
the October 1989 events bears the subtitle 'Wider den Schlaf der Vernunft'.5 As everyone knows, according to the pictorial dictum of the
painter Goya, *The Sleep of Reason Begets Monsters*. In the case of the GDR
the monsters were identical with tutelage, lies, oppression and inade-

quacy. Consequently, all that remained in reality of the 'socialist community' that had been propagated was a pale imitation, giving the disheartening impression of a cowed mass. This was where the opposition made its start — and triggered off a torrent-like social movement. Volker Braun has pointed out how closely the Utopian expectations of writers in earlier years coincided with the recent actual historical processes. He said: 'Wir erleben jetzt, wie rasch die Geschichte einigen unserer Hoffnungen nacheilt und unserem Zorn, unserem Hohn entgegnet mit der lächelnden Selbstverständlichkeit ihrer Wende'.[6]

It was also 'perfectly natural' that those energies should break through which ultimately caused the Berlin Wall to be opened, making 9 November 1989 a heavily symbolic date. The disappearance of the Wall epitomized the ending of the postwar era. Overnight, the 'antifascist dyke' lost its actual function as a prison for the Germans in the GDR. It was as if floodgates had burst asunder.

Inevitably, the qualitative leap to openness produced euphoria, causing surges of ecstasy in the general state of happiness. Suddenly the demonstrators' slogan was no longer 'Wir sind das Volk!' but rather 'Wir sind *ein* Volk'. The introduction of the numeral indicated a social process with momentous implications, a process of far-reaching structural change. In the face of the sluggish pace of renewal and the general instability of the situation, the people on the streets reorientated themselves and regrouped. It was evident that most of them were not prepared to summon up the patience to put their trust in the joint responsibility of two German governments. Consequently they joined their voices with ever increasing loudness in the call for national unity in one state. Who would hold such a decision against individuals who had for decades been obliged to endure the mismanagement of 'people's democracy' and the terror of the *Stasi*? The understandable desire to escape the ranks of the disadvantaged and to gain equal opportunities turned easily into an eagerness for unification which left little scope for reflection, examination or planning. Not a thought for the path of fundamental reform and systematic analysis of the past (Heiner Müller: 'Die Leichen müssen aus dem Keller'[7]); no thought either for the model of gradual rapprochement with the aim of confederating the two German states. The decisive factor was the understandable aspiration for the same material standard of living with immediately discernible consequences for the individual's own life. It would be pharisaical to criticize this attitude here in the

West, for the revolution was, as Monika Maron quite rightly emphasized, 'kein Aufbruch in die Utopie, sondern ein verzweifelter Sprung aus der Vergangenheit in die Gegenwart, aus einer autoritären kleinbürgerlich-feudalen Machtstruktur in eine offene bürgerliche Demokratie'.[8]

Unfortunately, however, this fundamental decision, understandable as it remains, was accompanied by changes which give one pause. The most striking phenomenon in this respect is undoubtedly the fact that the opposition figures who had been the first to build up the potential for resistance, thus initiating and carrying through the revolution at great personal risk, were then completely marginalized. Typically, in the Volkskammer elections of 18 March 1990 it was not the men and women of the peace and human rights groups who came to the fore, but the conformists and dependants of the Party dictatorship. These people, politically passive and silent in the past, occasionally even fellow-travellers (after all, the old CDU (East) emerged from the election as the strongest party), took possession of the public arena in the period following the fall of the Berlin Wall amidst much flag-waving. Benjamin Henrichs hit the nail on the head with his critical remark: 'Das Mitläufer-Volk wählte die Mitläufer-Partei und sprach sich damit selber frei.'[9] This development in the the GDR coincided with the interests of those who had long been averse to any policy of détente but had finally, with some reluctance, adopted one and were now looking to reap the fruits of other people's efforts. The *Allianz für Deutschland* was the product of a conservative coalition of interests. The spiritual fathers in Bonn and their helpmeets in the territory of the GDR joined their voices in glorious praise of the market economy. With historically tried and tested demagoguery they reduced the broad political spectrum to the crude antithesis: 'Freedom or Socialism'. The result of their action was pithily summed up by a cabaret performer: 'Die Wähler haben sich selber ver-kohlt.'[10]

We must not harbour any illusions about what all of this amounted to. Instead of reflecting on the various possibilities for unity available to the Germans within the universally invoked 'European family', the majority (the ruling coalition in Bonn and the elected 'accession'-alliance in the Volkskammer) clung to the spectre of the nation. They chose the one solution which, in a period of world history dominated by transnational and multicultural symbiosis, had to appear obsolete. This

'Deutschmark nationalism' was subjected to swingeing analysis by Jür-gen Habermas, although even he offered no orientation for the future.[11] The legitimate demand of GDR citizens for a better standard of living was by no means necessarily bound up with immediate accession to the Basic Law of the Federal Republic under Article 23.[12] Economic pressures and material needs, moreover, do not on their own provide a favourable basis for the unification of two states which had long been separated from each other and which had actually been in ideological competition, the one with the other. Obviously, the corrupt and washed-out GDR system was in no position to offer models which might be adopted by a future 'Republic of Germany'. However, since it is clearly more important to create unity not as quickly as possible but rather as effectively as possible, those people who had at last won the right to speak for themselves, should also have been given — and still should be given — the opportunity to define their own position.

This can only be done meaningfully through a self-critical examination of their own history. As matters stand at present, the neces-sary self-appraisal is simply being suppressed. We are familiar with this from the early years of the Federal Republic. Even at that time attitudes and actions were already determined by the motto: economic recovery, not *Trauerarbeit*. This has to raise questions. Is the GDR 'October revolu-tion', with all its democratic promise, to be retrospectively devalued? Was it all simply a matter of demonstrating that they were 'ready for the West'? Will we be able in future to dismiss the social achievements of the GDR lock, stock and barrel as a *quantité négligeable*? That would be a shame. The 'gentle revolution' was a much greater cause for hope than the forecast, sanctioned by the stock markets, of positively explosive eco-nomic growth. Let us hope that the solidarity of the revolutionaries of the first hour (already again victims of discrimination, their role virtu-ally forgotten) with others in the GDR who did not want simply to be taken over has not been lost without trace. There was never any question of a 'third way'. What was needed, however, was a process of reform shaped by mutually influential democratic evolution on both sides. This would certainly not have prejudiced the gross domestic product, but the East Germans would at least have retained their identity and the West Germans would at last have been able to earn the democracy they were given. Admittedly, there seems little chance of this now. And that is why we might feel inclined to echo the words of Schiller: 'Eine große Epoche hat das Jahrhundert geboren;/ Aber der große Moment findet ein kleines Geschlecht.'[13]

II The 'Sozialliterat' becomes an Independent Writer

Before discussing the situation of the writers, we must clear up the question of literature's social function. To do this it is necessary to survey the general cultural and political conditions. Different social systems create fundamentally different forms of literary life. While, according to the traditional bourgeois conception, the work of the writer should be kept free as far as possible from political influence, the 'people's democracies' attach the greatest importance to involving art and the artist in the planned, or at least postulated, process of social emancipation. It would be too schematic to reduce this antithesis to the simple formula of 'autonomy versus commitment', but obviously in the one case we are talking first and foremost about guaranteeing the freedom of art and, in the other, about a didactic perception of the work of art as a 'factor of production' in society.

Consequently, in the framework of a society which defines itself, in Marxist-Leninist terms, as 'on the road to socialism', a great deal is expected of the artist. He has a constitutive part to play in creating the necessary 'socialist consciousness' and developing a 'socialist community'. These, if anything, uncomfortable formulations reveal in themselves what is actually at stake, namely the enlistment of art for the socio-political programme laid down by the Party: aesthetics to order. With this clear purpose in mind, the doctrine of 'socialist realism' was implemented in the communist world during Stalin's time by Zhdanov, his art commissar, first in the Soviet Union and then elsewhere. It was intended, with the stipulation of concrete criteria such as mimesis, commitment, totality, popular characteristics, and exemplary character, to establish aesthetic maxims which, in the eyes of the Party, would guarantee 'positive, constructive art'. In practice, however, these led to nothing but dull edification, the glorification of an intrinsically lacklustre everyday life, and the stereotyped 'dawn of socialism'. With their requirement for unqualified affirmation, the totalitarian apparatchiks instantly succeeded in all but stifling that imagination so essential to creative and innovative processes. The history of the arts in the Soviet Union from the late 1920s onwards provides alarming evidence of the process of cultural deprivation. The practical consequences are easy to see: the public, brought up to think in 'socialist realist' terms, was totally deprived of the productive tension which exists between the experience of art and personal experience of life, while art, as a result, degenerated to become a travesty of itself. There is no doubt that 'socialist realism' has, as Manès Sperber rightly concluded, 'eine große Sache', that of art, 'bis zur Unkenntlichkeit entstellt'.[14]

The literature of the GDR must also be studied against such a background, since from the very beginning, in what was then the Soviet Zone of Occupation, course was set for a 'German socialist national literature'. This undertaking benefited at first from relatively good conditions. After the 'anticulture' of the National Socialists, a renewal under the auspices of antifascism seemed of necessity a sensible way forward. Success seemed all the more assured as authors were systematically recalled from exile and it was also announced that the 'bürgerlich-fortschrittlich' heritage would be maintained. If we add to this the noble aim of a 'transformation into a reading and literature-orientated society', it is easy to understand why a large majority of people, especially among the younger generation, had no reservations, initially, about identifying with this.

Cultural and political divergence led to separate developments in literature in the two parts of Germany which emerged as the product of the Cold War. But while the literature of the Federal Republic arrived at its specific features only slowly (towards the end of the 1950s), the GDR had at the outset mustered a considerable potential of artistic energies, on whose achievements the younger generation could draw as an organic process. The concept of art as a factor in a planned social development seemed about to be put convincingly into practice. Many people were already beginning to see the gulf between Utopia and history disappear.

Working in this atmosphere, authors had to combine their concept of the productive possibilities with their instrumental role for the Party. Typically, it was Christa Wolf who, not very long ago, emphasized: 'Natürlich frage ich mich, wie ich, schreibend, andere, produktive Bedürfnisse entwickeln helfen kann, die nur in innerlich unabhängigen, kritisch denkenden und verantwortlich handelnden Menschen entstehen.' And it seems almost self-evident that Christoph Hein should give a collection of essays the self-defining title of öffentlich arbeiten.[15] The location and the intended effect of the writer are here described positively. Thus literature under socialism was sustained by authors who regard themselves as 'Sozialliteraten'.[16]

But this is not the end of the story. This virtually perfect state of affairs, at least as far as the idea is concerned, proved to be increasingly precarious in practice. The drawbacks became more and more obvious. It is true that the 'socialist nation by the grace of Stalin' emphatically defended the great importance of art in shaping the life of society and accordingly favoured those writers organized in the *Schriftstellerverband*. In return for its support, however, the state party expected work which would be in accordance with its programme. Patronage and prescription went hand in hand. High prestige had ultimately to be paid for by conformity. Participants were in demand, and they found their place in the sun. However, supervision and tutelage do not constitute fertile soil for such basic requirements of artistic progress as creativity, readiness to experiment, and radicalness. In order to gain the necessary freedom, the writers affected had to circumvent the cultural and political maxims as best they could. That is why the history of GDR literature was always at once a history of latent protest and resistance to the Party's claim to direct. This produced a growing trend towards the 'unbediensteten Autor', as Volker Braun has put it.[17]

To trace here the subjective high-wire walks of individual writers in their endeavours for independence would lead us too far afield. We would have to mention virtually all successful GDR authors (including those successful in the West) — with the express exception of Hermann Kant! Wherever we begin, we come across more or less serious difficulties with the Party. Some chose cautious manoeuvring, others the arduous path of permanent conflict; yet others preferred to turn their backs on the GDR altogether. It is significant, in this connection, that from the time of the Biermann affair in 1976,[18] more than a hundred authors moved to West Berlin or the Federal Republic. It would be no exaggeration to say that around half of all GDR writers left the country of their birth. Every individual case is different, but a concern common to all may perhaps be found in one of Katja Lange-Müller's statements when, with her typical Berlin edge, she said: 'Ick hatte [...] det Jefühl, ick vejetier am Rande meines Horizonts. Det wir uns trennen, die DDR und ick, det beruhte auf beiderseitigem Interesse.'[19]

Under such constraints literature was bound to undergo modification. The countless individual discussions and debates of general principles did little to change the basic attitude of the SED political guardians of the cultural grail, although they did bring about a gradual reduction in aesthetic dogma. The conflict between the individual's perception of reality and the 'politischen Magie [...] von der künstlichen Steigerung des braven Ichs zu einem behaupteten WIR' (Volker Braun) was simply too obvious.[20] The main consequence of authorial detachment was that style became open, subtly diversified, individually shaped, and therefore more complex. However, it was undoubtedly a euphemism on Wolfgang Emmerich's part when he opined he could sense a 'Verschwinden der ästhetischen Doktrinen'.[21] Right up to the very end, Kurt Hager insisted that literature be given the 'necessary guidance'.[22]

Nevertheless, from the late 1960s, certainly from the 1970s, it was no longer possible to postulate homogeneity in GDR literature. Too many authors objected to betraying their 'Thema ans Schema' (Günter de Bruyn). The conclusion gained ground that 'Eigenstes, genau dargestellt, sich als Allgemeines erweist'.[23] A spectre was abroad the GDR: the spectre of the 'independent writer'. The Party reacted hesitantly. But the system of social and material privileges was losing its hold. Even the cunning apparatus of censorship and control lost its power of intimidation because of the ease with which dissentient texts could be published in the Federal Republic. The perverse machinery of obstruction could now only appear absurd, whatever form it took: expulsion from the Schriftstellerverband or a ban on publication, paper quotas, small print-runs or limited distribution by the LKG (Leipziger Kommissions-Groß-handel, the central body responsible for wholesale) — not to mention prosecution for 'propaganda hostile to the state' or 'establishing illegal contacts'. Clearly, the world of literature had its own wall and border fortifications. A large section of the 'Sozialliteraten' now considered it to be the real purpose of a writer's work to tackle the 'Deckgebirge der Verheißungen' (Volker Braun).[24]

This was what was meant by the authorial walk on the high wire: from conformity to critical distance. Some, such as the time-serving president of the Schriftstellerverband, Hermann Kant, preferred the easy going offered by the party line. Others, increasingly numerous, noted the risk this involved, 'aus der bewegten Zeit in eine stehende zu fallen'.[25] The necessary withdrawl was given its most rigorous formulation by Heiner Müller, when he wrote: 'Die Funktion von Kulturpolitik ist, Ereignisse zu verhindern. Aber Leben ist, daß sich etwas ereignet, daß etwas passiert. Und wenn nichts mehr passiert, dann ist es vorbei. Das ist der Punkt, wo die Systeme lebensfeindlich werden.'[26] With this Müller has outlined the position of the 'independent writer' with regard to life, revealing to us the coordinates within which every GDR writer had to work. Each had to find his or her own path somewhere between prescribed social commitment and necessary individual creative freedom.

It is demonstrably the case that the best artistic achievements occurred where it was possible to bring the two orientations into productive balance. The same synthesis created the conditions for contrary artists who wanted nothing to do with official apologetics and affirmatory adaptation. To leave no room for doubt: it was these writers, with their literary unruliness, who prepared the ground for the revolutionary process. It was surely no coincidence that in the discussions in the Gethsemanekirche on 7 October 1989 (thus, precisely on the fortieth anniversary of the founding of the GDR, accompanied by massive attacks on the population by both *Volkspolizei* and *Stasi*) the central issue was that of 'verweigerte Subjektwerdung'.[27] Some two decades previously, in 1968, Christa Wolf had made the claim that literature 'unterstützt das Subjektwerden des Menschen'.[28] Her postulate of 'subjektive Authentizität' did not fit in with the plans of the Party strategists; it gave an appearance of resistance or contained the potential for resistance.[29] At the end of March 1990, a GDR citizen wrote to the letters column of *Die Zeit* and gave a correct perspective on this assessment. Alluding to writers such as Hein, Heym and Wolf, he stated: 'Meine Freude [at *Die Zeit*'s literary supplement devoted to both German literatures] ist vor allem dadurch begründet, daß hier jene zu Wort kommen, die mit ihren Büchern unser Nachdenken, unsere kritische Sicht mitbewirkten und die auch in den Oktober- und Novembertagen sich deutlich artikulierten.'[30] There is nothing to add to this. The awareness that GDR reality could be extensively criticized was engendered first and foremost by the writers. Of course there were still the dutiful Party bards, from Kurt Bartel (alias Kuba) to Hermann Kant. Despite all their technical skills, they must now be worried about how they are to continue working, and rightly, since the official day of the socialist laureates is now irreversibly over. The future belongs to others, and that is heartening, for the categories in which we place art are still what they always were: good or bad, successful or failed experiment, authenticity or construct, transformation of present existence, imagination as reality.

III The Writers Pave the Way for a 'Revolution' without Writers

As I have shown, those authors who regarded their writing as a critical examination of GDR socialism's 'deformierte Realität',[31] contributed through their persistent burrowing to the gradual undermining of aesthetic doctrine. The steady drops, as always, wore down the stone. It was, admittedly, a lengthy process, a process accompanied by constant set-backs, above all a process involving far-reaching personal conflict. Even Brecht would have had enough to say on this score, given the problems of his struggle against the obsolete Stanislavsky method and with his critical treatment of the 'classical heritage' (his production of the *Urfaust*, for example, or his adaptation of *Der Hofmeister*). The clearest statement in this respect is undoubtedly the caesura, associated with their departure from the GDR, in the lives of Uwe Johnson, Peter Huchel, Wolf Biermann, Reiner Kunze, Hans Joachim Schädlich, Günter Kunert — to name but a few, particularly vehemently discussed individual cases as examples that prove the rotten rule. The Party was adept at 'cutting off the oxygen' of authors who were out of favour. Anyone who, in spite of this, did not want to leave the GDR needed great strength.

Christa Wolf has described vividly how those affected were treated: 'Es hat aus meiner Sicht bei uns jahrelang eine Anmaßung von Kritik und Theorie gegenüber Schreibenden und ihren Arbeiten gegeben. Es ist aber das eine, darum zu wissen, und etwas anderes, mit schwerwiegenden persönlichen Vorwürfen fertigzuwerden. Bei mir hat das dazu geführt, daß ich das eine oder andre Buch weniger geschrieben habe.'[32] And she was still a member of the SED when she said this. For 'difficult cases', Party membership was of little use. Her fellow writers Volker Braun and Heiner Müller could relate wierd and wonderful sagas about how their texts were (or were not) published and about the prevention and delaying of performances of their plays. The authors' paths to their public were indeed strewn with thorns.

And yet, undeniably, they had their effect. The poetry debates in the 1960s (following the now famous reading of December 1962 in the Akademie der Künste and the publication of the critical anthology *In diesem besseren Land* by Adolf Endler and Karl Mickel in 1966),[33] the controversy surrounding Christa Wolf's *Nachdenken über Christa T.* (published in 1968),[34] the extensive discussions of Ulrich Plenzdorf's *Die neuen Leiden des jungen W.* (1972), and the delayed publication of Volker Braun's *Unvollendete Geschichte*[35] did have a truly pioneering effect. Yet, for all that, the cultural functionaries retained their ideological taboos. They were too fixed in their views. They should have known better after their experience with Christa Wolf's *Nachdenken über Christa T.*, yet they continued to create critical storms over new works from her pen.[36] Given such an attitude, Hermann Kant's speech in September 1984 in which he called for a 'mutigere Literaturpolitik', must have seemed utter mockery.[37]

However, such Party restrictions, bans, censorship measures and obstructionist tactics are a source of implicit information about the influence exerted by literature on attitudes and ideas in GDR society. The reader's letter quoted above (p. 30) is one example among many. So the fears of those in power were not unfounded. There was, however, just one thing to which the advocates of the 'pure doctrine' were blind: namely, how rapidly the forces for social integration atrophy in these conditions. The Party specialists should have listened to Günter Kunert, who revealed the anomaly in official behaviour when he advanced the following view: 'Die Unterdrückung von Kritik, dem einzigen Korrektiv für die Funktionsfähigkeit von Gesellschaften [...] und die absolute Begriffsstutzigkeit für den erforderlichen Widerspruch, diesen Prüfstein der eigenen Theorie und Praxis, sie haben im Laufe von Jahren dazu geführt, daß jede abweichende Ansicht eo ipso als ein mit der "Waffe des Worts" vollzogenes Attentat gewertet wird.' His inevitable conclusion: 'Ein Denken, dem sich keine Hürde mehr in den Weg stellt, muß verflachen.'[38] This explains the reasons why a public starved of criticism kept an eager look-out for criticism in the guise of literature.

There is an accurate description of this complex set of circumstances; Monika Maron, not without (self-)critical reservations, has thrown light on the situation as follows:

> Die Schriftsteller in der DDR waren eine besonders verwöhnte Gruppe ihres Berufsstandes. Damit meine ich weniger die von der Obrigkeit gewährten Privilegien als eine allgemeine Verehrung, die ihnen zuteil wurde, selbst von Menschen, zu deren Lebensgewohnheiten das Lesen von Büchern nicht gehörte.
> Es brauchte nicht viel Mut, besonders nicht für die durch die Öffentlichkeit geschützten Autoren, um den Schein des Heldentums um sich zu entfachen. Und oft genügte eine halbe Wahrheit, um ihrem

Verkünder in einer Umgebung dummer und dreister Verlogenheit den
Ruf des Propheten zu verleihen.
Selbst wer der Zensur anheimfiel, wußte sich im andern Deutschland
um so aufmerksamer gelesen und auch im eigenen Land genossen als
die verbotene Frucht.
Ich fand Blumen an meiner Wohnungstür und Pralinen unterm
Fußabtreter mit ermutigenden Grüßen meiner Leser.
Jeder Schriftsteller in der DDR, sofern er nicht ein Apologet und
Nutznießer der stalinistischen Verhältnisse war, wurde getragen von
der wahrheits- und heldensüchtigen, zuweilen bedrängenden
Verehrung seiner Leser. Und wie fast jede lebenserhaltende Symbiose
in diesem Land durch den Mangel gestiftet war, so auch die zwischen
Lesern und Schreibern. In einem Staat, der den Mangel an bürgerlichen
Freiheiten zur Doktrin erhebt, sammelt sich die verbotene Öf-
fentlichkeit in den verbleibenden Rinnsalen der Kommunikation: in
privaten Zirkeln, in den Kirchen, in der Kunst. Der konspirative
Diskurs wird zu einer Form des Widerstands. Dies bescherte den
Schriftstellern und Künstlern der DDR ihre exklusive Bedeutung. Wie
selbstverständlich wuchs ihnen das Recht, sogar die Pflicht zu, im Namen der zum Schweigen gezwungenen Mehrheit zu sprechen.[39]

Monika Maron was not exaggerating. A public hungry for criticism was indeed seeking eagerly in literature for objective and, to that
extent, transferable critical material. This long quotation from a most
rewarding essay in Der Spiegel makes it clear to us, in relatively little
space, what the functional value of critical literature actually was in the
SED dictatorship. It acted as an alternative public forum, and this is why
books became objects of value in the GDR. People identified with their
subversive impulses. In the climate created by the Party's police state,
the resistant little seedling of criticism flourished and slowly but surely
grew into the strong plant of well-developed readiness to resist. The
gradual growth of critical consciousness in the closed (not to say, enclosed) society of the GDR took root initially in social fringe groups, especially amongst young people. Irrespective of their very different political opinions, they tended to gather under the wing of the church. This
'verbotene Öffentlichkeit' (Monika Maron) often drew on literary texts
for the terms and ideas of its protest.

Nobody from the West can really appreciate how avidly a readership on the look-out for critical guidance devoured texts, for example of
plays whose performance had brought the authoritarian censors onto
the scene. The incriminating phrases spread through the supposedly
democratic republic like wildfire. Examples are legion. Think of Volker
Braun's unassuming observation that the GDR was 'das langweiligste
Land der Erde' and his question, 'Kämpfen wir für eine Idee und nicht
für unser Fleisch? [...] Ist das eine Renaissance für Spießer?'. Then there

is Heiner Müller's telling characterization of '[die] schmutzige Praxis' as the 'Esserin der Utopien' and the comment of his work-brigade leader Barka on the building of the Wall: 'Gratulation zum Schutzwall. Ihr habt gewonnen eine Runde, aber es ist ein Tiefschlag.'[40] Such statements had an electrifying effect. Many a poem by Biermann, Braun, Kunze and Kunert provided the first spark for a frame of mind which rebelled against false consciousness. Even the very wording of Christa Wolf's: 'Die große Hoffnung oder über die Schwierigkeit, "ich" zu sagen'[41] was like the unleashing of an avalanche in its effect on social psychology, since an ideologically closed view of life was thus called into question. It was against such excesses of the 'subjective element' that the Party's cherished caviller Hans Koch fulminated in the columns of *Neues Deutschland* (occasioned by Ulrich Plenzdorf's *Die neuen Leiden des jungen W.*), setting against them the leathery lessons of a 'sozialistische Ethik' which, without a second thought, he said was 'dem geistigen Lebenselixier der sozialistischen Gesellschaft, der marxistisch-leninisti- schen Weltanschauung gemäß'.[42] One cannot but react allergically to this sort of thing — as did Plenzdorf's Edgar Wibeau.

The waves of agitation were occasionally felt as far as the Central Committee, but there everything had been pictured differently, more simply. As early as 1931 Ernst Bloch had said all there is to say about this when, in his essay entitled 'Poesie im Hohlraum', he noted: 'Der vulgäre Funktionär verhält sich [...] zur Imagination, gerade zur konkreten, wie ein Kommerzienrat sich zu seinem Sohn verhält, wenn er Lyriker werden will.'[43] What could just marginally be tolerated were 'non-antagonistic conflicts' susceptible of resolution. Irremediable contradictions were not to arise. The ultimate effect of this was what we might call a 'socialist *Biedermeier*' or a 'red hued *Gartenlaube*'.[44] Anything that went beyond this in either content or form was, essentially, achieved in spite of prevailing circumstances and tended to carry with it an implied resistance. This led to a situation in which authors who valued a critical leavening for their writing began to withdraw. It becomes clear from the example of Christa Wolf's route to art that this was at the same time a movement away from the Party. True authors simply need 'das wilde Prinzip Hoffnung'.[45]

Here one might modify Heiner Müller's phrase 'Praxis — Esserin der Utopien' and say that in the GDR literature proved to be the 'Ernährerin der Utopien'. Readers sought and found in the subtext of many works of literature the subversive impetus they so urgently desired. Book and stage accordingly acted as alternative forums for a public voice which was unwelcome and was kept down by force. 'Die Dimension des Autors' (to quote the title of a book by Christa Wolf) grew enormously in the process. Obviously the Party failed to realize that it was sitting on a time bomb; while literature acted as an essential pacemaker on the road to revolutionary protest against a dictatorially impoverished life and against the first duty imposed on every good Prussian socialist citizen from above to be calm and keep quiet.

This is why writers such as Christa Wolf and Stefan Heym, Helga Königsdorf and Christoph Hein appeared at the first mass protests. At the large demonstration on Alexanderplatz on 4 November 1989, Stefan Heym could call for 'einen Sozialismus, der des Namens wert ist' and actually be applauded, while Christoph Hein was able to second him by proclaiming to his 'lieben mündig gewordenen Mitbürgern': 'Die Strukturen dieser Gesellschaft müssen verändert werden, wenn sie demokratisch und sozialistisch werden soll. Und dazu gibt es keine Alternative.'[46] Only a short time later Heinz Czechowski was able express similar thoughts only in the subjunctive: 'Zöge sich die DDR aus eigener Kraft aus dem Sumpf, so wäre dies eine große historische Chance für das Entstehen eines neuen DDR-Bewußtseins.' And he concluded his observations in an obvious mood of resignation, adding: 'Doch scheint sie [the great historic opportunity] unwahrscheinlich angesichts der Defizite auf allen Gebieten.'[47] What had happened to bring about this change in mood?

Quite clearly, we are here witnessing a parallel development to the change in paradigm from 'Wir sind das Volk' to 'Wir sind *ein* Volk!', in the course of which a people which had found its own voice abandoned the writers to their Utopia. Even if some (Volker Braun, Stefan Heym and Christa Wolf are the obvious examples) still spoke out for 'eine eigenständige DDR', they met with no response from the masses.[48] Those who had originally sought guidance from the artists[49] were now acting autonomously. Where, at the original demonstrations, banners had carried such messages as 'Statt geistiger Qualen freie Wahlen', they now began to read differently: 'Wenn die D-Mark nicht zu uns kommt, gehen wir zur D-Mark.'[50] The shift in direction is obvious. The people wanted a rapid fusion of the two Germanys. However, this trend should not be condemned out of hand as a 'Wiedervereinigung im Aldi-Rausch' or a 'Jagd nach dem glitzernden Tinnef'.[51] Perfectly solid reasons can be adduced. People who were escaping from communism enforced by law were not interested in a new German Democratic Republic, as the majority of authors believed,[52] but rather in its quickest possible demise. Thus the men and women of letters, some of whom were even dreaming of a republic governed by *soviets* (Volker Braun: 'Kommt Zeit, kommen Räte'; Fritz Rudolf Fries: 'Alle Macht den Räten, wenn sie vernünftig handeln'[53]) found themselves on the periphery of society.

Once again, it was Monika Maron who provided an impartial diagnosis of events. Her clear-sighted analysis raises questions which her fellow writers would find difficult to answer:

> Jetzt, da die dünne Decke der Notgemeinschaft zerrissen ist, zeigt sich der tiefe Abgrund zwischen dem Volk und den Intellektuellen.
>
> Drängen die einen auf eine schnelle und praktische Verbesserung ihres Lebens, kämpfen die anderen um den Erhalt ihrer Utopie, was an sich kein Unglück wäre, würde die Utopie der einen — und zwar nur um ihres Bestands willen — das bessere Leben der anderen nicht bewußt opfern und 16 Millionen Menschen auch für die Zukunft zum Objekt einer Idee degradieren.
>
> Welche Zukunftsvisionen haben jene Literaten, die beschwörend vor dem Ausverkauf an den Kapitalismus warnen, obwohl sie wissen, daß der Ausverkauf seit Jahrzehnten stattgefunden hat? [...] Welche Solidarität soll verteidigt werden? Und wie steht es um das antifaschistische Ideal, dessen Fortleben an die eigenstaatliche Existenz der DDR gebunden sein soll?[54]

The contradiction is clearly stated. One group was indeed concerned with the 'Erhalt ihrer Utopie' and the other with the practical consequences and results of their sovereign action as a people. Since the writers were evidently disinclined to acknowledge how national identity here coincided with justified material demands, they 'missed the train', as Rudolf Augstein put it.[55]

The fact that political and social changes were and are thus taking place to the exclusion of literature, so to speak, is no cause for regret. The majority of writers certainly do not appear to be unhappy about it. They really have 'other worries', to quote a phrase. Nor do we have to look far for the reasons; they are obvious. With the opening of the Wall, the critical function of their writing automatically ceased for authors in the GDR. If the left-wing opposition groups, the groups who had actually set the revolutionary events in motion, were pushed into the background by the 'gentle revolution' and more specifically by the resulting surges of a patriotism thought long forgotten, this was all the more the case for those who had been 'mere' intellectual initiators of the changes. With the casting off of the communist dictatorship and the overnight disappearance of the Stalinist spectres the tasks of literature also changed abruptly. Because Utopia anticipates reality and establishes yardsticks for its dynamic movement, it cannot become involved directly in the course of reality. The success of the liberation has released literature to new perspectives.

Many people were shocked by the fact that, in the middle of a phase of national self-gratification ('our Helmut' in a swell of liberally distributed flags), Wolfgang Hildesheimer, always a clear-headed observer of the times, coolly tossed the following remark about developments generally in eastern Europe into the debate: 'Angesichts der Tatsache, daß die Natur stirbt, ist das nebensächlich.'[56] No less important is Heiner Müller's reminder, 'das Problem des Lebens in der Tiefe bleibt für die Welt bestehen.'[57] For literature and art in general, this is where the real challenges of the future lie; as Hans Mayer once said: 'Alle Literatur, auch die heutige, stemmt sich gegen den Tod.'[58] Thus it was only logical that Heiner Müller should make the following observation on the situation as it was developing: '*Hamlet* ist im Moment das aktuellste Stück in der DDR [...] Es beschreibt den Abgrund hinter jeder Politik.'[59] One can only agree.

IV The Undistinguished End of a Thoroughly Distinguished Literature

At present (summer 1990), extreme uncertainty is weighing upon writers in the GDR. The reactions to it are as varied as the reasons for it. We can make out three main tendencies.

For quite a few authors, our first group, the new situation has brought about an existential crisis. From one moment to the next, the premises for their lives, the determinants of Party function and thematic perspectives, have been removed. Since 31 March 1990 they have ceased to receive money from the state. Their future is now uncertain. It is inevitable that people in this position should be overcome by the fear of a normality in which they have to fend for themselves, as 'de-commissioned' writers. Those affected in this way feel threatened by painful ostracism. Their problem is that while petty-bourgeois GDR socialism promoted some art, it was exceedingly generous to mediocrity useful to the Party. In the free market, this is rarely the case. We may feel sorry for people who have suddenly been left to their own devices; from the aesthetic point of view, however, there is no call for sadness.

Others, our second group, including many of the best, are undergoing a real identity crisis. With Marxism-Leninism as the ideological basis of their entire socialization, they had with great effort worked out their own ethical position; subsequently, over many years, they had been engaged in critical conflict with their state, at high personal risk. Nevertheless, they identified with their society and now have to face hostility from it because they continue to hope for 'socialism with a human face'. They have had too much to bear. They have lost both the public they wrote for and the themes crucial to their work. Their Utopian expectations have been pushed back to kingdom come. At the same time there is the equally weighty factor that their work was determined primarily by moral and critical commitment and not necessarily by literary and aesthetic considerations (a problem we are familiar with from Heinrich Böll!). Now, however, they have to reorientate themselves artistically. Little wonder then that the productive and critical reappraisal of what was is now of crucial importance to them. And it is only natural that the total lack of response to their need causes them suffering.

Christa Wolf has intimated something of these worries in an interview with a West German journalist. 'Begreifen Sie,' she said 'wir haben viel Gemeinsames, ich betone das gerne. Aber wir haben auch etwas Eigenes; und sei es unser Versagen, das dazu gehört. Lassen Sie uns das, und lassen Sie uns das alleine aufräumen. Wir werden euch brauchen — aber wir möchten von euch nicht aufgebraucht werden.'[60] Volker Braun's view of developments since autumn 1989 is very similar: 'Es ist peinigend für mich, daß sich diese kurze Demokratie so schnell in die Obhut anderer Mächte flüchtet [...] Das ist eine intime Katastrophe dieser plötzlich lebendigen DDR.'[61] Anxiety is voiced when the gaze turns towards the West. 'Was soll geschehen?' asks Fritz Rudolf Fries, for example: 'Die Literaten zurück in den Elfenbeinturm? Die Literaten auf die Bestsellermärkte? Das ganze Deutschland, wenn es so aussähe wie die jetzige größere Hälfte, würde auch uns, den Schreibern dieses Landes, diese Alternative bescheren, die keine ist. Ist da nicht noch etwas?'[62] This seems to indicate that the main cause of their trepidation lies in the impending commercialization and even more in the threat that memory might be suppressed. These authors certainly realize the significance of making a change from one day to the next to a diametrically opposed system; they recognize the crippling effect failure to carry out a critical appraisal can have on political and cultural consciousness. A few lines from a poem by Helga Königsdorf speak with great immediacy of the 'mixed feelings' resulting from the change-round in their lives:

> [...]
> Fragt man uns
> Später
> Nach diesem Herbst
> Als auf den Straßen
> Bevor der Winter nahte
> Die Zukunft gewann
> Ach wir
> Die wir dann
> Im Gegenlicht die Augen schließen
> Wir werden müde sein.[63]

The reactions of the third group are characterized by a large degree of dissociation. Heiner Müller, for instance, provocatively claims to be disinterested, concentrating simply on his artistic work. The canny Saxon is only too well aware that this is purely wishful thinking, for he supplements his vision of aesthetic autonomy with a reference to a similar experience of Gustave Flaubert's: 'Ich habe ein schönes Motto gefunden in dem [...] Briefwechsel Flaubert/Turgenjew, wo Flaubert sich beklagt: Er habe sich so gemütlich eingerichtet in seinem Elfenbeinturm. Aber die Scheiße schwappt immer hoch.'[64] Thus even he has failed to make a clean break with the sphere of politics. However, it must be emphasized that Müller recognizes the necessity for a change of function in his fundamental significance as a writer. With reference to the depressing situation of art in the communist motherland, he observes: 'Viele Texte der jüngeren Sowjetliteratur haben sich mit aktuellen Problemen, mit Miseren und skandalösen Vorgängen beschäftigt. Jetzt brauchen sie das nicht mehr, denn das greift inzwischen die Presse auf. Durch diesen Prozeß wird Literatur wieder frei, sich ihrer eigentlichen Aufgabe zu widmen: die Wirklichkeit, so wie sie ist, unmöglich zu machen.'[65]

These are, in brief outline, three typical authorial reactions to the recent revolutionary occurrences. Clearly they lie between the two poles of stagnation and creativity. It is possible to place all writers and orientations somewhere between these two points. At least a broad scheme of the various tendencies should have become clear. But what general conclusions may we draw from this? Artists who allow themselves to be taken over pay with the loss of their capacity for artistic expression. For similar reasons, the artist's conscience forbids him to isolate himself in an ivory tower. Creative forces, if they are to communicate, presuppose consciousness based in recollection. To put it another way: without *Trauerarbeit*, there can be no artistic future.

Admittedly, here each individual can look only at himself or herself. Heiner Müller has provided us with a virtual paradigm for this in a poem significantly entitled 'Selbstkritik':

> Meine Herausgeber wühlen in alten Texten
> Manchmal wenn ich sie lese überläuft es mich kalt Das
> Habe ich geschrieben IM BESITZ DER WAHRHEIT
> Sechzig Jahre vor meinem mutmaßlichen Tod
> Auf dem Bildschirm sehe ich meine Landsleute
> Mit Händen und Füßen abstimmen gegen die Wahrheit
> Die vor vierzig Jahren mein Besitz war
> Welches Grab schützt mich vor meiner Jugend.[66]

There is no search here for a niche, no alternative is suggested. The author stands by his mistakes. He has overcome them productively, for his own benefit and to further his social possibilities. What Müller is striving for is 'die Mitteilung einer Befindlichkeit'. After all, he knows: 'Das ist reicher als eine Information [...] Denn es hilft, die eigene Befindlichkeit anders wahrzunehmen [...] Daran muß der Leser arbeiten, um es auf sich zu beziehen.'[67] Only if they adopt such an attitude as this can GDR writers develop a new creative programme for a literature which has lost both its function and its influence. Whether this will ever be realized is something we cannot predict.

V And now that GDR Literature has become History... ?
One thing is certain: GDR literature has become a historical phenomenon. Events since 9 November 1989 have, so to speak, cut the ground from under its feet. With the dissolution of the social and political framework of the dictatorship of one party over the people, the autonomous literary system in the GDR also came to an end. Different patterns of behaviour and a different mentality will indeed continue to be apparent there for some considerable time to come. However, it will not now be possible to speak of an independent 'socialist national culture' as understood by the SED. With the Party apparatus, every single prerequisite for an alternative culture has dropped away. To borrow a

metaphor from Volker Braun, we can say, 'auf den Hacken dreht sich die Geschichte um'.[68]

In practice the situation is such that the ministry of culture, the *Schriftstellerverband*, the Party publishing houses, the office for, believe it or not, 'propaganda through literature' (*Literaturpropaganda* in the actual title!) and the people's book trade — in short, all the institutions responsible for the production and distribution of books — are, for the time being, functioning simply as an interim measure. The end of the trade in licences between the two Germanys is imminent, and this will put a stop to the tiresome business of parallel German editions. The powerful publishing houses of the Federal Republic are lying in wait on all sides to ensure that they get their share in the approaching re-distribution. The situation also gives cause for alarm in respect of theatres, arts centres, the Johannes R. Becher Literaturinstitut in Leipzig and many other institutions. The whole area of culture in the GDR is currently in a vacuum.

Two events in March 1990 have proved instructive in this context: the spectral proceedings of the Leipzig book fair, its pavilion full of virtually deserted publishers' stands, and, to an even greater extent, the 'Extraordinary Writers' Congress' of 1—3 March in East Berlin. The book fair was undoubtedly the last in the old style. It would have been unreasonable to expect innovations. The second case is very different. After the long overdue resignation of Hermann Kant in December, this gathering of writers should have provided an opportunity to set things straight between colleagues. Unfortunately this did not occur. Instead, the assembled authors discussed matters relating to a new status and, primarily, to securing a livelihood once Party 'benefits' ran out. Only Stefan Heym found an appropriate expression for what this had really meant, and not one among the previously privileged objected to his 'Zuckerbrot und Peitsche'. However, what completely discredited the *Schriftstellerverband* on the moral plane was the slope-shouldered bonhomie with which its members acknowledged, by 'friendly applause', the message of greeting from its ex-president Hermann Kant. Wryneck-like, to use the image preferred in the GDR, he did not even shrink from asserting, 'daß in dem von ihm geführten Verband immer schon die Demokratie deutlicher sichtbar geworden sei als sonst irgendwo in der DDR, daß die Funktionäre keine Literaturpolizei gewesen seien und das der Präsident sein Amt immer als ein Ehrenamt verstanden und danach gehandelt habe. "Meine Interventionen", so Kant wörtlich, "sind belegt".'[69] Erich Loest, the former GDR writer now living in the West, rightly regarded this as 'Frechheit'. There were no advocates of self-critical retrospection, nor of forward-looking orientations. At the end, Christa Wolf finally plucked up the courage to make the crushing pronouncement: 'Man muß das wohl Verdrängung nennen.'[70] How true. Now, one thing at least is clear: any artistic talents will have to follow a different path from that of the *Schriftstellerverband*.

Typically enough, one writer did not put in an appearance: Heiner Müller. In contrast to Rainer Kirsch, the eventually-elected new president, who continued to speak of 'das Engagement für die gemeinsame Sache',[71] for Müller this has ceased to exist. Müller's credo is now: 'Das Produktive am Künstler in der Politik ist die Lust am Chaos [...] Es gibt keinen Dialog zwischen Kunst und Politik',[72] making him one of very few with completely open horizons for their work in future. His colleagues still have to face a great deal of hard work on their political and cultural consciousness.

However, let us not close our reflections on GDR literature with this disappointing swan song from a national congress which turned out thoroughly parochial. It will soon be assigned to oblivion. The literature of the GDR which has now come to an end, taken as a whole, was deserving of a more positive valediction. Looking back without anger, the overall achievement makes a surprisingly positive impression. As regards quantity, a banal literature of compromise and dross, a result of its Party allegiance, did indeed predominate, especially in the first two decades. However, by no means every author allowed himself or herself to be driven into a corner in this way. Like many of their colleagues in Poland, Hungary and Czechoslovakia, quite a number of GDR authors succeeded in wringing what have proved to be lasting works of literature from the post-Stalinist power system. The humane foundations laid under the influence of antifascism were undoubtedly helpful in this process. The ideational point of departure was correctly identified by Fritz Rudolf Fries when he drew attention to the following: 'Literatur in diesem Lande ist in ihren Absichten gestiftet worden von den Autoren der Emigration. Die ging bis 1945 und begann für viele ein zweites Mal mit dem "Fall Biermann".'[73] It was on these foundations, admittedly always in opposition to the Party leadership, that there developed, from the 1960s onwards, a literary movement of emancipation, the products of which will stand the closest scrutiny — and reading. Anyone requiring names here should refer to the lists of authors whose books have, for years, been published in the Federal Republic. In most cases this provides a pretty reliable indication of whether they are worthy of their status.

Let me reiterate: it was this literature that first put the SED-state to the test. As a body, the writers seismographically recorded social interrelations and states of political awareness in their texts. In simply doing this, they were contravening the clause in the old rules of the *Schriftstellerverband* whereby members had to recognize 'die führende Rolle der Arbeiterklasse und ihrer Partei'. Underlining the necessity of individual development within a movement encompassing the whole of society, critical authors deliberately renounced programmes and patent solutions, replacing them with their own often difficult and painful experience. Motifs of conflict and suffering came more and more to the fore in this process simply because this was the way things were. Thus through elements critical of society, matters of subjective interest made their impact of the consciousness of the reading public. And in this way, the readers gradually began to see self-realization as a vehicle for deviation from the Party line. In fact, it is possible to show that the presentation of individual fields of experience and imagination led automatically to the introduction of new forms of artistic representation. New forms and content completely undermined the Party's cultural agenda. It is purely to its subversive elements that GDR literature owes the large degree of that essential, universally necessary and universally appreciated vitality it undoubtedly contains. This is the direction which should be taken by all future work — with complete disregard for state, Party, and official aesthetics. In this way the writers can free themselves with a clear conscience from the idea of having to be a 'transmission belt' for a prescribed ideology. If they succeed in doing so, Heiner Müller's view will come into its own: 'Die Arbeit des Künstlers ist ein Privileg, weil sie ein Fest ist. Die Verstaatlichung des Festes oder seine Besetzung mit Ordnungsstrukturen widerspricht seinem Charakter, dem der Grenzüberschreitung.'[74] The wielders of political power tend to react allergically to those who break bounds. It is precisely this kind of counterbalance that we need, above all in the West. GDR authors who are experienced in the criticism of systems can be of assistance to us in this. The motto must therefore continue to be: a literature that transcends boundaries. The German 'October revolution' is behind us. What we need now is a revolution in the conditions of life. We must wait for the writers to show us the way to break these bounds.

NOTES

Translation by Sarah Brickwood and Arthur Williams.

1 *Die Zeit*, 29 December 1989. The literal translation of Gorbachev's remark runs, 'Dangers only await those who do not react to life' (see *Die Zeit*, 13 October 1989).

2 Both quoted from *Die Zeit*, 29 December 1989 ('Worte des Jahres').

3 The article by Christoph Hein is included in an anthology on the theme 'Für notwendige Erneuerung', *ndl*, vol. 38, no. 2, 1990, p. 186.

4 Heiner Müller: '"Nicht Einheit, sondern Differenz". Gespräch zur Revolution in der DDR', *Theater der Zeit*, no. 2, 1990, pp. 13—14; here p. 13. First published in *Deutsche Volkszeitung/die tat*, 24 November 1989.

5 *Oktober 1989. Wider den Schlaf der Vernunft*, Verlag Neues Leben, Berlin (GDR), and Elefanten Press, West Berlin, 1989. Volker Braun used the formulation 'Gegen den Schlaf der Vernunft' in one of two contributions to this collection (p. 153).

6 Volker Braun, interview of 18 October 1989 ('"Für notwedige Erneuerung", Dokumentation — Zweiter Teil', *ndl*).

7 Heiner Müller: *Zur Lage der Nation. Heiner Müller im Interview mit Frank M. Raddatz*, Berlin, 1990, p. 17. From a discussion on the theme 'Dem Terrorismus die Utopie entreißen. Die Alternative DDR'.

8 Monika Maron: 'Die Schriftsteller und das Volk', *Der Spiegel*, 12 February 1990, pp. 68 and 70; here p. 70. See also Helmut Peitsch's discussion of Maron's position, esp. pp. 176—7 below.

9 Benjamin Henrichs: 'Nothochzeit', *Die Zeit*, 23 March 1990.

10 *Scheibenwischer*, ARD broadcast, 22 March 1990.

11 *Die Zeit*, 30 March 1990.

12 Article 23 allows for the accession of the GDR, as individual *Länder* to the Basic Law, thus requiring no change to the constitution. It reads: 'Dieses Grundgesetz gilt zunächst im Gebiet der Länder Baden, Bayern [the list continues with the original *Länder* of the Federal Republic] In anderen Teilen Deutschlands ist es nach deren Beitritt in Kraft zu setzen.'

13 Friedrich Schiller: 'Der Zeitpunkt', *Sämtliche Werke in zwölf Bänden* ed. by Gustav Karpeles, Leipzig, no date, vol. 1, p. 286.

14 Manès Sperber, the foreword to Jürgen Rühle: *Literatur und Revolution. Die Schriftsteller und der Kommunismus in der Epoche Lenins und Stalins*, Frankfurt/Main, 1987, pp. 15—26; here p. 26.

15 Christa Wolf: 'Dankrede für den Geschwister-Scholl-Preis' (Munich, November 1987) in Wolf: *Ansprachen*, Darmstadt, 1988, p. 79; Christoph Hein: *Öffentlich arbeiten. Essais und Gespräche*, Berlin (GDR), 1987.

16 This was the title of one of the first accounts of GDR literature in the Federal Republic, Manfred Jäger: *Sozialliteraten. Funktion und Selbstverständnis der Schriftsteller in der DDR*, Düsseldorf, 1973.

17 Volker Braun: 'Rimbaud. Ein Psalm der Aktualität' (speech of 4 May 1984) in Braun: *Verheerende Folgen mangelnden Anscheins innerbetrieblicher Demokratie*, Frankfurt/Main, 1988, p. 118.

18 Wolf Biermann, song-writer and poet, was for many years banned from performing in the GDR until eventually, in 1976, he was refused re-entry into the GDR after a concert in Cologne. In the furore that followed many of the leading writers and intellectuals in the GDR came out in support of him.

19 Wolfgang Emmerich: *Kleine Literaturgeschichte der DDR*, rev. ed., Frankfurt/Main, 1989, p. 463.

20 Braun: *Verheerende Folgen...*, pp. 128f.

21 Emmerich: *Kleine Literaturgeschichte...*, p. 415.
22 In a television interview.
23 Günter de Bruyn: 'Der Holzweg' (1974) in de Bruyn: *Im Querschnitt. Prosa, Essay, Biographie*, Halle/Saale, 1979, pp. 331, 328.
24 Braun: *Verheerende Folgen...*, p. 125.
25 Ibid, p. 117.
26 Heiner Müller: 'Mich interessiert der Fall Althusser' (1981) in Müller: *Rotwelsch*, Berlin, 1982, p. 178.
27 This was drawn to my attention by my colleague Peter Peters. The expression was used in a special edition of the ARD programme *Brennpunkt*, 7 October 1989, entitled 'Reform oder Mauer? Gorbatschow in der DDR'.
28 Christa Wolf: 'Lesen und Schreiben' in Wolf: *Lesen und Schreiben. Neue Sammlung*, 3rd edn, Darmstadt, 1982, p. 48.
29 Christa Wolf: 'Die Dimension des Autors. Gespräch mit Hans Kaufmann', ibid, p. 75.
30 Letter from Gerhard Jahn of Karl-Marx-Stadt, *Die Zeit*, 30 March 1990.
31 Heiner Müller: 'Wie es bleibt, ist es nicht. Zu Thomas Brasch: "Kargo"' in *Rotwelsch*, p. 154.
32 Christa Wolf: 'Zum Erscheinen des Buches *Kassandra*' in Wolf: *Die Dimension des Autors. Essays und Aufsätze, Reden und Gespräche*, Darmstadt, 1987.
33 The reading in the Akademie der Künste was organized by Stephan Hermlin, who used the occasion to present Sarah Kirsch, Wolf Biermann and Volker Braun, among others, and who subsequently had to resign as secretary of the Academy. In the same year, Peter Huchel was relieved of his duties as editor-in-chief of *Sinn und Form*. The appearance of the poetry anthology by Endler and Mickel triggered off a fierce discussion which was pursued mainly in the FDJ magazine *Forum*. It was Endler who in 1971 again set off a debate on general principles, in the November edition of *Sinn und Form*, with his criticism of Hans Richter's conformist book *Verse, Dichter, Wirklichkeiten*. Similar controversies arose from the performance of Heiner Müller's adaptation of *Macbeth* in 1972.
34 See also the article by Elizabeth Boa (pp. 139—153 below, esp. p. 150) which, while it does not examine the controversy surrounding Nachdenken über Christa T., uncovers some of the challenging features of the book.
35 Braun's story appeared originally only in *Sinn und Form* (1975), putting it beyond the reach of the general public. It was not until 1988 that the text became available to the GDR public as a book.
36 The publication of *Kindheitsmuster* in 1976 was again the signal for a discussion of general principles (esp. in *Sinn und Form*, 1977). Wilhelm Girnus's harsh review of *Kassandra* (*Sinn und Form*, 1983) also caused a stir. Julian Preece, p. 311 below, points up the seminal influence exercised by Wolf's work in the late 1960s.
37 Cf. Emmerich: *Kleine Literaturgeschichte...*, p. 496. The same man, Hermann Kant, also played a role which hardly redounded to his credit in connection with the events subsequent to the exiling of Biermann (see Christa Wolf: 'Rede auf der Bezirksversammlung der Berliner Schriftsteller im März 1988', *Ansprachen*, pp. 87ff.). Typically enough, after the 'revolution', he did his utmost to put in a virtuoso performance as a weathercock before finally performing a vanishing act.
38 Günter Kunert: 'Wahrheit, Abstriche, Flugsand', *Die Zeit*, 5 August 1977.
39 Maron: 'Die Schriftsteller und das Volk'.
40 Quotations from the following: Volker Braun: 'Die Kipper', *Stücke I*, Frankfurt/Main, 1975, pp. 22, 47; Heiner Müller: 'Der Bau', *Stücke*, Berlin, 1975, pp. 139, 125, 130. Müller's play is teeming with critical remarks of this kind; to give but a sample: 'in unseren Büros ist der Abstraktionismus Fakt' (p. 119); 'Der Kommunismus ist was für die Zeitung' (p. 123); 'Der Plan, wenn er sich querstellt, ist ein Arschwisch' (p. 128); 'Und auf den Knien marschiert die Revolution' (p. 131).
41 Christa Wolf: *Nachdenken über Christa T.*, Darmstadt, 1971, p. 214.
42 Jürgen Wolf (ed.): *Materialien. Ulrich Plenzdorf: 'Die neuen Leiden des jungen W.'*, Stuttgart, 1980, p. 36.
43 Ernst Bloch: *Die Kunst, Schiller zu sprechen*, Frankfurt/Main, 1969, p. 30.
44 *Gartenlaube* — genteel family magazine.

45 The term is used by Christa Wolf ('Zum 80. Geburtstag von Hans Mayer', speech at the Akademie der Künste, West Berlin, March 1987, in *Ansprachen*, p. 42). She is, of course, taking up Ernst Bloch's famous phrase.

46 Charles Schüddekopf (ed.): *Wir sind das Volk. Flugschriften, Aufrufe und Texte einer deutschen Revolution*, Reinbek, 1990, pp. 207 (Stefan Heym), 208 (Christoph Hein).

47 Heinz Czechowski: 'Euphorie und Katzenjammer' in Michael Naumann (ed.): *Die Geschichte ist offen. DDR 1990: Hoffnung auf eine neue Republik. Schriftsteller aus der DDR über die Zukunftschancen ihres Landes*, Reinbek, 1990, p. 43.

48 For the appeal for an independent GDR, 26 November 1989, see Schüddekopf: *Wir sind das Volk...*, pp. 240f.

49 It seems that Christa Wolf, for example, was often asked for advice by those in the opposition, including the Leipzig demonstrators when there was the distinct threat that the order to shoot might be given.

50 Schüddekopf: *Wir sind das Volk...*, p. 206. The sense of the first example was echoed by a banner with the slogan 'Zensoren ab auf die Traktoren' (see *Oktober 1989...*, p. 169).

51 Naumann: *Die Geschichte ist offen...*, pp. 137 (Frank-Wolf Matthies), 72 (Stefan Heym).

52 Schüddekopf: *Wir sind das Volk...*, p. 202.

53 Ibid, pp. 15 (Volker Braun), 57 (Fritz Rudolf Fries).

54 Maron: 'Die Schriftsteller und das Volk'.

55 Augstein/Grass source *Der Spiegel* and TV; also published as Rudolf Augstein and Günter Grass: *DEUTSCHLAND, einig Vaterland? Ein Streitgespräch*, Göttingen, 1990.

56 *Die Zeit*, 2 February 1990.

57 Müller: 'Zur Lage der Nation', p. 55.

58 Hans Mayer: *Deutsche Literatur seit Thomas Mann*, Reinbek, 1967, p. 122.

59 Müller: 'Nicht Einheit, sondern Differenz', p. 14.

60 Interview with Fritz J. Raddatz: 'Das wehende Vakuum. Eindrücke von der DDR und der bitter-fröhlichen Beharrlichkeit ihrer Intellektuellen', *Die Zeit*, 15 December 1989.

61 Wilfried Mommert: 'Nachdenken über Deutschland. DDR-Autoren diskutieren auf Einladung von Walter Jens', *Aachener Nachrichten*, 26 February 1990.

62 Fritz Rudolf Fries: 'Braucht die neue Republik neue Autoren?' in Naumann: *Die Geschichte ist offen...*, pp. 53—7; here p. 56.

63 Helga Königsdorf: 'Im Gegenlicht' in Naumann: *Die Geschichte ist offen...*, pp. 83f.; here p. 84.

64 Fritz J. Raddatz: 'Das wehende Vakuum...'.

65 Müller: 'Zur Lage der Nation', p. 21.

66 Heiner Müller: 'Fernsehen' in *Oktober 1989...*, p. 31. 'Selbstkritik' is the third of the poem's three sections.

67 Heiner Müller: 'Nekrophilie ist Liebe zur Zukunft'. Heiner Müller in conversation with Frank Raddatz, 5th instalment, *Tansatlantik*, no. 4, 1990, pp. 40—5; here p. 45.

68 Volker Braun: 'Gegen den Schlaf der Vernunft' in *Oktober 1989...*, p. 154.

69 Monika Zimmermann: 'Sanftmütig. Die DDR-Autoren tagen', *FAZ*, 3 March 1990. See also notes 69 and 70.

70 Volker Hage: 'Drei Tage im März', *Die Zeit*, 9 March 1990.

71 Sibylle Wirsing: 'Lyriker und Realist', *FAZ*, 5 March 1990.

72 Müller: 'Nekrophilie ist Liebe...', pp. 40, 44.

73 Fries: 'Braucht die neue Republik...', p. 56.

74 Müller: 'Nekrophilie ist Liebe...', p. 41.

STEFAN HEYM:
A QUESTION OF IDENTITY

ROLAND SMITH

I Introduction

Stefan Heym returned to Germany, to what was now the GDR, in 1952, aged 39, in the expectation that, as a professional writer, he would be able to devote himself entirely to working for the cause of socialism. His main concern, he says in his autobiography, *Nachruf*, published in 1988,[1] was that, in a country where all the old social conflicts had been eliminated and Utopian conditions would henceforth prevail, there would be no place for the treatment of social and political issues which had provided the content of his work up to now and he would have to restrict himself to purely personal themes and settings.[2]

He had been three days in his new country when he discovered that this was not the case,[3] then, a few months later, there occurred the Uprising of 17 June 1953 and, with it, the subject of his first major work from within the GDR.[4] The course of the whole of his subsequent literary career was now determined and it will be the task of the present paper to trace something of his development. His early life and career will first be considered before going on to discuss three main issues: whether he is a German or an American writer, the importance of his Jewish heritage, and how far he can be considered a socialist author.

II Early Life and Career

He was born in 1913, Helmut Flieg, the first child of a middle class Jewish family in Chemnitz. They were, or thought they were, thoroughly integrated with the society around them and Heym describes how his father would admonish him and his younger brother to hold their heads up and their chests out during the regulation family Sunday walk, just as the members of every other self-respecting family did. A number of his uncles had served in the German Army during the Great War and, in common with the rest of the population, they all looked askance at the large numbers of 'Ostjuden' who had been flooding into Germany since before the conflict.

Like thousands of other Jewish people who had apparently been completely assimilated, the family did everything possible to conform, determinedly oblivious to the signs of trouble brewing around them in the later 1920s and it was not until 1931 that their first crisis occurred, precipitated by the young, precocious Helmut himself. He published a satirical poem on the 'successful export' of *Reichswehr* officers as advisers to Chiang Kai Shek's Kuomintang army, a forbidden topic in itself but, to make matters worse, he had done this in the local Social Democratic newspaper. It caused a tremendous furore and lead to his expulsion from the *Gymnasium*. He went to Berlin, to what was a still relatively liberal climate, where he stayed with relatives and took his *Abitur* the following year.

With the opportunities which the capital afforded, he began to frequent the literary café-society there, coming under the influence of such figures as Erich Kästner but, with the Nazi take-over and the burning of the Reichstag, it became increasingly obvious that nowhere in Germany was safe. What triggered his own flight was the arrest of his father back in Chemnitz as a hostage for himself, an early example of the Nazi practice of 'Sippenhaft', and the realization that the net was closing in on him too.[5] He therefore made his way to the Czech frontier, crossing by night on foot, and went to Prague where he stayed for two years, existing by means of his work for German-language newspapers in the Czech capital.[6]

In 1935 he was awarded a scholarship available to Jewish refugees for study in America and went initially to Chicago, where he wrote an M.A. thesis on Heinrich Heine, while continuing to contribute to Prague newspapers. In 1937, his scholarship having run out, he moved to New York to become the youthful editor of the *Volksecho*, a left-wing German-language newspaper. The whole enterprise was very much a shoestring operation, since the vast majority of German-Americans, if not active supporters of the Nazis, were impervious to any form of socialism and the whole enterprise foundered when the Nazi-Soviet pact of August 1939 was announced. Heym had no choice but to undertake a whole series of dead-end jobs, but he still managed to find the time to write, in English, his first major work, *Hostages*,[7] a powerful and surprisingly mature psychological study of the German occupation of Czechoslovakia. Orville Prescot, the then senior critic of the *New York Times*, called it one of the most significant novels to be published in the United States in 1942.[8]

By this time, America was itself embroiled in the War and Heym, having received American citizenship, was eligible for military service. He was called up in 1943, married an American woman of Polish-Jewish stock (unknown to him, a member of the Communist Party) and was enrolled in the Psychological Warfare Division of the US Army. In this unit he went through the Normandy Campaign, the Ardennes Offensive and the Battle for Germany, all of which feature in his bitter-sweet novel, *The Crusaders*, published in 1948.[9] It made the bestseller list, together with Norman Mailer's blockbuster of the war in the Pacific, *The Naked and the Dead*. The end of the War found Heym in Munich, where he was employed as leader writer on the official American newspaper, *Die Neue Zeitung*, but he found the attitude of the occupation forces increasingly frustrating. They seemed more concerned with running Germany as a successful enterprise and with their own material well-being than with rooting out the evil of Nazism in the German population. In addition, he was unhappy about their attitude to the Soviets, so he decided to resign his commission and return to the States.

The America of the later 1940s was, however, nothing like as welcoming as it had seemed in 1935. Even though *Crusaders* was a great success, the mood of the country seemed to have changed and when his next book, *The Eyes of Reason*,[10] dealing with the events in Czechoslovakia leading up to the Communist take-over, appeared in 1951 it was given a distinctly hostile reception.[11] This was just one manifestation of the general anti-left-wing climate in the country; racism and anti-Semitism were rife, fascist organizations were gaining in strength and McCarthyism was casting an ominous shadow across the land.[12] It seemed to Heym that what had happened in Germany in 1935 might be repeated here, so in 1952 Heym and his wife left the United States for Europe.

Their initial intention was to settle in Czechoslovakia, but in this they were to be disappointed, for if America had changed, so too had what was now known as the Czecho-Slovak Socialist Republic. The old happy-go-lucky atmosphere had been replaced by an impenetrable bureaucracy and a brooding Stalinism hung heavy in the air. In fact, as ex-Westerners, the Heyms were themselves in some danger, as the

Slansky show trial was in preparation,[13] but they were concious only of the frustration of having to chase all over eastern Europe to find a haven. When permission for them to settle was finally granted it came not from Prague but from Berlin, self-styled capital of the German Democratic Republic.

III A German or an American Writer?

Heym's arrival in Berlin in 1952 sparked off something of an identity crisis: was he a German or an American writer? He had had four novels published in America, all written in English and two of them bestsellers;[14] in addition, he had another English manuscript with him, with an exclusively American theme.[15] As a schoolboy in Chemnitz he had experienced anti-Semitism at the hands of neighbours and schoolfellows and had left Germany at some risk to life and limb in 1933. In America he had enjoyed the sweet smell of success in New York and been fêted as a literary lion at luncheon clubs all over the States, he had served with conviction in the US Army and the experience of being part of an occupying power had not left him with any great fellow-feeling for Germans. He decided therefore that, although willing to accept all the duties and obligations that citizenship of the German Democratic Republic would bring, he would continue to write in English. As he wrote in a letter at that time: 'Ich ziehe, obwohl der deutschen Sprache durchaus mächtig, das Englische vor, weil es konziser ist und besser geeignet, das auszudrücken, was ich zu sagen habe.'[16]

He was to continue to write the first version of a number of his works in English for another twenty years, and two of them, *The King David Report* (1973) and *The Queen Against Defoe* (1974), represent no mean linguistic feat, in that they involve the use of seventeenth- and eighteenth-century English style.[17] Walter Ulbricht indeed was to refer to him as 'der amerikanische Autor mit dem DDR-Paß'.[18]

Nevertheless, for all his affinity with English and particularly American style, we are still entitled to regard him as a German writer. All his early work, comprising short stories and non-fiction alike, was done in German, he translated his own middle-period novels into that language and his major works from the mid-1970s on have been written in German. In addition, the subject of the great majority of his books has been Germany, whether directly or indirectly.

However, it is much more difficult to place him as an East German author because, until the dramatic events of 1989, the great bulk of his work was never published in the GDR. Since his return to Germany he has published some two dozen works, the great majority of them dealing with historical or contemporary German themes but less than a quarter of these could appear in East Germany: of the seven major novels and the autobiography published between 1969 and 1989 only two works, *Der König-David-Bericht* (1973) and *Lassalle. Ein biographischer Roman* (1974),[19] could appear in East Berlin. The very first work he wrote in East Germany, *Fünf Tage im Juni*, was initially committed to paper in the same year as the events it describes, 1953, but it had to wait nearly thirty-seven years before it could appear in the GDR.

In West Germany, on the other hand, his works were published without delay and in 1988 Bertelsmann Verlag in Munich brought out a collected edition (*Werkausgabe*) of some fourteen volumes.[20] Not only were his books sold, he himself was in constant demand as a reader of his own work, as a contributor to newspapers and magazines, as a frequent guest at TV chat shows, and as a literary-cum-political guru in his own right. Given the East Germans' viewing habits, this meant that, in spite of the fact that very few of his works were available over there, he was very much in the public eye and ear. In 1985 he was able to say, with a mixture of bitterness and complacency: 'Ich kann wohl sagen, daß ich die bekannteste Unperson der Republik bin.'[21]

That this was no idle boast was shown by the fact that at the largest of all the demonstrations held in East Germany during the remarkable autumn of 1989, namely the one at Alexanderplatz in Berlin on 4 November, Heym should have been one of the four authors invited to speak, the others being Christoph Hein, Helga Königsdorf and Christa Wolf.[22] It was a fitting tribute for, more than any other GDR writer, Heym regarded the whole of Germany as his province and warned that the attempt to create two separate worlds was foredoomed to failure: 'Der Schrägstrich durch Deutschland markiert eine offene Wunde: wir können noch so viel Antibiotika darauf streuen, sie wird weiter eitern.'[23]

IV Heym's Jewishness

A further contribution to Heym's identity is that provided by his family background. While his parents did not regard themselves primarily as Jews but attempted to be just as German as their neighbours, Heym himself grew up in a climate where such factors were of ever increasing importance and could literally mean the difference between life and death. He himself exhibits a number of characteristics which we often associate with Jewish people, notably sheer vitality and power of survival, and these undoubtedly helped him make his way as a twenty-year-old exile, first in Czechoslovakia and then in America. The cosmopolitanism of the United States, with its model of the melting pot, made a strong appeal to him, coming as he did from the ever more intolerant, racialist Third Reich.

Heym has never displayed any sympathy for the ghetto-mentality depicted by many Jewish authors, not least the very few surviving in East Germany, such as Jurek Becker or Fred Wander.[24] Still less has he any use for the triumphant Zionism of a Leon Uris, having paid two visits to Israel but without gaining a very positive view of that country.[25]

Jewishness for him has two aspects, which are well illustrated in his novels *Der König-David-Bericht* (1972) and *Ahasver* (1981).[26] In the former case, it is the emerging monotheistic faith portrayed in the Books of Samuel and Kings in the Old Testament with its concept of a supreme, jealous God, summoning up great deeds of heroism and self-sacrifice but breeding also fanaticism and intolerance, and lending itself to manipulation and abuse by the powerful and unscrupulous. Here we have a model for later totalitarian régimes, with their insistence on absolute obedience and unswerving loyalty to higher authority, their witch-hunts, show trials and secret police.

Into this minefield there steps the unsuspecting figure of the historian Ethan Ben Hoshaja, whom King Solomon of Israel summoned ostensibly to write the official history of his great father, David, but in reality to provide a whitewash job which Solomon, as nasty a piece of work as they come, can then use to give himself and his régime the legitimacy he craves. It does not take Ethan more than a few days to discover that the great David he is supposed to commemorate in immortal words was in fact a cruel, bloodthirsty tyrant who destroyed practically everyone and everything he came into contact with. The problem of presenting David in a favourable light is, however, a minor one compared with the difficulty of extricating himself and his extended family from a land where, he now discovers, everyone's hand is against everyone else and where no one can be trusted. In the end Ethan does just manage to escape with his life but has to leave all his possessions behind, as well as two wives and one concubine.

Another aspect of Jewishness is the passive role of being a victim, which history has often demanded. Heym has very little time for the voluntary acceptance of the burden of the sins of others, as portrayed in Second Isaiah, but he is keenly alive to the danger of persecution. While still working for the US German-language press, he attended and reported on one of the very first concentration camp trials to be held after the War, that of a number of guards and supervisory staff of the camp at Belsen, arraigned before a British military tribunal in September 1945. The account he gave was quite factual and objective, but there can be no doubt that the revelations made must have come as a deep shock to him (he had, after all, lost almost all his wider family in the camps[27]) and made him highly sensitive to any hint of a resurgence of German nationalism.

In *Ahasver*, it is the image of the Jew as outcast which he seeks to portray. Ahasver is the Wandering Jew who, according to legend, refused Christ a last resting place and succour as the latter was groaning under the weight of the cross on his way to Calvary. As a punishment, he is condemned to everlasting pain and suffering, but in this life. Unable to find peace in death, he is the perpetual victim, appearing at key times in the history of the world and especially of the Jews — for instance, during their persecution at the time of the Reformation, or in the Warsaw ghetto in 1942. There now circulate reports that Ahasver has been sighted again at the end of the 1970s in Jerusalem, presumably presaging a further time of trouble because, with the build-up of nuclear weapons, Armageddon is at hand.

The action of the work occurs over two widely separated periods, the first one being that of the sixteenth century, when a young student and candidate for the ministry, von Eitzen, on his way to pay homage to Martin Luther and to further his own career, falls in with a certain Herr Leuchtentrager, a man of many parts, who soon becomes his guide, mentor and protector for the rest of his mortal life. This is, however, at the cost of his immortal soul, for Leuchtentrager is none other than the fallen angel, Lucifer, and at the end of the book he comes, together with Ahasver, to claim von Eitzen's soul. This is paralleled some four centuries later by a further plot involving Lucifer, only this time it comes in the form of a letter addressed to Professor Dr. Dr. Beifuß of the 'Institut für wissenschaftlichen Atheismus' in East Berlin from a certain Professor Jochanaan Leuchtentrager of the Hebrew University in Jerusalem. Beifuß is initially hesitant about involving himself in such correspondence but he is encouraged to proceed by the Ministerium für Hoch- und Fachschulwesen, which feels there might be some anti-Israeli mileage in it. In addition, it might help the GDR's credentials for the run-up to the Luther quincentenary, which was already being prepared in 1979.

As the correspondence develops, however, and Beifuß gets ever more deeply involved, his Party-minders grow uneasy about the whole affair, for dealings with the devil do not fit into any Marxist-Leninist categories; but by now it is too late, Beifuß is hooked just as firmly as von Eitzen had been all those years ago and once again Lucifer-Leuchtentrager and Ahasver come to claim their own, bearing Beifuß away over the Berlin Wall to the astonishment of the border guards stationed there.

Both of these works display a sureness of touch and a mastery in the ordering of material together with a stylistic dexterity which can make Heym worthy of consideration as a serious writer. They also display a quality which is often associated with Jewish life and culture, namely humour. In *Der König-David-Bericht*, for instance, there is a touch worthy of Woody Allen when the hero, Ethan, having been summoned to the court of King Solomon, has to present himself at the gate of Jerusalem. The captain of the watch asks him what his trade is and when Ethan replies that he is a historian the former makes a face: 'Historiker eh? Wir brauchen Steinmetzen, Maurer, Mörtelträger in Jerusholayim; sogar ein Schuster wäre von Nutzen, aber siehe, zu uns kommt ein Historiker.' Ethan demurs at this, but the captain goes on: 'Dieses Volk braucht eine Geschichte [...] wie ich ein Geschwür brauche an meinem Geschlecht.'[28]

Much of the humour in both of these works derives from the juxtaposition of the quaintly archaic and the startlingly contemporary. When, for instance, in the course of his researches into King David's background Ethan goes to question the witch at Endor about key figures in Israel's past, he is induced to take hashish. In the trance-like state thus brought about he beholds by the flickering light of the fire the shades of Saul, Samuel and David conjured up from the dead. He wakes up next morning with a naked witch in his arms and a bill: 'Einschließlich persönlicher Bedienung macht das vierundzwanzig Schekel.'[29]

Similarly delighful incongruities are to be found in *Ahasver* as the figures of Lucifer and the Wandering Jew stalk the streets of Berlin, Capital of the GDR, and cause chaos in a manner reminiscent of Bulgakov's saga of the devil at large in the Moscow of the 1930s in *The Master and Margarita*.[30] They come to join in the New Year's party at Prof. Dr. Dr. Beifuß's house, which is going with a real swing, and swing along with it until things are brought to a sudden halt by the disappearance of the host and these two latecomers coincident with the appearance of a large hole in the outside wall of the apartment. The *Volkspolizei* are sent for and suspect 'Republikflucht', so they in turn summon the *Stasi*, who confirm the fact of a 'real existierendes Loch' in the side of the building but are unable to take their enquiries any further, noting only the inexplicable smell of sulphur.[31]

V Stefan Heym and Socialism

While Jewish legend and mythology are important for Heym and have proved a fruitful source of inspiration for some of his best work, contemplation of his career leads to the conclusion that he belongs essentially to the line of Jewish thinkers, politicians and men of letters who have sought fulfilment for their Messianic drive in the attempt to establish a heaven upon earth through the various European socialist movements. It was, after all, the publication of an article in a Social Democratic newspaper which first brought him into conflict with the authorities and started him off on his geographical and intellectual odyssey at the age of seventeen. At the age of seventy-six, in December 1989, when most of his fellow citizens could not bear to hear the word, he could still write: 'Der Sozialismus ist vielmehr, oder sollte es sein, Freiheit, Gleichheit, Brüderlichkeit, plus soziale Gerechtigkeit, und er ist, wie Brecht sagte, das Einfache, das schwer zu machen ist.'[32]

Initially, when he first came to the newly founded GDR in 1952, it had all seemed straightforward. Having fought against Nazism and against fascism in all its forms both as a soldier and as a civilian, he would return to that part of Germany which had so completely purged itself of the evil and thus demonstrated its democratic credentials in an utterly convincing way. In this he was not alone:

Man darf nicht vergessen, daß die DDR in jener Zeit noch attraktiv war, und nicht nur für ausgesprochene Kommunisten; Linke der verschiedensten Schattierungen fühlten sich von ihr angezogen, Intellektuelle besonders; hier im Gegensatz zu der von den Amerikanern im Verbund mit recht zweifelhaften deutschen Gestalten verwalteten Bundesrepublik, experimentierte man mit neuen gesellschaftlichen Strukturen und suchte nach neuen Mustern menschlichen Verhaltens, oder gab zumindest vor, es zu tun, und die nur all-zu offensichtlichen wirtschaftlichen Schwierigkeiten, die Versorgungsmängel, und sogar die bereits beginnende Gängelei des Geisteslebens ließen sich glaubwürdig entschuldigen als Folgeerscheinungen des Hitlerkriegs; zum Teil waren sie es auch.[33]

Like Heym, such figures as Bert Brecht, Anna Seghers, Willi Bredel, Ernst Bloch, Ludwig Renn, Stephan Hermlin and Arnold Zweig had returned from exile because they had the conviction that they were engaged in a great and worthwhile enterprise and that, as creative writers and members of the intelligentsia, they had a key role to play in the collective adventure of creating a new society. In return, they could enjoy material advantages denied to the great mass of the population, together with special privileges, such as access to the ear of the highest in the land; and here Heym relates an incredible incident in his *Nachruf*.

One day in 1953, not long after the Uprising of 17 June, he was rung up by one of Walter Ulbricht's aides, who instructed him that the General Secretary wished to have informal contact with the people and would like Heym to help. The latter suggested that they meet and simply go for a stroll in the suburb of Köpenick, popping into a few shops and having a chat with passers-by. He stressed that Ulbricht must come in an unmarked car, without escort, and have no attendant flunkeys or bodyguards on their walkabout. He proposed that they meet outside Köpenick Town Hall. At the appointed day and time, however, a whole cavalcade of limousines appeared from which the General Secretary emerged to greet Heym then, instead of a tour of the streets, all they did was to make an inspection of the building, where Ulbricht gave the Bürgermeister and other members of the town hall staff a quick grilling, before sweeping out again and away in the cars.[34]

While such encounters must have enhanced the sense which GDR writers and artists had of their own importance in a way inconceivable in the West, there was a price to be paid for such privileges. This was the principle that he who pays the piper calls the tune, and it meant that all the songbirds whom the GDR maintained at such expense had to sing in harmony. The régime was rigid, dogmatic and inflexible, clinging anxiously to the Soviet model and requiring its authors to provide copy-book heroes for the population at large

This was a task for which Heym was uniquely unfitted, for all his heroes have faults, even if not actual feet of clay, and there was no way in which he could provide models on which others could pattern themselves.[35] His difficulties began with the work initially entitled *Der Tag X* and published, as mentioned above (p. 51), under the title *Fünf Tage im Juni*, for while Heym was quite willing to accept the official version that the Uprising was mainly the work of Western agents, he makes clear in the work that the Party was by no means blameless: the works' party-secretary, Banggartz, for instance, being portrayed as a contemptible man of straw, while the workers are loud in their complaints, though never, of course, rejecting the principle of socialism.

While progress on the publication of *Der Tag X* was stalled, Heym was by no means idle. He turned to the press. Divided Germany and particularly Berlin, with a front line between two world systems through the middle, made perfect territory for him, with his gifts as a journalist and polemicist. Before the Wall was put up, for instance, there was a great deal of illicit trade (in GDR law), with people from the GDR selling produce at relatively cheap prices in the West, in order to bring back luxury items for personal use or further trading. In his *Nachruf*, Heym relates that he would sometimes mingle with them, even pretending to be a smuggler himself, and describes how on one occasion he came across a young girl who had just been caught and was now waiting for the customs officials to deal with her. She asked him for the loan of a penknife and then, with tears streaming down her face, proceeded to cut to pieces a pair of shoes of the latest fashion which would have cost a fortune in GDR money: '"Die", sagt sie, und die, das sind die hinter der Tür, die sich mit ihr beschäftigen werden, "die sollen meine Schuhe nicht haben."'[36]

Such a cameo can convey much more than pages of the standard stodgy fare offered by the GDR press, but Heym, who was allowed to contribute a weekly column to the *Berliner Zeitung* under the title 'Offen gesagt' had to keep his journalist's impulses on a very tight rein. Even so, it was not long before he fell foul of authority. The occasion was the publication in April 1957 of the 'Göttingen Manifesto', a declaration by eighteen prominent West German physicists, including Max Born, Otto Hahn, Werner Heisenberg and Carl Friedrich von Weizsäcker, in which they appealed for the Federal Republic to renounce the use of any kind of nuclear weapon and declared their own refusal to cooperate in any related research. This was, of course, given full coverage in the GDR media, but it soon became apparent that nowhere in the GDR was a full copy of the text available. Heym therefore, after some correspondence with his readers, took it upon himself to publish the text, including the one crucial, missing sentence: 'Wir bekennen uns zur Freiheit, wie sie heute die westliche Welt gegen den Kommunismus vertritt.'[37]

As Heym saw it, this was precisely the part which gave the manifesto its impact, but the point was lost on the hierarchy, for whom protocol had been abused. After crisis meetings within the *Berliner Zeitung*, Heym was summoned to the august presence of Horst Sindermann, responsible for agitation and propaganda, who informed him that the Party would give permission for the column to continue, provided its author agreed to accept 'guidance'. This, for Heym, was tantamount to censorship, and he refused. In such a manner did his career as a journalist in the GDR come to an end; henceforth all his writing in this category would be published only in the West.

Inevitably, while his faith in socialism never wavered and he would stoutly defend the idea to his Western audience, his relationship with the authorities at home and with 'real existing socialism', as it came to be known, was subjected to increasing strain throughout the 1950s, 1960s and 1970s. The Berlin Uprising of 1953 had come as a great shock; it was followed by the Twentieth Congress of the Communist Party of the Soviet Union and the revelation of some of Stalin's crimes in 1956, the Hungarian Revolution later that year, the erection of the Berlin Wall in 1961, the invasion of Czechoslovakia in 1968, the policy of 'Abgrenzung' followed by the GDR in its relations with West Germany during the late 1960s and the 1970s, and the expulsion of Wolf Biermann in November 1976.

Since, for most of this time, Heym was denied the opportunity of expressing himself in the media of the GDR, he was forced to rely on West German and other foreign publications, and it was this which led to his being arraigned at the notorious Eleventh Plenum of the Central Committee, convened on 16—18 December 1965 specifically to discuss cultural matters.

In introducing this, Erich Honecker, presumably in his capacity as Central Committee Secretary for Security, made a wide-ranging attack on a number of East German writers, including Manfred Bieler, Wolf Biermann, Werner Bräunig, Heiner Müller and Stefan Heym. He accused them of arrogantly disregarding their primary function, which was to disseminate optimism and encouragement among the toiling masses of the GDR: 'Sie irren sich, wenn sie die Arbeitsteilung in unserer

Republik so verstehen, daß die Werktätigen die sozialistische Gesellschaftsordnung aufopferungsvoll aufbauen und andere daran nicht teilzuhaben brauchen, daß der Staat zahlt und andere das Recht haben, den lebenverneinenden, spießbürgerlichen Skeptizismus als alleinseligmachende Religion zu verkünden.' Not to be outdone, Walter Ulbricht joined in: 'Einige Kulturschaffende haben die große schöpferische Freiheit, die in unserer Gesellschaftsordnung für die Schriftsteller und Künstler besteht, so verstanden, daß die Organe der Gesellschaft auf jede Leitungstätigkeit verzichten und Freiheit für Nihilismus, Halbanarchismus, Pornographie oder andere Methoden der amerikanischen Lebensweise gewähren.' Heym himself was specifically mentioned by Horst Sindermann, who asked the rhetorical question: 'Woher kommt eigentlich der geistige Hochmut bei solchen Leuten wie Stefan Heym, an die Stelle der historisch gesetzmäßigen Führung durch die Partei der Arbeiterklasse eine Führung durch eine eingebildete Elitemission einiger Schriftsteller zu fordern?'[38]

Christa Wolf was the only person present to raise her voice in protest, but her objections were brushed aside and Stefan Heym, who of course was not a Party member, was summoned to the Ministry of the Interior the day after the conference finished to be solemnly cautioned by Minister Dickel against spreading disinformation about the GDR in West Germany and other foreign parts.[39]

There was no follow-up to this outbreak of neo-Stalinism, at least as far as Heym himself was concerned, though he was kept under surveillance for a time during the Biermann Affair, as were many others.[40] Heym, in fact, was able to make use of the experience he had gained through the summons to the Ministry of the Interior in his novel *Collin*, which was published in the West in 1979 and which constituted a far more direct and outspoken attack on persisting Stalinist practices in the GDR than anything he had previously written.[41]

The counterattack this time took the form of a visit by two customs officials, who 'arrested' his savings bankbook and took him in for questioning. He was subsequently tried at a court in Köpenick and found guilty of currency offences against the GDR by not disclosing the full amount of his earnings from the sale of his works in the West. He was fined 9,000 (East German) Marks, which he paid under protest because, he insisted, the real issue was not currency but censorship. In fact, this fine turned out to be a first-class investment, for the tremendous amount of West German media coverage of the affair helped the sale of his books in the Federal Republic enormously.[42]

Potentially much more serious was a new paragraph (no. 219) added to the penal code and obviously aimed at GDR writers publishing in West Germany. It provided for six-figure fines and for prison sentences of from two to three years and was so obviously targeted on one person that it became known as the 'Lex Heym'.[43] Had it been implemented, it would have seriously affected the fortunes (in both senses) of a number of East German writers; however, it was never applied, for, with the 1980s, remarkable changes were occurring internationally which were to send tremours throughout the GDR, well in advance of the final cataclysmic shock.

The consequence for Heym was a period of quiet after his brushes with authority. It was not however a time of repose, for during the 1980s he made full use of the opportunity to travel to the Federal Republic and to give interviews to the Western media; he was also able to address citizens of the GDR, though initially this was in churches only. In an interview with the foreign correspondent of the Italian Communist Party newspaper *L'Unita*, given in May 1989, he welcomed the arrival of Gorbachev and hoped it would mean an end to the Leninist concept of a 'Party of governesses':

> Gouvernanten aber praktizieren keine Demokratie; sie führen Aufsicht und strafen die Unbotmäßigen; und so nützlich sie auch eine Weile lang sein mögen, sie sind nicht fürs ganze Leben brauchbar. Vor allem gerät man mit den Methoden der Gouvernanten in einen bösen Widerspruch zum Zweck der Sache: Von ewig am Gängelband gehaltenen, kleinen Kreaturen kann man bestenfalls unkritischen Gehorsam erwarten, nicht aber, daß sie etwas so Kompliziertes wie den Sozialismus erfolgreich erbauen — der Sozialismus, hat sich herausgestellt, ist eine Aufgabe für denkende Bürger, nicht für eine Klasse Unmündiger.[44]

VI Heym's Place in GDR Literature

In a number of ways Heym's position is unique. He is the only author still alive who had produced a considerable *oeuvre* before the GDR was even founded, most of it of course in English. Unlike Brecht, he has survived long enough to build up a still more considerable corpus of work since his return to Germany and, unlike Anna Seghers, he has enhanced his reputation since that return. This second career of his spans virtually the whole of what we, presumably, will continue to call 'GDR Literature'.

Nor can there be any question of his having lost his touch as he has grown older. Such is his vitality that he has not only sustained a huge output of original work but, particularly during the 1980s, he has involved himself in public affairs through his journalism and his many public appearances to such an extent that many have come to regard him as the spokesman for literature and the arts. As already mentioned in this article, it is significant that Heym should have been invited to speak at the huge Alexanderplatz demonstration on 4 November 1989, together with two people whom many would regard as the most distinguished literary figures the GDR has produced, Christa Wolf and Christoph Hein.

When we survey the great quantity of Heym's own work, inevitably the question arises: has this been produced at the expense of quality? It must be admitted that there is no simple answer, his narrative flow being very strong but his power of characterization weak; he could, therefore, be dismissed as a mere potboiler. Great historical figures, such as Lassalle, appeal to him, but his approach is to show their feet of clay, rather than to bring out the special qualities which made them distinctive. His female characters in particular are lacking in clarity of outline and in internal realization.

The problem Heym faces as an author is the perennial one facing the historical novelist: how do you deal with the sheer mass of material needed for authenticity without suffocating the characters which must be created to make it all come alive? It is a difficulty Heym is never fully able to resolve, and one of the reasons is that he is as much a journalist as he is a creative writer. Reinhard Zachau makes precisely this point in his monograph on Heym, written in 1982: 'Das Ausformulieren von stilistischen Feinheiten, das Feilen an literarischen Formen, das Überarbeiten von Texten überhaupt erscheinen ihm auch bei den Romanen nicht als notwendig. Alles ist aus dem Augenblick entstanden und zur sofortigen Verarbeitung bestimmt.'[45] In other words, Heym does not regard his works as finished products but rather as contributions to a continuing debate, their purpose being to stimulate and provoke, rather as a good leading article in a newspaper might do. Konrad Franke makes much the same point in his work *Die Literatur der Deutschen Demokratischen Republik*: 'Der Schriftsteller Stefan Heym ist ein Journalist, veilleicht auch ein Unterhaltungsautor, der sich tarnt [...] der Unterhalter kaschiert seine Absichten mit Literatur.'[46]

The implication here, however, is that Heym is essentially a pop-ular writer attempting to achieve significance by latching on to large is-sues, something which both misunderstands the situation of the artist in a socialist society and Heym's own achievement in tackling tough themes. It is true that he did not settle in the GDR until the worst ex-cesses of Stalinism were over, but the neo-Stalinism operated by both Ulbricht and Honecker was difficult and dangerous enough for anyone intent on surveying the contemporary situation.

The above quotation from the work by Franke also seriously undervalues Heym's performance as a journalist. If we look at the stodgy fare provided by the media in East Germany over four decades, Heym's own contribution, brief though it was, positively sparkles.[47] To this extent we can argue that his journalism deserves just as much consideration as his 'serious' works of literature.

Where we can say Heym departs from the received notion of a serious author is the way in which he regards a work of art not as something complete in itself but as a contribution to a continuing dia-logue. In this he has something in common with socialist realism which also views the arts as one stage in a process. Whereas socialist realism sees it as the function of literature to create exemplary models and thus to act as a moulding force in bringing about a new society, Heym sees literature as essentially a stimulus, designed to provoke and bring about discussion. By such a criterion, the lack of polish and of fine writing in his work and his relative indifference towards the German language may not be the disadvantage it seems.[48]

However that may be, there can be no doubt that Heym has made an important contribution to the culture of what was the German Democratic Republic. When considering his situation vis-à-vis other writers there we have to remember that he arrived in the Republic already virtually fully formed as an artist. Since then he has gone his own way and remained very much his own man while yet being in-volved in the thick of the action; and he has stuck it out where numerous younger contemporaries, though born and bred in the GDR, found the action too much for them and fled to the West. He has made a unique contribution to the chapter entitled 'GDR Literature', which will surely remain for ever a part of the German literary heritage.

NOTES

1 Stefan Heym: *Nachruf*, Munich, 1988.
2 Ibid, p.534.
3 Stefan Heym: *Wege und Umwege. Streitbare Schriften aus fünf Jahrzehnten*, ed. by Peter Mallwitz, Munich, 1980, pp. 252—3.
4 *Fünf Tage im Juni*, published in West Germany (Munich) in 1974 and in what was still the GDR (Berlin) in 1990. The original title was *Der Tag X*.
5 Heym's father, who was a manic depressive, was not held for long but later committed suicide before his son could bring him and the family over to America.
6 Once he had crossed the Czech border, he changed his name to Stefan Heym, mainly so that he could remain in contact with his family without endangering them. See Heym: *Nachruf*, pp. 83—4.
7 Stefan Heym: *Hostages*, New York, 1942 (= *Der Fall Glasenapp*, Leipzig, 1958; Munich, 1976).
8 Heym: *Nachruf*, p. 223.
9 Stefan Heym: *The Crusaders*, Boston, 1948 (= *Kreuzfahrer von heute*, Leipzig, 1950; *Der bittere Lorbeer*, Munich, 1950).
10 Stefan Heym: *The Eyes of Reason*, Boston, 1951 (= *Die Augen der Vernunft*, Leipzig, 1955; Munich, 1950).
11 Heym: *Nachruf*, pp. 465—9.
12 The threat of McCarthyism was felt particularly by Hollywood scriptwriters and film directors. Heym relates how he attended a party in Manhattan to send off two of their number to face the Committee for Unamerican Activities. The experience caused him to think back to the farewell party for Carl von Ossietzky, editor of the left-wing periodical, *Weltbühne*, who had also gone to prison in some style but who was tortured by the Nazis, as a result of which he died in 1938 (Ibid, pp. 472—4).
13 Rudolf Slansky, Secretary General of the Czech Communist Party, was arrested in November 1951 on a charge of being a 'dangerous agent of imperialism' and, after a well-publicized trial which exhibited some markedly anti-Semitic features, executed in December 1952. See François Fejtö: *A History of the People's Democracies*, Harmondsworth, 1974, pp. 14—22.
14 These are the three mentioned in notes 7, 9 and 10 above and *Of Smiling Peace*, Boston, 1944.
15 Stefan Heym: *Goldsborough*, Leipzig, 1953; New York, 1954. Later published in German as *Die Liebe der Miss Kennedy*, Berlin (GDR), 1958, and as *Goldsborough*, Munich, 1978.
16 Heym: *Nachruf*, p. 584.
17 Stefan Heym: *Die Schmähschrift oder Die Königin gegen Defoe*, Zurich, 1970; Leipzig, 1974 (*The Queen against Defoe and Other Stories*, New York, 1974). *Der König-David-Bericht*, Munich, 1972; Berlin (GDR), 1973 (*The King David Report*, New York, 1973).
18 Heym: *Nachruf*, p. 730.
19 Stefan Heym: *Uncertain Friend*, London, 1969 (= *Lassalle. Ein biographischer Roman*, Munich, 1969).
20 Published by the Bertelsmann Verlag.
21 Stefan Heym: *Einmischung*, ed. by Inge Heim and Heinfried Henniger, Gütersloh, 1990, p. 151.
22 There were, in fact, other authors present, including Heiner Müller, plus representatives of the Church and the various reform movements. See Hubertus Knabe (ed.): *Aufbruch in eine andere DDR*, Hamburg, 1990, p. 314. See also Theo Buck's reference to this demonstration, pp. 35—6 above.
23 Heym: *Einmischung*, p. 40. See also Stuart Parkes's contribution, particualrly p. 198 below.
24 Fred Wander, born 1917 in Vienna, settled with his wife, Maxie, in the GDR in 1958. His book, *Der siebente Brunnen*, about his experiences in Auschwitz and Buchenwald, appeared in 1970 (Aufbau-Verlag, Berlin and Weimar), a year or so after Becker's *Jakob der Lügner* (1969, also with the Aufbau-Verlag).

25 Heym's first visit was in 1948, not long after the new state of Israel had been founded. He was disappointed on two counts: first, that Israel had not unequivocally declared itself a socialist state and thrown in its lot with the poeple's democracies and, secondly, that anti-Semitism had not disappeared from eastern Europe with the defeat of the Nazis. See Heym: *Nachruf*, pp. 445—52.

26 Stefan Heym: *Ahasver*, Munich, 1981.

27 In fact, he was later to discover that he had also lost a very close relative. During the latter part of his two years spent in Prague (1933—1935) he had a liaison with a Czech girl, Vera, who, unknown to him, had then borne his child, a girl, after his departure for America. This child had been adopted by a Jewish family and was gassed with them in Auschwitz. See Heym: *Nachruf*, p. 650.

28 Heym: *Der König-David-Bericht*, p. 22.

29 Ibid, p. 104.

30 Mikhail Bulgakov's *The Master and Margarita* was written in 1938 and published in English by Harvill in 1967.

31 Heym: *Ahasver*, p. 228.

32 Heym: *Einmischung*, p. 271.

33 Heym: *Nachruf*, pp. 542—3.

34 Ibid, pp. 574—7.

35 Heym was firm on this point right from the beginning. In an article for the *Berliner Zeitung*, 'Beobachtungen zum literarischen Leben in der DDR', published in July 1953, he wrote: 'Man muß den Leser dazu bringen, sich mit einer oder mehreren Figuren im Buch zu identifizieren; mit Figuren, die Leitartikel reden oder sich leitartikelhaft benehmen, kann man sich aber nur schwer identifizieren.' (Heym: *Wege und Umwege*, p. 279.)

36 Heym: *Nachruf*, p. 665.

37 Ibid, p. 622.

38 Manfred Jäger: *Kultur und Politik in der DDR*, Cologne, 1982, pp. 116—7.

39 Heym: *Nachruf*, pp. 709—12.

40 Heym recounts two meetings of well-known GDR authors during this period. The first, with Stephan Hermlin in the chair, decided on the wording of a letter of protest at the treatment of Biermann; the second, called by one of the Party leaders, Werner Lamberz, was an attempt to get the writers to retract, which very few did. Heym appears to have been not at all disconcerted by *Stasi* surveillance and made a close study of their techniques, which he made use of in his novel *Collin*. See Heym: *Nachruf*, pp. 799-811.

41 Stefan Heym: *Collin*, Munich, 1979.

42 Heym: *Nachruf*, p. 834.

43 Ibid.

44 Heym: *Einmischung*, pp. 224—5.

45 Reinhold Zachau: *Stefan Heym*, Munich, 1982, p. 11.

46 Konrad Franke: *Die Literatur der Deutschen Demokratischen Republik*, Munich, 1971, p. 322.

47 See for example Heym's essay about East German television published in *Stern* on 10 February 1977 under the title 'Je voller der Mund, desto leerer die Sprüche'. (In Heym: *Wege und Umwege*, pp. 404—14.)

48 Zachau: *Stefan Heym*, p. 12.

HEINER MÜLLER AND THE GERMAN QUESTION

AXEL SCHALK

> *Die Westdeutschen meinen, daß sie das bessere Los gezogen haben,*
> *[...] und von ihrem Standpunkt aus haben sie das auch. Die*
> *Mehrzahl der westdeutschen Bevölkerung findet ihre Identität im*
> *Standard der Deutschen Mark [...] Die eigentliche Gefahr für uns*
> *ist, daß die Westmark auch unser Standard wird.*
> (Heiner Müller: *Rotwelsch*, p. 56)

> *Die Partei [...] war zum Staat selbst, zum Inbild des Unabänder-*
> *lichen, Definitiven, Versteinerten geworden [...] das, je fester es*
> *sich etabliert hatte, desto mörderischer werden mußte.*
> (Peter Weiss: *Die Ästhetik des Widerstands*, III, p. 56)

I Writing in the Face of the Wall

Heiner Müller is one of the few contemporary authors whose work in its entirety reflects a radical and persistent preoccupation at both a theoretical and a literary level with the German Problem in its historical and contemporary manifestations. Not without good reason is the East Berlin author known as 'Deutschland-Müller'. It is peculiarly paradoxical that his case, even biographically, is an all-German one. First honoured in the GDR, where he was awarded the Heinrich Mann Prize in 1959, and repudiated like Bertolt Brecht by the Federal Republic of the Cold War years, he was then expelled from the GDR *Schriftstellerverband* in 1961, the year of the building of the Wall, in the wake of the wretched public debate about the performance of his play *Die Umsiedlerin oder das Leben auf dem Lande*.[1] Reprisals against his wife followed, to make her divorce the 'Schwein'.[2]

We may certainly regard Müller as a victim of the Stalinism of the 1960s: according to the testimony of the East German theatre producer Fritz Marquart, these were years of bitter poverty. Yet Müller never moved away from the state he lived in, for which he was explicitly writing.[3] Only in the late 1970s did his plays begin to be performed widely in the theatres of the Federal Republic, ensuring his public discovery. A wave of first performances followed, particularly at the Schauspielhaus in Bochum; an important trigger was the first performance of *Germania Tod in Berlin*, the key text on the German Problem, under the directorship of Ernst Wendt in Munich in 1978.[4] The 'rehabilitation' of a GDR author was thus achieved through the reception of his work in West German theatres.

Müller has always been dogged by the dilemma of German schizophrenia. It was only after the change in the political climate in the Soviet Union that he was accepted by GDR theatres, even then with great reluctance and too late: the high point came with his own, legendary production of *Der Lohndrücker* at the Deutsches Theater in East Berlin in 1987.[5] Now, after the opening of the Wall, he is caught in the vacuum of the GDR public's lack of interest. Marquart's production of *Germania* with the Berliner Ensemble, for example, and the electric performance of *Leben Gundlings Friedrich von Preußen Lessings Schlaf Traum Schrei* at the Volksbühne in East Berlin played to empty houses.[6]

We have to interpret the case of Heiner Müller in biographical terms and in terms of his work as an expression of the negative German-German dialectic. It redounds to his credit that he has always been able to rise above his personal difficulties to attain a dialectical, abstract distance, viewing the German Problem with the eyes of a Marxist who had to suffer the problems of 'real existing socialism' in the GDR. In December 1989, the GDR's wild, revolutionary month, Müller himself noted that his was a 'distanziertes Verhältnis zur DDR'.[7]

Even before the so-called 'change' came about, as one who was able in the 1980s to travel freely, Müller took up a position above any East-West antagonism — between the stools, as it were: 'on the Wall'. Because he was able to travel, his perceptions were all-German; however, in spite of his critical coolness, his political and ideological home remained the failed socialist experiment, the GDR: 'Ich stehe mit je einem Bein auf zwei Seiten der Mauer. Das ist vielleicht eine schizophrene Position, aber mir scheint keine andere real genug.'[8]

In spite of its Stalinism and its Prussian, goose-stepping mentality, the de facto existence of the GDR allowed Müller to think in Utopian terms, thus when he writes about Germany he is exploring the possibility of socialism, attempting to work at socialism. As a commuter across the border, Müller almost needed the Wall through Germany in order to formulate an ideologically unassailable mid-way position. In spite of its inhumanity, the Wall was for Müller, as becomes apparent from the interview with Sylvère Lothringer quoted above, a perceivable symbol[9] of the general schizophrenia of a world divided into two. Thus Müller's reflections on the problem of Germany and on the writer's position in Germany in the 1970s proceed on a global basis, from the division of the world. It was the East-West dialectic, the 'siebzigjährige kalte Krieg gegen die Sowjetunion'[10] (like Marxism, a fundamental premise for Müller's work) which had created the division and its Wall, 'ein Zeichen für die reale Situation, in der die Welt sich befindet'.[11] In this connection, Müller is a completely committed writer.

One of Müller's central poetic positions arises from the idea of the two realities. When the author's photograph is torn up in *Die Hamletmaschine* (1977), a key text for the 1970s,[12] it signals the negative dialectic in Müller's *oeuvre*. The author, who was allowed to cross the frontier of concrete and barbed wire, has a dual experience between Friedrichstraße and Bahnhof Zoo. Two civilizations mutually exclude each other, the failed attempt at Utopia and the cold, consumer society of the West: 'Man fährt da wirklich durch eine Zeitmauer.'[13]

Müller's experience of the division was quite different from Uwe Johnson's. Müller found writing within the 'Zeitmauer' productive at the poetic level; at least he did not practise his art in the GDR in any degree in order to produce merchandise but in order to be socially effective, in the hope of a 'new age'[14] - beyond any SED phraseology about 'real existing socialism'. In Johnson's case, the division led to a literature of conjecture and linguistic scepticism, to the attempt to re-think the concepts. In his 1961 text *Berliner Stadtbahn (veraltet)*, Johnson describes the difficulty of writing in a way not susceptible to ideological interpretation about the daily routine of travelling on the S-Bahn from one part of the city to the other. The border acts 'wie eine literarische Kategorie. Sie verlangt, die Sprache zu verändern'.[15] The very expression Berlin is euphemistic.

For Müller, the problem of the two German literatures simply did not arise; the only theme he admitted was the Stalinist tragedy of socialism as it was experienced by a whole generation, for example Thomas Brasch, as 'deformierte Realität'.[16] For Müller, writing and suffering because of concrete social circumstances were inseparably intermingled; the process described by Johnson is reversed in the case of Müller; GDR society is reflected within the topos of tragedy. The result of this was a stance of cynical distancing which exploited difference, the antagonisms in society, as the basis for productive writing. The brutal symbol of the

GDR dictatorship, the result of the division of the world, assumed a productive character which typified the tragedy of socialism in a surprising way: '[Die] Mauer [...] ist auch ein Denkmal für Rosa Luxemburg und Karl Liebknecht.'[17] It was Stalin's monument to them, since Stalinism had served to petrify their idealism, their undogmatic stance. The dialectical attitude examined the situation without succumbing to the emotional call for the removal of the Wall.

Germany, the 'pale mother' of Brecht's metaphor,[18] paid hommage to a malignant tradition, as Müller wrote in 'Panizza oder Die Einheit Deutschlands' in 1979. The intellectual, reflecting an all-German condition, was the scapegoat, 'Gotteslästerer und Staatsfeind'.[19] Müller's poetic position was, then, the result of a properly formulated concept of continuity, a historical view which was prefigured in Brecht. In his note on *Mutter Courage und ihre Kinder*, which no dogmatic Marxist could ever have countenanced, Brecht spoke of the Peasant Wars as the greatest 'Unglück der deutschen Geschichte'.[20] In this interpretation, the revolution came too soon, it was brutally suppressed; similarly the Thirty Years' War destroyed German national character. Again in 1848 Germany failed to make the European connection and the experience of history became one of opportunity missed. 'Und nun hängt das Land [...] zwischen Ost und West, und immer hat es Angst, keine Individualität zu haben.'[21] Müller drew the conclusion that the country had a death-urge. Germany history had to follow its own special path, leading to fascism and defeat in the War.

Writing about Germany therefore became an attack on a murderous continuity from which had issued two states which, armed to the teeth, marked the intersection of the two worlds. According to Müller, the GDR had the weaker position because it had lost the Second World War and had not had the benefit of Marshall Aid for its reconstruction. The 'deferred question', the 'Germany Question' became one of 'life and death' for Müller in the early 1980s at a time of tit-for-tat arming.[22] Maintaining the status quo could never be a solution. The consequence of this was the appearance in Müller's theatre of surreal images, images depicting German history (in a way reminiscent of Hans Henny Jahnn) as a slaughterhouse, images of an insane system of real and potential violence.

And yet the author rejected unification; he placed his hope in the third way as the 'große Bedrohung für den Westen und die große Hoffnung für unsere Seite', the GDR.[23] Thus writing about a country ensued from reflection and observation, the opposition to unification from poetic interest in conflict.

II Scenes from the German Chamber of Horrors

The five scenes of the play *Die Schlacht* can be regarded as Müller's first tentative approach to German history. The point of departure is typical for Müller: not only does he take fascism as his theme, death features in all parts of the scenario, which was created between 1951 and 1974. Germany is identical with terror, *Trauerarbeit* begins at the most extreme point in history, which is depicted as an act of self-dismemberment. In DIE NACHT DER LANGEN MESSER, Müller's metaphorical use of the English term to describe the night when the Reichstag was destroyed by fire, Müller's dialectic is demonstrated in its most extreme form: A. and B., two completely interchangeable figures, meet in a *Gestapo*, or is it a *Stasi*, cell. Theatre becomes a process of recollection which confirms place and time. The actual facts of the action, death in fascist Germany, stand in their own right:

> A. Ich sehs an dir: du hast es weit gebracht.
> Kriech in dein Fell, Hund, draußen bellt die Meute
> Und beiß dir deinen Anteil aus der Beute.
> [...]
>
> B. Ich hab geschwiegen im Gestapokeller.
> Als ich herauskam war der Tag nicht heller.
> Ihr seid an mir vorbeigegangen fremd
> Mein Blut war noch nicht trocken unterm Hemd.
> [...]
>
> *Zieht das Braunhemd an*
> Mein Kauf war, wo ein Hund ist ist ein Fell
> Das Braunhemd, rechtsum dreht das Karusell
> [...]
> Das war. Ich hab mir auf den Grund gesehn.
> Die Nacht der Langen Messer fragt wer wen.
> Ich bin der eine und der andre ich.
> Einer zu viel. Wer zieht durch wen den Strich.
> [...]
>
> A. Und als die Unsren in den Kellern schrien
> Die Langen Messer schnitten durch Berlin
> Hab ich getötet den Verräter, meinen Bruder, ihn.[24]

The theme of this short scene is fratricidal war, it thus uncovers archaeological strata. The prison scene also hints at the beginnings of historiography about Germany, for it quotes the fraternal feud between

Arminius and Flavus (AD16) as depicted by Tacitus. Death because of Germany is placed in historical context, the dialectic of murder is inescapable, theatre appears as a functional process, as machinery. It is Artaud combined with Brecht, it is about devouring and being devoured. As the death blow is being delivered, four soldiers lie in the snow eating a comrade, 'unser schwächstes Glied [...] Für den Endsieg'.[25] The petty bourgeois kills his wife and daughter, turning the picture of the *Führer* to the wall for a new 'beginning'; the butcher/SA-man murders the crashed American pilot. In *Traktor*, the play which is the continuation of *Die Schlacht*, Müller depicts the construction of the GDR in the symbol of a tractor-driver who loses a leg while ploughing a mined field. Previously a soldier who did not want to lay mines had been hanged. The processes of German history are shown in the abstract, figures serve as objects, marionettes of an insane system, pressed into a perpetual dilemma, bereft totally of the freedom of decision.

Müller's key text about the sufferings of German history, *Germania Tod in Berlin* (1971), places a comprehensive historical picture in the combined force-fields of past, present and a possible, desirable future. It describes an arc in images from the German revolution of 1918 to 17 June 1953, the Uprising in the GDR, when a political prisoner hears the troops marching in to the Internationale — 'Gesungen von Panzerketten'.[26]

Inherent in the horror which is the stuff of German history is a certain theatrical continuity à la Grand Guignol. The petrol-swigging Hitler has made Goebbels pregnant. The author has cynically turned on its head the oldest of all German myths, of the blonde Germania — she who watched over the Rhine. She appears as a midwife with gigantic breasts and helps the queer, infantile characters in the bunker to bear the child, the degenerate 'Contergan-Wolf'.[27] Müller exploits this bold image to describe the topos of politically perverted sexuality, cynically turning on its head fascist hate for anything that did not conform to their norms; Hitler and Goebbels thus appear as effeminate gays because they despised and persecuted homosexuals. Müller uses Hitler's language as a poetic instrument: 'Wolfsburg' was the name of the large industrial complex he founded to produce motor cars; intimates called him 'Wolf'; the young people he summoned as his last show of strength were called 'Jungwölfe'! Fascism, in Müller's theatre of provocation, 'brings forth' a deformed reality which has something to do with vampirism. The scarcely interpretable images aim, by means of the comic, to strip historical significance of its demonic features. Hitler and Goebbels are not the real, historical people, they are presented as counters in a game intended to demonstrate the insanity of terror. History and its protagonists are *used* in the play as illustrative material.

The Nibelungs meet at Stalingrad (or is it Etzels Hof?) and chop each other to pieces, fashioning themselves into a 'Monster aus [..] Menschenmaterial',[28] a device which creates a symbolic image and transforms the traditional theatre figure into a pupa. Mythic history pervades real history, the process is mechanical. When two clowns, in the BRANDENBURGISCHES KONZERT scenes, act out the anecdote about the miller of Sanssouci, in which Friedrich II assumes all the trappings of a hero, military music begins to play; the figures metamorphose into frontline soldiers. Müller is working to create a total picture of Germany from Prussia through the two World Wars to a possible apocalyptic future. Historic locations become nightmare landscapes in which Old Fritz rises again at a cold buffet for GDR activists: as a vamp bonking the workers. Action and dialogue are replaced by visual indicators of the situation; the theatre invents a language in which visual imagery provides a commentary. The opponent of Ulbricht, once imprisoned by the Nazis and also now doing time, reviews his version of history, which we can read as Müller's central statement on Germany:

> Die deutschen Kinder krochen aus den Bäuchen
> Der deutschen Mütter, rissen mit den Zähnen
> Den deutschen Vätern die deutschen Schwänze aus
> [...]
> Und soffen Blut, solang der Vorrat reichte.
> Und dann zerfleischten sie sich eins das andre.
> Zuletzt ersoffen sie im eignen Blut
> Weil es der deutsche Boden nicht mehr faßte.[29]

Müller is not making a case for historical pessimism, in fact each scene can be performed out of the context of the play as a whole. His theme is the constantly recurring German war, the self-destructive war of the Nibelungs. The theatre becomes a laboratory which, through the surreal presentation of the horrific, implies the possibility of change. History is in a cul-de-sac; 1918, 1953 — missed opportunities whose preconditions are laid open to discussion. It is precisely the latent comic elements, which rely on exaggeration for their effect and therefore can only become apparent through performance, that point up the nature of what is depicted as a process. The individual scene becomes a snapshot of *one* historical moment.

The setting for the images about Germany functions phantasmagorically, as theatre in the head, a visionary stream of consciousness. The cumulative title[30] of *Leben Gundlings Friedrich von Preußen Lessings Schlaf Traum Schrei* (1977) can be read programmatically. Müller works in extremes of paradox, the short scene assumes universal dimensions of simultaneity: the old, not yet disposed of, is still active in the new. Friedrich stands for the Friedrichs of the Prussians who made Ulbricht and Honecker possible. Through the stripping away of grammar, the figure in the theatre is absorbed into a traumatic process, showing the suffering of the intellectual caused by Prussia (Germany). The play, whose theme is the Enlightenment, the product of Kant's Prussia, missing its way, ends in a car dump in Dakota; Lessing sleepwalks amidst the scrap-metal of the post-industrial age. The Enlightenment has been alienated, in the Adornian sense of the word. The play has the sub-title EIN GREUELMÄRCHEN and depicts the objectification of the subject. Gundling/Friedrich/Lessing — intellectuals and power epitomize the history of suppression in Prussia (Germany). Stripped of their reality, historical figures, as products of the machinery of history, stand for a continuum of suppression. Müller's approach is at once radical and dialectical in that he has both the producer and the product of reactionary consciousness played by dual figures: Prussia/Friedrich and Gundling/Lessing. The apparatus of history erases the separation of reactionary and progressive attitudes. However, this does not indicate the impossibility of emancipation, rather the discursive drama fractures all the genres, Utopian liberty is located beyond the historical moment and beyond systems.

In the now famous dining-scene in the smokers' closet, a bear hugs Gundling and the officers piss on him — the intellectual is depicted as an idiot in a society which rejects him.

FRIEDRICH WILHELM *lacht*:

Nehm Ers als ein Exempel, was von Gelehrten zu halten. Und für die Regierungskunst [...] Dem Volk die Pfoten gekürzt, der Bestie, und die Zähne ausgebrochen. Die Intelligenz zum Narren gemacht, daß der Pöbel nicht zu Ideen kommt. Merk Er sichs, Er Stubenhocker, mit Seinem Puderquasten — und Tragödienkram. Ich will, daß Er ein Mann wird.[31]

Friedrich II has been trained to rule, he is the mirror-image of Gundling. The death of the intellectual in the apparatus of power represents the destruction, the degradation of human identity. The poetic working over of history argues through both form and content against the tying down of people as objects. Socialization processes, reflected in the Prussian chamber of horrors, lead automatically to a loss of individual existence. Müller presents variations on the 'Prussianization' of souls.

In the patricide at the PREUSSISCHE SPIELE there is a psycho-analytical concretization of desires. The context of suppression (father — son/intellectual) traces psychological and intellectual history. When Katte is executed, Friedrich, who identifies with him ('das war ich') becomes a militarist, the robotistic machinery of power operates deep in psychological strata. Childhood flows into kingship, identity into functional role-play, it is the emergence of the apparatchik. As this history of the Prussian psyche unfolds, one fragmented biography flows quite seamlessly into the next; the task here is the uncovering of the structures. The continuity ends in Pankow, at the Wall, in the death-strip; Friedrich, the instrument of history, prepares the way for the constraints of SED bureaucracy.

The central scene is played in a madhouse, a cynical characterization of the whole scenario: the whole of Prussia a gigantic madhouse, the 'Manifestation des gesamtgesellschaftlichen Zustands'.[32] This Prussian Hell is a commentary on the general condition of the production of death. A professor and his students on their rounds:

> Die Zwangsjacke. Ein Instrument der Dialektik [...] Eine Schule der Freiheit [...] Je mehr der Patient sich bewegt, desto enger schnürt er sich selbst, er sich selbst wohlgemerkt, in seine Bestimmung. Jeder ist sein eigener Preuße [...] Der Philosoph würde schließen, daß die wahre Freiheit in der Katatonie beruht [...] Die Konsequenz ist reizvoll: der ideale Staat gründet auf dem Stupor seiner Bevölkerung, der ewige Frieden auf dem globalen Darmverschluß [...] die Staaten [...] auf Kotsäulen der Vernunft.[33]

Kleist hacks a doll representing himself to pieces, Friedrich awards points for war mutilations and makes the peasants eat Prussian oranges (turnips), Voltaire looks on. Schiller, amidsts fits of coughing, recites his famous elegy 'Der Spaziergang',[34] Lessing (an actor in a Lessing mask,) speaks of the 'Sehnsucht nach Schweigen' and is mumified in the 'Lessingbüste'. The images have implications way beyond themselves, reporting the GRAMMATIK DER ERDBEBEN.[35] Prussia (Germany), the 'enlightened', 'ideal' state, takes the liberating reason that had developed within it and twists it until it has a negative function, reflecting the total German state of the suppression of the intellect, the petrification of visions. When Friedrich dies wretchedly ('krepiert') in the play,[36] Müller's history-machine brings forth the apparatus of files and records .

III The 'Weg der Panzer' — from Moscow to Pankow

Müller turns repeatedly to the historical paradox of the founding of the GDR and its 'rescue'. Stalin's tanks defeated the Nazis and thus created the conditions for the emergence of socialist states; Stalin's tanks overran the rebels in the GDR in 1953, Soviet troops marched into Hungary in 1956 and into Czechoslovakia in 1968. In an early text, from the 1950s, we read the following: SCHOTTERBEK, als er an einem Junimorgen 1953 in Berlin, unter den Schlägen seiner Mitgefangenen aufatmend zusammenbrach, hörte aus dem Lärm der Panzerketten, durch die preußisch dicken Mauern seines Gefängnisses gedämpft, den nicht zu vergessenden Klang der Internationale.'[37] The Utopia, which foundered on real conditions and the petrification of the parties, was born of force, by 'way of the tanks'. Here the GDR German dialectic becomes critical: the possibility of creating an alternative model of society holds at the same time, because of its creation and defence by military force, the seeds of its destruction. It finds encoded expression in *Die Hamletmaschine* as PEST IN BUDA; in his speech of acceptance for the Büchner Prize, which he called 'Die Wunde Woyzeck', Müller writes of 'der Panzerzug der Revolution, zu Politik zerronnen'.[38]

This problem has been taken up again by Müller in his latest texts *Wolokolamsker Chaussee I—V*, which echo the tragedies of antiquity in the classical might of regular blank verse.[39] He is seeking absolute objectification, as Lukács would have said, the totality of representation. *Wolokolamsker Chaussee*, the place where Hitler's aggression was brought to a halt in the battle for Moscow, is the metaphor for the consequences; as Müller views the situation, this is where the history of the GDR really begins. The dialectical question posed by the texts has been succinctly expressed by Günter Heeg: 'Das Arrangement wird abgesichert durch das Wissen, daß Lenins Frage 'Wer wen?' nicht nur der Roten Armee den Weg aus den Sümpfen vor Moskau nach Berlin wies, sondern auch die Spur bahnte, die die Panzer des 17. Juni und des August 1968 zogen.'[40]

In Parts I and II, RUSSISCHE ERÖFFNUNG and WALD BEI MOSKAU, Müller develops motifs drawn from a patriotic novel by Alexander Bek. A Soviet commander liquidates a deserter. Again the presentation of historical discourse is marked by interchangeability: 'In seiner Uniform mein andres ich.'[41] The pacifist stance becomes problematical in the face of danger, the non-observance of military codes, the anarchistic attitude. Only by the use of force, by the execution, can the resistance against the Nazi army be guaranteed. Again Müller throws light on the fundamental structures of the Stalinist use of force. The defence against fascism generates Stalinist terror on home territory, Auschwitz becomes the first step towards the gulag.

The themes of the sections that follow, Parts III—V, are the critical moments in the subsequent history of the Eastern Bloc: a split collective consciousness reflects the situation of those affected by the events of 1953 and 1968 when 'die Panzer unser letztes Argument [waren]'.[42] Weakness is compensated for in the use of force, the 'Panzer' also indicating the mental state of permanent defensive readiness. The VEB works' director stands against his deputy, hope become identical with the armour-plated consciousness, the senseless affirmation of the repressive structures:

> Und wo bleiben die Panzer dachte ich
> [...]
> Geburtshelfer der deutschen Republik
> Hab ich gesagt Stalin ist tot Heil Stalin
> Da kommt er das Gespenst im Panzerturm
> Und unter Ketten fault die Rote Rosa[43]

DAS DUELL cites once again the basic motif of what is on the surface a struggle between brothers made enemies by circumstance. Anyone attempting to think through and analyse these circumstances will founder on the objective dialectic.

In the fourth section, KENTAUREN, Müller alludes to Kafkas *Die Verwandlung*, whereby his 'Gregor Samsa', a bureaucrat, is trapped with terrifying humour in the thickets of his work, which is to produce enemies of the state. The 'dia/ Lektische' situation[44] transforms the mythic hybrid into an object-person with a Saxon accent, the writing desk produces the files-and-records fetishist, a machine (Müller's central image). Where the guarantee of order in the state provided by the 'wet-nurses', the 'T Vierunddreißig', an emancipatory dialectic is maintained in the round dance of the 'Totengräber':[45]

Unten ein Schreibtisch oben noch ein Mensch
Kein Mensch mehr eine Menschmaschine
[...]
Ich bin ein Vorgang legt mich zu den Akten[46]

DER FINDLING, Part V, explores the generational problems suppressed in the FDJ-GDR in favour of acclamatory celebrations. Referring back to Kleist's story of the same title, the text, written in 1987 (!), tells of a mother dying of cancer — the GDR. The milk from Stalin's steely wet-nurses could bring only death, the death of sons at the Wall, their heads filled with beat-music, the death of fathers 'im Zuchthaus Bautzen'.[47] The commander against the Red Army soldier, the director against his deputy, the bureaucrat as machine-man, fathers with the sign of the 'Panzerketten'[48] against sons, 'begraben immer wieder von der Scheiße'.[49] No socialist realist conformism this, Müller has drawn up a bloody balance-sheet 'der Proletarischen Tragödie im Zeitalter der Konterrevolution'.[50]

IV Writing on the Ruins of Utopia

It was no coincidence that Müller, after the performance of Der Lohndrücker, took the decision to embark on a Hamlet project. The rehearsals started at the Deutsches Theater in East Berlin in September 1989, the first performance took place in April 1990, after the change; Müller, the director, whose comments capture precisely the moment of change in the GDR, is locked paradigmatically in the problematical conditions between the two Germanys: 'Nun funktioniert dieses Stück ganz gut. Weil es ein Stück über eine Staatskrise ist, über den Riß zwischen zwei Epochen und über einen jungen Mann, der in diesem Riß steckt. Die spannende Frage am Ende lautet: Wer übernimmt den Staat? Wer ist Fortinbras?'[51]

The opulent production works by visual allusion: for example, the actor's presentation of Claudius as a grasping SED-man sporting a golden finger on his metal-clad hand, and, at the end of the play, the appearance of Fortinbras as a businessman in dark-blue suit and golden mask, the representative of capitalism arriving in the GDR. Yet the production is stylized as petrified scenery, with figures, who speak in slow-motion, hidden behind gauze, to be revealed at the end in the glaring light of a yellow desert-landscape slaughtering each other — it is a landscape from the end of time beneath the hole in the ozone layer. Müller's scenic comment also speaks through the unreality of the images of an intellectual helplessness, which hints at political action in a state of paralysis.

The figures are overtaken by the history they have suppressed, the appearance of Hamlet's ghost is accompanied by loudspeakers playing the crackling original recording of Stalin's funeral. Hamlet is to avenge Stalin. Once again we have the radical foreshortening of the epochs; Stalin lives on as a spectre.

The dizzy pace of German unification has also outrun Heiner Müller. In his poem 'Fernsehen' (1990), whose title alludes to the artificiality of developments, in the third section, SELBSTKRITIK, we read:

> Auf dem Bildschirm sehe ich meine Landsleute
> Mit Händen und Füßen abstimmen gegen die Wahrheit
> Die vor vierzig Jahren mein Besitz war
> Welches Grab schützt mich vor meiner Jugend[52]

The 'truth' of socialism is not posited as an absolute, but is rather discussed in a historical and biographical context, a subject has lost his identity, his hope. 'Youth' is placed in a metaphorical context and stands for the beginning of the work on the Utopia which lies buried beneath the ruins of the GDR. This contains the idea that there might be productive possibilities associated with the writer's own mistakes, a consideration which allows us to associate the author with the significant literary tradition of the universalist novel.

Peter Weiss, in his monumental work *Die Ästhetik des Widerstands* (1975—1981), took final account of Stalinism in similarly thought-provoking manner. In this fictional, idealized biography of a first-person narrator, who, as a Communist, fought in the Spanish Civil War and then worked with the underground against the Nazis, we have a precise depiction of the paradoxical situation: 'Da bewegte sich stets, gleichzeitig mit uns, eine andre Gewalt voran, eine Gewalt der Eindämmung.'[53] The persecuted are liquidated — by their own party, the illegal KPD and the Stalinist Soviet Union, the 'Land der Revolution', which has lost 'seine Würde'.[54] In the struggle against the German aggressors, the revolution devours its children. The individual people in Weiss's narrative experience the party they serve as an anonymous phantom; everyone who becomes involved in the historical process is in danger: 'Hinter dem Kampf gegen Unrecht und Ausbeutung stand der Kampf der Männer untereinander.'[55] But even Weiss indicates the ineluctable nature of the situation; the necessary commitment, even where it has developed out of idealistic attitudes, comes into conflict with the anonymous apparatus of a party which has become petrified in its alienation. As with Müller, here also there is an attempt at objective, reflective depiction of the author's political position. The discourse of history has, as it were, become autonomous, leaving those who would shape it far behind, crushed under its heels.

Heiner Müller's latest book, *Zur Lage der Nation* (April 1990), comprises a fundamental review of the position of writing in Germany after the 'change'. At the same time it is a sober analysis of forty years of SED régime which stands back from all forms of polemical score-settling (contrasting with what we find in the media) and eschews the frenzy of unification euphoria. As Müller views the situation, objective, empirically measurable reality had been officially replaced by falsified statistics. Instead of cool dialectical analysis, 'nur stalinistische Theologie' had predominated.[56] It is Marxism as substitute religion. Müller judges the turnabout in the GDR to be a revolution, with the GDR breaking out of the 'colonial' stage, Stalinism being substituted by nationalism. Events have substantiated Müller's works on Germany, 'the womb is still fertile'.[57] His poetic assault on the tradition of German chauvinism can be read now with new insight, his theatrical images from the German chamber of horrors acquire new dimensions on the streets of Leipzig with the placards declaring 'Der Jude Gysi muß weg'.

> Vergegenwärtigt man sich die erste Losung, in Leipzig: Wir sind das Volk... das klang ungeheuer gut. Völlig logisch, daß daraus schnell wurde: Wir sind ein Volk. Und daraus wird sehr schnell: Es gibt keine anderen Völker. Deshalb habe ich auch verstanden, warum Brecht immer so mißtrauisch war gegen das Wort 'Volk'. Er meinte, man müßte Bevölkerung sagen.[58]

Nor is this an arrogant, intellectual defamation of the anger on the streets; it is rather an expression of the unease felt at the new nationalistic intoxication. The old danger is again virulent, the social problems now emerging entail latent racism: 'Das nationalistische Vokabular und Instrumentarium ist immer abrufbar'.[59] Compensation is superseding analysis.

As he did before the 'change', Müller still perceives a vaccuum left by missed opportunities; however, while he himself does not assume the role of speaking for the people, he welcomes the fact that those who for forty years had been silent have now found their voice. Müller is also worried in this period of fundamental change because it is an inescapable fact that Hitler emerged victorious from free elections! Müller the Marxist holds fast to his sceptical hope, according to which he sees the 'masses' as having broken free 'aus dem Schatten Stalins mit einem Jahrhundertschritt'.[60] Yet the worry persists that people will now lose sight of the 'Mauer, die durch die Welt geht'[61] and which continues to exist.

For Müller, the difference between time and society, the conditions and the subject remains overt. On the ruins of a Utopia which at least existed in theoretical draft there has to be a redefinition of writing — now that, at least for Müller, the collapse of the GDR has removed the last alternative to consumer society. The 'theory' is lost from view, buried by historical events which were the consequence of Stalinist dialectic. The author again has the possibility of exploiting productively a historical situation which he rejects. If literature under the GDR dictatorship was a substitute for the press, for information, for criticism, it can now 'frei, sich wieder ihrer eigentlichen Aufgabe [widmen]', 'die Wirklichkeit, so wie sie ist, unmöglich zu machen'.[62] The house has collapsed upon itself, the work has to be started again from the beginning, the insistent counterfeit of conditions, taking up what Hans Henny Jahnn used to term the 'Querstellung'.[63] The vision of a literature which seeks to formulate Utopia develops anew for Müller at the moment when circumstances change. It becomes again possible to attempt autonomy in literature. This means leaving aside the discussion of symptoms, going beyond the documentary and making a fresh start, applying 'mythologische Genauigkeit' to the very 'Strukturen' themselves.[64]

Since his *Wolokolamsker Chaussee* texts, Heiner Müller has not published any literary work. This silence is his tacit literary response to the dynamic processes in Germany. His discourse is trapped in the dilemma of the events; theoretical premises, formulated in interviews, indicate a search for a new, yet not so new, definition of the writer's role and position: 'Mich interessiert der Gestus des Geschichtsschreibers [...] ein Dialog mit den Toten, mehr als mit den Lebenden [...] Das Drama war ja ursprünglich — jedenfalls die Tragödie — Totenbeschwörung und das hat jetzt noch Sinn [...] Das 'Neue' im Moment ist kein dramatischer Stoff [...] es ist kaum etwas an die Oberfläche gekommen, was ich nicht kenne.'[65] Clearly, at a moment in history when hope has petrified, Müller's poetics is developing a transcendental thrust. His 'conjuring of the dead' also involves *Trauerarbeit* for Stalinism, the removal of the 'corpses' rotting in the cellar. In the moribund GDR with the scramble to secure political positions, reflecting the 'Posten her' of Bert Brecht's Hitler chorals,[66] the process of forcing the past into the past has already begun. The ruins of the Wall, the old conditions are to be swept under the carpet. Work on the new remains dialectical, since the (repressed) past continues to have an effect in the present; literature is a process of rehearsal which, admittedly, has to capture the general difference, a long-term task: 'Die Befreiung der Toten findet in Zeitlupe statt.'[67] The spoilheap onto which the remains of the Wall are being cleared in Bernauer Straße, the place where most of those killed while attempting escape died, is a potential theme; it is the description of an archaeological landscape and its dead people. In Müller's draft, Stalin has to be 'liberated' from Stalin.

The West German press has started to settle scores with the Marxist writers of the GDR: 'Keiner ist frei von Schuld.'[68] German history repeats itself, intellectuals are again scapegoats. The *Experimenta 6* in Frankfurt/Main, which was devoted to the work of Heiner Müller, turned into public mud-slinging at him which had its origins in ignorance about his problematical German biography and about the substance of his texts. German history is catching up with Heiner Müller — in West Germany as well. The man with the cigar is being labelled a Stalinist and a servant of the system.

The campaign in the *Frankfurter Allgemeine Zeitung* and the *Frankfurter Rundschau* degenerated to a tasteless, indiscriminate, sweeping condemnation of Müller's aesthetics. There was talk of 'Held Heiner', of a 'Heroisierung',[69] which Müller himself would find suspect, and of making a monument of him. Bazon Brock brought up the expression 'Afterkunst und Spießerkram';[70] Peter Iden, the influential theatre critic of the *Frankfurter Rundschau*, ran down Müller's *Hamlet* as 'seltsam antiquiert', his aesthetics as 'zur Manier verkommen'. 'Heiner Müller ödet mich an.' His language was 'veraltet', his ideology 'verrottet', his aesthetics 'hinfällig', the man himself 'äußerst fadenscheinig'.[71]

The fact that who was or is a Stalinist is discussed and decided in the West shows up the typical absurdity of German-German behaviour on this theme. Once again the media have created a public view which is bereft of reflection and which can only demonstrate its total inadequacy when faced with a poetic *oeuvre* created over forty years of critical awareness. Writing in Germany — the experience of Büchner, Kleist and so many others is repeated. Müller's discourse, for which he needed the premise of the Germans' plight, is a commentary on the situation as it developed, engendering what is structurally an undogmatic literature of possibilities. The new historical situation makes a new reading of these texts possible — from a historical distance. A spirit of restoration is now taking over, the slogans of overblown criticism are designed only to increase sales. Since the 'change', Heiner Müller has been 'unmasked' as 'der große Einverstandene: der Außenseiter als der Affirmator' [sic],[72] the one who received prizes from the old men of the nomenclatura power-system.

In this German (self-mutilating) debate, which in fact confirms his position, our author has kept his head down: 'Es ist eine Zeit, wo man die Lehre begraben muß [...] möglichst tief, damit die Hunde nicht herankommen.'[73] The debate surrounding the Frankfurt *Experimenta*, which did involve some thoughtful defence of Müller, was the result of the unhistorical, imperial consciousness of the West German critical geniuses who slipped back into that hyper-German spirit which Heinrich Heine had found so dubious in his *Wintermärchen*. Suspects must be found and denounced, above all left-wing intellectuals — these are images of the enemy rooted in tradition. This debate, which was stirred up for reasons of fashion, to satisfy the media's gluttony for the new, the marketable, is yet another sign of the old dilemma; another opportunity has been missed to discuss the *substance* of theatre in East and West. Heiner Müller's assessment of the state of the nation is accurate: the West does not have a history, it has the Deutschmark.

Müller's essential subject is Germany. He treated it in radical paradoxes between text and text reduction and tackled it at its most painful points of fracture. His position is that of the outsider, his theme the broad connections which become apparent in the interwoven relationship of past and present. We may regard Müller as a paradigm for the case of the author caught between systems, the absurdity of the German problem is reflected in his biography, in his work, and in both his and its reception. His live theatre is too unwieldy to classify easily. He is searching, as Lessing did, for a new drama which looks towards a historical situation free of alienation, which seeks to remove the difference between subject and conditions, which believes in Utopia. Müller's most recent text speaks for the author; rarely emotional, it is the product of cool, rational despair:

Antigone: Hölderlins republikanischer Stuhl, brennend auf dem Scheiter-
haufen der Restauration. Gundling: die zerrissene Figur des stürzenden
Ikarus Lessing Kleist Friedrich der Große, oben links flattert das NEUE
DEUTSCHLAND, eine Zeitung ohne Leser einsames Bramsegel der sozialistischen Todgeburt. Hamletmaschine: der Hamletdarsteller ohne Gesicht, im
Rücken eine Mauer, sein Blick eine Gefängniswand. Bilder, deren Anspruch
keine Inszenierung einlösen konnte. Wegmarken durch den Sumpf, der sich
schon damals zu schließen begann über dem vorläufigen Grab der Utopie, die
vielleicht wieder aufscheinen wird, wenn das Phantom der Marktwirtschaft,
die das Gespenst des Kommunismus ablöst, den neuen Kunden seine kalte
Schulter zeigt, den Befreiten das eiserne Gesicht seiner Freiheit.[74]

NOTES

I wish to express my thanks to Dieter Stolz for providing the opportunity to write this article
and Christian Rochow for help with precise references in the text. AS.

Translation by Arthur Williams.

1   Heiner Müller: *Die Umsiedlerin oder Das Leben auf dem Lande*, West Berlin, 1975,
    contains the new version of the comedy entitled *Die Bauern*.
2   Heiner Müller revealed this in a discussion on 7 July 1988. See Wolfgang Storch (ed.):
    Explosion of a memory Heiner Müller DDR. Ein Arbeitsbuch, West Berlin, 1988, p. 226.
3   Heiner Müller rarely discusses details of his private life and experiences. I am grateful to
    Fritz Marquart for this information.
4   Heiner Müller: *Germania Tod in Berlin*, West Berlin, 1977.
5   Heiner Müller: *Der Lohndrücker* in Müller: *Geschichten aus der Produktion I. Stücke.
    Prosa. Gedichte. Protokolle*, West Berlin, 1974.
6   Heiner Müller: *Leben Gundlings Friedrich von Preußen Lessings Schlaf Traum Schrei.
    Ein Greuelmärchen* in Müller: *Herzstück*, West Berlin, 1983.
7   '"Es kommen viele Leichen zum Vorschein". Theater heute Gespräch mit Michael
    Merschmeier, Ulrich Mühe, Heiner Müller und Hilmar Thate', *Theater heute*, no. 12,
    1989.
8   Heiner Müller: 'Mauern. Gespräch mit Sylvère Lothringer' in Müller: *Rotwelsch*, West
    Berlin, 1982, p. 64.
9   The term used by Maurice Blanchot: 'Der Name Berlin (Le nom de Berlin)', *taz*, 13
    November, 1989.
10 Heiner Müller: 'BERLIN — EIN ORT FÜR DEN FRIEDEN. Rede während des inter-
    nationalen Schriftstellergesprächs 6 Mai 1987' in Frank Hörnigk (ed.): *Heiner Müller.
    Material, Texte und Kommentare*, West Berlin, 1989, p. 112.
11 Müller: 'Mauern...', p. 51.
12 Heiner Müller: *Die Hamletmaschine* in Müller: *Mauser*, West Berlin, 1978.
13 Müller: 'Mauern...', p. 49. Botho Strauß also exploits the motif of a wall offering different
    perspectives on time (see Arthur Williams, e.g. pp. 453, 455 below).
14 Ibid, p. 50.
15 Uwe Johnson: 'Berliner Stadtbahn (veraltet)' in Johnson: *Berliner Sachen. Aufsätze*,
    Frankfurt/Main, 1975, p. 10.
16 Heiner Müller: 'Wie es bleibt ist es nicht', *Der Spiegel*, no. 38, 1977.
17 Müller: 'BERLIN — EIN ORT...', p. 112.
18 Bertolt Brecht: 'Deutschland' in Brecht: *Gesammelte Werke*, vol. IX: *Gedichte 2*,
    Frankfurt/Main, 1977, p. 487.
19 Heiner Müller: 'Panizza oder die Einheit Deutschlands' in Müller: *Rotwelsch*, p. 180.
20 Bertolt Brecht: *Mutter Courage und ihre Kinder* in Brecht: *Gesammelte Werke*, vol. IV, p.
    1443. Heiner Müller: 'Der Weltuntergang ist zu einem modischen Problem geworden.
    Ein Gespräch mit Uwe Wittstock' in Müller: *Gesammelte Irrtümer. Interviews und
    Gespräche*, Frankfurt/Main, 1986, p. 179.

21 Müller: 'Der Weltuntergang ist...', p. 180.
22 Müller: 'Mauern...', p. 64.
23 Ibid.
24 Heiner Müller: *Die Schlacht. Szenen aus Deutschland* in Müller: *Die Übersiedlerin...*, p. 8.
25 Ibid, p. 9.
26 Müller: *Germania...*, p. 74.
27 Ibid, p. 63.
28 Ibid, p. 51.
29 Ibid, p. 73f.
30 See Genia Schulz: *Heiner Müller*, Stuttgart, 1980, p. 139.
31 Müller: *Leben Gundlings...*, p. 12.
32 Wolfgang Emmerich: 'Der Alp Geschichte. "Preußen" in Heiner Müllers "Leben Gundlings Friedrich von Preußen Lessings Schlaf Traum Schrei"', *Jahrbuch zur Literatur der DDR. 1981/83*, p. 142.
33 Müller: *Leben Gundlings...*, p. 26.
34 Friedrich Schiller: 'Der Spaziergang' in Schiller: *Werke in Drei Bänden*, Munich, 1966, pp. 714—8. Müller's critical attitude to German Idealism becomes clear from the way he presents what is one of the central lyrical expressions of it (e.g. ll. 39ff.: 'Jene Linien, sieh! die des Landmanns Eigentum scheiden,/ In den Teppich der Flur hat sie Demeter gewirkt./ Freundliche Schrift des Gesetzes, des menschenerhaltenden Gottes,/ Seit aus der ehernen Welt fliehend die Liebe verschwand,/ Aber in freieren Schlangen durchkreuzt die geregelten Felder,/ Jetzt verschlungen vom Wald, jetzt an den Bergen hinauf/ Klimmend, ein schimmernder Streif, die Länder verknüpfende Straße;/ Auf dem ebenen Strom gleiten die Flöße dahin.')
35 Müller: *Leben Gundlings...*, pp. 35—7.
36 Ibid, p. 33.
37 Müller: *Germania...*, p. 15 (SCHOTTERBEK).
38 Heiner Müller: 'Die Wunde Woyzeck' in Storch: *Explosion...*, p. 184.
39 Published in Heiner Müller: *Shakespeare Factory 1*, West Berlin, 1985 (*Wolokolamsker Chaussee I: Russische Eröffnung*) and *Shakespeare Factory 2*, West Berlin, 1989 (*Wolokolamsker Chaussee II: Wald bei Moskau*; *Wolokolamsker Chaussee III: Das Duell*; *Wolokolamsker Chaussee IV: Kentauren*; *Wolokolamsker Chaussee V: Der Findling*).
40 Günter Heeg: 'Der Weg der Panzer. Notizen zu einer geplanten Aufführung von Heiner Müllers "Wolokolamsker Chaussee I—V" in Storch: *Explosion...*, p. 138.
41 Müller: *Wolokolamsker Chaussee I*, p. 248.
42 Müller: *Wolokolamsker Chaussee III*, p. 30.
43 Ibid, p. 234.
44 Müller: *Wolokolamsker Chaussee IV*, p. 246.
45 Ibid, p. 243.
46 Ibid, p. 249.
47 Müller: *Wolokolamsker Chaussee V*, p. 251.
48 Ibid, p. 253.
49 Ibid, p. 255.
50 Ibid, p. 259.
51 Heiner Müller: 'Ohne Hoffnung, ohne Verzweiflung', *Der Spiegel*, no. 49, 1989. Many aspects of Müller's work as discussed in this article (his perception of time, the round-dance of history, the fragmented form, the nightmare scenes from Germny's past) are similar to motifs and techniques found in Botho Strauß, none more so than elements found in this particular quotation ('der junge Mann', 'Riß', 'zwischen zwei Epochen'). See Arthur Williams, pp. 449—65 below; esp. pp. 453—58.
52 Heiner Müller: 'Fernsehen', *Theater heute*, no. 12, 1989, p. 1.
53 Peter Weiss: *Die Ästhetik des Widerstands*, Frankfurt/Main, 1988, vol. I, p. 246.
54 Ibid, vol. III, p. 135.
55 Ibid, vol. III, p. 81.

56 Heiner Müller: 'Dem Terrorismus die Utopie entreißen. Alternative DDR' in Müller: *Zur Lage der Nation*, West Berlin, 1990, p. 21. Two other articles are quoted from the same volume: 'Plädoyer für den Widerspruch' and 'Das Jahrhundert der Konterrevolution'.

57 Bertolt Brecht: *Der unaufhaltsame Aufstieg des Arturo Ui* in Brecht: *Gesammelte Werke*, vol. IV, p. 1834.

58 Müller: *Zur Lage der Nation*, p. 85.

59 Ibid, p. 86.

60 Ibid, p. 81.

61 Ibid.

62 Ibid, p. 21. See also Karen Leeder's reference to Müller's view of 'Sehnsucht' as a revolutionary force, pp. 419—20 below.

63 'Diese Beharrlichkeit [...] das Unausweichliche einer Querstellung [...] entspringt nicht etwa einem Trotz, einer Manie bei mir, mich in Gegensatz zu einer mir bekannten Übereinkunft zu stellen, sondern einzig dem Wunsch [...] an die Veränderung des Menschen mitzuwirken.' Hans Henny Jahnn: 'Mein Werden und mein Werk' in Jahnn: *Werke und Tagebücher*, vol. VII, Hamburg, 1974, p. 306.

64 Müller: *Zur Lage der Nation*, p. 23.

65 Ibid, pp. 87ff. See also Julian Preece's reference to Uwe Johnson'd Gesina Cresspahl's communing with the dead, p. 316 below.

66 Bertolt Brecht: 'Hitler — Choral II' in Brecht: *Gesammelte Werke*, vol. IX, p. 445

67 Müller: *Zur Lage der Nation*, p. 24.

68 Ulrich Greiner: 'Keiner ist frei von Schuld. Deutscher Literaturstreit: Der Fall Christa Wolf und die Intellektuellen', *Die Zeit*, 27 July 1990.

69 Peter Iden: 'Aller für einen. "Experimenta 6" — eine Überdosis Heiner Müller', *FR*, 19 May 1990.

70 Quoted from Hendrik Markgraf: 'Haßtiraden und polemisches Gezänk. Ist Heiner Müller verbraucht oder experimentell? Eine Diskussion im TAT', *FAZ*, 31 May 1990.

71 Quoted from Helmut Schödel: 'Wir sind ein blödes Volk. Ein Heiner-Müller-Tagebuch zur Frankfurter "Experimenta 6"', *Die Zeit*, 8 June 1990, and Peter Iden: 'Am Ende. Müllers "Hamlet" als Finale der "Experimenta 6"', *FR*, 6 June 1990.

72 Gerhard Stadelmeier: 'Mumienstücke. "Experimenta" oder Wie Heiner Müller unters Drama kam', *FAZ*, 2 June 1990.

73 Müller: 'Dem Terrorismus die Utopie entreißen...', p. 24.

74 Heiner Müller: 'Kommentare zur Gesellschaft. Plakate von Gunter Rambow Frankfurt am Main' (unpublished manuscript, 1990).

KAST *RESURRECTUS*:

VOLKER BRAUN'S *BODENLOSER SATZ*

GISELA SHAW

I

In the early 1960s Benno von Wiese, at that time the foremost Germanist in the Federal Republic of Germany, wrote:

> Das Ästhetische als ein Werk der freien Einbildungskraft ist der erstaunliche Versuch des Menschen, eine Sphäre außerhalb von Raum und Zeit noch unter den Bedingungen von Raum und Zeit zu realisieren. Ja, ich möchte geradezu die etwas verwegene These aufstellen, daß eigentlich alle Dichtung von Rang, soweit sie sich selbst absolut versteht, bereits ihrem Wesem nach utopischen Charakter hat, auch wo sie keineswegs einen utopischen Inhalt zu ihrem besonderen Gegenstand gemacht hat. Denn es ist die Sphäre des Schönen, und insbesondere der Dichtung, innerhalb derer der Mensch auf seine Weise das Unmögliche begehrt und sich zueignet.[1]

Twenty years later Volker Braun declared: 'Poesie ist eine Gegensprache. Und ist sie weiter nichts: eine Grimasse.'[2] Indeed, no writer in the GDR has articulated his dream, his Utopia so aggressively and with such unswerving toughness as Volker Braun, using every means available to him as a writer — poetry, drama and prose. I would also argue that there is today hardly another writer who has placed himself so firmly in the German (and, increasingly, in the European) literary tradition, while developing it further in the process.

Volker Braun's most recent book, *Bodenloser Satz*, has just appeared (for the time being only in West Germany).[3] It was written in September 1988 — one year before the peaceful revolution in the GDR. In 1989 he was awarded, for *Bodenloser Satz*, the *Berliner Preis für deutschsprachige Literatur*, thus becoming its first recipient. It is a text which marks a new beginning in Braun's work, for it represents a sort of resurrection of the (almost) dead, a regaining of 'Poesie als Gegensprache'. Henceforth, there can be no fear that Braun is condemned to 'bloßes Grimassieren'.

For a number of years after 1976, Braun had been all but stifled by the feeling that he had been shunted onto the sidings of history by the silence imposed upon him.[4] The slim volume of texts from the years 1965—1986 *Verheerende Folgen mangelnden Ancheins innerbetrieblicher*

Demokratie, which was published in the GDR in 1989, provides eloquent testimony to the low ebb of these years. In relation to his own texts, the notes on Rimbaud and his work are of particular importance. Braun ackowledges Rimbaud as the 'Gewährmann meiner Erfahrungen' from the age of nineteen on.[5] In this context we find the following comments: 'Provinz, das ist der leere Augenblick. Geschichte auf dem Abstellgleis. Status quo. Was *uns* ersticken machen kann; aus der bewegten Zeit in eine stehende zu fallen.'[6] Or: 'In der Poesie erschöpft sich rapide die Hoffnung: der Realismus verbraucht die Illusionen. Unsere Desillusionierung, in der langsamen Revolution, erfolgt in der Zeitlupe. Wir haben, zähere Leute, mehr Hoffnung verbraucht.'[7]

During this time of stagnation, Braun's position as a writer seemed hopeless: 'Ich gehöre diesem Volk an, und ich bin doch ein Landstreicher: unbediensteter Autor. Das Privileg ist asozial.'[8] Volker Braun, the author, and Volker Braun, the pugnaciously committed citizen of the GDR, can hardly be separated the one from the other. If he had abandoned his home during these barren years, this would have been tantamount to abandoning himself. The way out which had been so obvious to others was never available to him: 'Freunde und Feinde warten auf meine endgültige Reise ins Aus, den Abgang vom Gerät. Sie sagen ihn voraus als die Konsequenz: die Zerreißprobe endet [...] Aber ich bin nicht nur das zerrissene Fleisch, ich bin es auch, der es zerreißt. Ich entkomme nicht, es sei denn über die eigene Grenze.'[9]

He was on a trip to Hungary when he heard that his *Hinze-Kunze-Roman*,[10] which he had just finished, had been rejected for publication. The relevant entry in his diary is illuminating:

> Nicht nur die satirische Prosa: auch die Gedichte, nichts scheint mehr druckbar. Da jetzt "alles darauf ankommt, den Sozialismus zu stärken", ist nur sein Lob gelitten. Byzantinische Ästhetik. Aber wenn das, was ich schreibe, "im Widerspruch zur Partei" steht, wie kann ich dann [...] wie kann ich dann Mitglied sein? Niemand fragt mich das, aber es ist unerträglich, diesen Widerspruch zu leben; eine bedeutende Kulturpolitik mitzutragen und ihr ein Ärgernis zu sein.[11]

He could see that a decision would soon be forced upon him: 'Wandeln — die Haltung ändern, die Art des Lebens. Noch bin ich eingemeindet in die Disziplin, die Hörigkeit. Noch übe ich Rücksicht, um der GEMEINSAMEN SACHE willen.'[12] But what would happen, were he to give up this common cause?

Slowly, Braun became convinced that nothing could be gained without self-liberation. He had to let 'den Anderen' in himself speak out, the alter ego who would not be intimidated by power structures.[13] But how was this to be achieved? The Party still remained the ultimate authority for him. Was he to take the step 'vom Genossen in der Partei zum Genossen außerhalb der Partei'?[14] The incipient breakthrough comes in *Die Übergangsgesellschaft* and *Transit Europa. Der Ausflug der Toten*,[15] which were written in 1982 and 1985—1986 respectively. The Communist Volker Braun was prepared to acknowledge that socialism, as it existed in his society, had betrayed its ideals and that a further revolution was necessary. This revolution had to emanate from the individual.

Bodenloser Satz marks the point at which Volker Braun crosses the threshold from heteronomy to freedom. He regains his upright gait.

I shall now undertake a discussion of *Bodenloser Satz* in the following sub-divisions:

— a brief outline of its plot
— the individual threads of the story
— the central conflict between Man/Male and Nature/Female
— the completion of the *Kast*-cycle
— continuity and innovation in Braun's view of the world and humanity in the context of German literary tradition.

II

The text comprises just over thirty generously printed A5 pages, all of which form one long sentence; it has one full stop — at the end. A prose monster with poetic and dramatic elements.[16]

The sentence divides into two quantitatively very unequal parts. In the first part, about four pages in length, the first-person narrator spends a night in a hotel. Lying in the darkness, alone in his double bed, half asleep, he has a dream-like vision. A woman is getting into bed beside him, snuggling 'an die brennende Linie meiner linken Seite' (p. 8).[17] His partner, who is feeling unwell, has withdrawn to another room, nevertheless he senses that she has sent him this visitor. She wants him to be released from the state of frozen rigidity, the 'Lebensstarre' (pp. 9f.), of which he has been for so long a victim.

The challenge is accepted. He, too, wishes to become 'der Andere', to be unfrozen, to be free and help her to be free as well. The dam is broken. In his dream, the night of love is followed by an awakening in a hotel in a city on the Rhine. Outside, narrow streets, obscene goings-on, the filthy waters of the river. A picture of aesthetic and moral repulsiveness.

The real awakening makes him see his environment with newly sharpened senses — this is not a country he can ever feel at home in.

In the second, main part of the sentence, the narrator finds himself back in his own country, more specifically in the Leipzig area, where for the second time in thirty years the natural landscape is to be sacrificed to lignite mining. He himself had been involved in the work of construction and destruction that had gone on before and was about to begin again. With his newly gained clear vision he watches, detached and yet with deep inner involvement.

A village is being evacuated. Anton, the Bürgermeister, announces and supervises the evacuation; the villagers pack their belongings; bulldozers are moving in; a young woman, Klara, starts a quarrel with Karl, the mining surveyor, pitting her moral strength against physical forces and ultimately winning him over. The text reaches its one and only moment of tranquillity when Karl, having fallen into a drainage ditch, is being helped out by Klara, who embraces him 'ganz ohne Grund' (p. 40).

III

This, then, is the plot in outline. In the main part of the sentence, it is interwoven with other threads of action and reflection. There are, for instance, flashbacks to the history of the land and its people which involve the narrator himself. He remembers events of thirty years previously when the young Republic was still in its pioneering stage and he had helped to drain the land, shovel in hand, as a member of a brigade of pipe-layers.[18] Amongst his tasks then had been that of moving the bodies of Russian prisoners of war from their mass grave (p. 23). Reflection on this process provides a glimpse of the country's history at a time which preceded the formation of the GDR.

Then, secondly, there are reflections on his own motivation for revisiting this spot. What is it that keeps him here, that binds him to this desolate area? The answer is: 'Ich will den Grund durchwühlen, der mich bleiben ließ' (p. 14). For, as he later admits, 'ICH KENN DAS LOCH IN

DER MAUER, die Republikflucht der Utopien in die Messer der Konsumschlacht, MIT ALLEN NEGERN WO DIE KOHLEN STIMMEN, der entnervte Besamer im Supermarkt' (p. 39).

He is filled with a sense of responsibility for what he himself has helped fashion; he is at one and the same time the accuser and the accused. Equally, the first person and the third person become interchangeable. The 'I' identifies with all main characters: with Karl, the mining surveyor, dividing up the land on his map (p. 19); with Klara, who is evacuated with her two children and who takes her revenge on Karl by forcing him to make her pregnant on the last strip of land not yet destroyed by the bulldozers (p. 32); with Anton, the Bürgermeister, who loyally carries out orders from above, though close to tears at the death of his village (pp. 29f.); — and with the SS-man who had forced Russian prisoners of war out of the waggons they had been transported in and had made them bury the dead and shoot those who had survived the journey. But the narrator is also his own victim: 'und ich spüre den Lauf der Pistole in meinem Genick [...] und sehe mein eigenes Gesicht in meines gerichtet [...] und ich falle unter den Greifern, unter das scharfe Schild der Rampe, das mich in den Sand planiert' (p. 26).

As the 'I' assumes the guilt and suffering of society, the way opens for a coming to terms with the country's history, for atonement and a new beginning 'in aller Unschuld' (p. 26).

IV

The history of this land and its people has been one of incessant struggles. Indeed, Man struggling for power appears as the driving force in history as such. Braun portrays these struggles by means of two metaphors. Firstly there is the struggle between Man and Nature. Man is intent on robbing Nature of its carefully guarded treasures. He comes armed with shovels, excavators, bulldozers, helmets — again now just as he did before. Thirty years previously, the 'Captain' had led up his troops (p. 20) and what the bankers and industrialists had not succeeded in doing, namely destroying the thousand-year-old forest, the heroes of peace and work had achieved. They knew not what they did.

When, in the 1980s, the second assault on the land is made, it is Karl, the mining surveyor, who takes command in the service of the Plan. The advances of his troops are reported triumphantly in the press: 'Kriegsberichte von der Kohlenfront, die Bürgermeister Anton sich laut

vorlas im leeren Büro, DIE EIMERKETTEN DER BAGGER DES FÖRDER-
VERBANDES HABEN DIE ORTSLAGE ERREICHT. DIE FÖRDERBRÜCKE
SCHWENKT IN IHR OSTFELD EIN. DER WENDERADIUS BESCHREIBT EINEN
FÄCHERFÖRMIGEN BOGEN, DER FAKTISCH DIE GANZE LANDSCHAFT EIN-
BEGREIFT' (p. 28). Ironically, the residual stocks of lignite for which the
village is being sacrificed will barely keep the power station going for
twenty hours (p. 37).

The struggle of blind, mindless Man with Nature is inseparably
linked with the struggle between the sexes. Woman is in harmony with
Nature and defends it. Her physical weakness goes with superior moral
strength. The Male is fought as the intruder and, ultimately, turns out to
be the loser (p. 33). His campaign will bring no more than short-term
gains. If he keeps up his assaults, Nature and Woman, the whole land,
will rise and the victims of history buried in it will band together 'zu
einem unwiderstehlichen Strom' (p. 38) and crush the robbers.

Karl is prepared to learn. He learns to see that salvation can spring,
not from reason or physical force, but from forgiveness and love alone,
love of the land, love between Man and Woman. Man needs to remember his original role as a friend, a brother and a protector of the weak.
On surveying his supposed enemy from the cabin of his bulldozer, all he
can see is

> dünne Reihen zärtlicher Pappeln, sachte aus dem Boden tretend, Gräser
> mühsam blühend auf der Asche, leichtsinnig schwache Gehölze, Birken vor-
> sichtig Fuß fassend und junge Eichen, wie zu einem Ausflug aufgebrochen
> auf den unauffindbaren Wanderwegen, arglos im frühen Nebel kamen sie auf
> ihn zu, unsäglich langsam und nicht die Anstrengung verleugnend, eine
> rührende Prozession mit dürren Bittgebärden, aufrecht, aber nicht
> kriegerisch. (p. 38)

As the land offers itself in friendship and peace, Klara receives the fallen
Karl with a similar gesture of pardon and of love 'ohne Grund'.

V

Bodenloser Satz fits in seamlessly with Volker Braun's four *Kast* stories,
each of which can be read as an account of a particular period in his life
as a human being, a Communist attempting to put into practice his
Utopian ideal and as an author.[19] In each of these stories, the protagonist, Kast, fails to fulfil his urgent desire to match up his own vision of
society with that propagated by the powers that be. Whether as a young
worker on the land, a student at university or a theatre producer, his

search for a marriage between the 'I' and the 'we', the individual and society, fails. This failure always manifests itself in his private life as well, his inability to establish a strong and lasting relationship with a woman as his equal partner.

In the last of these four stories, entitled 'Die Tribüne', the protagonist has taken on the post of party-secretary in a combine in order to make a contribution from a position of power. However, here, too, the picture of a centrally directed bureaucracy imposing its will on the individual kills any desire in him to take any further part in social developments. His marriage breaks down ('wir nahmen uns die Luft'[20]) hierarchical structures around him harden, his strength is running out. In helpless desperation he turns to his future readers:

> Diesen Liebesbrief notierend weiß ich, ihr werdet ihn zusehends beklommen lesen, und ich werde euch Satz für Satz in eine Geschichte hineinziehen (oder ihr werdet mit uneingestandener Hast hineindrängen), in der uns etwas geschieht, das ich jetzt nicht weiß; ja daß ich andere anwesend weiß in den Sätzen, auf meinen Fersen und unnachsichtig Offenheit fordernd, treibt mich tiefer in die Sache hinein und wird mich, der ich keinen Punkt zu machen weiß, soweit bringen, alles oder nichts mehr zu sagen[21]

This last report ends without a full stop. An anonymous editor simply adds a laconic note to the fragment after the protagonist has been found dead in his car following an 'accident' on the road. The dilemma remains unsolved. It is only fourteen years later that the thread is picked up again, in *Bodenloser Satz*. The narrator has now reached the point where the Gordion knot must be cut. The frankness which was not possible in 1974 can no longer be avoided. Thus Kast/Karl/Man does reach the point of salvation.

VI

Braun's myth of the eternal dialectical struggle between Man and Nature, Male and Female, lust for power and loving devotion, fits into an ancient literary and philosophical tradition. Which are his main precursors and models?

In all his writings, Volker Braun has remained loyal to his first mentor Bert Brecht, in whose theatre, the Berliner Ensemble, he had gathered his first experiences as a theatre producer. Other strong influences came from Georg Büchner's dramas and *Lenz* fragment[22] and from Goethe, in particular from Goethe's drama *Faust*.[23] Rimbaud and T. S. Eliot helped him articulate a sense of despair at the barrenness of his social environment during the 1970s and 1980s.[24] Greek mythology had always been an inspiration in his attempts to place his thoughts in a broader framework of meaning.[25] In recent years, his contemporary and fellow countryman Franz Fühmann (1922—1984) became important to him as someone desperately familiar with self-doubt and the sense of guilt that stems from having given everything to a cause that had betrayed his faith.[26]

When hell and purgatory became concepts applicable to his own experience, Dante's and Peter Weiss's works acquired increasing significance for him.[27] Understandably, his affinities with Weiss were close ones. Weiss, too, had been a Communist by conviction who had experienced the betrayal of his ideals and who had, in relentless intellectual and artistic effort, written his *Die Ästhetik des Widerstands* to combat his own despair as well as that of others. With Weiss in particular, Braun shares a keen interest in and sympathy with the suppressed and underprivileged and an absorption with the history of suppression and inequality. Like him he uses the aesthetic imagination as a revolutionary force, frequently resorting to a relentlessly forceful, even violent, style and unwieldy literary forms.

His involvement, indeed, identification with Weiss's thought and writing is evident in his having contributed to the slim volume *"Ästhetik des Widerstands" lesen*.[28] His contribution is a two-page piece entitled 'Traumnotiz' and is an account of a dream, or rather a nightmare.[29] He observes himself at a meeting surrounded by people who tell each other what they already know and who function purely by taking instructions from above without any thought of their own. The narrator suddenly finds the strength to speak up: 'ohne aufgefordert zu sein, nehme ich heftig das wort und spreche über die *Ästhetik des Widerstands* von peter weiss. ein satz, den ich also — wie mir im traum einfällt — im schlaf weiß: *wenn wir uns nicht selbst befreien, bleibt es für uns ohne folgen*.'[30] The meeting disperses and the narrator finds himself in a hostile, cold and dark landscape. Yet he feels a sense of joy welling up within him: 'das gebirge, das ich für unnahbar hielt, erkenne ich als die geronnenen und kommunen strukturen der geschichte. ich finde sie wie beschrieben, verwittert, grotesk. mich erfüllt plötzlich eine kalte ruhige freude.'[31]

Peter Weiss's three-volume work, written in unwieldy blocks of highly complex text, encompassing past, present and a Utopian future and attempting to rouse the reader to intellectual, moral and political resistance, served Braun as a source of great strength and inspiration. His *Bodenloser Satz* can be read as a modest offering of a disciple who sees himself also as at the same time an accused and an accuser; who wishes also to abandon all deviousness and opportunism and to allow the truth to come out.

This brief indication of Volker Braun's literary affinities would be less than complete without reference to a nineteenth-century German dramatist whose works, by and large, have enjoyed no great popularity in literary discussions in recent decades: Friedrich Hebbel (1813—1863). Hebbel was at odds with his bourgeois and tendentious social environment, a writer preoccupied with a brooding sense of guilt and self-doubt, yet he wrote with force, pathos and radicality.

No attentive reader of *Bodenloser Satz* will fail to notice that the characters in Braun's little book bear names that are identical with those in Hebbel's drama *Maria Magdalena*, subtitled 'bürgerliches Trauerspiel' ('domestic tragedy').[32] This goes with a striking similarity between each character pair. In Hebbel's drama, there are Klara, an innocent young woman, victim of male blindness and pigheadedness, and her brother Karl, the inconsiderate adventurer; we have Anton, the father, who is too old to understand the modern world and its seeming lack of morals;[33] finally, there is Leonhard, the 'geschickter Schreiber', who is ultimately responsible for Klara's suicide after she has discovered that she is pregnant.[34]

There can, therefore, be no doubt that Braun wishes us to read his text against, inter alia, Hebbel's *Maria Magdalena*. What is it that attracts him in Hebbel's works? The answer lies in their shared interest in and view of history. However, this does not preclude certain differences of opinion due to their very different social and intellectual environments. Hebbel saw the world as a process driven by the dialectical tension between guilt and expiation. Guilt, for him, was a result of individuals' unrestrained self-assertion which, while it is a necessary precondition for the historical process, at the same time causes destruction and suffering. The individual challenges the divine power, but is ultimately defeated. Hebbel's symbol for this dialectical process is the relationship between the sexes.

Hebbel's characters lack the freedom of will to avoid the pressures of historical necessity. They are incapable of change and have to submit to their fate. The author himself took great pains to explain this in his preface to *Maria Magdalena*:

> Das Drama, als die Spitze aller Kunst, soll den jedesmaligen *Welt- und Men-schenzustand* in seinem *Verhältnis zur Idee*, d.h. hier zu dem alles bedingenden sittlichen Zentrum, das wir im Weltorganismus, schon seiner Selbsterhaltung wegen, annehmen müssen, veranschaulichen. Das Drama [...] ist nur dann *möglich*, wenn in diesem Zustand eine entscheidende *Veränderung* vor sich geht, es ist daher durchaus ein Produkt der Zeit.[35]

This concept of history also determined Brecht's view of tragic conflict. However, Brecht introduced one major adjustment: his figures are capable of understanding, indeed they are obliged to understand that their seemingly hopeless situation can be altered, as it does not spring from a metaphysical constellation but is the product solely of conditions in bourgeois society. The individual is therefore challenged to change prevailing circumstances by revolutionary action. Brecht's characters are not seeking to provoke divine power. Their provocation is aimed at bourgeois society. His protagonists do undergo change: they learn to think and act rationally.

Interestingly, when, in *Bodenloser Satz*, Volker Braun draws on Dante, Goethe, Hebbel, Weiss and Fühmann, this also means that he is withdrawing from his former mentor Brecht and his spirit of enlightenment. For he no longer places all his trust in human rationality, but instead reinstates the irrational, the myth. In contradistinction to Brecht, he seeks salvation in the power of unfathomable, boundless love, an act of (secularized) grace.

However, as we know from Braun's *Kast* stories as well as from his *Unvollendete Geschichte*, such love is, by definition, never only an ending, but always also the beginning of new developments in the all-embracing dialectical movement. It cannot last, since it serves merely as a Utopia, whose realization occasionally, in great moments of our lives, comes within reach. In reading *Bodenloser Satz* which, as we know, does reach a full stop, we also need to remember the concluding narrator's comment in *Unvollendete Geschichte*: 'Hier begannen, während die eine nicht zuende war, andere Geschichten.'

VII

Volker Braun's *Bodenloser Satz*, appearing as it did in a period of unheralded upheaval in his country, marks a new beginning in his work — not in the sense of a rejection of what he had produced before, but rather in the sense of terminating a long period of uncertainty and existential doubt. As a human being, as a citizen, and as a poet, Braun has set foot on new territory. His narrator has gone through hell and has experienced a form of resurrection. However, there can be no doubt that the creation of a new society within the united Germany will bring with it new doubts, new grounds for rebelliousness and anger. It is no secret that Braun, like many of his fellow-writers and intellectuals, is anything but happy about the way history has moved for his country. He will most certainly continue to take a stand and carry on his struggle for a better, a more equal and a more humane society. What might have been lifted from him is the destructive self-doubt that has for so long hampered his creative energies.

NOTES

An early version of this text was translated by Arthur Williams.

1 Benno von Wiese: *Zwischen Utopie und Wirklichkeit. Studien zur deutschen Literatur*, Düsseldorf, 1963, p. 84f.
2 Volker Braun: *Verheerende Folgen mangelnden Anscheins innerbetrieblicher Demokratie. Schriften*, Leipzig, 1989, p. 101; written in 1983. The theme of 'Poesie als Gegensprache' is developed by Karen Leeder (pp. 413—24 below) and can be related also to figures discussed by Thomas Beckermann (Wolfgang Hilbig, esp. pp. 102—4 below, and Gert Neumann, esp. pp. 109—12) as well as to aspects of Botho Strauß (see Arthur Williams, esp. pp. 462—4 below).
3 Volker Braun: *Bodenloser Satz*, Frankfurt/Main, 1990.
4 This was the result of the expatriation of Wolf Biermann from the GDR and the subsequent disillusionment amongst those who had attempted to have this decision reversed. Braun had been one of the first to sign a petition addressed to Erich Honecker.
5 Braun: *Verheerende Folgen...*, p. 96.
6 Ibid, p. 101.
7 Ibid, p. 108.
8 Ibid, p. 102.
9 Ibid, p. 102f.
10 Volker Braun: *Hinze-Kunze-Roman*, Frankfurt/Main, 1985.
11 Ibid, p. 126f.
12 Ibid, p. 130.
13 An echo of Peter Weiss's method in *Die Ästhetik des Widerstands* (Frankfurt/Main, 3 vols, published in 1975, 1978 and 1981 respectively) of coming to grips with his intractable material. Cf. Thomas Beckermann's discussion of Monika Maron, esp. pp. 98—101 below.
14 Braun: *Hinze-Kunze*, p. 131.
15 Both included in Volker Braun: *Stücke 2*, Berlin, 1989.
16 Another (of numerous) indications of Braun's close reading of Weiss's *Die Ästhetik des Widerstands* and his strong sense of identification with this earlier Communist writer's dilemma as well as with his articulation of this dilemma in his literary works. See also Section VI (pp. 91—4 above).
17 Page references in the text are to the edition in note 3 above. This particular scene mirrors Christ's resurrection on Easter morning. Also Dante's *Divinia Commedia*.

18 See Braun's story 'Der Schlamm' in *Das ungezwungene Leben Kasts*, which was written in 1959 and was based on this earlier experience.
19 Volker Braun: *Das ungezwungene Leben Kasts*, Berlin (GDR), 1979. The stories were written in 1959, 1964, 1968 and 1974 respectively. The first three appeared initially only in the West (Frankfurt/Main, 1972), the fourth and final one was included in an expanded edition (1979) which was published in both Germanys.
20 Ibid, p. 178.
21 Ibid, p. 176. See also the references to the same story by Joseph Pischel (p. 118 below) and Julian Preece (p. 310 below).
22 In particular Braun's *Unvollendete Geschichte*, Frankfurt/Main, 1977.
23 See Gisela Shaw: 'The Striving of Man: Observations on Volker Braun's *Das ungezwungene Leben Kasts* in the Light of Goethe's *Faust*' in *GDR Monitor*, no. 13, Summer 1985, pp. 5—20.
24 See p. 86 above and Volker Braun: *Training des aufrechten Gangs*, Halle/Saale, 1979.
25 For example, the figure of Prometheus, the demigod who made man from clay, stole fire from Olympus, taught men the use of it and was punished by Zeus for his audacity, has always held a particular attraction for Braun, especially in his more daring and rebellious days (see, for example, the poem 'Prometheus' in *Wir und nicht sie. Gedichte*, Frankfurt/Main, 1970, p. 60; also in the GDR edition published in the same year in Halle/Saale). Similarly, Plato's parable of the cave helped him to clarify his thoughts in his later, more disillusioned phase (see 'Höhlengleichnis' in *Training des aufrechten Gangs*, pp. 60f.)
26 See also the article by Dennis Tate in this volume pp. 285—96 below.
27 See Weiss's 'Gespräch über Dante' where he comments: Hell, 'das ist die Lähmung, das ist der Ort, an dem es keine Weiterentwicklung gibt, an dem jeder Gedanke an Veränderung ausgeschlossen ist' (*Rapporte*, Frankfurt/Main, 1968, p. 149). See also Braun's note in *Verheerende Folgen*..., p. 124, where he confesses to having taken with him on his trip to Hungary in August 1984 (see p. 86 above) both Fühmann's *Zweiundzwanzig Tage* and Dante's *Divina Commedia*.
28 Karl-Heinz Götze and Klaus R. Scherpe (eds): *"Ästhetik des Widerstands" lesen*, Berlin, 1981.
29 Ibid, pp. 10—11. Also in *Verheerende Folgen*..., p. 73, under the title 'Traumtext'.
30 Ibid, p. 10.
31 Ibid, p. 11.
32 Written between 1839—1843, the play was to have been called 'Klara', but was then named after the sinner in the New Testament whose sins were forgiven 'for she loved much' (St. Luke VII, 47). Klara, in turn, served as a model for Gretchen in Goethe's *Faust*.
33 His notorious final exclamation: 'Ich verstehe die Welt nicht mehr!' (Act III, sc. xi) recurs literally in *Bodenloser Satz*, uttered by his counterpart Anton, the Bürgermeister (p. 30).
34 Leonhard is a partial self-portrait of Hebbel. The first-person narrator in Braun's text obviously shares this function.
35 This preface was written in 1844.

'DIE DIKTATUR REPRÄSENTIERT DAS ABWESENDE NICHT':
ESSAY ON
MONIKA MARON, WOLFGANG HILBIG AND GERT NEUMANN

THOMAS BECKERMANN

I Introduction

From the outset, the GDR wasted its chance of developing a separate, unmistakable literature of its own. On the one hand, the artistic doctrine of socialist realism, with its narrow-mindedness and its attachment to a simple nineteenth-century aesthetics, encouraged mediocrity and dis-qualified all other forms of writing by implying that they were ideologically unsound. On the other hand, and this was much more im-portant, a political and social reality developed which came to be in-creasingly rejected; however, because of the strict censorship of the media, this could only be articulated covertly in art. The consequence was a tendency to flee: into the uncommitted and idyllic, into archaism, into indirectness, and also, with increasing frequency over the last fif-teen years, to 'foreign parts'. The exile of the books was followed by the emigration and/or loss of citizenship of the writers. Another form of 'flight' was, however, also possible by means of the narrative techniques of contemporary world literature. It is appropriate at this time to under-take an analysis of the work of writers from the GDR from this point of view.

Already we can refute the cynical claim that literature in the GDR made no contribution to the current changes; it cannot be justified even on grounds of ignorance. Firstly, it is a mistake to expect of writers, of artists, that they should stand in the forefront of political movements. Their workplace is their desk, their struggle is fought out on writing paper. Thus the question is not whether a writer from the GDR might be suited for a leading political role, but rather what are his or her special literary qualities? Secondly, the more aesthetically radical an author's writing, the more critical of society, directly or indirectly, the resulting literature will be. And such aesthetic radicalism made an early contribu-tion to the unmasking of the whole system of 'real existing socialism' —

certainly earlier than we noticed, since our attention, in our reading, was focused exclusively on any small infringement of taboos. This literature is, in the best sense of the word, analysis of the contemporary situation; not the analysis carried out by politicians and men of practical action, but that of courageous, yet powerless literary writers.

Monika Maron, Wolfgang Hilbig and Gert Neumann, all born in 1941 or 1942, lived respectively in East Berlin, Meuselwitz and Leipzig when their first books, which had been rejected by publishers in the GDR, appeared in the S. Fischer (Frankfurt/Main) collection. Today, Monika Maron lives in Hamburg, Wolfgang Hilbig in Edenkoben, and Gert Neumann still lives in East Berlin, although he had permission to travel to the West for some time before November 1989. Hilbig's volume, *Stimme, Stimme. Gedichte und Prosa*, was in fact published in Leipzig in 1983, by the Reclam Verlag, and the Hinstorff Verlag in Rostock published Gert Neumann's *Schuld der Worte* in September 1989, having turned it down ten years earlier.[1]

II Monika Maron

Monika Maron's novel *Flugasche* (1981), which quickly brought her to public notice, was classified as a book about environmental problems or as 'women's literature'.[2] However, it is not the task of literature to set itself up in opposition to this or that deplorable circumstance, to the understanding of this or that role in society. The precondition of literature is a rejection on principle of each and every reality; it is this, and only this, that makes it possible to narrate the origins of existing reality, its future and all its unrealized possibilities.

The texts in Monika Maron's collection *Das Mißverständnis* (1982) were written before the publication of her first novel. Not trammelled by overarching structures, the author draws on her various narrative possibilities: documentary realism in 'Herr Aurich', which portrays social death preceding biological death; the seductive role-play of a powerful man with a woman who has no beliefs, in 'Audienz'; and above all parabolical sketches of the impossible in the two other stories and in the play 'Ada und Evald'.

In the titular text, 'Das Mißverständnis', a woman in Greenland wants to set off for the land of Northsouth with a man she meets by chance on a pillar of ice. The enterprise fails, but not because no such country exists; it fails because the man does not want to give up his familiar surroundings and activities, and because he finds a country where the snow is coloured intolerable. In the story 'Annaeva', a woman breaks out of a walled town, which stands there like a 'stille Festung' (p. 34), into an arid desert, because she can no longer put up with being 'der Erbe von nichts' (p. 35). In the town, with her friends and enemies around her, she cannot lead her own life and so she begins to feel like a 'Plagiat der Bücher' (p. 36). In this way she follows the boundary between dying and a hint of arriving (p. 41) and soon reaches the stage of extreme reduction: 'Sosein, dasein, nichtsein' (p. 42). This is followed first by a doubling of her personality ('ich bin der Wärter, ich bin das Tier. Ich bin zwei', p. 43) and then by its obliteration: 'Ich kann liegen bleiben und auf meine Zukunft warten, die ich selbst bin; die zwei, die ich bin, streiten lassen, bis ich selbst Niemand bin, der auf mich wartet' (p. 45).[3] Thus Monika Maron arrives, in this fragment, at the point from where all stories become possible; she has cast off the ballast of representative realism and gained the freedom to narrate.

What Josefa Nadler, in *Flugasche*, needs a whole book to achieve is already behind Rosalind Polkowski at the beginning of *Die Überläuferin* (1986) — the withdrawal from all relationships and connections. She sits in her room in the Pankow district of East Berlin, she has no needs, her legs are crippled, nobody misses her. It is a curious freedom: 'Sie könnte fortan bleiben, während sie fortging, und fortgehen, während sie blieb' (p. 13). But how can one get up and go, and to where, when one is crippled? Her movement is the freedom of thought and of recollection, to draft out the world through narration; it is the freedom of language and of representational form. Everything that is now narrated is of equal value and of equal importance.[4]

Rosalind recalls her past. The greatest catastrophe had come at the outset, with her birth, since she had not succeeded in dying at the right time. So death and dying (relating to her father, above all to her aunt Ida) run through the novel as its central theme. This 'mangelhafte Lust zu leben' (p. 16) contrasts with the desire for a life of her own, like her friend Clara Winkelmann succeeded in getting: Clara had never been able to hold even a trained mouse, but she had a child, and then hanged herself. Or like Martha Mantel, to whom stealing is second nature and who tells fantastic tales (for example, that her mother had died as a child, so another woman had given birth to her), and who had now gone off into the world to find her father. Men are different, they are sensible and speak in strange languages (both among themselves and to Rosalind); their favourite place is the local bar.

Clara and Martha simply do not take reality seriously, thus they are beyond the reach even of the representatives of law and order. Rosalind, who, by contrast, had tried hard to make herself useful, had had to fight her way through resistance, arrest and interrogation; she had fought through from 'Ich gehöre mir nicht' (p. 65) to 'Mein Ziel bin ich' (p. 64). Everything that helps her to progress has a subversive, oppositional effect on the rigid system, like incitement. Rosalind is, however, made inferior by male discourse (pp. 84, 110, 194) and also by the verbal demands of power, until she frees herself from them by responding to the Latin and Chinese of the men in Eskimo (p. 84) and by recognizing the interrogation as a 'Rollenspiel' (p. 65), thus turning it immediately on its head. This discourse does, however, not end with this simple negation; it now continues as a piece of theatre in her head, in which (in four interludes) the figures, who represent typical attitudes of mind, perorate, at times in rhyming couplets, on order, security, identity, family, and similar categories.

Hence Rosalind leads two lives: a public life in conventional frameworks and a secret life which is a defence against a thievish reality, a socially unproductive life which seeks to reestablish 'den unbenennbaren Zusammenhang der Dinge und unserer selbst' (p. 95). In the service of this life, narration takes every liberty: it changes from the past to the present tense, from the external perspective to the internal (sie/-ich); in the conflict between staying and leaving it intermingles passages of prose and dialogue, reflection and 'herabfallende Märchen' (p. 182), satire and Utopia. 'Niemand fragt: warum bleibst du, sagte Bruno, alle fragen: warum gehst du?' (p. 78). This is narration in a secret code which everybody can understand, in which everything also means something else. Rosalind wants to be as free as Clara, to go to find Martha again. But going in this sense turns everything on its head: Bruno has left Rosalind; later it becomes clear that she had separated from him a long time before, when she set out on her own path in search of the stranger who is one's own self, in order to stop being a 'Plagiat' (p. 101).[5] This dual life (the structures of real life are distinguished from her secret life with extreme clarity) is threatened in the long term by schizophrenia, by the conflict between mind and body.

The conclusion of this background story marks the caesura in the novel. Lamed, Rosalind sees her room as a prison cell, her four walls as one Wall. To get out into the open there remains one possibility: 'Und jetzt, sagt Rosalind, werde ich mit dem Kopf durch die Wand gehen' (p. 130). She aims for the railway station, the place of constant arrivals and goodbyes. But the way to it leads through a reality which becomes increasingly terrible. First she meets a man, once a Nazi, then a tram-conductor, who now pisses on her (p. 136). Then she comes across an ever-increasing number of wounded and dead from a struggle she knows nothing about, and a Wall rises up before her very eyes in the Eberswalder Straße (p. 192); an unexplained war breaks out — which might remind one of the events in Berlin and Leipzig before 9 November 1989 or of those in Peking, in Tianenman Square, the Square of Heavenly Peace. She watches as sentence of death is passed on Martha for crimes against the language, and meets a clone who regards himself as more important than his real original. This reality is alienated and murderous: the Wall is built all over again, a civil war is fought with great bloodshed, the rule of artificial man is proclaimed.[6]

Rosalind never reaches the station, but 'der Bahnhof ist überall' (p. 211). Wet foliage becomes stones, East Berlin becomes the Bowery in New York. And Rosalind changes into Martha, whom she approaches: 'Oder bin ich Rosalind; oder bin ich eine dritte' (p. 213). The sexual act is performed in filth, after a fleeting glimpse of harmony between the Individual/I and Nature ('für eine Weile glaubte ich, selbst der Regen zu sein und die Erde' p. 215) — and everything changes back to the familiar room in Pankow. Rosalind has never left it, but she has got closer to herself, and her journey was a journey through her reality. 'Den Mund weit öffnen und das Wasser in mich hineinlaufen lassen, naß werden, dachte sie, vom Regen naß werden, ja, das wäre schön' (p. 221).

The novel *Die Überläuferin*, whose title the writer knew was open to one-sided interpretation, is a radical book: it relies entirely on imagination, language and form, it shuns proximity to recognizable reality and yet it strives with the utmost accuracy to narrate movement in a time of deadly stasis.[7]

III Wolfgang Hilbig

Wolfgang Hilbig, who trained as a lathe and drill operative and worked for many years as a boilerman, taught himself from the classics of world literature available to him. In his prose works, as in the two volumes of poetry: *abwesenheit* (1979) and *die versprengung* (1986), he attempts from the outset to trace the cause of the dichotomy between the world and the self, sketching out his own situation as part of this process: a worker who writes, who recognizes his own inarticulacy and whose activity is regard by others with mistrust.

In the narrative essay 'Die Arbeiter' (in *Unterm Neomond*, 1982), he depicts the workforce as divided into three. Under the direction of the engineers, themselves invisibly instructed, the workers perform their various tasks without any appreciation of the connections between them, while the boilermen 'dienen der Arbeit der Arbeiter' (p. 33). The boilerman, thanks to his real situation, has an unimpaired view, he is able to develop a perception of and to describe the workers. Additionally, the boilerman, based as always on Wolfgang Hilbig himself and his own practical experience, is a boilerman who writes. In this essay there is a sudden change in narrative perspective from the distance of the third-person to a first-person view. Thus this boilerman recognizes that there is a 'Kampf zwischen der Sprache der Ingenieure und der Sprachlosigkeit der Arbeiter' (p. 36) which, because it never becomes overt, in turn intensifies the inarticulacy of the workers. 'Die Arbeit des Heizers aber ist Gedankenarbeit, sie trägt in all ihren Verrichtungen den Keim zu einer eigenen Sprache' (p. 36).

It is this 'eigene Sprache' that the author is constantly concerned about, a language in which he can express his own point of view and thus allow his personality to unfold.[8] And so he is soon faced with the following alternative: either the workforce recognizes 'daß wir, *die Arbeiter*, nichts anderes als dieser *Betrieb* sind' (p. 43) — this is prevented by the prevailing system and is something the boilerman cannot achieve on his own for all of them; or the boilerman, if he himself is to escape from this alienation, must quit his job — which is what happens in the story 'Der Heizer' (Wolfgang Hilbig himself became a freelance writer in 1981). A boilerman who has begun to write experiences a reality which becomes increasingly unreal to him; he is torn between the stated reality of the world in which he works and what he himself perceives. But what language is the writing boilerman to use in communications with his superior: that of the factory, in which case he will not be able express what he sees, or his own, which would mean a loss in credibility as a boilerman (p. 109)? A boilerman who writes and no longer wants to stoke the boilers arouses suspicion: 'Er redete es sich ein, aber dann hätte er die Stadt verlassen müssen, eigentlich hätte er das Land verlassen müssen' (p. 123). He has no choice, he has to hand in his notice, for 'er sah sich, wie so oft an diesem Morgen, als eine ganz erdachte und inszenierte, von einem lückenlosen System inszenierte Figur' (p. 133). In quitting his job, however, he also loses touch with himself, for he is the boilerman, the worker.

Living a dual life in this way, under constant pressure to make a decision, gives rise to anxiety: a result both of the lack of a defined social (and literary) position of his own and also of the power of the system, which fears the intelligence of a worker who writes. In 'Er', with a level of precision and an absence of emotion that remind one of Kafka's prose, Wolfgang Hilbig tells of an arbitrary arrest, towards which, despite many warnings, this He (*Er*) proceeds, unheeding and unwavering, as if he had become guilty of some unknown guilt. In the story 'Johannis', the first-person narrator sees that the destruction of his own language is the awful consequence of imprisonment ('an den sich ausdehnenden Abenden sind alle Kanäle eines *Untersuchungsgefängnisses* erfüllt von *unbeendeten Sätzen*' p. 65) and he is aware also of the growing aggressiveness that will not be turned against the system but against its victims: 'aber wir schrieben nichts und sprachen nichts, denn wir wußten, daß ein einziger, beliebiger Satz uns in rasende Bestien verwandeln mußte, daß wir uns aufeinander stürzen mußten' (p. 68). The 'Untersuchungsgefängnis' is the place of terror where the first-person narrator, when he is released, calls back to his fellow-prisoners: 'seid frei, ich wiederhole, seid frei ihr Toten... entflammt endlich, arbeitet nicht, arbeitet nie wieder auf den Höfen und in den Gärten einer Gewalt' (p. 68).

And the consequences of arrest are devastating. The first-person narrator in 'Die Einfriedung' knows that even though he has been allowed to go free he has been pronounced guilty (therefore has also become guilty?) and that he has now been sent back 'anwesend zu sein in einem Frieden, der mich kaltließ' (p. 73). In this freedom, he feels split up, divided between an innocent and a guilty person: 'und als ich entlassen war, war um mich der zwieträchtige Friede der Personen, in deren Existenz ich aufgespalten war' (p. 76). The duality, which comes close to that of the boilerman and the writer, again helps to rob the real of its reality, for everything that now happens is beset ultimately with ambiguity as to whether it involves the one or the other, so that they begin to relate to each other as ghosts: 'ich *erblickte* plötzlich eine fremde Figur, ganz ausgeliefert an das Chaos der aus allen Zusammenhängen gerissenen Trümmer, und diese Figur war ich' (p. 80f.). As the narrating figure is alienated from itself, so the narrator is forced into the third-person perspective; he tells of a figure wandering about among the ruins of meaning from its past, it sees through the illusory nature of these but keeps the truth about them to itself: 'die Sprache seiner Gedanken erwies sich ihnen gegenüber als hilflos, völlig unzureichend, es geschah ihm allein auf diesen Wegen, daß eine unterdrückte Person in ihm, in der er seine Wahrheitsperson vermutete, die Oberhand gewann und sich auf lähmende Art weigerte, die Dinge, die ihm begegneten, als die Welt anzuerkennen' (p. 87). His world, which others take to be a world of peace, now has a rent in it which can never be covered over even in the optimistic vision of a truly peaceful community: 'niemand erreichte diese sagenhafte Kultur, die keine Gefangenen mehr aufnahm' (p. 94).

In his later prose texts, which become increasing complex, Wolfgang Hilbig has made several references to his literary forebears, Edgar Allan Poe and Franz Kafka. In the story 'Beschreibung II' (in *Der Brief*, 1985), the first-person narrator, following the recommendation of his acquaintance F.S., presents himself at an exclusive hotel as the new waiter. There he is told that they do not know F.S., that he must mean Hands. The more the narrator denies knowing this Hands, the greater the suspicion becomes of a conspiracy. Of course, he fails to get the job. The narrator realizes too late that he has been and still is caught in a 'Konspiration der Macht' (p. 32), which fills him with horror. His invisible companion (his doppelgänger) accuses him of fundamentally wrong behaviour. 'Wirklich, Du hättest alle Hoffnungen, die sich an die Realität richten, schon vor Deiner Reise aufgeben müssen... Alle Möglichkeiten für Dich suchst Du zwanghaft und borniert in der Realität, als hättest Du irgendeinen schöpferischen Anteil an ihr' (p. 39).

Reality and the actions occurring in it are directed like a play by the controlling power, which seeks in this way to confirm its own existence. It does not describe itself, it requires description by another, second figure. When the first-person narrator is forced to recognize that he is not acting in his own right, but has assumed a role in the play of powerful reality, his security of perception is smashed. He had arrived on a ship; now he speeds by train on his return journey to Dresden to warn F.S. of his impending arrest, but this journey is described in such a manner that it is not clear what form of transport is being used: 'Ich glaubte, das Heck des Wagens, in dem ich mich befand, werde durch das Versinken des Bugs in Wellentälern aufgehoben' (p. 45). On his arrival in Dresden (the narrator now calls it 'Dreßden', for even this town has changed), the narrator is checked by the police. He is asked for his identity card and what his name is: 'Hands... wahrscheinlich... *Hands* mit D, wie in *Handlanger*' (p. 61). So to the police, who hand back his papers, he is called Handlanger; which is, of course, proof enough to them that he has assumed the role allocated to him. The narrator realizes that the controlling power is devoid of substance, a nothingness which is 'darauf angewiesen, sich dauernd Geschichten erzählen zu lassen, in denen sie wirkte' (p. 63). But the power is powerful. Not only does it split the personality of the first-person narrator, it also robs him of what he most dearly loves: there are no women in Dreßden, nor are there any anywhere else. (This, incidentally, is a motif Wolfgang Hilbig takes up again and develops in his story *Die Weiber*, 1987). In one of the large squares the narrator falls into an architectural trap. The walls of these monstrous buildings prove to be a stony sham, a stage set: 'dieser Ort, den sie Dreßden nannten, war die Hölle' (p. 73), for nothing now is as it had been for the narrator in the past. He suffers a 'Verlust jeglicher zweifellosen Wahrnehmung' (p. 74); all that he can do is to search for the way back out of this interminable nothingness. 'Wenn man sich selbst nicht kannte, mußte man sie [die Macht] noch um eins ihrer Gespenster betrügen' (p. 75).

'Ich bin nicht schizophren... viel eher noch wollte ich, ich wäre es,' says the first-person narrator at the beginning of the story 'Der Brief' (p. 83) to an invisible interlocutor. In this text, Wolfgang Hilbig pulls together the various themes of his writing and attempts to tie them in to a/his biographical context. The narrator immediately points out his enormous difficulties: nothing, not even the narrator himself, can guarantee the truth of the biographical detail (p. 83); even the language in which the biographical elements would be reported would not be his own, for his narrative language is 'eine so notorisch mit sich selbst entzweite Sprache geworden' (p. 84). Why is this?

The first part of this tale is a long fictitious dialogue or soliloquy in which the theme is indicated by 'Ich' with the concept of the *Arbeiter-Schriftsteller*. On the one hand, this term recalls the sympathy of the educated middle classes for the worker who also writes; on the other hand, it denotes precisely the situation of the first-person narrator in this story. He had been a worker and has now become a writer, i.e. he has left his class and thus given up his remaining security (p. 97). While the worker dreams of rising up the social ladder, as a rule he remains a worker or, and this is his fear, 'ein Schritt heraus aus der Sicherheit der Arbeitswelt bedeutet dann sofort: *Gefängnis*' (p. 100). It is precisely this fear, amplified by the proletarian anxiety about anything unknown, which makes the worker and 'Ich' homeless in society. 'Wenn wirklich Angst dabei war, als ich meinen Stand verließ und Schriftsteller wurde, so war es die schwer beschreibliche Angst, mit der man die warme Masse verläßt und in eine kalte, geisterhafte Welt eintritt, in der man seine Identität besetzen muß, um bestehen zu können' (p. 106).

The position as a social nonentity leads of necessity to 'einer inwendigen Spaltung' (p. 109), for the impulse to write which investigates itself must be able to withstand the gaze of literature regarding it from outside. The surface and the substrata of reality drift apart, bringing the writing worker, the worker seeking assurance of his self, to the growing recognition of the fantastic degree to which reality has governed and continues to govern him. The 'I' has a nightmare in which a doll is sawn up, and he is the doll — and it all happens in front of an onlooker/overseer whose eyes demand applause (p. 119).[9]

The first-person narrator, the *Arbeiter-Schriftsteller*, has to write his tales in a situation in which he can believe neither reality nor the explanations it offers; 'I' is 'sprachlos vor Zorn' about 'die Untat, die das Denken der angewandten Realität an mir begangen hatte' (p. 120). There is no place for him in society, he is inwardly divided, his greatest horror is the realization: 'Ich hatte mich überhaupt nicht in Gesellschaft darstellen können, weil ich mich nicht selbst dargestellt hatte. Denn ich war überhaupt nicht vorhanden' (p. 122).

His invisible interlocutor has by now noiselessly left the room, and 'I' goes outside into the half-light of the dawning day in search of a letter which he himself has written (p. 123). After what has been an essay-like monologue, the narrator tells the horror-story of C., who has been a worker and now writes. 'Er wollte sein vergangenes Leben wiederherstellen, selbst auch als Leben eines Arbeiters, jedoch in einer befreiten Form, daß es ihm zum Vorwurf einer selbsterschaffenen Autobiographie dienen konnte, die er zu schreiben hoffte' (p. 147). This C. searches feverishly, looking everywhere for his own letter, he falls in love with the postwoman, Kora Lippold, calls himself C. Lippold, and strikes the postwoman dead. C. disappears, and the narrator remarks laconically that C. has probably failed in his dual role-play of wanting to be and to remain both a proletarian and a writer, adding ironically that the texts left behind by C. were like contemporary prose, i.e. they corresponded to the sort of mediocrity, 'das der Klasse genehm ist, in die C. aufrücken wollte' (p. 162). It is, of course, no surprise that the first-person narrator has the same injury to his hand that C. had suffered when he murdered Kora Lippold, nor that the end of the tale consists of the letter both the narrator and C. had been searching for. In this letter C. Lippold reveals that he thinks he is the product of incest and is a vampire.

These ingredients: the peculiar blend of story and essay, of analysis of the present and depiction of the past, of rage and poetry, the use of the doppelgänger motif and of forgotten figures, the constant change in narrative perspective — this linking of them in a magical realism which wants all the time to tell two stories simultaneously with one and the same words — all of this makes up the significance of the novel which appeared in 1989, *Eine Übertragung*. The motifs are familiar: a worker who writes, a gratuitous arrest, the disappearance of people, the fracturing of reality etc; only this time they are extended further when the writer depicts a motiveless murder (which, in the end, is either not a murder at all, or it is one, but of a totally different nature). In a great epic sweep the first-person narrator relates his way step by step towards a narrative present, reports in a unique way the ripped-apart inner-life of an *Arbeiter-Schriftsteller*, the deformations resulting from investigative detention ('Untersuchungshaft') and the deadly petrification of totalitarian society. Gradually, as he tells the tale, he overcomes his self-hate, which 'dem Glauben an ein totales Erfassungssystem des Lebens entsprungen war' (p. 176). His power of perception has grown more acute, as has his criticism, which becomes serious in the sentence: 'Wir alle sind Kinder des Stalinismus' (p. 84). If it is true that materialism has destroyed subjectivity (p. 248), then the whole history and the social practice built around and on it is false, so that, in the end, 'der Materialismus' knows 'nur noch die Objektivität von Gewehrläufen' (p. 248f.). Page 284: 'Ja... dieser Ausgangspunkt der Ideologen ist der Gedanke, daß der Mensch a priori schlecht sei. Worauf man nun wieder nur mit der Diktatur antworten kann... Mauern, Entzug von Würde, Implantation von Schuld.'

In contrast to the ritual interrogation by the state authorities, which destroys people and their ability to speak, the whole novel is 'self-interrogation' with a dual objective: to unmask existing reality as the metaphor of a false ideology, a murderous nothingness (p. 140), and to narrate the story it tells as a metaphor for the process of finding oneself in a second existence. Beyond the enforced loss of reality, of perception, of language, the recognition that one is really alone becomes the precondition for art. Page 300: 'Er meinte damit plötzlich den Urgrund, das Grundprinzip dessen entdeckt zu haben, was Poesie genannt war: die Poesie war die Abwesenheit, wie sie denkbar konsequent, wie sie absolut zu verstehen war, nämlich als die Abwesenheit Gottes. Als die Abwesenheit einer Erklärung. Als die Abwesenheit auch der Klage.' Wolfgang Hilbig is relating the death of Stalin as the death of God.

The novel, as is to be expected, has a multi-layered ending. In respect of power, the first-person narrator is plainly a loser: he has recognized far too late both how trivial a role he has played in the game designed by the secret service and that everything in this game has followed the familiar pattern of a trivial detective story. This is expressed with great precision when he refers to 'die tödlichen Belanglosigkeiten' (p. 7). His inner story, however, of his own identity and his own language, results in the drawing back of the curtain, the revealing of a radiant picture of classic beauty (p. 332ff.) in which nothing happens and everything is: it is a view into the 'Jenseits aller bekannten Region' (p. 334). However, since the rent remains, since the journey from the provinces to East Berlin has, in fact, led back to the provinces, the narrator's powerful abgesang ends in 'Nacht, Macht, Raache, Acheron'.

IV Gert Neumann

If a definition of socialist realism had been set down and if, as a result of it, there had been a 'Bitterfelder Weg',[10] then there could have been no better expression of these than the text 'Die Reportagen' in Gert Neumann's *Schuld der Worte* (published in 1979; the texts span ten years from 1968 to 1978). This, the earliest text in the collection, contains a good indication of what we might regard as Gert Neumann's path to a different kind of literature. A writer goes to a lignite mine to report on an aspect of production; he is accompanied by a figure he calls Saquerieur, who represents his higher awareness of language and thus articulates what he cannot express. Naturally enough, he is 'der Meinung, jeder Mensch müsse sich im Sozialismus an seiner Verwirklichung beteiligen *können*' (p. 24), but he immediately recognizes a dual estrangement in his situation: the workers here are strangers to him and the language he brings with him becomes strange to him. 'Ich dachte das Wort *Arbeiterklasse*. Ich wußte nichts über dieses Problem, in der Hauptsache *kannte* ich dieses Wort, und ich konnte mich nicht entscheiden, *wem* es gehörte' (p. 23).[11]

Writing is not simply designation, for this would contribute to the disappearance of what is designated; designation, since it takes no account of the special features peculiar to what is designated, transposes it into a predetermined interpretational framework: 'zwar waren wir gesendet worden, um in der *Wirklichkeit* die Sätze zu finden, von denen es hieß, daß sie in der Wirklichkeit vorkämen: aber es war für uns leicht, über die Naivität eines solchen Auftrags zu lächeln' (p. 43). If the writer can proceed, therefore, on the basis that the workers, 'die Männer mit ihrer Arbeit und ihren Worten und ihren Gesten, tatsächlich, ihr eignes Leben behandelten' (p. 28), then, beyond the reality of the language (of the ideology) he has brought with him and behind the manifestations defined by it '[muß sich] eine andere Wirklichkeit verbergen, eine, die die Infantilität jener äußeren lächelnd gelten läßt' (p. 28). In this sense, a report is not simply the description of visible features, it is a 'Kampf um die Namen und Sätze' (p. 32) out of which shines that other reality, which can then avoid the guilt which arises 'indem alle versuchen *alles* zu erklären' (p. 33). Thus this writer, who hitherto simply stood around watching and waiting, defines his future writing as a dialogue in which the object can arrive at its name (p. 40). With this knowledge ('die Wörter hatten nun jene zweite Bedeutung' p. 45), speech becomes action — in contrast to silence, 'da das Nichtreden die im Schweigen geäußerten Banalsätze zur Philosophie erhebt' (p. 49). And, indeed, the two now talk to the worker, who sets his excavator in motion.

In his struggle against prescribed language (p. 62), in order to save himself and his subject from reconcilition with the commonplace and the inarticulacy this entails, Gert Neumann exploits the philosophy of language, engages in unprogrammed observation, and resists outside intervention. The new language, which has still to be found, is bound to be anarchic in relation to 'den geläufigen und bekannten Deutungen' (p. 81) and must have political consequences: 'Freilich sei immer von einem Sozialismus die Rede, doch dies geschähe aus Angst vollkommen ohne Wörter zu sein... Aber es gäbe, darüber, ja tatsächlich keine Wahl; die

Geschichte sei eines Tages demokratisch; und die Anarchie der Demokratie sei ja, hinlänglich, bekannt' (p. 99).

With this, however, Gert Neumann's difficulties as a writer are only just beginning. For he knows that 'die zweite Bedeutung der Dinge ohne Gestalt ist und ohne Nachricht' (p. 135), so that even literary works can fail to reach it. And, in keeping with the words of Jakob Böhme, which he has placed as a motto at the beginning of the volume, since he cannot write about something he himself is not, the implicit prerequisite for the legitimation of his future products as a writer is that he must become a worker. As a worker he recognizes, in the story 'Die Versammlung', that although the workers are inarticulate and dumb when set against the language of party conferences, they do have a voice available to them (in their silence), but they still have to discover it. 'Und aus solchen Gründen riefen wir laut, innen, etwas über die Notwendigkeiten unseres Handelns; dem es, zur Rettung vor der, so dauernden, Gegenwartslosigkeit, die als die einzige Wahrheit unsere Gegenwart beherrschte, gelingen mußte seine, es vernichtenden, Deutungen durch unsere Sprache, zu überwinden, "Wir sind doch Menschen!", riefen wir' (p. 106).

This largely unknown life, this way of thinking and speaking, is the subject of Gert Neumann's *Elf Uhr* (1981). This book, which is so complex that I can only indicate a few of its features, has no subtitle but it could be termed a novel in the form of a diary or an essay in the form of a novel. The entries are dated from 24 February 1977 through to 27 February 1978 and take as their theme the naming of 'die ganze, strahlende, Gestalt des menschlichen Elends, die im Sozialismus wie die Haut der Menschen zu sehen ist' (p. 5). The narrator works in the 'Konsument' store and tries at eleven o'clock every day to write some notes about himself and his work. 'Die Diktatur ist eine Interpretation der Welt; sie zerstört die transzendentale Struktur der Welt bei vollem Bewußtsein' (p. 17). It was to escape from positive and negative identification with this postulated truth and reality (he notes, incidentally, that even the simple, 'renowned' opposition is still bound by false thinking, pp. 170, 236) that the narrator deliberately took this particular job: 'Das Kaufhaus wählte ich, um die Tiefe und Notwendigkeit dieser Wirklichkeitsmetapher, mit der letztlich die gesamte Sozialismusstruktur begründet wird, zu prüfen' (p. 18).

To work and to write, this is the task he has set himself, and to do so not from the safe distance of his desk but in the immediate presence, so that the two can intermingle and, if this is successful, become one. His daily notes start with sentences like the following: 'Während meiner Arbeit an den Türen in der Küche' (p. 10). — 'Es ist stumm in die Gesichter der Menschen zu sehen, die die Etagen des Kaufhauses bevölkern' (p. 19). — 'Ich bin krank geworden' (p. 30). — 'Wie sehr mir meine Sätze zerfallen sind!' (p. 37). — 'Der Morgen findet im Keller statt' (p. 42). They report on repairs, the work of the salesgirls, the women shopping, the supervisors, smells and rumours. In this way a picture of daily life in the GDR is created and it could not be more accurate: a departmental head is demoted to transport work because he had requested permission to leave the country; 'der Morgen begann mit dem Terror eines Gesprächs über die gestrige Maidemonstration. An ihr hatte einer der Männer teilgenommen' (p. 62); there are sections about the sale of Polish jeans and about the party at the end of an 'ökonomischen, kulturellen Leistungsvergleichs zwischen den Brigaden', known as ÖKULEI, about discussions of Bahro's book *Die Alternative* and about Manfred Krug's leaving the country. 'Die Ausreise ist der Höhepunkt einer individuellen Erfahrung über die poetische Impotenz einer Gesellschaft' (p. 299).

However, the longer and the more closely the narrator looks at his material, the clearer becomes the lameness, the use of alcohol as an escape, the hate, the inarticulacy, and the search for some guilt or other which might make everything tolerable. These working conditions and working relations drive the workers to a state of psychological distress, serving only to destroy precisely this way of life and to prevent the realization of a positive reality (p. 81).[12]

At the same time this text is autobiographical in a most unusual way. The narrator tells how, in 1968, he had been expelled from the Johannes R. Becher Literaturinstitut and from the SED and also how he had had difficult and, ultimately, fruitless negotiations with a publishing house in the GDR about *Schuld der Worte*; he goes on to call the publishing house 'ein Instrument für den Bewußtseinsmord' (p. 86). In addition to this, and this is a story in its own right which runs through the whole book, he is constantly searching for an undisturbed and unobtrusive place to write, for the very act of writing makes others suspect him of being an informant.

'Eine Sprache muß verteidigt werden; jene, die täglich bis zur Un-kenntlichkeit zerstört ist' (p. 104). In view of these efforts, this struggle, it is no coincidence that, time and time again during the year, the narrator is taken ill. In the increasing gloom of reality ('Denn der Horizont für eine Wahrheit ist in der Realität, in der wir leben, vollkommen verdüstert, weil es keine Sprache gibt. Keine der Formulierungen kann sich zur Wirklichkeit erfüllen; das Volk ist der Wirklichkeit enteignet', p. 122), his only anchor is poetry, as a form of perception and as a language which defends the dignity of both writer and reader: 'Der einzige Ausweg, die zwiefache Wirklichkeitsdiktatur zu durchbrechen... ist der Nachweis von Poesieruinen in dieser Gegenwart' (p. 161, also pp. 177, 180). Given this conviction, the pain he feels when his book is exiled and he is refused permission to travel to his publishers in Frankfurt/Main is all the more acute. And so this writer, who in establishing his right to poetry refers to Büchner, Kleist, Hebbel, Kafka and Bernhard, comes to the conclusion (an inescapable consequence of a system killed by its rigidity): 'Denn, das Verhängnis ist vollkommen. Die Methode, die diese Gegenwart benutzt, um Wirklichkeit zu errichten, wird mit der jeweils entstehenden Realität identifiziert; und jede Freiheit des Individuums, an den Fragen der Wahrheit mit seinem eigenen Leben teilzunehmen, ist ausgeschlossen' (p. 187).

Any attempt at positive work and at positive language must fail at both levels. The workers smash and burn the objects they are supposed to collect from a warehouse; the narrator is asked by a wife to help her husband escape from the his pursuers (the *Stasi*?) and does so; people talk about a drunken Party-secretary, after a wedding-feast, being driven across country nailed up in a box used for transporting pigs — the fol-lowing day it had been found burnt out; A., a fellow-worker, suffers a fatal accident; and the sale of Romanian glassware all but ends in bloody chaos, an event in which the narrator was involved. Eventually, the *Ar-beiter-Schriftsteller* gives up his membership of a socialist brigade because he cannot be a worker and, at one and the same time, a writer 'in exile'; he quits his job. The dictatorship of reality and of realism forces him onto the sidelines.[13] 'Der Realismus, freilich, ist ein Verbrechen an der Würde des Menschen' (p. 290). — 'Es gab keine Sprache. Sie war ver-weigert. Die Handlungen weigerten sich Realität zu bedeuten' (p. 325). At one point the narrator makes the laconic remark: 'Dieses Manuskript ist, fraglos, ein Resultat der DDR-Realität' (p. 189).

That this was no fictitious crisis simply relating to the fictional narrator of *Elf Uhr* but was one suffered by Gert Neumann himself becomes clear when we consider that it was eight years before the appearance of his next book: *Die Klandestinität der Kesselreiniger* (1989). In the intervening period, since the state would not offer him employment, he worked in a Protestant hospital as a general handyman, and produced just a few texts: for example, 'Übungen jenseits der Möglichkeit' (1986), the difficult 'Brief an Adam Michnik' (1987), and 'Die Stimme des Schweigens', which was published privately in the GDR in 1988. Above all, however, he has been intensively involved with the new literature as the editor of the Leipzig unofficial journal *Anschlag*.

Die Klandestinität der Kesselreiniger, to which the author eventually gave the subtitle *Ein Versuch des Sprechens*, is both the consequence and expression of the discrepancy between postulated and actual reality, working and writing. At a time in which 'Willkür, Terror und Lüge durch die Ordnung des Gesetzes stattfinden' (p. 22), writing, as a dialogue with matters in the language, can exist only in secret. A factual example of such arbitrariness is the imprisonment of the narrator's son, who has been pronounced guilty simply because he was arrested. As a last attempt to escape falling silent as part of the decline of this society, the narrator breaks up the text about the arrest, which is at once report and reflection, with the pure poetry of sequences in which swifts fly about between blocks of houses, where people to come to their windows to watch.

However, the ruling power also threatens the *Abeiter-Schriftsteller*: he, the fitter, is obliged, with his friend and colleague Angel, to clean boilers, something which is permitted by existing labour law. They have the choice of doing as they are told or leaving — and they submit to the *'verwirklichten Diktatur des Proletariates'* (p. 53f.), which appears to them 'hier in der Gestalt eines machtblinden, christlich motivierten, Diktators' (p. 52). In this new, hidden workplace both thought and speech retreat into silence; a boilerman, for example, goes by talking to himself and is capable only of banality: 'So, das hätten wir... Ja, na klar' etc (p. 65). What Gert Neuman had previously called 'das Abwesende'[14] now becomes 'das Verschollene' (p. 78), and any kind of dialogue, even an 'oppositionelles Sprechen' between 'den alten Männern und meiner Generation' (p. 109) is described as totally impossible in the face of this 'real-sozialistischen Chaos' (p. 132). The chasm between them is unbridgeable.

The conception and writing of this book, which is designed as a grand elegy (p. 128) about a great social failure and which was triggered off by the sentence: 'Ich bin ein Trümmer der Verlegenheit' (p. 198), does not so much break off at this point, it breaks apart. New events are superimposed on old problems. The narrator is now actually given permission to travel to the West, but his manuscript is taken from him at the border; at the same time the opposition in the GDR begins to speak out, in spite of being kept massively under observation, both inside and in front of the Zionskirche in East Berlin (p. 142). The narrator returns, only to have to face grief at the death of Angel; his loneliness is great and the only way he can live with dignity is to continue to write. He quits his job, becomes really a free writer, and ends his book with unparalleled confidence: 'Mit der Frage nach der Zukunft des Sprechens möchte ich das Lesen grüßen: "Glatnata kokotschka proso synuwa."' — 'The hungry chicken dreams of millet'.

V Conclusion

Our three authors, who published their first books some ten years ago, have in common that they have been uncompromisingly radical in their refusal to bow to any diktat, in their thinking, in their writing, in their perceptions, in their social actions. This radicalism has led them to individual forms of narration in which they found the freedom to say everything they felt was necessary. This also explains why their books (with the two exceptions mentioned[15]) could not be published in the GDR at that time and why they were noticed by only a few people in the Federal Republic — they did not match the expectations of a readership attuned to traditional GDR literature.

These books have helped, no matter how far below the surface, younger writers (like Wolfgang Hegewald, Katja Lange-Müller and Bernd (Jayne-Ann) Igel[16]) to embark on the search for their own language and narrative form — exercising freedom of perception in relation to social realities and rejecting all spoon-feeding. This is an understanding of literature which has been taken further by authors in the unofficial literary journals (like *Anschlag, ariadnefabrik, mikado, schaden, verwendung* and *Zweite Person*) to the point of linguistic experimentation and to the interrelating of language with photography, the fine arts and music.

By recognizing the whole ideology and the practical political, social and economic system derived from it as a nothing (admittedly, a nothing with great power) and describing it as such, these writers contributed to what has happened in the GDR since 9 November 1989: the noiseless and total disappearance of this nothingness — although, and this must not be forgotten, thought and discourse will remain deeply affected by it.

NOTES

Translation by Arthur Williams.

1 References in the text are to the following works. Monika Maron: *Flugasche. Roman*, Frankfurt/Main, 1981; *Das Mißverständnis. Vier Erzählungen und ein Stück*, Frankfurt/Main, 1982; *Die Überläuferin. Roman*, Frankfurt/Main, 1986. Wolfgang Hilbig: *abwesenheit. gedichte*, Frankfurt/Main, 1979; *Unterm Neomond. Erzählungen*, Frankfurt/Main, 1982; *Stimme, Stimme. Gedichte und Prosa*, Leipzig, 1983; *Der Brief. Drei Erzählungen*, Frankfurt/Main, 1985; *die versprengung. gedichte*, Frankfurt/Main, 1986; *Die Weiber*, Frankfurt/Main, 1986; *Eine Übertragung. Roman*, Frankfurt/Main, 1989. Gert Neumann: *Die Schuld der Worte*, Frankfurt/Main, 1979 (Rostock, 1989); *Elf Uhr*, Frankfurt/Main, 1981; 'Übungen jenseits der Möglichkeit', *Neue Rundschau*, vol. 97, no. 2/3, August 1986, pp. 49ff.; 'Brief an Adam Michnik' in Thomas Beckermann (ed.): *Reise durch die Gegenwart*, Frankfurt/Main, 1987, pp. 343ff.; *Die Stimme des Schweigens*, Leipzig, 1988 (originally in *Neue Rundschau*, vol. 94, no. 1, February 1983, pp. 83ff.); *Die Klandestinität der Kesselreiniger. Ein Versuch des Sprechens*, Frankfurt/Main, 1989.
2 See also Ricarda Schmidt's discussion of *Die Überläuferin*, pp. 430—35 below.
3 Cf. Gisela Shaw's discussion of Volker Braun, esp. pp. 86—7 above.
4 See also Martin Kane's discussion of Monika Maron: 'Culpabilities of the Imagination', which draws on Gert Neuman's *Die Schuld der Wort* as discussed in the present article (in Arthur Williams, Stuart Parkes and Roland Smith (eds): *Literature on the Threshold. The German Novel in the 1980s*, Oxford, 1990. pp. 221—34).
5 The problem of the self as a 'Plagiat' also plays a role in the work of Botho Strauß. See Arthur Williams, esp. p. 459 below.
6 Cf. Axel Schalk's discussion of Heiner Müller's view of men reduced to automata, esp. pp. 72—4 above.
7 This problem, allowing for the change to a West German perspective, is central also to the work of Botho Strauß, particularly the long novel *Der junge Mann*. Cf. Arthur Williams: 'Botho Strauß and the Land of his Fathers: From *Rumor* to *Der junge Mann*' in Williams, Parkes, Smith: *Literature on the Threshold...*, esp. pp. 294—9.
8 Several contributions to this volume explore aspects of this problem. See, for example, Gisela Shaw (esp. pp. 85—6 above), Katrin Kohl (esp. pp. 342—50 below), Karen Leeder (pp. 413—24 below) and Arthur Williams (esp. pp. 462—4).
9 The destruction of the self in the shape of a doll or other image is reminiscent of aspects of Heiner Müller discussed by Axel Schalk, esp. pp. 67 and 73 above.
10 As a result of the Bitterfeld Writers' Conference of 1959 authors were encouraged to work in firms so that they could write more authentically about their experiences in the world of socialist production.
11 Katrin Kohl's analysis of cliché in writing (see note 8 above) is again relevant in this context.
12 Neumann here uses 'Wirklichkeit' which he differentiates, as a 'positive or good reality' still to be achieved, from the 'false (existing) reality' of 'Realität'.
13 Gisela Shaw (see note 3 above) draws our attention to a similar experience in the case of Volker Braun.
14 The title of this paper is taken from *Die Klandestinität der Kesselreiniger*, p. 14.
15 Hilbig: *Stimme, Stimme*; Neumann: *Schuld der Worte*.

16 Wolfgang Hegewald, b. 1952 in Dresden, moved to Hamburg in 1983, now lives in Bremerhaven. Hegewald has published: *Das Gegenteil der Fotografie*, 1984; *Hoffmann, Ich und Teile der näheren Umgebung*, 1985; *Jakob Oberlin oder Die Kunst der Heimat*, 1987; *Verabredung in Rom*, 1988. Katja Lange-Müller, b. 1951 in Berlin (GDR), has lived in West Berlin since 1984. Lange-Müller has published: *Wehleid — wie im Leben. Erzählungen*, 1986; *Kasper Mauser — Die Feigheit vorm Freund*, 1988. Bernd (Jayne-Ann) Igel, b. 1954 in Leipzig, lives in Markkleeberg. Igel has published: *Das Geschlecht der Häuser gebar mir fremde Orte*, 1989.

THE END OF UTOPIA?
THE CURRENT DISCUSSION ON GDR LITERATURE
AND THE CONTROVERSY SURROUNDING CHRISTA WOLF

JOSEPH PISCHEL

This article[1] is somewhat different from the other contributions to this volume both because its scope is limited to GDR writers within the territorial boundaries of the GDR and also because I find it difficult, as someone personally involved, to view the experience of the loss of Utopia from the cool distance implied in the use of concepts familiar in literary scholarship, like 'die Postmoderne' and 'Musealisierung der Geschichte'. Coming to terms with the loss of Utopia is even more difficult. Not only is there no conceivable future for a 'literature of the GDR' — even its past identity and integrity are being questioned. From Hamburg's *Die Welt* to West Berlin's *die tageszeitung*, in the *ZDF* Reich-Ranicki show and also even in the *DFF* 'Bücherrunde'[2] the representative authors of this country are being called to account: they had overwintered comfortably adapted in their niches; they had accepted privileges as bribes; they had been allowed to feign a small pseudo-public arena within the boundaries of an inwardness protected and monitored by the political powers; they had only ever worked *within* the system — and precisely this distinguished them from the real champions of civil rights like Václav Havel; they had persisted for far too long in the illusion of an autonomous third way for the GDR and had thus isolated themselves from the 'people's movement', which had had enough of left-wing intellectuals' plans to improve the world.

It is a remarkable but inescapable fact that these attacks are aimed at authors like Stephan Hermlin and Stefan Heym, Heiner Müller and Christa Wolf, Volker Braun and Christoph Hein, who provided important impulses for new thinking, indeed also for action, and who also gave the experience of life in this state and its crises, the awareness of 'congealed contradictions' and 'retarded developments', their most radical expression. Thus, for many readers, they became a source of moral and political orientation. Christa Wolf, on whom the attacks concentrated, spoke in March 1990 at the writers' congress of a deliberate campaign which 'mit der allgemeinen Totaldemontage der DDR auch die Literatur demontieren will, die in der DDR geschrieben wurde, und möglichst viele ihrer Autoren gleich mit'.[3]

Since if a community's identity is to find expression anywhere it must do so in literature, literature's representatives are to be stripped of their moral integrity. It is a perfectly logical position for the euphoric victors as they survey the worldwide collapse of real socialism to seek to reduce its history to the level of a 'whodunnit crime-story' and, with this in mind, to seek to neutralize its Utopian impulse.

It is incontestably true that the writers who are now at the centre of controversy sought with their critical findings and emancipatory demands not to remove the system but to improve it, and it is true that there was a price to pay for this limitation of aims: these writers will now have to come to terms with their 'blind spots' (as will literary scholarship as an institution, about which I say nothing here — nor about my own part in this). Obviously the forty years of dual German statehood have created a different scale of differentiation than is the case in other socialist countries. The majority of those who remained in the GDR (the majority even of those who emigrated or were expelled) held on till the very last, in spite of all their disappointment and disillusionment,[4] to the hope that the centralized, *politbburo*cratized power-structures could be broken apart through internal change or forcibly smashed from below, leading at last to the release of socialist forces which might be brought into step with their own ideas of human emancipation and enfrachisement and which might yet help to halt the catastrophic course of history towards the obliteration of the human race.

Admittedly, this holds good only for the generation that grew up with the GDR and knew strong personal commitment to the revolutionary changes of the 1950s and perhaps even of the early 1960s. Later generations were increasingly hesitant with their commitment, which was sometimes totally lacking.[5] The divisive tensions that writers had to suffer under such circumstances were charted by Volker Braun in his story 'Die Tribüne'. He says it was 'noch niemals so [...] daß einer *für* eine Gesellschaft ist — und doch zugleich sie mit derselben Energie *ändern* will wie in alten Zeiten. Das war wohl verrückt, und um verrückt zu werden. Und doch konnte man damit leben.'[6] Even then Braun's first-person narrator is still not able to cope with this tension. He drives his car into a wall: 'Das Genick war gebrochen, das Gesicht unkenntlich.'[7]

Why so many were unable, even to the very end, to find a way out of the dilemma presented by such unlivable alternatives and why we were never really frightened into action by literature's writing on the wall is really a matter for psychologists or sociologists, not for literary scholars. Experience is obviously not able to blot out the luminosity of Utopia, particularly not in the case of the generation that had emerged from the destruction of the War and fascism deeply disturbed and insecure and which had set out to find a radical alternative. There was widespread consensus in the early years of the GDR with their optimism in enlightenment and progress: the laws which governed the development of nature and society were recognizable or even established; it was possible on this scientific basis to organize the coexistence of individuals, of groups and of peoples according to a rational, humane model of society. Literature, as an important instrument in the broadening and changing of consciousness, became (and considered itself) obliged to support this methodical process of societal reform. The humane Utopia of a non-alienated, whole humanity was bound in with the 'real movement' towards socialism, which would enable it to take on concrete form. The legendary effect of Ernst Bloch on Christa Wolf and her generation did not, as is often stated, consist simply in the power of the Utopian principle to permanently break through the stagnation of the idea of socialism as an 'achievement' and to open up the possibility of forward progress in the movement of history; Bloch always related intellectual anticipation explicitly to this movement in its real historical context:

> Denken heißt überschreiten [...] Deshalb geht wirkliches Überschreiten auch nie ins bloß Luftleere eines Vor-uns, bloß schwärmend, bloß abstrakt ausmalend [...] Wirkliches Überschreiten kennt und aktiviert die in der Geschichte angelegte, dialektisch verlaufende Tendenz [...] Funktion und Inhalt der Hoffnung werden unaufhörlich erlebt, und sie wurden in Zeiten aufsteigender Gesellschaft unaufhörlich bestätigt und ausgebreitet. Einzig in Zeiten einer niedergehenden alten Gesellschaft, wie der heutigen im Westen, läuft eine gewisse partielle und vergängliche Integration nur abwärts.[8]

When, in her programmatic essay 'Lesen und Schreiben' (1968), Christa Wolf defended the Utopian dimension of literature against a concept of realism that was understood altogether too narrowly as mimesis, she demanded a literature which was at once revolutionary and realist, which would seduce and encourage the reader to the 'impossible'. At the same time she had constantly in mind a concrete point of reference: 'Die Prosa kann sich nur mit gedanklichen Strömungen und gesellschaftlichen Bewegungen verbinden, die der Menschheit eine Zukunft geben.'[9] And again, four years later: 'Das ist ja die Übereinstimmung im Grundsätzlichen, daß auch die sozialistische Gesellschaft das Ziel der Selbstverwirklichung ihrer Mitglieder hat wie die sozialistische Literatur.'[10] Even in her 1966 essay on Ingeborg Bachmann, that important step in the formulation of her own concept of prose writing, Wolf made a decisive distinction between herself and Bachmann: 'Literatur als Utopie [...] Utopie von welcher Grundlage aus? Tapferer, tief anrührender Entwurf eines neuen Menschen. Aber ein einsamer Entwurf, und nicht die Andeutung realer Schritte von der Misere ihrer Gegenwart weg zu dieser Zukunftsvision hin.'[11]

It was this increasingly disappointed hope that Utopia and the 'real movement' might proceed hand in hand and the extreme effort required to cope with this unlivable alternative which, in my view, constitute the identity and separateness of GDR literature — not just the specific experiences it reflects and its special role as a substitute public forum, as a source of help and advice in life, and as a point of moral and political orientation.

In both her essays and interviews, Christa Wolf tried right through to winter 1989 to hold on to the hope that the social and economic structures of socialism, despite their ossified and perverted nature, might yet offer better conditions for the realization of a system of human values which she delineated in terms like love, sisterliness, brotherliness and, above all, friendliness. Even after Wolf Biermann had been stripped of his GDR citizenship, when interviewers were trying to force her to radical consequences in this crisis situation and to pin her down to the idea of Utopia as a vanishing point, she invoked the special opportunities for literature in a society 'die nicht auf der Grundlage persönlichen Eigentums an Produktionsmitteln, nicht auf der Basis persönlichen Profitstrebens und Konkurrenzverhaltens produziert'.[12] She was never able at any time to see bourgeois society as a humane alternative. There were also in every series of sobering set-backs and disappointments always encouraging signs that Utopia and the 'real movement' might be brought into step. Gorbachev's vision of a world peace order without bombs and rockets was just such an underpinning of her own visions and conjurations, which had been for so long literally in the air. Sarah

Kirsch, visiting Mecklenburg at a fairly recent date, found only conflicting opinions and difficulties in communication on this point. She finds
her friends still 'stark mit dem alten Galimathias befaßt', still ready or,
perhaps, again prepared 'vom Kleister der Hoffnung zu zehren, an ein
Wunder zu glauben, das ausgerechnet von dort kommen sollte, wo
Heinrich Vogeler einstmals in einem Lager verscholl'.[13]

And yet Christa Wolf's general critique of civilization and rationalism has for a long time also been directed specifically at conditions
under real socialism. It was already apparent in the mid-1960s that she
had understood the contradictions of instrumental rationalism, the
'dialectic of enlightenment', in relation to the scientific and technological
appropriation of *Nature* and the ambivalence of technology. Manfred
Herrfurth (in *Der geteilte Himmel*, 1963) drafts out a technicalistic vision
of a conflict-free humanity, against which, admittedly, are set the daily
earthly efforts at moral responsibility. For understandable reasons, the
intention to enlighten, to design *society* according to a theoretical and
ideological model, is problematized here only hesitantly and covertly.
The consciousness of this inherent problem becomes increasingly sharp
from the time of *Nachdenken über Christa T.* (1969). In *Störfall* (1986), again
a form of writing on the wall, the monster of an exploding reactor and
the monstrosity of alienated conditions even under socialism are traced
back to the same mistaken belief, 'daß die Wissenschaften, der neue
Gott, uns alle Lösungen liefern werde, um die wir ihn angehen würden'.
Now the (much-quoted) question is: 'Treiben die Utopien unserer Zeit
notwendig Monster heraus?'[14]

This explains why *Der geteilte Himmel* represents Christa Wolf's
last attempt in literature to tie her humane system of values unambigu-
ously to socialist society. From that time onwards her literary findings
are generally negative, depicting unfulfilled expectations of emancipation (as in *Kein Ort. Nirgends*, 1979). Livable social forms combining the
individual *and* the communal, like those explored on Mount Ida by the
Trojan women and their children or reluctantly by the island dwellers in
Sommerstück (1989), are the exception: small human communities, the
family or groups of friends, always on the periphery, always
endangered, almost completely relegated to the mundane unheroic areas
into which women were always forced in the history of male-dominated
societies. Women's activities from the breast-feeding of a baby through
to the preparation of a banquet, demonstrable forms of human caring

and communication are presented as valuable alternatives to the system of 'male' values still prevalent in technical, scientific and economic rationality.[15] Literature is to function as 'research for peace' by making the description of the locations and landscapes of human relations so precise, so critical and so loving that people begin to regard them seriously as their 'home' and do not allow them to be destroyed: 'Ein Gespräch über Bäume, über Wasser, Erde, Himmel, Mensch — ein Versuch, der mir realistischer vorkommt als die strikte wahnwitzige Spekulation auf den Weltuntergang.'[16]

From the end of the 1960s, the Utopian impulse in Christa Wolf's thoughts and feelings derives less and less from theoretical and rational designs aimed at 'enlightenment', from systems and ideologies, and she turns increasingly to everyday, livable forms of individuality, communality, and solidarity. In 1977, she discovered, in Maxie Wander's collection of women's conversations, the 'Geist der real existierenden Utopie, ohne den jede Wirklichkeit für den Menschen unlebbar wird'. She experienced 'ein Vorgefühl von einer Gemeinschaft, deren Gesetze Anteilnahme, Selbstachtung, Vertrauen und Freundlichkeit wären. Merkmale von Schwesterlichkeit, die, so scheint mir, häufiger vorkommt als Brüderlichkeit.'[17]

There are numerous indications of how this hope in practical forms of non-violent, productive coexistence was nourished by experiences with the alternative and solidarity movements: the women's movement, the peace movement, the ecology movement, the church — in every case with people, 'die an dem Pol der Nichtmacht standen'.[18] At first, she tended to meet this type of person mostly among the '68' generation in western Europe, later she came across them increasingly in the GDR as well.

By the time of the Biermann affair at the very latest, Christa Wolf had given up the idea that the literary avant-garde could directly influence the *structures* which facilitate or prevent individuality *and* communality, that it could help vanquish the mega-machines, the monopoly monster and the bureaucracy monster, that it could outline alternative orders. By way of comparison, Volker Braun's observations and suggestions have remained directed at the *structures*: his 1977 essay on Büchner can now, in the light of our recent experiences, be recognized as a prophecy of visionary accuracy and yet it failed tragically to identify the course of history:

Solange eine Gesellschaft, sie mag mittlerweile wie immer heißen, auf Gewalt
beruht, nämlich solange es "die da oben und die da unten" gibt, bedarf es der
Gegengewalt, sie zu verändern. Zwar der Charakter dieser Gegengewalt mag
sich modeln, er mag feiner werden: oder in sozialistischen Staaten gar freund-
licher, aber mitnichten nachgiebiger. Es wird nicht der Hanf sein und nicht
die Laterne, nicht einmal der Streik und die Demonstration. Wo das Oben
und Unten sich nicht mehr in der archaischen Gewalt von *Klassen* gegenüber-
steht, aber doch die verschiedene Stellung der Individuen in der Pyramide
der Verfügungsgewalt anzeigt, geht der Kampf nicht mehr um den Platz an
der Spitze, sondern um die Zertrümmerung der Pyramide.

However, Braun's 'basis democracy' alternative was not attainable in
practice: 'Die Staaten, die fähig wären, ihre eigene Gegengewalt zu orga-
nisieren (mittels Volksvertretungen, Ausschüssen, Produktionsbera-
tungen, Grundeinheiten der Partei), befinden sich noch im Stadium des
Großversuchs: Die Massenproduktion von Demokratie ist noch nicht
freigegeben. Sie ist auch, obwohl das Ziel, ein Nebenprodukt — der
Jahrtausendarbeit, die vertikale Arbeitsteilung aufzuheben durch
Umwälzung der Produktionsweise von Grund auf.'[19] 'Jahrtausendarbeit'
is really nothing more than another word for Utopia. But then the 'real
movement', the 'Umwälzung der Produktionsweise von Grund auf'
which is now in progress, has taken completely the opposite direction.
Or, perhaps not? Is it just real socialism's methods of socialization that
have proved to be unproductive? Whatever the case, it is certainly going
to be difficult to support Utopian ideas by reference to this approach to
the philosophy of history and to link them firmly to specific social conditions. According to Christa Wolf, a new need for Utopian ideas must
develop, if it is to emerge at all, out of daily life and not out of theories.
For the foreseeable future it will be concerned probably above all with
individuals, with their identity, autonomy and enfranchisement, and
with their moral responsibility, which cannot be delegated to a group or
an institution. Inevitably, this must also involve an element of self-de-
nial, considering how insecure and susceptible to interference individual
identity and moral integrity have so far always proved to be when faced
with the apparatus and structures of the state. And yet this is no flight
into the private sphere; bearing in mind the disastrous continuities in
German behaviour patterns, the addiction to conformity and the implicit
trust in authority, it is rather the prerequisite for mature citizens in a
democracy — also when faced with new and seductive mechanisms of
manipulation.

It does therefore seem necessary to undertake a reappraisal of our
historical experiences in the light of Utopias, a recollection of history

which still strives to enlighten. In this respect, the voice of authors whose fundamental experience was the GDR will, for a long time to come, remain unmistakable in German literature — even if many might prefer to forget and suppress these experiences. How did these dreams of freedom, justice, humanity for all become — nightmares? Was it the fault of the Utopias, which were distorted only to the point of recognizability? Or is it precisely the Utopias that we must strive to preserve? Personally, I am aware of no medium of social communication that is better placed than literature to seek differentiated answers to these questions and to illuminate the 'blind spots' of our forgetting and repressing: the way dream and nightmare, hopes and illusions, personal integrity and opportunism, commitment and manipulation, 'achievements' and the perversion of them were almost inextricably interrelated.

In a speech in Hildesheim, where she was awarded an honorary doctorate in January 1990, Christa Wolf hinted at what it was that would now keep her writing:

> Wohin wird die Geschichte dieser vierzig Jahre geraten, die ja kein Phantom ist, aber bei ihrem Verschwinden Phantomschmerz hinterlassen wird? Wer wird die Trauer, die Scham, die Reue vieler Menschen, die ich aus ihren Briefen herauslese, in ihren Augen sehe und auch in mir selbst finde, noch öffentlich ausdrücken wollen, wenn alle mit der Verbesserung der materiellen Lebensbedingungen beschäftigt sein werden?[20]

What happened to us, what did we allow to happen, what did we ourselves cause to happen? — No writer can ever provide, or spare us, our own unqualified answers to these questions. Given her experiences with *Kindheitsmuster* (1976), we can certainly expect Christa Wolf, also in future, to set yardsticks for this imperative self-questioning and conscience-searching. Some will doubt whether cathartic shocks from empathetic identification will suffice in this case, whether this will not simply encourage new dimensions of repression between self-accusation and self-pity. 'Es gibt gute Gründe,' insinuated one critic in Hamburg's *Die Welt* on 3 May 1990, 'Christa Wolf zu mögen, wenn es in der deutschen Geschichte darum geht, die Wunde nicht zu berühren.' But the self-righteousness and malice of the columnists, of the new 'victors of history', can be excused only on the grounds that they were spared the tests and trials of a comparable life between unlivable alternatives.

The Utopia of human emancipation, as far as it was associated with the societal and economic prerequisites of socialist patterns of production, is dead. The removal of alienation by the really democratic control by the producers over the processes of production and therefore over the resultant human conditions, i.e. by means of democracy, proved to be unworkable within the power structures of a centralized *politburo*cracy. However, Christa Wolf does not expect this in a social market economy and a parliamentary democracy either. The hope of a third way, of an alternative, basis democracy was dashed in just a few weeks: between the mass demonstration in Berlin on 4 November 1989, that so rare historical moment of apparent concurrence between the artistic avant-garde and the 'Vernunft der Straße' (Christoph Hein), and the despairing appeal of 29 November 'Für unser Land'. In a reader's letter to the *Norddeutsche Zeitung*, a woman who in 'dark days of stagnation and resignation' had drawn courage from Wolf's books now reacted with an 'indescribable feeling of impotence and anger':

> Träume sind wichtig, ohne sie kann man nicht leben, aber leben kann man auch nicht allein von einem Traum. Wenn Traum und Wirklichkeit vermischt werden, wird es gefährlich. Die Chancen, Ihren Traum (damals auch meinen) zu verwirklichen, haben die Panzer 1968 in Prag niedergewälzt. Inzwischen hat sich viel verändert, und diese einmalige Chance ist vergeben. Geschichte wiederholt sich nicht.[21]

However, it is not just since the upheavals of the last few months that the relationship between the literary avant-garde and the 'people's movement' has been problematical. The contradictions and conflicts that are here at work are more complex and are not limited to any one system. In her 'Günderrode' essay of 1978, Christa Wolf had already taken account of the losses: 'Die rigorose Arbeitsteilung zeitigt ihre Ergebnisse. Die Produzenten der materiellen und der geistigen Werte stehen einander fremd an verschiedenen Ufern gegenüber, daran gehindert, gemeinsam lebbare Umstände hervorzubringen. Der Zerstörung, die nicht immer offensichtlich ist, sind sie alle ausgesetzt.'[22] A literature which was increasingly forced back on making itself heard and understood within an adminstratively restricted circle of communication could not escape destructive forces of this kind. It is a fact that the workers in Bitterfeld were unable to recognize their own ruin, their own needs and hopes in the crisis signals and emancipatory demands of important writers — not only because they were decreasingly their subject-matter, also because they found the increasingly complex forms of communication ever more difficult to penetrate. But, of course, the complaints about human deformation were also made on their behalf as well. And there is plenty to suggest that when the basis-democracy revolutionaries gave public expression also to the social concerns of the workers of Bitterfeld, they were encouraged by what they had read in books by GDR authors. It can hardly be a coincidence that Friedrich Schorlemmer, one of their representatives, made such frequent mention of Christa Wolf's books.

The concurrence between the literary and political avant-garde and the mass movement which was established with the revolutionary smashing of high-handed *politburo*cracy has to disintegrate again as soon as the struggle commences for value systems and political forms in which a historical alternative (a Utopia?) might be implemented. For the literary avant-garde, however, there is nothing new in this. Indeed, Christa Wolf herself has referred in positive terms to 'linke Melancholie', which for many today is a term of abuse. In doing so, she was assuring herself of her literary predecessors Hölderlin, Büchner and Tucholsky, and of her allies in the spirit of radical democratic thought Böll, Fried, Weiss, Grass and Jens. Christoph Hein also projected his present situation into the experiences of Tucholsky in a very similar way.

The authors, therefore, who are marked by hopes and disillusionment specific to the GDR will, like their colleagues in the Federal Republic, never break out of their minority position. Is it possible to speak, as did Christa Wolf, of an 'avant-garde ohne Hinterland'? Where would the front-line be in that case? Christa Wolf, although she never wanted to be satisfied with the notorious 'facts', seems to be preparing herself for a new reality. She knows that literature, once it is free of the enormous strain of providing a substitute public forum, will begin to play a comparatively marginal role. But it is most unlikely that she will be able in future to refrain from contributing her experiences to the process people face of coming to terms with their so radically changed circumstances. She will probe these for their effects on people with the same humane (Utopian?) demands that she has applied hitherto to the conditions of life. She will also want in future to keep alive the consciousness of the threat to the human race which, in the euphoria of national renewal, could perhaps for a time be pushed into the background.

NOTES

1 The article was originally presented as a paper at a colloquium held in the University of Rostock on 29—30 May 1990 with the title: 'Literatur und Zukunft — Die Zukunft der Literatur. Die Literatur der Bundesrepublik Deutschland in den achtziger Jahren'. It was subsequently published in *ndl*, no.9, 1990, pp. 138—47. We are grateful to Joseph Pischel for allowing this translation (by Arthur Williams) to be included in this collection. Some passages have been slightly modified to reflect changes in Germany since May 1990.

2 *ZDF* is the West German second television channel, *Zweites Deutsches Fernsehen*, DFF was the GDR television service, *Deutscher Fernseh-Funk*.

3 Christa Wolf: '"Heine, die Zensur und wir." Rede auf dem Außerordentlichen Schriftstellerkongreß der DDR' in Wolf: *Im Dialog. Aktuelle Texte*, Frankfurt/Main, 1990, p. 167.

4 'Disappointment and disillusionment'. In the original consistently *Ent-Täuschungen*, hinting at several layers of meaning, particularly 'betrayal', 'letting down' and 'disillusionment' as well as 'disappointment'.

5 The same point is made by Peter Graves, pp. 135—6 below.

6 Volker Braun: *Das ungezwungene Leben Kasts*, Berlin (GDR), 1988, p. 180.

7 Ibid, p. 191. Gisela Shaw (p. 91 above) and Julian Preece (p. 310 below) also refer to this story.

8 Ernst Bloch: *Das Prinzip Hoffnung*, vol. I, Berlin (GDR), 1954, p. 14.

9 Christa Wolf: *Die Dimension des Autors*, 2 vols, Berlin (GDR), 1986; here vol. 2, p. 35. Ricarda Schmidt (p. 435 below) also refers to Bloch's influence on Wolf.

10 Ibid, vol. 2, p. 309.

11 Ibid, vol. 1, p. 99. Elizabeth Boa offers a comparative study of aspects of Christa Wolf and Ingeborg Bachmann, pp. 139—53 below.

12 Ibid, vol. 2, p. 405.

13 Sarah Kirsch: *Allerlei-Rauh. Eine Chronik*, Stuttgart, 1988, p. 88. Peter Graves compares *Sommerstück* and *Allerlei-Rauh*, pp. 129—36 below.

14 Christa Wolf: *Störfall*, Berlin (GDR), 1986, p. 37.

15 Ricarda Schmidt (pp. 435—7 below) discusses *Sommerstück* as part of her exploration of 'The Concept of Identity in Recent East and West German Women's Writing'. See also Elizabeth Boa, esp. pp. 144—5 below.

16 Wolf: *Die Dimension des Autors*, vol. 2, p. 168. The idea of 'Gespräche über Bäume' is central to Axel Goodbody's discussion of *Ökolyrik*, pp. 373—96 below, esp. pp. 381—2.

17 Ibid, vol. 1, p. 197.

18 Wolf: *Im Dialog...*, p. 144.

19 Volker Braun: *Verheerende Folgen mangelnden Anscheins innerbetrieblicher Demokratie. Schriften*, Leipzig, 1988, p. 85.

20 Wolf: *Im Dialog...*, p. 161f.

21 *Norddeutsche Zeitung*, Rostock, 19 December 1989.

22 Wolf: *Die Dimension des Autors*, vol. 2, p. 115.

EAST-WEST MEMORIES OF A LOST SUMMER:
CHRISTA WOLF AND SARAH KIRSCH

PETER GRAVES

In the mid-1970s a group of East German writers and intellectuals used to spend the summer together in an isolated village in Mecklenburg, living in converted cottages and enjoying the weather, the wine, the seclusion, and each other's company. Among their number were Sarah Kirsch and Christa Wolf, two writers whose biographies were once closely intertwined but whom the pressures of GDR *Kulturpolitik* subsequently deposited on opposite sides of the East-West border. After the Biermann affair, when the question 'Warum bleiben?' forced itself upon even so critically loyal a citizen as Christa Wolf, she decided to remain in the GDR and overcome her 'Zweifel über die Wahl des Lebens- und Arbeitsortes' by means of literary productivity.[1] Sarah Kirsch, on the other hand, was subjected to treatment from the authorities which Christa Wolf later described as 'schweinisch',[2] and in August 1977, in her own words, 'mußte [...] das kleine Land/ Bei Nacht und Nebel verlassen [...]/ Und wieder frei sein'.[3] Each has since published her own account of their shared summers, Sarah Kirsch in *Allerlei-Rauh* (1988) and Christa Wolf in *Sommerstück* (1989).[4] Although both texts deal with the same events, it has been suggested by one commentator that nevertheless they are fundamentally different in tone and mood.[5] This is certainly true in so far as both are written in the light of their authors' subsequent experiences, and this lends a particular colouring which the author in each case is anxious to stress. Yet despite this, underlying the two works there is an almost identical pattern, one which is characteristic of this generation of GDR writers and which sets them apart both from their contemporaries in West Germany and from some of their younger colleagues in the East.

Of course there are certain obvious similarities between the two texts, as would be expected with descriptions of the same set of experiences, and one of the bonuses of reading them in parallel is the pleasure of recognizing a detail which is already familiar: the fish-soup, the apple-cake, the Greek music, the parties, the dressing-up, or (more balefully) the mole being eaten alive by maggots that is put out of its misery, or the fire that threatens the cottages but is mercifully extinguished. The main cast of characters too is essentially the same: apart from Sarah Kirsch and her young son, and Christa and Gerhard Wolf, both texts introduce one of the Wolfs' daughters, Annette, and her child, also Helga Schubert and Johannes, her husband, Maxie and Fred Wander, Carola Nicolaou and her Greek husband, Thomas. There is even Tilly the cat.[6] To be sure, in *Allerlei-Rauh* they are given their genuine names (a point to which we shall return), whereas in *Sommerstück* they have pseudonyms,[7] but they are equally recogniable, even on occasions down to their idiosyncrasies: Carola and her fastidious make-up, for example, Thomas and his love of antiques, or the fixation of Sarah Kirsch's son about all things military. In both texts too the authors acknowledge the presence of another writer possibly recording her own impressions of the summer. Sarah Kirsch tells of subsequent meetings with Christa Wolf in which they together recalled those months, and Kirsch 'sagte jedesmal, daß sie [Christa Wolf] alles darüber eines Tages aufschreiben müsse' (*A-R*, pp. 60—1). Wolf, for her part, introduces *Sommerstück* with a poem by Sarah Kirsch, 'Raubvogel', whose genesis we actually witness in the course of the narrative (*S*, p. 123).[8] She also narrates an incident when an argument breaks out over the interpretation of a poem, just published in a journal, which contains the line, 'Geh ich vom Sein des Hundes in das Sein der Katze' (*S*, p. 65). Although it is not labelled as such, this is also by Sarah Kirsch: it is taken from 'Tilia cordata', a poem which, together with 'Raubvogel', appeared in Kirsch's 1976 collection, *Rückenwind*.[9] Both these poems express the dominant note of that book, which is generally positive and confident, and to quote them here therefore reflects not only the generous spirit of mutual encouragement but also the hopeful mood which, at the time at least, infused the Mecklenburg gatherings.

However, both these texts, as already indicated, present retrospective accounts, and through the prism of the intervening years the experience looks somewhat different. The opening paragraph of *Sommerstück* is significant in this context. The very first words, 'Es war dieser merkwürdige Sommer' (*S*, p. 7), are in fact another quotation from Sarah Kirsch, although this one goes back much further. They are the title-line from a poem published in Kirsch's first solo collection, *Landaufenthalt*, in 1967.[10] The poem in question paints an affectionate picture of East Berlin one summer in the early 1960s, when the poet, disturbed by 'bösartige Reden fremder Radiostationen', prefers to leave her radio and go outside to enjoy the unpretentious charms of her own part of the city. There is an undoubted irony in Wolf's allusion here to a poem which is not only set in East Berlin but also demonstrates a quiet allegiance to the East German state, for it is precisely city-life and the pressures imposed by that same state which the friends in *Sommerstück* are fleeing. Furthermore, this quotation from a relatively obscure poem, inserted in such a way that the ordinary reader will not recognize it and certainly will not know the original context, constitutes what amounts to a secret message between the two women, the gist of which is to recall how their relationship has been marked by shifting positions, both geographically and politically. Until the time of the Mecklenburg summers they had, as it were, moved in tandem, but in the course of *Sommerstück* we hear of 'Bella's' decision to leave the GDR (*S*, p. 187), and the book's opening paragraph is of course written in the knowledge of that event. Indeed, having begun with a cryptic reminder of shared commitment, it finishes with the recognition of permanent distance, because now 'alles zu Ende ist': Steffi is dead, the houses have been destroyed, and Bella '[hat] uns für immer verlassen' (*S*, p. 7). The intervening decade turns a work that could have been an idyll into an elegy on, among other things, lost friendships. Towards the end of the book the narrator puts it in these words: 'Ein Jahrzehnt. Reden wir noch miteinander? Erreichen unsere Stimmen uns noch? [...] Steffis Stimme — haben wir sie noch im Ohr? Und Bella? Hört sie uns? Wir haben es nicht halten können' (*S*, p. 177).

In *Allerlei-Rauh* there are distinct echoes of these sentiments. We know that, whatever the circumstances under which it was made, Sarah Kirsch has never regretted her move to the West. 'Ich gedenke nicht am Heimweh zu sterben' was her defiant message,[11] and this is reaffirmed in *Allerlei-Rauh*, where she describes it as 'außergewöhnlich geschickt' that she landed in a tiny hamlet in Schleswig-Holstein, rather than having opted for the Danube, the Black Forest, 'oder gar geblieben zu sein, wo ich herkam' (*A-R*, pp. 18—19). This sense of distance from the East German state extends too to her erstwhile friends. They may still meet and talk, and indeed *Allerlei-Rauh* includes the account of a return visit by the narrator to the GDR to see them,[12] but the former intimacy and the old identity of purpose have gone: 'Die Gespräche flogen oftmals von einem zum anderen Gegenstand, um sich nicht auf das weite Feld conträrer Meinungen zu begeben, eine Kunst, die ich seit einiger Zeit den Freunden zuliebe gebrauchte'. 'Unfaßbar' above all for their visitor from the West is the fact that these GDR writers are 'wieder bereit [...] vom Kleister der Hoffnung zu zehren' (A-R, p. 88), this time in the context of Gorbachev's coming to power. The visit, in short, is like returning to a former life and finding the same people 'immer noch mit dem alten Galimathias befaßt. Es langweilte mich stark'. Her conclusion: 'Da bleibt keine Sehnsucht nach einer Vergangenheit' (A-R, p. 89).

In the light of this distance, which consciously informs both texts, it is perhaps not surprising that they can be seen as so unalike in temper and spirit. This, however, is a mistaken view, for they are narrating an identical experience, not just that of a shared summer but, much more importantly, the experience of having to come to terms with the shattering of ideals. In both Sommerstück and Allerlei-Rauh there is an underlying tension between the belief in, indeed a fleeting taste of, Utopian possibilities on the one hand, and on the other the struggle to fill the gap left when those hopes prove illusory. This has of course been Christa Wolf's theme ever since Nachdenken über Christa T.,[13] but its most poignant expression by far comes in Sommerstück, not least because in that work the autobiographical core is so thinly veiled. This is not the place to analyse Sommerstück any further under this aspect, since the point is not controversial.[14] More interesting in this context is to look again at Allerlei-Rauh and see the extent to which Sarah Kirsch, for all her disavowals, shows that same Utopian nostalgia as her former colleagues and, what is more, seeks to respond to its loss in surprisingly similar ways.

Allerlei-Rauh, no less than Sommerstück, is a work of autobiography. Like the patchwork cloak worn by 'Allerlei-Rauh' in the Grimms' Märchen of that title,[15] it incorporates a variety of material (direct narrative, reflection, dream, fairy-tale), and its focus is constantly shifting between different periods of her life. Indeed, the narrator herself puts it more drastically: 'Ich hatte mehrere Leben, die sich voneinander stark unterschieden' (A-R, p. 36). So she gives glimpses, among other things, of her childhood, shows scenes from her life in the GDR with its various upheavals (emotional rather than political), and intersperses it all with pictures of her present rustic existence in the depths of Schleswig-Holstein. Despite these changing backdrops, however, there is an emotional continuity, one which is marked by the effort to retain hope and a sense of purpose in human existence. As a child she had not found this difficult.[16] The daughter of a loving mother and herself possessed of a submissive, unquestioning temperament, she recalls that 'der einzige Auftrag am Anfang unzähliger Tage' was: 'Geh in die Sonne, und es war leicht, ihm zu folgen [...] Alles war gut. Es war das Leben der Schmetterlinge' (A-R, p. 93). Although not religious, she had developed her own 'Trostphilosophie' (A-R, p. 16) to guard against any intimations of mortality, and this served her well for years, withstanding even 'den ersten Bombenteppichen [...] und dem Anblick zerfetzter Leichen' (A-R, p. 92). Summing up the optimistic outlook of herself as a child, she writes: 'die lieblichen Erscheinungen, die sie allenthalben wahrnahm, gewannen über jegliche Trübsal in kürzester Zeit die Oberhand' (A-R, p. 92).

This facility always to look on the bright side must have proved an invaluable aid to survival in a state like the GDR, but with hindsight the narrator sees her Utopian aspirations as a delusion. Yet that does not mean that commitment to them was wholly without value. In 'Der Rest des Fadens', one of her best-known poems since leaving the GDR, Sarah Kirsch describes a kite escaping from the hand of the one who was flying it and who now, while the kite itself soars into the sky, is left with 'der Rest des Fadens, und daß wir dich kannten'.[17] However that may be interpreted in detail, it is clear that, although some past experience has finally become detached from the world of reality and is now irretrievably gone, an affectionate nostalgia for it can still remain.[18] This is very much the mood in which the Mecklenburg summer is approached, as something utterly delightful but ultimately unreal. It is in this light, therefore, that one should view the apparently genuine names the narrator gives to her characters, a decision seemingly corroborated by the advice offered in the text to Christa Wolf not to use pseudonyms in her version of the summer: 'Denn mit Mystifizierungen falscher Namen ist nichts gewonnen, wir müssen für uns selber gerade stehen, aus Christa kann ebensowenig Kitty werden wie aus Carola eine Cordula oder aus mir Bernhardine' (A-R, p. 61). There is quite clearly a playful element here, because Sarah Kirsch will have read Kindheitsmuster,[19] for example, and so be well aware of the reasons why Christa Wolf might wish to create a fictional persona for herself as a bridge to the past.[20] But what is more significant is that Sarah Kirsch does not in fact observe her own injunction. Although she may appear to do so, the appearance is already undermined by the impish announcement which has preceded the whole text: 'Alles ist frei erfunden und jeder Name wurde verwechselt' (*A-R*, p. 5). Thus the scene is set for a narrative of teasing ambiguity, in which the historical basis is constantly subverted as the text moves in free association from one location to another, the contours between the different modes of narration are blurred, fact blends into fiction, and reality dissolves into dream or fairy-tale. The effect of this is particularly marked when it comes to the Mecklenburg summer, a period which is vested from the start with an air of unreality: it is a time when 'die unwahrscheinlichsten Dinge geschahen', a time described variously as 'bezaubernd', 'verrückt', 'phantastisch', 'überwirklich' (*A-R*, pp. 62, 47, 58, 61, 48).

The narrator of *Sommerstück* has a similar memory as she recalls the 'Unwirklichkeitsgefühl' (*S*, p. 22) which seemed to imbue the whole experience, but now, ten cold years later, she too acknowledges that 'die Endlichkeit der Wunder feststeht, der Zauber sich verflüchtigt hat, der uns beieinander und am Leben hielt' (*S*, p. 7). In *Allerlei-Rauh* precisely the same words ('Zauber', 'Wunder') are used to describe this painful recognition, and they are linked even more explicitly with rejection of the naive idea that their little Mecklenburg community could ever have provided a model for wider social organization (*A-R*, pp. 98—9): 'Jetzt wirkte der Zauber, dem sie doch früher erlegen war, nicht mehr über Tage und Wochen. Die Zeit der Wunder war wohl verflogen, in der es ihr sogar möglich schien [...] an ein paar günstigen Stellen der Erde menschenfreundliche Reiche grob zu errichten.'[21]

This radical shift in perception was partly brought about by the pressure of external political events, but there is a deeper strand linking these two works, for each is marked by a growing awareness of the transience of life. The shadow of Chernobyl hangs over both texts,[22] but fearful as that is, it is only a symptom of a wider decay to which all are exposed, of which the death of Maxie Wander in November 1977 had been a sharp reminder. 'Die Vergänglichkeit wehte aus jeder Richtung uns an', we read in *Allerlei-Rauh* concerning an attempt to recapture the Mecklenburg experience at a time when Maxie was already 'mit letzten Dingen befaßt' (*A-R*, p. 77); and *Sommerstück*, which concludes with a long imaginary conversation between Ellen and Steffi (the Maxie Wander figure), is, as the narrator openly admits, a description of growing old (*S*, p. 215). The realization of human frailty obviously transcends all divisions into East and West, and in both women it creates what amounts to an existential crisis. Ellen talks of the 'Weltraumkälte, die hereinströmt', against which the 'Miteinandersein' of community had been inadequate protection (S, p. 202); the narrator of *Allerlei-Rauh* feels herself more and more as 'eine Fremde' on this 'Ascheplaneten', 'hierhin versprengt und lebenslänglich gefangen' (A-R, p. 98).

That is not quite, however, the end of the story. As Maxie Wander's doctor had said to his patient, 'Hoffnung und Leben sind dasselbe' (S, p. 204), and Christa Wolf has always managed to rescue some element of hope from even the direst situation. So, in the final chapter of *Sommerstück*, to accept the loss of Utopia and the reality of death and to translate that acceptance into art is presented as a positive, if somewhat fragile, outcome to the Mecklenburg experience. *Allerlei-Rauh*, whilst also seeming to teeter on the brink of despair, glossing over neither 'die Endlichkeit der Erde' (A-R, p. 109) nor the frailty of humankind, extracts comfort in the end by returning to where it began, the beauty of the Schleswig-Holstein countryside. Taking up the book's opening image of northern life as a slowly revolving kaleidoscope, the narrator concludes with a highly poetic picture of nature's changing rhythms, which permits her the final consoling thought, 'ich bin dem Wechselhaften eingebunden, es scheint mir lange zu gehn' (A-R, p. 109).

In Peter Schneider's *Der Mauerspringer* there is a character who, having left East Germany for the West, then strongly objects when anything about him is labelled 'typisch DDR'.[23] Although it would be similarly misleading to generalize from just two texts, *Sommerstück* and *Allerlei-Rauh* both reveal characteristics which, if not 'typisch DDR', are typical of a particular generation of East German writers. The very notion of Utopia, for example, has been an exclusively GDR phenomenon in postwar German literature, writers in the West being far more sceptical of any ideology claiming all-embracing solutions to political problems. But a similar scepticism has also been present in the younger generation of GDR writers. Christoph Hein, for instance, born in 1944, quite specifically rejected the role of 'Wegweiser' or 'Prophet', which is inherent in a Utopian posture,[24] and Bernd Wagner, four years his junior, referred to 'eine Art DDR-Messianismus' among some of his older colleagues.[25] The generation of Christa Wolf and Sarah Kirsch is therefore distinct in having embraced a Utopian hope not only based upon socialist values but also bound up so closely with the fate of the GDR.[26] As the true face of that state became more apparent, those values could only be preserved outside the public arena, and it was such groups as the Mecklenburg circle that sought to keep them alive, even if simply, in Christa Wolf's words, 'als Wunsch, als Vision, als Traum'.[27] It must be said that the dissolution of the dream has brought about in Sarah Kirsch a much more radical dismissal of what in *Allerlei-Rauh* she now calls 'die feige Flucht in die sanften Utopien' (*A-R*, p. 108), whereas Christa Wolf has suggested that even in a unified Germany there will still be 'ein Bedürfnis nach einem utopischen Denken',[28] albeit one based this time on reality rather than theory. Nevertheless both *Sommerstück* and *Allerlei-Rauh* portray the death of a very particular idealistic hope. The memory may linger on, but the gap left behind is equally painful on whichever side of the border one happens to be. Neither writer goes so far as Günter Kunert, who is an exception in proclaiming categorically that there is now 'für unsere Gattung keine Hoffnung mehr',[29] but the consolation which *Sommerstück* and *Allerlei-Rauh* feel obliged to offer at the end seems at best tenuous. This is above all a literature of disappointment. The wistfulness in the narrator of *Sommerstück* is therefore not surprising as she looks back to the Mecklenburg summer with some words which, in view of events since the text was written, can be seen as a wider epitaph on the romantic idealism which once fired a whole generation of East German writers: 'Unschuld alles. Die reine Unschuld, von heute aus gesehen. Unwiederbringliche Unschuld' (*S*, p. 98).

NOTES

1   Christa Wolf: *Ansprachen*, Darmstadt, 1988, p. 56.
2   *Der Spiegel*, 17 October 1977, p. 47.
3   Sarah Kirsch: *Erdreich*, Stuttgart, 1982, p. 44.
4   Sarah Kirsch: *Allerlei-Rauh*, Stuttgart, 1988; Christa Wolf: *Sommerstück*, Frankfurt/Main, 1989. References in the text are abbreviated: *A-R* and *S*. Ricarda Schmidt (esp. pp. 435—7 below) discusses *Sommerstück* in a different context. See also Joseph Pischel's discussion of Christa Wolf, esp. pp. 121—2 above.
5   Anna Chiarloni: 'Christa Wolfs *Sommerstück*', *GDR Monitor*, no. 21, 1989, pp. 39—48.
6   Among characters distinct to each text are the Wolfs' younger daughter, Tinka (who appears as Jenny in *Sommerstück*) and a second Helga (in *Allerlei-Rauh*), who is referred to as the 'andere sanftere Helga' (*A-R*, p. 74). This is Helga Paris, a professional photographer. One of the photographs she took during the Mecklenburg summer can be seen in Sarah Kirsch: *Erklärung einiger Dinge* (Munich, 1978, p. 64) and another in Therese Hörnigk: *Christa Wolf* (Göttingen, 1989, p. 162).
7   The Wolfs appear as Ellen and Jan, their elder daughter as Sonja and Sarah Kirsch as Bella. The Wanders are called Steffi and Joseph, Helga Schubert is given the name Irene and her husband Clemens, Carola and Thomas appear as Luisa and Antonis. Only Tilly the cat (although spelt Tilli in *S*) appears under his own name, a feature for

which some commentator will doubtless, in due course, produce a convincing explanation.

8 Christa Wolf has since said that neither writer knew the content of the other's text prior to publication: 'Als ihr Buch erschien, war mein Manuskript schon fertig. Sie wußte, daß ich daran arbeitete, aber wir kannten die Texte gegenseitig nicht' (Christa Wolf: *Im Dialog*, Frankfurt/Main, 1990, p. 150).

9 'Tilia cordata' did indeed appear in a journal (*Sinn und Form*, vol. 28, 1976, p. 583) before the publication of *Rückenwind* (Ebenhausen, 1977, p. 8). The line is slightly misquoted in *S* and actually reads: 'geh ich/ Vom Sein des Hunds in das der Katze'. Chiarloni ('Christa Wolfs *Sommerstück*', p. 40) falsely identifies the poem as 'Katzenleben', from Kirsch's 1984 collection of that title. This leads her to state that the summers described in *S* span the years up until the early 1980s (ibid., p. 41), an assertion which is chronologically impossible.

10 Sarah Kirsch: *Landaufenthalt*, Berlin (GDR), 1967. The West German edition, slightly altered, appeared under the title *Gedichte* (Munich, 1969). The poem appears on p. 67 of this edition.

11 Kirsch: *Erdreich*, p. 44.

12 'So befand ich mich nach sehr langer Zeit im Mecklenburgischen, einem Teil der Personage von ehdem froh gegenüber', of whom one is 'Christa Kassandra' (*A-R*, pp. 87f.). There are indications in the text that this visit took place in the year of Chernobyl (1986).

13 Christa Wolf: *Nachdenken über Christa T.* was first published by Mitteldeutscher Verlag, Halle/Saale, in 1968, but never reached the public. The first West German edition came in out 1969 (published by Luchterhand, Darmstadt)

14 One of the characters, contemplating Wolf and her generation, refers to 'ihre frühere Begeisterung, ihre heutige Enttäuschung' (*S*, p. 95), and that description sums up the emotional spectrum of the book.

15 The fairy-tale tells of a princess's attempts to escape her father's amorous attentions by ordering a cloak made of a thousand different animal furs in which she then runs away. It is variously translated as 'Thousandfurs' (*Grimms' Tales for Young and Old*, translated by Ralph Manheim, London, 1978) or 'Manypelts' (Jacob and Wilhelm Grimm: *Selected Tales*, translated by David Luke, Harmondsworth, 1982). Sarah Kirsch reworks the story within her own text (*A-R*, pp. 42—4, 101—5).

16 In both texts there is a very similar reaction as the narrator in each looks back on the child she once was: 'Ein Kind, das sie genau zu kennen meinte' (*S*, p. 76); 'ein Kind, das mir merkwürdig fremd ist, obgleich ich alles über es weiß' (*A-R*, p. 13).

17 Sarah Kirsch: *Drachensteigen*, Ebenhausen, 1979, p. 16.

18 There has been a lively controversy in *GDR Monitor* on the meaning of this poem. See Peter Shaw: 'The significance of the kite above the plains: a thorough interpretation of Sarah Kirsch's poem "Der Rest des Fadens"', and my rejoinder: 'The kite, the plains, and some further moralizing', *GDR Monitor*, no. 17, 1987, pp. 48—63, and no. 19, 1988, pp. 85—90.

19 Christa Wolf: *Kindheitsmuster*, Berlin (GDR), 1976.

20 It is certainly a mistake to infer from the comments in *Allerlei-Rauh* that Sarah Kirsch must be advocating some 'dokumentarisches Modell' (Chiarloni: 'Christa Wolfs *Sommerstück*', p. 40).

21 In *Sommerstück*, too, the narrator had expressed the hope that small groups of people might create 'bewohnbare Flecken [...] in denen Genuß, auch Lebensfreude sich erzeugen ließen' (*S*, p. 80).

22 When the narrator of *Sommerstück* says, 'Ich seh uns dahinschmelzen wie unter zu starker Strahlung, ein zeitgemäßes Bild, ich weiß' (*S*, p. 202), she clearly has Chernobyl in mind, as does the narrator of *Allerlei-Rauh* when she talks of 'das schwarze Frühjahr zuletzt, von dem alles gezeichnet nun war', a spring 'in welchem die Unheilbarkeit des Jahrhunderts sichtbar geworden ist' (*A-R*, pp. 88, 91).

23 Peter Schneider: *Der Mauerspringer*, Darmstadt, 1984, p. 20. See also the comments by Martin Kane on *Der Mauerspringer*, esp. pp. 360—1 below.

24 'Ich bin nich klüger als mein Publikum', he has said, 'ich kann über die Richtung des künftigen Weges nichts sagen. Ich würde das für viel zu anmaßend halten' (Krzysztof

Jachimczak: 'Gespräch mit Christoph Hein', *Sinn und Form*, vol. 40, 1988, pp. 342—59; here p. 347).

25 *Weimarer Beiträge*, vol. 25, no. 7, 1979, p. 46.
26 Joseph Pischel makes a similar point, p. 118 above.
27 Wolf: *Im Dialog*, p. 143.
28 Ibid., p. 162. Cf. also the conclusion to Joseph Pischel's discussion, esp. pp. 124—6 above.
29 Günter Kunert: 'Hat die Hoffnung noch eine Zukunft?', *Die Zeit*, 26 December 1986, p. 30.

UNNATURAL CAUSES: MODES OF DEATH
IN CHRISTA WOLF'S *NACHDENKEN ÜBER CHRISTA T.*
AND INGEBORG BACHMANN'S *MALINA*

ELIZABETH BOA

I Liberalism, Marxism and the Female Subject

Christa Wolf's *Nachdenken über Christa T.* was published in 1968 and Ingeborg Bachmann's *Malina* just three years later in 1971.[1] In comparing them now, I shall bear in mind both the historical conditions which obtained at the time of their writing and the very different situation some twenty years on: though both works reflect on the postwar division of Germany and Europe, the light cast by the political changes initiated in the late 1980s throw certain features of Wolf's novel into sharp relief, as does the comparison with *Malina*, notably a tension between critique of and accommodation with the GDR. But the analysis of the workings of social power which both works express will, I believe, remain relevant whatever the outcome of the unification of Germany and of the wider changes in Europe. As citizens of countries bounded until recently by Cold War borders, both writers associate the political divisions with divisions between individuals and with invisible boundaries within the psyche. Starting from comparable past experience of National Socialism but from different contemporary positions, both cast doubt on the dominant ideology of the postwar societies they inhabit, Bachmann on liberal individualism, Wolf on Marxist collectivism. Both detect surviving traces of fascism which they relate to patriarchal culture as a deep-rooted power-system which neither liberalism nor socialism has eradicated. Their work thus exemplifies the convergence towards feminist political analysis in women's writing on both sides of the East-West divide.[2] In what follows, I shall first relate the differing conceptions of subjectivity and gender in the liberal and the Marxist traditions to the experimentation in both novels with different ways of saying and writing 'I' and to the motif of doubles or alter egos. Then, through a comparison of the motifs of illness, madness and death, I shall use the radically feminist implications of *Malina* as a filter through which to read

Nachdenken über Christa T., looking also briefly back at *Der geteilte Himmel* (1963) and forwards to *Kassandra* (1983) to see how Wolf's work reads now in the light of the collapse of the GDR state.[3]

Liberalism posits emancipation from social constraints as its supreme value and an individualist teleology: inhering in every individual is a potential true self which under ideal conditions will freely unfold. The task of government is thus the negative one of removing constraints to individual self-development. Marx, by contrast, argues that 'das menschliche Wesen ist kein dem einzelnen Individuum innewohnendes Abstraktum. In seiner Wirklichkeit ist es das Ensemble der gesellschaftlichen Verhältnisse.'[4] I take this to mean that there is neither a universal essence from which humanity is alienated, nor a true self inhering in each individual. Rather, individuals develop through historically determined relationships with others. The ensemble of social relations need not imply monolithic stasis: changing social relations, pervaded by conflicts and contradictions, mean that individuals can make choices; though they cannot, in isolation, resolve personal conflicts which have social grounds, they can act together to change society and hence themselves. In sum, liberalism posits the enterprising individual as historical agent where Marxism stresses a social self and collective action. Both traditions do, however, share an emancipatory optimism, liberalism envisioning a linear progress towards ever greater freedom and civilization, Marxism a dialectical movement towards individual freedom under communism: 'An die Stelle der alten bürgerlichen Gesellschaft mit ihren Klassen und Klassengegensätzen tritt eine Assoziation, worin die freie Entwicklung eines jeden die Bedingung für die freie Entwicklung aller ist.'[5] But GDR orthodoxy turned the classical tag upside down, stigmatizing personal conflicts as subjectivism instead of recognizing in them the symptom of social ills, and so tended to move away from, rather than towards the ideal expressed in *The Communist Manifesto*.

Historically, both traditions marginalized women and addressed the woman question in a fundamentally similar way. To achieve emancipation women must adapt to the conditions of the male historical agents: that is the enterprising individual or the proletariat. In liberal society, middle-class women had to choose between enclosure as wife and mother within the domestic sphere or entry into the public sphere of education and a career, while working-class women were drawn into or excluded from the labour force as the economy demanded; in socialist countries it has meant entry into the labour force with state provision for child care. Latterly, a convergence has been evident as middle-class women in the West seek to combine motherhood and a career and working-class women have been forced financially to do likewise, albeit with less satisfactory state provision than in the socialist GDR, for example. Feminism challenges both traditions. The liberal programme is élitist (and ethno-centric) in ignoring class inequality (and racism) and simplistic in ignoring the cultural construction of gender. It is not that womanhood, as J. S. Mill put it, is 'an eminently artificial thing', a formulation implying that true womanhood might be rescued from social distortion, but that femininity and masculinity are historically changing social identities, not essential qualities: true womanhood or manhood and the true self are liberal delusions concealing the interests of white, middle-class men.[6] This mode of feminist critique is in keeping with the Marxist concept of social selfhood. But Marxism has its own gender-blindness in its stress on productive relations and relative neglect of reproductive relations so that the oppression of women is seen merely as an effect of class society which will, like the state, wither away on the victory of a united proletariat. To achieve this consummation women should join men in the class struggle, but no fundamental renegotiation of gender roles is envisaged. This classical position underlay GDR orthodoxy.

Women's marginality in both traditions gives rise to three senses of femininity: as limitation or exclusion from the public domain; as alienation from feminine desires as women adapt to a male-dominated public domain; and finally as the transcendence of such self-division. For some feminists, this third sense of femininity denotes less the gender of actual women, than a social transformation whereby the positive connotations of femininity would cease to be marginalized as impractical or imputed to idealized women through whom alienated male historical agents seek (and generally fail to find) solace. This kind of feminism posits the patriarchal construction of gender as the basis of power politics, which neither liberal nor socialist reforms have changed. Utopian femininity would overcome the division between women and men and between the private and the public, so transforming political practice and enabling the free development 'einer jeden' as of 'eines jeden'.

II Auto/biography

Nachdenken über Christa T. and *Malina* evoke the three senses of femininity through reflection on the position of women writing in the genres of biography and autobiography. The title of Christa T.'s fragmentary essay 'Die große Hoffnung oder die Schwierigkeit, "ich" zu sagen' (p. 164) sounds like an amalgamation of the titles of two of Bachmann's Frankfurt lectures, 'Literatur als Utopie' and 'Das schreibende Ich' (1959—1960). I am less concerned with possible influence, however, than with the political implications of such seemingly personal and aesthetic concerns. In 'Das schreibende Ich', Bachmann writes wryly of the assertive 'I' in memoirs of men of action like Churchill. Such an 'I' is 'vorgeschrieben' in the public record of history.[7] But most writers do not have such a singular, recognized 'I' at their disposal, Bachmann suggests. Writers are also readers and the written 'I' of autobiography has been possessed by many strange 'I's. Bachman's point recalls what Harold Bloom has called 'the anxiety of influence': writers feel caught in an intertextual web of discourse and unsure if their writing is truly theirs, as a Romantic poetics of authentic self-expression would require.[8] Bloom's anxiety of influence is a problem of intellectual paternity. His canon of great poets are the sons who, in the act of poetic creativity, usurp the fathers from whom they are descended. Bloom writes of poets, but the problem is as acute in the genre of autobiography which asserts the public claim to be the author of one's life. Modern literary autobiography arose in the eighteenth century as male intellectuals sought to overthrow feudal and patriarchal chains and to assert the rights of man, which were extended to women only after a century of struggle and a world war. In her lecture, Bachmann was not speaking specifically of women, but her novel *Malina* and Wolf's *Nachdenken über Christa T.* explore the peculiar difficulties women may experience in saying 'I'. *Malina* conveys the self-estrangement of a woman who feels her femininity as a role which is 'vorgeschrieben' in the double sense being of written in advance and imposed (inscribed and prescribed) so that when *Ich* says 'I', what speaks through her may be the weight of millennia of patriarchal culture: she is entangled in the web of patriarchal discourse. (The unnnamed narrator of *Malina* is designated simply as 'Ich' in the opening list of dramatis personae. p. 12) Christa T.'s difficulty arises ostensibly from a different context, a collectivist ideology which stigmatizes 'Subjektivismus' (p. 68) in men and women alike, but the novel has a feminist subtext with marked affinities with *Malina*.

Both novels convey the difficulty of saying and writing 'I' in a complex game with genres; both are hybrid between fictional biography and autobiography; in both two characters are also alter egos, of whom one occupies a more feminine, the other a more masculine position; in both the writing of auto/biography is a Utopian project which conveys critique of the liberal and socialist status quo; both have traces of actual autobiography. *Nachdenken über Christa T.* is ostensibly a fictional biography, but is also autobiographical in being as much about the narrator as about Christa T.: the narrator so identifies with Christa T. that it is often difficult to tell who the textual 'I' is. She constantly quotes from Christa T.'s diaries, a mode close to autobiography, except that the autobiographical 'I' is published whereas the diary-I remains private, unless some officious person publishes posthumously, as does the narrator here. Letters are an intermediate, dialogic form, though they may have a public addressee as in letters to the editor or to the President — Bachmann's *Ich* writes to the President (pp. 107, 141). Letters can be collected and published, of course, as in the fictional case of Wilhelm publishing Werther's letters. (Reduced to initials, the two W.s become alter egos.) The interview is a dialogic mode of saying 'I' which can then be published, though *Ich*'s interview is not a dialogue, but a battle between a journalist's determination to impose a persona on her and her resistance (pp. 88—101). Wolf's narrator invents an interview containing invented recollections of Christa T. in a effort to construct her version of Christa T. (pp. 47—51). Both novels present actual and imaginary conversations. *Malina* includes also one side of telephone conversations, as in Malina's sinister closing denial on the phone to Ivan of *Ich*'s existence (pp. 75f., 79, 149, 170, 337). Thus both novels fictionalize non-fictional modes of saying and writing 'I' and both include secondary invented utterances within their fictions. In what follows I shall look first at *Malina* and then at *Nachdenken über Christa T.* to bring out the political meaning of these formal devices.[9]

III Who killed *Ich*?

In *Malina*, a woman seeks to establish her subjecthood through that difficult act of writing 'I', which Christa T. saw as the great hope. Or to be more precise, Christa T. refers to *saying* where Bachmann's *Ich* tries to *write* 'I'. To write and publish is to intervene in the public domain. The American critics Gilbert and Gubar suggest that women suffer less from anxiety of influence, than from anxiety of authorship arising from a culture in which women were denied access to public discourse.[10] To publish is to step over the hidden boundary between the private and the public in a transgression of femininity, a step which women in the Romantic generation, for example, shunned, confining themselves to diaries and letters, for women who did publish were treated scurrilously by male critics.[11] To withstand the pressures of her public position as a famous writer, *Ich* needs a male alter ego, as the title of her autobiography, which is also a covert biography of Malina, indicates. (Bachmann was no doubt influenced by her experiences in Viennese literary circles where Ilse Aichinger was known as 'Fräulein Kafka' and Doderer referred to 'Der Bachmann'; the reception of *Malina* shows too that the scurrilous treatment of women writers continues.[12]) Malina is her protector against disabling feminine desires: in the second, nightmare chapter, Melanie, the honey-sweet daughter, dances with the Father as *Ich* sits humiliated until Malina comes to save her. Malina protects *Ich* both from the assaults of the Father who would stop her from studying and writing, and from the Melanie side of her, that feminine subjection to her lover Ivan, who wants *Ich* to write romances with a happy ending (the Mills-and-Boone mode of writing by women.) But the male double threatens to displace the woman altogether: Malina finally orders *Ich* to kill Ivan and his children, that is to kill the desires which threaten her writing. Rather than do that, *Ich* chooses to disappear, immured behind the wall of her room. The closing sentence reads: 'Es war Mord' (p. 337). Thus the reader is invited to ask 'who dunnit?' and can choose among the male trinity of the monstrous Father, the lover Ivan, and Malina, the alter ego. The first two demand that *Ich* conform to patriarchal femininity, Malina that she cease to be feminine at all.[13] *Ich*'s death is also a self-murder, as Christa Wolf has argued, for in this psycho-drama the main figures are also warring aspects of the self.[14]

To write 'I' as a woman is a political act contesting social oppression and psychic repression, which here fails. As the very model of an emancipated woman (*Ich* has a doctorate and is honoured by the State) she yet demonstrates the failure of liberal reform to address the underlying causes of women's subjection. This does not mean that *Ich* is the true feminine self and Malina a false masculine persona. Rather, it conveys how intellectual curiosity, practical rationality and emotional needs are constructed in ways which lead to conflict within individuals and between the sexes through a culture which splits such qualities along gender lines and through the division between the public and the private. This political claim, which I can only sketch here, comes out in the second chapter dominated by the monstrous Father (pp. 174—236). The title 'Der dritte Mann' (p. 174) is surely an oblique reference to the eerie blend of sexual charm and ruthlessness which Orson Wells lent smiling Harry Lime, the enterprising dealer in adulterated penicillin: fascism did not end with the war but continued in a new guise in the ruthless pursuit of profit which still underlies the traffic in licit and illicit drugs. Men are educated to follow the logic of the market come what may, to follow intellectual curiosity divorced from ethical concerns, to seek power over others and over nature, to pursue sexual domination and repress emotional needs. Women are educated to care for others, to value emotional attachment above intellectual curiosity, to fear self-assertion, to find sexual confirmation through adopting the position of an object of male desire. Male practicality is directed outwards at projects in the public sphere, female practicality at small-scale, interpersonal service. The divide comes out in Malina's job at the Army Museum, an institution documenting the blood-stained history of male intellectual curiosity, which continues apace in the age of technology — Ich's second meeting with Malina was at a lecture entitled 'Die Kunst im Zeitalter der Technik' (p. 18) — and, on the other hand, Ich's skill in cooking Austrian specialities for Ivan (p. 83).

Practical care for others, then, a feminine value in the interpersonal sphere, is stigmatized as impractical Utopianism in the public sphere, and women are not educated into the skills necessary to operate politically, but into a disabling emotionalism. Thus what is needed is neither a cult of irrationality nor separatist retreat, but a reconception of rationality to combat the massive unreason of scientific warfare and the rape of the planet. On the most pessimistic reading, Ich's murder suggests that it is impossible to intervene in the public sphere, here symbolized in the act of writing 'I', without donning a male persona and impossible to write *as a woman* outside of the patriarchal definitions. Less pessimistically, it expresses both a refusal to become assimilated entirely into Malina, an aspect of the self who survives but is not allowed to take over the first-person mode (the brief closing section is written in the third-person by a covert narrator who is neither Malina nor *Ich*) and a refusal to accept femininity as subjection to Ivan or to the Father, for whom the daughters are but dolls to provide pleasure or be eviscerated in the war-games. To be sure, an aspect of the self has been murdered, but the great hope is not dead. The emergent detective story of the last sentence invites the reader to pursue her enquiries and learn something, as the author too intended to do: *Malina* was to be the first part of a trilogy, not The End; within *Malina*, Utopian fragments point to what women cannot yet express in autobiography, a genre which, in the male canon, asserts achieved selfhood; and someone has published the unfinished autobiography and entitled it *Malina*, indicating the determination to survive, if not simply to be Malina.

IV The Fate of the Feminine in the GDR

The complex narrative technique deployed in *Malina* exemplifies what Sigrid Weigel calls 'der schielende Blick', the squinting double vision of women trying to see through deeply internalized gender conditioning.[15] The female writing subject has no fixed position. Unlike the singularity which Bachmann saw in Churchill's memoirs, there is constant movement back and forth across invisible boundaries within the subject. Such movement is dramatized through doubles: *Ich*, Malina, Melanie of the nightmares, the secretary Lina and so forth. Christa T. too is a divided character. The persona she presents conceals private concerns, as the narrator discovers on reading her diaries (p. 14). Like *Ich*, Christa T. oscillates between more masculine and more feminine roles. She begins as a tomboy: her cry of 'hooohaahoo' is a bold self-assertion against the femininity prescribed by National Socialism (p. 13). But more feminine traits emerge in the gift of flowers to the teacher and in her horrified pity during the traumatic events at the end of the war, experiences which threaten to stifle the tomboy (p. 15). Later, however, she refuses feminine enclosure as the village schoolmaster's wife and, like *Ich*, goes to university. But she is then, like *Ich*, deeply traumatized by unhappy love. She survives, however, seems to reach a happy ending of the sort Ivan wanted, but fails to live happily ever after. Happy love is almost as deadly to the writing 'I' as unhappy love: the vet's wife, unlike her younger self who refused to become the schoolmaster's wife, remains in her rural retreat and writes only fragments, comparable to *Ich*'s Utopian fragments, and, like the women of the Romantic age, she does not publish. That is the step into the public sphere which her alter ego takes for her posthumously, like the posthumous publication of *Ich*'s unfinished autobiography.

Christa T.'s roles are 'vorgeschrieben', as behavioural and literary parallels with the feudal, bourgeois and National Socialist past and the capitalist present convey. One parallel is the abuse of animals: Christa T.'s traumatic childhood memory of a man brutally dashing out a cat's brains against a wall is juxtaposed with her horrified response when one of her pupils in the socialist GDR steals and gratuitously smashes birds' eggs or when another bites the head off a frog to the evident delight of his classmates (pp. 24, 34, 106f.). Another parallel is implied both with the National Socialist past and with the capitalist world in the rationalist cult of efficiency — the boy who bit off the frog's head was hard-working and later condescendingly accuses his teacher of impractical idealism in terms similar to a cousin in the West attacking Christa T.'s socialist ideals (pp. 108, 123). The boy is a type who is still in demand, Christa T. comments (p. 108). The motif of impractical Utopianism set against efficiency, which in these examples is still couched in psychological terms, takes on full political point when it is associated with the Hungarian uprising of 1956 (p. 129). Thus a link is established between personal psychology and politics. Like *Ich*, Christa T. reacts with disabling emotion to such experiences, suggesting again that feminists should not elevate emotion over reason, but press for reconceptualization of what is considered rational; underlying the cult of efficiency is the thirst for power which is as much an emotion as Christa T.'s pity. — The collapse of the GDR state has since revealed the full irrational inefficiency of hierarchical authoritarianism.

There are also literary parallels with the past. These include Sophie La Roche's *Die Geschichte des Fräuleins von Sternheim* (1771) and Schiller's *Kabale und Liebe* (1784), both set in a still feudal world (pp. 114f., 65—9). In the first, a woman seeking autonomy in a male dominated world finally retreats into the rural idyll of marriage with Lord Seymour, a happy ending in ironic parallel to Christa T.'s life as the vet's wife. *Kabale und Liebe* explores the conflict between the social order and the individualism of the possessive sentimentalist, Ferdinand, implying a parallel between the social order of feudalism and the social order of the GDR, a point to which I shall return. Among Christa T.'s roles is the adulterous wife: she is a latter-day Madame Bovary (p. 150). Wolf's novel thus reflects back on Flaubert's *Madame Bovary* (1857) and the bourgeois novel of adultery, which Tony Tanner has described as the transgressive mode. Commenting on the socially displaced protagonists of the early English novel, Tanner notes:

> They thus represent or incarnate a potentially disruptive or socially unstabilized energy that may threaten, directly or implicitly, the organization of society, whether by the uncertainty of their origin, the uncertainty of the direction in which they will focus their unbounded energy, or their attitudes to the ties that hold society together and that they may choose to slight or break.[16]

Adultery has lost its transgressive power, but the motif is an ironic signal that the ties holding the GDR together hold only at the cost of repressing potentially disruptive, socially unstabilized energy, incarnated here in a woman, uncertain of the direction in which she should focus her unbounded energy. Unbounded energy takes the form in both novels under discussion here of erotic desire which loses focus: in the one, it is symbolized in the eerie, watery landscape of *Ich's Märchen*; in the other, it is stated directly by the narrator when she writes of Christa T.'s 'nächtliche, unbegrenzte Träume' (p. 65), her 'unverbrauchten Gefühle' (p. 152) or her 'gefährliche, gegenstandslose Verlangen' (p. 154).

Both novels, then, focus on the difficulty of saying or writing 'I' as a women, and in both femininity appears in the three forms which I outlined in the opening section: as limitation, as self-division and as Utopian aspiration. Both *Ich* and Christa T. began life under National Socialism with its cult of aggressive masculinity and true womanhood centred on the function of child-bearing. Both reject such a femininity and claim the right to education and to selfhood, *Ich* as a childless woman, Christa T. as a woman who loves her husband and children, but refuses reduction to the roles of wife and mother. For Christa T., then, the act of writing is a denial of femininity defined negatively as limitation, as it is also for *Ich*. But like *Ich*, Christa T. experiences conflict between feminine emotions and roles on the one hand and her wish for independent selfhood. And her feminine emotions become alienated as impractical desires which expand into 'unbegrenzte Träume' (p. 65) or 'gegenstandslose Verlangen' (p. 154). Such dreams and longings are doubly dangerous: they may disable the individual but also pose a potential threat to social stability. Just as *Malina* conveys the failure of liberal rights in capitalist Austria, then, Wolf's novel suggests that emancipatory measures in the socialist GDR have done nothing to change fundamentally the construction of gender along lines that lead to a greater oppression of women than of men and to a culture in which feminine feeling, which is idealized in interpersonal relations, is stigmatized as impractical in the public sphere — a point Wolf makes more forcefully in *Kassandra*. But in the earlier novel too, the cost of ignoring interpersonal domestic and sexual relations as distinct from collective relations in the political and industrial fields comes under critical scrutiny. Given the prevailing sexual culture, such a bias is a bias towards male interests, suggesting that the collectivist policies of the GDR are not leading towards 'die Freiheit einer jeden' as the condition of communism, but are reproducing an oppressive culture inherited from the past. The danger stands in tension with hope, however, for the unbounded dreams and unfocused longing convey also the third sense of femininity as the overcoming of division which here, as in *Malina*, is also expressed in Utopian fragments such as the sheet of paper with the tag 'die große Hoffnung oder Über die Schwierigkeit "ich" zu sagen' (p. 164).

V Who killed Christa T.?
Both authors warn of surviving fascist tendencies in socialist as in liberal society, but Wolf's warning is more muted. I want now to examine this muted warning conveyed in the doubles motif and in what Bachmann called *Todesarten*, modes of death,[17] and finally to look at the rising urgency of Wolf's warnings over the years. In *Malina*, the subject is divided into the feminine *Ich*, who is murdered, and the masculine Malina, who survives. Neither persona can be identified with the author, but the figure of a famous author does echo Bachmann's own position as a writer transforming her own experience. Likewise, the name Christa and the narrator's position as a writer gesture towards the author, Christa Wolf. Again, neither persona is the author, but together they reflect on the position of a woman writing in the GDR, which is shown to be not singular, but divided between Christa T., who dies, and the narrator, who survives. The narrator's biographical project is an effort to resurrect and publish Christa T.'s voice so signalling a movement away from repressive collectivism towards a truly communal 'we' which would promote individuality and dialogue between citizen and state: the wish to say 'I' need not be stigmatized as subjectivism. Publication will prove too that there was nothing fishy about Christa T.'s death: it was a natural tragedy, not the death of socialism. Seen through Bachmann-spectacles, however, Christa T.'s death was not perhaps as natural as the narrator

over-anxiously assures us it was. The narrator and Malina both represent survival though accommodation. Admittedly, Wolf's survivor is not distanced as a male character but enjoys the status of a first-person woman-narrator, a difference reflecting the difference between Bachmann's radical alienation from postwar Austria compared with Wolf's critical commitment to the GDR. But Wolf's narrator is not entirely reliable. The memory of Christa T. is fading and the narrator wields the power of the living over the dead: she can select and edit; she can suppress as well as publish. Unlike Malina, she is not implicated in the death of her alter ego and asks bitterly why her friend had to die: 'Ich hätte sie leben lassen' (p. 170). Why, then, did the author, who *could* have let her live, give Christa T. leukaemia and filter her voice only posthumously through the narrator? Before aids, cancer was *the* symbolic illness, and cancer of the life's blood is a subversive mode of death when set against the aesthetic of socialist realism which demands positive heroes and heroic deaths. Yet for all its subversive probing, *Nachdenken über Christa T.* is also a work of repression: repression of what could not be published in the GDR in 1968, but also perhaps of questions which the author could not ask without risking a catastrophic loss of faith in socialism as practised in the GDR. Seen through Bachmann-spectacles, the author murdered Christa T. in order to be able to go on living and publishing in the GDR.

VI The Madwoman in the GDR Attic

I should like finally to sketch stages in Wolf's critical accommodation with the GDR, not in a spirit of retrospective superiority: the GDR was a changing polity and careful judgements over decades should not be condemned now as appeasement. Rather, as Wolf herself conveys in essays on writers of the past, the reception of literature changes historically and Wolf's work too shifts in the light both of current events and of feminist consciousness. Wolf's first novel, *Der geteilte Himmel* (1962) repeats the plot of *Kabale und Liebe*: the heroine is torn between the demands of a father-substitute and a lover who rejects the social order and invites the heroine to flee with him to freedom. Just as Luise Miller's petty-bourgeois father in effect colludes with oppressive feudal power, so Rita's father-substitute in effect sustains oppressive state power and persuades Rita to do likewise: in the battle between fathers and sons, between love and filial piety, the paternal order prevails. In the eighteenth century, the romantic lover would have become in turn a despotic pater familias, for the new freedoms the sons claimed were not extended to wives and daughters; in the twentieth century, had Rita followed her lover she would have arrived in *Ich*'s world. Rita almost dies, not killed literally by poisoned lemonade, but torn between love for her enterprising lover and the internalized values of a paternalist state. How one evaluates her survival will depend on how one evaluates capitalist freedom as against socialist paternalism, and I have no wish to deny the difference between the GDR and the combination of feudalism and petty bourgeois patriarchy to which Luise Miller falls victim. But the heroine's adaptation to the conditions of the male historical agent, the proletariat, is a murder of the feminine: she must assume a Malina-like persona to survive. In *Nachdenken über Christa T.*, the claims for that free development of each, the Utopian ideal expressed in *The Communist Manifesto*, are more insistent in being embodied not in a man who flees West, but in a woman who stays to die; the division is not now geographical, but lies within the GDR which has failed to address patriarchal power relations. In *Der geteilte Himmel*, the heroine comes back to life to position herself singularly on one side of the divided sky under the guidance of a third-person narrator. In *Nachdenken über Christa T.*, the singularity of a live heroine has split to become a dead heroine and a live first-person narrator. In *Kassandra* (1983), the narrator-heroine indubitably will die and her voice fall silent. This effect is of course modified by the sheer existence of the novel and its essays. But the split has become so sharp that it cannot be accommodated within one text.

The finally singular position of the first novel gives way, then, first to the subversive, shifting positionality of *Nachdenken über Christa T.*, then to the sharp division between non-fiction and fiction. The 'I' of the lectures and essays was spoken in the West and published on both sides of the divided sky as the authorial 'I' of the famous writer, Christa Wolf, who has used her public inscription in the record of history to issue warnings to East and West. Conversely, the fictional end is more drastic than in the earlier novels: Kassandra dies an unnatural mode of death at male hands, butchered along with a woman from the other side. Gilbert and Gubar's title, *The Mad Woman in the Attic*, refers to Mrs Rochester, whose sane alter ego, Jane Eyre, survived and married in a dubious accommodation with patriarchy. Structurally, Christa T. is the madwoman in the GDR attic, just as *Ich*, in more directly Gothic manner, is immured in the West; Kassandra and Klytämnestra are further exemplars of the type in East and West. For a while, it looked as if the prisoners in the GDR attic might break out and find a third way. But the West German patriarchs and the lure of the Deutschmark have thrust such Utopian hope back to the margins, while the disappearance of the Cold War boundary has not killed off nationalism, racialism, nuclear weaponry, the marketing of licit and illicit drugs and all the other monsters inhabiting *Ich*'s psyche.

VII Post-mortem

In 1968, *Nachdenken über Christa T.* encoded a warning. The difficulties the novel encountered on publication suggest that the narrator did not suppress enough to satisfy the Party hacks, but in retrospect it could look now as if she had been too accommodating towards a state which deployed an oppressive apparatus to stifle criticism. In 1990, midway between the virtual and the actual death of the GDR, Christa Wolf published *Was bleibt*, a story written in 1979 and revised in 1989, which tells of a period at the end of the 1970s when she was kept under surveillance by the State Security Police.[18] *Was bleibt* is couched in autobiographical terms, yet is also designated an 'Erzählung', leaving the reader to discriminate between fact and fiction. As in *Nachdenken über Christa T.*, the narrator has a potential alter ego, a young woman who comes to visit her and who, so the narrator feels, will never again leave her: 'mein Gefühl verdichtete sich, daß dieses Mädchen meine Wohnung nie mehr verlassen würde' (p. 74). But on learning that the girl has spent a year in gaol as a dissident, the sense of intimate identification is threatened: '"Gefängnis" war das Wort, daß unsere Verwandschaft in Frage stellte. Es ließ sich nichts dazu sagen, nichts fragen' (p. 75). Thus the chastened narrator, a projected persona of the author, acknowledges the limits of her experience and of her courage compared with this younger woman.

The publication of *Was bleibt* unleashed a wave of criticism that Wolf had chosen to speak out so specifically only when the need was past; her earlier suppressions and silences, so one critic commented, were self-censorship freely undertaken; in the eyes of another they mark her out as a 'Staatsdichterin'.[19] The argument presented in this paper, originally written before the publication of *Was bleibt*, might seem to be in accord with such criticisms: the author killed off Christa T. in an act which, to use the words of the narrator, perhaps amounted to 'die Tote

[...] opfern zugunsten der Lebenden, die die ganze Wahrheit nicht brauchen kann' (p. 49). But a 'Staatsdichterin' would conceal rather than so reflect upon the ambiguities of her position, whereas Wolf constantly, and with rising urgency, thematized in her fictions the problematic and relative nature of her commitment to a society in which, *despite* the activities of the state, she saw the seeds of hope. The failure to publish *Was bleibt* in 1979 may have been a sacrifice of the truth for the benefit of the Christa Wolf who wished to go on living in the GDR, but it was closely followed by the Frankfurt lectures and the writing of *Kassandra* with its drastic ending, though even here the author still sought dialogue.[20] *Im Dialog*, the volume of essays and speeches produced in the year from March 1989 to March 1990 and published in April 1990, documents how, till the end, Christa Wolf was still looking for a dialogue of 'aller gesellschaftlichen Kräfte', in the effort to keep a 'sozialistische Alternative' alive, but the opening, retrospective essay of February 1990, 'Nachtrag zu einem Herbst', conveys a transformation of consciousness brought about at break-neck speed as the author moves from a position divided between public mediation and private fear (in essence still the narrative position of 1968) to recognition of irrevocable failure — 'Es *war* zu spät.'[21] But she refuses also to deny her own past hopes and dares to look forward to new dialogue, though the partners will have changed, and to a resurrection of Utopian thinking which may still spring from the unsolved contradictions and conflicts which marked the history of the now dead GDR. The need for such oppositional and creative thinking will remain as long as there remain the unsolved contradictions and conflicts produced by a patriarchal culture which transcends the East-West divide and which Bachmann and Wolf have critically illuminated. Let us hope, then, that Christa T.'s voice may outlive the death of the state which refused dialogue and of the accommodating narrator who died with it.

NOTES

1   Page numbers in brackets following quotations will refer to the following editions: Christa Wolf: *Nachdenken über Christa T.*, Darmstadt, 1971; Ingeborg Bachmann: *Werke*, Vol. 3: *Todesarten: Malina und unvollendete Romane*, Munich, 1982.
2   See Anna K. Kuhn: *Christa Wolf's Utopian Vision, from Marxism to Feminism*, Cambridge, 1988 on Wolf's move towards feminism. Joseph Pischel (p. 120 above) refers to differences in the approaches of Wolf and Bachmann to Utopian ideas.
3   Christa Wolf: *Der geteilte Himmel*, Munich, 1973; *Kassandra*, Darmstadt, 1983.

4   Karl Marx and Friedrich Engels: *Sudienausgabe in 4 Bänden*, Vol. I: Karl Marx: *Thesen über Feuerbach*, Frankfurt/Main, 1966, p. 140.
5   Marx and Engels: *Studienausgabe*, Vol. III: *Manifest der kommunistischen Partei*, p. 77.
6   John Stuart Mill: *The Subjection of Women*, Harriet Taylor Mill: *Enfranchisement of Women*, London, 1983, p. 38.
7   Bachmann: *Werke*, Vol. 4, p. 220.
8   Harold Bloom: *The Anxiety of Influence. A Theory of Poetry*, Oxford, 1973.
9   See Myra Love: 'Christa Wolf and Feminism: Breaking the Patriarchal Connection', *New German Critique*, no. 16, Winter 1979, pp. 31—53 on the interplay of speech and writing.
10   Sandra M. Gilbert and Susan Gubar: *The Madwoman in the Attic. The Woman Writer and the Nineteenth-Century Literary Imagination*, New Haven, 1984, pp. 3—44.
11   See Sigrid Weigel: 'Der schielende Blick. Thesen zur Geschichte weiblicher Schreibpraxis' in Inge Stephan and Sigrid Weigel: *Die verborgene Frau*, Argument-Sonderband, AS 96, Berlin, 1983, pp. 89—91 for examples.
12   See, for example, Friedrich Wilhelm Korff's review of *Malina*: 'Zu verstehen ist es freilich, daß eine unglückliche Frau gelegentlich gezwungen ist, ihr weibliches Minus als ein Plus der Literatur zuzuschlagen, unverständlich bleibt es aber, daß sie darin gleich so weit geht, ihr Unglück noch in Szene zu setzen, um es alsdann literarisch auszukosten', cited by Sigrid Töpelmann in Ingeborg Bachmann: *Ausgewählte Werke*, Vol. 3, Berlin (GDR), 1987, p. 629.
13   See Gabriele Bail: *Weibliche Indentität. Ingeborg Bachmanns "Malina"*, Göttingen, 1984 on the male trinity; also Elizabeth Boa: 'Women Writing about Women Writing and Ingeborg Bachmann's *Malina*' in Richard Sheppard (ed.): *New Ways in Germanistik*, Oxford, 1990, pp. 128—44.
14   Christa Wolf: *Voraussetzungen einer Erzählung: Kassandra. Frankfurter Poetik-Vorlesungen*, Darmstadt, 1983, p. 149.
15   Weigel: 'Der schielende Blick...', pp. 83—137.
16   Tony Tanner: *Adultery in the Novel. Contract and Transgression*, Baltimore, 1979, pp. 4f.
17   Ricarda Schmidt, who also discusses Christa Wolf (pp. 435—7 below), refers to Bachmann's *Todesarten* in connection with younger West German writers (p. 443).
18   Christa Wolf: *Was bleibt*, Frankfurt/Main, 1990.
19   Hellmuth Karasek: 'Selbstgemachte Konfitüre', *Der Spiegel*, no. 26, 1990, p. 162; Frank Schirrmacher: 'Dem Druck des härteren, strengeren Lebens standhalten. Auch eine Studie über den autoritären Charakter: Christa Wolfs Aufsätze, Reden und ihre jüngste Erzählung "Was bleibt"', *FAZ*, 2 June 1990. See also Helmut Peitsch's discussion of these reactions, pp. 173—5 below.
20   In his article Karasek attacks Wolf's decision to publish the *Kassandra* essays in the GDR at the cost of cuts rather than publishing only in the West.
21   Christa Wolf: *Im Dialog. Aktuelle Texte*, Frankfurt/Main, 1990, pp. 10, 14, 13.

WEST GERMAN REFLECTIONS ON THE ROLE OF THE WRITER
IN THE LIGHT OF REACTIONS TO
9 NOVEMBER 1989

HELMUT PEITSCH

I The Topos of Silence

Seven weeks after the opening of the frontier between the German Democratic Republic and the Federal Republic of Germany, the *Frankfurter Allgemeine Zeitung* (30 December 1989) published an article by Joachim Fest, a member of the editorial board, under the headline 'Schweigende Wortführer', accusing intellectuals of keeping silent about the 'national awakening': 'In Deutschland, Ost wie West, waren es [...] gerade nicht die Intellektuellen, die den 9. November oder was ihm voraufging und folgte vorbereitet und herbeigeführt haben.' The reference to silence as the typical reaction of the intellectual class, who, it is claimed, did not take part either 'gedanklich' or 'in der Empfindung', was also to be found in three other West German *Intelligenzblätter*,[1] *Der Spiegel*, *Die Zeit* and *die tageszeitung*.[2] As early as 10 November 1989 Ulrich Greiner, for example, stated in *Die Zeit*: 'Und alle Intellektuellen, hüben wie drüben, sehen mit schreckensweit geöffneten Augen: In Deutschland findet eine Revolution statt, und sie können sagen, sie sind nicht dabei gewesen', and Peter-Jürgen Boock noted in *die tageszeitung* on 17 November 1989 'einigermaßen verblüfftes Schweigen'.

The charge of silence comprises three distinct claims, and not just in the case of Joachim Fest. Firstly, unprepared writers had been taken by surprise by the events of 9 November. Secondly, they did not adopt a positive attitude. Thirdly, this reaction was true equally of writers in both the Federal Republic and the GDR. This paper sets out to show that all three claims are false, to explore the language and imagery of the debate and to offer some suggestions about what lies behind the distorted picture of the reaction of West German writers to the events of 9 November 1989.

II The Thesis of Surprise

The thesis of surprise rests on the assumption that before the collapse of 'real' socialism in the GDR writers had not reckoned with or even wanted 'so etwas wie [die] Wiedervereinigung',[3] any more than the citizens of the Federal Republic questioned in opinion polls. The lack of ambiguity in the rejection of re-unification by the majority of West Germans in polls taken in the 1980s[4] is matched only by the ambivalence of the role played by the writers in the neo-nationalist wave that preceded the intoxication of 9 November. Writers have contributed, certainly since 1979, in their works and public statements to something that in the 1980s was characterized by the fashionable term 'national identity'.[5] In contrast to the everyday perceptions of the majority of West German citizens which increasingly suggested a separate West German consciousness and tended increasingly to accept the existence of two German states for the indefinite future, among writers the so-called 'open German Question' gained renewed topicality. Long before 9 November, the number of novels, stories, poems and plays in which the 'German Division' was *the* theme had risen dramatically by comparison to the 1970s.[6]

Political scientists examining the increase in such publications in the mid-1980s came to the conclusion that the many books, essay collections and anthologies about Germany were generally of little relevance, because 'eine irgendwie geartete "Aktualität" der deutschen Frage im Sinne einer realistischen Möglichkeit zur Wiedervereinigung ist nicht gegeben'.[7] As far as they were concerned, it was merely a case of a 'literary renaissance' or, as Eckhard Jesse put it, of 'die (Pseudo-) Aktualität der deutschen Frage — ein publizistisches, kein politisches Phänomen.'[8]

It was, however, precisely this kind of 'realism' among political scientists and politicians, who, starting from the premise of the existence of two states, sought to continue the détente policies of the 1960s and 1970s and therefore dismissed reunification as mere rhetoric or declared the 'German Question' to be 'no longer open' (as did Willy Brandt, Oskar Lafontaine and Hans Apel in 1985), that was rejected by those writers who strove to bring the subject to the fore after 1979. These formed a growing minority among West German writers; their views can be categorized into three distinct groups which I shall call the 'Federal Republican' position, the '*Kulturnation*' position and the 'reunification rhetoric' position.

The Federal Republican position, which regarded as an accepted fact that there existed not only two states but also two cultures and ultimately two nations in the successor states of a Germany irrevocably destroyed in 1945, was articulated in 1979 in the anthology *Kein schöner Land*.[9] In spite of its nationalistic title, the volume dealt exclusively with the internal problems of the Federal Republic: alongside unemployment, hostility to foreigners and the limitation of democratic rights, it singled out the Federal Republic's lack of 'Selbstanerkennung', implying that upholding the claim to reunification was the country's 'Lebenslüge'. However, it was Dieter Wellershoff who was most often cited as the prime example of the Federal Republicans. He called Germany a '"Wort ohne Anwendbarkeit", denn Deutschland existiere nicht mehr. Damit sei die deutsche Nation im Begriff zu verschwinden. Hinter dem "realitätsmächtigeren" Leitbegriff' Bundesrepublik erscheint ihm Deutschland "kaum hörbarer Nachhall". Wellershoff sieht in der Bundesrepublik einen "akzeptablen politischen Lebensrahmen", der ihm Ersatz ist für das "verlorene Ganze".'[10]

The *Kulturnation* position involved the retention of the idea of an essentially cultural unity of the German nation and was based primarily on literature. Günter Grass's dictum of 1980: 'Einzig die Literatur [...] überwölbt die beiden sich grämlich begrenzenden Staaten'[11] became famous:

> Als etwas Gesamtdeutsches läßt sich in den beiden deutschen Staaten nur noch die Literatur nachweisen; sie hält sich nicht an die Grenze, so hemmend ihr besonders die Grenze gezogen wurde. Die Deutschen wollen oder dürfen das nicht wissen. Da sie politisch, ideologisch, wirtschaftlich und militärisch mehr gegen- als nebeneinander leben, gelingt es ihnen wieder einmal nicht, sich ohne Kampf als Nation zu begreifen: als zwei Staaten einer Nation.[12]

Grass's view was shared by the majority of writers, not least because of the effect created by the 'Teilverlagerung der DDR-Literatur in die BRD'[13] which took place after 1976. This process, which ultimately involved at least fifty authors (and possibly twice that number — see Theo Buck, p. 28 above), led to the reversal by literary experts and critics of the categorization of GDR literature as a special, discrete literature that had occurred in the late 1960s and early 1970s within the framework of the change to the policy of détente. Hans Mayer and Fritz J. Raddatz, who (in 1967 and 1972 respectively) had been the first, following the postulation of the existence of two states, to formulate the idea of two literatures, explicitly retracted this 'false thesis' in 1978 and 1979 respectively.[14]

By 1987, Dorothee Wilms, the Federal Minister for Inner-German Relations, could note with satisfaction in connection with attempts 'von der Aufspaltung [...] einer gemeinsamen deutschen Literatur zu sprechen' that things had of late become a great deal quieter.[15] In the 1980s most West German writers agreed with her thesis: 'Das Thema der staatlichen Teilung und die gemeinsame nationale Kultur verbinden die Literatur von hüben und drüben.'[16] '42 Jahre jüngster Geschichte können weder das Gericht [sic] eines Milleniums deutscher Literatur austarieren noch einen Schnitt machen und die Leistungen vorangegangener 1200 Jahre in die Bedeutungslosigkeit versinken lassen.'[17] In 1988, a school textbook on GDR literature commissioned by Frau Wilms's ministry was even able to declare the 'two literatures theory' 'eine politische Willens-erklärung maßgeblicher Kulturpolitiker der DDR',[18] which admittedly some critics in the West had taken on board out of pure opportunism,[19] but which from the outset had been contrary to the 'deutschland-politischer Konsens' of the parties represented in the Federal Parliament.[20]

The menacing undertone of the argument that anyone who recognized GDR literature as a discrete literature was an enemy of the constitution is characterstic of the reunification rhetoric of my third position. It can be explained by the compromise between recognition of the existence of two German states and the maintenance of the claim to reunification which the Federal Constitutional Court (in its verdict of 31 July 1973 on the Basic Treaty between the two German states) forced on the parties represented in the Federal Parliament as a consensus position. What was significant for literature here was not so much the claim that the Federal Republic was a continuation of (even if geographically it was only partially identical with) the German Reich, which was deemed not to have disappeared in 1945, but rather the subsuming of the concept of the *Kulturnation* under the goal of reunification. On Willy Brandt's 1970 formulation 'zwei Staaten einer Nation', the Federal Constitutional Court declared: 'Versteckte sich [...] hinter dieser neuen Formel "deutsche Nation" *nur* noch der Begriff einer im Bewußtsein der Bevölkerung vorhandenen Sprach- und Kultureinheit, dann wäre das *rechtlich* die Aufgabe einer unverzichtbaren Rechtsposition. Letzteres stünde im Widerspruch zum Gebot der Wiedervereinigung als Ziel, das von der

Bundesregierung mit allen erlaubten Mitteln anzustreben ist.'[21] Thus a development was institutionalized which accepted cultural and particularly literary factors as a basis for the argument that the Germans in both states belonged together in a single nation, but which at the same time linked this with the idea of state and political unity. That meant that the concept of the *Kulturnation* was from the outset seen exclusively as an argument against the recognition of two states and for the keeping open of the German Question within the public discourse of the Federal Republic. Whoever wished to speak legitimately about cultural unity had to do so with the goal of overcoming the existence of the two states.

The pressure of this threat of being categorized as an enemy of the constitution should not be lightly dismissed. However, only a few writers in the 1980s followed the path from the essentially literary concept of the *Kulturnation* to the political demand for reunification. Even in the case of Martin Walser, who did follow this path, the traditional 'Wiedervereinigungsnationalismus'[22] was accompanied by a rejection of reunification rhetoric: 'Das Wort Wiedervereinigung ist ein Adenauer-Wort, das können wir vergessen.'[23] In this way, Walser dissociated himself rhetorically from the 'Adenauersche Wiedervereinigungstrommel'.[24] And it is precisely this assertion of being non-rhetorical that seems to me to typify the *new* rhetoric of reunification. It presented itself as authentic, as subjective; reunification did not appear as an official political proclamation but as a quite personal question of individual identity, the expression of a feeling, as 'Geschichtsgefühl'[25] and 'Bedürfnis nach geschichtlicher Überwindung des Zustands Bundesrepublik'.[26] Although Walser, in his essays, put forward views enunciated by the Supreme Court judges and shared by the parties represented in the Federal Parliament (with the exception of certain sections of the Greens), he presented himself as an outsider who crusaded against the supposedly prevailing view and who was bitterly attacked by those in powerful positions in the media. Walser is the perfect example of the new nationalists of the 1980s described by Wolfgang Pohrt, whose views were based on Hannah Arendt's thesis that 'the enemy without' was in himself not sufficient for the nationalist, the latter needed 'den gemeinsamen Feind, der die vielen in Eins zwingt, im Land selbst'.[27]

To sum up: the blanket thesis of the silence of writers on the German Question before 9 November 1989 is untenable. On the contrary, it has to be said that the authors of the Federal Republic contributed in a great variety of ways to the new topicality of the subject. In view of the three different positions, however, neither is it possible to accept as generally accurate the proud claim of Hans Christoph Buch: 'Was Politiker versäumten, haben Schriftsteller wettgemacht' (*FAZ*, 27 February 1990), nor will the eulogy given to writers in general by the political scientist Reinhard Kühnl in 1986 stand up to close examination. According to Kühnl, who took Wellershoff as his example, the writers found it 'offenbar etwas leichter, die Realitäten beim Namen zu nennen'.[28]

III The Thesis of the Non-positive Attitude

It would be surprising if writers who had contributed so much to the debate before November 1989 had kept silent once the borders had been opened. At this point I come to the second aspect of Joachim Fest's thesis, that the writers had not adopted a positive attitude to the events of November 1989. At first sight, the reactions of writers corresponded to the three different positions that had developed in the course of the 1980s. November 9 acted as political litmus paper to test the positions on Germany which had been previously taken up or rejected within an essentially Utopian framework.

From the beginning, in newspapers and magazines, Martin Walser was allocated the role of the prophet whose predictions had been fulfilled. The Suhrkamp Verlag printed an expanded version of his *Über Deutschland reden* with an additional loose sleeve quoting Joachim Fest: 'Walser ist der einzige bedeutende Autor der Bundesrepublik, der die dramatische Gegenwärtigkeit der vielfach in die ungewisseste Zukunft verschobenen deutschen Frage anzusprechen wagte, *bevor* die politische Entwicklung sie bestätigte' (*FAZ*, 6 November 1989). Moreover, in an interview with Günter Grass, *Der Spiegel* added to this image of Walser by asking: 'Nur Ihr Kollege Martin Walser wird durch das Thema Deutschland um den Schlaf gebracht [...] Wie kommt es eigentlich, daß den Intellektuellen in der Bundesrepublik sowenig zur deutschen Frage einfällt?'. And the battleground for the impending polemics was marked out by *Der Spiegel* in the way Grass was built up into an antithetical figure to Walser: 'Das fehlende Interesse ist natürlich kein gutes Vorzeichen für Ihre Kulturnation' (20 November 1989).

As a consequence of this duality, a whole series of positions was lost to the attention of the media and thus had from the very first no chance of effective articulation: if Grass, who together with Walser had undermined the idea of a specific Federal Republican identity in the 1980s, now represented *the* 'Gegenposition zu Walser',[29] then the 'lunatic fringe' began on the other side of Grass, with the self-recognition of the Federal Republic. The raising of Walser to the position of an exception (which was, in any case, contradictory to the facts of literary life before 9 November) and the juxtaposing of Walser and Grass, effectively removing the common ground possible within the ambivalence of the concept of the *Kulturnation*, limited the scope for other authors' comments from the outset.

The hierarchical polarization of Walser and Grass contributed to an increasing limitation of the field of discussion; this became apparent, for instance, during a debate among writers in Berlin at which Walter Höllerer proceeded to place Grass outside the bounds of the current reunification discourse: 'Wir suchen eine Wiedervereinigung, die uns was bringt. Grass steht außerhalb des Vokabulars, in dem wir sind' (*FAZ*, 27 February 1990).

Höllerer's seemingly innocent formulation: 'eine Wiedervereinigung, die uns was bringt', contains hints of an image of the poet as the representative of the nation. It is an image which did not gain substance simply from reactions to 9 November, it was to achieve its political legitimation also as a result of events: a poets' Utopia had become historical reality. It was by the yardstick of this consensus between poet and people that comments by writers were subsequently measured. Any critical voice could be rejected as beyond the pale or condemned to silence. As early as December, for example, *Der Spiegel* was no longer prepared to print an article by Grass which sought to clarify the concept of the *Kulturnation* by locating it within the framework of two German states.[30]

A common line of argument emerged in the *Frankfurter Allgemeine Zeitung*, *Die Zeit*, *Der Spiegel*, and *Merkur* that tolerated almost no dissenting voices. It gained its uniformity not only in terms of personnel (through the writers who were regarded as legitimate spokespersons of the reuniting nation), but also through a network of concepts and images which became required usage in any attempted interpretation of current events. The ranks of the national tribunes, privileged as a result of their previous Utopian campaign for a united Germany, were extended by a small number of writers who changed their positions. Martin Walser, Günter Grass and Peter Schneider were joined in *Merkur* by

Dieter Wellershoff and in the *Frankfurter Allgemeine Zeitung* by Hans Magnus Enzensberger.

IV Images and the Interpretation of Events in the West

Which metaphors, terms and topoi were acceptable becomes particularly clear as soon as that sphere of outer darkness into which the Federal Republicans among the West German writers were banished is considered. On the radical Left, there was, for instance, the editor of *Konkret*, Hermann L. Gremliza whose collection of leading articles from the previous year: *Krautland einig Vaterland*, was passed over in determined silence by all those newspapers and periodicals which had devoted the greatest possible space in 1987 to his attack on Günter Wallraff.[31] To the right of him, Uwe Timm, Michael Schneider, Lothar Baier and Dieter Lattmann were only able to publish in the *Volkszeitung*, a publication whose existence until October 1989 had depended on advertising from the GDR and which only in April 1990 attempted a new start independent of the former SED and the West German DKP within a left-wing West Berlin publishing-house.

Three stages in the interpretation of 9 November can be differentiated on the basis of the major concepts and the images assigned to them: firstly, that of reunification 'dictated' by nature and history and by the people; secondly, that of the nation as a 'reality' — as opposed to a 'Utopia'; thirdly, that of 'overcoming the past'.

How rituals and the public discourse linked to them affect reluctant participants in public life was also shown by Gremliza in his description of the Federal Parliament in Bonn on 9 November. His commentary provides a satirical metaphor for the reaction of a broad red-green spectrum, including parts of the literary intelligentsia:

> Sie saßen nicht mehr und sie standen noch nicht. Wippend in der Hocke, den Hintern zehn Zentimeter überm Sitz, den Kopf hilfesuchend nach rechts und links und schräg hinten gedreht; so fing die Kamera sie ein, die Grünen im Bundestag, Sekunden zuvor hatten sich die Abgeordneten erst der Regierungsfraktionen, dann der SPD erhoben und das Deutschlandlied angestimmt. Sollte, durfte, mußte man jetzt auch aufstehen und mitsingen? Jeder, jede spürte, daß dies die Entscheidung war, an der sich vorbeizumogeln den eigenen und den Erfolg der Bewegung ausgemacht hatte. Weit und breit keine Nische, in die man sich hätte drücken können, wie es einst der Nazi Globke getan haben wollte, als der Eid auf den Führer geleistet wurde. Ach, wäre man doch vor fünf Minuten zum Pinkeln gegangen! Und so balancierten sie denn, endlose Sekunden lang, über den Sitzflächen zwischen Vaterland und Szene, Chuzpe und Scham, Freiheit und Sozialismus.[32]

That Gremliza's commentary: 'Zum dritten Mal in diesem Jahrhundert, nach 1914 und 1933, gab es in einem deutschen Parlament keine Parteien mehr'[33] caught the precise symbolic significance of the singing of the Federal Republic's national anthem can also be seen from an article in which the wife of the SPD's honorary chairman, Willy Brandt, referred to August 1914 in order to explain the stance intellectuals were expected to adopt at that moment: 'identification' — 'Von der Linken wird [...] verlangt [...] Einsicht zu nehmen in die Unwägbarkeiten der Volksseele.'[34]

As early as 1979 Martin Walser had indirectly invoked the 'spirit of 1914' when he complained that 'sich unsere Intellektuellen nach 1918 vom Volk getrennt und [...] seitdem die Erfahrung, die man im Volk, mit ihm oder durch es hatte, verdrängt [hatten]'.[35] In December 1989 he metaphorically praised the opportunity for 'speaking of the people again' as a regaining of biological strength, which had been lost in the past when only society had been spoken of: 'Jede Sprache, die sich nicht soziologisch sterilisieren ließ, verfiel bei uns dem entsetzlichsten Verdacht.'[36] The threatening virility of Walser's metaphors had already characterized the 1988 Munich speech in which he had attacked both the concept of Federal Republican constitutional patriotism and that of the *Kulturnation* as 'Wort[e] aus dem Abfindungslabor' smacking of 'Ersatz',[37] as 'einschlägig behäkelte Trostdecken über den Trennungsspalt'[38] and, even more viciously, as : 'polit-masturbatorischen Modeton'.[39] It was this emotional and irrational register that, as late as 1988, led many commentators to speak of Walser's descent to saloon-bar levels.[40] It typifies not only Walser's remarks on the internal enemies of the people, with which he identifies by his use of the first person plural; inevitably, it rears its ugly head again in the tetchy comments on European neighbours, who always appear as potential enemies: 'Zuerst richten wir uns jetzt das deutsche Zimmer ein, bevor wir vom europäischen Haus reden.'[41] This comment made on 11 November 1989, long before the relevant comments of Brandt and Kohl, rejects any idea of the four powers and the thirty-five CSCE states having a right to be involved in the regulation of relations between the Federal Republic and the GDR. In *Über Deutschland reden*, the reasoning behind this is found in the form of an attack on 'das Ausland', which makes 'West oriented' German 'intellectuals' appear as agents of the enemies of reunification:

Und das Ausland tut so, als sei ein nicht mehr geteiltes Deutschland eine Gefahr wie in der ersten Jahrhunderthälfte. In allen europäischen Ländern ist

das in den letzten 30 Jahren oft genug so formuliert worden. Es ist das Interesse des Auslandes, unter diesem Vorwand die deutsche Teilung unge-
mindert zu erhalten. Grotesk ist nur, daß im Inland, vor allem im westlichen
Inland, dieser Vorwand inbrünstig nachgesprochen wird. Am meisten von
Intellektuellen.[42]

Thus Walser's saloon-bar rhetoric creates the unity of the German people
by drawing a distinction between them and their internal and external
enemies. The groups defined as outsiders are the intellectuals as well as
foreigners. Walser himself, however, feels at one not just with the people
but also particularly with 'history'.

Walser makes particular reference to the role of television when he
addresses the way history is experienced: 'Jeder von uns hätte etwas anderes zu tun. Das Leben hat Konjunktur [...] Und schon ist man wieder
dabei und gafft und gibt zu, daß man das nicht versäumen darf. Eine
neue Rolle für Zeitgenossen: Zuschauerin und Zuschauer [...] Wir sind
Zeugen. Geschichte live. Das ist dann doch etwas anders als Politik.'[43]
Walser does not bear in mind that television reporting has always delivered interpretations along with its pictures. Whoever did not agree with
these interpretations of events by the media had to accept the criticism,
as, for example, did Günter Grass in the *Frankfurter Allgemeine Zeitung*,
that he had presumably not even 'gelegentlich auf den Bildschirm
geschaut' and therefore did not know 'was die Leute in diesen Tagen
bewegt': 'Oder interessiert ihn Volkes Stimme und Stimmung wenig?'
(14 November 1989). Only a few writers pointed in their comments to
the discrepancy between the presentation of history in the media and
their own experiences or the everyday comments of West German citizens. Uwe Timm, for instance, who 'experienced' November 9 in New
York on television, could not rediscover the momentous images he had
seen there in his conversations with West German citizens on his return
from the USA: 'Was mich überraschte [...] war [...] wie sachlich,
distanziert die Leute hier von der Wiedervereinigung redeten [...]
Nationale Besoffenheit, das zeigten nur die Fernsehbilder aus der
DDR.'[44]

Three metaphors in particular served to stylize the events following 9 November 1989 as 'history' moving towards the goal of reunification. The first was Willy Brandt's 'Zusammenwachsen dessen, was
zusammengehört',[45] the second Rudolf Augstein's 'Zug der deutschen
Einheit, der abgefahren ist',[46] and the third the force of the inexorable
river of time.

In the first stage of the reactions to 9 November, the view that the reunification of the German people as dictated by nature and history. Martin Walser set against the 'artificial nature'[47] of the inner-German frontier 'die millionenfachen Verwandtschaftsbeziehungen',[48] the brother 'der erwischt wurde und auch für uns den Kopf hinhielt'.[49] In the image of the family of the people biological nature and history became one; accordingly he read significance into the television pictures of November: 'Deutsche Geschichte darf auch einmal gut gehen [...] Leute, die einander nie gesehen haben, umarmen einander. Diesem Niveau muß Politik jetzt entsprechen.'[50]

At the time when the slogan 'Wir sind das Volk' had not yet been replaced at the demonstrations in the GDR by the sticker printed in the CDU headquarters in Bonn 'Wir sind ein Volk',[51] Walser had already, with his phrase 'deutsche Revolution', given the events an interpretation which made the focus reunification — rather than the democratization of society in the GDR. This thus expunged the ambiguity inherent in the comparison made frequently at the turn of the year between the ancien régime of Erich Honecker and that overthrown by the French Revolution which led to nationalism as well as democracy.[52] Walser's 'German Revolution' excluded from the outset a democratic reform of the second German state; other authors, who emphasized specifically German traits in the upheavals in the GDR tended to criticize these, for instance Günter Gaus, who was concerned about the 'moral rigorism' manifested in the way the politicians of the Honecker era were called to account; consequently he made the historical comparison with the Protestant Revolution.[53]

The stylization of history as an all-powerful, active subject brought up the problem of the relationship to the German past. In Walser's frequently used phrase of the 'einmal gut verlaufende' or 'gut gehende' German history,[54] the reference to the 'bad' past remains implicit. However, as soon as he goes into detail about what is bad in German history, it is Versailles and the Cold War that are blamed. Germany appears as the victim of foreign 'Sandkastenmonstren', who had tried to make 'ihre paranoiden Konstruktionen zu unserem Realitätsprinzip'.[55] When Walser speaks of ending the postwar period,[56] he means the reversal of 8 May 1945.

In contrast, the demise of the German nation-state is for Grass not only an irrevocable fact but also a political and moral obligation. Grass links the unified nation-state with Auschwitz and uses this as a decisive argument for clarifying his previous concept of the *Kulturnation*[57] as the 'Verzicht auf den Einheitsstaat im Sinne von Wiedervereinigung'. Ironically, it was during the Berlin Party Conference of the SPD which ratified the submission of the Social Democrats to Kohl's reunification policy that Grass appealed to the party's chairman, Hans-Jochen Vogel, personally and recalled the 'friedfertige [...] weil geschichtsbewußte [..] Deutschlandpolitik' of the SPD over many decades in the hope of a 'dritte Möglichkeit als Antwort auf die Deutsche Frage'.[58] The text of Grass's speech, with its juxtaposition of 'Dumpfheit des Einheitsgebots' and historical awareness, avoids the metaphors which predominated in the media and writers' statements at the end of 1989. Grass called to mind the possibilities of action which were excluded a priori in the system of metaphors used by the opposing side:

> Vereinigung als Einverleibung der DDR hätte Verluste zur Folge, die nicht auszugleichen wären; denn nichts bliebe den Bürgern des anderen, nunmehr vereinnahmten Staates von ihrer leidvollen, zum Schluß beispiellos erkämpften Identität; ihre Geschichte unterläge dem dumpfen Einheitsgebot. Nichts wäre gewonnen außer einer beängstigenden Machtfülle, gebläht vom Gelüst nach mehr und mehr Macht. Allen Beteuerungen, selbst den gutgemeinten zum Trotz, wären wir Deutschen wieder zum Fürchten. Weil von unseren Nachbarn mit berechtigtem Mißtrauen aus zunehmender Distanz gesehen, könnte bald wieder einmal das Gefühl des Isoliertseins und mit ihm jene gemeingefährliche Mentalität aufkommen, die sich aus Selbstmitleid als "von Feinden umringt" begreift. Ein wiedervereinigtes Deutschland wäre ein komplexgeladener Koloß, der sich selbst und der Einigung Europas im Wege stände.[59]

The reception of Grass's collection of essays underlined the impact made by the nationalistic metaphors. Whoever had stood aside and had now been 'left behind' by the 'D-Zug [der] deutschen Einheit', should 'at least keep quiet about it' (*FAZ*, 1 April 1990), because whoever 'set himself against' the '(zeit-) geschichtlichen Erfahrungen' (*Der Tagesspiegel*, 8 April 1990) only gets a 'bloody nose' for his troubles (*Rheinischer Merkur*, 27 April 1990), gets 'hinweggespült vom Volk' and thus 'history passes him by' (*Die Welt*, 26 April 190).

In the second stage of public discourse about 9 November 1989 and its consequences, the reality of the nation, which was supposed to be the premise for the inevitability of reunification, was played off against Utopian ideas. When in mid-December the new party system of the GDR began to take shape, the question of the relationship of the two states was narrowed down to exclude categorically the possibility that an autonomous GDR state might be preserved as a sort of red-green 'conservation area'. The public denunciation of Utopias served to exclude the idea of an independent development even for a GDR society that had been reformed root and branch.

In this there occurred a remarkable transformation which went unnoticed. Those writers who, before 9 November, had insisted on their right to a Utopia now began to support reality, while the advocates of the reality of the two German states turned to Utopian ideas. The apparent contradiction is resolved when we consider the concepts which were used to signify Utopias before and after 9 November: nation and socialism. On the very anniversary of the invasion of Poland, the former head of the cultural section of *Die Zeit*, Fritz J. Raddatz, invoking Rolf Hochhuth and Martin Walser, suddenly discovered the nation and its 'Neu-Vereinigung', for which the time had come:

> Ich lehne es ab, mir [...] ein Utopie-Verbot auferlegen zu lassen. Es ist ja nicht wahr, daß Geschichte von den Machern, den "Real-Politikern" vorangetrieben wurde [...] Es ist mir egal, wenn es hochmütig klingt; das Wort hat auch mit "hohem Mut" zu tun: Es wäre/es ist Sache der Intellektuellen, Sehnsüchte zu formulieren. Nicht die Wohnungsbauminister und Familienministerinnen [sic] haben 1956 und jetzt in Polen, 1956 und jetzt in Ungarn irgend etwas in Bewegung gebracht. Immer waren es die "Spinner", die Kolakowski und Czeslaw Milosz, die Lukács, Tibor Dery und Julius Hay. Wie es den Unterschied von Kunst zur Trivialkunst definiert, daß nicht der Horizont abgemalt, sondern hinter den Horizont gegriffen wird — so definiert sich der Unterschied des politisch handelnden Denkers zum kleinen Populissimus an seiner Kraft zur Utopie.[60]

A few weeks later Raddatz's successor at *Die Zeit*, Ulrich Greiner, used the same formula of the 'Recht auf Utopie' to rebut the attack of the *Frankfurter Allgemeine Zeitung* on writers: 'Weil nämlich diese Gesellschaft ohne den tätigen Widerspruch der Linken und der Sozialisten ziemlich finster aussähe. Zu den fälligen Modernisierungen und sozialen Zugeständnissen hat sie sich bequemen müssen — auch dieses Widerspruchs wegen.'[61]

It was again Martin Walser who set the tone for the prevailing use of language in connection with Utopias when, in the *Frankfurter Allgemeine Zeitung*, he presented Germany as a victim of the Cold War between the superpowers, who had divided it with the aid of the 'Polarisierungszwillinge Adenauer und Ulbricht': 'Schuld sind die zwei Wahrheitslager, die Religionsquartiere, die mit politisiertem Christentum und messianisiertem Marxismus die Verweltlichung der Welt für ein weiteres Mal verhinderten. Utopie sollte regieren, so blutig und böse wie immer. Jetzt möchte man endlich im Namen der Gegenwart Säkularisierung fordern.'[62]

Uwe Timm is one of the few left-wing writers to dismiss such polemics against the expression of Utopias as 'menschenverachtende, intellektuelle Selbstbefriedigung' (*Volkszeitung*, 9 March 1990). He combines this with both a historical assessment of the developments in the GDR and a revised evaluation of his own position vis à vis the society of the Federal Republic: 'Ich werde mich fragen, welche Illusionen ich mitgeschleppt habe, wo bei mir Wünsche die Wahrnehmung eingetrübt haben, wo die ökonomische Theorie entrümpelt werden muß, und vor allem, wie denn dieses Ziel aussieht, dieser Traum, daß es eine Gesellschaft geben müsse, in der dieser Widerspruch ausgesöhnt ist, die Freiheit und Gleichheit.' Since Timm refuses 'sich mit dem Widerspruch von Arm und Reich, Herr und Knecht, Ausbeutern und Ausgebeuteten [...] auszusöhnen [...] in den Stillstand der Geschichte einzuwilligen', he remembers in a more concrete way than those whose disillusionment remains abstract:

> Man muß sich daran erinnern, der Sozialismus in der DDR war eine Alternative zur BRD, eine zugegebenermaßen häßliche, bürokratisch aufgequollene Alternative, aber doch eine Alternative, und daß dieser "reale" Sozialismus trotz aller Erstarrung noch aus sich selber heraus wandelbar gewesen wäre, ist keine bloße Behauptung. Dafür steht die basisdemokratische Bewegung um das Neue Forum (was immer wieder vergessen wird), die Erneuerungsbewegung, die ja aus der Exekutive gekommen ist, die unter Gorbatschow begonnene Perestroika; die Demokratisierung der Gesellschaft, mehr Freiheit, sinnvolle, gesellschaftlich gesteuerte Produktionsprozesse, Gemeinschaftseigentum (nicht Staatseigentum), Abbau der Bürokratie. Darüber wurde ja nicht nur geredet, daran wurde in der DDR gearbeitet, in vielen Arbeitskreisen, Bürgerinitiativen, schließlich mit Demonstrationen.

This very real process of democratization in the GDR was subject, in the cultural and features pages of the West German press, to the accusation of Utopianism. Although at first sight (as in the Walser essay quoted) the present was given priority over the future, as was implied in the accusation that in all Utopian thinking, whether socialist or green-alternative, the present was being sacrificed to the future, in reality only a different kind of future was being postulated. The Federal Republic was being presented as the anticipated future of the GDR. The metaphor of the 'Naturschutzpark' referred to above (pp. 166—7), which was quickly popularized after its appearance in an essay by Dieter Wellershoff,[63] aimed to achieve acceptance of an inevitable wave of modernization: 'Alles spricht dafür, daß es in fortgeschrittenen Ländern zur parlamentarischen Demokratie und der Verbindung von freier Wirtschaft und Sozialstaat nur Varianten, aber keine vernünftige und lebenswerte Alternative prinzipieller Art gibt.'[64]

V The Loss of Utopia and the Role of the Intellectual

With the GDR elections the 'Streit über die Interpretation der Gefühle'[65] entered a new stage in as far as the conservative election victory effectively legitimized the 'semantic coups'[66] of the words 'nation' and 'reality' (achieved at the expense of democracy and Utopia) and, at the same time, put the creation of the new nation onto the ideological agenda.

The concept 'economic nationalism' or the metaphor 'Deutschmark nationalism' were suggested by critical observers of events to explain the election result. The former Green, now SPD member of parliament Otto Schily attracted the anger of television critics when in response to a request for his comments on election night he pulled a banana out of his pocket.[67]

In the face of such images and ideas, it was easy for Hans Magnus Enzensberger to express his suspicion that they represented cheap moralizing. The anti-Utopianism of the second phase of the debate was developed further in Enzensberger's contribution to the left-alternative *Kursbuch* (number 100) (in an article published, interestingly enough, in advance by the conservative *Frankfurter Allgemeine Zeitung* on 19 May 1990): 'Gangarten — Ein Nachtrag zur Utopie. Wenn ein Alltag anbricht, der ohne Propheten auskommt'. In his metaphor of the 'schwankender Gang', Enzensberger locates his essay in the middle between right- and left-wing Utopias, between nationalistic 'Rausch' and socialist 'Panik': 'Gemeinsam ist beiden Positionen, ohne daß sie sich dessen bewußt wären, die negative oder positive Fixierung auf den deutschen Einheitsstaat, Weihrauch oder Molotow-Cocktail, Hauptsache man hat es mit dem Altar des Vaterlands zu tun, als wäre dieses Möbelstück nicht längst zur anachronistischen Attrappe geworden.' By adopting the language of the critic of ideology who exposes the truth, Enzensberger promises his readers a 'non-ideological' view; this he identifies with the 'practical reason' of the 'Massen', a term which, like 'Geschichte', he coyly puts in inverted commas and which he categorically separates from states and their intellectual 'Eliten'. As his yardstick, Enzensberger takes 'Dorfbürgermeister', 'Schreiner', a 'hochherziger Helfer' (a doctor) as well as a 'trüber Spekulant' (a black-marketeer) in order to claim: 'Ganz im Gegensatz zur Hysterie ihrer "Eliten" hat die überwältigende Mehrheit der Deutschen, in einer äußerst zugespitzten und potentiell gefährlichen Situation, ein Maß an Einsicht und Vernunft an den Tag gelegt, das ihr kaum jemand zugetraut hätte [...] Insgesamt haben die "Massen" in ihrer unerschütterlichen Skepsis die Parolen der Wortführer einfach ignoriert.'

Enzensberger's panegyric on 'Gewöhnlichkeit' criticizes both nationalist and left-wing intellectuals for their distance from the people, as whose authentic spokesman he presents himself, even if he uses the terms masses and society rather than *Volk*: 'Eine weitere Gemeinsamkeit der verfeindeten Brüder im Geist ist ihre Verachtung für den niedrigen Materialismus, den der deutsche Mensch an den Tag legt, der Abscheu vor seiner Vorliebe für die D-Mark und für jenes entsetzlichste aller Übel, die "Fußgängerzone".' Enzensberger appears to defend this materialism against the moralizing criticism of intellectuals when, on the subject of the attitude of the masses towards the 'symbolic dimension' of society, he declares: 'So war das Brandenburger Tor gerade noch für ein kollektives Besäufnis gut, dem am nächsten Tag die dauerhafte Ernüchterung folgte.'

Enzensberger's critique is at once inaccurate: the common ground he claims between nationalists and their critics does not exist, for none of the nationalists has ever criticized the preference of the GDR citizens for the D-Mark; and it is dishonest: he extols the intellectuals' lack of influence and yet with his article he himself engages in the ideological interpretation of events. Instead of reflecting in a concrete way on his own position as a leading figure in the media debate, he denies the importance of intellectuals and politicians in the abstract; thus, on the one hand, he ascribes to himself a superior position both above and between the intellectual groupings, whilst, on the other hand, he claims to articulate not only what people really want but also what the course of history really is: 'Die Aussicht darauf, daß die Deutschen allmählich politisch erwachsen werden können, macht Politikern wie Intellektuellen offenbar schwer zu schaffen. Sie werden sich mit der banalen Tatsache abfinden müssen, daß die Demokratie ein offener, produktiver, riskanter Prozeß ist, der sich selber organisiert und der sich, wenn nicht ihrem Einfluß, so doch ihrer Kontrolle entzieht.'

In respect of the claim to represent the people — and history (shown in his metaphor of the maturing Germans), Enzensberger's stance is hardly different from that of Martin Walser, although he does shown more reserve towards some metaphors and concepts of the nationalist tradition. The spiteful malice towards certain intellectuals with different opinions is replaced in Enzensberger's case by a cynical denial of his own role as an intellectual.[68] At the same time, the populist nature of his nationalism drives him at the end of his essay to reverse the initial programmatic rejection of the Utopian metaphor of the 'aufrechter Gang' used by both the left- and the right-wing. If he was able to pass over the metaphorical significance of the Brandenburg Gate, in the case of the Trabant cars his critique of ideology flounders so that, by way of quotations from Bloch and Marx, he turns purely economic refugees into moral and political heroes. By presenting their motives as non-ideological, he believes he has satisfied his requirement of cynicism, but the acceptance of reality is presented as revoutionary through the ironization of Bloch and Marx quotations:

> Und was den aufrechten Gang betrifft, so haben ihn, taumelnd unter der Last ihrer Plastiktaschen, am ehesten jene vorgeführt, die sich, Staatsgewalt hin oder her, vor dem 9. November 1989 auf den Weg über die Grenzen gemacht und die Verhältnisse in Deutschland zum Tanzen gebracht haben. Mit der Gangart dieser Überläufer ist nicht das Millenium, sondern nur ein Alltag angebrochen, der ohne Propheten auskommt.

What Enzensberger achieved with this article was his own elevation to the very role of the 'Prophet dieses Alltags',[69] by which is meant the total integration of society and the end of history. The claim to be commenting in an unideological way, cynically playing off reality against all ideological interpretations, which are then ironized, is disproved by the very example Enzensberger chooses. The television pictures of the refugees who came to the Federal Republic after the opening of the Iron Curtain as a result of the billion-Deutschmark credits granted to Hungary and of the Federal Republic's practice of giving 'German' passports to GDR citizens — based on the legal fiction of the continuing existence of the German Reich at least within the frontiers of 1937, were (in view of these historical parameters) charged with an ideological significance which was hardly less compelling than that of the Brandenburg Gate.

As early as the summer of 1989, as Hans-Joachim Lenger emphasizes in his analysis of their reporting, the media had offered an interpretation of the significance of the wave of refugees which latched on to the fact that young fathers crossing the frontier with their families in their Trabants had used Churchill's V-for-Victory sign.

> Die Deutschen, das ist der Gehalt des nationalen Aufruhrs, wie er sich gegenwärtig in den Medien inszeniert, sollen geschlossen nicht nur die politische Nachkriegsordnung verlassen, die ihnen nach nationalsozialistischem Eroberungskrieg und rassistischer Vernichtungspolitik aufgezwungen werden mußte, sondern — und das reicht noch wesentlich tiefer — sich von der Verantwortung lossagen, die sie für beide tragen; das "Victory" signalisiert einen Sieg des Vergessens.[70]

Thus, not only does Enzensberger fail to reflect on his interpretation of the events; by taking over the cognitive framework created by the media, he expresses the same prohibition of criticism which, following the GDR election results, could be found everywhere in the press of the Federal Republic. By way of ironical polemics it attacked the 'prachtvoll-intellektuelle [...] Attitüde [...] die Motive der DDR-Wähler moralisch zu zensieren' (Reinhard Löw, *Die Welt*, 31 March 1990).

Through the prohibition on criticism of the opinions, attitudes or behaviour of the 'people' who make 'history', Enzensberger arrives at a determination of the role of the intellectual that has been formulated more succinctly by the neo-conservative American ideologue Irving Kristol than Enzensberger ever could, as left-wing radical terminology keeps intruding into his text. According to Kristol, it is the 'Aufgabe des Intellektuellen, [dem] Volk zu erklären, warum es recht hat, und den Intellektuellen, warum sie sich irren.'[71]

VI The Legitimate 'Voice of the People' — East and West

By way of his criticism of intellectuals, Enzensberger indirectly legitimizes the policy of the Federal Government as an authentic expression of the interests of the people and appeals directly to intellectuals to declare their approval of, their agreement with everything that, no matter what, will happen. How this demand can be made in an inquisitorial manner was shown by the journalist of the *Norddeutscher Rundfunk* who chaired the February 1990 discussion between Günter Grass and Rudolf Augstein. Not only did he ask Grass: 'Woher nehmen Sie eigentlich das Recht [...] zu sagen, liebe Bürger in der DDR und in der Bundesrepublik, stimmt nicht so ab, wie ihr wollt, sondern bleibt lieber in getrennten Staaten', he also immediately gave the answer himself, even though, at that time, no vote had yet been taken: 'Ihre Argumentation könnte ja

auch sehr elitär, sogar undemokratisch wirken, nämlich vor dem Hintergrund, daß es offenbar in beiden Teilen Deutschlands große Mehrheiten
für eine Wiedervereinigung in *einem* deutschen Staat gibt.'[72]

It was Uwe Timm who, almost casually, pointed out 'wie immer
häufiger mit wissender Dreistigkeit die DDR mit dem Nazi-Deutschland
gleichgesetzt wird' (*Volkszeitung*, 9 March 1990). This equation is manifested not only in the concept of totalitarianism but also in the metaphor
of the 'Stunde Null', which identifies the present and the future situation
in the GDR with that after the 'collapse' of 1945. In this way, the history
of the GDR is totally devalued and at the same time the history of the
Federal Republic presented as a paragon which the GDR must strive to
emulate. A whole series of popular slogans of the early postwar period
in West Germany has been resurrected and to a certain degree exported:
'verlorene Jahre', 'Nachholbedarf', 'Normalisierung' and, certainly the
most important, *Vergangenheitsbewältigung*.[73] A reporter from the Federal
Republic who travelled through the GDR and was intent on equating
1945 and the early months of 1990 in the GDR found 'Wut über all die
gestohlene Zeit', had the impression 'als sei es ein Land nach einem verlorenen Krieg', discovered 'hinter gestelzten Formulierungen sich [...]
demaskierende Sprachlosigkeit', a 'tragisches Lebensgefühl', and a
'Konsens [über] das Private' reminiscent of the Inner Emigration.[74]

The harsher tones among literary critics towards GDR writers can
be explained from the equating of socialism with fascism. Whereas in
November GDR writers had still largely been praised as pacemakers of
the democracy movement, after March they became candidates for 'denazification', as the question of the guilt they had incurred was called in
a discussion between journalists of the eastern and western editions of
die tageszeitung: 'Ein par [sic] Jahre westlicher Staatsbürgerkunde-Unter-
richt könnten gar nicht schaden, scholl es von der anderen Seite herüber.
"Ich habe den Eindruck, daß wir hier entnazifiziert werden sollen",
beschwerte sich der Ost-Kollege. "Ja, sicher!" riefen einige; "Genau
das."'[75]

Those West German writers who even once rejected this equation
of GDR socialism with fascism were subjected to the most swingeing
criticism — even if, like Peter Schneider, they had previously generally
identified fascism with Stalinism. After Christa Wolf's new book, whose
title *Was bleibt* was in itself a challenge, had been panned in *Die Zeit* on 1
June and in the *Frankfurter Allgemeine Zeitung* on 2 June 1990, Schneider

stated during a discussion organized by the GDR Akademie der Künste under the title '40 Jahre deutsch-deutsche Literatur — Versuch einer Bilanz': 'Es ist ja ziemlich ekelhaft, wie jetzt in den Feuilletons im Westen Leute, die nie etwas riskiert haben, DDR-Autoren vorwerfen, nie etwas riskiert zu haben. Das hat mit Literaturkritik überhaupt nichts zu tun. Das sind moralische Demontagen, die da passieren. Weil das aber so ist, sollte man dazu Stellung beziehen.'[76] The harshness of the subsequent polemic of the *Frankfurter Allgemeine Zeitung* critic Jens Jessen and of Frank Schirrmacher, the editor of its literary supplement, is particularly remarkable, for Schneider's questioning of the consensus is limited not only in scope but also to the defence of the right of literature to rework 'experience'.[77] The fact that it was Schneider's citing of Christa Wolf's statement: '40 Jahre kann man nicht so einfach wegschmeißen' that provided the bone of contention for Schirrmacher proves that 'wegschmeißen' was precisely what was demanded, a total condemnation of the 'kriminelle DDR'.[78]

This demand is expressed in system of metaphors common to the polemics of both Jessen and Schirrmacher that is based on a reworking of Christa Wolf's image of the still contagious 'Leichengift' of the 'verwesenden Mythos des sozialistischen Staates'. Jessen and Schirrmacher detect among West German writers the 'lähmenden Wirkungen des sozialistischen Leichengifts', because Schneider and Walter Jens (the latter had spoken during a discussion in Potsdam of the 'Spruchkammer-Mentalität' of West German literary criticism) '[sich] bereitwillig [...] vom totalitären Geist anstecken und auf schonende Sprachregelungen verpflichten ließen'.[79] Schirrmacher invokes the spirit of *Vergangenheitsbewältigung* in the Federal Republic: on the basis of Adorno's 'Erziehung nach Auschwitz' and the Mitscherlichs' *Trauerarbeit*, he polemicizes against 'Verdrängen und Vergessen'. In the process of constructing an inherent contradiction among intellectuals, he entangles himself in one; he creates a conspiracy theory in order to reproach intellectuals with it: 'Jene, die seit Jahrzehnten in der Bundesrepublik vor Verdrängen und Vergessen warnten, die "Trauerarbeit" forderten, zur schonungslosen Kritik drängten, weichen nun aus, fordern Zurückhaltung und Behutsamkeit und reden von "Hetzkampagne", wo Kritik sich äußert.'[80]

The rhetorical core is provided by the sickness metaphor: the death of socialism and the immunization of the society of the Federal Republic against criticism are the pre-condition for its health. Schirrmacher exaggerates both the influence of critical intellectuals in order to repudiate it and the possible influencing of the Federal Republic's culture by that of the GDR in order to prevent it. Through his negative examples he expresses the goal of his rhetoric: the immunization of the 'Legitimität des neuen Gesamtdeutschland' against criticism, which he equates with 'Verschwörungstheorien' and links with such (essentially critical) slogans as economic 'Ausverkauf', political 'Anschluß' and cultural 'Treibjagd'. Cynical accusations are directed at the small minority of West German writers who express opposition to the predominant viewpoint: 'Sie wollen keinen Streit und keine Offenheit und vielleicht keine Öffentlichkeit.'[81] The use of the concept of *Trauerarbeit* is hypocritical because it conflicts with his newspaper's attitude to the Nazi past: it was precisely the cultural pages of the *Frankfurter Allgemeine Zeitung* that had provided the platform for the conservative historians in their dispute with Jürgen Habermas during the *Historikerstreit*.

Though not intentionally, the head of the literature supplement of the *Frankfurter Allgemeine Zeitung* here also throws light on the thesis of the newspaper's editor, Joachim Fest, namely that intellectuals in East and West had been uniformly silent. Schirrmacher not only says what West German intellectuals must not say, if they want to avoid being considered as suffering from a deadly contagious disease spread by certain GDR intellectuals, he also clearly delineates those GDR writers who are accepted in the Federal Republic as legitimate spokespersons. The right to a public hearing is limited exclusively to those GDR writers who had moved to the Federal Republic before 9 November 1989. Jessen, in his turn, refers specifically to three authors whose presence would have made impossible a discussion like that at Potsdam, in which the former Deputy Minister of Culture of the GDR, Klaus Höpke had taken part: 'Man hätte nur Günter Kunert, Wolf Biermann oder Sarah Kirsch jenem Mann gegenüberstellen müssen, der sie einst terrorisierte und außer Landes trieb, und der ganze Spuk wäre verflogen.'[82]

The more the massive differences between West and East German writers came to the fore during the public debates attended by them in the months before the GDR elections,[83] the more stridently the media in the Federal Republic rejected the right of all the authors who had stayed in the GDR to 'contribute' (as the catchword of the election period had promised) either their expereince or their cultural identity to the process of union. Only those authors could count as legitimate spokespersons in pursuit of the goal of the unified Germany who, by settling in the Federal Republic, had made the latter the yardstick of what was desirable: 'Diejenigen, die von zu Hause fortgingen, blieben dennoch in Deutschland zu Hause.'[84]

At first sight a list of those former GDR writers allowed to publish lengthy statements in the *Frankfurter Allgemeine Zeitung* and *Die Zeit* might refute the view that those who had left the GDR had assigned themselves the leading role in the creation of opinion. This is because, alongside Wolf Biermann, Günter Kunert, Erich Loest, Monika Maron and Hans Joachim Schädlich, the voices of Rolf Schneider, Helga Schubert, Helga Königsdorf, Günter de Bruyn, Fritz Rudolf Fries and Renate Feyl made themselves heard. However, the articles of the authors remaining in the GDR were primarily polemics directed against the criticisms made by West German writers of the reunification policy of the Federal Government. Not all the GDR writers went so far as Monika Maron who, first of all in *die tageszeitung*, then in *Der Spiegel*, and finally in *Rheinischer Merkur*, declared: 'Ich habe mehr Angst vor Piwitt und Grass als vor Höpcke und Kant' (2 March 1990).[85]

Those who had moved were assigned an authority, as victims of Stalinist terror, which marginalized criticism within the Federal Republic of their internal role. Although Lothar Baier normally writes in the *Frankfurter Rundschau* and *die tageszeitung*, only the *Volkszeitung* published his rejoinder to Monika Maron's and Rolf Schneider's 'Abrechnungs- und Vergeltungswut'. Baier expressed scepticism about their attacks, which had characterized writers in the Federal Republic and the GDR as out of touch with the world and the people, asking 'welch merkwürdige Idee von Volksgemeinschaft hinter einem Gesellschaftsbild stecken mag, in dem die für moderne Gesellschaften charakteristischen Spannungen nicht vorgesehen sind — zumal die zwischen der Bevölkerungsmehrheit und der kleinen Gruppe der literarischen Intellektuellen?'. At the same time he questioned Maron's and Schneider's 'häßlich auftrumpfenden Realismus', which polemicizes against Utopias:

> Es macht immer noch einen Unterschied, ob man die Realität im Februar 1990 anerkennt, die besagt, daß die Option für eine weiter selbständige DDR oder gar für einen "dritten Weg" keinerlei Aussicht mehr hat, oder ob man laut und triumphierend mit den Wölfen heult, nur weil sie in der Mehrheit sind. Demokratie heißt nicht nur Sieg der Mehrheit, sondern auch Recht der Min-

derheit auf Gehör und Anerkennung, heißt auch Schutz der Minderheit vor
der siegestrunkenen Mehrheit.

Baier turned Maron's title in *Der Spiegel*, which spoke of the 'neues Elend
der Intellektuellen', against all-German conformism under the guise of
radical criticism: 'Ein Elend sehe ich eher darin, wenn Intellektuelle Dis-
sens nicht mehr ertragen und sich auf die Seite der Mehrheit flüchten,
die sich dann auch noch schlecht agitatorisch zum "Volk" erklären.'[86]

GDR authors contributed principally two claims as indirect arguments for reunification: firstly, that 9 November had liberated literature
in the GDR from its previous function as a substitute for a political public sphere and had thus brought about a 're-literization' as a movement
away from politics; and, secondly, that the literary unity of the *Kulturnation* had always remained intact and there had, therefore, never been a
GDR literature.[87]

Even where GDR writers who had remained in the GDR did make
such comments totally denying their own literary past by submissively
subsuming it within West German literature of the 1980s, effectively de-
politicizing it and emphasizing its national qualities, and thus conform-
ing to the criteria of a future all-German literature, one feature that characterized the statements of those who changed countries was missing:
the demoralizing personal polemics in which everyone hit out at everyone else and, whenever possible, landed blows below the belt, giving
rise in the West German press to the picture of *the* typical GDR writer as
someone who 'eitel, geschwätzig und absichtsvoll seine Ängste feilbietet
und keine Sekunde vor sich selber erschrickt'.[88]

The desire to preserve elements of the literary culture of the GDR
in a united Germany was negatively interpreted not only politically as a
lack of *Vergangenheitsbewältigung*, but also economically as the attempt to
preserve privileges. The tone of moral indignation in which this mixture
of economic and political suspicion was expressed, contrasted starkly
with the paean of praise that had otherwise greeted the materialistic self-
interest shown by GDR citizens. Only where material interests were unequivocally linked with the ideology of the social market economy of the
Federal Republic, were they viewed as sacrosanct by the writers on cultural matters at the *Frankfurter Allgemeine Zeitung* and *Die Zeit*. Where
this interest took the form of questions about social security (whether in
welfare-state or, even worse, socialist terms), it was counted as unclean.
Thus we read in *Die Welt* of 12 May 1990: 'Die DDR-Schriftsteller werden

lernen müssen, daß Freiheit den Verzicht auf staatliche Hofsänger-Privilegien bedeutet; wer eine Datscha will, muß sie sich in Zukunft auf dem Buchmarkt erarbeiten.'

Since the election result an interpretation of the Brechtian dichotomy between 'Fressen' and 'Moral' has established itself among those very authors who are critical towards reunification, which in my view emanates from their preverse trend of mystification that idealizes sacrifice in the Federal Republic and selfishness in the GDR. This new mystification arises from a national way of thinking which states that both in the Federal Republic and in the GDR there will be, on the one hand, winners and, on the other, losers as a result of reunification. Because these opposite groups in both German states may no longer be considered within the categories of classes and social strata but only mystified in national terms, Peter Schneider is able to claim: 'Im Westen gibt es keinen Grund dafür, die Vereinigung zu wollen. Das von Kohl ist kitschiger Nationalismus. Im Osten hingegen ist es anders. Es gibt wichtige wirtschaftliche Gründe, die Leute haben keine Lust, sich für ein drittes Experiment herzugeben, sie wollen ihren Anteil am Wohlstand, und das sofort' (*taz*, 22 January 1990). 'Nun [...] hätten die Leute eben das Geld gewählt. Im Ausland sehe man die Deutschen meist "viel zu romantisch und unterstellt Gefühle, wo wir Deutschen nur noch rechnen"' (*FR*, 21 March 1990).

Günter Grass's comment in *Die Zeit* of 11 May 1990: 'Geld muß die fehlende, übergreifende Idee ersetzen. Harte Währung soll mangelnden Geist wettmachen' is no different in its description of the apparent state of affairs, only in its evaluation. — The conflict hinted at within the question about how the reunification process is to be evalutated from the standpoint of the Federal Republic (expressed by Schneider as 'kitschiger Nationalismus' and by Grass as 'Geld [ohne] Geist') echoes the supposed opposition between materialism and idealism.[89]

VII Concluding Summary

It is in the nationalistic mystification of ideas and interests that I see the answer to my initial question about what lies behind all the talk of the intellectuals' silence — something that has been shown to be clearly false by what has been documented here. The preparation of 'national renewal' which was cultural and Utopian, the predominance of positive comments in the *Intelligenzblätter* and the commitment of former GDR authors to a purely literary unity of the nation are 'selectively forgot-ten'[90] because there are still dissenting voices. Behind the supposed silence lies the fact that what is being said is not exclusively what is desired. The creation of the category of silence is therefore to be under-stood as an attempt *to impose* silence.[91]

Through the elimination of positions that deviate from what is to be regarded as in the national interest, it is ensured that views can only be articulated in a certain way and linked to certain interpretations. Above all, the interests of the rest can be subordinated to those of the rulers, as expressed within the dominating ideas.

Through the accusation against writers that they have remained silent up to now, they are presented with a task to fulfil in the future. They are to make up for their omissions as quickly as possible. Martin Walser, for instance, criticized his colleagues for lagging behind politi-cians and above all historians.[92] The philosopher Helmut Dubiel explained this tardiness in terms of the way that especially writers had shown themselves to be 'verführbar' by the ideas of socialism.[93] The chairman of the Historical Association of the Federal Republic spoke in the *Frankfurter Allgemeine Zeitung* of the way there was a need for 'Arbeit an der mentalen Infrastruktur' of the new, united Germany,[94] and that paper's arts editor, similarly a historian, insisted (in *Merkur*) on the 'Teilhabe der Intellektuellen' necessary to ensure the success of re-unification.[95]

That a positive contribution to the 'legitimation' of the incipient larger Federal Republic is expected from writers, in as far as they have previously been critical of reunification, was made particularly clear by Karl Heinz Bohrer in his *Frankfurter Allgemeine Zeitung* article of 13 Jan-uary 1990. While its title: 'Warum wir keine Nation sind', seemed to take the misgivings into account, the subtitle: 'Warum wir eine werden soll-ten' hinted at the new function literature was to have. Bohrer's line of ar-gument shows the impossibility of maintaining a differentiation between an innocent economic nationalism and a dangerous German spirit. Bohrer links a primarily economic motivation for reunification arising out of the necessity for modernization with the cultural aspect that arises from the 'tiefere geistige Dimension der Völkeridentität [...] der psy-chisch-intellektuellen Verfaßtheit der Deutschen'. What is kept separate by foreign observers like Richard J. Evans and Conor Cruise O'Brien[96] is linked together by Bohrer. In this, the cultural and literary argument even acquires the decisive role, because it is only on the basis of the supposed unity of culture that Bohrer is ultimately able to define the nation as 'kulturelles Gedächtnis'.

That this culturally based national identity is anything but innocent is shown not only by Bohrer's eulogy of 'unsere spezifisch irrationale Tradition' but also by his use of the word 'harmlos' as a derogatory term. His ultimate argument against the existence of two German states is the resultant 'Stillegung' of German history 'ins Harmlose'. The way that Bohrer presents, as a warning example of how a German can forget his Germanness, the case of a supporter of the Greens who conceives of a future Federal Republic as an 'ökologisches Schweden', is reminiscent of Enzensberger's Sweden report, which accused the Swedish Social Democrats of trying in schools to prevent or even eradicate pride in the battles of Gustavus Adolphus. And it is reminiscent also of Walser, who repeatedly cites Holland as a horrific example of the loss of a sense of history. He, too, uses 'harmlos' as a negative concept.

In 1982 Bohrer gave the negatively 'harmless' Germans an example to follow. In his article 'Falkland und die Deutschen. Vom Ethos der Mainzelmännchen. Eine Polemik' (*FAZ*, 15 May 1982), he criticized the lack of understanding among West Germans, particularly intellectuals, for British policy 'den Krieg nicht bloß anzudrohen, sondern damit Ernst zu machen': 'Von Beginn an ist eigentlich nicht verstanden worden, daß auch dieser Krieg [...] seine sonore Symbolik haben kann: Instinkte der alten Großmacht, parlamentarische Metaphern, die plötzlich verpflichtende Bedeutung herstellen, zum Beispiel die Bedeutung von "Prinzipien", die nationale Identität als das große Über-Ich, ja sogar das mystische Element der Ehre — auf einen Begriff gebracht: Spiritualität.' Against this cultural paragon of national identity, the inhabitants of the Federal Repubic are shown in a negative light. They appeared to Bohrer as the 'westdeutsche Händlernation', which had no 'sense of the past and its symbols' and to which 'every form of struggle was taboo': 'Die winselnde Harmlosigkeit — wo wäre sie psychoanalytisch sprechender, repräsentativer dargestellt als in den Symbolfiguren des Zweiten Deutschen Fernsehens, jenen uns gleichen Kreaturen, die als Mainzel-Männchen das Nachkriegs-Gartenzwerg-Bewußtsein einhechelten.'

Bohrer is not the only one who uses the old anti-British cliché of a nation of shopkeepers against the West Germans, who are no longer the heroes as which the German people had been depicted in the hostile stereotype of the imperialist era. Enzensberger's anthology of reports from the postwar era, whose appearance coincided with its end, calls the Federal Republic in an equally derogatory way, albeit ironically, a nation of shopkeepers:

> Daß die Besiegten von damals, die Deutschen und die Japaner, sich heute als Sieger fühlen, ist mehr als ein moralischer Skandal; es ist eine politische Zumutung. Natürlich wird unser Führungspersonal nicht müde zu beteuern, daß wir unterdessen alle friedlich, demokratisch und zivil geworden seien, mit einem Wort: brav, und das Merkwürdigste an dieser Behauptung ist, daß sie zutrifft. Diese Mutation hat die Deutschen zu dem gemacht, was sie einst anderen nachsagten: zu einer Nation von Krämern.[97]

In his 1982 article, evoking the contrast between heroes and shopkeepers within ideological terms reminiscent of 1914, Bohrer went on to state expressly what the example of the British in the Falklands taught: 'Die Westdeutschen werden wieder lernen müssen, daß ihre eigene geschichtliche Katastrophe oder Desillusionierung in der Niederlage den Wert des "Patriotismus" keineswegs relativiert: oder sie laufen weiter einer politischen Lebenslüge nach.' In 1990, he sees in the union of the two Germanys the chance of regaining the lost or fogotten German heroic identity, 'wenn die Ursache des Erinnerungsverlustes, die Trennung von DDR und BRD als sebständige Staaten, aufgehoben wird, wenn das Jahr 1945 als Nullpunkt des traumatischen Erinnerungsverlustes verschwindet, wenn die gemeinsame Zeit vorher angenommen ist'.[98]

These examples show that the cultural legitimation of the new, bigger Germany is inevitably linked with the praise of danger and aggressiveness.

There is no such thing as innocent 'DM-Nationalismus';[99] it is always, not least because of the activity of writers, not only 'emotional aufgewertet', as Habermas writes, but also imbued with ideological meanings which link interests and ideas. Habermas has spoken of an 'obszöner Code', as if naked interests were visible, and differentiated this correctly from the 'Sprache der Stukas'. Yet acquiescence in what Habermas calls the 'Politik des Alleingangs',[100] which has been transmitted by West German writers, involved silence about or the playing down of the economic interests of the ruling class in the Federal Republic, which became apparent, but only indirectly, in the suppression of antifascism and the regeneration of the ideas of 1914 through the appeals to the ideal of sacrifice. Clarity like that shown by Friedrich Christian Delius is a rare exception:

> Das Peinliche für alle Intellektuellen ist, daß nicht die Ideen, sondern die Ökonomie die Zukunft, auch die deutsche, diktiert. Das hat Marx zwar schon gesagt, aber damit wollen sich die Kopfarbeiter Ostwestlinks nicht abfinden. Das ist begreiflich, niemand möchte gern zum Affen des Kapitals und der Politik werden. Also gibt es, vereinfacht, zwei natürliche Reaktionen; die einen, die mit ihren Gedanken dem Kapital mitlaufend vorauseilen — und die andern, die zwar nicht bremsen können, aber den Widerstand suchen, in Kunst, Meinung oder Praxis.[101]

NOTES

Translation by Stuart Parkes.

1   The term used by Claus Koch in his useful analysis of the West German press: *Die Intelligenzblätter der Deutschen*, Berlin, 1989.
2   See Rudolf Augstein: 'Das tolle Jahr 1989' in *Spiegel-Spezial*, II/1990, p. 15; Gunter Hofmann: 'Die Einheit, die spaltet', *Die Zeit*, 23 February 1990; Walther Müller-Jentsch: 'Hokuspokus', *taz*, 13 January 1990.
3   Jürgen Habermas: *Die nachholende Revolution*, Frankfurt/Main, 1990, p. 206.
4   See, for example, *Die deutsche Frage*, published by the Niedersächsiche Landeszentrale für politische Bildung, 2nd ed., Hanover, 1982, p. 422f.
5   Karl Dietrich Bracher: 'Das Modewort Identität und die Deutsche Frage', *FAZ*, 9 August 1986.
6   On the matter of relevance see my article: 'Die problematische Entdeckung nationaler Identität. Westdeutsche Literatur am Beginn der 80er Jahre', *Diskussion Deutsch*, vol. 18, no. 96, 1987, pp. 373—92; similarly critical are Thomas Steinfeld and Heidrun Suhr: 'Die Wiederkehr des Nationalen: Zur Diskussion um das deutschlandpolitische Engagement in der Gegenwartsliteratur', *The German Quarterly*, no. 62, 1989, pp. 345—56; more superficial and more positive is Thomas Koebner: 'Von der Schwierigkeit zu sagen, wer wir sind. Die Suche nach der nationalen Identität in der deutschen Literatur heute', *Neue Rundschau*, vol. 100, no. 1, 1989, pp. 96—118. For a discussion that goes beyond literature, see Karl-Rudolf Korte: 'Deutschlandbilder — Akzentverlagerungen der deutschen Frage seit den siebziger Jahren', *aus politik und zeitgeschichte*, 15 January 1988, pp. 45—53.
7   Wilfried von Bredow: *Deutschland — ein Provisorium*, Berlin, 1985, p. 136.
8   Eckhard Jesse: 'Die (Pseudo-)Aktualität der deutschen Frage — ein publizistisches, kein politisches Phänomen', *Neue politische Literatur*, supplement 3 ed. by Wolfgang Michalka: *Die Deutsche Frage*, Wiesbaden, 1986, p. 51.
9   *Kein schöner Land. Deutschsprachige Autoren zur Lage der Nation*, ed. Uwe Wandrey, Reinbek, 1979. The dust jacket describes 'die Mängel in der Gesellschaft als eine Herausforderung' and the preface declares the object of the critique to be 'damit dieses Land, das nicht das schlechteste ist, ein schöneres, freieres wird' (p. 13).
10   Helmut L. Müller: 'Der "dritte Weg" als deutsche Gesellschaftsidee', *aus politik und zeitgeschichte*, 7 July 1984, p. 35, quoting Dieter Wellershoff: 'Deutschland — ein Schwebezustand' in Jürgen Habermas (ed.): *Stichworte zur "Geistigen Situation der Zeit"*, vol. 1: *Nation und Republik*, Frankfurt/Main, 1979, pp. 77—9.
11   Günter Grass: *Kopfgeburten oder Die Deutschen sterben aus*, Darmstadt, 1980, p. 154.
12   Ibid., p. 15.
13   Karl-Wilhelm Schmidt: 'Grenzüberschreitungen. Über Leben und Literatur ehemaliger DDR-Autoren in der Bundesrepublik' in Helmut Kreuzer (ed.): *Pluralismus und Post-*

modernismus. Beiträge zur Literatur- und Kulturgeschichte der 80er Jahre, Frankfurt/Main, 1989, p. 152.

14 See Theo Buck, who speaks of the 'teilweise erstaunlichen Bekundungen der Schriftsteller zur Frage der kulturellen Einheit' ('Deutsche Literatur, deutsche Literaturen? Zur Frage der Einheit der deutschen Literatur seit 1945' in Heinz Ludwig Arnold: *Bestandsaufnahme Gegenwartsliteratur — Bundesrepublik Deutschland, Deutsche Demokratische Republik, Österreich, Schweiz*, Munich, 1988, pp. 183—92; here p. 190), and, by contrast, Jörg Schönert, whose approach is unemotional and analytical: 'Identität und Alterität zweier literarischer Kulturen in der Bundesrepublik und DDR als Problem einer interkulturellen Germanistik' in Alois Wierlacher (ed.): *Das Fremde und das Eigene. Prolegomena zu einer interkulturellen Germanistik*, Munich, 1985, p. 220.

15 Dorothee Wilms: *Beiträge zur Deutschlandpolitik*, Bonn, no date (1988), p. 96.

16 Ibid., p. 98.

17 Ibid., p. 97.

18 Günther Rüther: 'Die geteilte Literatur — ein Bindeglied der geteilten Nation' in Rüther (ed.): *Kulturbetrieb und Literatur in der DDR*, Cologne, 2nd ed., 1988, p. 20.

19 Ibid., p. 15.

20 Ibid., p. 10.

21 *Juristenzeitung*, no. 18, 1973, p. 590; see also Erhard Hexelschneider and Erhard John: *Kultur als einigendes Band? Eine Auseinandersetzung mit der These von der "einheitlichen deutschen Kulturnation"*, Berlin, 1984, p. 88.

22 Jürgen C. Heß: 'Westdeutsche Suche nach nationaler Identität' in Wolfgang Michalka: *Die Deutsche Frage...*, p. 38.

23 Martin Walser: *Über Deutschland reden*, rev. ed., Frankfurt/Main, 1989, p. 110.

24 Ibid., p. 58.

25 Ibid., p. 92.

26 Ibid., p. 23.

27 Wolfgang Pohrt: *Endstation. Über die Wiedergeburt der Nation*, Berlin, 1982, p. 125.

28 Reinhard Kühnl: *Nation — Nationalismus — Nationale Frage. Was ist das und was soll das?*, Cologne, 1986, p. 109.

29 See the general review by Volker Hage based on this juxtaposition: 'Kein schöner Thema weit und breit', *Die Zeit*, 9 March 1990.

30 See '"Gegen meinen Willen setzt bei mir so eine Art Absonderung ein." Ein Gespräch mit Günter Grass', *Neue Gesellschaft/Frankfurter Hefte*, vol. 37, no. 8, 1990, p. 702.

31 See *Konkret*, no. 10, 1987.

32 Hermann L. Gremliza: 'No deposit, no return (Dezember 1989)' in Hermann L. Gremliza: *Krautland einig Vaterland*, Hamburg, 1990, p. 42.

33 Ibid.

34 Brigitte Seebacher-Brandt: 'Die Linke und die Einheit. Unwägbarkeiten der deutschen Geschichte', *FAZ*, 22 November 1989.

35 Walser: *Über Deutschland reden*, p. 17. See Stuart Parkes, esp. pp. 190 and 199—201 below, for a discussion of Walser's earlier attitude.

36 Ibid., pp. 116f.

37 Ibid., p. 90.

38 Ibid., p. 84.

39 Ibid., p. 85.

40 See, for example, the report in *FR*, 8 December 1988, which spoke of 'gefährliche Nähe zum gesunden Volksempfinden'.

41 Walser: *Über Deutschland reden*, p. 115.

42 Ibid., p. 84.

43 Ibid., p. 116.

44 Uwe Timm: 'Von der Schönheit subventionierten Schnittblumen', *Volkszeitung*, 9 March 1990.

45 *Die Zeit*, 17 November 1989.

46 Rudolf Augstein and Günter Grass: *DEUTSCHLAND, einig Vaterland? Ein Streitgespräch*, Göttingen, 1990, pp. 78—80.

47 Walser: *Über Deutschland reden*, pp. 121f.

48 Ibid., p. 123.

49 Ibid., p. 116.
50 Ibid., p. 126.
51 See Lutz Hoffmann: '"Ein Volk" statt "Das Volk". Hintergründe einer semantischen Korrektur', *Blätter für deutsche und internationale Politik*, vol. 35, no. 4, 1990, p. 488.
52 Compare the political commentaries in *FAZ*, 2 and 13 November 1989 with the later ones in the cultural sections on 23 and 29 December 1989 and 3 January 1990. On the fear of the new 'jacobins' see: Rolf Schneider: 'Notizen nach dem Umbruch in der DDR: Viele Lügen, viele Tränen', *FAZ-Magazin*, 16 March 1990, p. 30 and also the earlier articles in *FAZ* by Helga Königsdorf and Helga Schubert on 4 and 24 January 1990 respectively.
53 See his 'Rede an die Deutschen in der DDR' held in the East Berlin Friedrichstadtkirche on 19 December 1989 and published in *Blätter für deutsche und internationale Politik*, vol. 35, no. 3, 1990, p. 316; similarly Klaus Harpprecht, who tried to combine the two historical comparisons: 'Nun müssen sie tapfer beweisen, daß sich auch unter uns, den Deutschen, Aufklärung und Religiosität, Reformation und Revolution endlich, endlich miteinander versöhnen. Das ist der entscheidende Umbruch. Er macht wahrhaft Epoche.' (*FAZ-Magazin*, 29 December 1989, p. 21.)
54 Walser: *Über Deutschland reden*, pp. 115 and 126.
55 Ibid., p. 122.
56 Ibid.
57 Dieter Stolz, pp. 207—22 below, discusses Grass's concept of Germany in some detail ('"Deutschland — ein literarischer Begriff": Günter Grass and the German Question').
58 Günter Grass: *Deutscher Lastenausgleich*, Frankfurt/Main, 1990, p. 11. Both Stuart Parkes (p. 191 below) and Dieter Stolz (pp. 211—2 below) comment on Grass's involvement with the SPD.
59 Ibid., pp. 10f.
60 Fritz J. Raddatz: 'Deutschland, bleiche Mutter. Ein Plädoyer für die deutsche Einheit', *Die Zeit*, 1 September 1989.
61 Ulrich Greiner: 'Utopie-Verbot. Die deutschen Intellektuellen und das deutsche "Volk"', *Die Zeit*, 8 December 1989.
62 Martin Walser: 'Vom Stand der deutschen Dinge', *FAZ*, 5 December 1989; also in Walser: *Über Deutschland reden*, p. 121.
63 Dieter Wellershoff: 'Befreiung und Modernisierungsschub. Zur Revolution in der DDR', *Merkur*, vol. 44, no.1, 1990, p. 72.
64 Ibid.
65 Habermas: *Die nachholende Revolution*, p. 159.
66 Arnuf Baring, *FAZ*, 7 June 1990.
67 See Hellmuth Karasek: 'Mit Kanonen auf Bananen', *Der Spiegel*, 26 March 1990, pp. 56f.
68 On this point, see the criticism of Hauke Brunkhorst: 'Populärer Maoismus. H. M. Enzensberger und keine Wende', *FR*, 2 June 1990. Earlier, attention was drawn to this tendency by Jochen Schimmang (explicitly a 'former Maoist'), but without mentioning Enzensberger by name: 'Eine Art Hingerissenheit, eine sehr intellektuelle, die auch etwas von Identifikation mit dem Aggressor hat, herrscht vor darüber, daß das Volk gehandelt hat, als habe der leibhaftige Mao uns noch einmal daran erinnert: "Die wahren Helden sind die Massen und nur die Massen."' ('Die Wiederkehr des Weltgeistes. Unsystematische Anmerkungen zum neuen Glauben an die Geschichte', *Merkur*, vol. 44, no.4, 1990, p. 342.
69 See, for example, the emphatic repetition of Enzensberger's key terms by the editor of a 'trendy magazine' in the survey 'Spinnt Gorbatschow' conducted by a similar journal: 'Gorbatschow ist weder ein Diktator noch der "gute Onkel". Er ist ein "Organisator des Rückzugs" (Enzensberger). Dieser moderne Herrschertypus hat keine andere Aufgabe, als verpfuschte Utopien und marode Herrschaftssysteme auf möglichst unschädliche Art zu beenden. Ein Staatsmann als Entsorger.' (Matthias Horx, editor of *Pflasterstrand*, in *Tempo*, no. 5, 1990, p. 16) In other Western countries, too, Enzensberger was regarded as a representative spokesman. For example: *Time International*, Special Issue: Germany Toward Unity, 25 June 1990, pp. 20f. and p. 87, where under the title 'Rigmarole'

it published a shortened version in English of his articles 'Die Helden des Rückzugs' and 'Gangarten'.

70 Hans-Joachim Lenger: 'Nicht sonniger Süden, sondern freier Westen. Zur Soziologie eines nationalen Aufruhrs', *Blätter für deutsche und internationale Politik*, vol. 34, no. 12, 1989, p. 1518.

71 .Quoted by Arthur Heinrich and Klaus Neumann: 'Die provisorische Republik', *Blätter für deutsche und internationale Politik*, vol. 35, no. 5, 1990, p. 267.

72 Augstein, Grass: *DEUTSCHLAND, einig Vaterland?*, p. 75.

73 See 'Von deutschem Jubel über die eigene Unzulänglichkeit. Günter Gaus im Gespräch mit Karl B. Bredthauer', *Blätter für deutsche und internationale Politik*, vol. 35, no. 5, 1990, pp. 531—3.

74 Mark Siemons: 'Von neuen Menschen und alten Gedanken. Die DDR im Frühling; Dialektik, Markt und die Invasion der Sinnvermittler', *FAZ*, 12 May 1990.

75 Volker Zastrow: 'Linke Verdrängung. Deutsche Szene; Ost-*taz* und West-*taz* im Kalten Krieg', *FAZ*, 20 June 1990.

76 'Vierzig Jahre kann man nicht einfach wegschmeißen', *Volkszeitung*, 15 June 1990. There is confirmation of the existence of this view in the review by Matthias Altenburg (*Stern*, 25 June 1990), where the play on words in the phrase 'finaler Todesstuß' betrays the intention, and also in Hellmuth Karasek's resumé of the various negative reviews (*Der Spiegel*, 25 June 1990: 'Selbstgemachte Konfitüre: SPIEGEL-Redakteur Hellmuth Karasek über die Diskussion um Christa Wolfs Erzählung *was bleibt*). Even though Karasek tones down the 'denazification court whitewash' comparison directed by Frank Schirrmacher against those seeking to exonerate Christa Wolf (Schirrmacher speaks of an 'als untauglich erweisener [...] Persilschein' and sees Wolf not as an 'autoritärer Charakter' but as 'eine ins Innerliche emigrierte Autorin' — drawing on the metaphor from the Nazi era), he nevertheless intensifies the attack on Christa Wolf, not least when he calls her a 'symbol of co-existence' and through this demands from West German readers 'Scham über eigenes Verhalten' in the past towards GDR literature: 'Es ist ein Abschied von Gestern, in dem wir alle damals Heute spielten, als sollte es ewig währen.' The same line is taken in Ursula Eschenig's review in *Der Tagesspiegel* (24 June 1990). It is true that she attacks the 'many' who are only really concerned with 'die Generalabrechnung mit den Schriftstellern und Intellektuellen der DDR' but her warning against the 'vorschnelle [...] selbstgerechte Siegerpose' incorporates Karasek's requirement of the reader's self-criticism towards attitudes to literature adopted during the period of détente: 'Auch wir haben zu manchem geschwiegen und die Schriftsteller der DDR in einer stillschweigenden Übereinstimmung in einem Schonraum gelassen.' By contrast, see Uwe Koch who, in his 'Literaturkritik im Zeichen der Sieger' (*Volkszeitung*, 22 June 1990) provided the first critical reaction to the reception of Wolf's story.

77 See also Elizabeth Boa's comments on *Was bleibt*, pp. 152—3 above.

78 Frank Schirrmacher: 'Hetze? Die zweite Stunde Null', *FAZ*, 18 June 1990.

79 Jens Jessen: 'Auch tote Götter regieren. Streit der Intellektuellen auf einer Tagung in Potsdam', *FAZ*, 16 June 1990.

80 Schirrmacher: 'Hetze?...'.

81 Ibid.

82 Jessen: 'Auch tote Götter...'.

83 See Maja E. Gwalters in the *Neue Zürcher Zeitung*, 6 March 1990, who concluded 'daß hier der Prozeß des Zusammenwachsens dessens, was laut einem politischen Schlagwort zusammengehört, womöglich steiniger als in der Wirtschaft sein wird'. Even in the *FAZ* (14 May 1990), Michael Scheffel admitted on the occasion of a PEN-meeting in Kiel that 'die Köpfe eben doch auf ganz unterschiedliche Weise geformt [worden seien]'.

84 Hans Joachim Schädlich: 'Tanz in Ketten. Zum Mythos der DDR-Literatur', *FAZ*, 28 June 1990.

85 Theo Buck discusses Monika Maron's article in *Der Spiegel*, esp. pp. 24, 32—3 and 36 above. Stuart Parkes (p. 193 below) indicates something of Piwitt's stance.

86 Lothar Baier: 'Intellektuelle unter sich. Kündigt die Abrechnungswut unter DDR-Schriftstellern das geistige Klima des neuen Deutschlands an?', *Volkszeitung*, 30 March 1990.

87 For a rare critical voice responding to such statements, see Hans-Jürgen Schmitt: 'Das Zentralkomitee liest nicht mehr. DDR-Literatur im Umbruch', *Literaturmagazin*, no. 25, 1990, pp. 20 and 24.
88 Frank Schirrmacher: 'Sorgen', *FAZ*, 31 March 1990.
89 Foreign observers of the developments between the two Germanys also seem to operate within the alternative: idealism or business. Thus, in Great Britain the new German nationalism is interpreted either as economic nationalism or as a recurrence of the unchanging German spirit. A value judgement is linked with this kind of description. The first appears harmless, the second dangerous. See, for example, Richard J. Evans: 'Promised Land?', *Marxism Today*, no. 4, 1990, pp. 18—19, and Conor Cruise O'Brien: 'Beware the Reich is reviving', *The Times*, 31 October 1989.
90 On this concept, see the methodologically stimulating study by Karen Ruoff: 'Rückblick auf die Wende zur "Neuen Subjektivität"', *Das Argument*, vol. 25, no. 142, 1983, pp. 802—20.
91 See Frank Deppe: 'Die Intellektuellen, das Volk und die Nation', *Blätter für deutsche und internationale Politik*, vol. 35, no. 6, 1990, p. 710.
92 Walser: *Über Deutschland reden*, pp. 57—9.
93 Helmut Dubiel: 'Linke Trauerarbeit', *Merkur*, vol. 44, 1990, pp. 483f.
94 Christian Meier: 'Allianz der Ängste', *FAZ*, 7 June 1990.
95 Gustav Seibt: 'Zyklus von Erniedrigung und Überhebung. Norbert Elias' "Studien über die Deutschen"', *Merkur*, vol. 44, 1990, p. 334.
96 See note 89 above.
97 Hans Magnus Enzensberger: 'Europa in Trümmern. Ein Prospekt', *Die Zeit*, 1 June 1990.
98 Karl Heinz Bohrer: 'Und die Erinnerung der beiden Halbnationen?', *Merkur*, vol. 44, 1990, p. 185.
99 Habermas: *Die nachholende Revolution*, p. 205.
100 Ibid, p. 206.
101 Friedrich Christian Delius: 'Der Westen wird wilder. Die Intellektuellen und die deutsche Frage: Die Claims werden abgesteckt', *Die Zeit*, 2 February 1990.

'LEIDEN AN DEUTSCHLAND':
SOME WRITERS' VIEWS OF
GERMANY AND THE GERMANS SINCE 1945

STUART PARKES

In an interview in *Die Zeit* published in September 1989, the literary critic and survivor of the Holocaust, Marcel Reich-Ranicki, when questioned about Jewish self-hatred, countered by referring to the Germans: 'Es gibt noch ein Volk auf Erden, das sich selbst leidenschaftlich haßt. Das sind die Deutschen.'[1] He went on to refer to Heinrich Mann's veneration of all things French and Italian, interpreting this as an irresponsible anti-German attitude. It would have been easy for Reich-Ranicki to offer earlier examples of this phenomenon, not least the comments by the poet Friedrich Hölderlin, whose denunciation of the Germans has possibly become the most famous of all such diatribes: 'Barbaren von Alters her, durch Fleiß und Wissenschaft und selbst durch Religion barbarischen geworden, tief unfähig jedes göttlichen Gefühls, verdorben bis ins Mark zum Glück der heiligen Grazien, in jedem Grad der Übertreibung und der Ärmlichkeit beleidigend, dumpf und harmonielos, wie die Scherben eines weggeworfenen Gefäßes.'[2] Some years later, in his conversations with Eckermann, even Goethe commented on the killjoy German police whose authoritarian behaviour turned natural youthful exuberance into adult philistinism.[3]

In the case of Hölderlin at least, it would be difficult not to apply Reich-Ranicki's category of self-hatred. Elsewhere, however, it is a term that has to be viewed sceptically, since hatred of Germany has been one of the many terms of abuse hurled at certain writers and intellectuals by those who might just as easily be accused of the opposite: the kind of nationalism that refuses to accept any criticism at all. Thomas Mann, to whom it must have appeared that nothing much had changed, was one of the first to be subjected to the accusation of being anti-German in the early postwar years, not least because of his novel *Doktor Faustus* and the accompanying essay 'Deutschland und die Deutschen', originally a speech given in the United States. Specifically, after Mann had criticized the literature written in Germany between 1933 and 1945 as carrying the stench of blood and shame, his fellow writer Frank Thiess accused him of 'Haß gegen die Deutschen'.[4]

Given Thomas Mann's status, especially in comparison to that of Thiess, it is hard to take the accusation of hate very seriously. Mann himself, in the title given to those parts of his diaries published in 1946, spoke of 'Leiden an Deutschland'.[5] By taking this term for its title, this essay presupposes that Mann's concerns have continued to be relevant, or rather that other writers have experienced similar feelings.[6] As lack of space inevitably prevents exhaustive reference to all such expressions of concern made since 1945, it will concentrate on examples that appear particularly significant in a specific historical context, starting with the immediate postwar period, which, not surprisingly, was for many Germans a time to contemplate the factors which could be seen as having led to the tragedies of the recent past.

In the first years after 1945, concern with National Socialism dominated consideration of the themes Germany and the Germans, and it has continued to cast its shadow on nearly all writers' statements on this topic. However, the debate started before 1945 when Mann's 'Deutschland und die Deutschen' took up where others had left off.[7] Mann concentrates on the flawed intellectual tradition of his native country, which he traces back to the Reformation and the teachings of Luther. The Reformation is seen as having isolated Germany from its European neighbours, whilst Luther's theology is considered as lacking a political dimension, being solely concerned with spiritual liberation. The later German tradition Mann attacks is Romanticism. This propagated solely a nationalistic concept of liberty with no place for democratic values; at the same time, it maintained the speculative idealism of Luther. Specifically, Mann views Romanticism as a manifestation of the German quality of 'Innerlichkeit', in which abstract speculation takes pride of place over concern for social and political questions. This in turn leads to a rejection of the political values of the Enlightenment and of the French Revolution: 'Die Deutschen sind ein Volk der romantischen Gegenrevolution gegen den philosophischen Intellektualismus und Rationalismus der Aufklärung.'[8] His overall conclusion is that this tradition has made the Germans a non-political people, typically because of their unwillingness to accept the expediency and compromise that politics inevitably involves. Mann's attempt to explain the course of German intellectual history and its negative consequences is, in the light of its erudition, anything but a crude anti-German tirade. It is an attempt to explain rather than to condemn. If it is open to criticism, it is because it is too speculative, with the interpretation of German history leaving out economic and sociological factors. Indeed, the same thing can be said of much that was written at this time, as Hans Magnus Enzensberger pointed out when, introducing a selection of post-1945 writing, he noted the concentration on the abstract at the expense of direct consideration of present circumstances.[9]

Much of the postwar debate took place in the plethora of periodicals (many of them short-lived) that sprang into being at that time. In the first edition of *Frankfurter Hefte*, the co-editor and former Buchenwald inmate, Eugen Kogon, came to similar conclusions about the Germans as Thomas Mann, speaking of a propensity towards the ideal that can cause the acceptance of false creeds. He says of the German people: 'Schweifend im Reich der Phantasie, unerschöpflichen Plänen, vielen Empfindungen und Träumen hingegeben, sieht es in jeder Konkretisierung eine Beeinträchtigung des Hohen und Idealen. Wie es dem Irrglauben aus Glaubensüberfülle verfällt, so auch leicht einer realen Bindung, die gar nicht einmal aus ihm stammt.'[10]

A little later, in his magazine *Ost und West*, a journalistic attempt to counter the increasing divisions between the two parts of the country, Alfred Kantorowicz spoke of the traditional dichotomy between Germany's writers 'mitsamt ihren Träumen, Visionen Erkenntnissen'[11] and the ordinary citizens. He demanded a new kind of intellectual élite to give leadership to the German people. What is noteworthy is that both the Catholic Kogon and the Marxist Kantorowicz place so much stress on the world of the intellect. Intellectual or spiritual failure, albeit in somewhat different ways, is seen as responsible for the rise of National Socialism. Both also seek some form of spiritual renewal, a hope destined to be frustrated at a time when the majority were primarily concerned with physical survival and subsequently the enjoyment of the new prosperity.

As the hopes for a new German beginning after 1945 began to fade, not just in the face of the economic miracle but also before the stark realities of the division of the country and the Cold War, it is not surprising that there should develop an increasing impatience with speculation about Germany and the Germans. It is also logical that this feeling should have surfaced particularly around the time of the building of the

Berlin Wall when German politics appeared to be in an impasse — and among a younger generation of writers who felt alienated from the materialistic society around them. Hence in 1964, originally in *Encounter*, Hans Magnus Enzensberger, at that time dubbed Germany's 'Angry Young Man', asked the question 'Am I a German?' and began his answer by stating: 'I have never really understood why nations exist.'[12] He goes on to suggest that the division of Germany proves that nationality is a shaky principle on which to base judgements of character. Turning to the question of Auschwitz, he claims that it is more a proof of what the human race is capable of than a product of a 'hypothetical German collective soul'.[13]

Even if this last statement is contentious, it is clear that Enzensberger at this time is no apologist of German nationalism. It is rather a case of refusal to think in national terms at all, as another essay of the same period shows: 'Versuch, von der deutschen Frage Urlaub zu machen'. Here he speaks of German as an anomaly and, dismissing the claims of Ludwig Erhard that the Germans count again in the world, adds 'wir gelten [...] ungefähr soviel wie auf dem Jahrmarkt das Kalb mit den zwei Köpfen'.[14] Surprisingly, in the light of his more recent statements (several of which are discussed by Helmut Peitsch, esp. pp. 159—67 above), Martin Walser appeared to be saying something similar to Enzensberger in the 1960s. His series of essays 'Ein deutsches Mosaik' not only shows impatience with discussions of the German Question but also in its first sentence points out that his grandfather did not know he was a German.[15] Walser though does not go on to deny the existence of Germans but rather expresses the hope that European unity will make German nationhood an easier burden for the individual.

Alongside this impatience with the German Question (another part of Walser's mosaic entitled 'Und am Abend das Ost-West-Gespräch' satirizes the ritual of polemical discussion of the subject with the use of 'und' stressing the stereotyped nature of such discussions) some writers turned their interests more to the Federal Republic. Instead of simply criticizing that state,[16] they began to look for more of an insider role. In an essay 'Skizze zu einem Vorwurf', Walser criticized fellow-intellectuals for their distant attitude: 'In welche Verlegenheit brächten uns ein Staat, eine Gesellschaft, die uns einlüden zur Mitarbeit.'[17] This essay was originally written for a volume *Ich lebe in der Bundesrepublik*, which was seen by one critic writing years later as showing the greatest degree of identification by intellectuals with their state there had ever been.[18] In fact, it reflects more a grudging willingness to be involved in the development of the Federal Republic than any total identification, at least in a good many cases.

Enzensberger's contribution to the same volume, although extreme, cannot be called untypical. Entitled 'Schimpfend unter Palmen', it includes vitriolic comments on Düsseldorf cafés (this city no doubt being used solely as an example), which are compared to hell, and there is also the wonderful aphorism: 'In den beiden streitigen Haufen Deutschland leben teilweise Leute teilweise.'[19] It is only in a postscript that Enzensberger speaks of leaving Rome, where the article was written, and returning to the Federal Republic. This new willingness to involve himself in the life of the Federal Republic is apparent in his readiness to contribute to Walser's volume *Die Alternative oder Brauchen wir eine neue Regierung?*, in which a number of writers expressed their support for the Social Democrats in the 1961 elections — another sign of their changing role, although again it must be stated that Enzensberger is far from wholehearted in his support.[20]

It was, incidentally, with contributions to this volume that Günter Grass first emerged as a supporter of the SPD and began to play an active part in politics. Since then Grass has undoubtedly become the German author who has devoted most attention to political questions, some would say in a rather simplistic manner and to the detriment of his literary talents.[21] Not least because of his biography, the experience of Danzig and the subsequent expulsion, it is not surprising that he should have been particularly concerned with the concept of Germany and the nature of the Germans. Like Thomas Mann, his starting point has frequently been cultural. Speaking to an Israeli audience in 1967, he sought to explain the crimes against the Jews in terms of an unchanging German character, as described in the writings of Jean Paul and Wilhelm Raabe. With its literary emphasis and neglect of historical and economic factors (it is surely inadequate simply to link both the Federal Republic and the Third Reich to the 'heiter umspielte und ironisch umzäumte Dämonie' described by the two authors[22]), Grass's explanation fails to convince, although the difficulties of speaking in such a setting should not be underestimated.

Grass went on to develop the theme of Germany in the 1980 work *Kopfgeburten*, where the nature of the genre allows for a fuller treatment.

The main fictional element of the work, the anguishing of a young couple about whether to have a child, is not just a reflection of the demographic concern referred to in the full title *Kopfgeburten oder Die Deutschen sterben aus* but a framework for comments on the nature of the German identity. There are comments on all kinds of perceived German characteristics: obstinacy, the love of order, the need to achieve and many others besides. Grass even speculates on the nature of a world in which the Germans would have been as prolific as the Chinese. His main questions are: 'Wer sind wir? Wo kommen wir her? Was laßt uns deutsch sein? Und was, zum Teufel ist das: Deutschland?'[23]

Some clearcut answers to this kind of questioning were given in the years preceding the appearance of *Kopfgeburten*. The tendency towards identification with the Federal Republic as outlined above began to diminish in the 1970s, initially not least because of the decision taken by the federal and state governments in early 1972 to ensure that those applying for positions in the public service were loyal to the constitution — the step that came to be known as the 'Radikalenerlaß'. Several writers, including Alfred Andersch, Uwe Johnson and Wolfgang Koeppen, wrote a letter of protest to the 'Präsidium des Bundestages' that recalled previous events in Germany, particularly the exclusion of Jews from a whole series of professions by the Nazis: 'Die Handhabung eines inhaltlich überstimmten Radikalismusbegriffs ist verfassungswidrig. Wie die Praxis zeigt, dient sie in der Bundesrepublik fast ausschließlich zur einseitigen Diskriminierung linker Staatsbürger, während alte und neue Nazis unbehindert die Staatsapparate durchwuchern. Dieser Vorgang hat in Deutschland ominöse historische Beispiele.'[24]

The continuity, at least in personnel, between the Nazi Reich and the Federal Republic is also the theme of Peter Schneider's *...schon bist du ein Verfassungsfeind*, which besides being an account of a young teacher's attempts to be accepted as a public servant, contains documentary sections about the role of the former Nazi judges in determining the democratic loyalties of the next generations. Despite the obvious incongruity of this and the frequency with which it is pointed out, Schneider sees little hope for change: 'Bestimmte Rufe hört der deutsche Wald einfach nicht, er schweigt.'[25] The metaphor of the forest recalls aspects of the German Romantic tradition referred to by Thomas Mann.

In the years after the 'Radikalenerlaß' it was the methods used to combat the terrorism of the Red Army Faction that were seen as a further revival of unhappy German traditions. Peter Paul Zahl, who himself was imprisoned for terrorist activities, concedes that many of what he sees as the unpleasant features of the Federal Republic (his list covers about a page and ranges from road-deaths to television violence) are found in other countries but in a different way: 'Aber nicht in dieser Massierung. Aber nicht mit der Penetranz. Aber nicht mit so bösen Traditionen. Aber nicht mit dieser tränenseligen Geschichtslosigkeit.'[26] What is striking is the continued relevance of the past for a writer born in 1944 and therefore enjoying, in Chancellor Kohl's terms, as used during his visit to Israel in 1984, 'die Gnade der späten Geburt'.[27]

Zahl's comments appear to be in the tradition of Hölderlin, as do a number of others found in a volume entitled *Deutschland, Deutschland* that appeared in 1979, ironically enough in Austria. This collection contains forty-seven contributions from writers from both German states. Simply entitling his essay 'Deutschland', Klaus Stiller takes issue with those who, in the tradition of Goethe and Schiller, have difficulty with the concept of Germany, saying: 'Ich behaupte nicht, daß es Deutschland nicht mehr gäbe. Ich weiß genau, wo es ist.'[28] Stiller bases his knowledge not on geography but on what he sees as the unhappy German qualities that came to the fore in the 1970s in the antiterrorist campaigns. The same phenomena concern Angelika Mechtel as she seeks to reconcile the idyll of her rural Bavarian home with present and past nationality: 'Ich bin nur ein Zufall, zufällig diesem Land zugefallen'.[29] Like Enzensberger, she would like to cast off nationality, although she realizes this is impossible. A similar wish is expressed very directly by the younger Ludwig Fels, who simply states: 'Meine Anwesenheit ist ein Versehen.'[30]

Not all the critical comments made during the late 1970s fit the pattern of those just described. Hermann Peter Piwitt, in an essay 'Einen Kranz niederlegen am Hermannsdenkmal', bemoans a lack of German nationhood and castigates the Germans for an insipid cosmopolitanism, together with a tendency to destroy all that is beautiful: 'Sie können nicht einmal mehr stolz sein auf ihre Heimat, sie haben eine einzige Produktionsanlage daraus gemacht, in die sie, von ihren Reisen und Beutezügen, die Kulturen aus aller Welt heimschleppen. Die Küche griechisch, das Kleid aus Indien, Wandschmuck und Weltanschauung aus Fernost.'[31]

The Left, too, is criticized for its lack of national identification. In the same volume, Reinhard Lettau from his American vantage-point inveighs against what Stiller refuses to accept, a German lack of identity. The title of his piece 'Deutschland als Ausland' refers not only to his own situation but also to the country itself, where, like Piwitt, he sees much that is indigenous being suppressed. He, too, refers to eating habits but concentrates primarily on the language, bemoaning the way educated citizens speak with a mixture of French and English words. This not surprisingly provokes sorrow in a writer: 'Nachdem dieses Volk fast alles, was an ihm schön, leibenswürdig und zart war, verraten hat, verlernt es nun auch seine Sprache.'[32]

This kind of complaint is not new; one needs only think of Lessing's championing of the German language against the then dominant French. Nor is the other element in Piwitt's and Lettau's strictures: the positive ideal of Germany that lies behind them. This is the other major recurring factor that is visible in writers' concerns about Germany and the Germans since 1945, not least because of the division of the country. Many of them set the vision of a united country against the depressing reality of a division that for a long time seemed permanent.

Some of the earliest attempts to fight the spectre of division came in the periodical *Der Ruf*, whose co-editor Hans Werner Richter became the convenor of the *Gruppe 47* once the magazine had been banned. In an article entitled 'Deutschland — Brücke zwischen Ost und West', Richter puts forward the ideal of a German state that will incorporate elements of the Eastern and Western systems; he speaks of socializing democracy and democratizing socialism. The plea for German unity is, however, in no sense nationalistic; the writers of *Der Ruf*, not least Richter's fellow editor Alfred Andersch, believed with some justification that a united Germany was a pre-condition for a united Europe.[33]

Writers' pleas for German unity became more intense as the reality of division became fully apparent with the foundation of the two German states in 1949. 1951 saw the appearance in the Federal Republic of a volume entitled *Wir heißen Euch hoffen. Schriftsteller zur deutschen Verständigung*, in which writers expressed their concern about division, frequently in a rhetorical manner with scant regard to political facts or even ideals. Thus, in the postwar controversy, Walter von Molo sought to express the idea of unity despite division in a kind of sub-Goethean rhetoric: 'Die Sonne geht nicht nur auf und unter, sie geht ständig auf und unter, immer wechseln Tag und Nacht, dazu sind der Osten und der Westen nötig, sind sie in Einheit da. Der Wechsel ist das Dauernde,

Naturgesetze der Einseitigkeit gibt es nicht: überall ist alles gedoppelt und doch Einheit!'[34]

Many of the contributions to the volume are from GDR writers, a reminder that the ideal of unity was not in conflict with the official policy of the day. Johannes R. Becher in a poem compares Germany with a single heart that cannot be divided, whilst another verse contribution by Rudolf Leonhard consists of a rhetorical appeal to his fellow-countrymen:

> Deutschland ist keine Länder,
> Deutschland ist ein Land.
> Deutsche, zerreißt die Ränder,
> Deutsche, bindet die Bänder,
> jeder mit seiner Hand.[35]

On a practical, political level, one is inclined to ask how this appeal might have been followed, whilst aesthetically one may question the crude alliterations in the third and fourth lines. During the first decade after the war many intellectuals harboured the ideal implied by Richter of a neutral Germany belonging neither to the Western nor to the Eastern camp. It is an ideal that again came to prominence during the turbulent events of 1989—1990 with, for instance, the GDR writer Helga Schubert expressing her hope for 'ein einheitliches, friedliches und neutrales Deutschland,'[36] which is very much in line with the postwar period. At the end of the 1950s and in the early 1960s, however, division and re-armament meant that such ideals appeared futile and irrelevant. This was the time when Uwe Johnson came into prominence. Not only the theme of division in his early novels, which seems to parallel Enzensberger's impatience with the national question referred to above, but also his concern with the aesthetic problems of writing about division earned Johnson accolades as the chronicler of divided Germany. Specifically, Johnson seeks to create a way of writing that reflects the complications of the division of Germany. Traditional narrative is ineffective in as far as it assumes that geographical location and personal identity can be taken for granted. The titles of Johnson's first two novels *Mutmaßungen über Jakob* and *Das dritte Buch über Achim* suggest the impossibility of this, the reason being the division of Germany, which means that only surmise and uncertainty are possible across a frontier that itself beggars description. Thus, at the beginning of *Das dritte Buch über Achim*, after the use of the (at first sight) unproblematical word 'Grenze', the narrator feels obliged to add: '[ich] kann [...] nichts anders als ergänzen', something that then takes up two pages of complex prose, because the frontier is synonymous with 'die Entfernung: den Unterschied'.[37] Significantly the message of Johnson's third novel *Zwei Ansichten*, incidentally a less satisfactory work in that it reverts to a more traditional narrative style, is that the two parts of Germany, symbolized by the two major protagonists B. and D., who break off their relationship, are destined to remain separate.

If political unity seemed impossible after the construction of the Berlin Wall, this did not prevent writers from thinking about nationhood in different terms. In so doing, they were to some degree following the example of Goethe and Schiller, both of whom were sceptical about Germany as a political entity and preferred to encourage their compatriots to achieve distinction by espousing the ideals of Weimar Classicism. The apparently insurmountable barriers to unity led in earlier eras to the resurrection of such concepts as the *Kulturnation*, which at times appeared relevant again in view of post-1945 divisions. In *Kopfgeburten*, Günter Grass suggests a museum straddling the two halves of Berlin, in which all Germans might view their common heritage, although he admits (reasonably enough at the time of writing) that such a project is impossible.[38] Another project mooted by Grass, this time in the 1960s, was similarly Utopian, the building of new towns in the Federal Republic that would re-create the lost Oder-Neiße territories; inevitably, one of these was to be Neu-Danzig. The following passage shows clearly how far Grass had let his imagination run away with him: 'Traditionelle Industrien, wie früher in Breslau, Danzig, Königsberg, sehe ich Fuß fassen. Und vielleicht werden die aussterbenden Dialekte, Gerhart Hauptmanns Schlesisch und mein geliebtes Danziger Platt, grotesk gemischt mit friesischer und bayrischer Mundart, eine Renaissance erleben.'[39]

Generally though, Grass remained close to the mainstream idea, expressed for a long time by his political mentor Willy Brandt, that Germany consisted of one nation living in two states.[40] Although in the early 1970s GDR politicians, obsessed with the idea of total separation from the Federal Republic, even rejected this idea of common nationhood, it is interesting to note that it was not anathema to all GDR writers. In his contribution to *Deutschland, Deutschland*, Rainer Kirsch, whilst accepting the political division of Germany for the foreseeable future, expresses his wish to maintain the sense of nationhood and sees a particular role for writers in the project: 'Als Staatsbürger bleiben wir der

Nation verpflichtet, um sie, schreibend oder sonstwie handelnd, für möglich bessere Zeiten mit allem auszurüsten, was sie als Teil einer künftigen Weltgemeinschaft braucht.'[41] Now that German unity has come, it remains to be seen if there is any hope for Kirsch's internationalist ideals.

In the light of this new unity, it may seem that such concepts as *Kulturnation* have become irrelevant or can be dismissed as nothing more than abstract constructs, which may have provided some kind of comfort in the days of division but which bore no relationship to the real political aspirations of the German people. Whatever the truth of such a view, it must be pointed out that some time before the events of 1989, many writers had returned to the theme of political division and the German Question. One immediate reason for this was the decision to station medium-range American missiles in the Federal Republic. The early 1980s were marked by a growing fear among writers that there would soon be a new kind of unity for the Germans — the unity of nuclear obliteration. This fear led to two meetings in Berlin in 1981 and 1983 in which writers from the two German states, meeting together semi-officially for the first time since the early postwar years, discussed ways of securing peace.[42] For some, this meant the rejection of division. Klaus Stiller, for instance, criticized the Germans in both East and West for identifying too strongly with their respective superpower and neglecting common interests. He concludes pessimistically: 'Es gibt kein Rezept für die Rettung einer Bevölkerung, die ihre Identität nur aus dem jeweiligen Zufallstaat bezieht und nicht sieht, daß sie wenigstens geographisch sich selbst am nächsten wäre.'[43]

This inability to identify with one or other of the German states was not just confined to a writer like Stiller, who as a resident of West Berlin might see things in a different perspective. In a major publication to commemorate thirty years of the Federal Republic edited by Jürgen Habermas, Dieter Wellershoff, an older writer with memories of a single German state, expressed the difficulty he had in identifying emotionally with the Federal Republic, which he compared with a 'Verein'. In explanation of his feelings towards the Federal Republic, he added: 'Eine objektlos gewordene, aber unübertragbare Liebe zu Deutschland hindert mich daran, diesen Staat, der sich zunächst selbst als Provisorium verstand, anders zu erleben als einen akzeptablen politischen Lebensrahmen und dieses restliche, arg geschrumpfte Land für das verlorene Ganze zu halten.'[44]

There is no suggestion here that unity might one day be on the agenda, nor is there the emotional reaction to division found elsewhere. Such metaphors as that of the 'open wound' are conspicuously missing. This was even used, surprisingly enough, in the light of his unenthusiastic reaction to the events of 1989, by Stefan Heym in 1983 when he stated; 'Der Schrägstrich durch Deutschland ist eine offene Wunde; wir können noch so viel Antibiotika darauf streuen, sie wird weiter eitern.'[45] Although he indicated no clear path to unity, he also stated that division could not be regarded as permanent when viewed in the framework of Marxist dialectics. Again, such a statement appears to be in conflict with Heym's championing of the GDR's separate identity in 1989.

In the case of Wellershoff, as the above quotation shows, despite the apparent realism of his essay he was not someone who happily accepted division. It is by no means surprising that, unlike Heym, he was enthusiastic about the events of 1989. An article in the January 1990 edition of *Merkur*, whilst by no means nationalistic, holds out the ideal of unity, albeit to be achieved over a longer period than has turned out to be the case.[46]

In the early 1980s the theme of division also came to the fore in works of fiction. One such work, Stefan Heym's *Schwarzenberg*, reflects the views quoted above, although it concentrates primarily on an alternative vision rather than the reality of division. The novel is set in an enclave of Germany, which by chance is left unoccupied at the end of the war. An independent German administration is set up there which is presented as a possible model for the single democratic socialist state that might have been formed after 1945. The constitution worked out by the main protagonist, for instance, starts from the proposition of the *Grundgesetz* that: 'Alle Staatsgewalt geht vom Volke aus' but then adds a major element of plebiscitary democracy and the demand that public servants should earn no more than factory workers, both frequent demands of radical socialists. The fictional Utopia is, however, short-lived; in keeping with historical fact, the brief period of independence gives way to occupation.[47]

Another novel with a similar all-German theme, Dieter Lattmann's *Die Brüder*, is primarily a chronicle of division within a family, the two brothers of the title living in the two German states. As a work of fiction, it is top-heavy with political debates, its main interest being the way in which it reflects the prevalent feeling of the early 1980s that many West Germans had cut themselves off from the East and had developed their own mental wall, which was as much a barrier as the concrete one in Berlin.[48]

This concept of a self-imposed wall is reflected in the title of a 1985 essay by Peter Schneider, 'Über das allmähliche Verschwinden einer Himmelsrichtung'.[49] He complains that many Westerners, not least left-wing intellectuals, prefer to ignore events in the East, especially those that deserve criticism. Particularly in *Der Mauerspringer*, which appeared in 1982, Schneider provides an example of a younger writer who addressed himself to the problems of division in the early 1980s. This partly documentary work propagates the ideal of German unity, albeit not necessarily in a political form. Towards the end, there is a strong plea for the retention of a German identity, not least through the medium of a common language. Schneider refers back to the time of the formation of the German language to drive home his point: 'Und wie vor 1000 Jahren kann der Versuch, eine gemeinsame deutsche Sprache zu sprechen, nur mit einer Weigerung anfangen, mit der Weigerung, das Kirchenlatein aus Ost und West nachzuplappern.'[50] Previously, the narrator has complained that whenever he speaks with a GDR colleague, neither partner can escape the influence of his respective state, no matter how independent-minded they each consider themself to be.[51] As with Grass, some kind of cultural unity seems to be Schneider's ideal.

The writer who went beyond the cultural dimension by seeing in it the basis for political unity and who has arguably gained most attention in the recent national debate is Martin Walser, who was born, like Grass, in 1927 and is therefore old enough to have some memory of a united Germany. The question that has to be posed in connection with Walser is quite simply whether this one-time apparently archetypal left-wing intellectual and sometime supporter of the DKP has turned into a nationalist, who is happy to debate the German Question with the CSU, with whom, in his own words, he spent a pleasant afternoon in early 1989. Before attempting to answer this question, it is advisable to recall some of his statements since the comments in the 1960s referred to above. These, it was noted, did not reject nationality in the way that Enzensberger appeared to be doing; equally, when supporting the DKP, Walser did not exclude a national dimension, albeit largely a West German one, when he demanded, only partly in jest, that West German Communists should support their own national team on the occasion of any football international between it and the Soviet Union.[52] It should also be remembered that Walser had always championed his native region of Lake Constance so that his new 'nationalism' seems some kind of extension of that feeling. It was, however, in the late 1970s that Walser began making more frequent comments about the national question. Over the last decade, he has articulated his ideas more in expressions of vague feelings and speculations than concrete political statements. In the essay 'Händedruck mit Gespenstern', he concedes that he is only reflecting a personal sentiment that may not be shared by others.[53] Moreover, from the 1977 essay 'Über den Leser — soviel man in einem Festzelt darüber sagen soll', where he states: 'wer von Wiedervereinigung spricht, zementiert die Spaltung',[54] up to a 1989 interview with the *tageszeitung* following the appearance at the CSU meeting referred to above, he has consistently rejected the term 'Wiedervereinigung'.[55]

Where Walser takes up the national theme in fiction, in the 1987 novel *Dorle und Wolf*, there is a similar preponderance of emotional commitment to the ideal of unity. Thus Wolf is a GDR spy in Bonn, but not out of a true political commitment to his native state but because he wants the gap between the two Germanys to be reduced. One way this can be achieved is by the transfer of technological data so that the GDR might catch up a little in the economic field. Yet his actual spying is only a concrete manifestation of his psychological unwillingness to accept division. When he sees West Germans, he feels that they lack something; they are 'lauter Halbiente',[56] as indeed are the citizens of the GDR. The basis for this belief is that despite material success, nobody in the Federal Republic seems happy — a somewhat sweeping assertion. Clearly, Walser's character is indulging in speculation that is as whimsical as his refusal to play Schumann's piano music with both hands as long as Germany remains divided. Incidentally this leads to a Hungarian neighbour, who is a mathematician, deducing the truth (shades of Rubik's Cube!) and revealing it to Wolf in one of the best passages in the novel, in which Walser brilliantly captures Hungarian German.[57]

Can one conclude in the light of this that Walser's apparent nationalism is as eccentric and ineffectual as his character's espionage, which, as the West German authorities have long since discovered his activities, only provides the GDR with disinformation? Although Walser has, as shown, constantly rejected the rhetoric of 'reunification' and stated after his discussions with the CSU that he could offer no practical advice about how unity might be achieved, such a conclusion would be mistaken. There are times when Walser is guilty of expressing himself in a manner reminiscent of the extreme Right. In the 1985 essay 'Tartuffe weiß wer er ist', he blames the rise of Nazism largely on the Versailles Treaty, as many overt apologists of Nazism do, and sees a parallel in the post-1945 situation: 'Der deutsche Rassismus hätte sich ohne die Minderwertigkeit, zu der die Sieger Deutschland verurteilten, nicht zum Wahn gesteigert [...] Wenn aber Hitlerdeutschland [...] durch Versaillesdiktat entstand, dann ist der zweite Krieg eine Folge des ersten. Aber der Sieger reagierte wieder nicht viel vernünftiger, als der zu Züchtigende war: Deutschland wird geteilt. Und das soll jetzt gefeiert werden.'[58]

A similar type of argument, which amounts to blaming the victim rather than the murderer, is found in the 1988 essay 'Über Deutschland reden' that provoked such controversy in Die Zeit. Here it is the antifascists who are blamed for neo-fascism because their campaigns kept the subject alive. It is small wonder that Jurek Becker felt particularly incensed by a claim which to him and others seemed to justify Walser's own self-apolegetic aphorism: 'Wer beim Deutschland-Gespräch nicht unter sein Niveau gerät, hat keins.'[59] At the same time, Walser does appear to have retained his awareness of Nazi crimes. The volume Über Deutschland reden does contain the 1979 essay 'Auschwitz und kein Ende', which makes clear that forgetting the past is neither possible nor desirable.

A simple summing-up of Walser's contribution to the debate on Germany and the Germans would be to say that it is both confused and confusing. It might indeed be possible to sum up the whole debate since 1945 in a similar way when one considers some of Grass's esoteric ideas and how someone like Klaus Stiller, on the evidence of the two statements cited above, has been capable of such contrary emotions towards Germany. Obviously, there is no simple common denominator, unless one were to conclude that in most of their comments on Germany writers have been far removed from the political reality of the day and taken up esoteric stances. Indeed, this was the accusation levelled by Monika Maron at those who, after the events of 1989, seemed unhappy at the prospect of German unity. She criticizes them for neglecting the economic needs of the GDR's population in favour of more socialist experiments, whose possible failure would not affect them in their materially privileged position.[60]

The most recent debates on the German Question go beyond the scope of this essay. Nevertheless Maron has raised a key question about the relationship between writers and the rest of society that can be asked in connection with many of the comments referred to here. In their criticism of the Germans, are writers guilty of wishing to follow Brecht's suggestion to the SED after the 1953 East German uprising: that the Party should elect a new people?[61] Others too, including the prominent social scientists Helmut Schelsky and Kurt Sontheimer, have accused German writers of élitist arrogance in their relations with other social groups.[62]

To come to a generalized conclusion of this kind though would be extremely rash, given the variety of comments made about Germany and the Germans since 1945. What is significant is simply the fact that so much attention has been given to the subject. This reflects not just the problems of the past but the uncertainties of the position since 1945, which the events of 1989 clearly confirmed. In view of the moral dimension, it is fully justified that writers and intellectuals should be so concerned, not as lofty instances or as the 'conscience of the nation' but, as Grass has always seen his role, and Böll did too, as critical concerned citizens. As for the German Question itself, one can perhaps hope that it will wither away, as a unified German state takes its position in a united Europe in the peaceful manner hoped for by so many writers after 1945.

Someone who sought to encourage this in a lecture delivered in December 1989 was the philosopher Peter Sloterdijk. He rejects all kinds of nationalism ('wiedersehen ist besser als wiedervereinigen"[63]) and urges the Federal Republic to show more self-confidence. In general Sloterdijk exudes optimism about the future. In his concluding paragraph, he asks rhetorically: 'Wann waren die Deutschen zuletzt so wenig häßlich wie heute? Wann haben sie zuletzt sowie in jüngster Zeit durch gute Nachrichten die Weltneugier erregt?'[64] Others take a less sanguine view. Ralph Giordano, a writer born in 1923, has continued to warn against nationalist hubris, not least because of his own background: his mother was Jewish — the family's sufferings are recounted in his autobiographical novel Die Bertinis.[65] His non-fictional work Die zweite Schuld places an obligation on those too young to have been involved in Nazi crimes. Specifically, the second guilt lies in the way the Federal Republic has never faced up to the past; for the past to be overcome, the next generation, however much without direct moral or judicial guilt for National Socialism, must face what their forebears did and unreservedly espouse democratic principles.

Giordarno's comments are no more motivated by hate than those of Thomas Mann. His description of his own relationship to Germany is particularly revealing. He admits to having contemplated emigration at the end of the War but was emotionally unable to take such a step: 'Ich bin [...] angenagelt an dieses Land, ans Deutsche. Es fragt mich nicht, was ich möchte, es hält mich fest, hoffnungslos und ohne jede Aussicht auf Änderung. Es hat mir meine Unlösbarkeit eingerichtet — wo immer ich auch hinginge, sie käme mir überall nach.'[66]

After the different approaches of Sloterdijk and Giordano, it seems appropriate to conclude with two contrasting statements by the same author reflecting the two attitudes towards Germany and the Germans that have been reflected in this essay. They were, however, not made over a period of years but appear within three pages of each other. The volume *1989 oder Ein Moment Schönheit* is a collection of Helga Königsdorf's writings which are largely taken from that momentous year and given the descriptive sub-title 'Eine Collage aus Briefen, Gedichten, Texten'. The arrangement is largely chronological. After a letter dated 15 December 1989 there is a poem that begins:

> Deutschland einig Vaterland
> Denk ich an dich in der Nacht
> Bin ich um den Schlaf gebracht
> Wie sie wieder stolz skandieren
> Fehlt nur einer noch zum Führen
> Und wir sind nun sicher baldig
> Wieder kühn und sehr gewaltig.[67]

This poem with its literary echoes is, in itself, a kind of collage and the simple structure and rhyme scheme contributes to the direct, worrying message. By contrast, the next text, dated 16 December 1989, contains the following sentence in connection with the events of 1989: 'Zum erstenmal kann ich auf das Wort "deutsch" stolz sein.'[68] Such a juxtaposition underlines once again that national questions continue to arouse strong but confused feelings in Germany — 'Leiden an Deutschland' continues.

NOTES

1   Marcel Reich-Ranicki: 'Ich bin kein Deutscher, und ich werde es nie sein', *Die Zeit*, 15 September 1989, p. 61.
2   Friedrich Hölderlin: *Sämtliche Werke*, Stuttgart, 1957, vol. 3, p. 153.
3   Quoted from Hans Chistoph Buch (ed.): *Tintenfisch 15. Thema: Deutschland*, Berlin, 1978, p. 143.
4   Frank Thiess in Klaus Wagenbach, Winfried Stephan, Michael Krüger (eds): *Vaterland, Muttersprache. Deutsche Schriftsteller und ihr Staat von 1945 bis heute*, Berlin, 1979, p. 49.
5   Thomas Mann: *Leiden an Deutschland*, Frankfurt/Main, 1946.
6   It is interesting to note that when Wolf Biermann, whose experience of both German states has led him to write frequently on German themes, was awarded the *Friedrich-Hölderlin-Preis* of the town Bad Homburg von der Höhe, the jury spoke of his 'Leiden an Deutschland' in the tradition of Hölderlin and Heine. See Franz Josef Görtz, Volker Hage, Uwe Wittstock (eds): *Deutsche Literatur 1989. Jahresüberblick*, Stuttgart, 1990.
7   Many writers seeking to explain at the time the rise of National Socialism concentrated on intellectual and cultural factors. In both Irmgard Keun's *Nach Mitternacht* and Ödön von Horváth's *Jugend ohne Gott* (both first published in 1937), the intellectual characters, although opposed to the Nazis, have nothing to set against them.
8   Thomas Mann: 'Deutschland und die Deutschen' in *An die gesittete Welt. Politische Schriften und Reden im Exil*, Frankfurt/Main, 1986, pp. 117f.
9   See, for example, the following comment: 'Im großen und ganzen flohen die Intellektuellen, statt kaltblütig zu konstatieren, was der Fall war, in die Abstraktion. Nach der großen Reportage sucht man vergebens. Dafür findet man, neben philosophischen Erörterungen zum Thema der Kollektivschuld, endlose Beschwörungen der abendländischen Tradition.' (Hans Magnus Enzensberger: 'Europa in Trümmern', *Die Zeit*, 1 June 1990, p. 53.)
10 Eugen Kogon: 'Gericht und Gewissen', *Frankfurter Hefte*, vol. 1, no. 1, 1946, p. 33.
11 Alfred Kantorowicz: 'Marginalien', *Ost und West*, vol. 2, no. 1, 1948, p. 89.
12 Hans Magnus Enzensberger: 'Am I a German?', *Encounter*, vol. 22, no. 4, 1964, p. 16.
13 Ibid., p. 18.
14 Hans Magnus Enzensberger: *Deutschland, Deutschland unter anderem*, Frankfurt/Main, 1967, p. 47.
15 Martin Walser: *Erfahrungen und Leseerfahrungen*, Frankfurt/Main, 1965, p. 7.
16 A typical example of a swingeing criticism of West German society is Rudolf Hagelstange's essay 'Endstation Kühlschrank. Maß und Vernunft frieren ein' (*Die Kultur*, vol. 6, no. 112, 1958, pp. 1—2). He accuses West Germans of only being interested in the material to the exclusion of higher things.
17 Walser: *Erfahrungen...*, p. 32.
18 H. Koopman: 'Die Bundesrepublik Deutschland in der Literatur', *Zeitschrift für Politik*, vol. 26, no. 2, 1979, pp. 161—78.
19 Hans Magnus Enzensberger: 'Schimpfend unter Palmen' in Wolfgang Weyrauch (ed.): *Ich lebe in der Bundesrepublik*, Munich, 1961, p. 30. By way of contrast to the tone adopted by Enzensberger, Weyrauch's introduction contains an emotional justification of the publication which shows a commitment to the Federal Republic: 'Ich liebe meine Heimat. Weil ich sie liebe, sorge ich mich um sie. Weil ich mich um sie sorge, habe ich diesen kleinen und unvollständigen Band zusammengestellt und herausgegeben.' (Ibid., p. 7)
20 Martin Walser (ed.): *Die Alternativen oder Brauchen wir eine neue Regierung?*, Reinbek, 1961.
21 This is the thesis of Ronald Hayman's monograph *Günter Grass* in the Contemporary Writers Series (London, 1985, especially p. 74).
22 Günter Grass: *Über das Selbstverständliche*, Munich, 1969, p. 129.
23 Günter Grass: *Kopfgeburten oder Die Deutschen sterben aus*, Darmstadt, 4th edn, 1983, p. 33.
24 Wagenbach et al: *Vaterland...*, p. 288.
25 Peter Schneider: *...schon bist du ein Verfassungsfeind*, Berlin, 1975, p. 49.

26 Peter Paul Zahl: 'Die dauernde Ausbürgerung' in Buch: *Tintenfisch 15...*, p. 121. Zahl shot at a policeman whilst trying to escape arrest in December 1972. He was sentenced to fifteen years imprisonment, of which ten were served (an unusually high proportion).

27 A most scathing criticism of this phrase has been made by Ralph Giordano, whose logic it is impossible to fault. He says that those who use the phrase can only mean 'daß sie unterm Hakenkreuz nicht anders gehandelt hätten als ihre Eltern und Großeltern'. *Die zweite Schuld oder Von der Last, Deutscher zu sein*, Munich, 1990, p. 328. Hella Ehlers also refers to this phrase, p. 238 below.

28 Klaus Stiller: 'Deutschland' in *Deutschland, Deutschland. 47 Schriftsteller aus der BRD und der DDR schreiben über ihr Land*, Salzburg, 1979, p. 267. Stiller, who made his reputation as a socio-critital writer, was born in Augsburg in 1941 and now lives in Berlin.

29 Angelika Mechtel: 'Deutschland, drinnen und draußen' in *Deutschland, Deutschland...*, p. 203. Mechtel was born in Dresden in 1943 and now lives in Bavaria. Her prose is marked by grotesque, surreal elements.

30 Ludwig Fels: 'Und hier ist das Märchen zu Ende' in *Deutschland, Deutschland...*, p. 58. Fels, who was born in Treuchtlingen in 1946, has written poems and novels as well as shorter prose works.

31 Hermann Peter Piwitt: 'Einen Kranz niederlegen am Hermannsdenkmal' in Buch: *Tintenfisch 15...*, p. 18. Piwitt was born in Hamburg in 1935. He has written a number of novels.

32 Reinhard Lettau: 'Deutschland als Ausland' in Buch: *Tintenfisch 15...*, p. 121. Lettau, who was born in Erfurt, is known as both a critic and a writer of fiction. This sentence would appeal to Botho Strauß; see Arthur Williams, esp. p. 464 below.

33 See Hans Schwab-Felisch (ed.): *"Der Ruf". Eine deutsche Nachkriegszeitschrift*, Munich, 1962.

34 Walter von Molo: 'Ja, wir müssen uns retten' in Georg Schwarz and Carl August Weber (eds): *Wir heißen Euch hoffen*, Munich, 1951, p. 33.

35 Rudolf Leonhard: 'Unser Land' in Schwarz, Weber: *Wir heißen...*, p. 43.

36 Helga Schubert: 'Wo soll man anfangen? Die stille Liebe zur Heimat DDR', *FAZ*, 24 January 1990, p. 29.

37 Uwe Johnson: *Das dritte Buch über Achim*, Frankfurt/Main, 1964, p. 9. *Mutmaßungen über Jakob*, Frankfurt/Main, 1959. *Zwei Ansichten*, Frankfurt/Main, 1965.

38 Grass: *Kopfgeburten*, p. 120. Grass's ideas are explored by Helmut Peitsch (esp. pp. 165—7 above) and Dieter Stolz (pp. 207—22 below).

39 Grass: *Über das Selbstverständliche*, p. 36.

40 This was the formula adopted by Willy Brandt as Federal Chancellor as he sought to reconcile his *Ostpolitik* with the constitutional requirement of seeking German unity. For instance, in his 'Bericht zur Lage der Nation' of 28 January 1971 Brandt said: 'Die deutsche Nation bleibt auch dann eine Realität, wenn sie in unterschiedliche staatliche und gesellschaftliche Ordnungen geteilt ist' (quoted from *Bericht der Bundesregierung und Materialien zur Lage der Nation 1971*, published by the Bundesministerium für innerdeutsche Angelegenheiten, Bonn, 1971, p. 9. A major part of the *Ostpolitik* was the search for some kind of accommodation with the GDR; this was achieved by the treaty of 1972.

41 Rainer Kirsch: 'Wertschätzung der Umfelder' in *Deutschland, Deutschland...*, p. 146.

42 Private meetings had previously taken place between West German and GDR writers with Grass playing a major role. See Grass: *Kopfgeburten*, pp. 46—7.

43 Klaus Stiller: *Zweite Berliner Begegnung. Den Frieden Erklären*, Darmstadt, 1983, p. 84.

44 Dieter Wellershoff: 'Deutschland — Eine Schwebezustand' in Jürgen Habermas (ed.): *Stichworte zur "Geistigen Situation der Zeit"*, Frankfurt/Main, 1979, vol. 1, p. 88.

45 Stefan Heym: 'Die Wunde der Teilung eitert weiter', *Der Spiegel*, 7 November 1983, p. 66. See also Roland Smith, pp. 47—62 above, for a discussion of Stefan Heym and his German identity (esp. p. 51 in this context).

46 Dieter Wellershoff: 'Befreiung und Modernisierunsschub. Zur Revolution in der DDR', *Merkur*, vol. 44, no. 1, 1990, pp. 70—4.

47 Stefan Heym: *Schwarzenberg*, Munich, 1984.

48 Dieter Lattmann: *Die Brüder*, Frankfurt/Main, 1985.

49 Peter Schneider: *Deutsche Ängste*, Darmstadt, 1988, pp. 54—64.

50 Peter Schneider: *Der Mauerspringer*, Darmstadt, 1984, p. 109.
51 Martin Kane, p. 361 below, refers to the same passage.
52 Martin Walser: *Wie und wovon handelt Literatur?*, Frankfurt/Main, 1973, p. 112.
53 Martin Walser: 'Händedruck mit Gespenstern' in Habermas: *Stichworte...*, vol 1, pp. 39—50.
54 Martin Walser: *Wer ist ein Schriftsteller?*, Frankfurt/Main, 1979, p. 99.
55 Martin Walser: 'Es war ein sehr sympathischer Nachmittag bei der CSU', *die tageszeitung*, 16 January 1989.
56 Martin Walser: *Dorle und Wolf*, Frankfurt/Main, 1987, p. 54.
57 Ibid., p. 112.
58 Martin Walser: *Geständnis auf Raten*, Frankfurt/Main, 1986, p. 68.
59 Martin Walser: *Über Deutschland reden*, Frankfurt/Main, 1988, p. 80. Jurek Becker answered the original essay in *Die Zeit* (3 November 1988) with a highly critical contribution: 'Gedächtnis verloren — Verstand verloren', *Die Zeit*, 18 November 1988, p. 61. For a fuller treatment of Walser's 'nationalism' see Helmut Peitsch: 'Martin Walser — eine exemplarische Biographie', *Theater Zeitschrift*, no. 25, 1988, pp. 75—85, and no. 26, 1989, pp. 110—21.
60 Monika Maron: 'Der Schriftsteller und das Volk', *Der Spiegel*, 12 February 1990, pp. 68—70.
61 Bertolt Brecht: 'Die Lösung' in Wagenbach et al: *Vaterland, Muttersprache...*, p. 120.
62 See Kurt Sontheimer: *Das Elend unserer Intellektuellen*, Hamburg, 1976, and Helmut Schelsky: *Die Arbeit tun die anderen*, Munich, 1977.
63 Peter Sloterdijk: *Versprechen auf Deutsch. Rede über das eigene Land*, Frankfurt/Main, 1990, p. 82.
64 Ibid.
65 Ralph Giordano: *Die Bertinis*, Frankfurt/Main, 1985.
66 Giordano: *Die zweite Schuld...*, p. 362.
67 Helga Königsdorf: *1989 oder Ein Moment Schönheit*, Berlin (GDR), 1990, p. 112.
68 Ibid., p. 115.

'DEUTSCHLAND — EIN LITERARISCHER BEGRIFF':
GÜNTER GRASS AND THE GERMAN QUESTION

DIETER STOLZ

Hier wird er von der Weltpresse ausgefragt: Germany's Günter Grass, er antwortet nicht als Sprecher der Regierung, aber auch nicht als Privat-Schriftsteller, sondern als Staatsbürger mit besonderer Reputation [...] Seine zähe Allergie gegen deutsche Verstiegenheit stiftet Vertrauen gegenüber Deutschland.
(Max Frisch: *Tagebuch 1966—1971*, pp. 332—3)

I 'Kein schöner Thema weit und breit'

Haven't we heard all this before? The burning question now occupying everyone's waking hours is Germany, though no two people will give the word the same meaning. Is 'Germany' a geographical, an economic, or a political concept? Or is it no more than a literary idea? Is 'Germany' nowadays a piece of history? A chimera born of Romantic yearning? Or is it the future name of a new federal state in a united Europe? The notorious German Question has challenged the most thoughtful minds for more than three centuries. As Grass writes in *Das Treffen in Telgte*, where he looks back to the end of that other total war on German soil in the seventeenth century, 'solange ist jede Geschichte her, die in Deutschland handelt' (VI, 6).[1]

The wishful thinkers would dream of a bright and blessed future, while the sleep of others would be troubled, like Heine's, by gloomy night thoughts. Both Germans and non-Germans have suffered from the answers, which have all too often promised redemption from misery only to bring violence and death in their train. The German poets and thinkers have always bewailed their unhappy experiences with all their respective 'alternative Germanys' and the seemingly ineducable Germans.[2] They have lain abed at night tormented by the catastrophic course of German history, by their disappointment at revolutions which failed to take place. Their loyalties were split between a political patriotism for their difficult Fatherland and a love of the *Kulturnation* encapsulated in the literature of their mother tongue. Hoffmann von Fallersleben was not the first to add new verses to the never-ending song of Germany; and, as Tucholsky might have said, only a republic totally bereft of good sense would choose von Fallersleben's *Deutschlandlied* once more as its national anthem.

Germans are once again asking themselves (with Grass): 'Wer sind wir? Wo kommen wir her? Was läßt uns deutsch sein? Und was, zum Teufel, ist das: Deutschland?' (VI, 165). 'Kein schöner Thema weit and breit' is how *Die Zeit* entitles its first ever all-German literary supplement.[3] Just in time to catch the Leipzig Book Fair, five of the most popular East and West German authors bundled together their essays, speeches and interviews on the German Question; the combined result, so writes their reviewer, resembles a Round Table of literati, straddling the borders and as compelling as any live television debate. And, of course, there has been no shortage of studio discussions, brought for no extra charge (like an encore to the publications) into German homes and living rooms, then rushed into print with the greatest of haste to be sold for hard Deutschmarks.[4] The marketing experts were among the first to leap abord Helmut Kohl's reunification express.

The Faustian 'Kopfgeburten' of German writers are by no means an endangered species. They are conceived between dream and nightmare in the connubial bed of poetry and *Realpolitik*. Even though their words have never counted for very much in the world of politics, writers are still rehearsing their well-formulated uprising. Their appeals, however, are evidently bought by the wrong people and what, without them, 'doch nicht gehört worden wäre' (VI, 134), might just as well have remained unsaid. This was true at the poets' meeting in Telgte 300 years ago and has remained true to this day. This is the German *Misere*, the all-German tragedy as it has been from the very beginning.

This at least is how our 'Zeitgenosse' (IX, 921), Günter Grass, an active participant (having been made 'ungeheuer beredt'[5] by political developments) in all of these discussions, sees the situation. He has been familiar for a number of years with the dangers such partisan interventions have for his literary work: 'Die dem Schriftsteller gemäße Distanz droht verlorenzugehen; seine Sprache sieht sich versucht, von der Hand in den Mund zu leben; die Enge jeweils gegenwärtiger Verhältnisse kann auch ihn und seine auf Freilauf trainierte Vorstellungskraft einengen; er läuft Gefahr, in Kurzatmigkeit zu geraten.'[6] Nevertheless, the never-weary Sisyphus (to borrow one of Grass's own metaphors; X, 323) still manages to push forward his twin beer mats of literary integrity and political commitment, though now and again they may appear to stick together (IV, 542). The literary manuscript brooks no compromise, whereas political activism in speeches, discussions and articles depends on (often dirty) compromises (IX, 158), where every second subjunctive has to be left out. Grass finds it 'manchmal schwierig, aber es geht' (IV, 542), though the difficulties inherent in this bold 'dual-track action' are impossible to systematize.[7]

At the end of his recent Frankfurt lecture, to which he gave the highly charged title 'Schreiben nach Auschwitz', he writes à propos of this question: 'Auch das Nachdenken über Deutschland ist Teil meiner literarischen Arbeit. Seit Mitte der sechziger Jahre bis in die anhaltende Unruhe hinein gab es Anlässe für Reden und Aufsätze. Oft waren diese notwendig deutlichen Hinweise meinen Zeitgenossen zuviel der Einmischung, der, wie sie meinten, außerliterarischen Dreinrede. Das sind nicht meine Besorgnisse.'[8] He thus hints strongly that all of his writing should be assessed with regard to the German Question — as a counterdiscourse of political speeches and literary stories. With this very ambitious wish in mind, I shall divide my discussion into two sections, devoted repectively to the nightmares and the wishful dreams of Günter Grass, writer and citizen, for whom 'Utopie und Melancholie Zahl und Adler der gleichen Münze sind' (IV, 545).

II The Stuff of Nightmares: A Unitary State for Single-minded Germans

> Sicher, es stimmt, daß wir kein geschriebenes Mandat haben, uns in politischer Sache wie Wortführer aufzuführen. Aber es stimmt auch, daß wir als Autoren in Deutschland Erfahrungen gemacht haben [...] Das waren auch in der Regel Autoren, die sehr früh Entwicklungen zum Schlimmen vorausgesagt haben und denen niemand zugehört hat.
> (Günter Grass: 'Nachdenken über Deutschland. Gespräch mit Stefan Heym', 1984)

Grass thinks of himself (all too) happily as a 'Berater in Sachen Politik'[9] and he has lately been addressing the political and moral conscience of his fellow citizens once again. Sometimes he comes perilously close to a point he once criticized in others, namely 'die Anmaßung, Gewissen der Nation zu sein' (IX, 158). But he is certain of nothing as much as of his own lack of power and his ignorance of political forces, since experience has taught him repeatedly that even his 'manifestos' are not listened to by the people who matter (VI, 128—36). In order to counter his political impotence and express 'ein leises "dennoch"' (VI, 71), the writer is obliged to articulate painful truths in the current debate on reunification, however much they run against the grain of the spirit of the time (IX, 925). It was no coincidence that Grass chose the etching, *Westfälischer Friede II*, to adorn the cover of his recent anthology of essays,[10] as he wanted to underline the connections between the Baroque and the present situation. In *Das Treffen in Telgte* he had depicted baroque poets who still dreamt of immortality though the historical situation was precarious. He was confident that 'wenn man sie steinigen, mit Haß verschütten wollte, würde noch aus dem Geröll die Hand mit der Feder ragen' and that it was only with the poets that 'was deutsch zu nennen sich lohne, ewiglich aufgehoben [sei]' (VI, 134).

However, it is not the immortality of poetry which is at issue now, but rather the galloping pace of political history, which has without doubt already overtaken many of the speeches and essays under discussion. For this reason, rather than any academic predilection for chronology, and certainly avoiding the pompous tone of a 'Lehrer für Deutsch und also Geschichte' (IV, 15), I am obliged to return to Grass's beginnings; it is the only way to do justice to his prodigious authorial memory and to reveal, with due attention to the shifts and developments in his emphasis, how remarkably consistent his approach to the German Question has been.

On his first foray beyond the bounds of literature, where he ventures out of the safety afforded by the devices of poetry and fiction, he published his reaction to an 'Ungedicht', entitled 'Deutscher Schwur' (by R. A. Schröder), which as a boy he had been made to recite (IX, 932—4). This antipoem reawakens the nightmare of his youth, which he spent under a régime which committed unspeakable crimes in the name of his generation and its future (IX, 163). He writes:

> Wer als Dreiunddreißigjähriger vom zehnten bis zum sechzehnten Lebensjahr Gelegenheit hatte, dieses Gedicht anläßlich Morgenfeiern, Weihestunden, beim Fahnehissen, im Zeltlager nahe dem Lagerfeuer, in Jungvolk- und Hitlerjugenduniform nach chorähnlicher Melodie, mit Todesschauern im Rücken oder sonstwo halb zu singen, halb in den Ostwind zu sprechen, wird gewiß heute noch aus unruhigem Schlaf aufschrecken und nicht frei von kaltem Schweiß "Deutschland, fallen wir Haupt bei Haupt" ins stockdunkle Schlafzimmer schwören. (IX, 933)

The all-German trauma has remained to this day a central theme in Grass's work as a poet, playwright and novelist. He is able neither to repress the horror, nor to overcome it; it is ever-present, even though occasionally and for a short while other images of terror may displace it.

Only a few months later, on 14 August 1961, deeply affected by the building of the Berlin Wall, Grass wrote an open letter to Anna Seghers,[11] then chairman of the GDR *Schriftstellerverband*, imploring her to act because 'heute stehen Alpträume als Panzer an der Leipziger Straße, bedrücken jeden Schlaf und bedrohen die Bürger' (IX, 34). He warned of the temptation to embrace irrational solutions and appealed to his East German colleagues to defend themselves publicly, to reject the division of Germany and to recognize the violent measures for what they were, namely the actions of a dictatorship which had only thinly disguised itself with the Utopian mantle of communism. The latter was a dream which he did not dream himself, but which he respected, as he respected all other dreams (IX, 33f.). The reactions from East Germany to the appeal were resoundingly negative: the Cold War had left its mark on writers too. Grass regarded the division of Germany as disastrous from the start, but he realized that it was now being extended systematically to all levels of the two societies (IX, 228). The two states, both built on sand and with neither pausing for a moment's self-reflection after 1945, stood inimically opposed to each other, each eager to prove itself the model pupil of its respective power bloc (IX, 147f.). In his Büchner Prize acceptance speech in 1965, Grass noted angrily that since the disturbances of June 1953 'zwölf Jahre angeblicher Politik der Stärke' had been nowhere more successful than in the confirmation of the existence of the 'Gegenstaat'. West Germans combined 'unverbindliche Lippenbekenntnisse zur Wiedervereinigung' with 'die törichte Spekulation, es wünsche sich die Bevölkerung der DDR nichts sehnlicher, als von Ludwig Erhards CDU regiert zu werden' (IX, 149). The result was that their neighbours in Rostock, Leipzig, Weimar and Magdeburg turned away from the West with bitterness and disappointment.

From the mid-1960s Grass took to the campaign trail in order to breathe life into 'die ideologische Versteinerung, hier wie drüben' (IX, 233).[12] He counselled his compatriots to follow the path of enlightened reason, or (as he expresses it in verse) 'ich rate Euch, Es-Pe-De zu wählen' (I, 198). According to Grass, the Social Democrats were the only party with a mature national consciousness which had prevented them from ever falling victim to nationalist hysteria (IX, 115). Grass is the declared opponent of all abstract ideas and absolute claims and he abhors sudden revolutionary leaps forward (IX, 425). Placed in the midst of an unholy configuration of tried and tested answers to the 'berüchtigt-berühmte Frage nach der Nation' (IX, 222f.), he asks, 'was ist des Deutschen Vaterland?' (IX, 99).

The first part of his response was unambiguous, as he dubbed re-unification 'ein sinnentleerter Begriff, den wir, wollen wir glaubwürdig werden, streichen müssen' (IX, 225). Both German guilt and post-1945 German borders had to be accepted unconditionally by the Germans if there was to be any chance of reconciliation between the two German states and their joint set of neighbours. But there was the rub. It had always been precisely such points which had caused the Germans enor-mous problems. Their lack of 'Nationalgeist' (IX, 147) and national iden-tity, a result of the peculiar course of their ideological history, had meant, says Grass, that they had perched precariously between the ex-tremes or swung from one all-or-nothing position, from one either-or postulate to another (IX, 162). Grass believes that his fellow countrymen 'haben das Maß nicht finden können. Zwischen Nationalismus und Separatismus liegt jedoch unsere einzige und selten genutzte Möglichkeit: die Konföderation oder der wirtschaftlich feste, politisch und kulturell lockere Bund der Länder' (IX, 230). But the material and intellectual conditions necessary for the attainment of such an objective (which might incidentally be exemplary for a federal Europe) were lacking in Germany, for 'wer hier eine Wiedervereinigung träumt, wird sich an Realitäten sehr bald wachstoßen' (IX, 426).

By the end of the 1960s, a new nightmare, 'der wie viele deutsche Alpträume, Chancen birgt, Realität zu werden,' was already torturing him. A coalition of the two extremes 'deutschnationale Rechte plus sta-linistische Rechte' might be in a position 'die Spottgeburt einer Nation in die Welt [zu] setzen, deren furchterregende Existenz durch das wach-sende Selbstverständnis der Deutschen verhindert werden möge' (IX, 233). Nationalism was still virulent in Germany, 'der Brautgarten des Ir-rationalismus' (IX, 457): what Brecht wrote of Hitler, that the womb from which he crawled was 'fruchtbar noch',[13] was still true of both German states. Grass saw how military offensives were simulated using model soldiers, past wars won belatedly on the military drawing-board, bor-ders rolled back eastwards once more, as sermons for the salvation of a united Germany resounded from the political pulpits, awakening un-controllable nationalist feelings (IX, 225). He never missed an opportunity at this time to warn, in his 'politische Gegenreden', against a regression to nineteenth-century notions of national statehood (IX, 233), the re-emergence of irrationalism in German politics (IX, 341), and the disastrous militaristic policies which had twice failed the German 'Groß-Vaterland' in this century (IX, 454).

'Deutschland ist nur zwangsweise, also immer zu seinem Schaden, eine Einheit gewesen,' says Grass, 'das singuläre Deutschland ist eine Rechnung, die nie mehr aufgehen möge; denn genau gerechnet ist Deutschland eine kommunizierende Mehrzahl' (IX, 235). He concluded that the fateful idea of national statehood as the condition for unification had to be forgotten once and for all (IX, 443), announcing uncategorically three years later that 'es wird keine Wiedervereinigung geben: keine unter den Vorzeichen unseres Gesellschaftssystems, keine unter kommunistischen Vorzeichen. Zwei deutsche Staaten deutscher Nation, die gegensätzlicher nicht gedacht werden können, müssen lernen, nebeneinander zu leben und miteinander die Hypotheken gemeinsamer Geschichte zu tragen' (IX, 418f.). Thus his rejection of a unified state as a home for the forgetful Germans was already total at this point. Instead he favoured a federation consisting not only of the two German states, but also of the German *Länder*. In the spring of 1990 he called this 'eine Möglichkeit, die den Deutschen befriedigend sein könnte und unseren Nachbarn keine Angst machen müßte'.[14] The well-founded nightmare vies with the carefully thought out, but still wishful dream.

Since the time of his earlier comments the historical situation, which Grass followed closely, has changed beyond all recognition. Yet our author has found no reason to revise his stance, remaining obstinately loyal to his own arguments. His recent contributions to the reunification debate have been packed with self-quotation, as he rehearses his same old answers to the German Question, paraded under provocative newspaper headlines calculated to shock his readers. It seems almost as if nothing had really happened, or as if he would have preferred it had nothing happened. He writes once more, in February 1990, 'Alptraum steht gegen Traum'.[15] The wishful dream is inspired by the reasonable and well-balanced German whose knowledge of his country's recent history makes him an advocate of a German confederacy, and again such a dream is contradicted by the nightmare of a unified state, a freakish deformity which is the product of a forced enlargement. The re-birth of an isolated, fear-inspiring Fatherland (this time round out of the spirit of the Deutschmark) is something Grass still regards as a horror story, or rather as a badly directed western with an inevitably unhappy ending.

Aid will only be granted to the East if West German conditions are met, since 'die westliche Ideologie des Kapitalismus, die jeden anderen Ismus ersatzlos gestrichen sehen will, spricht sich wie hinter vorgehalter Pistole aus: entweder Marktwirtschaft oder...'[16] A Fatherland built with blood and iron, driven by the German will to ever greater power must never again, says Grass, revoking Bismarck, be placed in a position of control. For it is still a real and fearful prospect that such a creation would once again steer us all, to the sound of German brass, to rack and ruin.

These very real fears, which he shares with many others at home and abroad, cannot be dismissed lightly: his worries are genuine; his anxieties easy to understand in view of what he experienced in his youth. Yet it is still legitimate to point out that his rhetoric seems questionable, to say the least, and that he either re-states the obvious or invites polemic almost for the sake of it. His arguments contain few subtle differentiations between past and present.[17] His main point against the 'Verlangen nach Wiedervereinigung' is especially problematical as he contends that 'gegen jeden aus Stimmung, durch Stimmungsmache forcierten Trend, gegen die Kaufkraft der westdeutschen Wirtschaft — für harte DM ist sogar die Einheit zu haben — ja, sogar gegen ein Selbstbestimmungsrecht, das anderen Völkern ungeteilt zusteht, gegen all das spricht Auschwitz, weil eine der Voraussetzungen für das Ungeheure, neben anderen älteren Treibkräften, ein starkes, das geeinte Deutschland gewesen ist'.[18] No route towards unity can skirt round this terrible stigma in German history, it is an immovable obstacle of shame which will bar all moves to reunification. 'Wer gegenwärtig über Deutschland nachdenkt und Antworten auf die Deutsche Frage sucht,' he insists, 'muß Auschwitz mitdenken. Der Ort des Schreckens, als Beispiel genannt für das bleibende Trauma, schließt einen zukünftigen deutschen Einheitsstaat aus. Sollte er, was zu befürchten bleibt, dennoch ertrotzt werden, wird ihm das Scheitern vorgeschrieben sein.'[19]

It is difficult to judge at this stage whether this bold contention is an appropriately moral reaction to Kohl's over-hasty, and therefore mistaken policy for Germany, or whether Grass is using German war crimes simply for rhetorical purposes.[20] Certainly, his fears must be

taken seriously. They make him tireless in his search for new ways forward for Germany, now that everyone else has discovered the all-
redeeming *voie noble* to unity. What he misses is a 'third way', a route
'which tries to answer the German Question by turning to other sources
in German history than, of all things, Bismarck'.[21] He still advocates instead 'the dream of democratic socialism with a human face', a dream
which might still have a world-wide future; the way in which 'alles, was
mit diesem Traum auch nur annäherend zu tun hat, weggebügelt und
ein regelrechtes Traumverbot ausgesprochen wird' he finds quite
nauseating.[22]

  Grass refuses to be bound by any such banning orders and continues to explore his own dreams. For a writer, language is a means of
crossing boundaries and Grass carries on searching for a third possibility, which might yet serve as an answer to the Germans' national
predicament. He still believes this to lie in the attempt to become a
'Kulturnation in konföderativer Vielfalt',[23] which is, he stresses, 'in
diesem Fall der dritte Weg, den ich vorschlage'.[24]

III A Vigilant Daydream: Nationhood born of and nurtured by Culture

> Ich sagte: "Unsere Nachbarn in Ost und West werden eine Bal-
> lung wirtschaftlicher und militärischer Macht in der Mitte Eu-
> ropas nie wieder dulden nach der Erfahrung zweier Weltkriege, die
> dort gezündet wurden. Doch könnte die Existenz der beiden
> deutschen Staaten unter dem Dach eines gemeinsamen Kultur-
> begriffs unseren Nachbarn verständlich und dem National-
> verständnis der Deutschen angemessen sein." Eine Illusion mehr?
> Literatenträume? Ist meine Behauptung, die ich [...] wie ein när-
> rischer Wanderprediger vortrug — es hätten sich die deutschen
> Schriftsteller, im Gegensatz zu ihren separatistischen Landes-
> herren, als die besseren Patrioten bewiesen — nur eine Trotz-
> gebärde?
> (Günter Grass: *Kopfgeburten oder Die Deutschen sterben aus*,
> 1980)

Grass delves back a long way in German history, oblivious to the
changes in government and cultural policies in either East or West, in
order to give his proposal for a third way some substance. In 1965 he
had already made the appeal: 'Wer Ohren hat, höre: Bevor es überhaupt
eine deutsche Nation gab, gab es seit Klopstock und Lessing, eine
deutsche Literatur' (IX, 114). He quotes other writers and philosophers
of renown in support of his thesis: Schubart, Stolberg, Bürger, Moser,
and repeatedly Herder; many others were to follow, recently even

Uhland and Schelling. For a craftsman of language aware of his literary lineage: 'Deutschland ist, hundert Jahre vor Bismarck, durch deutsche Schriftsteller und Philosophen, die den Geist der Aufklärung durch dieses Land wehen ließen, kraft der Sprache geeingt worden' (IX, 114).

To this day Grass has found no more appropriate way to define the German nation than to resuscitate the all-embracing idea of 'Kultur'. He reiterated this view in his *Financial Times* interview in December 1989, where he pleaded for 'two confederated states, one cultural nation'. As German political unity has now failed twice, a modified version of Herder's *Kulturnation* (things have, after all, moved on since the eighteenth century) enables him both to abandon the obsolete notion of national statehood and to fill the 'national vacuum' (IX, 454), that ideological black hole, which makes many young people in particular potentially susceptible to right-wing dogma.[25] As an entity it would obviate the need to create a nation state, assume the burden of responsiblitiy for German history, and take account, for instance, of the failed parliamentary efforts in the Frankfurt Paulskirche in 1848, as well as join together the many strands of German culture. He goes as far as to say that it is the last remaining way for the Germans to conceive of themselves as a nation, since they now know that everything except their culture could be divided.[26]

The practical problems associated with this proposition hardly need to be spelt out. We must ask Günter Grass whether it is possible to limit the concept of nationhood in this artificial way to the cultural sphere and whether such a creation based on a common language and literature really would be a national panacea which would always prevent 'worse' happening. His vague concept of nationhood would, if it became reality, entail a host of political and economic repercussions (and events in the GDR provide only the latest example to remind us of this), not that anybody could even have dreamed of those all that time ago in the 1970s, when German writers launched their cultural counter-offensive in a period of ideological stagnation. In common with many others, who also put themselves forward as self-confident national advocates, Grass articulated in many of his texts the idea that contemporary German literature bore a special responsibility for the cohesion of Germany. His imaginary meeting of the baroque poets in Telgte, an impressive literary memorial to the *Gruppe 47*, is devoted to this same theme. Here his discourse on the German Question reached a degree of literary accomplishment which he has not equalled either before or since, as on this occasion he deliberately makes his art the measure of his formulations (VI, 71).

In this 'Gegengeschichte' for chaotic times the discussion focuses on poetological questions rather than political ones: language is not merely the medium of expression, it is an overriding theme of the text. Grass reformulates his cultural patriotism and his belief that 'einzig die Dichter [...] wüßten noch, was deutsch zu nennen sich lohne. Sie hätten "mit vielen heißen Seufftzern und Zähren" die deutsche Sprache als letztes Band geknüpft. Sie seien das andere, das wahrhaftige Deutschland' (VI, 70). The quotation is from the 'leidiges Manifest', which the baroque poets intend to send to their princes but which in the end is consumed by fire before it can be disseminated. While their hasty attempt to contribute to the political debate from the social periphery is destroyed unread, their immortal literary works will survive. Only by writing poetry can poets register resistance to the passage of time, but it is an act of resistance which is peculiar to them.[27] The moral renewal, for which so many of them had hoped so fervently, fails to materialize; the peace negotiations at the end of the Thirty Years' War merely serve as preparation for yet more wars. If seen as a metaphor for the situation in a war-ravaged Europe after 1945, Grass's text implies that politicians in neither part of Germany noticed that Germany continued to exist, bound together by a common language and, not least, by the literature written in that language, both so resilient as to withstand the political division.[28] The attempt to create an autonomous national literature in the GDR failed, just as the Federal Republic failed to prevent its citizens' taking an active interest in GDR writing.

In the 1970s writers from the respective sides came closer together, as they by-passed the cultural bureaucrats in Bonn or East Berlin and established a dialogue with each other, their works exploring common themes and concerns.[29] Even though the politicians ignored the initiative, the primary objective was reached, just as it had been three hundred years earlier in Telgte:

> Fortan könne sich jeder weniger vereinzelt begreifen. Und wen zu Haus Enge zu bedrücken, neuer Jammer einzuholen, der falsche Glanz zu täuschen, wem das Vaterland zu schwinden drohe, der möge sich der heilgebliebenen Distel im Brückenkopf vor Telgtes Emstor erinnern, wo ihnen die Sprache Weite versprochen, Glanz abgegeben, das Vaterland ersetzt und allen Jammer dieser Welt benannt habe. Kein Fürst könne ihnen gleichen. (VI, 134)

The seventeenth-century poets' meeting and the regular gatherings in East Berlin between 1973 and 1978, where writers read from their manuscripts and discussed literary questions (closely following the model of the *Gruppe 47*), proffer the same clear message. Whereas in all other respects the Germans have always split everything into two: 'Körper und Seele, Praxis und Theorie, Inhalt und Form, Geist und Macht' (VI, 249), their writers have displayed unity and exercised tolerance and solidarity. Grass, who took part in these discussions, has good reason to claim that the common indivisible culture serves as the roof to an otherwise divided household. German writers are the upholders of that culture:

> Nehmt sie alle, wenn ihr am Sonntagnachmittag (und sei es beim Puzzle) Deutschland sucht: den toten Heine und den lebenden Biermann, Christa Wolf drüben, Heinrich Böll hier, Logau und Lessing, Kunert und Walser, stellt Goethe neben Thomas und Schiller neben Heinrich Mann, laßt Büchner in Bautzen und Grabbe in Stammheim einsitzen, hört Bettina, wenn ihr Sarah Kirsch hört, lernt Klopstock bei Rühmkorf, Luther bei Johnson, beim toten Born des Gryphius Jammertal und bei Jean Paul meine Idyllen kennen. Von Herder bis Hebel, von Trakl bis Storm. Pfeift auf die Grenzen. Wünscht nur die Sprache geräumig. Seid anders reich. Schöpft ab den Profit. Denn Besseres (über die Drahtverhaue hinweg) haben wir nicht. Einzig die Literatur (und ihr Unterfutter: Geschichte, Mythen, Schuld und andere Rückstände) überwölbt die beiden sich grämlich abgrenzenden Staaten. (VI, 250)

If the Germans are ever to understand themselves properly as a *Kulturnation*, they will have to look to the poets rather than to the politicians.[30]

This opposition between ever cooperative writers and unimaginative, ineducable politicians, which has lately become rather a commonplace, is the *leitmotif* of an unpublished speech, entitled 'The German Languages', which Grass gave in English during a tour of Asia in 1979.[31] He acknowledges that the subtitle might easily have been 'Deutschland — ein literarischer Begriff' (VI, 142) and claims that 'Germany today — and not for the first time — can only be grasped as a literary concept'. After the failure of the one-sided policies pursued in both German states, only literature can make any claim to be all-German, as it ignores obsolete political borders. Contemporary literature is the only real mirror of societal developments: while politicians follow a programme of short-sighted crisis-management to secure material prosperity and their own positions of power, writers have made essentially more far-sighted efforts to do away with the clichés of yesteryear and to break up the inhuman frontier systems. Grass believes:

Even political answers are no longer sought from parliaments but from lite-rature. That is the reason why the policy of détente between the two block systems and between the two German states, which has been stagnating for years, is continued in thought by the German writers alone. To the annoyance of the politicians, they are carrying on, beyond the ideologies in vogue, a dia-logue of an all-German kind which defines the concept of the nation solely from its cultural traditions, free from the usual power claims, Culture [...] is expected to accomplish spiritually what politics fails to achieve in everyday terms.

Only writers have faced up to their responsibilities towards history with any degree of honesty; it has been left to them to keep the wounds open, to expose contradictions, to correct omissions and to register doubts with regard to simplified explanations and to display scepticism to-wards ideological 'isms' of any hue or colour. This is the tradition, which stretches from Logau and Lessing via Herder and Heine to Böll and Biermann, to which Grass believes himself to belong.

For Grass 'writers have always been the better patriots. Patriots and at the same time cosmopolitans,' whose

call for unity did not mean accumulation of power. Their longing for great-ness never strove for domination, their riches were the cultural varieties of the German people [...] [Their fatherland's] wealth is not threatened by infla-tion [...] its power is not oppressive, it imparts knowledge and frees the imagination. Its capital is the German language, and with it you can practise usury.

For years Grass has been demanding a 'Nationalstiftung deutscher Kul-tur' for precisely this reason, 'damit wir uns endlich begreifen, damit uns die Welt anders und nicht mehr als fürchterlich begreift,' and in order that the Wall, 'der Widerpart aller Kulturen', should be penetrated at least at one point. He anticipated the objections: 'Aber das geht doch nicht! höre ich rufen [...] Lächerlich, zwei Staaten einer Nation. Auch noch Kulturnation. Was kann man sich dafür schon kaufen?! Ich weiß. Es ist nur ein hellwacher Tagtraum. (Eine Kopfgeburt mehr)' (VI, 251f.). It is nothing new for the Germans, who have always demanded the impossible, to disregard their writers' dreams.

A few years ago Grass dreamt of a She-Rat, who had never noticed that Germany was divided, but who regarded it 'als Ganzes gefundenes Fressen' (VII, 249). After the nightmare of the third and final world war, his fatherland had disappeared wholly from the poisoned earth and he could only recite (with the She-Rat): 'es war einmal ein Land, das hieß Deutsch' (VII, 96). And yet, even this 'katastrophales Buch in einer katastrophalen Zeit' (X, 360) had had to be written to prove that 'die

Schriftsteller sind nicht totzukriegen'. They are 'Ratten und Schmeißfliegen, die am Konsens nagen und die Weißwäsche sprenkeln' (VI, 250). Grass is able to contrive to draw literary strength from his lack of political power, only because he knows that 'die Tradition unserer Literatur diesen ohnmächtigen Trotz fordert' (VI, 252).

IV Will a Grey Story counter the Dream become Reality?

> *Es träumt sich nicht mehr recht von der blauen Blume. Wer heut'*
> *als Heinrich von Ofterdingen erwacht, muß verschlafen haben [...]*
> *Der Traum eröffnet nicht mehr blaue Ferne. Er ist grau geworden.*
> *Die graue Staubschicht auf den Dingen ist sein bestes Teil.*
> (Walter Benjamin: 'Glosse zum Surrealismus')

The unity of Germany as a *Kulturnation* was the stuff of bold literary dreams in the 1970s; now in 1990 the notion has been overtaken by rapid political change. Other ways forward have replaced 'reunification through literature', as against all expectations the Berlin Wall became first porous and then was torn asunder. In all areas of life things that had been separated but belonged together could now grow together again, as Willy Brandt famously phrased it.[32] What began as a brave in- itiative on the part of writers left them far in the rear once the borders were opened. They have now been forced on the defensive and the chances of culture offering the answer to the German Question are slim indeed. The self-proclaimed realist, Rudolf Augstein, told Grass: 'der Zug ist abgefahren, Sie sitzen nicht mit drin'; and Grass could only retort with a counter assertion that 'der Zug ist noch nicht weg',[33] even though by that time all the evidence pointed to the contrary. Granted: there is to this day 'kein subalternerer Hohn als den auf den Dichter, der in die politische Arena herabsteigt' (IX, 113), but should a writer, who never- theless responds to the challange, really make it so easy for his political opponents?

We have come full circle. The poets' Cassandra-like cries fall on deaf ears and the never-ending German story continues its absurd course. The fact is that the 'other Germany' voted first with its feet then with the ballot box and that the right-of-centre *Allianz für Deutschland* won the GDR elections with West German CDU slogans straight out of the 1950s. The first successful revolution on German soil has already devoured its children, but Grass refuses to allow any reality to shake him out of his wishful dreams. As a writer shunted off to the political side-lines, he has been immeasurably disappointed by post-revolution developments in the GDR, which has wrenched itself free from the clutches of one ideology only to fall into the embrace of another. Grass, in contrast, remains unswervingly loyal to his old arguments and, in a vain attempt to salvage what is already beyond salvation, refuses to swim with the tide of change. If he really believes in his influence on public opinion then he is quite voluntarily leaving it to other contemporaries, less dreamy than he, to set the course for the future, namely the right-wing demagogues and fast-moving economic ideologues, who know already exactly the direction the reunification train is to take. The 'wandering preacher', buried in thought, walking the tightrope between self-styled provocation and desperate gestures of defiance, is faithful to his familiar scepticism, which is doubtlessly in many ways well-founded.[34] He reminds his compatriots of the hang-over which will inevitably follow the the emotional all-German carousal; he even goes as far as to put the whole German Question itself into question by urging that parochial German concerns must not cloud the greater issues, nor endanger the idea of a European Germany and the dream of a united Europe (IX, 488).

At the reunion meeting of the *Gruppe 47*, held in Prague in May 1990 at the invitation of the writer President Václav Havel, Grass read from his latest manuscript, *Totes Holz*, whose theme is environmental destruction. Only if we learn to look at ourselves for a moment from the outside can Germany's problems be put into an appropriate focus, since 'von China, Indonesien und Indien aus gesehen, schrumpft der alte Kontinent auf Spielzeuggröße, gibt die "deutsche Frage" endgültig ihre Drittrangigkeit preis'.[35] The real problems which confront the globe remain untouched by such small-time worries and 'in a few months time, the euphoria will have died down and we will be faced with these problems without an answer. The contaminated and poisoned air knows no boundaries.'[36] We have every reason to fear that he will be right, but at present politicians are in no mood to listen to Utopian ruminations, which seek to go beyond their easy solutions and eurocentric view of the world.

Such obstacles are unfamiliar to the writer, as in his literature he can afford to deal uncompromisingly with the paradoxical and contradictory twists of reality. His are other levels of difficulty, cumbersome blocks of material to be shaped into aesthetically viable forms. In literature both writer and reader can find fantastic escape routes, learn of third ways (I, 92) or even third breasts (V, 6). The writer refutes claims to absolute truth and does away with binary oppositions by insisting with the peasant woman who passed on the two versions of the flounder's tale in *Der Butt*, that we must take 'dat een un dat anner tosamen' (V, 412). He renounces black and white ideological answers and casts a veil of greyish ascetic doubt over multi-layered realities, celebrates grey masses (I, 145), and most importantly, 'angeekelt vom christlich-marxistischen Hoffungsquark' (IV, 212) greets any idea which promises a final resting place for Sisyphus's stone with peals of laughter.

Without advocating ostensible escape routes myself, the retreat to the ivory tower or the flight to an artificial paradise, I think it conceivable that Grass's extra-literary interventions may soon be followed by a more ambivalent, literary treatment of German questions: shaded with lead-grey melancholy and tinged with all the nuances of these too, too German cares - 'eine alte Geschichte will ganz anders erzählt werden'. [37] It may be that in his literary texts a wondrous regiment of women may again emerge, like Heine's French mistress, to chase away his 'Nachtgedanken' with a smile.[38] For distance, both temporal and spatial, is requisite in order to write of these matters — a commodity which up till now has been in short supply.

It is still permitted to dream of good spirits in politics and, in any case, the rude awakening usually comes soon enough; although, as Thomas Mann knew, for the Germans it has always come too late.[39] Yet for the writer more than anyone else there is an alternative to 'politische Gegenrede', namely radical aesthetic opposition, the return to the Utopia of fiction, the virgin sheet of paper which demands to be spotted with the contradictory dreams born of his creative imagination. Grey prospects? Literature, faced with a myriad of third ways, makes the impossible possible. The end of the story can be kept open...

NOTES

Translation by Julian Preece.
1   Günter Grass: *Werkausgabe in zehn Bänden* ed. by Volker Neuhaus, Darmstadt, 1987. References in the text by volume and page number are to this edition of works by Grass.
2   These ideas and the traditions associated with them are discussed in Helmut L. Müller: *Die literarische Republik. Westdeutsche Schriftsteller und die Politik*, Weinheim, 1982; see especially pp. 17ff., 48, and 167.
3   *Die Zeit*, 9 March 1990.

4   Rudolf Augstein and Günter Grass: *DEUTSCHLAND, einig Vaterland? Ein Streitgespräch*, Göttingen, 1990.
5   Grass in an interview with *taz*, 12 February 1990, p. 10: 'Da wird ein regelrechtes Traumverbot ausgesprochen'.
6   Günter Grass: 'Frankfurter Poetik-Vorlesung. Schreiben nach Auschwitz', *Die Zeit*, 23 February 1990, pp. 17—19.
7   For discussions of the relationship between literature and politics in Grass's work see, for example, Volker Neuhaus: *Günter Grass*, Stuttgart, 1979, pp. 125ff.; Otto F. Best: '"Doppelleben" zwischen Evolution und ewiger Wiederkehr. Überlegungen zum postgrastropodischen Werk von Günter Graß [*sic*]', *Colloquia Germanica*, vol. 15, 1982, pp. 111—21; and Müller: *Die literarische Republik...*, pp. 206ff.
8   Ibid.
9   Günter Grass: *Deutscher Lastenausgleich. Wider das dumpfe Einheitsgebot. Reden und Gespräche*, Frankfurt/Main, 1990, p. 46.
10 *Deutscher Lastenausgleich...*
11 Jochen Wittmann also refers to this letter in his discussion of the reception of Grass in the GDR (pp. 273—83 below, here p. 276).
12 Grass's most extensive statement on the division of Germany: 'Eine kommunizierende Mehrzahl' (1967), IX, 223—35.
13 Bert Brecht: *Der aufhaltsame Aufstieg des Arturo Ui* in Brecht: *Gesammelte Werke*, vol. IV, Frankfurt/Main, 1977, p. 1834.
14 Grass: *Deutscher Lastenausgleich...*, p. 44.
15 Günter Grass: 'Kurze Rede eines vaterlandslosen Gesellen', *Die Zeit*, 9 February 1990, p. 61.
16 Ibid.
17 See the response by Jens Jessen: 'Leichtfertig. Günter Grass über Auschwitz', *FAZ*, 15 February 1990.
18 Grass: 'Schreiben nach Auschwitz'. See also Augstein, Grass: *Deutschland, einig Vaterland?...*, p. 57.
19 Grass: 'Kurze Rede eines vaterlandslosen Gesellen'.
20 See Jessen: 'Leichtfertig...' and Wolfram Schütte: 'Voneinander Lernen lernen. Auf einem deutsch-deutschen Schriftstellertreffen im Literarischen Colloquium', *FR*, 27 February 1990, p. 10 (especially the views of Johano Strasser and Dieter Wellershoff.
21 Grass in an interview with Andrew Fisher in *Financial Times*, 4 December 1989: 'A third way for Germany?'.
22 Grass, *taz* interview, 12 February 1990.
23 Grass: 'Kurze Rede eines vaterlandslosen Gesellen'.
24 Augstein, Grass: *Deutschland, einig Vaterland?...*, p. 89.
25 Günter Grass: 'Deutschland — zwei Staaten — einer Nation?' (1970), IX, 447—57. See also Müller: *Die literarische Republik...*, p. 166; Andreas Roßmann: 'Die Einheit — eine (literarische) Fiktion?', *Deutschland Archiv*, no. 6, 1981, pp. 568f; Grass in conversation with Wolfram Schütte: 'Die liegengebliebenen Themen', *FR*, 29 January 1980.
26 See Grass: *Deutscher Lastenausgleich...*, p. 33, and Wolfgang Werth: 'Kommentare zur Lage der Nation. Ein Grass-Hearing in München', *SZ*, 30 May 1979.
27 Several other contributions to this volume examine related themes. See, for example, Thomas Beckermann (pp. 97—115 above, esp. pp. 102—3 and 109—14), Katrin Kohl (pp. 339—56 below, esp. pp. 347—50) and Karen Leeder (pp. 413—24 below). While he shares this view, Botho Strauß's stance is less optimistic (see Arthur Williams, esp. pp. 461—4 below).
28 Werth: 'Kommentare zur Lage der Nation...'.
29 See, for example, Hans Mayer: 'Literatur heute im geteilten Deutschland', *Politik und Kultur*, no. 4, 1978, pp. 3—21, esp. p. 19; also Grass: *Deutscher Lastenausgleich...*, pp. 33—9, and conversation in *FR*, 29 January 1980.
30 Grass, conversation in *FR*, 29 January 1980.
31 Günter Grass: 'The German Languages', unpublished manuscript of a speech given in English in 1979 which he has kindly made available to the present author. Grass kept the English deliberately simple. Here p. 4.

32 Willy Brandt's words on the opening of the border: 'Wir sind jetzt in einer Situation, wo wieder zusammenwächst, was zusammengehört'.

33 Augstein, Grass: *Deutschland, einig Vaterland?*..., pp. 62 and 78.

34 Günter Grass: 'Was rede ich. Wer hört noch zu', *Die Zeit*, 11 May 1990, p. 71.

35 Grass: 'Schreiben nach Auschwitz'.

36 Grass: *Deutscher Lastenausgleich*..., p. 17.

37 Grass: 'Schreiben nach Auschwitz'.

38 The final stanza of Heine's famous poem, which opens 'Denk' ich an Deutschland in der Nacht,/ Dann bin ich um den Schlaf gebracht', reads: 'Gottlob! durch meine Fenster bricht/ Französisch heitres Tageslicht;/ Es kommt mein Weib, schön wie der Morgen,/ und lächelt fort die deutschen Sorgen.'

39 The reference is to Thomas Mann: 'Deutschland und die Deutschen' in Mann: *An die gesittete Welt. Politische Schriften und Reden im Exil*, Frankfurt/Main, 1986, pp. 117f.

ERINNERUNGSARBEIT GEGEN VERGESSEN UND 'ENTSORGUNG': ON THE TREATMENT OF THE EXPERIENCE OF GERMAN FASCISM IN PROSE WORKS OF THE LAST DECADE IN THE FEDERAL REPUBLIC

HELLA EHLERS

I

The German past, concern with it and the treatment of it, has, in the perspective of the reality of the GDR, caught up with the present and the debate about the future of the Germans, if not of Europe and beyond, in a most depressing manner. Under this pressure from of recent political events, and given our impression of them, it is relevant to inquire with renewed vigour into the intellectual, moral and emotional contribution made by literature to our ability to deal with historical phenomena, our ability to maintain of our sensitivity to the dangers of the deformation of humanity in and by fascism — our ability to preserve humanitarian values. Literature can show us models of resistance, it can inspire and strengthen our confidence in our own individual potential for resistance.

I am convinced that our capacity as human beings to shape the future depends today essentially on our ability to learn in the ethical and political direction of antifascism. What I have to say, therefore, to make my position clear, has to do with that literature which aims to offer the reader a level of receptivity to antifascist models; that is, I am concerned with the guidance and aid to life today that might be gained from such texts.

Although this discussion will concentrate on selected texts of the 1980s, it must be remembered that the literature of the FRG has, in all phases of its development, put down clear markers for the critical treatment of war, fascism and the immediate postwar period. Wolfgang Borchert, Heinrich Böll, Siegfried Lenz, Günter Grass, Wolfgang Koeppen, Alfred Andersch are just a few of the names I might mention here. It is, however, possible also to observe a new approach since the mid-1970s. We must ask to what extent this new approach consists solely in the large number of relevant texts, whether the 'old' theme is simply being attacked through new or changed formulations of the questions, or whether it is the result of the emergence of a new generation of writers (born between 1933—1945) and the fact that this problem is seen by them (and beyond them, more generally) as unresolved. This generation is bound through the experiences of their childhood to the fascist period; these experiences exerted lasting influence on their subjective awareness, their social attitudes and their perceptions of values.

The 'Rückgewinnung von Historizität'[1] indicated a desire to understand expressed in the face of the contradictions, of the fundamental disappointments and of the continuing hope for the future felt by this generation, all of which seemed explicable essentially out of the history of their 'fathers', of the nation. The question must be asked whether this literature has any validity as a counter to historical pessimism and irrationalism. It seems inevitable that the search for the roots of their own lives must involve relating these roots to the German fascist past. This is the reason why so many texts are autobiographical in character. Jürgen Habermas has referred to these relativities in the following way:

> Mit jenem Lebenszusammenhang, in dem Auschwitz möglich war, ist unser Leben nicht etwa durch kontingente Umstände, sondern innerlich verknüpft. Unsere Lebensform ist mit der Lebensform unserer Eltern und Großeltern verbunden durch ein schwer entwirrbares Geflecht von familialen, örtlichen, politischen, auch intellektuellen Überlieferungen — durch ein geschichtliches Milieu also, das uns erst zu dem gemacht hat, was und wer wir heute sind. Niemand von uns kann sich aus diesem Milieu herausstehlen, weil mit ihm unsere Identität, sowohl als Individuum wie als Deutsche, unauflöslich verwoben ist.[2]

The 'revival' of interest in fascism can also be understood as an opening up to a historical sphere which demands the investigation of the question, in its most extreme form, about the possibilities of preserving and defending humanity (or losing it) within the frameworks of both individual and societal thought and action. My own observations show that a large portion of contemporary prose is concerned both with the problem of the personal guilt of individuals, with the way they/we respond to it and also with the 'Verstrickung der Söhne und Töchter'[3] in the 'Unterlassungshandeln ihrer Eltern und Großeltern';[4] it is a question about the continuing moral and social responsibility of our contemporaries today.

In texts which thematize fascism, the urge to remember dominates as a point of departure and emerges also as an aesthetic factor in the shaping of structures. Recollecting, keeping the memory alive enables the narrator to pursue a consciously directed process against forgetting. In many instances this process is an attempt at communication, at dialogue with the reader. The silence, the concealment through silence is forcibly breached. Dialogue is taken up with the fathers, the parents at this late point in time, when, often, they are already dead. The communicative objective is pursued in respect both of the figures in the books and of the reader. Questions, discussions, inquiry, reconstruction, remembering prove to be the most essential forms of action for the literary figures. Action in the real sense is, in part, reduced to movements in time and space or it is simply recollected.

Quite unmistakably, a major influence has been exerted on the literature of historical recollection by the techniques and tools of psychoanalysis. Repressing, not expressing, concealing, forgetting, denying, remembering, mourning, grieving, feeling guilt, losing identity — all are dominant themes and motifs of recent literature are also all fundamental categories in psychoanalysis. One decisive advantage of the psychoanalytical approach lies, in my opinion, in the way it seeks always and inexorably to make the subjective processing of historical discontinuities the precondition for society's relationship to history. Subjective *Trauerarbeit*, then, requires enlightenment about phenomena of social psychology if it is to be objectivized; in the same sense, aesthetic enlightenment can also make the 'Aufarbeitung von Vergangenheit'[5] possible. And there are differences in the consistency with which the psychoanalytical approach has been pursued in the literatures of the GDR and of the FRG.[6]

Underlying the German concept *Trauerarbeit* is an active element whose objective is not the reduction of the individual's sense of his or her own value, but rather the enhancing of their sensitivity to contradictions and discontinuities and to their own position within them. 'Die Trauerarbeit ist das auffallendste Beispiel für die mit der Erinnerung verbundenen Schmerzen [...] ein Erlebnis von Rissen und Wunden im Selbst des Trauernden.'[7]

In the current literary debate about fascism, there are, for me, two broad areas to examine: firstly, where writers give expression to the experience of historical continuity and insist on the force of moral responsibility for ensuring that fascism cannot be repeated, and, secondly, where the search for individual identity is a process of definition and demarcation in respect of one's relationship to and position vis-à-vis national history. In the first section I shall refer in particular to *Exerzierplatz* by Siegfried Lenz and to *Ein Unglücksfall* by Wolfdietrich Schnurre. The second section is subdivided into two parts, relating to texts which examine the world of children and young people in the fascist period (Gert Hofmann: *Unsere Eroberung* and *Veilchenfeld*), and the relationship between the generations (the so-called *Vaterbücher*, in particular Christoph Meckel: *Suchbild. Über meinen Vater*, Peter Schneider: *Vati*, and Gert Heidenreich: *Die Gnade der späten Geburt*).[8]

II

The relatively unbroken continuity in the existence of conditions in the Federal Republic (in terms of structures, personnel and intellectual frameworks) which make fascism possible is a source both of subjective consternation and of the impetus to write. In this context, apart from Siegfried Lenz and Wolfdietrich Schnurre, I should mention writers like Peter O. Chotjewitz, Eva Demski, Peter Härtling, Gert Hofmann, and August Kühn.[9] In many cases the motivation for writing is directly recognizable as uneasiness about the present. The degree to which past and present are interwoven becomes apparent in compositional features.

In his novel *Exerzierplatz*,[10] as in his earlier works, Siegfried Lenz goes in search of credible alternative worlds: having lost their former homeland in Silesia, the eccentric Karl Zeller and his assistant, the homeless, parentless Bruno take positive action and by dint of their work together in Zeller's tree nursery discover a sense of their own value and a new meaning in life. Zeller becomes a symbol for an individual person who conserves nature and reflects on the original abilities of human beings. Through the figure of Zeller, Lenz is able to show that a person's home is where he or she can perform meaningful, life-preserving work. In this way, Lenz's figures attempt to overcome and assimilate the past, to transcend it in the Hegelian sense. The failure of the attempt is presented as the logical consequence of a chain of events to which the individual is exposed as he struggles on, because he is endowed with moral integrity. The model might sound archaic, but it appears to the reader as the most reasonable and natural reaction to historical experiences. Past and present meet on the 'Exerzierplatz' as value-systems with irreconcilable orientations; the author gives the alternative model of thought and action no chance of success; it remains the Utopia of imaginable resistance. Hope resides in the morality of the individual.

Just as Gert Hofmann in his novel *Unsere Vergeßlichkeit* makes the basic motif of his narrative the danger of experience becoming transitory as a consequence of forgetting, so in Wolfdietrich Schnurre's novel *Ein Unglücksfall*[11] Rabbi Lesser Lovinski offers the following reason for his report on the death of master glazier Karl Goschnik during the rebuilding of the synagogue in West Berlin: 'Um dem Gleichmut keine Chance einzuräumen. Auch dem Gleichmut der anderen. Denn wer wird sich noch Goschniks erinnern?' (p. 8). Transience was indeed there in Jewish cemeteries for all to see; transience and oblivion were displayed in physical terms by the ruins of the synagogue in the middle of the business quarter which bounded them in and thus also placed them out of bounds: 'Sie hatte sich zusammengezogen. Sie war in sich reingekrochen, wie irgend so n vorsintflutliches Tier, das sich in sein Jahrtausend geirrt hat und sich nu auflösen möcht und zurück in die Vergangenheit will und sie beschwört und sich schon hinduckt zum Sprung; doch s kommt nich mehr hoch, denn die Gegenwart hat es zu Stein werden lassen' (p. 21). The glazier himself regards fundamental refusal as the only possibility of working against forgetting: 'aufhörn, fleißig zu sein müßt man können, das wär ne Tat. Aber man kann s nich. Denn dann müßt man ja auch aufhörn, vergessen zu wollen. Und nur das soll er im Augenblick ja, unser Fleiß: uns das Vergessen erleichtern' (p. 20).

Ein Unglücksfall reports, from an extraordinary narrative position, the ineradicable tragedy in the life of Karl Goschnik. With the fascist seizure of power, he takes over the business at the request of his master Avrom Grünbaum. As the threat to the lives of the Jews increases, Goschnik hides Avrom and his wife Sally in his cellar out of reach of the Nazis. However, when he is conscripted, he is no longer able to fulfil his protective role. Sally and Avrom feel that they have been doubly forgotten, robbed of their humanity; they see their suicide, by freezing to death in the snow-filled cemetery beside the grave of their prematurely deceased daughter, as salvation. Goschnik hopes for a chance of personal atonement when he begs Rabbi Lovinski to give him the task of glazing the mizrah window. A moment after he finishes his task, Goschnik tumbles from his scaffolding, destroying the window and suffering a mortal injury. In the hope of picking up the threads of guilt and of their own weakness, Goschnik, in a state between unconsciousness and death throes, and the rabbi (Avrom) tentatively revive what they had once experienced and said. Goschnik is made aware that reparation, atonement in the simple sense, is beyond reach, is therefore self-deception. Goschnik has all the features of a figure representing integration, mediation, the attempt at reconciliation between Jews and Gentiles; his thoughts and actions are moral, determined by healthy human understanding. This is true for both time-levels. His attempt to make recompense is presented literally as work; Zeller and Bruno also perform *Trauerarbeit* in the same sense.

The framework for the novel consists of the rabbi's report on the rebuilding of the synagogue, Goschnik's death, and the rabbi's reflections on his intention to quit his office. Between these come Goschnik's fevered memories, mainly monologues, indirect dialogues. Frequent changes of narrative perspective (rabbi / Goschnik / Avrom-Sally / authorial narrator), frequent shifts and leaps in time mean that the text is highly structured. This enables as many elements as possible from within the horizons of the figures to be summoned as 'contemporary' witnesses in the search for truth. The figures of Goschnik and the rabbi are set against each other as a contrasting pair who at the same time complement each other. They emerge as two different models of the way historical experience can be processed. Correspondingly, they have quite distinct levels of discourse. By dint of his intellect and his calling, Lovinski tends to favour philosophical reflection and thus lends Goschnik's recollection of events general relevance in relation to the experience of fascism; Goschnik alone could never achieve this. Lovinski comments on Goschnik's words, contradicts him and never spares him, as indeed Goschnik never spares himself. — The dialogic element, the posing and answering of questions, predominates in the text and by dint of its inconclusiveness makes demands on the reader's powers of discrimination, thus involving her or him in the dialogue.

Ein Unglücksfall aims to shake the reader both by the tragic events depicted and by the emotional power of the depiction. The cognitive process encapsulated in the contrasting complementarity of the two interlocutors is concerned with Goschnik's conflict, but it cannot now be experienced by him; it is therefore aimed more properly at the reader. Thus, the strength of the figure of Goschnik lies in his direct humanity, in his ability, against all indications, to preserve both his sensitivity and his will to act. Goschnik dares to resist and yet at the same time adapts to prevalent circumstances. He fails because of his isolation and because of his historical and political naiveté about the annihilation of the Jews; he fails also because of his mistrust of self-satisfaction. Through Goschnik then, Schnurre is pleading for active humanity: and at the same time he shares the objective of the rabbi's *Trauerarbeit*: to keep alive the memory by writing. The rabbi performs that act of witness that has central significance in Schnurre's political design.[12] To the author, writing represents the 'einzige akzeptable Form der Sühne'; it is a form of conscience-searching about his own experiences and those of his generation. 'Wenn ich meine Zeugenschaft verleugnete, meine Chronistenfunktion nicht wahrnähme, wozu schreibe ich dann?'.[13]

III

I turn now to the second broad area under discussion, the investigation of the past as a *search for identity*. The interest in the historical dimension finds expression here as the interest of the first-person narrator in himself or herself, in the individual's journey through life.

III.i

In one series of texts, the first-person narrator or a medial narrator explores the world and conflicts of children and young people in the fascist period. Attention is concentrated on everyday things, on easily surveyed spaces, on the psyche of the figures. We can observe this tendency in works by such authors as Heinrich Böll, Tankred Dorst, Gert Hofmann, August Kühn, Hanns Josef Ortheil, Klaus Stiller, and Jochen Ziem.[14] Achieving a historically adequate understanding of the period becomes problematical where the first-person perspective of the child is consistently maintained and where the view of what was experienced, limited by dint of age, is not relativized or extended by any change of perspective and yet associations of which the youngster would necessarily have been oblivious are introduced to give objectivity.[15]

In certain respects Gert Hofmann, in those of his books written from the child's point of view, is an exception here.

Schauplatz meiner Werke [...] ist der Menschenkopf, der, da es ein moderner Kopf ist, ein übersichtlicher und heikler, von allen Seiten bedrängter [...] mit sich selbst und den anderen tödlich entzweiter Kopf ist. Davon handele ich. Dabei ziehe ich es vor, daß das, was ich über ihn sagen möchte, die anderen Köpfe [der Leser oder Hörer] [...] ohne großen technischen Aufwand erreicht, der lenkt dabei womöglich nur ab. Um die Verformungen und Entstellungen unserer Köpfe — meines, deines, unser aller — aufzuzeigen, habe ich keine

Modulation oder Fiebergeräte, sondern, nach alter Schriftstellerart, die Sprache nötig, die unverstellt und nackt sein darf.[16]

Hofmann seeks out the causes of and background to patterns of behaviour hidden in patterns of speech, he shows how the patterns established during childhood ('Kindheitsmuster') assimilate the rules of the game through patterns of language. The story *Veilchenfeld* and the novel *Unsere Eroberung*[17] are of interest here.

Unsere Eroberung presents the experience of children in the little township of L. on 8 May 1945, the day of the 'conquest'. The children of whipmaker Imbach, 12—13 year old boys, and the somewhat older son of a factory worker want to go into the town to see the conquerors and to find out '[was sich] eben so verändert hat'. The action comprises their walk through the town and the constant clash between the depressing, grotesque images of the adult world and the children's viewpoint and insight. In this way misunderstandings are laid bare which prepare the ground for disastrous behavioural norms (the bigotry of those with possessions, lies, concealing the truth, narrow-mindedness, violence). Hofmann holds up our language to us for closer examination. The children's vivid, symbolic language provides a richer range of meaning than that proffered by any superficial report of experience. Through the way it is represented, what has been seen, heard, spoken acquires the qualities of a model, a parable of basic human behaviour. The encounters with grown-ups, which take place (with obvious symbolism) in the abbatoir, the church and the theatre, are intended to bring home the significance of experiences which individuals have not yet been able to internalize. All of the happenings and observations are presented in a first-person-plural perspective, but the dimensions of this first person plural remain open: it includes (at least) two children and both the reader and the author — who might conceivably have comparable experiences to contribute. The children speak with one voice, think with one mind. For the reader, the appeal arises from the discrepancy between what the children actually see, recount, what they comprehend (or do not comprehend) and what stands behind the happenings, behind the language-patterns. The historical distance from that time and the uninterrupted continuity in the existence of thought- and speech-patterns (clichés, formulae) constrain the reader to critical self-reflection.[18]

In his story *Veilchenfeld*, the author again uses a child-narrator to experience and recount events and again the frequent use of the first person plural indicates collective experiences. The setting for these fragmentarily recollected episodes, pictures, conversations, dreams is the adult world of a small town. The Jewish Professor Veilchenfeld does not become the centre of the story because of the evidential value of his life of suffering. What interests the author is rather how it can be possible for a human being to be gradually destroyed right in the midst of a community of other human beings. He is interested in the behaviour, the action and inaction, the speech- and thought-patterns of the townspeople. The young lad registers his observations faithfully, without prejudice and without making direct value judgements. Silence, indifference, cowardice, selective ignorance and fear are denounced as forms of behaviour which are of service to fascism.

The way parents, without reflection, drew their children into their culpability is revealed in the rules of behaviour enunciated by the mother:

> Wie die Dinge liegen, solltet ihr ihn auf der Straße lieber nicht mehr ansprechen, sagte die Mutter immer, wenn wir an ihm vorbei waren. Und grüßen, fragten wir die Mutter, sollen wir ihn noch grüßen? Nein sagte die Mutter, auch nicht grüßen. Sondern wir sollten so tun, als kennten wir ihn nicht, als sei er schon nicht mehr vorhanden. Und wenn er grüßt? Mein Gott, rief die Mutter und warf die Arme hoch, so taktlos wird er wohl nicht sein. (p. 9)

The tone of the story remains unemotional, designatory throughout. Hofmann's strategy for the discovery of reality follows the unprejudiced observation, directness, neutrality and naiveté of children, which allows what is perceived to emerge in completely unadulterated form.

III.ii

I now come to my other model of the search for individual identity. In the so-called *Vaterbücher*, the search for the self is a laborious, largely contradictory process which examines critically the guilt or complicity of the fathers. The process of comprehending the individual's own identity through learning to understand the fathers' identity (and it is mostly an autobiographical process) here acquires a historical framework. By examining the person to whom the individual has related most closely for so many years, she or he hopes to draw closer to her or his own past, to the point of origin of their own socialization. To some extent it is possible to deduce from the social position of the father figures in fascist society what their class stood for in that society and also to learn something about the way values have been communicated within the family. Compared with the tendency towards *Vatermord* common in German Expressionism, the forty- and fifty-year-old authors of the 1980s vacillate between 'Annäherung und Ablehnung, Anziehung und Abstoßung'.[19] Thus, according to Michael Schneider, the wave of *Vaterbücher* which started in the early 1980s bears witness to 'einer tiefgreifenden Störung im Verhältnis der Generationen, die offenbar spezifische historische Ursachen hat und weit über jenen klassischen (ödipalen) Konflikt hinausgeht, der jedes Generationsverhältnis zu bestimmten Zeiten mehr oder weniger prägt'.[20] While the figure of the son in Peter Härtling's *Nachgetragene Liebe*,[21] at the end of the novel, summarizes his motivation for going back to his roots: he wanted to understand his father, to stop having to defend himself and to read the traces left behind by his father. His conclusion: 'Ich fange an, dich zu lieben' (p. 168). Thus the denial and rejection of the guilt-laden generation of the fathers, which, at the end of the 1960s, had been violent and uncompromising, changed in the 1970s and early 1980s, with the development a certain readiness to come to terms, to a critical, yet productive attitude to the historical failure of the parental generation. It would, however, in my view, be inappropriate to characterize this new approach as a process of reconcilitation with the fathers, if only because this would imply a lack of differentiation between the many and varied ways in which it has been articulated.[22]

The attempt to get closer to the fathers occurs most frequently at a time when the latter have just died. Death seems to remove the fear of contact. The intimate, mostly posthumous discussions arising out of and centring on recollection and memory are complemented and objectivized by reference to diaries, letters, information from third parties and documents of the time. Fathers from many social groups are represented: petty bourgeoisie, civil servants, white collar workers, intellectuals, representatives of National Socialism. What is not represented is the proletariat. — It would be instructive to make a comparison at this point, although we cannot pursue this in the present context, with the depiction of generational problems in *Die Ästhetik des Widerstands* by Peter Weiss.[23]

The list of *Vaterbücher* is very long,[24] I have selected just two for discussion here which contain views of the 'father problem' that are less well represented elsewhere: Christoph Meckel's *Suchbild. Über meinen Vater* and Peter Schneider's *Vati*.

Meckel's *Suchbild*[25] is conceived as an attempt to get closer to the poet Eberhard Meckel. Here again biographical detail forms the basis for reflection. The narrator is caught in an uncompromising polemic with the aesthetic position of his father and out of this he arrives at a definition of his own position in terms of his attitude to life in general and to his art. While his father remained unaware of his role as a conservative middle-class intellectual under Hitler's fascism, the son seeks to uncover the actual dangers inherent in a view of the world and an understanding of art which is dedicated to and limited to the power and dignity of the mind, to 'eternal' values. Meckel depicts the limitations of a bourgeois belief in the intellect, which '[sich] verkroch in die Jahreszeiten, im Ewigen, Überzeitlichen' and could not escape assisting the rule of fascism. This constitutes a critique of an attitude of mind which is ahistorical and anthropological. The narrator's motivation for writing seems to lie in the relevance for us today of a basic attitude which is shown, from the antifascist point of view, to be untenable. At the same time I see Meckel's *Suchbild* as a contribution to the debate about two essential questions: How should a critical examination of fascism be conducted in art? Are certain philosophical and aesthetic concepts unsuitable a priori to expose the character and essence of fascism?

The slim volume by Peter Schneider, *Vati*,[26] differs in some respects from the the other *Vaterbücher*. Here the first-person narrator is an adult when he first comes face to face with his father, the fascist doctor, director of a euthanasia programme, who had escaped to South America. A critical comparison of experiences is still possible between them. Thus the story presents the attempt at communication with the 'meistgesuchter Mann der Welt' (p. 29). The narrator, however, strives to achieve communication at three levels: with a friend (in the form of a fictitious dialogue), through this also simultaneously with the reader, and with his father.

The reconstruction of the meeting, the recollection of events from childhood, snippets of dialogue with his father are complemented in essayistic passages which constitute an attempt above all at a polemical discussion of the various relationships of the 1968 generation to their fathers. Rather than any polemic with his father, the purpose of these passages seems to be the justification of individual decisions vis-à-vis the norms of the individual's own generation. The search for an individual identity seems to fail because of the dominance of his father, because the ideology the latter has lived out is unshakeable, even though he is now limited to an insular existence and any effect he seeks to have misfires as he becomes a caricature of himself. His growing son had become aware, from signs he was at first unable to understand, that a secret was attached to his name. His surname and his nickname stood 'für ein Vergehen, das ich gar nicht begangen hatte' (p. 15). Long before he knew why, he had sensed that he had been 'schuldig geboren'.[27]

The difficult process of gaining access to his own identity is accompanied by the fictitious dialogue with his former fellow-student, to whom the narrator feels obliged to explain and defend himself and whom he knows to hold positions contrary to his own. Only this friend is given no individual qualities. He serves simply as a symbol for the 'patricide' variant in the narrator's own generation. This friend had declared his own father dead when, in some archives, he had come across an article written in 1943 in which his father had set out his fascist views. To the narrator, this 'endgültige Lösung des Vaterproblemchens' seems 'lieblos und vorlaut' (p. 29). The absurdity of the break with the father proclaimed in this way, coupled with the acceptance of the monthly cheque from him, is met by the narrator with swingeing irony — and a touch of self-pity: 'Es war mir, als hätte ich allein und als einziger eine Last zu tragen, von der ihr alle nur geredet habt. Mit dem Ausbruchsversuch von 68 [...] habe ich sympathisiert. Die Hoffnung aber, ich könnte mich durch ein paar hastig erlernte Zitate von Mao und Che Guevara von meinem Vater befreien, war mir nie erlaubt' (p. 29).

In an essay published almost at the same time as *Vati*, 'Im Todeskreis der Schuld',[28] a critical analysis of positions assumed by participants in the *Historikerstreit*, Schneider draws some conclusions about the limits and limitations of antifascism in the context of the student movement and of left-wing terrorism and its supposed proximity to fascist methods and patterns of thought. As he sees it, the left-wing movement had been able to be so radical in its anti-authoritarian revolt against their 'fathers' only because they had reduced fascism as a concept to 'allgemeine und übertragbare sozialökonomische Strukturmerkmale.' In Schneider's view, this had meant that they had defamed political opponents indiscriminately and had, thus, never been forced '[sich] mit dem jeweils konkreten und persönlichen Schuldanteil der

Väter auseinanderzusetzen und folglich mit unserer Verstrickung als deren Söhne und Töchter'. Hence his conclusion: 'dieser Antifaschismus war weder historisch noch emotional erarbeitet'.

Within the limited possibilities of the genre, Schneider's story is an attempt to open himself up sensitively to the responsibility of the younger generation and to make himself aware of the difficulty of gaining freedom for the self. What predominates in the story is the illumination of the emotional, the psychological structure of the relations between father and son; the presentation of them is sober, laconic. When the narrator receives his father's address it is 'like a wound' (p. 8) in his head; first and foremost, he promises himself healing from the confrontation. Although 'nicht hinfahren wäre zweifellos bequemer gewesen' (p. 7). This desire on the narrator's part to communicate with the reader is shown also in the way he displays the sources of friction in the conflict with his father, for he is aware, even as he sets out on the journey to meet his father, of the differences between them, he wants '[ihn] zur Rede stellen, ihn dazu bewegen, sich vor einem deutschen Gericht zu verantworten [...] ich wollte durch ihn erlöst werden — oder mich und die Welt von ihm erlösen' (p. 31). Their identities are superimposed in flashes of illusion: 'Ich lag im Bett meines Vaters an seiner Stelle und wartete auf meine Verfolger' (p. 51). The methods of presentation are chosen to indicate the son's fear that, apart from secondary similarities in features which betray the close relationship, he might also have inherited social attitudes with many more implications: his father's view of the world, his ethics, his approach to science, his awareness of élites, his concept of culture and so on.

He defends himself against this suspicion, on the one hand, by fleeing and, on the other, by making himself aware of his fear '[durch die] wissenschaftlichen Erläuterungen des Vaters intellektuell überrannt zu werden'. However, the son's vulnerability begins to show and the narrator's reaction is to resort to near caricature: he reports fragments of the father's speeches, their content and the speaker's behaviour, painting the primeval forest scenery as a stage-setting for the presentation of the father's attitude of mind, which emerges as a relic from the past. '"Ach Vati, deine Substantive!" — mehr ist mir in meiner Erschöpfung nicht eingefallen' (p. 53).

The critical analysis here has implications far beyond the text itself; its concern is with the reader and his or her *Trauerarbeit*.[29] I hold the view that, because of its chosen subject (a high-ranking Nazi as the father), the pronounced internalization of the debate and the narrator's patent social responsibility, Schneider's story helps our subjective attempts at overcoming the past to acquire historical dimensions. This is also helped by the way the father's conservative position in philosophy and attitude to life shows current conservative thinking in a different light by extending it backwards in time. The dispute with the father's ideology becomes the reponsibility of the reader. Put in more radical terms, the story constitutes an open polemic against the idea of the 'Gnade der späten Geburt'. It achieves its effect, in my view, by the (sometimes conflicting) combination of narrative and essayistic elements. It was this idea of the 'Gnade der späten Geburt', because it enabled the younger generation to feel that they were free of blame and free of all limitation on thought and action, that caused some writers to provide a literary antidote to the idea, among them Gert Heidenreich, in particular in the titular story of his collection *Die Gnade der späten Geburt*.[30]

Heidenreich regards it is as a prerequisite for a meaningful future existence that the generations work towards mutual understanding:

> Sich der eigenen Geschichte und der daraus folgenden individuellen wie sozialen Konsequenzen zu versperren, ist die für den Einzelnen wohl am schwierigsten zu erkennende, in ihren politischen Folgen zugleich am schwersten wiegende Form der Resignation. Der qualitative Widerspruch zwischen Trauer und hoffnungsloser Traurigkeit wird politisch wirksam: Die Unfähigkeit zu trauern mit ihrem für die Eltern gnädigen Effekt der Verdrängung verleitet die Kinder zu einem geschichtslosen Dahintaumeln unter der Devise "alles egal"; sie fallen damit, von den Älteren preisgegeben, in die allseitige Bezugslosigkeit. Dieselben Älteren, die diesen Zustand mit verursachten, beklagen dann vehement die Orientierungslosigkeit und Mangel an Sinngebung bei den Jüngeren.[31]

IV

There is hardly a subject, in my view, where it is more necessary to elucidate the relevant texts both in terms of the literary process itself and also in terms of the social context which has given rise to this literature and in which this literature will have its effect, than in the case of texts which explore the location of the individual in fascism and the way the individual later seeks to come to terms with this. To me, some reference to this context is absolutely essential, if we are to throw light on the communicative process between literature and other forms of the societal consciousness. By way of conclusion, I offer a summary of my position in the following six points:

1. The late 1970s and early 1980s saw an intensification of the debate about matters to do with the nation, 'national identity', the 'German Question'. History as a discipline gained in public importance, historical awareness took on a strong national orientation.

2. Here I shall rely on a quotation from Christoph Hein's speech in November 1989 to the Berlin branch of the *Schriftstellerverband*:

> Der Westdeutsche Historikerstreit von 1986, in dem auch eine Um- und Neubewertung des Faschismus und seiner Verbrechen und Ursachen des Zweiten Weltkrieges versucht wurde, hatte [...] Auswirkungen auf die westdeutsche Gesellschaft. Nach diesem Streit [...] gelang es einer Partei, die als rechtsradikal und sogar faschistisch eingeschätzt wird, in der Gesellschaft Fuß zu fassen [...] Ich erwähne dies, um auf den Zusammenhang einer Gesellschaft mit ihrer Betrachtung der Geschichte, zumal der jüngeren Geschichte, zu verweisen.[32]

3. Nationalist, neofascist ideologies and political groups are gaining in acceptance. This is, however, a tendency not limited to the FRG: In France, Le Pen gained 11% of the votes in the 1984 parliamentary elections; right-wing intellectual potential is growing in the Soviet Union, and it is a fact that can no longer be ignored in the GDR, where the *Republikaner* have been in existence officially since the beginning of 1990, when they founded a local association in Leipzig.

4. I used the term 'Entsorgung' (disposal, particularly the disposal of dangerous or toxic waste) in relation to the critical debate about fascism. Helmut Peitsch, in his article 'Die problematische Entdeckung nationaler Identität',[33] refers to the original use of *Entsorgung* by Dolf Sternberger. Jürgen Habermas uses the term in his essay 'Entsorgung der Vergangenheit' as his point of departure for his critical attack on the re-working of history in the FRG.[34] In adopting this concept from the ecological sphere for use in relation to the way historical experiences are treated, the implications of the idea of 'waste disposal' are addressed, as they must be if there is to be a view of the past which does not diminish the Germans' feeling for their own national value. *Entsorgung* implies that the historical responsibility of future generations for the crimes of fascism is removed even for the individual.

5. It is my view that literature can only bring new meaning to the critical debate about the past when it is guided by responsibility for the future.
— Gert Heidenreich argues that literature must think 'phantasievoll auf

Humanität hin', in order to save generations of children from 'einem geschichtlosen Dahintaumeln'.[35]

6. I have sought quite deliberately to replace the usual concept of 'overcoming the past' (*Bewältigung der Vergangenheit*) by that of 'active recollection' (*Erinnerungsarbeit*). My aim was to focus on the idea that this is a process. — Stephan Hermlin used a metaphor for this process which I find quite convincing:

> Ich habe mich zu allen Zeiten gegen die These von der bewältigten Vergangenheit gewandt. Vergangenheit kann allenfalls so bewältigt werden, wie Sisyphus seinen Stein den Berg hinaufrollt. Der entgleitet ihm immer wieder, und er muß von vorn beginnen. Das ist das Schicksal der Antifaschisten — Sysiphus zu sein und einen unablässigen Kampf zu führen, der nie aufhört. Der einzelne Mensch mag aufhören, dann müssen die nächsten die Verantwortung weitertragen.[36]

NOTES

Translation by Arthur Williams.

1   Gerd Fuchs, quoted in Uwe Naumann (ed.): *Sammlung 4. Jahrbuch für antifaschistische Literatur und Kunst*, Frankfurt/Main, 1981.

2   Jürgen Habermas: 'Vom öffentlichen Gebrauch der Historie. Das offizielle Selbstverständnis der Bundesrepublik bricht auf', *Die Zeit*, no. 46, 1986, pp. 12f.

3   Peter Schneider: 'Im Todeskreis der Schuld', *Die Zeit*, no. 14, 1987, pp. 65f.

4   Habermas: 'Vom öffentlichen Gebrauch...'.

5   Theodor W. Adorno: 'Was bedeutet: Aufarbeitung der Vergangenheit' in Adorno: *Eingriffe. Neun kritische Modelle*, Frankfurt/Main, 1963, pp. 125ff.

6   The GDR's understanding of itself as an antifascist state (which was enshrined in the law) meant that the individual could be spared any individual, internalized need to relate to the historical responsibility of the Germans. This was detrimental to the subjective process of experiencing and coming to terms with this reponsibility and could not be compensated by a presupposed definition of the collective self.

7   Alexander Mitscherlich: 'Die Unfähigkeit zu trauern — womit zusammenhängt, eine deutsche Art zu lieben' in Mitscherlich: *Gesammelte Schriften IV. Sozialpsychologie 2* ed. by Klaus Menne, Frankfurt/Main, 1983, p. 78.

8   The original article contained a brief section on Jewish identity. The recollections of Jewish victims of fascism and our memories of them have a particular role to play in the debate about the problems of identity and, narrated in the perspective of the victims, serve to highlight through alienation (in the Brechtian sense) the failings and responsibilities of every German today. Saul Friedländer, in his essay 'Die Last der Vergangenheit' (in Wolfgang Wippermann (ed.): *Der konsequente Wahn. Ideologie und Politik Adolf Hitlers*, Munich, 1989) investigated comparatively the divergent 'Entwicklung deutscher und jüdischer Gedächtnisstrukturen in bezug auf die nationalsozialistische Epoche' and the drastic reversals within them. The period upto about the end of the 1950s or the mid-1960s was dominated in the Jewish world by relative silence about the annihilation of european Jewry. It was only in the mid-1960s that a clear interest in the history of the holocaust developed among the Jewish diaspora in the context of the struggle in America of other minorities for the preservation of their own particular ethnic qualities. The 'Shoah' became a crucial factor in Jewish identity. The following texts are of relevance here: Inge Deutschkorn: *Ich trage den gelben Stern*,

Cologne, 1978; Fania Fenelon: *Mädchenorchester in Auschwitz*, Frankfurt/Main, 1980: Ralph Giordano: *Die Bertinis*, Frankfurt/Main, 1985; Edgar Hilsenrath: *Nacht*, Cologne, 1978; Ilse Koehn: *Mischling zweiten Grades*, Reinbek, 1979; Valentin Senger: *Kaiserhofstr. 12*, Darmstadt, 1978.

9   Peter O. Chotjewitz: *Saumlos*, Königstein/Ts., 1980; Eva Demski: *Hotel Hölle, Guten Tag*, Munich, 1987; Peter Härtling: *Felix Guttmann*, Darmstadt, 1985; Gert Hofmann: *Die Denunziation*, Darmstadt, 1979; *Veilchenfeld*, Darmstadt, 1986; *Unsere Vergeßlichkeit*, Darmstadt, 1987; August Kühn: *Wir kehren langsam zur Natur zurück*, Munich, 1984.

10 Siegfried Lenz: *Exerzierplatz*, Hamburg, 1985. The edition available to the author was published by the Aufbau-Verlag, Berlin (GDR), 1986.

11 Wolfdietrich Schnurre: *Ein Unglücksfall*, Munich, 1981. The edition available to the author was published by the Aufbau-Verlag, Berlin (GDR), 1983.

12 I want to draw attention, without further comment, also to the imagery of the novel, which constitutes an additional link between past and present.

13 Peter Sandmeyer: 'Schreiben nach 1945. Ein Interview mit Wolfdietrich Schnurre', *Literaturmagazin 7*, Reinbek, 1977, pp. 191—202.

14 Heinrich Böll: *Was soll aus dem Jungen bloß werden*, Bornheim, 1981; Tankred Dorst: *Die Reise nach Stettin*, Frankfurt/Main, 1984; Gert Hofmann: *Unsere Eroberung*, Darmstadt, 1984, and *Veilchenfeld*; August Kühn: *Jahrgang 1922 oder Die Merkwürdigkeiten im Leben des Fritz Wachsmuth*, Munich, 1977; Hanns Josef Ortheil: *Hecke*, Frankfurt/Main, 1983; Klaus Stiller: *Weihnachten*, Munich, 1980; Jochen Ziem: *Der Junge*, Munich, 1980.

15 An attempt was made to create a synthesis between the life-stories of individuals and the representation of objective historical processes by Max von der Grün in *Wie war das eigentlich? Kindheit und Jugend im Dritten Reich*, Darmstadt, 1979.

16 Gert Hofmann: 'Hörspiel und Literatur. Rede anläßlich der Verleihung des "Hörspielpreises der Kriegsblinden 1982"' in Hans Christian Kosler (ed.): *Gert Hofmann: Auskunft für Leser*, Darmstadt, 1987, p. 33f.

17 References are to the edition published by the Aufbau-Verlag, Berlin (GDR), 1985.

18 The technique here is close to that examined in some detail by Katrin Kohl, pp. 339—56 below.

19 Sylvia Adrian: 'Im Brachland der Gefühle. Ein Rückblick auf die deutsche Literatur über Vaterfiguren' in Volker Hage and Adolf Fink (eds): *Deutsche Literatur 1981. Ein Jahresüberblick*, Stuttgart, 1982, pp. 241—7. See also Julian's Preece's discussion of aspects of this phenomenon, esp. pp. 303—8 below.

20 Michael Schneider: 'Väter und Söhne, posthum. Das beschädigte Verhältnis zweier Generationen' in Schneider: *Den Kopf verkehrt aufgesetzt oder Die melancholische Linke*, Darmstadt, 1981, pp. 8—64; here p. 9.

21 Peter Härtling: *Nachgetragene Liebe*, Darmstadt, 1980 (edition used: 1982). Ian Huish (pp. 243—52 below; esp. pp. 248—51) discusses Härtling's works from an angle closer to that of section III.i (pp. 231—3) of the present essay.

22 Cf. positions depicted by Michael Schneider in 'Väter und Söhne, posthum...'.

23 Peter Weiss: *Die Ästhetik des Widerstands*, Berlin, 1983.

24 I should like to draw attention to just a few: Siegfrid Gauch: *Vaterspuren*, Königstein/Ts., 1979; Peter Härtling: *Nachgetragene Liebe*; Roland Lang: *Die Mansarde*, Königstein/Ts., 1979; Ruth Rehmann: *Der Mann auf der Kanzel*, Munich, 1979.

25 Christoph Meckel: *Suchbild. Über meinen Vater*, Düsseldorf, 1980.

26 Peter Schneider: *Vati. Erzählung*, Darmstadt, 1987.

27 These problems are confronted at a greater aesthetic distance in the work of Botho Strauß, particularly in *Rumor*. See Strauß's appeal for a past of his own as discussed by Arthur Williams, p. 452 below.

28 Peter Schneider: 'Im Todeskreis der Schuld', *Die Zeit*, no. 14, 1987, pp. 65f.

29 For an analysis which takes a totally different approach to *Vati* see Gordon Burgess: '"Was da ist, das ist [nicht] mein": The Case of Peter Schneider' in Arthur Williams, Stuart Parkes and Roland Smith (eds): *Literature on the Threshold. The German Novel in the 1980s*, Oxford, 1990, pp. 107—22.

30 Gert Heidenreich: *Die Gnade der späten Geburt. Sechs Erzählungen*, Munich, 1986.

31 Gert Heidenreich in: *Und sie bewegt sich doch... Texte wider die Resignation*, published by the Fischer Taschenbuchverlag, Frankfurt/Main, no date.

32 Christoph Hein: 'Rede auf der Versammlung des Bezirksverbandes Berlin des Schriftstellerverbandes der DDR, 14. September 1989', *ndl*, no. 1, 1990, p. 147. Since, in this context, Hein deliberately directs his attention solely to the negative effects of the 'new evaluation', I want to add the following. The *Historikerstreit* caused a polarization both among West German historians and within West German society, thus arousing antifascist potential among the intellectuals, which has found expression in such publications as: *Historikerstreit. Die Dokumentation der Kontroverse um die Einzigartigkeit der nationalsozialistischen Judenvernichtung*, Munich, 1987; Reinhard Kühnl (ed.): *Vergangenheit, die nicht vergeht*, Cologne, 1987; Hilmar Hoffmann (ed.): *Gegen den Versuch, Vergangenheit zu verbiegen*, Frankfurt/Main, 1987. Between summer 1986 and the end of 1987 there was a growning number of pubications in the West German press (above all in *FAZ, Die Zeit, Merkur, Die historische Zeitschrift, Blätter für deutsche und internationale Politik*) as well as both radio and television programmes on the (re-) evaluation the fascist German past. In addition, a number of conferences and colloquia were held by historians on the problem of the historical evaluation of the National Socialist period in the public consciousness (the three most notable were held in June 1986 at Römerberg, Frankfurt/Main: 'Politische Kultur heute?', in October 1986 in West Berlin: 'Wem gehört die deutsche Geschichte?', and in January 1987 in Frankfurt/Main: 'Auschwitz, Buchenwald, Dachau — Verdrängen oder Bewältigen?'). The first foundations for what became a vehement series of exchanges were laid in publications by the historians Ernst Nolte (West Berlin), Michael Stürmer (Erlangen) and Andreas Hillgruber (Cologne). The fact that these exchanges became the Historiker*streit* as which they as known, and that the indubitably divergent views held by both academics and journalists were meaningfully differentiated in relation to this theme is due in the main to the unequivocal interventions of the Frankfurt philosopher and sociologist Jürgen Habermas. The contentious points were: the imperialist aggression of Hitler's Germany was interpreted as a preemptive war (Hitler had simply anticipated Stalin's intentions); the question of the originality, uniqueness and singularity of the crimes of German fascism, in particular of its anti-Semitism and genocide against the Jews, was reopened and subjected to a thorough revision by the way it was answered (Nolte mounted a general attack on historical fact and attempted, in principle, a reassessment of the perpetrators and their victims); it was generally possible to recognize the objective (in the relativization of historical fact and the historicization of the crimes of fascism) of classifying fascism as part of the normal processes of universal history; the view was propounded that the history of the Third Reich had been written largely by the victors in the war and had thus become a negative myth (the emphasis on the absolute necessity of a reevalution of historical events from a *national* point of view, i.e. by German historians). See also my article: 'Der "Historikerstreit" im Widerschein der konservativen geistigen Wendepolitik der 80er Jahre' in Wilhelm-Pieck-Universität: *Neues Denken und Reformpolitik in der BRD und in Hamburg am Übergang zu den neunziger Jahren. Materialien des XI. Wissenschaftlichen Kolloquiums der Forschungsgruppe 6, "Regionale Imperialismusforschung" der Sektion Marxismus-Leninismus am 21./22. September 1988*, Rostock, 1989.

33 Helmut Peitsch: 'Die problematische Entdeckung nationaler Identität. Westdeutsche Literatur am Beginn der 80er Jahre', *Diskussion Deutsch*, vol. 18, no. 96, 1987, pp. 373—92.

34 Jürgen Habermas: 'Entsorgung der Vergangenheit' in Habermas: *Die neue Unübersichtlichkeit*, Frankfurt/Main, 1985.

35 Heidenreich in *Und sie bewegt sich doch...*

36 Stephan Hermlin: 'Dies ist das Schicksal der Antifaschisten: Sisyphus sein', interview in *Junge Welt*, 16 September 1988.

THE ADULT WRITER IN A CHILD'S WORLD:
SOME REFLECTIONS ON
PETER HÄRTLING AND THE *KINDERROMAN*

IAN HUISH

I

When Leo states at the opening of *The Go-Between* that 'the past is a for-eign country',[1] he is immediately inviting the reader to share a sense of the topography of past and present. In many of Peter Härtling's novels, and notably in the *Kinderroman: Krücke*, published in 1987,[2] there is a search, a journey, which involves a return to the past. The past as a place which may be re-discovered is, of course, an idea that has been repeat-edly explored in literature, and one that seems particularly to appeal to our own age: Proust's monument to the past and to recalling that past, *A la recherche du temps perdu*,[3] rightly stands as a central work of the twen-tieth century. This is also the century in which psychoanalysis has high-lighted the crucial importance for our subsequent development of the world that we live in as children. It is the task of analysis to give back the key to that 'foreign country'; often it is the self-imposed task of the writer to lead the reader back into the lost world of childhood.

This may be done in a variety of ways: for example, writing as a child with a child's perceptions, where Jona Oberski's brilliant recollec-tions of his very early childhood in a concentration camp come to mind;[4] writing about children from an adult perspective, as in Horváth's novel *Jugend ohne Gott*;[5] using the framework narration device, as L. P. Hartley does in *The Go-Between*,[6] to exploit the double perspective of child and adult; juxtaposing scenes with adults and scenes with children, as in Wedekind's tragic drama of childhood and adolescence *Frühlings Erwachen*;[7] or, in the deceptive way that some writers of children's books approach the subject, making the sun shine on farmyards full of good-natured animals and happy children who are permanently on holiday. It is, I suspect, this latter category that Härtling had in mind when, with children of his own, he began to write for children:

Es gibt eine Literatur für Kinder, deren Verlogenheit kränkend ist. Die Welt wird verschönt, verkleinert, bekommt Wohnstubengröße [...] Als ich dann meinen Kindern vorlas, ärgerte ich mich über manches Buch. Ich fing an, Kinderbücher zu besprechen. Und ich stellte fest, daß die Literatur überaus aufmerksame, spontane, kritische, phantasievolle Leser nicht ernst nahm. Das war der Anstoß: Versuch es selber, meckere nicht über andere.[8]

Härtling writes in his *Kinderromane* of children who have lost their parents, of children who feel themselves to be outcasts and of handicapped children. The realities of Härtling's own childhood, the death of his father (in 1945) in a Russian prisoner of war camp and his mother's suicide the following year,[9] ensured that he had no cosy, over-protected image of the child's world, and he has repeatedly stressed the importance of writing honestly about difficult topics.[10] *Das war der Hirbel*, his first *Kinderroman*, which appeared in 1973 when its author was forty years old and father of four, deals with a mentally retarded child in a home for handicapped children.

The novel went on to be a best-seller not only in Germany but in a large number of other countries, including Japan. Clearly it crossed cultural frontiers and dealt with a topic that was as valid in the oriental as in the occidental world. Its popularity is particularly significant when we remember that for Germany the treatment of mental handicap still had uncomfortable echoes, as the extreme nature of two early reviews perhaps suggests. They also typify reactions in the West German press, which oscillated between proselytizing praise: 'Man müßte dieses Buch zur Pflichtlektüre machen und es über Eltern und Grundschullehrer an die Acht- und Zehnjährigen im Land verteilen [...] Dieses Kinderbuch darf nicht nur in den Kinderzimmern von fortschrittlichen Eltern verschwinden: Dieses Kinderbuch muß von allen Kindern gelesen werden.'[11] And outraged sensibility: 'Härtling hat an einer Falldarstellung, obgleich sie sich an Kinder richtet, nichts gemildert. Es wird klar, daß Hirbel keine Chance hat. Schon der Titel klingt wie ein Nachruf. Man sollte Kinder, zumal sensible, mit diesem Buch nicht allein lassen.'[12]

Hirbel may be handicapped, but he is no lame duck, no pathetic object of the reader's sympathy. Härtling achieves the desired aim of making Hirbel's character the true subject of the story by letting us feel not only his frustrations and rages but also his manipulative power and mischief. The following episode, in which the reader is allowed to share Hirbel's seemingly magical hypnotic powers, is a good example of this. The janitor at the children's home, Herr Schoppenstecher (*nomen est omen* since he is a heavy drinker) is Hirbel's particular enemy and takes it upon himself to find Hirbel at fault for anything that goes wrong. Hirbel has watched one of the other boys 'hypnotizing' one of the five rather repulsive chickens kept by Herr Schoppenstecher. He decides that he, Hirbel, can go one better!

> Hirbel hatte vor, alle fünf Hühner aus Rache zu 'hypnotisieren'.
> An einem Freitag entschloß sich Hirbel zur Tat. Herr Schoppenstecher war weg, Frau Schoppenstecher litt an Asthma und lag im Bett. Die Hühner waren ihr auch gleichgültig. Sie gehörten ihrem Mann.
> Hirbel ging in den Stall und fing ein Huhn nach dem anderen, legte es auf den Rücken, und am Ende lagen fünf Hühner schön aufgereiht völlig regungslos da. Hirbel hatte sie hypnotisiert. Während er die Hühner fing, hatte er Angst, jemand könnte wegen des Gegackers kommen. Er hatte Glück. Es kam niemand.
> Herrn Schoppenstecher, als er mit dem Lieferwagen zurückkam, fiel nicht gleich auf, was mit seinen Hühnern geschehen war [...] erst am Nachmittag, als er die Hühner füttern wollte, sah er das Unglück. Er lief durchs Haus, schrie: Man hat sie umgebracht! Alle umgebracht![13]

Here Härtling reverses the power situation to such an extent that we almost begin to feel a glimmer of pity for the brutish, bullying and alcoholic Schoppenstecher; certainly we are allowed to participate fully in Hirbel's victories and his sense of *Schadenfreude* both on this and on other occasions. Of course Hirbel does not ultimately win against the authorities, nor against his handicap, but like Jules Renard's Poil de Carotte many years before him and Christopher Nolan's Joseph Meehan some years later, it is neither the handicap nor the victimization that we remember, but the dignity with which a very real human being experiences his sufferings, and the subtle and effective ways in which he learns to combat those sufferings.[14] That Peter Härtling should have chosen a child suffering from a concrete handicap as the hero of his first *Kinderroman* is a powerful means of expressing a sense of deprivation: of what most children consider to be a normal upbringing.

II

Härtling has now written seven children's novels in all, but before writing *Das war der Hirbel* and in the years since then he has also written poetry, novels and critical articles, as well as introductions to a vast range of other people's work.[15] Much of his own writing has been autobiographical fiction and fictionalized autobiography: at times it is difficult to disentangle the two. Yet it seems to me that the autobiographical material in the *Kinderromane* is an essentially positive element, for whereas the adult writer writing for an adult audience will often veil and distort the relationship between fiction and reality, through stylistic devices and narratorial games, Härtling suggests that children cannot be duped and played with so easily: 'Verschleiern kann man aber bei Kindern nicht: die merken das sofort. Kinder sind ein tolles Publikum. Die besondere Schwierigkeit bei Kinderbuch-Autoren ist eben, Zusammenhänge einfach, schlüssig und anschaulich zu schreiben.'[16]

This last sentence would seem to point up a problem that Härtling found particularly tricky in his next *Kinderroman*, one of his most successful, *Oma*, published in 1975 and awarded the *Deutscher Jugendliteraturpreis* in the following year. Interestingly, it comes a little closer to Härtling's own autobiography than Hirbel had done, in that the boy Kalle loses both of his parents in a car crash when he is only five years old. Kalle is taken in and taken on by the magnificently robust Oma of the title, Frau Erna Bittel, a woman to be feared by bureaucrats, schoolteachers and school bullies, but herself terrified of flying, of betraying her own vulnerability, and not averse to fairly regular nips at the schnaps bottle. Despite the immense success of this book it seems to me a less satisfying work, in that each chapter ends with a narratorial comment from Oma, as if the author felt he had failed to communicate her feelings in the body of the text. By comparing and contrasting youth and age in this way it does give the reader a double perspective, but the narrative unity is thereby destroyed. When writing about children's emotions Peter Härtling is sure-footed, and seldom is there a false note (Kalle's perceptions of the old woman are beautifully apt and poignant), but Oma's own observations ring less true. If the past of childhood is a foreign country, but one that can be re-discovered, the future of old age is a land not yet charted that can only be fantasized about.

The chapter 'Oma besucht eine Freundin im Altersheim' illustrates the problem quite clearly. The writing, while we experience the visit through Kalle's eyes, is powerful and moving, never tumbling into sentimentality; Oma's little homily, on the other hand, reads too much like a moral message, even (or perhaps especially) for a child — the gist of it has, in any case, been discreetly implied in the preceding passage.

> Es war viel zu heiß in dem Raum. Es roch muffig und ungelüftet. Kalle schwitzte. Er zog seine Jacke aus. Er stellte fest, daß auch Oma schwitzte, denn sie setzte nach einer Weile sogar den Hut ab. Er hörte nicht auf das Gespräch der beiden alten Frauen. Oma erzählte viel von ihm, Frau Wendelin von ihrem einzigen Sohn, einem Flieger, den sie im Krieg verloren hatte; blutjung, sagte sie immer wieder, blutjung.

Kalle beobachtete die alten Leute an den runden Tischen. Die meisten ver-
hielten sich ganz normal. Aber manche lächelten oder grinsten seltsam vor
sich hin. Redeten mit sich selbst. Einigen mußte eine Schwester beim Essen
helfen. Und andere saßen auf ihrem Stuhl, reglos, als wären sie schon tot.
Kalle fürchtete sich nicht vor ihnen. Es war jedoch eine Welt, die ihn be-
klommen machte, die ihn nichts anging.
Bei der Heimfahrt sprachen sie lange nichts.
Dann sagte Oma [...] Das Alter wird dann schrecklich, wenn man vor lauter
alten Leuten das Leben rundum nicht mehr sieht, weißt du. Das ist alles. Aber
die Welt hat ja Angst vor dem Alter. Und du auch, Kalle.
Kalle dachte wieder an die Hitze, an den Mief, an die Beengung, die ihn
bedrückt hatten. Er gab Oma recht und fand, sie sei eine tolle Frau.

Then, perhaps not inappropriately in 'heavy type', comes Oma's *envoi*, as
is the case at the end of all chapters except for the last one of the book:

**Ganz gut, daß der Kalle einmal gesehn hat, wie das ist: so viele alte Leute
auf einem Haufen, in einem Heim.**
**Nein, dahin wollte ich auch nicht. Nicht für die Welt. So alt komme ich mir
auch nicht vor.**
**Genau genommen ist daran natürlich der Kalle schuld. Hätte ich den
Burschen nicht zu versorgen, würde ich meine Wehwehchen pflegen, jam-
mern, den Nachbarn auf die Nerven gehn. Also ist Kalle im Grunde meine
Medizin.**[17]

A taste of medicine for the reader too, and one that vitiates the power of
the chapter.

The problem is one that clearly brought about much discussion
between the author and his publisher Hans-Joachim Gelberg, who tells
us in a *Werkstattbericht* published in 1979 that they could not see how to
make Oma 'unverfälscht eine alte Frau', with her own voice, 'ohne die
erzählerische Sicht des Kalle zu verlassen [...] Wie soll ein Kind begreifen, was Oma wirklich fühlt?'[18] The result was that, with the Oma-
monologue, Härtling created not a bridge but an artificial wall between
the two worlds of youth and age, hindering a free flow of perceptions.
This can be irritating, but it does not ultimately destroy the playful
portrayal of the power-struggle between Oma and Kalle; nor does it dis-
colour the presentation of a child coming to terms painfully yet confi-
dently with the inevitability of sickness, aging and death only five years
after losing his parents.

Härtling's fundamental position is one of respect for the feelings of
which children are capable. This is, perhaps, most clear when he writes
about children in their own world, rather than, as in the novels discussed in this article, children in the adult world. Thus, for example, his
admonition in 'das ist kein vorwort', the introduction to *Ben liebt Anna*, is
a timely reminder not only that he writes love-stories but also that

children experience such love-stories much earlier than adults remember:

> Manchmal sagen Erwachsene zu Kindern: Ihr könnt gar nicht wissen, was Liebe ist. Das weiß man erst, wenn man groß ist.
> Dann haben die Älteren eine Menge vergessen, wollen mit euch nicht reden oder stellen sich dumm.
> Ich erinnere mich gut, wie ich mit sieben Jahren zum ersten Mal verliebt war. Das Mädchen hieß Ulla. Es ist nicht die Anna in diesem Buch. Aber wenn ich von Anna erzähle, denke ich auch an Ulla.
> Ben hat Anna eine Weile sehr lieb gehabt. Und Anna Ben.[19]

Thus, in what is one of the few stories in which Härtling deals with something other than a so-called 'schwarzes Thema', we are again reminded of how well Härtling is able to remember and re-create the joys and sorrows of those first glances and touches. Indeed, he has talked repeatedly of the quality of 'Erstmaligkeit' in childhood experiences, and of the importance of capturing this in writing: 'Diese Erstmaligkeit [soll man] nicht bloß respektieren, sondern hüten und pflegen. Wie viele erste Male gibt es in jeder Kindheit, in jeder Jugend!'[20]

III

It is in his most recent *Kinderroman*, *Krücke*, that Härtling has perhaps produced one of his most accomplished portrayals of childhood. Certainly it is a book as much for an adult as for a child reader. *Krücke* is the novel which, written when its author was in his fifties, comes closest to actual autobiographical material, and yet this material is handled with the greatest degree of artistic detachment. When asked in a recent interview: 'Ist das Kind in Ihnen in irgendeiner Buchfigur besonders ausgeprägt?' Härtling responded by mentioning Thomas, the boy in *Krücke*.[21] It is the first *Kinderroman* in which he returns (more than forty years later) to the time of his own grim losses, and re-enters the destroyed world of a child whose father had fallen at Voronezh and who has become separated from his mother in the crush at Kolin railway-station. The journey which leads eventually to reunion with his lost mother begins when he is twelve years old, and takes him through Czechoslovakia, Austria, Swabia and Bavaria on trains that meander, break down, divide and grind to a halt. As Krücke points out to him:

> Überleg dir mal, Tom, wie viele Züge gleich dem unseren jetzt auf Fahrt sind. Von Osten nach Westen, von Norden nach Süden. Vollgestopft mit Menschen, die irgendwo ankommen wollen. Aber das Irgendwo hat noch nicht einmal einen Namen. Da ist es gut möglich, daß so ein Zug vergessen wird,

aus den eilig zusammengestellten Fahrplänen verschwindet, für immer auf einem Abstellgleis landet.[22]

By using the *train* rather than the human being as the wanderer a stróng yet emotionally neutral symbol is created for rootlessness; the search is for a home, a mother-country, a place where there will be security and stability. Härtling's approach to this story, which focuses, unlike the other *Kinderromane* I have mentioned, on a boy very close to his own age in 1946, was to demonstrate the evolution of interdependence between a highly independent, self-sufficient adult, Krücke, and the helpless, lost child who arrives in Vienna to find that the only address he had been given is reduced to a doorway in front of a bomb-site. The man's nickname and dependency on the crutches from which it derives underline admirably that he is, in fact, no more self-sufficient than the young lad who turns to him for help. They come from very different worlds and arrive back after the war with very different expectations, but they discover together the need for trust and dependency in a rare and unusual friendship. The start of that friendship is, however, less than auspicious:

> Hau ab, sagte der Mann, ohne daß sich seine dünnen Lippen bewegten [...]
> Hau ab, wiederholte der Mann und hob drohend die eine Krücke. Mach 'ne Mücke.
> Was, fragte Thomas, was soll ich machen?
> 'Ne Mücke, wiederholte der Mann. Wenn du es so besser verstehst: Verkrümele dich, verpiß dich, zieh Leine! Ist das klar?[23]

The exchange reflects all the exhaustion, suspicion and disillusionment felt by the one-legged *Heimkehrer*, Eberhard Wimmer. It is left to the child to make the initial overtures, to show, to teach trust. Once again Härtling lets the apparently weaker, more defenceless person show the way; in this sense Tom becomes the crutch for Krücke. The boy senses that there is more to this man than his words alone suggest: 'Er hatte auch den Eindruck, daß es der Einbeinige nicht so ernst meinte.' And a little later, after yet more gruff words from the 'Einbeiniger', 'Thomas entspannte sich. So wie es aussah, hatte er beinahe gewonnen. Nun mußte er nur noch abwarten und jedes falsche Wort vermeiden'.[24] The child wishes to enter the adult's world, sensing at once that Krücke's hostility is only a defence; the adult, even more hurt and vulnerable at this stage, wishes to keep his world closed. The child's needs, hunger, exhaustion and desire for companionship, do not take long to disarm the adult and remind him of his own needs: 'Es hat keinen Sinn, daß wir uns belauern und bekriegen, was. Wir sind beide arm wie die Kirchenmäuse, obwohl ich noch nie eine arme Kirchenmaus gesehen habe. Das kommt davon, daß ich selten in Kirchen gehe.'25

Common territory is established which is initially mapped out solely according to the physical needs of the two protagonists. Härtling wisely avoids any early expressions of emotion between the two: 'Hilf mir den Tisch hinaustragen, forderte der Mann. Hier drinnen ist es zu stickig. Und die Stühle bring nach.'26 They eat in silence, Krücke says he will talk after eating, as there is something important he has to say. Will this be the start of a beautiful friendship? Of course not; when Krücke does speak it is firstly to say: 'Du stinkst. Du stinkst wie ein Geißbock, wie eine Tonne Jauche, wie ein Biber. Du stinkst, mein Junge, nach Dreck, nach Schweiß, nach Kohlenfeuer, nach Kellerschimmel. Wann, frage ich dich, hast du zum letzten Mal deine Sachen ausgezogen und gewaschen?'27

Smells feature prominently in all of Härtling's stories and here especially so; they are the kind of smells that children are well acquainted with, and Härtling does not shy away from the smells of stale urine and excrement either. In most children's literature they remain strictly taboo. But because they feature here so naturally, as of course they do for children and adults alike in spite of our manic denial of them most of the time, there is no sense of revulsion, but rather one of relief. Just as the oral and the anal feature so strongly in the opening of *Im Westen nichts Neues*,28 a novel which also portrays the development of comradeship *in extremis*, so here Härtling establishes the basic relationship between Krücke and Thomas firmly on bodily functions.

As the novel progresses, the journey through the ravaged cities of Austria and Germany continues; all the while the friendship between the two unlikely companions develops and deepens, with Thomas becoming more like a young adult and Krücke increasingly resembling a recalcitrant adolescent. As time goes on, Krücke allows Thomas to gain access to his world, a world that has now been destroyed: his years as a student, interrupted by the War, his experiences on the Russian Front, his amputated leg, his homecoming. In doing this, incidentally, Härtling discreetly introduces a good deal of historical background material. Hitler, the concentration camps, the SS, all receive a brief but telling mention. They are references which are likely to encourage the child-reader to ask further questions, of both parents and grandparents: What had they done in the War? Had their experiences been like those of Thomas or of Krücke? What did they know of the SS? And what about their friends and neighbours?

Almost imperceptibly Krücke's attachment to his young protégé becomes one of dependency, much as he pretends to the contrary. For a brief time he is even dilatory about looking for Thomas's mother: he does not want to lose this new-found friendship. This is demonstrated in a touching and painful scene where the boy overhears Krücke and his girlfriend Bronka discussing him in the next-door room while he is thought to be asleep. Bronka is urging Krücke to get the boy into a home, if his mother cannot be found. Krücke's monosyllabic, unenthusiastic responses betray the pain that he feels at these suggestions. Bronka presses on:

> Von Tag zu Tag wird es dir schwerer fallen, dich von dem Jungen zu trennen. Oder hast du womöglich vor, ihn mit nach Deutschland zu nehmen? Willst du ihn dir als Reisegepäck aufhalsen? [...] Nein! schrie Thomas. So dürften sie nicht über ihn sprechen. Wie über ein Gepäckstuck, das sie irgendwo abstellen wollten [...] Nein, schrie er noch einmal, gegen seine Angst, gegen seine Wut.
> Krücke stand schon in der Tür. Ein paar Schritte hinter ihm Bronka. Sie preßte die Faust gegen den Mund, als wollte sie alles, was sie gesagt hatte, zurückstopfen.[29]

A child is peering into an adult world and knows himself to be excluded from it. As a result of this eruption Thomas is taken into the discussion by the two adults; they apologize to him and ensure that he is no longer excluded from any talk about *his* future and *his* return home.

IV

Thus, with this novel, Härtling has not only returned to the land of his own childhood, coming to terms with his past and his losses; he has written a story that may help German (and non-German) children to visit a foreign country that is also their country, the Germany of 1945. Härtling makes it clear in the preface to *Krücke* that he consciously set out to write a novel for children against what he calls the 'böses Sprichwort' *homo lupus hominem*: 'Ich habe mein Buch gegen dieses Sprichwort geschrieben. Es ist Krücke und Thomas gewidmet, die uns die Botschaft hinterließen, daß der Mensch auch des Menschen Freund ist.'[30]

The title of Härtling's next novel *Der Wanderer*,[31] which is not a *Kinderroman*, indicates a theme similar to that of *Krücke*, but that story is conflated with and subsumed in the stories of all those other victims of

National Socialism, and it reaches back, moreover, to embrace other wanderers from other times: Schubert, Hölderlin, Heine and many more. In the final pages of the novel Härtling's 'Wanderer' has become a composite figure, one who has finally come to terms with the past and so has arrived in the present: 'Er kam zur rechten Zeit. Er kam heim. Und er zog eine andere Unsterblichkeit vor als Faust — namenlos und doch genannt: Kömmling.'[32]

NOTES

1 L. P. Hartley: *The Go-Between*, Harmondsworth, 1958, p. 7.
2 Peter Härtling: *Krücke. Roman für Kinder*, Weinheim, 1987. *Krücke* is the seventh work by Härtling described as a *Kinderroman* or *Roman für Kinder*, the others being: *Das war der Hirbel* (1973), *Oma* (1975), *Theo haut ab* (1977), *Ben liebt Anna* (1979), *Alter John* (1981) and *Jakob hinter der blauen Tür* (1983); all published by Beltz & Gelberg, Weinheim.
3 Marcel Proust: *A la recherche du temps perdu* ed. by Pierre Clarac and André Ferré, with an introduction by André Maurois, 3 vols, Paris, 1954; in English translation by C. K. Scott Moncrieff and Stephen Hudson: *Remembrance of Things Past*, 12 vols, London, 1941.
4 Jona Oberski: *Kinderjaren*, The Hague, 1978.
5 Ödön von Horváth: *Jugend ohne Gott*, Amsterdam, 1938.
6 In particular pp. 7—21 and 263—81.
7 Wedekind termed *Frühlings Erwachen*, written in 1890 when he was 26 and first performed in 1906, 'Eine *Kindertragödie*'.
8 'Fünf Überlegungen beim Schreiben von Kinderbüchern' in Hans-Joachim Gelberg (ed.): *Peter Härtling für Kinder*, Weinheim, 1989, p. 22.
9 Härtling was born in Chemnitz (which became Karl-Marx-Stadt and is now Chemnitz again) in 1933. His father was a lawyer. Härtling's novel, *Nachgetragene Liebe* (Darmstadt, 1980), explores his relationship with his father. See also the article by Hella Ehlers in this volume (esp. p. 234).
10 See, for example, Peter Härtling: 'Von den Anfängen zwischen Himmel und Erde', *FAZ*, 17 December 1988.
11 Horst Brandstätter in *Stuttgarter Nachrichten*, 19 September 1975.
12 Ursula Valentin in *FAZ*, 11 December 1973.
13 Härtling: *Das war der Hirbel*, p. 36.
14 Jules Renard: *Poil de Carotte*, Paris, 1894; Christopher Nolan: *Under the Eye of the Clock*, London, 1987.
15 Works of note by Härtling not discussed in the present context include: *Das Familienfest oder Das Ende der Geschichte* (Stuttgart, 1969), *Zwettl. Nachprüfung einer Erinnerung* (1973), *Eine Frau* (1974), *Hölderlin* (1976), *Die dreifache Maria* (1982), *Felix Guttmann* (1985) and *Waiblingers Augen* (1987); all except the first published by Luchterhand, Darmstadt. See also notes 2 and 9 above.
16 'Unverschleierte Realität', interview with Peter Härtling in *Nürnberger Nachrichten*, 15 December 1973.
17 Härtling: *Oma*, pp. 85—6.
18 'Wie die "Oma" entstanden ist...; Ein Werkstattbericht' in Gelberg: *Peter Härtling für Kinder*, p. 64.
19 Härtling: *Ben liebt Anna*, p. 5.
20 Härtling: 'Von den Anfängen...'.

21 'Wir Dichter brauchen eure Phantasie', interview with Hannelore Daubert, in Gelberg: *Peter Härtling für Kinder*, pp. 14—21; here p. 19.
22 Härtling: *Krücke*, p. 103.
23 Ibid, p. 16.
24 Ibid, p. 17.
25 Ibid, p. 19.
26 Ibid, p. 20.
27 Ibid.
28 Erich Maria Remarque: *Im Westen Nichts Neues*, Berlin, 1929 (in English translation by A. W. Wheen: *All Quiet on the Western Front*, London, 1929). For example, p. 6: 'Dem Soldaten ist sein Magen und seine Verdauung ein vertrauteres Gebiet als jedem anderen Menschen. Dreiviertel seines Wortschatzes sind ihm entnommen, und sowohl der Ausdruck höchster Freude als auch der tiefster Entrüstung findet hier seine kernige Untermalung [...] Für uns haben diese Vorgänge den Charakter der Unschuld wiederenthalten durch ihre zwangsmäßige Öffentlichkeit [...] Nicht umsonst ist für Geschwätz aller Art das Wort "Latrinenparole" entstanden; diese Orte sind die Klatschecken und der Stammtischersatz beim Kommiß.'
29 Härtling: *Krücke*, p. 46f.
30 Ibid, p. 5.
31 Peter Härtling: *Der Wanderer*, Darmstadt, 1988.
32 Ibid, p. 132.

'ABER WO BEFINDE ICH MICH?':

THE NARRATOR'S LOCATION AND HISTORICAL PERSPECTIVE
IN WORKS BY SIEGFRIED LENZ, GÜNTER GRASS
AND JOHANNES BOBROWSKI

ANTHONY WILLIAMS

I

The West German writers Siegfried Lenz and Günter Grass (born in 1926 and 1927 respectively) and the GDR writer Johannes Bobrowski (1917—1965) came from territories which once constituted part of eastern Germany. Grass spent his early years in and around Danzig, Lenz grew up in Lyck, Masuria, in the south of East Prussia, and Bobrowski, who hailed from Tilsit to the north of East Prussia, was brought up, as he put it, 'auf beiden Seiten der Memel'.[1] An experience common to these regions was that of the relations between Germans and other national groups living in these areas and close by;[2] these relations, whether in the more distant or more recent past, provide a theme for all three writers. The imprint of their home landscapes and townscapes on their memory and imagination is so great that descriptions of these feature prominently in their work; moreover, landscape may be used metaphorically, relating to the events portrayed, to the history which is represented.[3]

This essay will concentrate on differences in approach to similar historical subjects between novels by Lenz (*Heimatmuseum*) and Grass (*Die Blechtrommel*) on the one hand, and a number of prose works by Bobrowski on the other.[4] It will also embrace depictions of landscape and the natural realm which contribute to the interpretations of history presented and which can exemplify dissimilarities in historical perspective. It is of course true that literary compositions like the ones under discussion ultimately represent the world or a particular epoch as the authors experienced it or as they understand it. Differences in approach to similar historical subjects are also doubtlessly connected with the courses the lives of these authors took in the period after the Second World War: Lenz and Grass became resident in the Federal Republic and

Bobrowski in the GDR,[5] which had implications for the authors' attitudes towards the world about them as seen from their vantage points in these two societies. Lenz and Grass grew critical of many aspects of the developing West German state in the Adenauer era. They still felt that there was a place for them in a liberal society as committed writers and intellectuals, however ineffective they might feel on, as it were, the periphery of society. In the 1960s both, though careful to distinguish between their roles and responsiblities as authors and citizens,[6] strove to move a little towards the centre of society by actively supporting the main opposition party in the Federal Republic, the SPD, in election campaigns. The attitude of Lenz and Grass towards the other German state was one of almost total disfavour: not only was the society there no better than their own, it was in many repects worse, illiberal, allowing little scope for critical writers and intellectuals.[7] Bobrowski basically identified with the main political direction and goals of the GDR,[8] referring to his 'Position eines bewußten Bürgers unserer Republik, die Position eines Sozialisten'.[9] He shared the GDR's radical criticism of the 'Bonner Staat'[10] in the Adenauer era, especially with regard to factors like anti-communism,[11] clericalism,[12] revanchism[13] and 'restaurative Erscheinungen'.[14] But it is also true that there were moments when Bobrowski's commitment to GDR society wavered;[15] his solidarity did not preclude his criticizing distortions of truth in public life or discrepancies between socialist ideal and reality.[16]

However, this essay is concerned more with the narrators of the works in question than with their authors. A central reason for this is that, especially in the case of *Heimatmuseum* and *Die Blechtrommel*, it is difficult to assess on the evidence purely of the texts the precise relationship between authors and narrators, and some caution would have to be exercised in attempting to deduce the attitudes of the authors from those of the narrators. Both *Heimatmuseum* and *Die Blechtrommel* are examples of 'Rollenprosa'.[17] Bobrowski's narrators, by contrast, are usually close to the author himself; the authorial voice frequently speaks through the narrators.

II

The question of a link between a narrator's location and the view of history presented by a work can be illustrated by a reference to the beginning of Bobrowski's *Levins Mühle*. In this novel about a crime committed by a German against a Jew in West Prussia in the late nineteenth century, the narrator opens his report by reflecting on whether it is right and proper for him to tell this story and to convey his interpretation of the events.[18] The narrator's grandfather, motivated by business considerations and anti-Semitic prejudice, is responsible for the destruction of Levin's mill, and the initial suggestion is that the narrator might be reluctant to render his account because of the shame it would bring on his family. And there were those who did object to the version of history presented in the novel, particularly in West Germany, including members of Bobrowski's own family.[19]

That the narrator goes ahead with his story, and states that it is 'anständig' to do so,[20] suggesting that Germans must face up to the fact of what their forefathers did — with the determination that such things must never happen again and that there must be a radical change in Germans' relations with the peoples of eastern Europe. Moreover the narrator probably believes that there does exist in his present location, which may be identified as East Berlin, a readiness to think constructively about the past. Certainly we deduce that in the narrator's opinion his interpretation of events, placing the blame on Germans, and especially on the social, economic and political circumstances which enabled Germans like the narrator's grandfather to oppress Jews and also Poles, whilst likely to cause some resentment in certain circles in West Germany, will find favour in the socialist society and culture of the GDR: 'Ob etwas unanständig ist oder anständig, das kommt darauf an, wo man sich befindet — aber wo befinde ich mich? — [...] Ich sitze — das ist die Beantwortung der Frage: Wo befinde ich mich? — einige hundert Kilometer Luftlinie westlich von jenem Weichseldorf.'[21] To this extent, then, there is a link between the narrator's location and the picture of history he conveys. Location is to be understood literally, as a geographical place, but also metaphorically, in terms of a viewpoint adopted that is central to, or in some way characteristic of, the society and culture in which the individual resides.

From this same geographical and ideological standpoint, which is present in many of his prose works, Bobrowski's narrators present a pattern of events, often in a specific social context, with regard to the relations of Germans and the peoples of eastern Europe over the course of many centuries, 'seit dem Auftreten des Ritterordens bis in die jüngste Vergangenheit'.[22] The most conspicuous feature of this pattern, which derives both from Bobrowski's study of history and his own experience, is the recurrence of German guilt in these relations.

Up to a point this historical conception is corroborated by comments of Lenz's narrator Zygmunt Rogalla in *Heimatmuseum*. With regard to the history of East Prussia itself Zygmunt also indicates the key, negative role of the Teutonic Knights, 'die meine Leute [the 'Pruzzi'] unterwarfen'.[23] In his account too the tradition of German nationalism leads in Nazism to the deserved forfeiture of this territory ('ein selbstverschuldetes Unglück'[24]). As in some of Bobrowski's works, notably 'Dunkel und wenig Licht',[25] the movement to restore the pre-war boundaries of Germany is a target of the narrator's criticism in *Heimatmuseum*, where it is shown to represent a continuation of the discredited ideological and political tradition of German nationalism. Despite these similarities, however, Lenz's narrator does not go so far as to impose any general pattern on history in the manner of Bobrowski, whose narrators concentrate exclusively on the aggression and guilt of Germans in their relations with other peoples in the area. What Zygmunt presents is an endless series of cruel, destructive acts from all sides and parties: Teutonic Knights, Lithuanians, Tartars, Swedes, Poles and Russians, as is apparent in the following passage where history is expressed in landscape. A topographical feature conjures up events of the past in the mind of the narrator, and the impressions conveyed include, in the example of the 'ernsten Kadikbüschen', an imagined reaction of landscape to the occurrences:

> Wer auf dem Schloßberg stand, der konnte gar nicht anders, der mußte ihn gleich zur Verteidigung einrichten; man geriet kaum dazu, die Wälle und die Holzwehren hochzuziehen und das Tor zu verrammeln, als auch schon auf der Landenge die in den weißen Mänteln auftauchten, dekorativ zwischen den schwarzen reglosen Seen, vor den immer matten Silberpappeln; und gerade hatte man ihnen die Mäntel rot befleckt, als es zwischen den ernsten Kadikbüschen zu wieseln begann, es huschte und flitzte da nur so vor litauischen Bogenschützen, die sich einen Jugendtraum erfüllen wollten. Viele konnte man sich als Angreifer aussuchen: Tataren auf zottigen Rennern, unglückliche Schweden, immer wieder besessene polnische Kavallerie und schließlich auch Samsonows verzagte Schützen.[26]

In the First World War landscape testifies to destruction which, as the narrator emphasizes, stems equally from both parties to the conflict, for the artilleries of the rival German and Russian armies together inflict damage on the Masurian landscape: 'Die Bäume, ich muß bekennen, mir taten damals die Bäume leid, die da dutzendweise in die Knie gingen oder nach einem einzigen Hieb die Kronen verloren, tragende Obstbäume und legendenreife masurische Eichen. Wie sie rasiert wurden, geknickt, verdreht, aufgeklaftert!'[27] Here the involvement of landscape in the events of history is much stronger and more immediate than in the case of the 'solemn' juniper shrubs. The narrator, in his recollection of the spectacle of destruction and out of his own response to it, endows the trees not merely with human attributes, but with the degree of human sensitivity which enables them to suffer acts of war.

The divergence in the picture of history conveyed by Zygmunt Rogalla and Bobrowski's narrators is connected with their locations and ways of thinking. The sense of belonging to a particular political and cultural community and the security within it experienced by Bo-browski's narrators[28] contrasts with the tentative and uncertain nature of Zygmunt Rogalla's position in the period leading up to and during the time of narration. Far from identifying with West German society he feels ill at ease in it, choosing to locate the revived Masurian folk mu-seum 'in der Abgelegenheit von Egenlund',[29] on the periphery of society therefore. He is critical of the rise of former Nazis to social prominence; and the intention of revanchists to take over the museum and use it to press home their case, distorting historical evidence if necessary, prompts Zygmunt to destroy the museum and, thereby, to withdraw totally from public life. Being bandaged up in a hospital bed as a result of burns received in the fire encapsulates Zygmunt's situation at the time of narration: he is cut off from the world.

In a certain sense isolation characterizes Zygmunt's position both before and after the destruction of the museum. In his criticism of much that goes on around him, unlike Bobrowski's narrators in *Levins Mühle* and elsewhere, he does not adopt a political and ideological stance that elucidates the world in terms of opposing social forces of which *one* could be wholeheartedly embraced and supported. Zygmunt lies between the political and ideological camps, in a 'no-man's land'.

Zygmunt's expression 'Niemandsland' has more than one applica-tion. His preoccupation with the folk culture of the past constitutes a search for roots and a secure identity, an escape from his immediate so-cial and cultural environment, 'einer Landschaft aus Zement' in which the individual appears 'namenlos und auswechselbar'.[30] But here too he finds himself in a no-man's land — between the past and the present. The government representative who opens the folk museum in Egen-lund stresses that those promoting the culture of the former homeland should also be integrated with the community of the present. That Zygmunt does not succeed in this is not simply due to his own failing but, as we have seen, to features of the society in which he resides. An opposite case is provided by the narrator of Bobrowski's 'Das Käuzchen', who is also concerned with the landscape and culture of his former home, the borderland between East Prussia and Lithuania: his preoccupation is part of a new identity which embraces both the past and the present and is grounded in a firm commitment to GDR society. The closing sentence: 'Und ist der Ort, wo wir leben' refers to both the former and present homes of the narrator and his wife.[31]

The folk culture of the old homeland provides a moral and intellectual station which is narrow, remote and precarious in relation to the world at large. And when Zygmunt feels obliged to destroy the museum he enters a state of extreme disorientation, for he is deprived of his life's work and purpose. He is, as it were, left rudderless and without a compass 'in der unsicheren Stille des Niemandslands'.[32] From this vantage point the historical world appears as essentially irrational, too complex to be perceived in terms of a clearly structured interpretation as offered by Bobrowski's narrators. 'Geschichte', maintains Zygmunt, is a 'Sumpf', a 'Morast', 'ein dunkler, trügerischer Tümpel', which can never be illuminated 'bis auf den Grund'.[33] And the overwhelming tendency of the opaque historical world (confounded by few exceptions) is destructive: 'Vergangenheit: sie gehört uns allen, man kann sie nicht aufteilen, zurechtschleifen; das verwächst doch miteinander, verschränkt sich, das bestätigt sich gegenseitig in Habgier, Macht und Niederlagen — manchmal, aber sehr selten, in Vernunft.'[34]

While Zygmunt repeatedly expresses scepticism about any theory as a means of understanding and elucidating life: 'In jeder Theorie steckt die Enttäuschung ihres Urhebers über die Unwilligkeit des Lebens, sich planvoll zu schicken',[35] Bobrowski's narrators are clearly conversant, for example, with the social and historical theory of Marxism and draw on this to highlight factors contributing to particular historical developments. Unlike Bobrowski's narrators, Zygmunt does not discern an underlying, or essential pattern to the violent and destructive events of history. If a principled taking of sides, as in the case of Bobrowski's narrators, produces a clearly structured picture of history (embracing and pointing up, where appropriate, the relationship between nationality and class) and presents the historical world as comprehensible and changeable, a principled withdrawal from the world on the part of Lenz's narrator renders the realm of history, at any rate with regard to forces which move it, inexplicable and beyond human comprehension.

III

Oskar Matzerath's narrative in *Die Blechtrommel* is comparable to Zygmunt's concerning the connection between location, vantage point and view of life and history. The opening of the chapter 'Beton besichtigen — oder mystisch barbarisch gelangweilt', which culminates in the slaying of Roswitha, includes this description: 'Die steinerne Menagerie der weltberühmten Kathedrale spie, vom Menschentume angeekelt, ohne Unterlaß Wasser auf die Pflastersteine.'[36] Here Oskar, as he recalls the wartime scene in France, imposes his impressions on, in this case, the townscape, and in such a way that the resultant witness of Rheims Cathedral to the affairs of men and the destruction of war embodies his own vantage point of deliberate remoteness from the world.

Oskar's residence in a mental institution at the time of narration constitutes a conscious withdrawal from West German society, though as a result of experience accumulated both before and since 1945.[37] He is disaffected from the Federal Republic of the 1950s, in which renewed prosperity and respectability, accompanied by a social and cultural environment of coldness and impersonality, have been erected on the unsubstantial foundation of an unresolved past, as evidenced, for example, by revanchism towards Poland. But his retreat is also motivated by resignation (partly out of awareness of the guilt he himself has incurred over the years) and fear, for he looks upon his hospital bed as a haven and, once in it, is at pains to preserve his 'zwischen weißen Metallstäben geflochtene Stille'.[38]

In certain respects Oskar's 'Stille' here resembles the 'Stille des Niemandslands' of Zygmunt's situation. Oskar too stands between the ideological and political fronts; he is not 'at home' in any belief or philosophy.[39] Although, unlike Zygmunt, Oskar claims to have found in his hospital bed not only a refuge but also a yardstick ('Mein weißlackiertes metallenes Anstaltsbett ist also ein Maßstab'[40]), he is neither free from fear in his enclosed and isolated location, nor is the yardstick sufficiently sensitive to alleviate his disorientation in relation to the world at large.

From the vantage point of his hospital bed, Oskar has the sense that the world is hostile and threatening, dictated by forces which cannot be controlled. These forces are influential in individual life and in the life of society, in the present as in the recent past. As the novel progresses, Oskar increasingly encapsulates these forces in the metaphysical image of the 'Schwarze Köchin'. The last page in particular summarizes the horrific and painful experiences in the public and private spheres portrayed during the course of the novel; all of these are now attributed to the influence of the 'Schwarze Köchin', to whose evil power Oskar, with his release from the mental institution imminent, is about to be exposed totally: 'Fragt Oskar nicht, wer sie ist! Er hat keine Worte mehr. Denn was mir früher im Rücken saß, dann meinen Buckel küßte, kommt mir nun und fortan entgegen.'[41]

Such all-consuming, but unspecific dread goes hand in hand with a picture of history as a destructive realm in which fundamental causal factors are not discernible in psychological, social or political terms. If for Zygmunt the historical process is irrational since underlying causes cannot be perceived, are inaccessible to reason, from Oskar's vantage point the forces behind life and history are brought into focus (and are symbolized eventually by the 'Schwarze Köchin'), but they cannot be identified in a concrete sense. Certainly in the description of landscape about to be examined, the passing reference to the dreams of combatants as a motivating force in history does not serve by itself as a sufficient explanation for the historical catastrophes evoked:

> Links und rechts lag hinter den Deichen immer dasselbe, wenn nicht flache, dann gehügelte, schon abgeerntete Land. Hecken, Hohlwege, eine Kesselkuhle mit Ginster, plan zwischen Einzelgehöften, geschaffen für Kavallerieattacken, für eine links im Sandkasten einschwenkende Ulanendivision, für über Hecken hetzende Husaren, für die Träume junger Rittmeister, für die Schlacht, die schon dagewesen, die immer wieder kommt, für das Gemälde: Tataren flach, Dragoner aufbäumend, Schwertritter stürzend, Hochmeister färbend den Ordensmantel, dem Küraß kein Knöpfchen fehlt, bis auf einen, den abhaut Masoviens Herzog [...][42]

Here the landscape of West Prussia gives rise in the narrator's imagination to a never-ending chain of battles. The culmination of the whole passage, beginning some seven lines after the extract quoted, is a reference to the attack of Nazi Germany on Poland. With regard to historical parallels and prefigurations this event is set not in the context of other instances of German guilt (which would accord with the pattern of history presented by Bobrowski's narrators[43]) but in the framework of violent episodes in the region involving not just Germans as aggressors, but other peoples too, such as the Tartars.[44] In this respect Oskar's evocation of history in the West Prussian landscape coincides with the picture of history conjured up in Zygmunt's mind by the Schloßberg in the Masurian landscape, with cruel and destructive acts stemming from representatives of many nations. In Oskar's account the history of centuries is condensed into a rhythm of destruction; the construction of the second sentence, which continues for a further ten lines after the extract quoted, emphasizes the factor of rhythm. Here there is no hope of change; no end to the historical rhythm of violence is foreseen.[45]

IV

In Bobrowski's works landscape is not only the scene of, and gives testimony to, man's inhumanity to man, it may also stand out against this feature of the historical world and, in doing so, provide a perspective of change. A comparison between a passage from *Die Blechtrommel* and one from Bobrowski's 'Dunkel und wenig Licht' illustrates this key difference in the picture of history conveyed through descriptions of the realm of nature. On the surface the two episodes in question, involving ants in *Die Blechtrommel* and a fly in 'Dunkel und wenig Licht', express a similar idea. Creatures of nature are unmoved, unimpressed by destructive historical events or tales of them. In *Die Blechtrommel* neither the arrival of the Soviet soldiers in Matzerath's cellar nor even the killing of Matzerath deflects the ants from their everyday activities: 'Bei all dem Geschrei wirkte beruhigend, daß sich die Ameisen durch den Auftritt der russischen Armee nicht beeinflussen ließen.'[46] In 'Dunkel und wenig Licht' the fly goes slowly but surely about its business, unperturbed by the stories in a West Berlin bar concerning the 'heroic' endeavours of the German army in the Second World War. The juxtaposition is clearly a source of consolation for the narrator, who is disturbed by the tales of war and the revanchist tendencies they represent: 'Ich beobachte ja übrigens schon längere Zeit eine Fliege. Sie ist bis zu halber Höhe an P's Glas hinaufgekrochen, langsam und stetig, als gehörte sie hierher. Jetzt steht sie schon eine ganze Weile an dem gleichen Fleck. Vorhin war sie immer, aber auch ruhig und ohne Eile, um eine kleine Bierlache neben dem Untersatz herumspaziert.'[47]

At a deeper level the difference between the two passages is still more significant. If the ants provide some reassurance for Oskar, indeed a kind of model for the distance and lack of involvement with regard to historical events he himself aspires to, the natural world, in the example of the ants, does not give the reader any such comfort.[48] In their attraction to 'jener aus dem geplatzten Sack rieselnde Zucker', which has lost 'nichts von seiner Süße',[49] they exhibit tendencies analogous to those followed by human beings in the private and public spheres of life, where, as a number of episodes in the novel indicate, the pursuit of, or more correctly indulgence in, these tendencies results in destruction or self-destruction.[50] The link between human and insect world is made apparent in this juxtaposition: 'Die hatten nur Kartoffeln und Zucker im Sinn, während jene mit den Maschinenpistolen vorerst andere Eroberungen anstrebten'.[51] To this extent, then, the realm of nature is similar to the human and historical world, and the spectacle of the ants strengthens, rather than undermines, the sense that life is subject to strong irrational impulses to whose sway there are no exceptions and from which there is no escape.[52] In 'Dunkel und wenig Licht' the fly's steady progress, likewise the canal at the wartime scene itself, unimpressed by the German efforts to conquer the whole of Europe, retaining its air of permanence and normality,[53] are images which create the sense that the Nazis' activities are not only unlawful and unnatural, but above all short-lived. The endurance, stability and persistence of the world of landscape and nature, in its contrast with what goes on in and around it, suggest that though the historical epoch, embracing the actions of the Nazis and the potential violence of their successors, the revanchists, may be destructive, it is also transitory; the circumstances and influences prevailing in it need not last, it does not have to represent man's ultimate historical condition.

The testimony of landscape to history in Bobrowski's works is in many repects more diverse than in *Heimatmuseum* and *Die Blechtrommel*. It is true that Zygmunt and Oskar, with the aid of landscape descriptions, could be said to present a view of the relations of the peoples in eastern Europe which is not particularly restrictive or selective, in that they focus on violence perpetrated by representatives of many nations; but landscape in the hands of Bobrowski's narrators, notwithstanding their concentration on a historical pattern of German guilt in these relations, contributes to a picture of history and of the historical process which has more sides to it than the by and large bleak and unchanging image conveyed by Zygmunt and Oskar. A number of features of landscape's testimony to history may be identified in accordance with the multifaceted representation of history by Bobrowski's narrators.

Landscape bears witness to violence and oppression, but it may also testify to resistance and hence illuminate the active force in human beings. Landscape may contribute to the highlighting of social factors in, or the social context of, historical events. Landscape is 'parteilich', to use the appropriate Marxist term; it takes sides in its testimony. And, as the example from 'Dunkel und wenig Licht' has already indicated, landscape may testify to history as a process of change, may give expression to a perspective of change. All these features of landscape's testimony to history reflect important strands of thinking in the socialist society and culture of which the author was part[54] and where many narrators are explicitly or implicitly located.[55] As compared with Zygmunt's and Oskar's reflections on history through landscape, in Bobrowski's works landscape testifies to history more directly and with a greater variety of means. Whilst in *Heimatmuseum* and *Die Blechtrommel* we have the sense of the narrator's voice speaking through landscape about history or the narrator imposing his view of history on landscape, it is as if Bobrowski's narrators often allow landscape to speak for itself.[56]

Nowhere is this last point clearer than in the opening section of the autobiographical story 'Ich will fortgehn'. Here the depiction of the Russian landscape evokes both violence and resistance to violence. The personified river Volga expresses the suffering inflicted on the Soviet people in the Second World War: 'und hatte eine Stimme, in der die Stimmbänder festgezogen waren und schnarrten'.[57] The action of 'festziehen' is normally applied to objects and used here in conjunction with a sensitive organ of the human anatomy like the voal cords, it helps to constitute a harrowing metaphor; the cracked, hoarse tones of the river suggest perhaps the moans of a tortured person. The atmosphere of violence is intensified by the short, cryptic sentence: 'Und Stroh schwamm vorüber', which conjures up the debris of destruction. But in the first half of the sentence, where the first-person narrator recalls the Volga, the river displays the strength and constancy that were eventually to repel the Nazi invader: 'Und da war der Strom, lehmgelb, langsam und sehr stark.' Furthermore the river as metaphor represents not only an active force but also one which is social; the narrator's description of its colour ('lehmgelb') indicates that it is of one body with the surrounding landscape, which is 'lehmig'.[58]

Landscape helps to present history as the interplay of competing forces and, moreover, through its quality of 'Parteilichkeit', plays a significant role in conveying the narrator's evaluation of a given action and the parties involved. Landscape is not passive or neutral with regard to the events it witnesses, but active and partisan. This can be exemplified by another river testimony to history, this time in 'Die Seligkeit der Heiden' which, exceptionally, does not treat the general theme in Bobrowski's works of the crimes of the Nazis and their predecessors in German history, but does embody the characteristic focus on the social context of historical developments. In this story the river Dnieper near Kiev demonstrates the conflict involving Prince Vladimir and the ordinary people over the introduction of Christianity at the expense of the traditional religion of the Slavs in tenth-century Rus: 'und, weit draußen, die über das Ufergewächs hinaufspringen, die Schnellen, die aufeinander zustürzen und ihre Wasser übereinanderwerfen'.[59] The rapids are made up of forces constantly clashing against each other; they constitute an image, therefore, of unavoidable, furious struggle. In the end, when Prince Vladimir is victorious and the people have to bow to his will, the river is in disarray and inconsolable, no matter how much the birds may appear at pains to calm it: 'Wirbel, über denen Vögel dahinschießen, als sollten sie die Fluten besänftigen'.[60] With its 'harten, kurzen Lauten',[61] the river seems to express its own anguish and to indicate the agony of those (the mass of the people) whose cause it espouses. The active and partisan witness not only of the river, but also the wind and earth, to the unfolding conflict is a key factor in the narrator's presentation of the story's events in terms of class struggle and class domination, his portrayal of Christianization as ideological and political suppression by the feudal state.

If in 'Die Seligkeit der Heiden' despotism prevails, the opposite is the case in 'Boehlendorff'; or rather it is landscape which illuminates the prospect of change and the triumph of the ordinary people and Boehlendorff's humanistic ideals. Boehlendorff's desire for a just social order brings him into conflict with the ruling German manorial nobility in the Baltic Provinces of Russia in the early nineteenth century and leads him to seek common cause with the exploited inhabitants of the 'undeutschen Dörfer'.[62] As in Levins Mühle national suppression, here by Germans of Latvians, is presented as social oppression. Boehlendorff, however, isolated and increasingly deranged, takes his own life, his endeavours apparently fruitless. But during Boehlendorff's funeral, landscape conveys a prophetic message. A dramatic interplay between light and darkness envelops the sky, a spectacle, as the narrator specifically points out, watched by 'die Leute' as if to see what the future holds for them: 'Der Lichtschein hat sich dem finsteren Himmel über das Haupt geworfen, ganz hoch steht er, und beginnt zu stürzen, jetzt, zu sinken, und breitet sich von oben her über die ganze Verfinsterung aus, über den harten Himmel.'[63] Light, symbolizing Boehlendorff's ideals in harness with the social aspirations of the Latvian working people and exemplifying man's active force, overcomes and disperses darkness, representing oppression and obscurantism. And as if to indicate the revolutionary rather than evolutionary character of the historical change foreshadowed, light gains the upper hand over a grim and uncompromising opponent only as a result of a violent struggle.

V

In the different ways shown, landscape in Bobrowski's works may contribute to the interpretation of history which a narrator wishes to put across. In this it fulfils a similar function as in *Heimatmuseum* and *Die Blechtrommel*. However, in this role, landscape in Bobrowski's works is more conspicuous and its testimony to history more diverse. Thus Bobrowski's narrators, in contrast to Lenz's Zygmunt and Grass's Oskar, place emphasis on the possibility of change and on the active force in human beings, and this is reflected in landscape's testimony. All the works examined are convincing in their own terms; it is issues connected with these terms which this essay has sought to compare and contrast. All three writers acknowledge the importance of Germany's recent past in their own lives, and themes arising from this experience are at the heart of their literary compositions. To this extent they are, as writers, of one nation. But the findings of this investigation indicate that the establishment of two separate societies and cultures in Germany in the lifetime of these authors has had an influence on the ways in which these themes are presented, at any rate in the works examined. In this sense the latter could be taken to support the notion of 'zwei Literaturen einer Nation'.[64]

NOTES

1 Johannes Bobrowski: 'Lebenslauf' in Gerhard Rostin, Eberhard Haufe and Bernd Leistner (eds): *Johannes Bobrowski. Selbstzeugnisse und neue Beiträge über sein Werk*, Berlin (GDR), 1975, p. 14.

2 See Siegfried Lenz: 'Ich zum Beispiel: Kennzeichen eines Jahrgangs' in Lenz: *Beziehungen. Ansichten und Bekenntnisse zur Literatur*, Munich, 1972, pp. 9—31 (here p. 15); Ekkehart Rudolph: 'Interview mit Günter Grass' in Rudolph (ed.): *Aussage zur Person. Zwölf deutsche Schriftsteller im Gespräch mit Ekkehart Rudolph*, Tübingen, 1977, pp. 83—100 (here p. 84); and Bobrowski: 'Lebenslauf', p. 14. While Bobrowski's experience of these relations was enhanced by regular visits to his maternal grandparents, who had a farm in Willkischken on the Lithuanian side of the border, Lenz and Grass could witness them within their own family circles (see Ekkehart Rudolph: 'Interview mit Siegfried Lenz' and 'Interview mit Günter Grass' both in Rudolph (ed.): *Protokoll zur Person. Autoren über sich und ihr Werk*, Munich, 1971; respectively pp. 95—105 (here p. 96) and pp. 59—72 (here p. 60)).

3 With regard to the use of landscape as metaphor in relationship to history, there is a reference to Bobrowski's works in a passage of Grass's *Hundejahre* (Darmstadt, 11th—16th edn, 1963, p. 80). Significantly it comes in the middle of an episode which evokes a brutal crusade of the Teutonic Knights against the Lithuanians in the fourteenth century (the subject of the military campaigns of the Teutonic Knights against the Baltic peoples, beginning in the thirteenth century, is frequently treated in Bobrowski's works): 'aber erst im Juli drauf sahen sie [die Deutschherren — during the campaign against the Lithuanians] wieder jenes Flüßchen [die Szeszupe], das heute noch der Dichter Bobrowski dunkel besingt'. In 1963 Bobrowski completed his autobiographical piece 'Das Käuzchen', in which he acknowledges Grass's reference, following closely the words quoted, as if to underline their significance: 'Oder besinge noch immer dunkel, wie Graß sagt, das Flüßchen Szeszupe' (Johannes Bobrowski: *Gesammelte Werke*, ed. by Eberhard Haufe, 6 vols, Berlin (GDR), 1987; hereafter, references by volume and page number are to this edition. 'Das Käuzchen', IV, 77—8; here 77). Grass attaches the adverb 'dunkel' to the verb 'besingen' and thereby alludes to the fact that 'dunkel', as an attribute of landscape, is a recurrent metaphor in Bobrowski's works, appropriate to the violent nature of the events which have taken place; it is no less appropriate to the crusade against the Lithuanians as depicted in *Hundejahre*.

4 The dates of composition and of first publication respectively of the fictional works under consideration are: Lenz, *Heimatmuseum*, 1976-1978, 1978; Grass, *Die Blechtrommel*, 1955—1959, 1959; *Hundejahre*, 1959—1963, 1963; Bobrowski: 'Das Käuzchen', 1962—1963, 1965; *Levins Mühle. 34 Sätze über meinen Großvater*, 1962—1963, 1964; 'Dunkel und wenig Licht', 1964, 1965; 'In eine Hauptstadt verschlagen', 1964, 1965; *Litauische Claviere*, 1965, 1965; 'Die Seligkeit der Helden', 1963—1964, 1965; 'Boehlendorff', 1964, 1965.

5 The divergent experiences of the three authors depend to a certain extent on age. Unlike Lenz and Grass, Bobrowski participated in the second World War from beginning to end as a member of the *Wehrmacht*. Throughout the Nazi period he was an active Christian and, from 1934, belonged to the Confessional Church in Königsberg, an association which would certainly have strengthened his intellectual independence of Nazism. Thus, when he entered the War his views were well formed, and his experiences confirmed them, adding only a sense of his own guilt. He was a prisoner of war in the Soviet Union from 1945—49, and this served to bring him closer to Marxist socialism, with which he had been familiar from the early 1930s (see Johannes Bobrowski: 'Fortgeführte Überlegungen', IV, 158—60). His return to what had become the GDR involved a conscious commitment to society there. Lenz and Grass were drafted into the War before their seventeenth birthdays in 1943 and 1944 respectively. Participation in the war and the revelation of the true nature of Nazism, whose ideology had influenced them as children and adolescents, caused shock and disillusionment (See, for example, Lenz: 'Ich zum Beispiel...', pp. 23—7, and Grass's comments in a conversation with Heinrich Vormweg quoted in Heinrich Vormweg: *Günter Grass*, Reinbek, 1986, pp. 23—6). Lenz deserted in Denmark and was taken prisoner in northern Germany by the

British; Grass became a prisoner of the Americans in the west of Germany. That Lenz and Grass arrived in the area which became the Federal Republic was as much by accident as by design and was not the result of a principled choice. And just a few years after the war both Lenz and Grass were embracing ideas which are recognizably part of the intellectual and literary culture soon to be identified with the Federal Republic. (See Lenz: 'Ich zum Beispiel...', p. 29, and Günter Grass: 'Ich klage an' in Grass: *Über das Selbstverständliche. Reden, Aufsätze, Offene Briefe, Kommentare*, Darmstadt, 1968, pp. 71—83; here 72f.)

6 See Lenz's essay 'Elfenbeinturm und Barrikade. Schriftsteller zwischen Literatur und Politik' in Siegfried Lenz: *Elfenbeinturm und Barrikade. Erfahrungen am Schreibtisch*, Hamburg, 1983, pp. 9—31, and Günter Grass: 'Vom mangelnden Selbstvertrauen der schreibenden Hofnarren unter Berücksichtigung nicht vorhandener Hofe' in Grass: *Über das Selbstverständliche...*, pp. 105—12; here p. 112.

7 See, for example, Günter Grass: 'Was ist des Deutschen Vaterland?' in Grass: *Über das Selbstverständliche...*, pp. 37—49; p. 43: 'O bärtiger, großer Marx! Was haben sie dir dort angetan?/ In welchem Gefängnis würdest du dort sitzen?' It is interesting in this context to consider the GDR reception of Grass's work as analysed by Jochen Wittmann (pp. 273—83 below).

8 Johannes Bobrowski: '"Die Koexistenz und das Gespräch." Rede bei einer Tagung des Präsidiums des Hauptvorstandes der CDU mit Kulturschaffenden in Weimar', IV, 449—55.

9 Ibid, p. 452.

10 Ibid, p. 454.

11 Bobrowski: 'Fortgeführte Überlegungen', p. 160.

12 Bobrowski: '"Die Koexistenz und das Gespräch"...', p. 454.

13 Johannes Bobrowski: '"Positionsbestimmungen". Ein Interview von Eduard Zak', IV, 489—93; here 492.

14 Johannes Bobrowski: '"Kultur — die Vermenschlichung der Verhältnisse." Ein Interview der *Neuen Zeit*, IV, 494—5; here 495.

15 See, for example, the poem 'Vorsorge' (August 1964), which suggests isolation and despair, pointing to the poet's past homeland as a safe haven (I, 209).

16 See, for example, the poem 'Das Wort Mensch' (June 1965), which castigates the abuse by officials of what for the poet are legitimate 'official' values of GDR society. (I, 217).

17 Grass uses this term with reference to *Die Blechtrommel, Katz und Maus* and *Hundejahre*. See 'Günter Grass über seine Werke' in Gudrun Uhlig (ed.): *Autor, Werk und Kritik. Inhaltsangaben, Kritiken und Textproben für den Literaturunterricht*, 3 vols, Munich, 1969—72, vol. 1, pp. 93—4; here p. 93. We may, however, perceive a connection between the authors (Lenz and Grass), writing from a 'critical distance' to developments in society, and the positions adopted by their narrators (Zygmunt and Oskar), who consciously opt out of society at the time of narration. The withdrawal of the narrators is a more radical and absolute response to the world than that of their creators. Lenz uses the term 'kritische Distanz' in '"Was kann man schreibend für den Frieden tun?" Ein Gespräch zwischen Gustav Heinemann und Siegfried Lenz' in Hans Jürgen Schultz (ed.): *Der Friede und die Unruhestifter. Herausforderungen deutschsprachiger Schriftsteller im 20. Jahrhundert*, Frankfurt/Main, 1973, pp. 335—44; here p. 339.

18 Johannes Bobrowski: *Levins Mühle. 34 Sätze über meinen Großvater*, III, 7—223; here 9.

19 Bobrowski received letters from West Germany which 'did him the honour', as he put it, 'meine Haltung oder mein Buch als eines Deutschen unwürdig zu bezeichnen' ('Positionsbestimmungen...', p. 492).

20 'Nun steht noch an, glaubhaft zu machen, daß die Geschichte erzählt werden soll, weil es anständig ist, sie zu erzählen, und Familienrücksichten keine Rolle spielen' (Bobrowski: *Levins Mühle...*, p. 10).

21 Ibid, pp. 9f.

22 Johannes Bobrowski: '"Meinen Landsleuten erzählen, was sie nicht wissen." Ein Interview von Irma Reblitz' (IV, 478—88; here 481).

23 Siegfried Lenz: *Heimatmuseum*, Hamburg, 1978, p. 14. See p. 165 for Zygmunt's explanation of the name 'Pruzzi'.

24 Ibid, p. 569. Cf. Bobrowski's reference to this 'Landschaft, die mit allem Recht verloren ist' ('Notiz für Karl Schwedhelm/Süddeutscher Rundfunk', IV, 327).

25 Johannes Bobrowski: 'Dunkel und wenig Licht', IV, 118—26.

26 Lenz: *Heimatmuseum*, p. 20f.

27 Ibid, p. 150.

28 This is expressed most explicitly in 'Das Käuzchen' and 'In eine Hauptstadt verschlagen'. In the closing lines of the latter, the narrator looks forward to resuming his full, varied and productive life in East Berlin following a trip to Stockholm, where the social and cultural environment of a modern capitalist society has unsettled him (IV, 141—4; here 143f.).

29 Lenz: *Heimatmuseum*, p. 621.

30 Ibid, pp. 120 and 348.

31 Bobrowski: 'Das Käuzchen', p. 78.

32 Lenz: *Heimatmuseum*, p. 655.

33 Ibid, p. 427f.

34 Ibid, p. 419f.

35 Ibid, p. 407.

36 Günter Grass: *Die Blechtrommel*, Darmstadt, 12th edn, 1965, p. 393.

37 Oskar has carefully fostered the impression that he is the murderer of Schwester Dorothea and also that he is mentally deranged; his consequent committal to a mental hospital for observation amounts to the implementation of his resolve for remoteness. However, his stay is to be only temporary: as he finishes his narrative new evidence has come to light which points conclusively to Schwester Beate as the murderer; Oskar will soon have to leave the hospital.

38 Grass: *Die Blechtrommel*, p. 10.

39 Ibid, p. 168: '[...] da ich weder im Sakralen noch im Profanen beheimatet bin, dafür etwas abseits in einer Heil- und Pflegeanstalt hause.'

40 Ibid, p. 9.

41 Ibid, p. 711.

42 Ibid, p. 27.

43 See, for example, Johannes Bobrowski: *Litauische Claviere* (III, 225—332), where a parallel is drawn between the violent deeds of the Teutonic Knights and those of the Nazis in Lithuania (esp. p. 273).

44 Compare Oskar's portrayal (Grass: *Die Blechtrommel*, pp. 468 and 475—8) of the recent and older history of Danzig through the testimony of the townscape itself, as his recollections of the city burning in 1945 cause him to picture its fate in previous conflict-ridden epochs. The emphasis is on the many nations which have contributed to the recurrent cycle of reconstruction and destruction.

45 See John Reddick: *The 'Danzig Trilogy' of Günter Grass*, Oxford, 1975, p. 11. Other useful secondary literature includes Reddick: 'Vom Pferdekopf zur Schnecke. Die Prosawerke von Günter Grass zwischen Beinahe-Verzweiflung und zweifelnder Hoffnung' in Heinz Ludwig Arnold and Theo Buck (eds): *Positionen im deutschen Roman der sechziger Jahre*, Munich, 1974, pp. 39—54, and 'Vergangenheit und Gegenwart in Günter Grass' "Die Blechtrommel"' in Bernd Hüppauf (ed.): *'Die Mühen der Ebenen.' Kontinuität und Wandel in der deutschen Literatur und Gesellschaft 1945—1949*, Heidelberg, 1981, pp. 374—97; Frank-Raymund Richter: *Die zerschlagene Wirklichkeit. Überlegungen zur Form der Danziger-Trilogie von Günter Grass*, Bonn, 1977, and *Günter Grass. Die Vergangenheitsbewältigung in der Danziger-Trilogie*, Bonn, 1979; Noel Thomas: *The narrative works of Günter Grass. A critical interpretation*, Amsterdam, 1982.

46 Grass: *Die Blechtrommel*, p. 471.

47 Bobrowski: 'Dunkel und wenig Licht', p. 123.

48 Oskar draws inspiration from the ants at the scene itself and to a certain extent at the time of narration as well. But as narrator Oskar is aware also of the dark implications of the episode; they are central to his view of life and history from the vantage point of his hospital bed.

49 Grass: *Die Blechtrommel*, p. 474.

50 The deaths of Agnes Matzerath and Herbert Truczinski, for example, result directly from falling victim to powerful appetites and urges. At the beginning of the chapter following Herbert's death, 'Glaube Hoffnung Liebe', which represents the growing prominence of the Nazis and culminates in events of the *Kristallnacht*, Oskar establishes a connection (by linking together the word 'Unglück', p. 229, and the seductive power of Niobe) between the private fate of Herbert and the public fate of Germany. Violent and destructive acts are frequently presented by Oskar as themselves the perpetrators yielding to an irresistible 'Versuchung' (p. 25). Like the nationalistic fire-raiser Joseph Koljaiczek, the nations involved in the history of Danzig are portrayed as gratifying a destructive impulse; even subsequent reconstruction is described in terms of 'sich im Wiederaufbau austoben' (p. 478), suggesting that this, in turn, is paving the way for indulgence in the next bout of destruction.

51 Ibid, p. 471.

52 At the end of the novel it is significant that Oskar links the activity of the ants with the 'Schwarze Köchin': 'Oskar [...] sah Ameisen zu und wußte: das ist ihr Schatten, der sich vervielfältigt hat und der Süße nachgeht' (p. 711). The ants' episode, in its connection with the fate of characters like, for example, Agnes Matzerath, Herbert Truczinski, or Joseph Koljaiczek, points to subjective channels whereby the 'Schwarze Köchin', as the overall symbol of the forces to which life and history are subject, exerts control over human beings in private and in public.

53 'Lieber Himmel, den Kanal wird es nicht stören [...] diesen nicht, der ist ordentlich, hat seine Geheimnisse: Schlamm und tote Hunde und Fahrradrahmen' (Bobrowski: 'Dunkel und wenig Licht', p. 123f.).

54 The most important strands for Bobrowski are Marxism, Christianity and humanism. See my article: 'Some thoughts on historical perspective in Bobrowski's prose works', *GDR Monitor*, no. 14, Winter 1985/86, pp. 1—13.

55 Herr Fenske, the first-person narrator of 'Dunkel und wenig Licht' and citizen of West Berlin, has in the main a similar approach and similar concerns as Bobrowski's other narrators, and it is substantially the case that the author's 'local' viewpoint has been superimposed on his West Berlin narrator in this story.

56 The article by Ian Hilton (pp. 401—11 below) explores related themes in relation to the poetry of Heinz Czechowski.

57 Johannes Bobrowski: 'Ich will fortgehen. Erzählung für sieben Stimmen', IV, 61—7; here 61.

58 Ibid.

59 Johannes Bobrowski: 'Die Seligkeit der Helden', IV, 91—6; here 95.

60 Ibid, p. 91.

61 Ibid.

62 Johannes Bobrowski: 'Boehlendorff', IV, 97—112; here 106.

63 Ibid, p. 111f.

64 Christoph Hein's idea is quoted in Volker Hage: 'Freiheit mir graut's vor dir. Über die DDR im Jahre 1968 — und heute: Christoph Hein's Roman "Der Tangospieler"', *Die Zeit*, no. 13, 24 March 1989, special literature supplement pp. 1—2; here p. 1. (See also p. 17 note 1 above.)

THE GDR AND GÜNTER GRASS:
EAST GERMAN RECEPTION OF THE LITERARY WORKS
AND PUBLIC PERSONA

JOCHEN WITTMANN

Very few public figures, if any, have of late had more to say on the question of Germany than Günter Grass. Whatever the subject of debate: division, unity, or a possible third way (an option which Grass interpreted as a confederation of the two German states), his name has remained in the headlines. This paper reverses the focus of attention: not what Grass has had to say about Germany, but what the eastern Germans had to say about Grass is what here comes under scrutiny. The East German reception of Grass's work can be divided conveniently into four phases, as critics blew alternately hot and cold in appreciation and condemnation, switching from cautious approval to scandalized rejection, from chilly rebuff to renewed tentative approbation.

It was none other than Heiner Müller who set the ball rolling with a relatively long review of Grass's first volume of poetry, *Die Vorzüge der Windhühner*, which he slated mercilessly from start to finish.[1] Unlike Majakovski, wrote Müller, Grass did not benefit from 'die Perspektive der sozialen Revolution' and it followed that his surrealist poems represented an attempt 'den naturwissenschaftlichen Blick zu diskreditieren, nachdem er auf die Gesellschaft gerichtet worden ist'. He concluded categorically: 'Die Gedichte von Günter Grass sind rhythmisch kraftlos, Assoziationsreihen ohne Struktur. Was bleibt, ist Highbrow-Pornographie. Aufgabe der Dichtung bleibt die Verteidigung des Menschen gegen seine Verwurstung und Verdinglichung. Leute wie Grass haben uns und wir haben ihnen nichts zu sagen.'

Müller had not minced his words. However, his criticism was not aimed solely at Grass, it formed part of an attack upon all lyric poetry which refrained from proclaiming a 'postives Menschenbild' and which employed moreover 'formalist', namely surrealist, techniques. And it was, perhaps, similar verse that Johannes Bobrowski may have wanted to defend against such blanket condemnation when he published a review of the same collection of poems two months later. The tone and thrust of his critique were quite different. He certainly took issue with what he calls a 'kunstgewerbliche Neigung', as evident in the choice and use of images, but assessed the collection on the whole positively, concluding his review with the prediction that 'Grass [ist] aber eine Begabung, auf die man achten sollte'.[2]

A third GDR author, Hermann Kant, registered his view on the publication of *Die Blechtrommel* in 1959. He found it impossible to accept 'die Kot-, Eiter-, und Spermaphantasien', which in his opinion were the chief characteristics of the novel. He aimed his critical fire against Oskar Matzerath, the narrator, a 'physisches und psychisches Monstrum',[3] whose narrative perspective consumed itself in obscenities and rendered him incapable of raising his gaze above the 'beschränkter Horizont einer geschickt kolorierten Kleinbürgerwelt'. Kant acknowledges that Grass makes a stand against 'Faschisten, Revanchisten, Ostlandreiter und heuchelnde Kleriker', but laments his total lack of idealism, since 'zwischen dem Nein zum Vergangenen und dem Ja zum Neuen und Zukünftigen liegt für Grass eine ungeheure Kluft'.

For the period from 1956 to 1966, the first phase in the reception of Grass's work in the GDR, these three reviews are representative in the way they express at once explicit reservations and cautious approval. While they may rap Grass on the knuckles, they deem such a reproof to be sufficient. While certain aspects of his work may be rejected outright, his status as a West German author of some repute means that his voice is both heeded and commented upon.

A central category for GDR *Germanistik* in the early 1960s was what was referred to as the 'Menschenbild'. Literary figures were supposed to be depicted playing active roles within the historical process. If, on the other hand, a disoriented individual appeared to be confronted by a chaotic world, or if he was portrayed as the victim of blind fate, this was deemed a 'Signatur der Verfallskunst',[4] a consequence of 'staatsmonopolistischer Kapitalismus', which resulted in turn in the 'millionenfache Degradation, Verkrüppelung, Vereinstigung und Verdummung des Menschen'.[5] These were the criteria which were used to assess all of Grass's early novels and it hardly needs to be said that when they were employed he could not score very well. He was accused of depicting only misshapen, distorted, or grotesque characters. The 'monstrosity', Oskar Matzerath, was proof enough that the figures in his novels were 'alle absonderliche, absurde, verkrümmte, verkümmerte

Kleinbürgerexistenzen, die Grass als "das" Menschenbild ausgibt'.[6] He did not measure the 'Blechtrommler an einem humanistischen Gegenbild, sondern macht ihn selbst zum Maß aller Dinge'.[7]

The conclusion drawn from this line of argument (that Grass lacked any sort of idealism) was indeed quite correct. It was said that he never progressed from 'eine nörgelnde Kritik',[8] and that 'die wertende Analyse ist seinem Standpunkt fremd'.[9] It is certainly the case that Grass never presumed in his early novels to draft a detailed Utopia, preferring instead to proffer his own brand of historical pessimism. This never met with approval in the GDR; the author's reservations towards notions of historical progress were spotted immediately and these formed the burden of the charges brought against him. It was claimed that he neglected historical reality, that his 'Dingperspektive muß die Gesetzmäßigkeit der Geschichte verwischen',[10] and that he was able to discover 'keine Kausalität, keine Kontinutät in der Geschichte'.[11]

There was some praise mixed in with these criticisms, but it was not so much the literary quality of his works which was extolled (though that was not ignored either) as the critiques of fascism, militarism, anti-Semitism and Adenauer's Biedermeier restoration, which the works contained. Critics credited him with a 'beißende Ironie'[12] and applauded him for 'eine Fülle ungemein scharfer Beobachtungen, auch eine Anzahl kritisch-satirischer Episoden von entlarvender Beweiskraft'.[13] As a representative of a 'kritisch-oppositionelle Literatur in Westdeutschland',[14] he was certainly held in some esteem, but, as we have seen, this appreciation was never unalloyed. Günter Cwojdrak finds that even though '[es] gelingen ihm ausgezeichnete Einzelschilderungen, die soziale Beweiskraft haben, so bleibt aber auch seine Kritik begrenzt'[15] and since he obviously has neither a clear social standpoint, nor a 'Begriff von der Zukunft, der Hauptlinie der historischen Entwicklung', his criticism of West German society must needs remain half-hearted.[16]

Günter Grass is regarded in this first phase of his reception as a serious representative of 'westdeutsche bürgerlich-oppostionelle Satire',[17] an author who, despite clear reservations about him, enjoys a degree of official recognition because of his refusal to conform. During the period before the politicization of West German literature non-conformity was understood as the tentative refusal to enter into a 'Dienstverpflichtung' with 'der restaurative Staat'[18] and was thus seen as a worthy, though hardly exemplary, oppositional stance. As long as

Grass fitted this description he was certain of attracting critical attention and some degree of good-will. It was thus possible for him to be invited to the Fifth German Writers' Congress in East Berlin in 1961 where he was permitted to make a highly critical statement, claiming that while artistic freedom may be under threat in the West, in the East it simply did not exist. Even after his public letter of protest to Anna Seghers in August 1961, condemning the building of the Berlin Wall and exhorting her as chairman of the GDR *Schriftstellerverband* to do the same,[19] he did not fall completely out of favour with the GDR authorities. He was invited in 1964 to speak at the Seventh Conference of the Weimar Academy, where once more he courted controversy with his hosts.

The decisive turning point occurred in 1966 with the première of his play, *Die Plebejer proben den Aufstand*, where he interprets the troubles of 1953, which were officially regarded in the GDR as a fascist counter-revolution, as a workers' uprising, which 'der Chef' (undeniably based upon Bertolt Brecht) refuses to support. This was too close to the mark. In *Neues Deutschland*, the official organ of the SED, he was immediately charged with being a lackey of reactionary forces,[20] and elsewhere he was denounced as 'anticommunist'.[21] He had now earned himself a new label which would accompany him until the 1980s.

In the second phase of East German Grass reception, from 1966 to 1970, the accusation of anticommunism served as an excuse not only for bitter attack, but also for denying him his previous status as a progressive West German author worthy of respect. Yet the play itself was more the pretext for this course of action than the cause of it, for as West German literature in general became increasingly concerned with politics, so GDR scholarly interest was directed more and more towards writers whose work could be regarded as either socialist or, to borrow the jargon of the day, 'humanist'. Nonconformity was no longer held in the same high regard and authors were preferred who took up a clear position.

Grass was now repeatedly accused of refusing to choose between the two sides. A Russian Germanist announced with aggressive insistence that there was no third way, claiming that Grass's satire lacked 'ein postiver Ausgangspunkt und die Orientierung auf positive gesellschaftliche Ideale'.[22] Since Grass had 'keinen festen ideologischen Standpunkt', he was susceptible to an ugly anticommunism, whereas it was incumbent upon an artist to decide where he stood and 'heute, angesichts der Existenz zweier deutscher Staaten, gilt das erst recht'. Open season had been declared as far as Grass was concerned. On the occasion of his public letter to Antonín Novotny, President of Czechoslovakia, *Neues Deutschland* seized the opportunity to describe his appeal as an example of the 'verstärkten ideologischen Aggressionsakte des Imperialismus' and declared that the former non-conformist writer, as a 'Fürsprecher der Konterrevolution', to have degenerated to 'vollkommen antikommunistischen Positionen'.[23]

The political role which Grass played in both public life and election campaigns during the 1960s came under ever heavier fire. *Neues Deutschland* printed an article which contained the denunciations made by the Secretary-General of the Hungarian Writers' Union,[24] and in the East Berlin newspaper *Volkswacht* his electioneering, where he pleaded for reforms rather than revolutions, was once more rebuked.[25] His literary output also met with rough treatment from reviewers. In a discussion of his verse collection *Ausgefragt*, he was accused of vilifying the 'Widerstand gegen eine Notstandsgesellschaft' which other West German writers, such as (presumably) Heinrich Böll, Erich Fried, Peter Weiss and Günter Herburger, had displayed.[26] But the death knell of Grass's reputation was sounded by Heinz Plavius à propos of his play *Davor*, which was said to show that Grass not only performed 'Zutreiberdienste für eine Gesellschaft' which was becoming 'ihrem Wesen nach autoritär und neofaschistisch', but that he was reponsible for 'eine Denunziation der Kräfte, die sich gegen diesen Prozeß wehren'. Grass's activity amounted to 'Ablehnung durch Geschwätz; Ästhetisierung der Widersprüche durch Vernebelung des Massenbewußtseins'. As a result it was impossible to count him any longer as belonging to the opposition, since he had unmasked himself totally 'mit diesem Engagement an eine falsche Politik und an eine falsche Ideologie', incurring the loss of 'aller linken Ehrenrechte'.[27] Plavius continued his mud-slinging a year later when he summarily concluded: 'Der ganze Grass — ein Spieler, ein Hasardeur, dem Frieden und Verständigung, Demokratie und Freiheit nicht mehr als Jetons sind, seinen Gewinn zu machen. Wir aber sagen dazu: rien ne va plus...'.[28]

With these comments the wheel had turned almost full circle and we were back to the point where Heiner Müller had decided that '[Grass hat] uns und wir [ihm] nichts zu sagen'. In the years that followed, a doctoral dissertation on Grass's conception of history[29] and an important article on his relation to the East German writer Johannes Bobrowski[30] were allowed into print, but after that all public discusion of his work and persona came to an end — the book was, indeed, closed.

The third phase of Grass reception, from 1970 to 1979, can be defined only by the fact of its non-existence: his books were no longer reviewed; his public utterances no longer criticized; his literary significance simply ignored. This ice-age in Grass's East German fortunes falls strangely enough in a period of general thaw as regards GDR *Germanistik* as a whole. The change of SED leadership in 1971, when Honecker replaced Ulbricht, brought with it a re-orientation in cultural policy. Honecker's announcement that 'auf dem Gebiet von Kunst und Literatur [könne] es keine Tabus geben'[31] provoked all manner of frank critical debates during the 1970s on the relation between literature and society. Whereas up to the beginning of that decade 'die entscheidende Wertungskategorie für die Literatur der BRD der Realismusbegriff bzw. der sozialistische Realismus gewesen war',[32] afterwards the notion gradually gained currency that so-called modernist ways of writing might also perform a socialist function. Critics no longer believed that aesthetic techniques were themselves components of ideology, but instead accepted that the various functions of literature allowed for a variety of asthetic perspectives.

Honecker had, of course, appended to his remark dismissing all taboos, that this only applied 'sofern die feste Position des Sozialismus nicht verlassen werde'. Even though the transposition of ideology into literature no longer had to take place within the confines of socialist realism, literature was still closely linked to ideology. A politically unreliable author like Grass was consequently still persona non grata. Critics preferred to deal with writers whom they could describe as 'humanist' or 'democratic', and authors such as Martin Walser, who was close to the DKP in the 1970s, or Peter Weiss, were the subjects of detailed monographs. Furthermore interest had shifted from writing which might be described as 'bürgerlich-kritisch' to 'die Reportage- und Dokumentarliteratur' produced by such figures as Günter Wallraff.[33]

In the period from 1970 to 1979 Grass merited attention of one critic only. After investigating 'antihumanism' in West German literature for her doctoral thesis (1971), Ursula Reinhold discussed (1976) the degree to which West German writing might be regarded as having moved 'durch Thema und Wirkungsabsicht in den Zusammenhang der antiimperialistischen Bewegung'.[34] With such a critical brief she could hardly ignore Günter Grass, although there was never any doubt that he would receive very short shrift.

Reinhold's charge against Grass in both discussions is his negative response to left-wing committed literature of the late 1960s. She accused him of helping maintain the establishment and of launching attacks against progressive authors; his political pragmatism might be summed up as consisting of 'demagogy' and 'empty rhetoric'.[35] Since his 'volle und bewußte Eingliederung in das herrschende System', he had developed 'eine Angst vor eindeutig demokratischen Positionen'[36] which was in turn associated 'mit einer militanten Haltung gegenüber konsequenten Kommunisten und Demokraten'. This entailed that: 'Bei Günter Grass [wird] der Antikommunismus aus einem ideologischen Vorbehalt zu einem bewußt eingesetzten Politikum, das besonders gegen die demokratischen Bestrebungen im Lande angewandt wird. Er hilft, jede Oppositionsbewegung gegen das herrschende System und jede Bemühung um wirkliche Veränderungen zu diffamieren'.[37] The former anarchic rebel was now a supine conformist whose political decline in turn accounted for the 'Niedergang des Epikers Günter Grass', due to his inability to perceive 'gesellschaftliche Realitäten'.[38]

This critical opinion held sway until 1979 when an essay by the literary scholar, A. Karelski, appeared in a Soviet monthly and was translated six months later in the East Berlin magazine, Kunst und Literatur.[39] Karelski's argument was based upon philosophical enquiry, since he investigated the changing Weltbild in Grass's oeuvre and tried to determine the author's ideological and philosphical position in its respective phases. He decided that Grass began as a rebel whose early novels were consistently 'anti-idealistic' and even 'nihilistic'. From the mid-1960s onwards Grass was ready to reach compromises and his public support for the SPD brought in its train conformism and in part even anti-communism. With the publication of Aus dem Tagebuch einer Schnecke (1972) he underwent a further change, becoming a stoic and a melancholic, and his pessimistic view of history now took on both private and absurd aspects. This was a sign of 'eine Art privater Renaissance', as by way of concentrating on the private and the sensuous Grass attempted to confront the tragic dimension of world politics with a residue of optimism.

Despite its questionable division of Grass's work into the above phases, this article contains an extensive and thorough examination of Grass's philosophical concepts. Despite Karelski's political and ideological reservations he leaves his readers in no doubt as to the artistic quality of Grass's fiction. The article's publication in the GDR ended the period of isolation and commenced a fourth and now final phase in Grass's reception there. Beginning with tentative advances on the part of the critics, this culminated in the publication of some of his books, reviews of them appearing in the press, and permission for him to give public readings in Leipzig and Berlin. This change of course was helped by Grass lending his vociferous support for disarmament and détente in East-West relations during the early 1980s and by his working together with East German writers such as Heym, Kant and Hermlin in the Peace Movement.[40] The most fundamental of the political objections had now been removed and despite the ideological differences which remained, Grass was no longer a taboo subject of discussion.

Reproaches of anti-idealism and anticommunism continued to be levelled at Grass, but his books were no longer damned utterly. On the contrary, he became the subject of detailed critical studies. It had become, after all, impossible to continue to ignore the leading role which he played in West German literary life; it was now inconceivable that his name should be passed over in the most ambitious GDR history of German literature when the last volume, devoted to West German literature, came out in 1983.[41] In this he received a similar amount of attention to writers such as Böll, Walser, Eich and Enzensberger, and a careful analysis of his *oeuvre* up to *Das Treffen in Telgte* (1979) was undertaken — although naturally political considerations still determined its basic tenor and slant. Grass's development from rebel to conformist'and his political statements of the 1970s were regarded as all that was needed in order to arrive at an adequate idea of what his work was all about. At the same time essential literary features, which had indeed remained constant since his literary début, were identified and his refusal to commit himself to a fixed ideological position in the *Danziger Trilogie*, his 'Ideologiefeindlichkeit', was explained with reference to the intellectual climate of the 1950s. Grass's pessimistic view of humanity and his cyclical idea of history were identified as characteristic also of his later texts and not merely his early novels. Even though the watchword 'anticommunism' was not avoided, the criticism remains slight; despite very clear ideological objections to what Grass says and stands for, the authors refrain from attacking him directly. Instead of which there is even explicit praise for the literary accomplishment of his novels and he is extolled for his 'Lust am sinnlich-farbigen Erzählen',[42] his 'epische Fabulierkunst' and his artistisches Vermögen'.[43]

After what amounted to Grass's official rehabilitation it was then possible (in 1984) for two of his books to be published for the first time. *Katz und Maus* had an initial print run of 18,000 and *Das Treffen in Telgte* more than twice that number — and both disappeared quickly from bookshops. Three years later his most important novel, *Die Blechtrommel*, was made available to the East German public and when, just a few months later, it was necessary to print a second edition, *Neues Deutschland* wrote that it counted 'aufgrund seiner poetischen Ideen und seiner Sprachkultur zu den wichtigsten Werken der Literatur unseres Jahrhunderts'.[44] Thus, thirty years after Grass achieved fame and recognition in the West, he finally made a breakthrough on the eastern banks of the Elbe.

As this brief survey has shown, Grass's East German reception was influenced above all by political and ideological interests. Although, in my opinion, it is wrong to judge a work of literature according to whether the author holds socialist views, I must concede that some of the conclusions reached by East German scholars and reviewers about the content of Grass's work are significant. It was precisely their ideological perspective which made them focus their attention upon essential philosophical features and I should like to illustrate this by looking at the way *Die Blechtrommel* was received.

Grass's first novel did not become the object of detailed research in the Federal Republic until rather more than a decade after it was published, thus the doctoral theses written by Brode, Just, Schneider and Richter[45] are all influenced to some extent by the image of Grass in the late 1960s, when he had already established himself as a committed writer and as an election campaigner. As a direct consequence the novel was treated in these theses as a piece of 'committed literature'. Whether they took the book as a panoramic critique of the petty-bourgeoisie, or whether they interpreted it as an historical chronicle, there was never any doubt that it belonged to the category of socially critical literature. In these circumstances, other aspects, such as the Existentialism typical of

1950s, which is of such crucial significance for *Die Blechtrommel*, were not considered for a single moment.

This did not change until 1980 when, in *Kopfgeburten*, Grass informed the world in words which could not be misconstrued that Camus and his philosophy of the Absurd had been of decisive influence.[46] Critics now recalled his comments made in 1973 à propos of *Die Blechtrommel*, when he said that it had not been 'gesellschaftliche Verpflichtung' which had motivated him.[47] For the first time articles appeared which investigated the themes of Existentialism, historical pessimism and anti-idealism in this novel.[48] Such topics had been discussed much earlier by the East Germans, since their ideological approach with its emphasis upon the 'image of man' and the 'image of the world' constituted in effect an appraisal of the novel's *Weltanschauung*. Gerhard Dahne's thesis of 1970 anticipates much West German research by ten or fifteen years and provides a summary of the essential aspects of historical pessimism, the elements of the absurd, and the consistant anti-idealism.

Yet it must also be said that even though East German scholarship presented these results at a very early stage, it was not able to reach a fair assessment of their importance. Their fundamentally idealist precepts, which demanded a positive image both of the world and of man, enabled them to register all shades of historical pessimism with the accuracy of a seismograph recording earth tremors, but they could only react with hostility towards them. The idea, for instance, of a view of history which was anti-Hegelian and not oriented towards progress was deemed to lie simply beyond the bounds of reasoned discussion. Existentialism was dismissed as the expression of Western intellectual impotence, or, even worse, it was decried as decadent. East German literary scholars recognized quite correctly the fundamental suspicion of all ideologies as an essential characteristic of literature in the immediate postwar period, but they assessed such scepticism as a sign of philosophical immaturity.

Thus East German studies appear at one and the same time to be both extremely up-to-date and old-fashioned. If their comments on central philosophical features in Grass's work provide a stimulus to a discussion which is only just beginning in the West, then their conclusions are reminiscent of nothing so much as the 'Lebenshilfe' *Germanistik* of the 1950s. They provided an accurate description of the philosophical profile of Grass's work, but no acceptable interpretation of it. The discrepancy between precise observation and an inability to understand remains, or, to adapt the words of Goethe, 'zum Sehen geboren, zum Schauen *nicht* bestellt'.[49]

NOTES

Translation by Julian Preece.

1   Heiner Müller: 'Die Kröte auf dem Gasometer', *ndl*, vol. 5, no.1, 1957, pp. 160—1.
2   Johannes Bobrowski: 'Die Windhühner' in Gert Loschütz (ed.): *Von Buch zu Buch — Günter Grass in der Kritik* (Neuwied, 1968, p. 165); originally in *Das Buch von drüben*, Berlin (GDR), March 1957, p. 69. Anthony Williams (esp. pp. 255—6 above) also discusses the difference in approach between Bobrowski and Grass.
3   Hermann Kant: 'Ein Solo auf Blech', *ndl*, vol. 8, no. 5, 1960, pp. 151—6.
4   Irene Charlotte Streul: *Westdeutsche Literatur in der DDR*, Stuttgart, 1988, p. 78.
5   W. Jopke: 'Bemerkungen zum Menschenbild der gegenwärtigen bürgerlichen Philosophie' in W. Eichhorn et al. (eds): *Das Menschenbild der marxistisch-leninistischen Philosophie*, Berlin (GDR), 1969, p. 43.
6   Günter Cwojdrak: *Eine Prise Polemik. Sieben Essays zur westdeutschen Literatur*, Halle/Saale, 1965, p. 109.
7   Ibid, p. 108.
8   Hans Jürgen Geerdts et al. (eds): 'Zur Problematik der kritisch-oppositionellen Literatur in Westdeutschland (H. E. Nossack, G. Grass, Chr. Geißler, P. Schallück)', *Wissenschaftliche Zeitschrift der Ernst-Moritz-Arndt-Universität Greifswald*, vol. IX, 1959—60, pp. 357—68; here p. 361.
9   Arno Hochmuth (ed.): *Literatur im Blickpunkt. Zum Menschenbild in der Literatur der beiden deutschen Staaten*, Berlin (GDR), 1965, p. 256.
10 Ibid, p. 253.
11 Cwojdrak: *Eine Prise Polemik...*, p. 102.
12 Hochmuth: *Literatur im Blickpunkt...*, p. 232.
13 Cwojdrak: *Eine Prise Polemik...*, p. 105.
14 Geerdts: 'Zur Problematik der kritisch-oppositionellen Literatur...', p. 357.
15 Cwojdrak: *Eine Prise Polemik...*, p. 107.
16 Ibid, pp. 113f.
17 Werner Neubert: 'Das Groteske in unserer Zeit', *ndl*, vol. 13, no. 1, 1965, p. 105.
18 Dorothea Dornhof and Frank Wecker: 'Die Literatur der Bundesrepublik Deutschland in der Geschichte der DDR-Germanistik', *Zeitschrift für Germanistik*, vol. 10, no. 3, 1989, pp. 336—52; here p. 340.
19 Günter Grass: 'Und was können Schriftsteller tun? An die Vorsitzende des Deutschen Schriftstellerverbandes in der DDR, Anna Seghers' in Grass: *Werkausgabe in zehn Bänden*, ed. by Volker Neumann, Darmstadt, 1987, vol. IX, pp. 33—4. See also Dieter Stolz who relates this letter to Grass's nightmare about Germany (p. 211 above).
20 H. Konrad: 'Dramatische Dienstleistung auf "drittem Weg"', *ND*, no. 15, 1966.
21 'In der Sackgasse des Antikommunismus', *Der Morgen*, 21 January 1966; also in Loschütz: *Von Buch zu Buch...*, pp. 144f.
22 Irina Mletschina: 'Tertium non datur', *Sinn und Form*, vol. 18, no. 4, 1966, pp. 1258—62; here pp. 1261f.
23 *ND*, 17 September 1967. See also Günter Grass and Pavel Kohout: *Briefe über die Grenze. Versuch eines Ost-West-Dialogs*, Hamburg, 1968.
24 'Der Irrtum des Günter Grass', *ND*, 13 November 1969.
25 Dieter Fricke: 'Herr Grass, springende Schnecken und das westdeutsche Hotelfrühstück', *Volkswacht*, 7 July 1970.
26 Gerhard Wolf: 'Besprechungen', *ndl*, vol. 16, no. 9, 1968, pp. 164—70.

27 Heinz Plavius: 'Geschwätz verhindert Taten', *ndl*, vol. 17, no. 8, 1969, pp. 173—8.
28 Heinz Plavius: *Zwischen Protest und Anpassung. Westdeutsche Literatur, Theorie, Funktion*, Halle/Saale, 1970, p. 56.
29 Gerhard Dahne: *Zur Problematik des Geschichtsbewußtseins im Werk von Günter Grass*, Greifswald, 1970.
30 Günter Hartung: 'Bobrowski und Grass', *Weimarer Beiträge*, vol. 16, no. 8, 1970, pp. 203—24.
31 Erich Honecker: 'Schlußwort auf der vierten Tagung des ZK der SED', *ND*, 6 July 1972.
32 Dornhof, Wecker: 'Die Literatur der Bundesrepublik...', p. 338.
33 Irene Charlotte Streul: 'Literatur der Bundesrepublik in der DDR', *Frankfurter Hefte*, vol. 33, no. 8, 1986, pp. 714—8
34 Ursula Reinhold: *Antihumanismus in der westdeutschen Literatur*, Berlin (GDR), 1971; *Literatur und Klassenkampf*, Berlin (GDR), 1976 — also published as *Herausforderung Literatur*, Munich, 1976 (here p. 7).
35 Reinhold: *Herausforderung...*, p. 30.
36 Ibid, p. 162.
37 Ibid, pp. 248f.
38 Ibid, pp. 252f.
39 A. Karelski: 'Rebellion, Kompromiß und Melancholie im Werk von Günter Grass', *Kunst und Literatur. Zeitschrift für Fragen der Ästhetik und der Kunsttheorie*, vol. 28, nos 2 and 3, 1980, pp. 162—80 and 299—308.
40 See Dieter Ulle and Klaus Ziermann: 'Friedensbewegung und Kultur', *Weimarer Beiträge*, vol. 32, no. 8, 1986, pp. 1237—60.
41 Hans Joachim Bernhard et al: *Geschichte der Literatur der Bundesrepublik Deutschland*, Berlin (GDR), 1983.
42 Ibid, p. 194.
43 Ibid, p. 518.
44 Quoted from *Westfälische Rundschau*, 9 September 1987: '*Neues Deutschland* würdigte Grass und *Die Blechtrommel*'.
45 Hanspeter Brode: *Die Zeitgeschichte im erzählenden Werk von Günter Grass. Versuch einer Deutung der "Blechtrommel" und der "Danziger Trilogie"*, Frankfurt/Main, 1977; Georg Just: *Darstellung und Appell in der "Blechtrommel" von Günter Grass*, Frankfurt/Main, 1972; Irmela Schneider: *Kritische Rezeption. "Die Blechtrommel" als Modell*, Frankfurt/Main, 1975; Frank-Raymund Richter: *Die zerschlagene Wirklichkeit. Überlegungen zur Form der "Danziger-Trilogie" von Günter Grass*, Bonn, 1977.
46 See Grass: *Werkausgabe*, vol. VI, p. 212.
47 Ibid, vol. IX, pp. 624—33 ('Rückblick auf *Die Blechtrommel* — oder der Autor als fragwürdiger Zeuge. Ein Versuch in eigener Sache').
48 See especially Werner Frizen: 'Zwei Schelme im Unterricht', *Mitteilungen des deutschen Germanistenverbandes*, vol. 30, no.3, 1983, pp. 1—19; and '*Die Blechtrommel* — ein Schwarzer Roman?', *arcadia*, vol. 21, no. 2, 1986, pp. 166—89.
49 The opening lines of the song of Lynkeus der Türmer in Goethe's Faust, part II, act V: 'Zum Sehen geboren,/ Zum Schauen bestellt,/ Dem Turme geschworen,/ Gefällt mir die Welt.'

THE SUFFERINGS OF 'KAMERAD FÜHMANN':
A CASE OF DISTORTED RECEPTION
IN BOTH GERMAN STATES

DENNIS TATE

Franz Fühmann's story 'Marsyas' provides one of the most painful reading experiences in the postwar literature of the two German states. Written in 1977, it is included in Fühmann's collection of reworked themes from Greek myth, *Der Geliebte der Morgenröte* (1978).[1] It recounts the sufferings of Marsyas, the satyr who challenges Apollo, the god of artistic creation, to a musical contest, in which his talents on the double flute are judged against those of Apollo on the lyre. The adjudicating panel of the Muses, naturally biased towards the establishment figure rather than his rival from the backwoods, declares Apollo the winner. Apollo then exercises the victor's right to demand a forfeit from Marsyas, and bewilders his well-intentioned opponent by ordering him to be flayed, in retribution for his arrogance in having issued the challenge in the first place. This punishment is an unspeakably cruel one, described by Fühmann's narrator in unrelenting graphic detail. Marsyas is systematically skinned alive, without even the prospect of death as a release from his pain, since he, like Apollo, even if on a lowlier plane, is one of the Immortals:

> Wolfslicht, und aus der Waldtiefe traten zwei Skythen, Männer des Nordens, auch Apollons Gefolge, Darmsaiten und Messer in den Händen, schmale Klingen aus Eisen, in Firnwasser geschliffen.
> Marsyas sah ihnen neugierig zu, wie sie herankamen, mit unhörbaren Tritten, und er verstand selbst dann noch nicht, als sie ihn, Arme und Beine in die Schräge zerrend, packten und, Kopf nach unten, als zottiges Xi, an zwei schwarzstämmige Fichten banden.
> Die Därme schnitten in die Gelenke.
> Kopfabwärts könne er aber nicht aufspielen, ächzte er. — Er versuchte zu lachen; es mißlang. — Die Flöte lag unter dem pendelnden Schädel [...]
> Erst als die Skythen seinen Balg, von den Leisten her aufzuschlitzen begannen, begann Marsyas zu begreifen, und sogleich ging alles im Heulen unter. — Er war unsterblich.
> Die Skythen schälten ihn aus der Haut, zuerst die Beine, beidseitig, vom Schritt her: die Schenkel, die Knie, die Waden bis zu den Wulstansätzen der Hufe, in denen Leder und Knorpel verschmolzen sind.
> Ins heulende Warum tropfte Blut.[2]

On a figurative level the story demonstrates the impossibility of Marsyas changing his nature. The question asked of him as his suffering intensifies: '[Kann er] denn nicht aus seiner Haut?',[3] has colloquial connotations which imply that some people at least are able to undergo significant personality change and survive the experience. Yet the force of Fühmann's story is to expose such assumptions as an illusion. 'Marsyas' suggests that there is no possibility of denying one's inner self and of entering into compromise with the powers-that-be as a way of avoiding suffering. Fühmann's primary purpose in writing it was to create a metaphor for the situation of the professional writer measuring his talents against the ultimate artistic criterion which the figure of Apollo represents. It also reflects his profoundly-held conviction that significant creative writing only arises from totally disciplined, self-lacerating effort. The force of 'Marsyas' is heightened, however, by two more personal aspects of the context in which it appeared: it was an expression of Fühmann's feelings in the aftermath of the GDR's 'Biermann Crisis', and he dedicated the story to Heinrich Böll.

Fühmann was one of the most prominent GDR authors involved in the protest against the expatriation of Wolf Biermann in November 1976, an action which brought him into direct conflict with the SED leadership and exposed him, not for the first time, to the kind of ruthless authoritarianism displayed by Apollo in his story.[4] 'Marsyas' demonstrates that Fühmann was no longer prepared to enter into the loyal compromise with official cultural policy which had, on many occasions in the 1950s and 1960s, undermined his creative intentions. The fact that Fühmann also dedicated his story to Heinrich Böll, on the occasion of the latter's sixtieth birthday, indicated both deep respect and a strong sense of literary kinship, evidence that for Fühmann, by 1977 at the latest, there was only one German literature worth the name: the one which linked him with Böll in moral opposition to repressive state authority in both the Federal Republic and the GDR.[5]

This pointer to the process of cultural convergence developing over the 1970s appears to contradict Christoph Hein's reference, in the interview which has provided the focus for this volume, to the continuing existence in the second half of the 1980s of two separate German literatures.[6] On closer examination, however, it accords quite precisely with the distinction Hein drew on that occasion between the experience of his generation, born in the 1940s and later, and that of the generation to which both Fühmann and Böll belong. Hein argued that the work of this older generation (Fühmann was born in 1922, Böll in 1917) could still be viewed in the context of a single German literature, since they shared 'einen gemeinsamen Hintergrund, eine gemeinsame Geschichte' — by implication, the Hitler years, their direct involvement in the Second World War, and their experience of the ideological polarization which led to the Cold War and the division of Germany. Hein also made the stimulating suggestion in this context that Böll, in terms both of his biography and of the focus of his work, could easily also have been an East German author: 'Daß Böll in Westdeutschland lebte, war sicherlich nicht zufällig, aber es wäre denkbar, daß er in der DDR gelebt und gearbeitet hätte'.[7]

The striking thing about both Hein's assertions and Fühmann's sense of kinship with Böll (to which he also referred in his interview of 1980 with Margarete Hannsmann[8]) is that it has only been possible relatively recently to consider the work of this older generation in terms of the parallels between their experience and the development of their creative writing. A detailed comparative study of Böll and Fühmann would be a fruitful exercise in itself, although it falls outside the scope of this paper. The more general point arising from Hein's comments relates to their implications for the reception of an East German author like Fühmann. They point to the misguidedness of literary critics in both German states in assuming that the ideological division of the nation locked authors in their respective states into irreconcilable creative positions, from the Cold War until at least the 1970s. The case of the distorted reception of Fühmann in both states suggests something akin to an unholy alliance of literary critics and publishers, in the face of a growing body of evidence in his creative writing, from the mid-1950s onwards, of the kind of literary quality and critical independence which transcends political boundaries.

Fühmann, of course, personally sowed the seeds of the distorted reception of his work through his adoption of a high-profile propagandist role in the GDR during the Cold War. Almost immediately after his return from captivity in the Soviet Union at the end of 1949 he took over the responsibility for cultural policy in the National-Democratic Party (NDPD), which had been created especially to cater for middle-class converts to the antifascist cause like himself, and by 1953 he had produced a collection of 'Aufbaulyrik' under the title *Die Nelke Nikos*, which ranks amongst the most embarrassingly simplistic of the Stalin era. By 1956 he was on the executive both of the NDPD and of the GDR *Schrift-stellerverband*, as well as being a member of the 'künstlerisch-wissenschaftlicher Rat beim Ministerium für Kultur'.[9] Then, in the late 1950s, he was one of the few established authors prepared to gather the first-hand experience needed to write about the GDR's industrial revolution — in his reportage *Kabelkran und blauer Peter*, published in 1961 (even if the results were not quite what the Party intended when it promulgated the 'Bitterfelder Weg'). This public role also extended to forthright attacks on the cultural life of the Federal Republic, for example in a pamphlet directed against the spate of unrepentant memoirs of Hitler's generals (*Die Literatur der Kesselrings*, 1954) and in a reportage exposing the impoverished state of popular culture in West Berlin ('Ich stieg am Bahnhof Zoo aus'[10]).

Fühmann was, however, also fairly unique amongst the authors who first came to prominence in the GDR, as one of the survivors of what he called the 'Stalingrad-Jahrgang'[11] and in the breadth of his cultural knowledge, from Greek myth and the German classics right up to the modernism of Rainer Maria Rilke and Georg Trakl.[12] He was sufficiently older than, say, Günter de Bruyn (b. 1926), Christa Wolf and Heiner Müller (both b. 1929) to have read widely before being subject to the 'Gleichschaltung' of Nazi cultural policy, and was therefore not a *tabula rasa* uncritically exposed to Stalinist dogma in the GDR's early years in the way Wolf described herself in her essay 'Lesen und Schreiben'.[13] Although this fairly sophisticated literary awareness over and above the utilitarian ambitions of Soviet socialist realism caused Fühmann immense guilty anguish, it did mean that he was aware of the need to extend the range and improve the quality of GDR literature from a relatively early stage of the Cold War. He tentatively sought to introduce the imagery of allegedly 'decadent' Expressionists such as Trakl, Georg Heym and Gottfried Benn into some of his poetry, while his early short stories, based on his war experience, contain passages of stream of consciousness and dream analysis which betray a close interest in the unmentionable Sigmund Freud and a basic knowledge of modernist narrative techniques. By the early 1960s Fühmann was so completely immersed in the work of another ideologically dubious modernist, the sculptor and dramatist Ernst Barlach, that he was able (in his story 'Barlach in Güstrow', 1963) to recreate the latter's existential crisis of

1937 sufficiently vividly as to raise the question whether this kind of persecution of intellectuals had really come to an end with the destruction of the Third Reich.[14]

This range of innovative writing, which, despite its obvious flaws, was aiming to build on the achievements of earlier twentieth-century literature rather than conventional socialist realist models, was encouraged by discerning fellow-authors in the GDR such as Stephan Hermlin, Georg Maurer and Louis Fürnberg, but was undertaken in almost total isolation from West German cultural life in the 1950s. There are no indications of Fühmann seeking literary contacts in West Berlin or further afield before the 1960s, no doubt because of a strong ideological desire to avoid doing anything to weaken his total commitment to the GDR,[15] and yet his early work could have been of considerable interest to Western readers with even a partially open mind to Fühmann's view of the Third Reich and its continuing legacy in postwar Germany.

This is where the attitudes of critics and publishers in the Federal Republic to politically active GDR authors such as Fühmann became crucial. If they were not prepared to look beyond the ideologically threatening façade, then important new elements in a far from monolithic GDR literature were going to be missed. Fühmann appears to have suffered more than most of his colleagues from the West's almost total failure until the 1970s to look seriously at the work of GDR authors.[16] Although he was introduced to West German readers in 1960 through the inclusion of his story 'Das Gottesgericht' in the anthology *Auch dort erzählt Deutschland: Prosa von 'Drüben'*,[17] edited by Marcel Reich-Ranicki, the general impression the interested minority in the West would have gained of him was more likely to have been determined by Reich-Ranicki's essay 'Kamerad Fühmann' in his influential volume *Deutsche Literatur in West und Ost* of 1963.[18]

'Kamerad Fühmann' is a curious essay which, in terms of its patronizing title, its entirely justifiable dismissal of Fühmann's earlier poetry, and its conclusions, presents Fühmann as an incorrigible propagandist for the SED régime. In Reich-Ranicki's words: 'Wie einst der begeisterte Rückkehrer aus der Kriegsgefangenschaft ist auch der reife und mehrfach preisgekrönte Dichter folgsam. Er hört nicht auf, der Propaganda der DDR zu dienen. Vergeblich wird man in seinen Arbeiten die leisesten Anzeichen der Unzufriedenheit oder gar der Revolte finden.'[19] Yet a few pages later we find considerable praise for

Fühmann's war-stories, relating to their narrative power and diversity, which go far beyond the limits of the official view of realism and caused him to be publicly rebuked in 1959 in the journal of the *Schriftsteller-verband, neue deutsche literatur*. Then individual sections of his autobiographical cycle *Das Judenauto* (1962) are rated 'vortrefflich' and 'meister-haft'; the title-story is 'eine in ihrer Art vollkommene Kurzgeschichte, die keinerlei Vergleiche in der deutschen Gegenwartsliteratur zu scheuen braucht'.[20] But this is all forgotten again in a dismissive conclusion which implies that, once officially criticized for going too far, Fühmann will always fall back into line.

Perhaps Fühmann was unlucky that the cultural East-West frictions following the building of the Berlin Wall in 1961 again drew him into public defence of the régime's actions, in response to an open letter from Günter Grass and Wolfdietrich Schnurre.[21] This conflict led to the refusal of the S. Fischer Verlag to proceed with what would have been the first all-German anthology of prose since the division of the nation, under the editorship of Klaus Wagenbach, which would have included Fühmann's story 'Das Judenauto', and to which Fühmann himself was now firmly committed.[22] Only when Wagenbach became a publisher in his own right in the middle 1960s was he able to make good some of the damage caused in previous years to cultural understanding between the two German states, by producing two all-German anthologies, both of which included stories from Fühmann's *Das Judenauto*: the *Atlas, zusammengestellt von deutschen Autoren* (1965), featured 'Die Berge herunter', his account of the annexation of the Sudetenland in 1938, as a contribution to the volume's unifying themes of *Heimat* and identity, while the highly successful *Lesebuch: Deutsche Literatur der sechziger Jahre* (1968) finally brought the title story of Fühmann's collection to a wider Western audience.[23] In the same year in which Wagenbach's *Lesebuch* appeared, the Swiss publisher Diogenes achieved the breakthrough of making *Das Judenauto* in its entirety available, as Fühmann's first book to appear in the West, a full fifteen years after his literary debut in the GDR.

As publishers began to take GDR literature in general seriously, a limited amount of catching up with Fühmann's earlier work was attempted, with a selection of his war-stories of the 1950s and early 1960s also being provided by Diogenes in 1970, under the title *Die Elite*, and the complete collection of his short prose, *König Ödipus*, appearing as a

Fischer paperback in 1972. Reich-Ranicki's ambivalent role in this belated process of reception is further accentuated by his response to *König Ödipus*: as literary editor of *Die Zeit* he drew special attention to it by taking the unusual step of reviewing the East German edition shortly after its appearance in 1966; yet the review itself is again predominantly negative, presenting Fühmann as a long-standing conformist whose work is still somehow readable when it is ideologically unpalatable, and who is only just showing signs of political independence and stylistic maturity, on the evidence of his two most recent stories, 'Die Schöpfung' and the title-piece 'König Ödipus'.[24] By 1973, when Fühmann's self-critical examination of his earlier life, *Zweiundzwanzig Tage oder Die Hälfte des Lebens*, was published in the GDR, his acceptance into the ranks of the authors of all-German status was finally acknowledged by its simultaneous publication in the Federal Republic, this time by Suhrkamp.[25]

Although Fühmann continued to have his major works published in both German states up until his death in 1984 and beyond, his reputation in the Federal Republic has never properly recovered from the distorted earlier reception which Reich-Ranicki's essay exemplifies. No serious study of his work was carried out there in the 1970s. The first general accounts of literature in the GDR, such as F. J. Raddatz's *Traditionen und Tendenzen* (1972), which discusses Fühmann's work under the heading 'Märchen-Irrationalität', broadly accept the 'Kamerad Fühmann' approach to his career thus far, while Eberhard Mannack attaches no importance to Fühmann's work prior to *Zweiundzwanzig Tage* in his *Zwei deutsche Literaturen?* (1977), a book which specifically sets out to rebut the notion of entirely separate literary developments in the two German states.[26] No single publisher has taken over responsibility for his entire work in the way Hinstorff has done in the GDR since the early 1960s: his West German readers still have to search hard today amongst the lists of Luchterhand, Suhrkamp, Hoffmann & Campe and dtv to find his main fictional and essayistic work, while his modern versions of classical epics are more widely scattered again amongst the minor publishers. There is still nothing in the West to compare with the nine-volume *Werkausgabe* Hinstorff has assembled since 1977, which devotes separate volumes to aspects of Fühmann's work still virtually unknown there, such as his high-quality translations of the work of Czech and Hungarian poets, his film-scripts, and his fascinating attempts to find a suitable prose form for the transcription of dreams.[27] This highly incomplete awareness of

Fühmann's work has severely hindered the task of reassessment and means that assumptions can still be made that virtually everything written by Fühmann before the 1970s is of negligible interest today. The recent monograph by Uwe Wittstock in the 'Autorenbücher' series, for example, is predicated on the belief that Fühmann's serious literary career only begins after his existential crisis of the late 1960s, when he almost died from alcoholism, with the writing of *Zweiundzwanzig Tage*. We still find Wittstock adhering remarkably closely to Reich-Ranicki's assessment of Fühmann's earlier work, well over twenty years on.[28]

Turning to the East German reception of Fühmann, it may seem natural to assume (on the basis of his much-quoted expressions of support for the SED régime, in his writing about events such as the international Youth Festival of 1951, the Hungarian Uprising of 1956 and the GDR's tenth anniversary in 1959,[29] which led Reich-Ranicki to dub him 'Kamerad Fühmann') that he enjoyed the full confidence of its cultural politicians and could publish at will. The situation was in fact much more complex: as a middle-class intellectual only converted as a prisoner of war to the communist cause, he constantly had to justify both his style of writing and his chosen subject-matter to ideological masters rigidly committed to socialist realism on the Soviet model. The only reviews of his early poetry to appear in the GDR were the largely sympathetic ones provided by his fellow-authors Georg Maurer and Anna Seghers,[30] while his prose debut with *Kameraden* (1955) faced considerable hostility from reviewers unaccustomed to war literature with unheroic protagonists,[31] and his first collection of stories, *Stürzende Schatten* (1959), was, as mentioned above, given a very hostile reception in *neue deutsche literatur*.[32] Fühmann had a difficult time with his East German publishers too, having to break his links with the NDPD's publishing house Verlag der Nation after abandoning his role as the Party's spokesman on cultural policy in 1958, and coming into serious conflict with his other early publisher, Aufbau-Verlag, over its insensitive editing of *Das Judenauto*,[33] before finding a more congenial base with Hinstorff.

As a result, his earlier work had a more marginal impact on readers in the GDR than is normally assumed, while his later work, from the 'Biermann Crisis' onwards, was generally published in small editions and conspicuously ignored by all East German media except the prestige cultural journals. There were also a few celebrated cases of stories being prevented from appearing there, most notably 'Der Mund des

Propheten' of 1982, Fühmann's contribution to the antinuclear debate, which highlighted the Biblical origins of the phrase 'Schwerter zu Pflugscharen', adopted by the GDR's unofficial peace activists as their slogan.[34]

The serious reception of his work in the GDR only began in the 1960s, largely thanks to the efforts of the Rostock-based Germanist Hans-Joachim Bernhard, who published a succession of discriminating essays over a period of ten years or so, taking initial stock of Fühmann's pioneering achievements.[35] (It seems no coincidence that Bernhard's recognition of Fühmann's importance developed from his major research preoccupation with West German literature in general, and — another pointer to the potential of a closer comparison of the two authors — Heinrich Böll in particular, exemplified in his study *Die Romane Heinrich Bölls: Gesellschaftskritik und Gemeinschaftsutopie*, published in 1970.[36]) During Fühmann's existential crisis of the later 1960s, however, after he had publicly dissociated himself from the 'Bitterfelder Weg' and resigned from the executive of the *Schriftstellerverband* in protest against the repressiveness of SED cultural policy,[37] public awareness in the GDR of his literary development was largely managed by Werner Neubert, the editor of *neue deutsche literatur* newly appointed after the SED's cultural crackdown at the end of 1965.

Neubert, a professor in Marxist-Leninist cultural theory and aesthetics in Potsdam, evidently saw it as his role to present a sanitized Fühmann to readers in the GDR. In a series of interviews and reviews in *neue deutsche literatur* published over the period 1966—1975 Neubert, focused exclusively on Fühmann's work as an adaptor of Greek myth, the *Nibelungenlied*, and Shakespeare for younger readers, without ever hinting at the political circumstances which had brought about this radical shift of creative orientation.[38] And when he produced an assessment of Fühmann's work as a whole, as part of a collection of essays marking the GDR's twenty-fifth anniversary in 1974, it proved to be an ideologically bloated attempt to argue that Fühmann's overriding concern over the previous quarter-century was to attack his bourgeois origins and bourgeois culture in general. A brief sample of Neubert's style should suffice to indicate the primitive level at which some prominent literary critics were still operating during the earlier part of the Honecker era:

[Fühmanns] geistige Auseinandersetzung mit den Stationen seines Lebens [entfaltet sich] als Abrechnung mit den Stationen reaktionär-ahumanistisch gewordener Bürgerlichkeit und deren weltanschaulich-geistigen, philosophischen und negativ-ästhetischen Wurzeln, insofern kulturelle Bildung betätigt wurde als Bestätigung elitären Anspruchs, Flucht in idealen Schein und schließlich in den Irrationalismus der Vorläufer des Faschismus [...] Für seine Generation hat Franz Fühmann gezeigt, daß nur der schonungsloseste, tatsächlich mit allem ideologischen 'Gepäck' vollzogene Ausstieg aus dem antihumanen System des Imperialismus-Nationalismus-Militarismus die künstlerische Aussage der objektiven Epochenwahrheit ermöglicht.[39]

In an evident attempt to rebut Reich-Ranicki's mocking use of the epithet 'Kamerad Fühmann', Neubert went to self-defeating lengths in the section of his essay devoted to *Kameraden* to explain the new ethical force concepts like 'Kameradschaft' had attained in the GDR after being cleansed of the taint of fascist ideology.[40] Furthermore, Neubert's concerted effort to view Fühmann's development as entirely different from that of his bourgeois counterparts in the West led him to treat Fühmann's writing about his childhood in the Sudetenland and about his war years as a thematic block unaffected by his subsequent experience of the GDR.

The fact that Fühmann had begun in the early 1960s to ask serious questions about whether there had actually been a revolution of values in the nominally socialist GDR, in stories of everyday life such as 'Strelch',[41] is rapidly passed over as an exaggerated anxiety on his part. The irony of Neubert's reassurance that 'die marxistisch-leninistisch verstandene und betätigte Kulturrevolution' is making steady progress[42] is that, at the time his essay was published, Fühmann was focusing his creative attentions predominantly on the *continuing* failure of the Party leadership to create a socialist democracy, in his stories 'Drei nackte Männer', 'Spiegelgeschichte', and 'Bagatelle, rundum positiv'.[43] Small wonder, then, that Fühmann had devoted his speech at the GDR Writers' Congress in November 1973 to the subject 'Literatur und Kritik' and the need for drastic reforms in the practice of literary criticism, in order to produce 'eine potente Kritik statt einer prinzipiell positiven, eine sachkundig engagierte, unbequeme, gnadenlose Kritik, eine Kritik, die aufdeckt statt zudeckt und zuspitzt statt abstumpft, eine Kritik, die uns zu schaffen macht, die uns anspornt, die uns durch Gedankentiefe und Maßstäbe fordert, kurzum: die uns ernst nimmt und an der Potenz der Literatur interessiert ist.'[44]

In the later 1970s the quality of Fühmann criticism in the GDR began to show signs of the kind of improvement he was asking for at this uniquely open Writers' Congress. Sigrid Damm's lengthy review in 1976 of *Erfahrungen und Widersprüche*, the first collection of Fühmann's essayistic work, set a new standard in sympathetic articulation of his political and aesthetic criticisms of the status quo, while the joint commentary by Jacqueline Grenz and Karen Hirdina in 1980 on *Die dampfenden Hälse der Pferde im Turm von Babel* retained much of the subversive quality of this ostensible 'Kinderbuch'.[45] Yet there was no attempt in his lifetime (in the way that there has for most of the GDR's established authors) to produce a monograph for the series *Schriftsteller der Gegenwart* (or elsewhere, for that matter), and thus initiate a fundamental reassessment of his work which would balance his undoubted achievements in illuminating the experience of the Third Reich against his never-ending battle with cultural politicians to permit an authentic portrayal of the failings of socialism. Only since Fühmann's death has this process been initiated by Hans Richter, one of the GDR's older school of Germanists who has progressively shown more sympathy in his essays for Fühmann's role as a precursor of *glasnost*.[46] Richter is now engaged in producing the long-overdue monograph, although it cannot now appear before the demise of the GDR itself.

The widespread failure of literary commentators on Fühmann's creative writing to appreciate its originality was obviously a source of considerable suffering to him, but he rarely alluded to it directly in his many essays and interviews. His most open reference to the bitterness caused by this prolonged misunderstanding comes in his interview of 1981 with Horst Simon, the chief editor at Hinstorff:

> Von Natur aus neige ich gar nicht zum Pessimismus: ich sehne mich wirklich nicht danach, mich hinzustellen und zu bekennen, ich sei gequält und traurig und so. Ich möchte arbeiten, etwas schaffen, hervorbringen, nachdenken, analysieren, auch durchaus 'mit Lachen die Wahrheit sagen', aber eben die Wahrheit. Ich bin auch nicht in dem Maße verletzlich, wie es andere sind, was natürlich kein Wertmaßstab ist. Ich glaube schon, robust zu sein, und ich erziehe mich auch ein bißchen dazu. Aber wenn ich mal so zurückschaue auf die letzten fünfundzwanzig Jahre, dann waren's vorwiegend schmerzliche und bittere Erfahrungen, dem Wesen nach Enttäuschungen, Abbau von Hoffnungen, ein immer mehr wachsendes Gefühl, ohnmächtig zu sein und mit dem, was man will und macht, wenig gebraucht zu werden. Philosophisch ausgedrückt heißt das dann wohl: die Diskrepanz zwischen Ideal und Wirklichkeit.[47]

If there were any remaining doubts regarding the autobiographical core of Fühmann's story 'Marsyas', then this statement provides powerful confirmation that his inspiration was an intensely personal one. The pain so graphically depicted in Fühmann's portrait of the mythological artist is quite clearly also his private anguish at not being adequately appreciated as a creative writer in either German state.

Despite his original partisan motivation, Fühmann became, both through the thematic focus of his writing and through the originality of his self-expression, an author of all-German importance, a worthy East German counterpart to Heinrich Böll. And yet, because of the distorting effects of the German division and the failure of critics in both states to look at his work as a whole and to acknowledge its development, essential features of his writing still have to be grasped in both states. Fühmann may have suffered more in this respect than, say, Christa Wolf, who performed similar propagandist functions in the 1950s, because he also established his creative career in that worst phase of the Cold War. He may even be the regrettable exception in terms of the extent of the distortion his work has suffered in both states. But his is certainly an urgent case for investigation, as the division of Germany comes to an end and the task of reassessing the cultural history of the past forty years begins.

NOTES

1   Reprinted in Franz Fühmann: *Irrfahrt und Heimkehr des Odysseus, Prometheus, Der Geliebte der Morgenröte und andere Erzählungen*, Rostock, 1980, pp. 353—68.
2   Ibid., pp. 361f.
3   Ibid., p. 363.
4   In his interview of 1980 with Margarete Hannsmann, Fühmann stressed that, while 'Marsyas' was not a 'politische Schlüsselgeschichte', contemporary political events had left their mark on it: see Franz Fühmann: *Essays, Gespräche, Aufsätze 1964—1981*, Rostock, 1983, pp. 449f.
5   For the wider context of intellectual rapprochement over the 1970s, see my article "The "other" German literature: Convergence and cross-fertilization' in Keith Bullivant (ed.): *After the 'Death' of Literature: West German Writing of the 1970s*, Oxford, 1989, pp. 176—93.
6   Krzysztof Jachimczak: 'Interview mit Christoph Hein', *Sinn und Form*, vol. 40, no. 2, 1988, 342—59; here p. 358. See also p. 17 note 1 above.
7   Ibid., pp. 358f.
8   See Fühmann: *Essays, Gespräche, Aufsätze*, p. 441, where he refers to his view of Böll, from about 1970 onwards, as 'Vorbild und — mutatis mutandis — Muster der Möglichkeit literarischer Kritik an der eigenen Gesellschaft'.
9   See Erich Loest: *Bruder Franz: Drei Vorlesungen über Franz Fühmann*, Paderborn, 1986, pp. 9f. (quoting from Hilde Weise-Standfest (ed.): *Schriftsteller der Deutschen Demokratischen Republik und ihre Werke*, Leipzig, 1956).
10 *Sonntag* vol. 13, no. 49, 1958, pp. 3 and 7. An excerpt has been reprinted in Helmut Peitsch and Rhys W. Williams (eds.): *Berlin seit dem Kriegsende*, Manchester, 1989, pp. 70—2.
11 See Franz Fühmann: 'Mein Erstling' (text of a broadcast on Westdeutscher Rundfunk in 1973), *Sinn und Form*, vol. 41, no. 2, 1989, pp. 273—9; here p. 273.

12　See, for example, the references to his childhood reading in his interviews with Josef-Hermann Sauter, *Weimarer Beiträge*, vol. 17, no.1, 1971, pp. 33—53, esp. pp. 41f., and with Margarete Hannsmann, in *Essays, Gespräche, Aufsätze*, pp. 430—8.

13　Christa Wolf, *Die Dimension des Autors: Essays und Aufsätze, Reden und Gespräche*, Darmstadt, 1987, pp. 472—8.

14　First published under the title 'Das schlimme Jahr', in Ernst Barlach: *Das schlimme Jahr: Grafik, Zeichnungen, Plastik, Dokumente*, ed. by Franz Fühmann, Rostock, 1963, pp. 7-72. Reprinted in Fühmann: *Erzählungen 1955—1975*, Rostock, 1977, pp. 219—81. See my articles 'Franz Fühmann als Lyriker und Förderer der Lyrik in der DDR' in John L. Flood (ed.): *'Ein Moment des erfahrenen Lebens': Zur Lyrik der DDR*, Amsterdam, 1987, pp. 51—72, and '"Subjective Authenticity" in Franz Fühmann's early prose writing' in Margy Gerber (ed.): *Studies in GDR Culture and Society* 10, Lanham, 1990, pp. 135—50.

15　In 1960, for example, Fühmann refused permission to Peter Jokostra and Ad den Besten to include selections from his work in the anthologies of East German poetry they were each compiling, on the grounds of their political hostility to the GDR. (This correspondence is included in Section 150 of the Fühmann Archive in the Akademie der Künste in East Berlin.)

16　The general neglect of GDR literature in the Federal Republic over this period is summarized by J. H. Reid in his *Writing without Taboos: The New East German Literature*, Oxford, 1990, pp. 2f.

17　Munich, 1960, pp. 144—63. Reprinted in Fühmann: *Erzählungen 1955—1975*, pp. 49—71.

18　Marcel Reich-Ranicki: *Deutsche Literatur in Ost und West*, Munich, 1963. Reference here is to the paperback edition, Reinbek, 1970, pp. 269—77.

19　Ibid., p. 272.

20　Ibid., p. 277. *Das Judenauto*, Berlin (GDR), 1962, was reprinted as part of the *Werkausgabe* in *Das Judenauto, Kabelkran und blauer Peter, Zweiundzwanzig Tage oder Die Hälfte des Lebens*, Rostock, 1979, pp. 7—172.

21　See Klaus Wagenbach (ed.): *Vaterland, Muttersprache: Deutsche Schriftsteller und ihr Staat seit 1945*, Berlin, 1979, pp. 184—8.

22　See Wagenbach's afterword to the more modest volume which emerged from this crisis: *Das Atelier: Zeitgenössische deutsche Prosa*, Frankfurt/Main, 1962, pp. 148—51. Fühmann's correspondence of 1961 with Wagenbach and the Fischer Verlag is also included in Section 150 of the Fühmann Archive.

23　See Klaus Wagenbach (ed.): *Atlas, zusammengestellt von deutschen Autoren*, Berlin, 1965, pp. 67—79, and Wagenbach (ed.): *Lesebuch: Deutsche Literatur der sechziger Jahre*, Berlin, 1968, pp. 22—8. Fühmann's first appearance at a major literary event in the West appears to have been as part of a GDR delegation at the annual meeting of Gruppe 47 in West Berlin in November 1965, although he did not give a reading from his work there. See Reinhard Lettau (ed.): *Die Gruppe 47: Bericht, Kritik, Polemik. Ein Handbuch*, Darmstadt, 1967, pp. 209—17.

24　First published in *Die Zeit*, 31 March 1967. Reprinted in Marcel Reich-Ranicki: *Literatur der kleinen Schritte: Deutsche Schriftsteller heute*, Frankfurt/Main, 1971, pp. 190—7.

25　Reprinted in *Das Judenauto, Kabelkran...*, pp. 281—506.

26　Fritz J. Raddatz: *Traditionen und Tendenzen: Materialien zur Literatur der DDR*, Frankfurt/Main, 1972, pp. 311—6; Eberhard Mannack: *Zwei Deutsche Literaturen?*, Kronberg, 1977, pp. 31f.

27　Franz Fühmann: *Gedichte und Nachdichtungen* (1978), *Simplicius Simplicissimus, Der Nibelunge Not und andere Arbeiten für den Film* (1987), *Unter den Paranyas: Traum-Erzählungen und -Notate* (1988), all published by Hinstorff, Rostock.

28　Uwe Wittstock: *Franz Fühmann*, Munich, 1988. I have examined some aspects of Wittstock's assessment in my article '"Subjective Authenticity"...' (see note 14).

29　See 'Weltfestspiele 1951' in *Die Nelke Nikos*, Berlin (GDR), 1953, pp. 49—78; 'Die Demagogen' in *Die Richtung der Märchen*, Berlin (GDR), 1962, pp. 155—9; and 'Zum erstenmal Deutschland' in *Das Judenauto, Kabelkran...*, pp. 162—72.

30 In *ndl* vol. 2, no. 4, 1954, 142—9, and *Der Schriftsteller*, no. 13, 1955, 8—10 respectively. (Seghers's article is reprinted in Klaus Jarmatz (ed.): *Kritik in der Zeit: Der Sozialismus, seine Literatur, ihre Entwicklung*, Halle/Saale, 1970, pp. 360—6).

31 Berlin (GDR), 1955; reprinted in *Erzählungen 1955—1975*, pp. 7-48. For its reception see Alfred Könner, *Sonntag*, vol. 11, no. 3, 1956, p. 8, and Dieter Wuckel, *Der Deutschunterricht*, no. 12, 1958, 597—603, see Hans-Joachim Bernhard's article 'Franz Fühmann's Novelle "Kameraden"', *Weimarer Beiträge*, vol. 11, no. 3, 1965, pp. 380—9.

32 Berlin (GDR), 1958; reviewed by Rosemarie Heise, *ndl*, vol. 7, no. 8, 1959, 32—4.

33 See Fühmann's afterword to *Das Judenauto, Kabelkran...*, pp. 517f.

34 First published in Hans-Jürgen Schmitt (ed.): *Franz Fühmann: Den Katzenartigen wollten wir verbrennen. Ein Lesebuch*, Hamburg, 1983, pp. 141—53. It only appeared posthumously in the GDR in Franz Fühmann: *Das Ohr des Dionysos: Nachgelassene Erzählungen*, Rostock, 1985, pp. 18—30.

35 'Nationale Thematik in der Erzählung' (= *Böhmen am Meer*), *ndl*, vol. 11, no. 5, 1963, pp. 152—5; 'Franz Fühmanns Novelle "Kameraden"', (see note 31); 'Franz Fühmann' in Hans-Jürgen Geerdts (ed.): *Literatur der DDR in Einzeldarstellungen*, Stuttgart, 1972, pp. 316—37; 'Meermotiv und Menschenbild: Bemerkungen zur Lyrik und Prosa Franz Fühmanns' in Konrad Reich (ed.): *Trajekt 5: Franz Fühmann zum 50. Geburtstag*, Rostock, 1972, pp. 6—32; 'Über den Grund des Scheiterns' (= *Zweiundzwanzig Tage*), *ndl*, vol. 22, no. 1, 1974, 121-8.

36 Berlin (GDR), 1970.

37 Fühmann discussed these personal problems frankly in his interview with Winfried F. Schoeller in *Den Katzenartigen wollten wir verbrennen*, pp. 350—84, esp. p. 363; see also his 'Brief an den Minister für Kultur' in *Essays, Gespräche, Aufsätze*, pp. 7—16.

38 'Klassik — neu erzählt: Werkstattgespräch mit Franz Fühmann', *ndl*, vol. 14, no. 12, 1966, pp. 99—102; 'Neu erzählen — neu gewinnen: Arbeitsgespräch mit Franz Fühmann', *ndl*, vol. 18, no. 12, 1970, pp. 68—75; 'Der Nibelungen Lesbarkeit', *ndl*, vol. 20, no. 6, 1972, pp. 155—7; 'Schrieb Shakespeare für Kinder?', *ndl*, vol. 21, no. 2, 1973, pp. 144—6; 'Ernste Schöpfung — schöpferisch und heiter' (= *Prometheus*), *ndl*, vol. 23, no. 6, 1975, pp. 129—32.

39 'Zur Ideologie und Psychologie des Werkes von Franz Fühmann' in Klaus Jarmatz et al. (eds): *Weggenossen: Fünfzehn Schriftsteller der DDR*, Leipzig, 1975, pp. 267—98; here pp. 268f.

40 Ibid., pp. 270—6.

41 First published in *König Ödipus: Gesammelte Erzählungen*, Berlin (GDR), 1966; reprinted in *Erzählungen 1955—1975*, pp. 347—75.

42 'Zur Ideologie und Psychologie', pp. 282f.

43 Published separately in the West under the title *Bagatelle, rundum positiv*, Frankfurt/Main, 1978; in the GDR included in *Erzählungen 1955—1975*, pp. 473—522.

44 Fühmann: *Essays, Gespräche, Aufsätze*, p. 75.

45 See *ndl*, vol. 24, no. 6, 1976, pp. 147—63, and *Sinn und Form*, vol. 32, no. 4, 1980, pp. 884—92 respectively.

46 Richter's essay on Fühmann's study of Georg Trakl, *Vor Feuerschlünden* (1982), in his *Werke und Wege: Kritiken, Aufsätze, Reden*, Halle/Saale, 1984, pp. 133—44, marks the beginning of a systematic analysis of Fühmann's works. See also 'Bruchstücke einer offenen Konfession: Zu Franz Fühmanns Essayistik' in Siegfried Rönisch (ed.): *DDR-Literatur '83 im Gespräch*, Berlin (GDR), 1984, pp. 33—40; 'Vermächtnisse Fühmanns: Zum postum Erschienenen' in *DDR-Literatur '86 im Gespräch*, 1987, pp. 199—214; 'Der Filmautor Franz Fühmann' in *DDR-Literatur '87 im Gespräch*, 1988, pp. 219—30.

47 Fühmann: *Essays, Gespräche, Aufsätze*, pp. 475—93; here p. 479.

'1968':

LITERARY PERSPECTIVES

IN POLITICAL NOVELS FROM EAST AND WEST

JULIAN PREECE

> Lutz: *Der große Traum ist aus* —
> Johannes: *Nichts ist aus!*
> Lutz: *Natürlich! Die Zeit der großen Einheit ist vorbei. Spätestens*
> *seit die Russen in Prag einmarschiert sind. Und wer weiß, wann*
> *die Chinesen irgendwo einmarschieren.*
> Johannes: *Die Chinesen machen das nie!*
> Lutz: *Den Russen hast's es auch nicht zugetraut.*[1]

I Introduction

1968 is the mid-way date between the Allied victory over Nazism in 1945 and the collapse of the postwar European order in 1989. On both sides of the Iron Curtain, whether in Dubcek's Prague or in Dutschke's Berlin, it was a year of violent unrest followed by defeats for the reformist or radical Left. It was no coincidence that the Stalinist régimes in eastern Europe faced one of their severest tests, namely that presented by the independent socialist government in Prague and student protest in Warsaw, at the same time as restorationist governments quelled students' rebellions in France and the Federal Republic of Germany. In both power blocs the threat to established authority came from a Marxist-inspired Left which sought, in related though thoroughly different ways, to renew Marxist political theory and praxis. There, however, the points of comparison seem to cease: Dubcek or Dutschke; the Prague Spring or the Parisian May — the two experiences are marked in the main by otherness and mutual incomprehension.

However, there is a relatively small group of German writers who, in one way or another, were exceptions to this rule. One novelist who not only experienced both sides of the divided Germany but was also able to identify with what happened in each was Peter Weiss. Yet in effect he had no real roots in either the Federal Republic or the GDR, since he had Swedish citizenship and had lived in Stockholm since emigrating from Nazism in the 1930s.[2] His rather more cosmopolitan perspective led him to find common factors and a decade later he viewed the internationalist aspect of the revolts and their joint failure as most important:

> Es ging nicht mehr allein um das deutsche Problem, es ging um eine Abwendung von der patriarchalisch-autoritären Ordnung, es ging um die Bestimmung des imperialistischen Terrors, wie er sich entlud über Vietnam. Was sich in diesem Jahr, in Paris, in Prag, auf den Straßen der Metropolen aller Länder ereignete, kündete eine grundsätzlich veränderte Lebenshaltung an. Heute, zehn Jahre später, haben wir die Folgen der Zerschlagung dieses Aufschwungs zu tragen.[3]

Uwe Johnson, Max Frisch and Irmtraud Morgner are three further writers of importance who were able to rise above the more common preoccupation with events in their own countries.

Johnson was exiled from his native Mecklenburg in the GDR from 1959 until his death 25 years later and he lived in Britain for the last decade of his life. This enabled him to stand somehow above or beyond the divide, but like the central figure in *Jahrestage*,[4] Gesine Cresspahl, he only really takes the East, Prague and the consequences for socialism in East Germany, with any seriousness.

Morgner presents a variation of this view. She was the only GDR novelist to give any attention to the West as the beginning of her fantastical, feminist satire, *Leben und Abenteuer der Trobadora Beatriz*, is set in France.[5] Trobadora Beatriz, a twelfth-century minstrel and poet who fails to find recognition in her own epoch because of her sex is awoken after some eight hundred years of fairy-tale slumber on 6 May 1968. She had been sent to sleep in order to await a time of greater justice for women and she still yearns on her return to waking life for 'eine dritte Ordnung. Die weder patriarchalisch noch matriarchalisch sein sollte, sondern menschlich' (p. 29). Her experience of revolutionary Paris, particularly the machismo of its male ideologues, leaves her partially disappointed while whetting her appetite for the promised land of 'real existing socialism' in East Germany, which is warmly described to her. The brief episodes in France underline how the Western experience was by no means completely alien to an East German writer, as what began to happen in Paris might be completed in the GDR: patriarchy at least was one form of oppression which united an otherwise divided Europe.

Frisch (who is of course Swiss and thus theoretically neutral) was cynical about Western concern for the fate of the reformists in Czechoslovakia, stressing that an Eastern Bloc version of 'socialism with a human face' may potentially serve as a model for the West. The suppression of the Czech experiment would serve the interests of both East and West:

> Die neuen Männer in Prag sprechen nüchtern, aber ihr Versuch ist kühn, Sozialismus zu entwickeln in der Richtung seines Versprechens. Ob ihnen das Gelingen gegönnt wird? Zu vermuten, daß dieser Versuch nichts anders bedeute als eine reuige Rückkehr in den Kapitalismus, wäre ein Irrtum, jede Zustimmung in diesem Sinn zudem ein schlechter Dienst, nämlich genau die Auslegung, die die Feinde der Demokratisierung haben möchten, um sie unterdrücken zu können. Noch mehr von diesem Beifall für Dubcek (hier und in der Bundesrepublik) ist Denunziation — aber nicht ahnungslos; "ein Sozialismus mit menschlichem Gesicht", das können sich unsere Machthaber nicht wünschen.[6]

Whether Western governments actively connived in Dubcek's downfall, or whether they might have done more to help him, are matters open to speculation, but the news of 21 August 1968, that Soviet tanks had rolled into the Czech capital, was certainly a devastating blow to those in West Berlin and Paris who had taken to the streets in April and May.

Frisch's comments stand out, like the novels by Morgner and Johnson, as exceptions to the general rule,[7] as in the main the two sides failed to understand each other. This is nowhere more in evidence than in the literatures of the two Germanys. Yet the speed with which East German intellectuals and writers were dispatched to the sidelines after November 1989 was anticipated by what happened twenty years previously to their counterparts in the West. Distance from the mass of the population is certainly an important theme in the novels of the West German student movement, which became a minor genre in the decade that followed, though it is wrong to say that disappointment at the failure of '68 led directly into the 'new inwardness' which marked much of the literature in the years that followed: politics remains at the centre of writers' concerns. Two generations of West German authors were influenced decisively by the turbulent events and the backlash which they provoked from the authorities. While those who had already achieved recognition (Heinrich Böll, Günter Grass, Hans Magnus Enzensberger) reassessed their political stance, the work of those who came to prominence in the wake of the unrest (Peter Schneider, Uwe Timm, Bernward Vesper, Peter Paul Zahl) was shaped by the writers' experience of it.

Böll became both more radical and more politically involved, motivated particularly by his revulsion at press and popular reaction to the terrorist Baader-Meinhof gang. His *Die verlorene Ehre der Katharina Blum: oder wie Gewalt entstehen und wohin sie führen kann* (1974) is a strong campaigning text with all the strength and moral rigour of an old-fashioned satirical pamphlet, while in *Fürsorgliche Belagerung* (1979) he makes a gentler plea for understanding between the generations caught up in the sometimes bloody conflict.[8] Like Grass he strives to understand the sons as well as the fathers — and unlike Grass he devotes equal time to the mothers and daughters as well. His indignation and sense of moral right, however, have a much clearer political thrust in all his novels after *Gruppenbild mit Dame* (1971) than in his earlier work.[9]

What was probably most significant for West German writers in the late 1960s was that, once they abandoned their literary manuscripts and stepped onto the political rostra,[10] they were forced to focus their attention upon the effectiveness of their words and actions — or lack of it. While Enzenberger discussed the 'death of literature',[11] others demanded revolutionary action rather than poems — even revolutionary poems. Frisch describes the dilemma which more moderate writers encountered in his *Tagebuch 1966—1971*. He refuses, for instance, to sign any more public declarations or appeals, convinced that they achieved nothing. On the day the news of the Prague invasion reaches him he can do nothing except carry on with what he would have done had nothing occurred. He quotes Kafka's diary entry on the outbreak of the First World War: "'2. August (1914). Deutschland erklärt Rußland den Krieg. — Nachmittag Schwimmschule'" (p. 179).

In East Germany there could never be any question about the political importance of literature, which in turn lent authors both prestige and influence — at least until November 1989. The GDR authors I shall discuss in this paper, Stefan Heym, Volker Braun, Christa Wolf and Christoph Hein, all still called for reform in November 1989 and all deal in their literary prose either explicitly or implicitly with the invasion of Prague by Warsaw Pact forces in August 1968. Unlike dissidents in other East European countries they remained to the end socialist critics of the communist régime and although the government may often have wished they would simply go away or shut up, all were ultimately loyal to the idea of a workers' and peasants' state on German territory: all learnt to live with the cynical and brutal crushing of what, in retrospect, was the last serious chance for East European socialism.

For Hein in *Der Tangospieler*, one of the last major East German texts to be published before the autumn of 1989, the Prague Spring is a very powerful metaphor for political and social hope, providing a backdrop to the narcissistic deliberations of his central figure, the historian Dallow. While East German literature of the early years had presented exemplary figures and exemplary resolutions to problems, Hein, in common with many other writers of his generation, does the very opposite in both *Der fremde Freund* (1982) and now in *Der Tangospieler*.[12] Dallow's lack of interest in the events in Prague, which are avidly followed by all his contemporaries, is, however, ultimately vindicated once the Soviets have regained control, as his failure to reach any degree of political awareness after his arrest and imprisonment leads eventually to his reinstatement in his old university post.

Der Tangospieler is an old-fashioned historical novel in the way that Hein sets his story twenty years in the past (Spring to August 1968) in order to depict themes of interest in the late 1980s. The text hints very strongly that only such characters as Dallow, devoid of all emotional depth and intellectual integrity, will flourish and be happy in post-1968 society. After Czechoslovakia has been occupied by Warsaw Pact forces (including the National Peoples' Army of the GDR), Dallow's successor is sacked for chance comments he made to students while still ignorant of the latest turn of events. Dallow is summoned back to take his place and on the eve of his reinstatement he settles down with a bottle of vodka to watch a silent television screen. The novel ends with a powerful image:

> Er [...] sah dem stummen Film seines Fernsehgeräts zu, der Soldaten zeigte, die von der Bevölkerung begrüßt und offenbar von Armeegenerälen besucht wurden. Frauen mit kleinen Kindern auf dem Arm warfen Blumen zu den auf ihren Panzern sitzenden Soldaten, andere Bilder zeigten Prager Bürger in freundschaftlichem Gespräch mit den Soldaten. Dallow trank in kurzer Zeit die Flasche aus, stellte den Fernseher ab und ging ins Schlafzimmer. Bevor er sich auszog, prüfte er die Klingel des Weckers und stellte ihn dann. Er wollte am nächsten Morgen pünktlich im Institut sein. (p. 217)

II The West German View

In West Germany the rebellion was directed against a consumerist and strictly hierarchical society, created by a parental generation who had all but denied, suppressed or ignored its part in Nazi barbarism. Family conflict and misunderstanding between the generations are overriding themes in the literature dealing with the student movement. In *Örtlich betäubt* by Günter Grass (1969) the seventeen-year-old schoolboy, Phillip Scherbaum, is sarcastically contemptuous of his father's allegiance to democracy: 'Mein Vater war natürlich kein Nazi. Mein Vater war nur Luftschutzwart. Ein Luftschutzwart ist natürlich kein Antifaschist. Ein Luftschutzwart ist nichts [...] Jetzt ist mein Vater Demokrat, wie er früher Luftschutzwart gewesen ist.'[13] The inability of Uwe Timm's hero, Ullrich in *Heißer Sommer*,[14] to communicate with his parents, and the intense awkwardness between parents and offspring in Böll's *Fürsorgliche Belagerung*, are further typical examples of this profound malaise which separated the generations.

Michael Schneider regards this conflict as specifically German, recalling 'daß die meisten meiner Altersgenossen ein ziemlich belastetes Verhältnis zu ihren Eltern hatten; daß sie selten mit Liebe, viel häufiger dagegen mit Geringschätzung, einem trotzigen Gleichmut oder mit Verachtung über ihre Erzeuger sprachen; ein Phänomen, das ich in dieser Ausprägung in keinem anderen Land beobachtet habe'. He believes that personal factors influenced the 1968 protest at least as much as social circumstances or political events and concludes 'daß hinter radikal-demokratischen Kampfzielen dieser Bewegung (Protest gegen Verrat der Sozialdemokratie in der Großen Koalition, gegen die vergreiste Universitätsverfassung, gegen den amerikanischen Vietnam-Krieg u.a.) noch ganz andere subjektive Triebkräfte und Sehnsüchte standen'.[15]

The National Socialist past makes a conspicuous intrusion into *Die Reise* by Bernward Vesper, once lover to Gudrun Ensslin and father of her child and whose own father was the Nazi poet, Will Vesper.[16] Ensslin became, along with Andreas Baader and Ulrike Meinhof, one of the most important members of the *Rote Armee Fraktion* and her commitment to violence emerged like theirs from the same milieu as produced Vesper's autobiographical novel. His childhood experience was extreme, as his father continued to hold Nazi views openly after the war, but the son's feelings towards him were characterized by a curious 'Haßliebe': he and Ensslin had at one time even intended to edit his father's collected poems.[17]

Die Reise is intended as a representative work, its posthumous publication only reinforcing its status as the 'testament of a generation'. Vesper clearly places his left-wing attitudes as growing out of family conflict, as a revolt against what remained of Nazism in postwar family life: 'Meine Geschichte zerfällt sehr deutlich in zwei Teile. Der eine ist an meinen Vater gebunden, der andere beginnt mit seinem Tod. Als er starb, flüsterte ich ihm noch den namen "Gudrun" ins Ohr, die ich gerade kennengelernt hatte' (p. 39). He writes of 'die eiskalte Gewalt der Erziehung, der Domestizierung' and that 'der Aufstand geschieht gegen diejenigen, die mich zur Sau gemacht haben [...] die Rebellion gegen zwanzig Jahre im Elternhaus, gegen den Vater, die Manipulation, die Verführung, die Vergeudung der Jugend, der Begeisterung, des Elans, der Hoffnung' (p. 55).

Contemporary West Germans were able to identify both with his childhood in Adenauer's Germany and his inner battle with his father, which led eventually to a posture of total opposition to society.[18] Vesper displays chilling contempt for the citizens who surround him, whom he describes as 'die Vegetables', 'faschistoide Deutsche' (p. 54), and his frustration and anger are at times so great that he wants to mow them all down. Whereas Vesper eventually internalized his rebellion, some of his erstwhile friends took a different step and joined the 'armed struggle', the psychological and emotional motivation for which is described in this autobiographical 'Romanessay'.[19]

Böll's Rolf Tolm, on the other hand, son of a successful but liberal industrialist, and who himself 'fast Bankdirektor geworden wäre, wenn er nicht, ja, wenn er nicht Autos angezündet und Steine geworfen hätte' (p. 166), is now in resigned, rural retreat. He ponders on 'diese mörderische mythische Logik' (p. 159) with which his former friends plot their campaigns against the rest of society (Böll's '6 gegen 60,000,000'[20]), and imagining that for the terrorist, such as Bewerloh, his ex-wife's new companion, rational argument must have ceased to influence political behaviour. For the revolutionary who has turned to terror, the enemy is 'diese Hydra mit vielen Köpfen', and he, a latter-day Siegfried, 'würde alle diese Köpfe abzuschlagen versuchen [...] das war mit dem Wort Kapitalismus nicht mehr gedeckt, war mehr, mythisch' (p. 159). For his brother Herbert, whose own insurmountable difficulty is how to begin to combat 'dieses System, das "anderswo", sehr weit weg lag', 'das System' is 'das Nichts', 'die etablierte Nichtigkeit' (p. 121). This is a political and personal dilemma which confronts all the revolutionary characters in West German novels dealing with radical protest, its beginnings and aftermath. It accounts also for the 'decentred realism', common to most of these novels, as they are unable to reproduce more than a fragmentary, partial picture of political reality. The political centre, which might feasibly have been reached or affected through mass participation, for instance, remains beyond the individual's experience or field of vision. Consequently political targets are confused, or have a purely symbolic or metaphorical value, as Johnson's Gesine Cresspahl realizes only too well.

Three days after the Easter attempt on Dutschke's life,[21] Gesine telephones her old schoolfriend, 'die rote Anita', in West Berlin to make sure she is all right amid the reported scenes of street violence. Gesine has woefully misunderstood the situation (of course Anita is safe) and she takes time to comprehend why the demonstrators should be shouting 'Ho-Ho-Ho-tschi-minh!', asking, 'und wieso Ho-tschi-minh? Geht es nicht um den Anschlag auf Herrn Dutschke?' Anita explains, 'um Rudi Dutschke, und um Herrn Professor Springer. Der soll es mit seinen Zeitungen gemacht haben.' When hero, target and cause of the rebellion are so unconnected, no wonder its aims are uncertain, its chances of success slim. Gesine summarizes her impression after Anita has explained once more: 'Der Präsident der Republik Nord-Viet Nam als Symbol des revolutionären Befreiungskrieges, ein Zeitungsverleger als Symbol der Unterdrückungsmacht' (p. 988). For Gesine the true struggle is taking place in the East, where the stakes are high, the consequences real, while the Western students are little more than play-acting.

Johnson spent his entire career honing a narrative method which exemplified an author's incapability of depicting anything like a rounded, Lukácsian totality. His narrator's vision is always fractured and in both *Mutmaßungen über Jakob* (1959)[22] and *Jahrestage* this is evidently a consequence of (apparently) opaque political realities. Böll's literary form in *Fürsorgliche Belagerung*, constructed from a series of limited, individual perspectives with a confusingly large array of characters, but reminiscent in its use of suspense even of television thriller or detective drama, also correctly reflects political circumstances. Yet in the true tradition of these genres Böll neatly ties up all his loose ends in the final chapters and thereby succeeds in providing a human solution which effectively by-passes the political problem. Johnson is more rigorous and consistent, since Gesine is involved both personally and politically; the political defeat of the reformists in Prague will be a personal catastrophe.

Lenz, the hero of Peter Schneider's novella, the classic of the activist student movement, is a frenetic revolutionary, who has desperate, violent fantasies when his desires for happiness are not fulfilled.[23] After he has experienced moments of idyllic rapture during an excursion to the countryside, 'alte vergessene Wünsche wurden in ihm wach' and he feels that 'er hätte den Asphalt aufreißen mögen' (p. 23). Yet he later chastises a friend for seeking personal emancipation from throwing a stone at a demonstration. He claims that the time for such (self-indulgent) feelings and actions must be over, that 'die Demonstrationen müßten Ausdruck einer viel breiteren und langfristigeren Arbeit werden', and that a protester must ask himself 'ob es politisch interessant und nützlich sei, seine persönliche Angst vor der Anwendung von Gewalt zu überwinden' (p. 24). Isolated, spontaneous acts of protest serve only the individual's personal and usually adolescent ends, such as those of Grass's Scherbaum, who wants to burn his own dearly-loved dog, the dachshund Max, in front of the Café Kempinski on Berlin's Kurfürstendamm because in Vietnam 'Menschen verbrennen jeden Tag langsam' (p. 225). The element of self-sacrifice is paramount, and Scherbaum only refuses to immolate himself because he claims Berliners are more likely to take notice of a burning dog than a burning human being. His teacher, the juvenile, apolitical anarchist Störtebeker from *Die Blechtrommel* (1959), persuades him that his action would be an escape, an expression of 'aktive Resignation' (p. 192), thus an admission of desperation and political helplessness. Scherbaum gives up his plan, eventually convinced of his existential rather than political motivation, and instead goes on to study medicine, thus aligning himself (in Grass's field of metaphor) with the forces of a reformist and (for Grass), even prophylactic social democracy.[24]

Despite manifest inadequacies, hypocrisy and maladjustments in West German society, all rendered that much sharper and less easy to accept if judged as a legacy of Nazism, there was no mass revolutionary movement in the late 1960s to absorb such as Vesper, Scherbaum, Lenz, the brothers Tolm, or Uwe Timm's Ullrich. The intellectuals' alienation from a mass base, which in turn created a gulf between their political aspirations and those of the majority of the population, was apparently total. This is the cause of Lenz's revolutionary and emotional crisis. He begins to realize that his conceptual knowledge of politics, however sophisticated it may be, is divorced from his own private experience. In discussion he notices that 'er rede lauter blabla, lauter braves, vorgekautes Zeug' (p. 9) and at the meeting of his 'Betriebsgruppe', where workers and students discuss a passage by Mao Tse-Tung, he cannot help feeling that 'der Text ist so weit von unserer aktuellen

Erfahrung weg, daß man ihn, unabhängig von einem persönlichen Zustand, mit völlig fremden und willkürlichen Erfahrungen füllt' (p. 30).
How it is that 'Eindrücke' and 'Empfindungen', such as one may experience on a journey or during a day at work, are transformed into
'Begriffe', or whether there is any meaningful relation betweeen the two
at all, comes to obsess him. What distinguishes Lenz from the satirical
gallery of figures he encounters is his sometimes naive, but nevertheless
genuine search for political authenticity, and his need of a politics free of
all cant and dogma, which should be founded upon his own real, lived
experience. Like *Heißer Sommer* and *Örtlich betäubt*, *Lenz* is a modern
'Bildungsroman' of sorts and the hero learns to slow down his frantic
pace through his urban environment and after his journey to Italy to
achieve 'das richtige Tempo für meine Wahrnehmungen, für die
Verknüpfung meiner Wahrnehmungen mit meinen Erkenntnissen' (p.
75). Whereas previously he had been unable to integrate into a West
Berlin factory, and he had failed to overcome 'den Widerspruch zwischen den Klassen privat durch eine Liebesgeschichte' (p. 46), now after
his return from Italy, 'da er die Bedürfnisse der Studenten und Arbeiter
[...] jeden Tag offen vor sich sah, zweifelte er nicht an den Begriffen, mit
denen er sie ausdrückte' (p. 83). Like Scherbaum and Ullrich he arrives
at a solution which may be private but which still upholds the meaning-
fulness of political action. In the closing sentences of the book, when his
condescending intellectual friend, B., announces his departure for Latin
America and thus escape from the mundane, daily round of political toil
in his own country, he asks what Lenz now intends to do —
'"Dableiben", erwiderte Lenz' (p. 90).[25]

III The East German View

In Prague the conflict was not between generations but between a native
populace eager for reform and an alien power which destroyed their
hopes with military force. What happened in Prague was of exemplary
importance for all East European countries but especially for a country
like the GDR whose intellectuals had believed, by and large, in the
legitimacy of their own government, which was a party to the military
intervention. Neither the government, nor the population in the GDR
was in any doubt as to the international significance of what was
happening on their southern border.

Two prominent East German dissidents, the disgraced physicist Robert Havemann and the political theorist Rudolf Bahro, refer to the events in Prague as representing an exemplary liberation from the Stalinism of the past. Havemann believed it to be a 'grandioser Versuch eines radikalen und kompromißloser Durchbruch zur sozialistischen Demokratie', which, if it had succeeded, would have borne comparison to the Russian Revolution itself, since for the first time socialism was combined with democratic individual freedoms.[26] Ten years later Bahro, who was imprisoned for these views, remained convinced that 'das 1968 entfesselte soziale Potential' had not disappeared and that it would 'zunächst durch passive Resistenz — weiter gegen den inadäquaten Überbau rebellieren'.[27]

Their fellow dissident, the novelist Stefan Heym, recognizes in his memoirs that it was 'ein Kampf, der [...] weit über die böhmischen Länder hinaus wirken wird' (p. 738), the consequences of which might reach as far as 'die sandigen preußischen Niederungen, in denen noch immer der Stock herrscht, mit dem der König die Bürger geprügelt' (p. 755).[28] He describes a visit to Budapest and a discussion of the 1956 Hungarian Uprising in the same chapter where these remarks occur, implying clearly that the two revolts against Soviet orthodoxy and authority belonged together. His wife is violently ill after hearing the terrible news that Warsaw Pact forces had marched into their ally's territory and she loses along with her health 'nun auch der Glaube' in a truly socialist society (p. 757). Yet Heym, the author of a remarkably balanced literary account of 17 June 1953, when Soviet tanks fired on striking workers in East Berlin, and *Collin*, where he chronicles the considerable repercussions of the Hungarian Uprising in the GDR, fails in his novels to give the experiment in 'socialism with a human face' any special treatment.[29] Although he had written *5 Tage im Juni* shortly after the events it describes, the text was extensively revised for publication (in the West) in 1974; even so, there is little sense that Prague was also in his thoughts. His omission is instructive, as it indicates that although there is no evidence for a lack of East German solidarity with Dubcek's régime, 1968 was not necessarily a date of great significance in the internal history of East Germany. All three, Heym, Havemann and Bahro, continue their opposition after Prague has been occupied.

Three prominent authors who do concentrate on the events, however, Erik Neutsch, Volker Braun and Reiner Kunze, offer an interesting range of literary and political standpoints.[30] Their three portrayals correspond to three modes of behaviour open to East German writers: support for the régime (Neutsch); outright opposition (Kunze); or qualified critique and determined, but constructive commentary (Braun). In February 1990, as a curious postscript to that beloved East European practice of rewriting history, Neutsch withdrew the fourth volume of his mammoth chronicle, which aims to encapsulate the entirety of GDR history, as he could no longer defend the orthodox interpretation he gave to the upheavals in Czechoslovakia. The novel could no longer be read in the Staatsbibliothek in East Berlin.

In the section 'Café Slavia' of *Die wunderbaren Jahre*, Kunze reports on the humiliations visited upon Czech friends once the old order has been restored. His vignettes and anecdotes devoted to the violence done by ideology on human lives, particularly those of the young, are a savage indictment of official policy in both the GDR and Czechoslovakia, and he was expelled from the *Schriftstellerverband* as a result.

Braun's reaction is more difficult, as he deliberately refuses to take sides. While his central figure expresses evident disappointment when he hears the news bulletin, his reponse is intended as 'dialectical' and Braun's prose as a challenge to his reader's perceptions and ideological beliefs. Kast and his colleagues are rehearsing an experimental play (hence 'Die Bretter' or 'Die Bühne' of the title) which has just such an interreaction between audience and performers (or reader and text) as its principal theme. The reader or audience is not served up with a prepared and easily digestible set of answers — that is not the sense of 'didactic' writing at all. Kast is revolted by the Western broadcasters who suddenly shed 'Wasser und Rotz zugunsten des wahren Sozialismus' (p. 114), and could certainly not contemplate quitting his socialist home to emigrate westwards, as many Czechs were forced to do. His 'yes' to GDR socialism comes, however, despite this setback. He has previously asked in a discussion, whether because '"die Menschen jetzt ihre Geschicke bestimmen und sich nicht mehr den Gegebenheiten beugen"', this also means they now have to deny 'die Gegebenheiten' altogether (p. 111). He refuses that path, which is the one taken by the authorities, but ultimately accepts the invasion of the CSSR as a 'Gegebenheit' that he has to live with and understand.[31] This was the line adopted by the vast majority of critical (and perhaps not so critical) writers.

For GDR literature, however, the year 1968 may have been a watershed for a different reason, as Christa Wolf wrote her programmatic essay, or manifesto, for a new kind of socialist literature, 'Lesen und Schreiben', and published her second novel, *Nachdenken über Christa T.*, which met with a tumultuous and troubled reception.[32] Both texts mark an important ceasura not only in her own literary career but also in the literary history of the country, as they express a timely liberation from the dogmatic strictures of socialist realism. Wolfgang Emmerich, in his influential literary history of the GDR, argues that from the late 1960s East German literature underwent a process similar to modernism in the use of new techniques and formal experimentation, and J. H. Reid more recently concludes that now 'the unique individual becomes the focus of interest' (p. 61).[33]

It is not by chance that these shifts in attitude and focus coincided with the beginning of the Brezhnev years of social and ideological stagnation, a period which was initiated by the invasion of Czechoslovakia. The major new prose writers of the next decade, Ullrich Plenzdorf, Klaus Schlesinger, Christoph Hein, Hans-Joachim Schädlich and Jurek Becker, all stand in Wolf's debt. The fractured social existence of individuals now becomes the object of writers' attention, a change which can be noted in the shift of emphasis in Braun's next prose text, *Unvollendete Geschichte*.[34] Both Plenzdorf and Wolf write about dead people who have failed, who are victims, at least metaphorically, of day-to-day socialism;[35] Hein's and Becker's figures might as well be dead, as they are anaesthetized to their environments, without hopes or aspirations, stripped of the ability to form human friendships.[36] Becker's Gregor Bieneck loses his youthful poetic spirit, which the publishing authorities had always seen as subversive, without even realizing his loss. His employers succeed in neutering him, as he produces anodine, ideological scripts: the deception of the authorities is in fact self-deception. Schädlich's title, *Versuchte Nähe*, taken from a piece describing the party leader's befuddled distance from his people, is an apt epigraph to the whole prose collection, where a lack of humanity and warmth between individuals, and particularly between individuals and representatives of the authorities, are dominant themes.[37] His texts may seem unremittingly bleak, but, rooted in everyday, social life, they are redeemed by a very strong sense of how the characters' lives may be made different. All these writers, but especially Hein and Becker, rely upon an underlying

Utopian notion, namely a comparison between the ideal claims of socialism and reality as portrayed in the literary text.

If there is now at last a classic account of East Germany and 1968, it is Hein's *Der Tangospieler*, where the antihero and central character is confronted with the chance to express at least support for the Prague experiment and its defeat. His self-seeking opportunism means that he fails to see the significance of what is happening even after he has been unjustly sent to prison. He was sentenced to twenty-one months for an act he committed unwittingly and for which, by the time he is released, he would no longer have been punished. When he returns to everyday life in Leipzig in the early spring of 1968, 'man ist ein Stück weiter gekommen', and the authorities would no longer think to arrest him for playing piano as accompaniment to a satirical song performed by an amateur student group.

For Dallow the whole experience has caused a personal crisis in his hitherto empty, but successful life. He is no longer valued by either his colleagues or by his institution and would have to debase himself (by working for the *Stasi*) in order to regain his old post. It is evidently not for ideological reasons that he refuses their offer. Yet the anger and resentment which he quite naturally feels are not channelled in any useful or productive direction. His previous friendships, like his early marriage, now prove to have been extremely shallow, his work as an historian mechanical, as he had always been told what subjects to research and how to go about them. His reaction is to seduce a whole series of women he picks up in bars and clubs, though he endeavours never to spend the night with any of them, never to leave his telephone number or arrange another meeting, since 'er fürchtete die morgendliche Enttäuschung, den Anblick des abgeschminkten und ihn erschreckenden Gesichts' (p. 56). Erotic pleasure and sexual power, often with a suggestion of sadomasochism, are the only things which interest or motivate him in the slightest. The only woman for whom he seems to have some feelings, although he regards her too as little more than a sex object, comes to regard him as a self-indulgent, self-pitying intellectual, whose personal crisis is a result of social and male privilege. The difference between the two of them, she gestures, is that she has to work to support her small child, whom she is bringing up single-handedly.

Dallow's experience in prison has merely brought out feelings which must have been latent in him before: it has taught him nothing.

He compares himself to 'eine elektrische Eisenbahn' which has been taken off its rails and which now has to be redirected, 'damit das Spielzeug weiter den endlosen, weil als Schlaufe angelegten Schienenstrang gleichmütig abfahren konnte' (p. 117). When this is done effectively at the end of the text all his problems are over. Hein seems to be suggesting that Dallow, like the impassive Claudia in *Der fremde Freund*, is a typical product of GDR socialism — a figure whose features Hein has exaggerated for dramatic impact. What makes Dallow even more frightening than Claudia is that there is no sense of personal loss or deprivation, which characterized the heroine of the earlier novella. Whereas Claudia is a chronically unhappy figure who develops a tough outer skin to protect herself from her own feelings and from emotional involvement with others, Dallow is merely superficial.

References to Prague, discussions overheard in cafés, conversations at a party, punctuate the narrative with deliberate regularity, as the text covers the exact span of the Prague Spring. When an acquaintance insists that 'so oder so ist doch jeder engagiert', Dallow replies that, '"was da in Prag passiert, kümmert mich so viel". Er schnipste mit den Fingern' (p. 159). For an historian to have such an attitude seems almost incredible, but that is precisely Hein's point, as he draws his reader slowly and subtly from a position of identification with Dallow at the beginning of the text, where his refusal to work with the *Stasi* seems commendable, to one of inevitable criticism, even condemnation, towards the end.

Finding no other employment possibilities open to him, he moves to work on a Baltic island as a waiter. His sex life quickly resumes its previous frantic pace and he continues to ignore all news reports from the outside world. His hedonism and sadistic selfishness now expressly account for his indifference when news of the invasion of Czechoslovakia reaches him. The unnamed girl he has spent the night with is distraught at the radio announcement, but for Dallow her distress only increases her attraction as an erotic object. The symbolism is heavy-handed, but effective:

> Dieses halbnackte weinende Mädchen mit den dicken Beinen, die ihren Kopf gegen den Fensterflügel lehnte und einer emotionslos wirkenden Radiostimme lauschte, über deren Rücken in fast regelmäßigen Abständen ein Zittern lief und die mit hilflosen Gebärden der Hand sich die Tränen abwischte, erregte Dallow. Er ging zu ihr, nahm ihr das Laken weg, das sie vor der Brust hielt, und trug sie zum Bett. Sie ließ es willenlos geschehen, und er schlief mit ihr, während der Radiosprecher ein zweites, heroisch klingendes Kommuniqué verlas (p. 210).

He returns from the island as the happy beneficiary of changed circumstances, rather than bemused victim of a malign political fate. His colleague and replacement at Leipzig University has been sacked for remarks made on 21 August, the day the tanks rolled into Prague. Unaware of the recent news, he had repeated the now abandoned party line that there would be no foreign intervention in Czechoslovakia, rehearsing the official reasons to his assembled students; someone shopped him immediately to the authorities; Dallow returns to take his place, oblivious to what has just happened, but happy that he is once more needed. The most disturbing aspect of *Der Tangospieler* is that, given the arbitrary, ideological ruthlessness of his society, Dallow's indifference is ultimately more reasonable and his behaviour more appropriate. In the end it is he who is vindicated, since he not only gets the job, but (so it seems) the girl of his dreams as well. It is a selfish and empty character such as he who flourished in late GDR society and Prague '68 is a metaphor for general hopes and aspirations which were betrayed and whose betrayal not only created such as Dallow but enabled them to prosper.

Uwe Johnson's Gesine Cresspahl is Dallow's exact contemporary, though the two could hardly be more different both morally and politically. The reports from Prague, which she reads in the *New York Times*, come to dominate her thoughts and reawaken 'Kinderhoffnungen von vor zwanzig Jahren' (p. 866). Born in Mecklenburg in 1933, she was a citizen of the German Democratic Republic for the first three and a half years of its existence until she 'dahin ging, wo ein anderer Pfeffer wächst' (p. 464) and emigrated to the West, the story of which is told in *Mutmaßungen über Jakob*. After working at the NATO Headquarters in West Germany she is now an emigrée in New York employed by an American merchant bank. Somehow she is still a determined socialist; her hopes have been nurtured in exile, just as those of Morgner's *Trobadora Beatriz* were kept alive in absence. Johnson is 'der Genosse Schriftsteller', who chronicles each day from 21 August 1967 to 20 August 1968, the day before Gesine is due to arrive in Prague on a mission from her bank and the day before Dubcek's brave defiance is trodden under heel. That date is the *telos* to *Jahrestage*.

About nine tenths of the very long text (1,891 pages in all) are devoted to Gesine's reconstruction of her personal history, which becomes also the history of twentieth-century Germany and which she either dictates into a tape recorder for the future benefit of her daughter, Marie, or recounts to Marie directly. Gesine is obsessed by her past, which determines not only her interest in the current events of 1967—1968, but all her actions and attitudes. She is initially sceptical about what is happening in Czechoslovakia, remarking on 20 January, 'daß die K.P.C. in der Tat sich selbst "demokratisieren und humanisieren" will? Die Worte kenne ich. Reichlich abgetragene Schuhe' (p. 620). But her attitude quickly changes and a fortnight later she believes, 'es könnte dennoch ein Anfang sein', 'es könnte ja ein Sozialismus anfangen, mit einer in Kraft gesetzten Verfassung, mit der Freiheit zu reden, zu reisen, über die Verwendung der Produktionsmittel zu bestimmen, auch für den Einzelnen', 'für den würde ich arbeiten, aus freien Stücken' (p. 690). The supreme irony of her intentions, which is not lost on her, is that she will work for the capitalist West in lending the Czechs money for economic expansion and that her employer, de Rosny, is motivated solely by financial return on his bank's investments.

Gesine is interested, like every other foreign observer, in the international significance of the reforms. The socialist hopes of her youth, which had been betrayed by Stalinist machinations, arrests, denunciations and rigid, authoritarian dogma in the GDR she had known fifteen years previously, may now be given a chance. The last one and a half volumes of the novel (some 600 pages), which lead up to her journey to the CSSR, are devoted to the beginnings of the East German state and the opportunism and violence which characterized its inception. The narrative past, the deficiences of socialism in East Germany in the early 1950s, catches up with the narrative present, the defeat in Prague: the novel's structure means that the two sequences run parallel. The betrayal of her father, initially made mayor of Jerichow by the Soviet authorities and then dispatched to the concentration camp of Fünfeichen, is matched by the betrayal of the SPD by the Communists in creating the SED through an enforced merger of the two parties. Gesine's preparations for the journey are peppered with moments of excitement and anticipation: 'wenn ihr wissen wollt, was an Sozialismus möglich ist zu unseren Zeiten, lernt Tschechisch, Leute!' (p. 1447) — and worries which foreshadow the impending doom, such as those on 12 July when she remarks 'die *Pravda* erwähnt Ungarn. Das kann sich anhören wie Panzer' (p. 1538).

Her fiancé, D.E., also a native of Mecklenburg, a heavy drinker, defence industry expert, quietly envies Gesine's deep-seated conviction, her sense of moral right and her active attachment to her past, from which she draws her stubborn energy and determination. His own attitude is characterized by resignation, 'eine Haltung, die längst auf den individuellen Protest verzichtet hat und damit auf eine grundlegende Veränderung der Verhältnisse' (pp. 340—1). But because of their common background he understands how she thinks, unlike native Americans. In his letter of proposal he enumerates qualities which she still possesses, but which he lacks: she has 'eine rundum belebte Vergangenheit, Gegenwart mit Toten' while his past and background no longer mean anything to him;[38] for him his job is merely 'eine Funktion', which he carries out with no sense of commitment and no sense that he could achieve any degree of commitment; whereas she might be accused of a fascination with the dead (in her mind, she has conversations with people long since deceased). D.E. recognizes, 'für Dich gibt es immer noch wirkliche Sachen: den Tod, den Regen, die See' (p. 817). A belief in socialism is part of her 'belebte Vergangenheit': 'Du hast nie aufgegeben. Es versteht sich, daß ich es bei mir selbst unglaublich fände. Dir gebe ich recht. Immer noch nicht hast Du es satt, die Versprechungen des Sozialismus beim Wort zu nehmen [...] Wäre das Naivität, auch auf diese andauernde Lehraufgabe fiele ich herein mit Vergnügen; es ist aber Hoffnung' (p. 818).

In the *New York Times* she reads daily reports of murders, rapes, and violent robberies, accounts of slaughter in Vietnam, riots by American Blacks and demonstrations by students in Paris and Warsaw, next to reports from West Germany covering the trials of Nazi war criminals, the Federal Government's 'Notstandsgesetze', or the accusations against Federal President Lübke that he had helped to build concentration camps. The political assassinations of Martin Luther King, Bobby Kennedy and the shooting of Che Guevara also attract her eye. The past dictates her present interest in current affairs; it is a highly selective, limited picture of world events, but for a short while Prague is the only good news in the paper.

The motivations for civil unrest and protest in the West, whether in the USA, Paris or West Berlin, are quite foreign to Gesine, who learnt her politics in a fledgling socialist state and in the Cold War of the 1950s. Student protests are either devoid of all deeper seriousness, tactically inept, or pointless expressions of misguided idealism: they achieve nothing. She displays open contempt for Hans Magnus Enzensberger, when in a notorious public letter he lists his reasons for abandoning a post at an American university in order to travel to revolutionary Cuba (pp. 794—803, also 737f. and 769). His polemic is crude, full of rhetorical pathos and confident, easy answers, making banal comparisons between American imperialism and the Third Reich and drawing expressly upon Manicheanism to explain the American 'böser Blick', which he claims is recognizable all over the globe. The Manichean reference betrays a hasty use of binary oppositions, black and white, good and evil, which Gesine sees as typical of Western, or West German intellectuals.

Grass was also angered by Enzensberger and for similar reasons, but while Grass preferred dogged campaigning for small changes,[39] Gesine reviles the dramatic gesture because the hot-headed idealism which inspired it is both self-indulgent and self-destructive. Her American friend is puzzled by her reaction:

> Aber Ihnen, da Sie eine Deutsche sind, hat er gewiß ein Beispiel setzen wollen.
> Naomi, deswegen mag ich in Westdeutschland nicht leben.
> Weil solche Leute Wind machen?
> Ja, solche guten Leute. (p. 803)

Gesine's political work begins with mundane actions which have some chance of relieving suffering or injustices: she gives subway tokens (though never money) to beggers; she welcomes her daughter Marie's disadvantaged black school-mate to their home; she devotes herself to Marie's education and upbringing, attention which Gesine herself did not receive as a child; she gives Anita, her own former schoolfriend, practical help in smuggling someone out of Eastern Europe by getting hold of a valid passport. She feels contempt, on the other hand, for the dreadful Carpenters who give money to civil rights' campaigners but who do not want blacks living in their own neighbourhood.

A more sympathetic foil is provided by a fellow European, Annie Killainen, whose attitude is one of active protest and who takes refuge in Gesine's flat with her three children after her husband has beaten her for participating in an anti-Vietnam demonstration. Gesine will not go onto the streets to demonstrate because such an action would achieve nothing. She argues with herself, or with the voices in her head, exclaiming, 'Beweist es mir! Beweist es mir! Zeigt mir, wie ich einem einzigen helfen könnte, zuverlässig! sofort!' (p. 583). Since it is impossible to do anything to stop the war, it is better to do nothing: 'Ich könnte einen Leserbrief an die *New York Times* schreiben; ich könnte fürs Leben ins Zuchthaus gehen wegen eines erfolglosen Attentats auf den Präsidenten Johnson; ich könnte mich öffentlich verbrennen. Mit Nichts könnte ich die Maschinerie des Krieges aufhalten um einen Cent, um einen Soldaten; mit Nichts' (p. 894). The democratic options, open to any citizen in a free society, are just as useless as violent or terrorist actions. Nevertheless she is determined to go to Prague.

If the import of *Jahrestage* can be quickly summarized, it may be reduced to two things: it is a novel against all easy, ideological answers and it concerns a correct, moral attitude to politics, which if carried over into the political realm, must be not only intellectually consistent, but produce tangible results. It ends with defeat, as there is nowhere where she can lead 'ein richtiges Leben, in einer richtigen Zeit, mit den richtigen Leuten, zu einem richtigen Zweck' (p. 899), though critics who stress the bleakness of the ending forget that Marie (at least) will survive to continue her mother's fight.

IV Conclusion

This brief survey of German political novels and prose which deal with the events, emotions and political consequences of 1968, must conclude, to return to the theme of this volume, that there are at least two German literatures and that they have only occasionally attempted dialogue. The difference in political experience in the two states was almost too great for there to be sensible comparison. Hein and Schneider depict two classic examples of this extreme divergence; and Johnson demonstrates that the gulf is difficult to bridge. If there is something which unites such a diverse group of writers from East and West Germany, it is that political hopes, when articulated, have come from the Left, but that the failures of that same Left, particularly in the land where socialism was tried, have cast a very long shadow. When in *Die Glücklichen* by Peter Paul Zahl, that compendious novel of West Berlin left-wing sub-culture, the picaresque rogue and leftist polymath, now head of a one-parent family, leaves his Kreuzberg haunts to travel West through the 'Soviet Zone', he cannot help exclaiming to the ubiquitous poster of Karl Marx, 'Oh Charly. Was hamse mit Dir gemacht? O Charly, O Charly, der du da hangest an allen Plakaten.'[40]

NOTES

1 Volker Ludwig and Detlef Michel, *Eine linke Geschichte*, 4th version, Grips Theater, Berlin, 1987, p. 71.

2 The phenomenon of the writer as displaced citizen is reflected in the lives of the many authors who were unable to make either part of Germany their home. The Jewish writers, Elias Canetti, Paul Celan, Erich Fried, and Jakov Lind, all chose, like Weiss, to remain abroad after the defeat of Nazism. Wolfgang Hildesheimer chose to live in Switzerland after exile in Palestine and England, as did Thomas Mann after his return from the United States. The same phenomenon is reflected in the works of Günter Grass, Siegfried Lenz and Johannes Bobrowski, whose origins in the lost eastern provinces are reflected in much of their writing (see also Anthony Williams's discussion of this theme, pp. 255—67 above), and by the choice of the Austrian Ingeborg Bachmann to live in Rome. Similarly, many of the East German authors who were forced to settle in the West preferred to reside in the in-between city of Berlin (West).

3 Peter Weiss: *Notizbücher 1971—1980*, vol. 2, Frankfurt/Main, 1981, p. 681.

4 Uwe Johnson: *Jahrestage. Aus dem Leben von Gesine Cresspahl*, Frankfurt/Main, 4 vols published respectively in 1970, 1971, 1973 and 1983.

5 Irmtraud Morgner: *Leben und Abenteuer der Trobadora Beatriz nach Zeugnissen ihrer Spielfrau Laura. Roman in 13 Büchern und sieben Intermezzos*, Berlin (GDR), 1974.

6 Max Frisch: *Tagebuch 1966—1971*, Frankfurt/Main, 1972, p. 112.

7 Another, rather different, exception is provided by Günter Grass and Pavel Kohout: *Briefe über die Grenze. Versuch eines Ost-West Dialogs*, Hamburg, 1968.

8 Heinrich Böll: *Die verlorene Ehre der Katharina Blum*, Cologne, 1974; *Fürsorgliche Belagerung*, Cologne, 1979.

9 Heinrich Böll: *Gruppenbild mit Dame*, Cologne, 1971.

10 See also Stuart Parkes, esp. pp. 190—1 above.

11 Hans Magnus Enzensberger: 'Gemeinplätze, die neueste Literatur betreffend' in Enzensberger: *Palaver. Politische Überlegungen (1967—1973)*, Frankfurt/Main, 1974, pp. 41—54.

12 Christoph Hein: *Der fremde Freund*, Berlin (GDR), 1982; *Der Tangospieler*, Berlin (GDR), 1989. See also Gisela Shaw: 'Christoph Hein: The Novelist as Dramatist manqué' in Arthur Williams, Stuart Parkes and Roland Smith (eds): *Literature on the Threshold. The German Novel in the 1980s*, Oxford, 1990, pp. 91—105.

13 Günter Grass: *Werkausgabe in zehn Bänden*, ed. Volker Neuhaus, Darmstadt, 1987, vol. IV, p. 157.

14 Uwe Timm: *Heißer Sommer*, Munich, 1974.

15 Michael Schneider: 'Väter und Söhne, posthum. Das beschädigte Verhältnis zweier Generationen' in *Der Kopf verkehrt aufgesetzt oder Die melancholische Linke. Aspekte des Kulturzerfalls in den siebziger Jahren*, Darmstadt, 1981, pp. 8—64; here p. 54. See also Hella Ehlers's discussion of the *Vaterbuch* phenomenon, esp. pp. 233—8 above.

16 Bernward Vesper: *Die Reise. Romanessay. Ausgabe letzter Hand*, Frankfurt/Main, 1977.

17 See Heinrich Böll: 'Wohin die Reise gehen kann. Über Bernward Vesper, *Die Reise*' in *Es kann einem bange werden. Schriften und Reden 1976—1977*, ed. Bernd Balzer, Munich, 1985, pp. 206—11. Also Stefan Aust: *Der Baader-Meinhof-Komplex*, Hamburg, 1985.

18 See Michael Schneider: 'Über die Außen- und Innenansicht eines Selbstmörders. Notwendige Ergänzungen zu Bernward Vespers *Die Reise*' in Schneider: *Der Kopf verkehrt...*, pp. 65—79.

19 See also Alfred Andersch's short story 'Jesuskingdutschke' (in Andersch: *Mein Verschwinden in Providence*, Zurich, 1971), set during the Easter demonstration outside the Springer Haus. Two of the three students have fathers who had endured the concentration camps in the Third Reich and who are both sympathetic to their student offspring and want their children to continue their own struggle.

20 'Will Ulrike Meinhof Gnade oder Freies Geleit?' in *Ende der Bescheidenheit. Schriften und Reden 1969—1972*, ed. Bernd Balzer, Munich, 1985, pp. 222—29; here p. 226.

21 Dutschke was the leading figure in the Sozialistischer Deutscher Studentenbund. On 11 April (Maundy Thursday) 1968 he was shot three times by a young neo-Nazi, Josef Bachmann. He survived and publicly forgave his would-be assassin. He died of his injuries some eleven years later. The protest demonstrations that followed the attack were among the most violent West Berlin had seen. They centred on the headquarters of the Springer press in Kochstraße, Kreuzberg. See Ulrich Chaussy: *Die drei Leben des Rudi Dutschke. Eine Biographie*, Darmstadt, 1983, and also Andersch: 'Jesuskingdutschke'.

22 Uwe Johnson: *Mutmaßungen über Jakob*, Frankfurt/Main, 1959.

23 Peter Schneider: *Lenz. Eine Erzählung*, Berlin, 1973.

24 Alfred Andersch's 'Jesuskingdutschke' again provides an interesting parallel. Marcel realizes that he could have staved off the blow which badly injured his friend by quickly knocking flat the policeman who delivered it. He did not do so out of fear of being beaten to a pulp himself. At the end of the story he withdraws to concentrate on his academic work. This is another personal, private solution to a public dilemma and suggests that violence and non-violence (whether inspired by fear or principle) will both lead equally to the students' defeat. Marcel's father is also pessimistic: '"Ob det jut is, det ihr so wenich überlecht? Ick gloobe, ihr wißt janich, mit wem ihr euch da anlecht. Der Rudi Dutschke hat's bestimmt nech jewußt." Leo beobachtete wie das KZ-Trauma seinen Vater förmlich schüttelte. "Vater," sagte er, "et hilft allet nischt. Wir müssen unsere Erfahrungen alleene machen." " Ick weeß schon," erwiderte sein Vater, wieder gefaßt. "Nur det ihr jetzt in eure Niederlaje looft, det steht fest."' (p. 144)

25 For the positive sense of the ending, see Michael Schneider: 'Peter Schneider: Von der Alten Radikalität zur neuen Sensibilität', in *Die lange Wut zum langen Marsch. Aufsätze zur sozialistischen Politik und Literatur*, Reinbek, 1975, pp. 317—29.

26 Robert Havemann: 'Sozialismus und Demokratie. Der "Prager Frühling" — Ein Versuch, den Teufelskreis des Stalinismus zu durchbrechen' in *Die Stimme des Gewissens. Texte eines deutschen Antistalinisten*, Reinbek, 1990, pp. 150—6.

27 Rudolf Bahro: *Die Alternative. Zur Kritik des real existierenden Sozialismus*, Berlin, 1990, p. 11. (First published in 1979).

28 Stefan Heym: *Nachruf*, Munich, 1988.

29 *5 Tage im Juni*, Munich, 1974; *Collin*, Munich, 1979.

30 Erik Neutsch: *Der Friede im Osten. Viertes Buch. Nahe der Grenze*, Halle/Saale, 1987; Volker Braun: 'Die Bretter' (1968) later renamed 'Die Bühne', part three of *Das ungezwungene Leben Kasts*, Berlin (GDR), 1971; Reiner Kunze: *Die wunderbaren Jahre. Prosa*, Frankfurt/Main, 1976.

31 Gisela Shaw comments that 'his confidence in having finally found a mission that caters for totality of experience is not shattered' ('The Striving for Man: Observations on Volker Braun's *Das ungezwungene Leben Kasts* in the light of Goethe's *Faust*' in *GDR Monitor*, no. 13, 1985, pp. 5—20; here p. 10. Both Gisela Shaw (p. 91 above) and Joseph Pischel (p. 118 above) refer to 'Die Bretter'.

32 Christa Wolf: 'Lesen und Schreiben' in *Aufsätze und Prosastücke*, Darmstadt, 1972, pp. 181—220; *Nachdenken über Christa T.*, Halle/Saale, 1968.

33 Wolfgang Emmerich: *Kleine Literaturgeschichte der DDR: 1945—1988*, 5th edn, Frankfurt/Main, 1989; J. H. Reid: *Literature without Taboos. The New Writing in East Germany*, Oxford, 1990. Reid continues that 'instead of social conflicts, in whose resolution the individual becomes integrated with society, private topics, those of love, personal identity, alienation, come to the fore' (p. 61).

34 Volker Braun: *Unvollendete Geschichte*, Frankfurt/Main, 1979.

35 Ullrich Plenzdorf: *Die neuen Leiden des jungen W.*, Rostock, 1973. See also Elizabeth Boa's analysis of 'modes of death', pp. 139—53 above.

36 Jurek Becker: *Die Irreführung der Behörden*, Rostock, 1973.

37 Hans-Joachim Schädlich: *Versuchte Nähe*, Reinbek, 1977.

38 Cf. Gesine at this point with Heiner Müller as discussed by Axel Schalk, p. 79 above.

39 Grass, campaigning for Willy Brandt, exclaims: 'Guck mal der lustige Enzensberger: hüpft bubenhaft einfach nach Kuba und ist fein raus, während du hier Schönwetter zu machen versuchst für die Dynamisierung der Kriegsopferrente und für die Anerkennung für Tatsachen, die schon vor Jahrzehnten Moos angesetzt haben' (*Werke*, IV, p. 335).

40 Peter Paul Zahl: *Die Glücklichen. Ein Schelmenroman*, Berlin, 1979, p. 489.

'EIN SCHWIERIGES GESPRÄCH':
THE CORRESPONDENCE BETWEEN MONIKA MARON
AND JOSEPH VON WESTPHALEN

ANDREA REITER

For a period of thirty-five weeks in 1987—1988, the internationally renowned West German weekly newspaper Die Zeit *ran a 'public' correspondence between Joseph von Westphalen, a freelance journalist based in Munich, and the East German novelist Monika Maron. The authors' letters, each about 800—900 words long, appeared in alternate issues of the newspaper's colour supplement,* ZEIT-magazin, *and were subsequently collected in book form.[1] The dating of the letters in the text refers to their first publication; since the period covered is less than a year, only the month and day are indicated (i.e. 3 July = 3 July 1987; 11 March = 11 March 1988).*

I

Correspondence between writers or other persons in the public limelight is by no means a rarity.[2] But in an age in which communication can be accelerated by telephone, radio and electronic mail, letters written in a traditional way may seem anachronistic. To turn to this apparently superseded genre thus requires a special occasion or the interest of a third party. The obvious occasion for the correspondence between Maron and Westphalen was the thawing of the political climate in the Eastern Bloc countries. It was to be expected that the West German public would be interested in the reactions to this by the citizens of the GDR. Although Gorbachev and his reforms are discussed at a relatively late stage, the correspondence lasts just long enough to include Maron's reaction to the demonstrations in East Berlin (January 1988) marking the sixty-ninth anniversary of the assassination of Karl Liebknecht and Rosa Luxemburg.[3]

The problems underlying such a correspondence surface in the letters themselves: 'ein schwieriges Gespräch', as the editor of the book version entitles her postscript. Westphalen, however, does not seem to be too concerned about the anachronism, but rather flirts with the idea that this public exchange will boost his reputation as a writer.[4] It is only the fact that the letters are published immediately, making them special within the genre, that he considers disadvantageous, particularly when talking about private matters (17 July). He pities people who no longer write letters (14 August). He observes, almost in the same breath, that it is 'ein bißchen überzüchtet', 'beim Briefschreiben übers Briefschreiben zu schreiben' (14 August); but he cannot help doing so himself periodically, if only because he is searching for a way to begin a letter.

Maron, too, is reminded of the anachronism of writing letters, but only after eight months of correspondence. She terminates her part of the exchange by pointing out that East Berlin and Munich have finally been connected by telephone. Maron is honest enough to admit that she is abandoning a dialogue which had for some time only existed as a formality (4 March). To be fair, she has repeatedly voiced her dissatisfaction about the progress of her correspondence. Her partner, however, seems to be surprised and sorry (26 February).[5]

Although both Maron and Westphalen try in earnest to establish a genuine dialogue, eventually it is bound to fail. Each undertakes a trip at roughly the same time — Maron spends eight weeks in the USA (letters from 27 November to 15 January), Westphalen four weeks in Moscow (letters of 4 and 18 December),[6] and the delay caused by this (which the reader of the ZEIT-magazin can infer from the content of the letters) turns the dialogue into two monologues. Although neither Maron nor Westphalen expresses this verbally, both anticipate the reversal of place with a great deal of interest. Nevertheless Westphalen, who did not enjoy his trip to Moscow all that much, is not too pleased with his role as a 'Reiseschriftsteller': 'Die Abschilderung von Eindrücken kommt mir so brav vor. Wenn ich an unsere letzten Briefe denke, habe ich das Gefühl, daß wir uns nur wie wortlose Urlauber Berge von Farbfotos zugereicht haben' (29 January).

II

What, then, is the true reason for the failure of this dialogue? By the very end, the reader realizes that the two writers have run out of ideas. In her final letter Maron points to her 'lack of ideas', in consequence of their radically different temperaments. Westphalen's reaction seems to support this hypothesis. He stylizes the unsatisfactory course of the correspondence in the same consensus-seeking fashion which is characteristic of his previous letters as a virtue of resistance to the kind of 'Dialog' which has become fashionable in political discourse: 'es ehrt uns [...] daß wir bockig monologisiert haben' (11 March).

Are the difficulties in this communication attributable, as Maron suggests, simply to the incompatibility of two personalities? Much seems to support her view. Presumably, the dialogue between the writer from the East and the journalist from the West was doomed to fail at the outset, when the editors of the ZEIT-magazin accepted Joseph von Westphalen's choice of Monika Maron, thus pitting a female representative from the East against a male from the West.[7] The tension is increased by the fact that Westphalen is allowed the first and the last word in the correspondence. From his opening letter he acts the part of Western *animateur*. Entangled in an old-fashioned net, he repeatedly pushes his partner into a typical woman's role. He is polite enough, however, to leave the decision about formal or informal address to her: 'Neigen Literaten in der DDR zum Duzen oder zum Siezen?' (13 July).

Maron's reaction is surprising: She makes it clear that she perceives the GDR 'Gewerkschaftsdu' and 'Minderheitendu' as degrading, compared with the Western 'therapeutische Alternativdu' and the 'Englischdu', and thus as unacceptable in the dialogue with a Western colleague (10 July). She thus argues explicitly in political terms in justifying her preference by referring to an aspect of the GDR society which she loathes. Westphalen's assumed 'male' role becomes apparent even more strongly in his repeated remarks that, unfortunately, it is not love letters which are being exchanged (14 and 28 August 1987). Though Maron ignores these allusions without comment, her characteristic reactions to similar statements of Westphalen's would suggest that she is annoyed by this sort of remark as well (see especially the letters of 2 and 30 October).

Maron's angry replies become understandable if one considers the position of women in the GDR society. The emancipation of women was set down in the socialist constitution and, at least as far as employment was concerned, was to a great extent realized. But although the GDR had the highest employment rate of women,[8] economic equality of the sexes was, until late in GDR history, used as a feeble disguise of the actual disadvantage of women and their underrepresentation on the political scene.[9] In a highly developed, feminist literature, the women writers of the GDR have fought for their emancipation.[10] With her novels *Flugasche* (1981) and *Die Überläuferin* (1986), Maron is firmly rooted in this tradition.[11] Why, then, the vitriolic counterattack? Would it not have sufficed to inform Westphalen about the position of the woman in the GDR and leave it at that? Possibly there is more to Maron's anger. Does she, however subconsciously, defend a certain view of life? She does not simply refuse to be pushed into the typical female role: she refuses to be treated as a representative of the East. She vehemently rejects Westphalen's attitude as 'Animier-Partner', and does not want to watch him in his 'literarischen Negligé' (30 October).

Westphalen's letters confirm her impression that a dialogue between the 'Westmensch' and the 'Ostmensch' is doomed to fail simply because of the inequality of the partners. 'Deutsch-deutsche Gespräche', she claims, are characterized by a 'rhetorische Einseitigkeit' according to the pattern 'Der Westmensch fragt, der Ostmensch antwortet' (24 July). This pattern means that the GDR citizen will always be viewed as weak and subordinate, existing in the consciousness of her Western counterpart only as an exotic creature. The position of women in society is not all that different; so Maron, while fending off Westphalen's sexism, is able to teach him a political lesson at the same time.

Although Westphalen seems to think of the GDR citizen as a 'special animal', an attitude which he has to reconsider when he first meets Maron in person in Munich,[12] he also defends himself against the label of a typical 'Westmensch' (31 July). This is supported not least by his refusal to visit the GDR: he does not want to be a voyeur (17 July). If this attitude is not exactly that of the typical representative of the West, it nevertheless seems prevalent among Western intellectuals. Fritz Raddatz, who spent his childhood and part of his early employment in the GDR, testifies to this in a report on a trip to East Berlin on the occasion of the Wall being breached. He was ashamed of his role of the 'inquisitorial reporter', which he considered as indecent and dishonourable.[13]

The 'rhetorische Einseitigkeit' of the German-German conversation is by no means accidental; it is based on the fact that the GDR citizens were much better informed about the West, through Western media, than the average West German was about the East.[14] This at least was still true at the time of this correspondence. Referring to the topic of television, Maron observes: 'Würde sich ein Westmensch die Disziplin abnötigen, auch nur drei Tage hintereinander unsere Aktuelle Kamera (Beginn 19.30 Uhr) zu sehen, wüßte er über die Absurdität unserer

Verhältnisse mehr, als man ihm in einem vielstündigen Gespräch vermitteln kann' (24 July). This general reproach directed at the third person is doubtlessly meant for Westphalen and is understood by him as such. In his defence, however, he points out that Maron's criticism is misdirected, since the broadcast which she mentions cannot be received in Munich. On the basis of the prevailing rules of the free market, this need not be evidence of West German apathy (31 July).

This section of the correspondence is interesting for another reason: it is one of the few in which Maron has to accept criticism. And this brings me to the style of the dialogue. Maron argues in an aggressively intellectual way; her replies to Westphalen's letters are sharp and stern. His suggestion, for example, that the modification of the well-known motto of the peace movement 'Schwerter zu Pflugscharen' to 'Schwerter zu Bierdosen' might have originated in the GDR (28 August) is turned down laconically: 'Der Slogan 'Schwerter zu Bierdosen' kann nicht aus der DDR stammen, weil es in der DDR kein Dosenbier gibt' (4 September).

Throughout the correspondence, Maron seems to adopt a defensive role in her position of a critical GDR citizen, hitting back even when not attacked personally. It is thus not surprising, that she never allows herself to take up a new topic, or to be the first to discuss it. In the debate about Gorbachev, for instance, she does not immediately answer Westphalen's 'längst angebrachte Westfrage an die Ostfreundin: Sag, wie hältst Du's mit dem neuen Kurs?' (28 August), but in the following letter asks him for his opinion on the matter (4 September).

Her reactions compel Westphalen to be forever modifying his casually phrased assertions, to weaken and to relativize them. His caution in political matters concerning the GDR is guided by the fear that his West German compatriots might label him a right-winger. Every now and then he makes a somewhat forced attempt to point out a comparable shortcoming in the Federal Republic by disregarding the danger of comparing completely different things. While it is relatively harmless to assert that the ambivalent 'Landgefühle der Städter' are 'ziemlich systemübergreifend' (14 August), other comparisons are unacceptable. When, for instances, he relativizes Western press freedom by likening the effect of the free market upon it to censorship in the GDR (25 September), Maron is quick to point out in her following letter that he is trying to compare apples with oranges: 'Die Freiheit, als Autor einen herrschenden Markt zu bedienen, hat man wohl überall, die habe ich hier auch, und hätte ich sie mir genommen, wäre ich vielleicht schon Staatspreisträger' (2 October).

Westphalen compares with the eyes of a West German. Westphalen's attitude towards the GDR reveals a short-range thinking which, according to Günter Gaus, who spent six years in East Berlin as the first director of the *Ständige Vertretung der Bundesrepublik* (1974—1981), is typical of most West Germans:[15] he projects West German circumstances onto the situation in the GDR.[16] Where direct comparison is not possible, Westphalen's urge to compare does not prevent him from making indirect comparisons. He parries Maron's criticism of Western German prejudices against GDR citizens, especially as far as their appearance is concerned, with the statement that he abhors anti-Semitic prejudices (11 September): compared with the mockery of Jewish stereotypes (so his argument runs) Maron is criticizing a rather harmless offence. This argument characterizes Westphalen as a typical liberal representative of 1968 generation in West Germany, for whom anything that even remotely hints at traditional anti-Semitism is still taboo.[17]

Wherever, on the other hand, Westphalen abandons his struggle for a just evaluation of the GDR (i.e. an evaluation which cannot be easily taken over by the political Right) he comes over as condescending and didactic. This is particularly true of his boast about the advantage he enjoys as a Western journalist in having access to information in matters concerning recent publications: 'Würde mich interessieren, was Sie von diesem Buch [Martin Walser's *Dorle und Wolf*] halten. Aber das geht ja wieder nicht. Ich nehm an, Sie sind nicht in der Lage, dieses oder ein beliebiges anderes Druckerzeugnis ohne die Gnade der guten Beziehungen in einem Buchladen zu bestellen' (25 September). Westphalen's condescension is bound to backfire time and again, being based on a serious misconception of his partner. Maron has indeed read the book. Because of her position as a writer and her contacts with the West, she does not fit into the picture which Westphalen seems to have of the typical GDR reader of books. Even where he points out Maron's advantage of her limited access to Western printed media, he comes over as condescending: at least she does not have to put up with the critical opinion of the readers of *Die Zeit* (23 October).

Maron also attributes the limited success of the correspondence to a multiplicity of inadequately (i.e. insufficiently) discussed topics. From the outset, Westphalen showers his partner with questions: his letters are characterized by an abrupt shifting from one topic to another. However reluctantly, Maron has to bear with him. According to Gaus this manifests another difference between East and West Germans: in the GDR there is less 'Smalltalk',[18] the tone is more serious, and people have more time for conversation. Conversation among friends is of paramount importance, being one of the most important 'niches' in GDR society.[19]

III

Although Monika Maron complains about her Western correspondent treating every problem as a political one, and declaring every difference between them 'zum Unterschied zwischen Ost und West' (30 October), it is she who insists repeatedly on the peculiarity of the East. She is aware of her inability to escape politics even when reporting about a purely private incident.[20] Commenting on a holiday in her country home, she writes: 'Ich wollte Ihnen heute einen ganz anderen, weniger politischen Brief schreiben. Es gelingt mir nicht' (7 August 1987). Political matters (army manoeuvres, in this case) cannot be escaped. The 'niches', those preferred places 'der Menschen drüben, an den[en] sie Politiker, Planer, Propagandisten, das Kollektiv, das große Ziel, das kulturelle Erbe — an dem sie das alles einen guten Mann sein lassen' (as Günter Gaus rather crudely defines them[21]), are, like the rest of life in the GDR, marked by the social and political situation.

While GDR citizens retreat into their niches,[22] trying to escape politics at least temporarily, Westphalen constantly feels obliged to prove his political awareness. As a Western journalist he lives in a politicized world. Nevertheless, he falls back into the private personal sphere more quickly than Maron. Letters to the editor of Die Zeit criticize his lack of political acumen. He justifies his style by pointing out that private letters thrive on 'Sichgehenlassen' and on 'übler Nachrede', and that they please the public only if their authors are either dead or famous. But neither he nor Maron is dead, nor is he, at any rate, famous (9 October).

Still, political themes do crop up in the dialogue. Their handling by the two writers corresponds pretty much to the political system in which they have been brought up. What occurs first to Westphalen, when he considers the border between the two Germanys, is, typically, his attitude towards customs officials. Whereas he is annoyed by them in Western countries, he denies himself the same resentment where GDR officials are concerned: 'Ich denke nur deswegen nicht so schmutzig über Eure Zöllner, weil dies die schmutzigen Gedanken unserer Reaktionäre sind' (3 July). He collects his border experience on holiday or on business trips to West European countries. His attitude towards border officials depends on whether they search him for smuggled goods: 'Wenn ich nach Süden fahre, denke ich immer, wieviel besser doch die Italiener aussehen als die Deutschen, wenn aber dann einer von denen mich bittet, den Kofferraum zu öffnen [...] dann sehe ich in seiner adretten Uniform nur noch das Faschistische' (3 July). He does expect the formalities at the border between East and West (which he plays down as 'absurd' and 'exotic', and in the end 'halb so wild') to have a totally different meaning for his Eastern counterpart. For once she agrees with him: the most obvious difference is that, for the people in the East, the border is associated first and foremost with the lack of mobility and impossibility to travel. Her observation that this perception, which is based on the political circumstances, spills over into other spheres of life via metaphors is more significant (10 July). The impermeability of the border from the eastern side, moreover, creates dreams and desires, whose occasional fulfilment (through the granting of the odd travel permit) establishes barriers within the population which contradict the principle of a classless society. Maron's view about the border is necessarily expressed in an emotional way, although the source of her emotions differ from Westphalen's. In what he calls 'unsere gemeinsame Grenze', as it is customarily referred to, she can only see division.

Maron protests against comparisons between the two Germanys for fear of repeating familiar clichés. In particular, she objects to the slight differences which Westphalen attributes to the treatment of bureaucracy by the citizens in the two countries. Even if it is true that the GDR citizens treat their civil servants in a cunning way she says, this is no compensation for the 'Gründung von Bürgerinitiativen oder einer grünen Partei, [auch] eine organisierte Frauenbewegung mit eigenen Publikationsmöglichkeiten läßt sich durch keine Pfiffigkeit ausgleichen' (4 September). In this way, she sets the record straight.

While Westphalen's judgements are inherently subjective and emotional, an expression of his gut reaction, Maron argues in a more rational, intellectual way. This difference in their approach to a topic can also be observed in their attitude towards the new Soviet leader, Mikhail Gorbachev. Obviously, his reforms were bound to rouse quite distinct reactions in the East and the West. Their perception by the two correspondents, however, does not merely differ on political grounds, but confirms their differences in personality. What they share is a certain amount of prudence when talking about the international political situation (11 and 18 September). Nevertheless, both struggle for a judgement that turns out to conform to their political view of the world. Westphalen likes Gorbachev personally: even if he admits that this is not a political argument, he considers it an important statement. While he is interested in the personal aura of the new Kremlin chief, Maron is more concerned with his effect on the GDR. She admires Gorbachev and hopes that his example will shake her compatriots out of their political apathy and make them demand changes in their own country. In her interviews with Western journalists she complains about the lack of a fighting spirit among her fellow citizens, a stance which puts her in accordance with Western critics of the GDR like Martin Ahrends, who speaks of the 'Blüten des Stillstandes' in the GDR.[23] This Western polemic, however, tells only half the story: the reverse of the coin is the appeal of the GDR's retarded civilization upon Western tourists.[24] Maron's first letter diagnoses this 'neue Art von Heimatliebe oder nostalgischer Neugier', which Western tourists suffer from when searching for 'richtige Dörfer', 'angesichts deren man seufzen darf: ach ja, wie in meiner Kindheit' (10 July).

In order to appreciate Maron's expectation in Gorbachev one has to understand that her criticism of the GDR has focused on the political apathy of her compatriots. Even in her prose (and especially in her first novel), she tries to get at the roots of this problem. Only for a short while, prior to the demonstrations in Berlin in January 1988, does she begin to sound optimistic: 'das Wort Zivilcourage scheint wieder einen Sinn zu bekommen' (18 September). After the demonstrations she considers this hope as being confirmed and wishes that the courage of the demonstrators might have a multiplying effect (19 February). In an interview which she gave Volker Hage for Die Zeit[25] four months later on the occasion of her move to Hamburg, however, her optimism seems to have sunk to zero. Again she condemns the 'Lustlosigkeit' of the GDR citizens, which even the writers cannot or do not want to change. No longer does she consider Gorbachev to be the hoped-for model, but sees in him rather the source of a depression: 'Es ist ganz hausgebrautes Zeug, was da getrunken werden soll. Da sieht man es schon gar nicht mehr ein, stellt aber fest, daß man nicht gelernt hat, sich zu artikulieren und zu reagieren.'

What caused this pessimism was Maron's 'Kontroverse mit Hermann Kant', which the interview alludes to. The then president of the *Schriftstellerverband* expressed cautious optimism about the abolition of censorship in the GDR,[26] making it quite clear, however, that this did not mean the government's abstinence from its shaping role. Maron was to experience immediately exactly what this meant: the prospect of having *Flugasche* finally published by the Aufbau-Verlag after an eight-year delay was crushed by the veto of the chief editor, who condemned her correspondence with the Western journalist as 'unappetitlich'.[27] Even about the events of November 1989 Maron remains guarded, not least because the euphoria about the newly-won freedom touches the roots of her socialist identity.[28]

This takes us back to the correspondence and the controversy about the correspondents' self-perception as writers. Although Western politicians often parry criticism from writers with verbal attacks, Westphalen thinks that a writer's actual impact is minimal: 'Auch der angriffslustigste Literat kann nicht viel mehr tun, als die zu ärgern, die er nicht mag' (9 October).[29] He attributes this ineffectiveness of literary action to the 'freiheitlich demokratische Grundordnung' which provides a role even for the polemical writer, who merely has to slip into it, to the delight of the public. By thus absorbing attack and counterattack, Western society reduces this verbal battle to a kind of social game.

But 'real existing socialism', as Maron's difficulties in publishing her novels testify, distributes its roles in a different way. Thus she can legitimately continue to regard 'Widerstand für eine Existenzform der Literatur und die Literatur für eine Existenzform des Widerstandes' (16 October). Resistance, a term which Westphalen only uses in inverted commas, retains its original existential meaning for Maron. While GDR writers were relatively privileged, this was conditional upon their role in society: while it is true to say that the state offered them every kind of social benefit, the price they paid for this was high, only when they accepted the rules of the political game could they hope to enjoy the security offered by the social safety net (2 October). Failing that, they had to struggle on their own and their work became 'Selbstbehauptung im weitesten Sinn'. They had to defend 'was [sie] für richtig und wichtig erkannt hat[ten], gegen alle Angriffe, manchmal auch nur gegen die Realität' (16 October). Thus Christa Wolf's assertion of 1964 still applies, namely that the quality of GDR literature lies in its very consciousness of conflict, the fact that it produces 'neuartige Konflikte [...] produktive Konflikte'.[30]

The resistance expressed in and by GDR literature assumed additional relevance in its function as journalism. Since East German journalists 'entweder in falschen Tönen trällern oder ganz und gar schweigen' (30 October), serious writers had to take over their part as well.[31] Maron herself is a good example of this idiosyncrasy in GDR literature: at the centre of her partly autobiographical novel *Flugasche* is a young female journalist who gets herself into trouble when trying to publish a truthful report about the pollution caused by an outdated lignite-fired power station in Bitterfeld. She resigns from her job to pre-empt being sacked. The novel ends with indications that she is trying to pursue her cause as a serious writer.

The function of literature to compensate the lack or poor quality of information also had an impact on the reader. The rigorous censorship of the book market and the limited number of books published annually[32] both contributed to the extraordinary status of literature in GDR society. The fact that some books might be read 'von hundert Leuten' (24 July) makes Western writers jealous, as Westphalen subsequently confirms: he would not be surprised if some of them even toyed with the idea that 'die DDR sei womöglich die bessere Hälfte' (31 July). Reviews, on the other hand, are a different matter. Whereas those published in *Die Zeit*, for example, have a multiplying effect in the West, for the GDR writer it is 'das Schlimmste, was [ihm] passieren kann [...] im *Neuen Deutschland* gelobt zu werden' (24 July).

Resistance as a form of existence for GDR writers and artists was, at the time that Maron wrote about it, to be taken literally. To be hampered or prevented from publishing books, as Maron herself experienced, was only the most harmless form of disciplining by the government. Imprisonment and exile (Wolf Biermann in 1976 and more recently Freya Klier and Stephan Krawczyk in 1989) were the upper end of the scale. Without compromising Maron had stood her ground for a long time until June 1988, when she finally gave in and left the country of her own accord on a three-year visa.

Without knowing about her intention to leave the GDR, West-phalen refers to her in connection with 'inner emigration' (11 March). Her view about this category is not known. But, in June of the following year she indicated to Volker Hage that she had overcome her separation from East German life some time ago.[33] Whether this actually means a form of inner emigration remains doubtful. In any case, the expression is laden with too many associations and denotes too limited a historical situation to be left without further comment.[34] Furthermore, both Maron's novels and her interviews contradict this label. She openly op-posed the prevailing discourse in the GDR (this is especially true for *Die Überläuferin*). Her interview in the *Süddeutsche Zeitung*, which she gave shortly before commencing the correspondence with Westphalen, would suggest that she does not consider herself to be an 'innere Emigrantin'. The problems presented, especially in *Die Überläuferin*, where she adopts a distinctly experimental narrative technique,[35] are in her view not speci-fic to the GDR but concern the borders which lie 'innerhalb unserer Zivi-lisation'. She would leave the GDR if she could hope to escape these problems.[36] She has always refused to conform, when she was a student and later during her career as a journalist.[37] Even the political pressure from her family could not bend her.[38] She never allowed herself to see other than that 'der Kaiser keine Kleider hat' (19 February).

The situation of the inner emigration could be applied, with reser-vations, to some of Maron's fellow writers in the GDR, particularly those who reacted to Wolf Biermann's exile in 1976 by using historical subjects as political camouflage.[39] At no time did Maron permit herself even the most subtle of arrangements with the authorities of the GDR. If it really was the 'Tugend des Ostens', 'unauffällig und umso unangreifbarer anders zu denken als es offiziell erwartet wird', as Martin Ahrends thinks,[40] this did certainly not apply to Maron. She never made any compromises. Like the 'Löwe, der nach einem Urlaub im Dschungel nun wieder in den Zoo zieht, wo ihm die tägliche Mahlzeit und ein sauberer Käfig gewiß sind' (15 January), her own description of her feelings on her return from the USA, she cannot but perceive her situation in terms of a mutually exclusive 'either/or'. It seems to have been this 'Löwen ex-perience' which finally determined that she should leave the GDR, at least temporarily.

IV

Maron believes that 'die Sucht, die physischen Verschiedenheiten in Ost und West als endgültiges Ergebnis einer politisch-biologischen Mutation anzusehen, wurzelt eher im Westen als im Osten' (4 September), implying that the existence of two German languages is merely a cliché. Her view is rooted in her observation that a special GDR German is often associated with the influence of Russian, as in the word 'Datsche' for holiday home. According to her observations, however, very few people in the GDR actually use this expression. Moreover, she thinks that GDR German is 'ebenso durch die Computertechnologie und durch die Rockkultur geprägt wie überall, folglich wird sie von Anglizismen überflutet, wie überall.' The difficulties in conversing with her West German partner, which keep their correspondence going over long stretches, seem to contradict this categorical assertion. A possible reason for the difficult communication between two people actually speaking the same language could obviously be the fact that two very different personalities are exchanging ideas week by week in a limited space. This format seems destined to arouse conflict. But is it indeed only due to the 'verschiedene Temperamente', as Maron suggests in her final letter of 4 March that the communication between the journalist from the West and the novelist from the East fails? If this were the case, they should have come to a certain consensus within the eight months of their correspondence. The fact that this does not come about indicates that there were more fundamental differences of a linguistic nature.

The question of address referred to above (p. 323) suggests two different political views — Westphalen's 'Protokollfrage' challenges Maron's self-perception: she rejects the 'Minderheitendu' and the 'Gewerkschaftsdu'. This difference of perception indicates the division between the political blocs, which is revealed also in the argument about 'Pluralduzen'. Westphalen is annoyed when, by her use of the singular possessive pronoun in 'Ihr Herr Löwenthal', his partner appears to identify him with this well-known television personality. His protest is rooted in the fear of being associated with the political Right. However, his suggestion that they use the plural possessive when referring to representative figures is rejected by Maron on the grounds that 'Pluralduzen' reminds her of the formula '"unsere Menschen", diese viel gebrauchte Bezeichnung meiner hohen und niederen Regierenden für das Staatsvolk der DDR' (24 July). Apart from being an indication of

Maron's strong sense of individuality, her aversion to the use of the plural in address thus also seems to signal the existence of a specific GDR German.

A more subtle difference in German usage can be seen in the treatment of irony. Westphalen assumes, or even fears, a lack of agreement about this linguistic device in his first letter. Maron, however, does not seem to notice it initially. Eventually, he finds his fears confirmed by Maron's violent attacks: 'Liebe Monika Maron, daß mein letzter Brief Sie so sehr verärgert, hat mich überrascht. Ich gebe zu, das war kein Glanzstück, die Ironie war mühsam [...] Ein etwas frozzelhaftes Spiel mit Klischees, meinetwegen, und ich kann verstehen, wenn dieser Ton nervt' (11 September).

Westphalen's irony is not only reminiscent of the postmodern interpretation of the term, as a distancing from an expression whose meaning has become trivial through overuse,[41] as exemplified in the following comment: 'die Parodie der reaktionären Wendung bleibt uns oft als letzte verlegene Möglichkeit der Benennung' (3 July); he uses it as a literary crutch to hobble over unfamiliar territory (e.g. the nature of GDR society) and to bolster his diminishing personal security as his quick-witted partner delivers him one intellectual blow after another.

The irony of the 'Westmensch' hardly knows any taboos, at least they do not correspond with those of the 'Ostmensch'. As a writer in the GDR, especially one who was critical of the political régime, Maron does not tolerate jokes. She thus rejects Westphalen's assertion that a 'Schmießfliege' (he was quoting the term used by Franz Josef Strauß of a writer who attacked him), 'und wenn sie noch so böse summt', is 'ein fester Bestandteil des biologischen Kreislaufs [...] [und] hat keine Möglichkeit, Widerstand zu leisten' (9 October; Maron's reply: 16 October).

Westphalen, for his part, considers himself not only as misunderstood by Maron but complains about the seriousness with which she places him ' in die vernagelte Ecke derer [...] die bei den Buchstaben VEB brüderliche Glanzaugen kriegen und die Unverschämtheit besitzen, von hier aus in der DDR alles halb so schlimm zu finden' (23 October). Towards the end of this letter, however, he puts it all down to the view that there are different 'ironies' in operation in the East and in the West, attributable to the 'asymetry' between the GDR and the Federal Republic which influences both language and literature. If Westphalen had taken to heart what Günter Gaus said in 1983: 'Ironie, gar Selbstironie ist der Tonfall der Ketzerei. Dabei ist das, an dem der westliche Ironiker frevelt, keineswegs der Kommunismus',[42] he could have saved himself and Maron a lot of trouble.

As her prose testifies, Maron herself is not entirely without a sense of irony.[43] Although she does not give her opinion on Westphalen's concept of a split irony, her reflection confirms Gaus's position. Her own irony belongs to a different context. In the 'Briefwechsel' it is a bitter one, an expression of her powerlessness as far as the limitations imposed on a writer by the government are concerned. In two letters she comments ironically about how yet another of her numerous travel applications has been turned down, having planned to meet Westphalen in Munich. She tried to look on the bright side of things: 'Für unsere Korrespondenz ist das sicher von Vorteil, sonst erzählen wir uns in einer Nacht bei einigem Wein alles, was wir uns in der nächsten Zeit schreiben wollen. Und was machen wir dann?' (24 July). She counters Westphalen's surprise at how easily she can accept the authorities' refusal to grant her permission for a 'Lesereise in den Westen' with the observation:

> Ich sage mir, daß die Behörde, ob sie will oder nicht, mir in jedem Fall Gutes tut. Läßt sie mich reisen, freue ich mich, kann ich in öffentlichen Lesungen um Gunst der Leser buhlen, treffe Kollegen und sehe die Welt. Läßt sie mich nicht, zwingt sie mich, die ich zur Faulheit neige, zu kontinuierlicher Arbeit, so daß ich zum höheren Ruhme meines Landes ein neues Buch schreiben kann, das der gleichen Behörde um so schneller zur Begutachtung (die bisher immer als Mißachtung ausfiel) vorliegt, je seltener sie mich reisen läßt. Dann, hoffe ich, stöhnt die Behörde und klagt: Hätten wir sie doch reisen lassen, dann müßten wir jetzt nicht ihr Buch ablehnen. So lebt sie. Und Sie wollen mit mir Mitleid haben? Bedauern Sie die Behörde.' (7 August)

Maron's irony thus boosts a self-confidence weakened by political circumstances. It helps her to overcome the governmental chicanery, which she can otherwise do nothing about; it is a kind of self-defence with a fundamentally existential meaning, and not least a weapon which allowed her to remain in the GDR for such a long time.

In his letter of 23 October, Westphalen writes that 'dieselben deutschen Wörter werden von uns verschieden besetzt'. It remains questionable to what extent this obviously true observation, which locates the difference between the language spoken in the two Germanys in usage, not in vocabulary,[44] is an actual measure of the difference.

The 'Deutsch-deutscher Briefwechsel' suggests that the difference between the two German idioms does not remain at the surface, but points to two individual forms of existence, which have emerged within the forty years of the GDR, differing in many respects. A spoken language functions as a barometer of the political system. The people in the two Germanys are influenced more by the social and political system than they are prepared to admit. What is a question of style in the West, or a writer's personal nuance, could often assume a serious existential meaning beyond the frontier.[45]

Although language and literature are not the central themes of this correspondence, in its course they turn out to be the main bones of contention. To be sure, the literatures of the two Germanys have come closer together in the last twenty years;[46] but if the area of investigation is shifted to the conditions of production and reception, differences become immediately apparent. The same is true for language: lack of agreement is attributable to usage. In the main, it is sociological difference which is responsible for difference between the two cultures. It was the same sociological difference which caused the dialogue between the journalist from the West and the writer from the East to break down. Recent events, however, have turned this exchange of letters into a document of a historical situation which is already in the process of change.

NOTES

Translation by Andrea Reiter, with the assistance of William Drabkin.

1   Monika Maron and Joseph von Westphalen: *Trotzdem herzliche Grüße. Ein deutsch-deutscher Briefwechsel*, with a postscript by Antonia Grunenberg, Frankfurt/Main, 1988.

2   See, for example, the recently published extensive correspondence of Thomas Mann with other writers ed. by Hans Wysling, Frankfurt/Main, 1988.

3   The correspondents were merely given the guideline that their letters should be about everyday topics. Their political and intellectual orientation is quite accidental. (I owe this information to a personal communication of 12 December 1990 from the editors of the *ZEIT-magazin*.)

4   Cf. the description of a letter by Thomas Mann in Westphalen's letter of 14 August 1987.

5   Financial considerations were probably also a factor in the length of the correspondence.

6   Westphalen's trip to Moscow was organized by the editors of the *ZEIT-magazin*, as a response to Maron's trip to the USA (personal communication; see note 3).

7   According to the editors of *ZEIT-magazin* (see note 3) the choice of Joseph von Westphalen and Monika Maron was quite arbitrary. However, they were hoping for a male/female combination.

8   See Günter Gaus: *Wo Deutschland liegt. Eine Ortsbestimmung*, Hamburg, 1983, p. 216.

9   See Susanne Mayer: 'Nun kommen wir. Feministinnen in der DDR', *Die Zeit*, no. 8, 16 February 1990.

10 See Sara Lennox: 'Nun ja! Das nächste Leben geht aber heute an. Prosa von Frauen und Frauenbefreiung in der DDR' in: Peter Uwe Hohendahl and Patricia Herminghouse (eds): *Literatur in der DDR in den siebziger Jahren*, Frankfurt/Main, 1983, pp. 224—58.

11 Ricarda Schmidt, pp. 426—31, discusses *Die Überläuferin* from a related point of view.

12 The meeting took place between the letters of 21 and 28 August.

13 *Die Zeit*, no. 51, 15 December 1989.

14 See also Gaus: *Wo Deutschland liegt...*, p. 62.

15 Ibid, p. 86.

16 Ibid, p. 101.

17 See, for example, the the controversy about the posthumous staging of Rainer Werner Fassbinder's play *Der Müll, die Stadt und der Tod* in Frankfurt/Main in 1985. The documentation appears in Heiner Liechtenstein (ed.): *Die Fassbinder-Kontroverse oder Das Ende der Schonzeit*, Königstein/Ts, 1986.

18 Gaus: *Wo Deutschland liegt...*, p. 166.

19 Ibid, p. 165.

20 Gaus's observation (Ibid, p. 165) that the citizens of the GDR like to talk about private matters does not apply to Maron.

21 Ibid, p. 160.

22 Martin Ahrends talks about a 'DDR-spezifischer Druck' which made 'einen DDR-spezifischen Gegendruck reifen'. 'Der Widerstand, der nirgends hinaus konnte, befestigte sich in sich selbst, lernte, politische Nahziele loszulassen und sich als Lebensweise zu begreifen.' (Martin Ahrends: 'Das große Warten oder Die Freiheit des Ostens. Ein Nachruf aufs Leben im Dornröschenschloß', *Die Zeit*, no. 47, 17 November 1989.

23 Ibid.

24 See also Gaus: *Wo Deutschland liegt...*

25 'Alles zu wenig, alles zu spät. Steht die Kulturpolitik der DDR vor einer Wende? Kontroverses von Monika Maron und Hermann Kant, ein sensationeller Text von Johannes R. Becher', *Die Zeit*, no. 25, 17 June 1988.

26 See *Die Zeit*, no. 25, 17 June 1988. Kant is censured by Theo Buck, pp. 28—9, 32 and 40—1 above. See also Stuart Parkes, pp. 3—4 and 11 above.

27 For Westphalen, the correspondence also had consequences: because of his attack upon the *Bundeswehr*, he was no longer invited to publish in *Die Zeit* (personal communication from Thomas Beckermann).

28 See 'Ich war ein antifaschistisches Kind', *Die Zeit*, no. 49, 1 December 1989; also published in Hans-Jürgen Wischnewski et al: *Reden über das eigene Land: Deutschland 7*, Munich, 1989, pp. 67—85.

29 See also Joseph von Westphalen: *Warum ich trotzdem Seitensprünge mache. Fünfundzwanzig neue Entrüstungen*, Zürich, 1987.

30 Christa Wolf: *Die Dimension des Autors. Essays und Aufsätze, Reden und Gespräche 1959—1985*, Darmstadt, 1987, p. 405.

31 See also Hermann Weber: *Geschichte der DDR*, Munich, 1985, pp. 453—4.

32 See Dieter E. Zimmer: 'Lermontows Werke, Honeckers Leben. Ein Streifzug durch die Buchhandlungen und die Verlagslandschaft der DDR. Es droht das Ende einer seltsamen Buchkultur', *Die Zeit*, no. 9, 23 February 1990.

33 *Die Zeit*, no. 25, 17 June 1988.

34 See Charles Hoffmann: 'Opposition und Innere Emigration. Zwei Aspekte des "Anderen Deutschlands"' in Peter Uwe Hohendahl and Egon Schwarz (eds): *Exil und Innere Emigration. II. Internationale Tagung in St. Louis*, Frankfurt/Main, 1973, pp. 119—40.

35 Thomas Beckermann discusses *Die Überläuferin* from this angle, pp. 98—101 above.

36 *SZ*, 6 March 1987. Her eventual move to Hamburg shows that this statement is not quite true.

37 Cf. Maron: *Die Überläuferin*.

38 Cf. Maron: 'Ich war ein antifaschistisches Kind'.

39 See Wolfgang Emmerich: 'Der verlorene Faden. Probleme des Erzählens in den siebziger Jahren' in: Hohendahl and Herminghouse: *Literatur der DDR...*, p. 180.

40 *Die Zeit*, no. 47, 17 November 1989.

41 See Umberto Eco: *Nachschrift zum "Namen der Rose"*, Munich, 1987.

42 Gaus: *Wo Deutschland liegt...*, p. 123.

43 Two examples will illustrate the point. The biography of the narrator's parents in *Die Überläuferin* (Frankfurt/Main, 1986, p. 80: 'Rosalinds Eltern, der Vater gelernter Dreher, die Mutter Telefonistin, nach dem Krieg und der Gefangenschaft des Vaters beide Neulehrer, hatten sich unter äußerster Anstrengung das notwendige Häuflein Wissen für ihren neuen Beruf angeeignet und in den folgenden Jahren auf Parteischulen und ähnlichen Bildungseinrichtungen erweitert, wo sie die Wissenschaft von der neuen Weltanschauung nach wechselnden Katechismen erlernten.' And in *Flugasche* (Frankfurt/Main, 1981, p. 41), where Josefa comments on the devious sale of obsolete tombstones and the resultant paving of the footpaths in Wetzin: 'Wetzin jedenfalls bekam gepflasterte Bürgersteige, die für mich inzwischen zum Inbegriff nützlicher, wahrhaft atheistischer Denkmäler geworden sind.'

44 Cf. Martin Ahrends: 'Kleine DDR-Sprachschule', *Die Zeit*, no. 9, 23 February 1990.

45 Katrin Kohl, pp. 339—56 below, explores these aspects of language in the two Germanys.

46 See Wolfgang Emmerich: 'Gleichzeitigkeit. Vormoderne, Moderne und Postmoderne in der Literatur der DDR' in Heinz Ludwig Arnold (ed.): *Bestandsaufnahme Gegenwartsliteratur. Bundesrepublik Deutschland, Deutsche Demokratische Republik, Österreich, Schweiz*, Munich, 1988, pp. 193—211.

COMMON GERMAN LANGUAGE IN CONTEXT: CLICHÉ AND QUOTATION IN EAST AND WEST

KATRIN KOHL

I

In 1973 Erich Honecker stated: 'nicht Sprache und Kultur [haben] die Grenze zwischen der DDR und der BRD gezogen [...], sondern die unterschiedliche, ja gegensätzliche soziale Struktur der DDR und der BRD'.[1] If we take the 'contrasting social structure' to be the result of differing ruling ideology and political identity, Honecker's distinction identifies the factors which gave rise to the continuing debate concerning the number of 'German literatures' between 1945 and 1990.[2] Whether one considers there to have been one German literature or two during this period must depend on the extent to which emphasis is placed on the differing social and political context of literature in East and West Germany, the common cultural heritage, or the common language. The debate is founded in a long tradition, given Germany's late political unification, and it runs parallel with the less contentious issue as to whether the literatures of Austria and Switzerland have distinct identities.

Although the political identity of the GDR remained politically controversial throughout the country's existence, many factors encouraged seeing its literature as distinct from that produced in West Germany: notably the rigidity of the frontier, the firm centralized control over literary output especially during the 1950s and 1960s, the high degree of politicization of society and literature, and the relatively homogeneous society. Where the permeable frontiers between the Western German-speaking countries permitted open cultural interaction and unlimited communication between writers and readers, the Iron Curtain drew an effective barrier between East and West. Distinctions between Western national literatures using the same language are perhaps marginal when viewed in the light of the ideological and economic disparities between East and West. Peter Paul Zahl once commented that 'die Zeit der Nationalliteratur ist [in den entwickelten Kapitalistischen Ländern] endgültig vorbei, zerschlagen vom Weltmarkt',[3] implying a crucially different basis for literature in the two political systems. The governments of the FRG, Austria and Switzerland show relatively little interest in literature, and writers wield correspondingly little political power through their literary work; public attention tends rather to centre on the mass media. The absence of central political control permits a pluralistic literary landscape, although control is exerted by market forces. In the GDR, by contrast, the Party evinced a marked interest in literature, since literature was assigned the function of supporting Marxist values. Owing to public acknowledgement of the power of literature, GDR writers showed greater confidence in the power of their writing than authors in the Western German-speaking countries. Publication was determined by political judgements rather than market forces. All these factors contributed to a separate development for GDR literature. By the 1980s, political control over literary content, style and form was rather less specific and severe than in the early years, and television, especially, had made the border between East and West seem less absolute; but the generation of *Hineingeborene* could no longer look back on a shared history with West Germany. It had grown up with a different evaluation of the common cultural heritage, and in a more or less closed speech community.

With regard to the political and social context of literature, and its motivation and role, it is clearly appropriate to view the literature written in the GDR as distinct from that written in the West, despite some degree of overlap (writers who moved to the West, publication of East German works in the West etc.). The cultural and linguistic aspect, however, deserves closer scrutiny. In the following, I propose to examine some uses of quotation and cliché in East German poetry, with reference to the West. Quotations from German literature up to 1945 provide an overt manifestation of the joint cultural heritage. Clichés (a term which I use broadly to include all types of fixed collocation, including idioms) are segments of every-day language that are neither structurally fundamental, nor limited to the basic lexical elements. They are integral to idiomatic use of a language and tend to be peculiar to that language. Both quotation and cliché may be identified as chunks of 'received language', quotations being attributable to particular writers (or speakers), while clichés are handed down by the users of the language as 'quotations' from common parlance. Quotations and clichés offer both evidence of shared cultural and linguistic traditions in East and West, and evidence of the differing contexts and the extent to which those contexts influence interpretation.

II

The GDR (like the FRG) considered itself heir to the *whole* of the German cultural heritage: 'angesichts des Traditionsverlustes der Bourgeoisie im Imperialismus [... gehört] unser gesamtes künstlerisches Erbe [...] zu den Voraussetzungen, zur Entstehung und zur Ausarbeitung des Marxismus.'[4] However, only certain aspects of the tradition were singled out as worthy of forming part of the heritage: the GDR, according to Honecker again, is 'die staatliche Verkörperung der besten Traditionen der deutschen Geschichte'.[5] The choice varied according to the changing political constellation, with the debate between writers and the state on the value of various models playing a vital part in the GDR's literary history.

Although the cultural heritage of East and West may be considered the same up to 1945, the value assigned to it subsequently in the two German states differed in line with diverging political contexts. The literary scene in the GDR was more cohesive, with a strong ideological framework providing a firm basis for communication between writers and their readers, in some ways analogous to that offered by the Bible in the sixteenth and seventeenth century. The literary tradition was seen to have the purpose of relating productively to the present. A somewhat crass example is Ulbricht's interpretation of Faust's vision of mankind at the end of *Faust* part II. Ulbricht sees Faust's dream of a 'freies Volk' on 'freiem Grund' as a prefiguration of the GDR, whereas the description of the neighbouring mire points forward to the FRG:

> Ein Sumpf zieht am Gebirge hin,
> Verpestet alles schon Errungene;
> Den faulen Pfuhl auch abzuziehn,
> Das Letzte wär' das Höchsterrungene.[6]

So although the two states could look back on a common literary tradition, the perceived significance of that tradition varied in accordance with the differing ideologies.

This difference is evident in the role of quotations in poetry. The end of *Faust* may serve as an example:

> Alles Vergängliche
> ist nur ein Gleichnis;
> Das Unzulängliche,
> Hier wird's Ereignis;
> Das Unbeschreibliche,
> Hier ist's getan;
> Das Ewig-Weibliche
> Zieht uns hinan.[7]

Oskar Pastior alludes to these well-known lines in 'hier hat es die rosen an',[8] a poem that plays on quotations and expressions with 'Wort'. It starts with a quotation from Eichendorff's 'Wünschelrute',[9] and continues by recalling the Faustian lines 'Denn eben wo Begriffe fehlen,/ Da stellt ein Wort zur rechten Zeit sich ein'.[10] The end of *Faust*, already suggested in 'hinan!', then reappears in the third stanza, together with an allusion to John 1.1, 'Im Anfang war das Wort':

> schläft eines in allen dingen
> zwei ist eines auf vorderwort
> und nicht neben anderes haben
>
> ein es — ein es: im essigkrug
> hinan! ein gutes zur rechten
> hat worteswort — alles export
>
> es in die länge war am anfang
> das ledig wörtliche zieht es
> in faust und wenigkeit höher
>
> [...]

Pastior's use of literary models here is characteristic of the way in which he plays with the reader's expectations in order to loosen stereotyped thought-patterns: he is concerned primarily with language, with relationships between sounds and words, and with the thought-patterns relating to language. The reader is given enough familiar word-combinations to evoke a sense of recognition and logical meaning, but that meaning is then fragmented in such a way as to engender new fluid patterns.

Volker Braun's 'Gemischter Chor'[11] focuses less on general patterns of language and thought than on political and social reality, and views of that reality:

GEMISCHTER CHOR

Das Unverfängliche
Gibt uns kein Gleichnis;
Das Unzulängliche

Hier wirds E r r e i c h n i s.
Das fein Geplante
Ist doch zum Schrein.
Das Ungeahnte
Tritt eisern ein.

Braun's poem is based directly on the Goethean model. He works with the notion of predictability suggested in Goethe's lines, but changes the focus from metaphysical realms to the existing social context. Where Goethe's 'das Unzulängliche' refers to the general human condition, Braun gives it specific political significance, highlighting the discrepancy between ideal and practice, between official rhetoric and actual conditions. 'Das Geplante' (one of the key concepts of the GDR's economic order[12]) is called into question, and with it the positive view of a definite imminent future asserted by official sources. Braun subverts the notion of a fulfilled eternal plan suggested by Goethe *and* by official GDR rhetoric: not 'das Geplante' is inevitable but 'das Ungeahnte'. In the dialectical interplay between the Goethean model and Braun's reworking, a static assumption thereby becomes a dynamic issue.

With Pastior's poem, knowledge of the political and ideological context does not help us understand the poem. We need to look rather at the linguistic and literary structures with which he operates. By contrast, Braun's poem demands to be read with reference to the conditions and ideology of the GDR. Braun modifies tradition to make a political point, encouraging a more critical and realistic view of actual conditions in order that the reader may aspire to a fuller realization of Marxist ideals than is provided by the status quo. Where Ulbricht draws on *Faust* to bolster the régime, Braun uses it to call into question one of the prime official assumptions. As with Ulbricht, though, literary tradition is used 'productively' to address current problems and aspirations.

Concern with the present was generally manifest in the choice of literary models in the GDR, and the choice tended to be more homogeneous there than in the FRG. In the early years — dominated by Georg Lukács — Weimar Classicism had pride of place, in line with the official emphasis on humanist values. There then came a period in which writers turned to Romanticism and Hölderlin to justify their insistence on the right of the individual to develop his or her full potential, in accordance with Marxist doctrine. However, despite the focus on the individual, the argument was essentially socio-political.

In the West, quotations from the literary tradition tend not to have the same public significance. In 'Gedicht',[13] Jürgen Theobaldy quotes from Hölderlin's 'Hälfte des Lebens' ('woher nehme ich'[14]), and uses the Klopstockian word 'Mittler'[15] to highlight his personal predicament as a poet who has no firm mental framework or 'message':

> Aber woher nehme ich diesen Glauben,
> in der Wahrheit selber zu schreiben, rein, in
> klaren Versen, und wenn gebunden, woran?
> Keine Siege leuchten aus den Entwürfen.
> Klagen und Erwartungen, Fragen höre
> ich, erregtes Sprechen, ich rede selber,
> sonst auf nichts bezogen, auf keinen Glauben,
> nicht auf Götter, denen ich Mittler wäre.
> [...]

This may be seen as characteristic of poetry in a society which has no collective social aspirations and which can therefore offer the poet no clearly defined social role. The only firm point of reference is the self: 'ich rede selber,/ sonst auf nichts bezogen'. Theobaldy's poem is not concerned with a public debate, and in that respect the prevailing ideology is less significant for a reading of the individual poem than it is with the poem by Volker Braun.

During the 1980s, there were in fact indications that in the GDR, too, the social purpose of poetry was becoming less clearly defined. Where in the late 1960s, Christa Wolf's *Nachdenken über Christa T.* had epitomized the concern of writers to make the public sphere accommodate private needs, in the 1980s the younger generation of poets (notably the Prenzlauer Berg poets) tended rather to explore private spheres and experiment with their poetic medium. In an interview with Ursula Heukenkamp, Uwe Kolbe claimed: 'meine Generation hat die Hände im Schoß, was engagiertes Handeln betrifft'.[16] Although it is questionable to what extent this provocative statement can be regarded as representative, it points to a debate concerning not just the appropriate form, but also the very existence and nature of political engagement. Favoured topics in the 1980s were local life, personal friends, life in the city, and love. Correspondingly, the choice of literary models tended to be more diverse and personal than previously. For example Steffen Mensching, in his poem 'Hotelzimmer-dämmerung',[17] quotes in French from Rimbaud as cited by Walter Benjamin,[18] and sets himself in the tradition of Paul Éluard;[19] he quotes in English from Mick Jagger,[20] and he also cites Goethe.[21] The conclusion incorporates Hamlet's 'To be, or not to be':[22]

> [...]
> vielleicht, sage ich, vielleicht kann ich treu
> bleiben, vielleicht, denn
> zwischen den Dingen ist Platz für zwei
> oder x ungeahnte Möglichkeiten
>
> wie heißt du willst du mit mir
> schlafen darf es etwas
> mehr sein oder nicht sein das ist hier
> die Frage
>
> ich küsse den Konjunktiv dir auf die Stirn
> der eisenbeschlagene Stiefel tritt gegen die offene
>   Tür, doch im Türspalt
> steht dein nackter Fuß, mit sanfter Gewalt
> eroberte Zwischenräume,
>
> mehr, sagst du, trauen sie uns nicht zu,
>
> ich sage, daß sie sich bloß nicht irren,
>
> in diesem Licht ist vieles möglich

Mensching here opens up a private poetic space of love that has the power to exclude the violently intrusive external system. Instead of referring to the humanist values of Weimar Classicism or, in reaction, to the inward-looking subjectivism of the German Romantics, Mensching draws on a wide variety of sources, with emphasis on Symbolist, Surrealist and Pop poets. Although the choice of literary models in the 1980s tended to be both less homogeneous and less politically sensitive than in the early years of the GDR, Mensching's choice has political force: an alternative culture is being proclaimed, one which is neither confined to East Germany nor to the Eastern Bloc, one which is dynamic rather than prescribed and predetermined, and one which cannot be harnessed to material productivity. However, the poem must be read with reference to its East German context if it is to communicate its public, political significance.

The poems considered so far suggest that the significance of literary tradition differed in East and West. This does not, of course, hold true uniformly. Two poems concerned with global issues show how quotations may fulfil a similar role even when the provenance of the poems diverges: Braun's 'Material VI: Die Mummelfälle'[23] from the cycle 'Der Stoff zum Leben' and Walter Höllerer's 'Untergrund'[24] highlight modern destruction of nature by recalling Romantic nature worship through quotations from favourite German nature poems and songs, and references to fairy-tales. Braun quotes the line 'Der Wald steht schwarz und schweiget' from Claudius's 'Abendlied',[25] and cites Eichendorff's line 'In einem kühlen Grunde'.[26] The destruction of the natural environment is traced through *Rübezahl*, the legendary spirit of the *Riesengebirge*, and references to Hölderlinian purity:

> Über die Felsen fällt das reine Wasser
> Über die Füße, *reine Freude*
>   die Natur
> Mummelt in ihren Bart
>   grün
> Die Augenweide, Farn und Lattich, der Wald
> Steht schwarz und schweiget immer noch
> Wär ich ein Lyriker, mit blankem Vers
> Wie wollte ich
>   aus den Fichten
> Tritt der bärtige Alte mit der Keule
> *Vergiß nicht deine Rede*
> [...]
>   Ich schreibe meine Sätze
> Ins Reine, Wasser Wald, aussterbende
> Worte, die ich hege, *im Umkreis*
> *Von 100 m ist jede Verschmutzung*
> Der Alte verschwindet zwischen den Fichten
> Der Bart ist ab.
>   In einem kühlen Grunde
> Steht meiner (wenn ich nichts mehr sage)
> Heimat Haus: der kommunale Schutt
> In dem ich mich ergehe mit den An-
> Verwandten

Höllerer's poem similarly harks back to *Rübezahl*, and to other figures and creatures from mythology:

> UNTERGRUND
>
> Es tickt und tickt im Untergrund.
>
> Es fährt dahin, daher von Ort zu Ort im Untergrund.
> Statt Pilzen sprießt Rakete aus dem Wald.
>
> Statt Blocksberg, Hexensabbath: Sprengkopf-Untergrund.
> Und Erdgas nach Befruchtung ruft, vom Himmel hoch.
>
> Entsorgung sorgt sich, tickt und tickt.
> Chemie im Wasser tickt im Untergrund.
>
> Und kommt Atom geflogen, setzt sich auf Atomkraftwerk,
> auf Brennstab-Aufbereitung und Atommüll-Untergrund.

Wer hat dich hier, du schöner Wald, so sehr durchwühlt,
nicht Wildschwein, Fuchs und Dachs
und auch nicht Rübezahl und Schöne Lau und Drachenbrut.

MX und SS 20, Pershing sitzt im Märchenwald,
im Westerwald, im Sauerland, im Fläming auch, wer weiß, demnächst,

und warte, balde bist auch du —

Tritt leis, es tickt. Es zuckt ungut.
Es schuftet, ächzt, rumort im Untergrund.

Höllerer quotes from Luther's Christmas carol 'Vom Himmel hoch',[27] and Goethe's lines 'Warte nur, balde/ Ruhest du auch',[28] as well as the children's song 'Kommt ein Vogel geflogen',[29] while the reference to the *Westerwald* together with the phrase 'du schöner Wald' recalls the refrain 'O du schöner Westerwald' from the patriotic 'Westerwaldlied'.[30] Whereas Braun's poem is located in the Polish *Riesengebirge*, Höllerer's straddles the Iron Curtain, as indicated by the juxtaposition of US and Soviet missiles,[31] and by the geography: the *Westerwald* and *Sauerland* in the FRG, the *Blocksberg* (assuming that it refers to the *Brocken*) on the border, and the *Fläming* in the GDR. Braun also, however, bridges the political boundary, ironically accommodating his Western readers in a note about the poem's location: 'Mumlava vodopad im Riesengebirge. Das Gedicht könnte auch Der Mummelsee heißen; Rübezahl wäre dann ein baden-württembergischer Grüner'.[32] Both poems use quotations to enhance the reader's awareness of a current political issue, and in both, the German cultural past serves as evidence of a time when nature was intact and the future of mankind secure, highlighting an all-German and indeed global political issue.[33]

In these poems, political and ideological boundaries recede before the greater issue of the survival of mankind. Consequently the common literary heritage of East and West Germany is invested with similar significance and serves a common purpose. Notwithstanding such examples, however, use of the cultural tradition emerges primarily as a factor that distinguished poetry in East and West, and as an aspect of poetry that needs to be interpreted in relation to political context.

III

With language, it becomes more difficult to draw a dividing line between two literatures. The German language served consistently as the medium for everyday communication in both German states. Linguistically, it is often hard to distinguish poetry written in the GDR from that written in the FRG or indeed Austria or Switzerland. Honecker's statement that the border between GDR and FRG is not based on linguistic differences was confirmed by the eminent East German linguist Wolfgang Fleischer, who stated in 1987: 'Es gibt kein besonderes "DDR-Deutsch" [...] Allerdings existiert die deutsche Sprache in der DDR auch nicht unberührt von den spezifischen Verhältnissen und vor allem von den damit verbundenen Benennungs- und Kommunikationsbedürfnissen [...] Sie befindet sich dadurch in einer spezifischen *Situation* und wird durch diese Situation geprägt.'[34] There are few ideologically neutral phrases that could be identified as 'typically East German' or 'typically West German'.[35] Fundamentally, grammar and lexis remained the same in East and West, although there were significant context-specific lexical divergencies stemming from differing ideologies and political and social conditions. Consequently Fleischer refers to '[die] deutsche Sprache in der DDR'.[36]

Volker Braun's poem 'Gespräch im Garten des Chefs'[37] reveals its geographical and political provenance by the reference to Neulobeda (a district of Jena), and by the words 'Klassenkampf', 'Sozialismus', and particularly 'Plankorrektur'. The opening of Johann Rist's hymn 'O Ewigkeit, du Donnerwort' is transformed into 'Klassenkampf — o Donnerwort', a parody which gains its significance from the political context.[38] The fixed collocations, however, are by no means specific to East German:

> Nicht daß uns die Worte fehlen —
> Sie hängen uns aus dem Hals
>
> Na na, sagte er
> Und verschwand schon halb auf der Treppe
>
> Aber sie klingen verquollen
> Pappig, redaktionelle Knödel.
> Man macht sich noch einen Begriff
> Worum es gegangen war
> Und steckt längst in der Kreide
> Auf dem Verhandlungsweg, in der Plankorrektur.
> Klassenkampf — o Donnerwort
> Nur zur Verrechnung.
>
> Komm zur Sache, Freund.
>
> Ja gewiß, aber bitte! aber gern
> Ergreifen wir noch

Die Initiative, beidarmig
Und ziehen das Lebensniveau
An den Haaren herbei. Aber warum
Franst das Bewußtsein aus
In Neulobeda? Ansteckhoffnung
Auf dem Ehrenkleid, rostige Andenken
An die Zukunft.
Der Sozialismus, nur noch eine Metapher
Aber wofür?

Ich weiß nicht, wovon du redest.

[...]

Vielleicht war die Frage
Die große Frage Werwen
Eine Nummer zu klein, und die Schrecken
Von denen wir zehren
Sind nicht mehr das Wahre. Dergutemensch
Denkt an sich, selbst zuletzt.
Wenn die Wahrheit, Asche im Mund
In eure Türen fällt
Werdet ihr sie wissen.

Du bist ja nicht mehr zu retten
Rief er, aus seinem Bunker.

The following collocations are all part of West German idiom, and are recorded in the West German *Duden*:[39]

mir fehlen die *Worte*
etwas hängt jmdm. zum *Hals* heraus
sich einen *Begriff* machen (*Duden*: ich kann mir keinen rechten *Begriff* davon machen)
worum *geht* es
in der Kreide stecken (*Duden*: bei jmdm. in der *Kreide* stehen/sein/sitzen)
nur zur *Verrechnung*
zur *Sache* kommen
die *Initiative* ergreifen
etwas an den *Haaren* herbeiziehen
die große *Frage*
eine *Nummer* zu groß
das ist nicht das *Wahre* (*Duden*: das ist das einzig *Wahre*)
an sich selbst zuletzt denken (*Duden*: sie denkt an sich selbst *zuletzt*)
(mit der *Tür* ins Haus fallen/jmdm. die *Tür* einlaufen)
nicht mehr zu *retten* sein

Idiomatically, there is nothing to distinguish the conversation in the poem from one between West Germans. Nevertheless there are subtly different resonances for East and West German readers. The idiom 'die Initiative ergreifen' has a political connotation specific to its use in the GDR: 'Initiative' has been described as 'eines der "aktivierenden" Wörter der innenpolitischen Propaganda'.[40] And in the GDR context, the phrase 'an sich selbst zuletzt denken' attains political rather than moral significance: the question of whether the individual 'denkt an sich selbst zuletzt' or 'denkt an *sich*, selbst zuletzt' forms part of the debate concerning the individual's duties to, and rights in socialist society. In order fully to communicate with the reader, Braun's poem thus demands to be placed in its political context, despite the fact that the linguistic substance hardly reveals itself as 'East German'.

The poem 'Auch ich bin nicht ganz dicht' by Mensching[41] similarly relies on the reader's familiarity with conditions in the GDR. The poem grows out of the cliché 'nicht ganz dicht sein' (common to East and West German) which Mensching takes literally. He links it with a quotation attributed to Heraclitus, 'everything flows',[42] in a highly physical celebration of sexual intercourse:

> Auch ich bin nicht ganz dicht, wie du
>   sondre ich
>   Flüssigkeiten ab,
> Schweiß, Spucke, Tränen, Blut und einen andren Saft
>   dazu.
> Mein Ego hat ein Loch,
> faß rein, hab Mut, ja, das tut gut, nur zu, vergiß dich, du,
>   und das Tabu,
> o panta rhei, du gehst heraus aus dir, ich geh dazwischen,
>   ja dazwischen.
> Wer wie wir zwei so undicht ist, kann sich so schön
>   vermischen

This is a powerful love poem for any German-speaking reader, but in order to communicate politically, it calls for a reader familiar with the background: in a state which sought to suppress sexuality and make its literary treatment 'taboo', explicit celebration of the sexual act gains a significance that differs from that which it has in the more permissive Western societies.

The poems cited so far all depend for their effect on the reader's awareness of political context, whether or not they disclose their origin through the language used. With others, though, the context has less immediate bearing on their interpretation. The sentimental (and eminently popular) poems by Eva Strittmatter, for example, are for the most part barely affected by their social and political context. The experience conveyed in a poem like 'Einsicht'[43] is so clichéd that the poem transcends political differences and is likely to communicate similarly with East and West German readers:

Als ich zwanzig war und leben mir schwer,
Da dachte ich, es wird leichter werden.
Mit dem Alter kommt auch Weisheit her.
[...]
Und nun? Nun bin ich schon fünfzig Jahr,
Und leben ist schwer, wies mit zwanzig nicht war.

Neither the sentiments not the linguistic expression mark out this poem as East German. Eva Strittmatter regards her poetry as a 'drug' that provides relief from normal existence.[44] Instead of engaging with day-to-day social and political conflicts, she seeks to transport herself and her readers into a realm of personal experience that calls for simple identification rather than mental or imaginative activity. It ceases to matter what society the reader is escaping from, although assessment of the poem may need to take account of its intended readership.

Where Eva Strittmatter's poems operate in a stereotyped realm of sentiment that is independent of political borders, other poems written in the GDR transcend those borders through the German language. They have no obvious links with their context, and are not significantly illuminated by reference to context. They differ from the poems by Strittmatter in their effect: rather than drawing the reader into personal experience, these poems with their intriguing use of language stimulate the reader into questioning what the poem is 'about', and draw attention to the relationship between language, the mind, and the world in which we live. These questions are not specific to a political system, and are therefore equally effective for readers from East and West.

In the poem 'Rede-Wendungen' by Kito Lorenc,[45] there is no linguistic clue to its provenance, and no obviously East German resonance. The poem consists entirely of modified idioms, each making up a line. The idioms are 'turned against' their conventional usage:

REDE-WENDUNGEN

Ich steh auf Messers Schneide
knietief in der Kreide
als fünftes Rad am Wagen
und will ein Schnippchen schlagen.

Auf dem Zahnfleisch krieche
ich in Teufels Küche.
Der Teufel malt mich an die Wand
und legt mir Feuer in die Hand.

Ich sauf im Sitzen Tinte,
werf Korn in meine Flinte,

> streu Puder auf mein Haupt und jag
> die Katze aus dem Klammersack.
>
> Und wie's mich juckt, so kommen
> die Felle angeschwommen
> mit Zähnen auf den Haaren,
> die noch voll Suppe waren.
>
> Kaum hab ich einen blassen Dunst
> der Tuten- und der Blasenkunst,
> da beißt die Maus den Faden ab,
> der ich den Marsch geblasen hab.

The idioms, all of which are listed in the West German *Duden*,[46] have no immediate political connotations, although the prominence of the writer's *ich* and the choice and modification of the idioms might invite the reader to interpret the poem as a statement concerning the writer's role in the GDR. It is precarious: 'Ich steh auf Messers Schneide', and he serves no useful purpose, being '[das] fünfte Rad am Wagen'. But he does have a degree of subversive power: '[ich] will ein Schnippchen schlagen' and 'Der Teufel [...] legt mir Feuer in die Hand'. Such an interpretation, however, is supported by little other than the knowledge that the poem originated in the GDR. More pertinent is the fact that it was written for children. By playing on stock phrases, Lorenc encourages an irreverent and critical attitude to convention in general. This is not limited to a particular type of society or political system.

Heiner Müller's miniature play *Herzstück*,[47] included here because of its brevity and linguistic density, takes the dead metaphor 'Herzstück' literally, interpreting 'Stück' as drama. He elaborates on the idiom with clichéd expressions that include the word 'Herz': 'jemandem sein Herz schenken' (the verb is here replaced by the more flowery phrase 'zu Füßen legen'), 'reines Herz', 'Herz aus Stein', and 'mein Herz schlägt nur für dich':

HERZSTÜCK

EINS Darf ich Ihnen mein Herz zu Füßen legen.
ZWEI Wenn Sie mir meinen Fußboden nicht
      schmutzig machen.
EINS Mein Herz ist rein.
ZWEI Das werden wir ja sehn.
EINS Ich kriege es nicht heraus.
ZWEI Wollen Sie daß ich Ihnen helfe.
EINS Wenn es Ihnen nichts ausmacht.
ZWEI Es ist mir ein Vergnügen. Ich kriege es
      auch nicht heraus.
EINS *heult*

ZWEI Ich werde es Ihnen herausoperieren. Wozu habe ich ein Taschenmesser. Das werden
wir gleich haben. Arbeiten und nicht ver-
zweifeln. So, das hätten wir. Aber das ist ja
ein Ziegelstein. Ihr Herz ist ein Ziegelstein.
EINS Aber es schlägt nur für Sie.

Müller's piece dramatizes elements of the German language that are in no way specific to the GDR, giving them a life of their own which is independent of political context. In this respect *Herzstück* is similar to a poem such as the following by the Austrian Ernst Jandl:[48]

> the pig has left me
> in the stitch — das
> schwein hat mich im
> stich gelassen

As with *Herzstück*, an idiom is taken literally, the effect here deriving from the literal translation into English. The linguistic medium itself is primary, rather than its message.

Several GDR poets looked to Western concrete poetry in the 1980s. For example, Elke Erb dedicated her poem 'Kleine Tippfehler-Fogle'[49] to Ernst Jandl. In the poem 'Ein Schuldgefühl'[50] she works with visual connections that run counter to ordinary linear reading patterns.

EIN SCHULDGEFÜHL

NUR WEIL DIE SCHULD

AN DEN TAG TRITT

Man
hat de
n Mond
angebiss
en. Er h
ängt am
Himmel. V
ielleicht
sieht
es
k
ein
er. V
ielleicht
halten sie
ihn für una
ngebissen —

DA IST

The poem is based on the phrase 'an den Tag kommen/treten' and the association day — night — moon, playing with words and images without tying them into a definite context. The permutations characteristic of Western concrete poetry[51] were similarly taken up in the 1980s. The poem 'willelei' by Stefan Döring[52] consists of permutations of the stereotyped expressions 'jemandem etwas zu sagen haben' and 'machen, was man will':

> **willelei**
>
> ich habe euch nichts zu sagen
> ihr habt mir nichts zu sagen
> ihr macht was ihr wollt
> ich mache was ich will
>
> niemand hat uns was zu sagen
> wir haben niemandem was zu sagen
> wir machen was wir wollen
> niemand macht was er will

Although the poem may be interpreted as treating the relationship between the self and society, the variations and contradictions created by the permutations keep the meaning fluid and allow it to be related to any self in any society. The poem »geld oder leben«[53] (the alternative proposed in the title recalls the threat of an archetypal bank robber) consists of hackneyed phrases that include 'Geld' or 'Leben', but substitutes 'Geld' for 'Leben' and vice versa. By making his readers complete the phrases in accordance with linguistic convention, Döring encourages exploration of the relationship between money and life, and cracks open stereotyped thought-patterns:

> »geld oder leben«
>
> um am geld zu bleiben
> muss man sein leben verdienen
> aber das reicht nicht aus
> denn das ist ja kein geld
> wenn man nur so wenig leben hat
> sein geld zu fristen
> und wenn nur ab und zu
> leben ins haus kommt
> und kein gespartes vorhanden
> macht das geld keinen spass
> denn es gibt immer etwas
> wofür man sein leben hingeben möchte
> und hat man keins fängt man an
> leben zu stehlen

um sein leben zu spielen
und überhaupt
fürs leben alles zu tun
oder die leute fragen
woher hat der sein leben
wenn er keins verdient
bekommt ers geschenkt
wer verschenkt auf die dauer sein leben

Although the clichés may suggest differing associations in East and West, the effect of the poem is likely to be similar in both economic systems: rather than conveying a definite message that is determined by context, the poem encourages creative play with words that encapsulate the foundation of existence.

In the poems cited above, language provides an avenue to processes of thought. Instead of being a rhetorical means to a utilitarian end, it may become an end in itself. This would be analogous to Hinze's discovery in Volker Braun's *Hinze-Kunze-Roman* that 'es gab nichts außer ihnen selbst, was ihrem Leben Sinn gab'.[54] Such poems neither reveal the political context in which they were written, nor do they demand to be read with reference to that context. This poetry is not designed to affect the political status quo directly, although it may be regarded as political in the sense that it marks the poets' refusal to participate in the role assigned to them by the state, and refusal to 'produce' politically useful artefacts. Where the poetry by Eva Strittmatter discourages mental activity and encourages the reader to escape into an apolitical realm of private sentiment, these poems demand, and create, an active reader who is challenged to explore habits of language, thought, and ultimately action. The emergence of concrete poetry in the 1980s is a phenomenon that is specific to the GDR, and it gains a political significance there that differs from its status in other German-speaking countries. The poems as such, however, are directly accessible to any German-speaking reader without recourse to political and social background, since the East German idiom remained largely unchanged by the GDR's political isolation from other German-speaking states.

Viewed from the socio-political angle, there can be no doubt but that GDR literature is distinct from the literatures produced at the same time in other German-speaking countries; and the significance of the literary heritage varied in accordance with the differing ideological value placed on culture. With regard to the common German language, however, one might adapt Wolfgang Fleischer's phrase of 'die deutsche

Sprache in der DDR' to literature: 'die deutsche Literatur in der DDR'. This would allow for a variety of classifications cutting across state boundaries, in an era when two German literatures are becoming one.

NOTES

1 *ND*, 29 May 1973.
2 On the topic of German literature(s) see, for example, Theo Buck: 'Deutsche Literatur, deutsche Literaturen? Zur Frage der Einheit der deutschen Literatur seit 1945' in Heinz Ludwig Arnold (ed.): *Bestandsaufnahme Gegenwartsliteratur. Bundesrepublik Deutschland, Deutsche Demokratische Republik, Österreich, Schweiz*, Munich, 1988, pp. 183—92.
3 Peter Paul Zahl: *Ergreifende oder ergriffene Literatur. Zur Rezeption "moderner Klassik"*, Frankfurt/Main, 1978, p. 75. Zahl's verdict offers a modern angle on Goethe's proclamation concerning the advent of 'Weltliteratur' to replace the narrow concept of 'Nationalliteratur' ('Gespräch mit Eckermann', 31 January 1827, *Goethes Werke. Hamburger Ausgabe*, ed. by Erich Trunz, vol. XII, 8th edn, Munich, 1978, p. 362).
4 Johanna Rudolph: *Lebendiges Erbe. Reden und Aufsätze zur Kunst und Literatur*, Leipzig, 1972, p. 151. Cited by Jürgen Schröder: 'Die DDR und die deutsche Klassik' in Jens Hacker and Horst Rögner-Francke (eds): *Die DDR und die Tradition*, Gesellschaft für Deutschlandforschung, Jahrbuch 1981, Heidelberg, 1981, pp. 57—74; here p. 57.
5 Autorenkollektiv (Leitung: Ernst Diehl): *Grundriß der deutschen Geschichte. Von den Anfängen der Geschichte des deutschen Volkes bis zur Gestaltung der entwickelten sozialistischen Gesellschaft in der Deutschen Demokratischen Republik. Klassenkampf — Tradition — Sozialismus*, 2nd edn, Berlin (GDR), 1979, p. 9. Cited by Peter J. Lapp: 'Der politische Stellenwert der Traditionspflege in der DDR' in Hacker, Rögner-Francke: *Die DDR und die Tradition*, pp. 11—34; here p. 11.
6 Goethe: *Werke*, vol. III, p. 348, ll. 11559—62. See Schröder: 'Die DDR und die deutsche Klassik', p. 58.
7 Goethe: *Werke*, vol. III, p. 364, ll. 12104—11.
8 Oskar Pastior: *Lesungen mit Tinnitus. Gedichte 1980—1985*, Munich, 1986, p. 71. Quoted with kind permission of Carl Hanser Verlag, Munich.
9 Joseph Freiherr von Eichendorff: *Sämtliche Werke*, ed. by Wilhelm Kosch et al., vol. I/1, Regensburg, 1908, p. 134.
10 Goethe: *Werke*, vol. III, p. 65, ll. 1995—6.
11 Volker Braun: *Langsamer knirschender Morgen. Gedichte*, Frankfurt/Main, 1987, p. 7. Quoted with kind permission of Mitteldeutscher Verlag, Halle-Leipzig.
12 See Hans H. Reich: *Sprache und Politik. Untersuchungen zu Wortschatz und Wortwahl des offiziellen Sprachgebrauchs in der DDR*, Munich, 1968, pp. 173—7.
13 Jürgen Theobaldy: *Die Sommertour. Gedichte*, Reinbek, 1983, p. 10. Quoted with kind permission of Jürgen Theobaldy.
14 Johann Christian Friedrich Hölderlin: *Sämtliche Werke. Große Stuttgarter Ausgabe*, ed. by Friedrich Beißner, 6 vols, Stuttgart, 1946—61, vol. II/1, p. 117. Compare Theobaldy, ll. 1—4, with Hölderlin, ll. 8—14. Later in the poem (l. 14), Theobaldy also cites the words 'ins Offene' from 'Der Gang aufs Land' (Hölderlin: *Sämtliche Werke*, vol. II/1, p. 84).
15 See, for example, Friedrich Gottlieb Klopstock: *Der Messias*, I. 21, in Klopstock: *Werke und Briefe. Historisch-kritische Ausgabe*, vol. IV/I, ed. by Elisabeth Höpker-Herberg, Berlin, 1974, p. 1.
16 *Weimarer Beiträge*, vol. 25, no. 7, 1979, p. 46.
17 Steffen Mensching: *Tuchfühlung. Gedichte*, Cologne, 1987, pp. 29—31. Quoted with kind permission of Mitteldeutscher Verlag, Halle-Leipzig.

18 Ibid, p. 29, ll. 21—3. The quotation is identified in the poem and in a note (p. 97). Rimbaud forms the subject of an essay by Volker Braun: 'Rimbaud. Ein Psalm der Aktualität', *Sinn und Form*, vol. 37, no. 5, 1985, pp. 978—98. See also Karen Leeder's discussion 'Poesie ist eine Gegensprache', pp. 413—24 below, which takes Braun's essay as its starting point.

19 Ibid, p. 29, ll. 12—13.

20 Ibid, p. 30, l. 7. The quotation is identified in a note (p. 97).

21 The lines 'eine neue Liebe/ ist wie ein neues Leben' (ibid, p. 30, ll. 4—5) recall the title of Goethe's poem 'Neue Liebe, neues Leben' (Goethe: *Werke*, vol. I, p. 96).

22 *Hamlet*, Act III, Scene i.

23 Braun: *Langsamer knirschender Morgen*, pp. 40—1. Quoted with kind permission of Mitteldeutscher Verlag, Halle-Leipzig.

24 Walter Höllerer: *Gedichte 1942—1982*, Frankfurt/Main, 1982, p. 222. Quoted with kind permission of Suhrkamp Verlag, Frankfurt/Main.

25 Matthias Claudius: *Sämtliche Werke*, ed. by Jost Perfahl, Munich, 1968, p. 217.

26 Eichendorff: *Sämtliche Werke*, vol. I/1, p. 438.

27 Gerhard Hahn (ed.): *Die deutschen geistlichen Lieder*, Tübingen, 1967, p. 44.

28 From 'Ein gleiches [Wandrers Nachtlied]', in Goethe: *Werke*, vol. I, 10th edn, 1974, p. 142.

29 See, for example, Anne Diekmann and Willi Gohl (eds): *Das große Liederbuch*, Zurich, 1975, p. 108.

30 See, for example, F. J. Breuer (ed.): *Das neue Soldaten-Liederbuch. Die bekanntesten und meistgesungenen Lieder unserer Wehrmacht*, Mainz, n.d., p. 71.

31 MX and Pershing are US missiles, while the SS 20 is a Soviet missile.

32 Braun: *Langsamer knirschender Morgen*, p. 91.

33 Similarly, Braun's poem 'Material VII: Der Frieden' from the cycle 'Der Stoff zum Leben' cites graffiti slogans familiar to West German readers: 'STELL DIR VOR ES IST KRIEG UND KEINER/ GEHT HIN' and 'ENTRÜSTET EUCH' (ibid, p. 42).

34 Wolfgang Fleischer et al.: *Wortschatz der deutschen Sprache in der DDR*, Leipzig, 1987, p. 29.

35 A comparatively rare example is *vor Ort*, identified by Fleischer as 'offensichtlich aus dem Sprachgebrauch der BRD übernommen' (ibid, p. 40). Volker Braun uses this phrase in his depiction of Kunze's visit to the West in *Hinze-Kunze-Roman*, Frankfurt/Main, 1985, p. 90.

36 Fleischer: *Wortschatz...*, p. 15.

37 Braun: *Langsamer knirschender Morgen*, pp. 11—12. Quoted with kind permission of Mitteldeutscher Verlag, Halle-Leipzig.

38 For Rists's hymn see, for example, *Evangelisches Kirchengesangbuch*, Evang.-Luth. Kirche in Bayern, Munich, n.d., pp. 397—8, no. 324.

39 Günther Drosdowski et al.: *Duden. Das große Wörterbuch der deutschen Sprache*, 6 vols, Mannheim, 1976—81. *Duden* takes account of the German language in the GDR as well as in Switzerland and Austria. However, none of the phrases are identified as specific to East German — as is the case, for instance, with 'Plaste (DDR ugs.)'. The headword of each collocation is italicized.

40 See Reich: *Sprache und Politik...*, p. 102.

41 Mensching: *Tuchfühlung*, p. 72. Quoted with kind permission of Mitteldeutscher Verlag, Halle-Leipzig.

42 See Georg Büchmann: *Geflügelte Worte. Der Zitatenschatz des deutschen Volkes*, 34th edn, ed. by Winfried Hofmann, Frankfurt/Main, 1981, p. 254.

43 Eva Strittmatter: *Heliotrop. Gedichte*, Berlin (GDR), 1983, p. 49.

44 See the poem 'Gram', ibid, p. 88.

45 Kito Lorenc: *Wortland. Gedichte aus zwanzig Jahren*, Leipzig, 1984, p. 102. First published in *Die Rasselbande im Schlamasselland*, Berlin (GDR), 1983. Quoted with kind permission of Kinderbuchverlag, Berlin. This poem supplies the title for Alexander von Bormann's article 'Rede-Wendungen. Zur Rhetorik des gegenwärtigen Gedichts in der DDR' in Christine Cosentino, Wolfgang Ertl and Gerd Labroisse (eds): *DDR-Lyrik im Kontext, Amsterdamer Beiträge zur neueren Germanistik*, vol. 26, 1988, pp. 89—143.

46 Etw. steht auf des *Messers* Schneide; bei jmdm. [tief] in der *Kreide* stehen; fünftes *Rad* am Wagen; jdm. ein *Schnippchen* schlagen; auf dem *Zahnfleisch* gehen; in *Teufels* Küche kommen; den *Teufel* an die Wand malen; für jmdn./etw. die *Hand* ins Feuer legen; in der *Tinte* sitzen; die *Flinte* ins Korn werfen; sich *Asche* aufs Haupt streuen; die *Katze* aus dem Sack lassen; jmdn. juckt das *Fell*; jmdm. sind die *Felle* davongeschwommen; *Haare* auf den Zähnen haben; ein *Haar* in der Suppe finden; keinen [blassen] *Dunst* von etwas haben; von *Tuten* und Blasen keine Ahnung haben; da beißt die *Maus* keinen Faden ab; jmdm. den *Marsch* blasen.

47 Heiner Müller: *Herzstück*, Berlin, 1983, p. 7. Quoted with kind permission of Rotbuch-Verlag, Berlin.

48 Ernst Jandl: *idyllen. gedichte*, Frankfurt/Main, 1989, p. 186. Quoted with kind permission of Luchterhand Verlag, Frankfurt/Main.

49 Elke Erb: *Kastanienallee. Texte und Kommentare*, Salzburg, 1988, p. 65.

50 Ibid, p. 17. Quoted with kind permission of Residenz Verlag, Salzburg.

51 See, for example, the anthology *Konkrete Poesie*, Stuttgart, 1972, which includes permutations by Claus Bremer (p. 27), Eugen Gomringer (p. 59), Franz Mon (p. 102) and Timm Ulrichs (p. 138). See also Konrad Balder Schäuffelen's poem '46mal augen' (p. 125), which consists of clichéd phrases with 'Auge'.

52 In Egmont Hesse (ed.): *Sprache & Antwort. Stimmen und Texte einer anderen Literatur aus der DDR*, Frankfurt/Main, 1988, p. 91. Quoted with kind permission of S. Fischer Verlag, Frankfurt/Main.

53 Ibid, p. 90. Quoted with kind permission of S. Fischer Verlag, Frankfurt/Main.

54 Braun: *Hinze-Kunze-Roman*, p. 87.

WAS THE WALL A LAUGHING MATTER?
SOME REFLECTIONS ON THORSTEN BECKER'S
DIE BÜRGSCHAFT

MARTIN KANE

I

Despite Brecht's implication that, by and large, comedy has been more successful in tackling the ills of the world than tragedy: 'im allgemeinen gilt wohl der Satz, daß die Tragödie die Leiden der Menschen häufiger auf die leichte Achsel nimmt als die Komödie',[1] the perennial German problem (along with its postwar manifestation in social, political and cultural schism) is, by and large, not a subject which has invited or received a lighthearted approach. Few writers have been tempted to explore the potentially droll side of matters when writing about a divided Germany and to investigate, for instance, what the grotesque phenomenon of a wall which until recently bisected a city as effectively as a knife through cheese — dividing one ideology from another, separating people and ways of life of natural affinity, and invariably the subject of sententious and solemn platitudes — might in fact yield in the way of the comic.

There have been exceptions, of course, and from both sides of the divide. Hermann Kant's laid-back 'Grenzgänger', Robert Iswall, exposes the shortcomings he finds in the 'absurde Fremde' of West Germany[2] by casting (to humorous effect) a caustic and ironical gaze over a selection of bizarre and, for him, representative capitalist eccentrics or scoundrels. Who could fail to be amused by the Nestroy actor with white luggage and cat whom Robert meets on the train back to Berlin, or not raise a smile at the spectacle of his brother-in-law Hermann Grieper who, on the basis of smuggling gypsies during the Third Reich for exorbitant fees, assembles a reputation as a 'Widerstandskämpfer', claiming that by forging tobacco coupons he had destroyed 'die Wirtschaftspolitik des Regimes'.[3]

From his perspective on the other side of the Wall, a relentless observer of German division such as Peter Schneider can also harvest lighter moments from a troubled situation. A resident for twenty years of what he calls the 'siamesische Stadt', Schneider, in his tale *Der Mauer-springer*,[4] (in truth a loosely connected collection of several different tales, anecdotes and reflections) provides us with an account of a divided city beset by what one critic has called 'Anfällen von Ordnung und Anfällen des Absurden'.[5] Into the second part of this description one might wish to slot the antics of the East Berlin youths (already elevated to mini-legend by Stefan Heym's version of the same events, 'Mein Richard'[6]) who repeatedly sneak over the Wall to satisfy their passion for westerns in Kurfürstendamm cinemas; or the unemployed West Berliner, Kabe, who on fifteen occasions clambered over it from West to East, motivated more it seemed by gymnastic challenge than by any need to ventilate a sense of political outrage.

These examples from Kant and Schneider of the ways in which humour may be found in the situation of a divided Germany need also, of course, to be put in the total ideological or socio-psychological context of the works in which they appear. Schneider with that earnestness of purpose which has characterized his endeavours as a political essayist (most recently in the volume *Deutsche Ängste*[7]) tries to weld the loosely linked episodes, experiences and extended observations which constitute *Der Mauerspringer* into a coherent mosaic which will make some sense of the fragmented chaos of a divided Berlin. Prefacing his tale with some perceptive comments on the role that the Wall has played in the West German consciousness, he argues that, after the outrage which its erection initially provoked had ebbed away, it had become a symbol for a detested social system, the mirror on the wall which day to day confirmed West Germans in the belief that their half was the fairest of the two Germanys. But how far does the comic element in the stories which Schneider has collected (as opposed to his own encounters and reflections in the book) help us to understand this monstrous symbol? The escapades already described are certainly amusing by-products of the existence of the Wall, but they only partially illuminate its real significance (the perplexity from East and West confronted with Kabe's hilarious and hair-raising obsession cracks, for a moment, the iron-faced ideological certainties of both sides). But the most useful insights come from elsewhere in the book: from Schneider's productively fraught relationship with Pommerer, an East German novelist who, despite his Marxist commitment, is constantly engaged in a running battle with the authorities on matters of petty censorship, and Robert, a forcibly expatriated dissident now living in West Berlin, who finds little difficulty in reconciling a fascination with the baubles of capitalism (fast and flashy cars) with a paranoid dislike of it as a political system. Through Schneider's confrontations with these two communist intellectuals, one on each side of the Wall, we gradually see how profound the divisions really are. More than thirty years of mutual propaganda, in which each of the two Germanys had drawn a sense of identity from stressing its difference from the other, had left a mark which went even deeper than that which operated at an official political level. Schneider speculates, after one of his bruising encounters with Robert, that were the formal national barriers to suddenly melt away, the arguments about which was the preferable system (and how history has borne him out) would still go on in bar and drawing room: 'Die Mauer im Kopf einzureißen wird länger dauern, als irgendein Abrißunternehmen für die sichtbare Mauer braucht [...] wir können nicht miteinander reden, ohne daß ein Staat aus uns spricht.'[8]

If it would seem, then, that whereas the humour in Schneider's book is a welcome, but somewhat incidental part of the author's purpose, it occupies in Kant's novel a much more central ideological function. Here, the ability to poke fun at certain aspects of West German society is clearly meant to signal a certain self-confidence, a coming-of-age, a setting of the seal on the establishment of the GDR as a state with a distinctive identity of its own. Any judgement, however, on whether this humour, and the superiority of the socialist system in the East over the capitalist system in the West it was meant to underpin, were ever anything more than whistling in the dark, must await a fundamental reappraisal of *Die Aula* in the light of the subsequent collapse and demise of the GDR. The novel may well remain a monument to what its author, in an interview in *Der Spiegel* in August 1990, described as a 'Schimäre', a forlorn remainder of what might have been, of dashed beliefs in a 'Gesellschaft [...] die so sei, daß niemand sie gegen eine andere tauschen wolle'.[9]

II

These preliminary reflections bring us to Thorsten Becker, an author who, in his first two books, *Die Bürgschaft*[10] and *Die Nase*[11] (both described as 'Erzählungen'), demonstrates, in his talent for freewheeling narrative boisterousness, an entirely original approach to the question of the two German cultures.

The titles of both of these works seem to point us in the direction of literary joke and allusion. The first fulfils the anticipation it arouses, the second — whether intentionally or not is unclear — leads us up the garden path. *Die Bürgschaft*, as rapidly becomes apparent from the second page, takes its cue and central episode from Schiller: 'Als Schüler des Schiller-Gymnasiums mußte ich die Ballade von der Männertreue auswendig lernen', and transplants his 'Die Bürgschaft' to the circumstances of East Berlin and a divided Germany. *Die Nase*, on the other hand, has nothing remotely to do with Gogol's bizarre short story. Its attempt to repeat the classical connection, this time on the basis of Goethe's *Wilhelm Meister*, fails to build on the promise of its author's sparkling debut and will not be the subject of discussion here.

Works of fiction conceived as elaborate literary jokes may well end, of course, as somewhat solemn monuments to their author's ingenuity: spun out too long, the wit is liable to get crushed. There is nothing of this about Thorsten Becker's first prose work, which in 1986 succeeded in winning its author the *Frankfurter Allgemeine Zeitung*'s 'Preis für Literatur'. In Schiller's poem the tyrant Dionys grants his thwarted assassin Damon a stay of execution to enable him to reunite his sister with her husband. As a pledge of good faith he must leave behind a friend, who will be crucified should he fail to return. Not only does Damon redeem the pledge — as Goethe pointed out, somewhat implausibly overcoming floods, heat and marauding bandits to return in the nick of time ('In der Bürgschaft möchte es physiologisch nicht ganz zu passieren sein, daß einer, der sich an einem regnigen Tag aus dem Strome gerettet, vor Durst umkommen will, da er noch ganz nasse Kleider haben mag.'[12]), but succeeds, by his display of loyalty, in softening the face of tyranny: Dionys begs to be included in the bond of friendship between the two men: 'Und die Treue, sie ist doch kein leerer Wahn,/ So nehmet auch mich zum Genossen an,/ Ich sey, gewährt mir die Bitte,/ In eurem Bunde der dritte.'[13]

The account which Thorsten Becker's narrator gives us of his first confrontation with Schiller in the late 1960s: 'Die Schillerbüste in der Aula war von Primanern mit Ketchup und Verbandszeug in ein Pop-Art-Objekt umfunktioniert, mit roter Farbe war dahinter an die Wand gesprüht: Schiller ist tot' (p. 6), prepares us for an irreverently relaxed approach to 'Die Bürgschaft' in which the implausibilities of the original will find their counterpart in further and deliberate implausibilities. Beginning on the transit route to West Berlin, in that no-man's-land between two quite different worlds which, we are informed, is the only place in Germany, 'den die Bundesrepublikaner fürs Erzählen haben' (p. 5), Becker's amiable parody unfolds its purpose slowly, mischievously releasing an initial scatter of red herrings. In fact, it is the recently emigrated 'DDR-Bürger' known as 'Glatze', tippler, raconteur extraordinary, and former youth boxing champion, to whom the narrator has given a lift, who does most of the talking. He whiles away the journey with Rabelaisian tales of drunken escapades involving shattered HO windows,[14] stolen alcohol and salami, and improbably forbearing officials: 'Nun geht in der DDR das Verständnis für den Trunk bis hoch in die Behörden' (p. 15). His flood of anecdotes (which can only confirm the narrator in his ambition to become better acquainted with the cultural and subcultural side of life in the GDR) proves, however, to be a diversionary preamble to the nub of the tale. Glatze, in this first part of Becker's triptych (subtitled: 'Vaterland und Muttersprache'), merely provides the link to the story's main thread and the East Berlin set-designer Schlitzer, a 'Don Giovanni im Kostüm des DDR-Bürgers', whom the narrator gets to know amidst the faded bohemian splendour of the 'Wiener Café' and with the help of massive consumption of alcohol and disputations over the state of contemporary culture.

Typical, in this opening section, of the exuberance which characterizes the whole of Becker's narrative is, on the one hand, the rapid intercutting between affable observation of dialogue and action in the time-warp GDR décor and setting, and, on the other, access to the author's richly stocked imagination or 'Gehirnzirkus' (to use an expression of George Grosz). Associative recollection, for instance, in which an argument about Proust leads to reflections on East Berlin productions of *Rameaus Neffe* (points of comparison here, *en passant*, with Bob Dylan and Frank Zappa interviews), *Leonce und Lena* and *Dantons Tod*, merge uninhibitedly into the recollection of his father's predilection for 'Herrenwitze' of dubious taste and a watch-swapping episode which represents, in his friendship with Schlitzer, 'ein materielles Siegel der Initiation in einen edleren Stand menschlicher Beziehung' (p. 47). For Schlitzer this means soliciting the help of the narrator in easing his way to a commission with a theatre in the West. For the reader, it marks the point at which the tale prepares to move into the realm of the distinctly fanciful. The request to use one of Schlitzer's erotic drawings as an illustration for a book he is just about to publish, introduces the narrator to the frustrating realities of the cultural scene in the GDR. Schlitzer reluctantly declines; unauthorized use of his work could jeopardize his plans for a trip to the West. Ignoring the possible consequences, the narrator nevertheless surreptitiously pockets the drawing, intending to remunerate his friend at a later point. After the appearance of his book, he returns somewhat guiltily to East Berlin to settle his debt, with the 300 Deutschmarks stuffed, not like the dagger in the opening lines of Schiller's ballad, 'im Gewande', but in his sock. He is promptly arrested and makes the acquaintance of 'Kommissar Lärisch' of the 'Staatssicherheit',[15] who proves to be the benign counterpart of Schiller's tyrannical despot. Improbability begins to escalate as Lärisch responds to the narrator's delinquency by first inviting him to 'ein paar Gespräche über Marxismus-Leninismus' (p. 72), and then by giving him the opportunity to redeem his peccadillo. Schlitzer will be permitted an extended trip to Vienna if the narrator will stand as guarantor of his return. The bargain (and point of contact with Schiller) is that should Schlitzer be seduced by the charms of the West, the narrator will forfeit his passport and identity and spend the rest of his days as a citizen of the GDR.

Quite by design of course, Thorsten Becker has devised a wildly preposterous scenario. And yet such are the stylistic verve and vitality with which this perfectly outrageous tale is told that the invention sticks. It has always been open for fiction to create its own rules, and they, we note, are in no way necessarily bound by what we know, or imagine we know, is likely to happen in 'real life'. Reality is not always most authentically caught in faithful reproduction of what is, and what is not, possible; the outrageously improbable, as here in *Die Bürgschaft*, can also be an avenue to the truth.

In fact, this aspect of the book gave few of its first reviewers any problems. There was distinctly less enthusiasm, however, about the authorial interventions and intellectual excursions which are interwoven with the main thread of the tale. These drew critics to different sides of the barricades. Marcel Reich-Ranicki was tempted to an unusually enthusiastic response: 'Jawohl, sein Debüt ist ein kesser Sieg, ein kleiner und schöner Triumph', although the impact of this high praise was modified somewhat by the faintly self-justificatory remark at the conclusion of his review: 'Wer nicht den Mut zur Übertreibung hat, der mag Buchhalter oder Apotheker werden, als Kritiker ist er fehl am Platze.'[16] Martin Ebel on the other hand, while giving Becker credit for the 'hübsche Idee' of making of Schiller's ballad an all-German 'Schelmenstück', delivers a harsh verdict (repeated by other commentators) on Becker's immodest way with the erudite reference: 'Zweifellos ist Becker ein gescheiter Kopf, aber es ist eine kalte, eine gewissermaßen intelligenzelnde Gescheitheit nicht ohne einiges Imponiergehabe; allzuoft geht die Laune des Verspielten in die altkluge Phrase über, geht die frech-naseweise Pirouette im weltweise tönenden Aphorismus auf.'[17] This is a rather uncharitable view of one of the principal strands of the book's underlying dynamic — the uninhibited interweaving of narrative with authorial elaboration and discursiveness. From the opening pages, for instance, Glatze's roistering anecdotes rub shoulders with the narrator's slightly tongue-in-cheek deliberations on the problematic relation between 'Dichtung' and 'Wahrheit' and on Schlegel's dictum that a certain Romantic freedom is binding on all German writers. Simultaneously, in the veritable potpourri of these opening scenes, the 'deutsch-deutsche Geschichte' on which the narrator is embarked seeks disputatious connection with Wolfgang Pohrt's arguments on the nature of German nationalism, straying thence by leaps and bounds to fleeting observations on the aestheticization of politics and Fritz Lang's *Hangmen also die*.

This feature of *Die Bürgschaft*, its particular brand of braggadocio intellectual pyrotechnics, will remain a question of individual taste: some readers will doubtless regard it as intrinsic to the overall wit of the book; others will want to dismiss it as vulgar showmanship. What, on the other hand, it is difficult to fault, is Becker's ability to evoke milieu and setting. As East Germany as once we knew it comes gradually to be subsumed in the picobello uniformity of its western neighbour, we may well come to be grateful for what Becker has pinned down of those corners of seedy charm which have always been an endearing aspect of the GDR. Not perhaps for the descriptions of the gastronomic horrors of the GDR motorway 'Raststätte' which he does so well, but certainly for his preservation of the unique, irresistible ambience of certain East Berlin drinking dens:

Das Lokal war eine große dunkle Berliner Buttike, ein Fossil aus ganzdeutschen Zeiten, wie sich dergleichen im Westteil der Stadt nur als Tankstelle der äußerst deklassierten Alkoholisten im Wedding und in Kreuzberg hie und da hat erhalten können. Hier aber war es ein vollebendiges Organ des sozialen Körpers, das um diese frühe Nachmittagsstunde bestens besucht war. Wir fanden nur mit Mühe und durch Unterstützung des Kellners einen Tisch im Hinterraum. Auf der von den Jahren mit einer dicken Schicht von Rauch und Schmier überzogenen Tapete hingen Reproduktionen holländischer Meister, von derselben Patina verziert. Ich saß an der Wand und konnte an ihr entlang tief in den Gang hineinsehen, von welchem die Wirtschaftsräume abgingen. Das aus den verschiedenen Türen auf den Gang fallende Licht und der Blick durch die offene Tür eines Vorratsraums am Ende des Ganges gaben ein ganz ähnliches Versprechen von Unendlichkeit wie auf der Reproduktion, die mir vis-a-vis hing, wo der Amsterdamer Maler seine perspektivischen Spiele mit den Durchblicken in verschachtelte Höfe und Stuben trieb. Die Farbigkeit der beiden Ansichten aber stach völlig voneinander ab. Die ganz unvertönte Grelle der Palette aus Schkopau, die originale Farbenwelt, mit der allein schon die nationale Identität der DDR bewiesen ist, habe ich leider nie auf Gemälden wiederfinden können. (pp. 32—3)

As we have seen, it is part of the narrative licence Becker has allowed himself, to propel his story forward on the wheels of chance and coincidence. And so it is with the narrator's enforced, but not unwelcome stay in East Berlin. A fortuitous meeting and the renewal of an earlier brief acquaintanceship with Knut Kallrath, an East German director of international reputation, gives him the opportunity to consolidate his stay and to revive a passion, born and nurtured as a drama student in West Berlin, for Shakespeare's *Richard II*. It just so happens (once again the sheer charm of the tale persuades us to turn a blind eye to this element of contrivance) that Kallrath is to direct the play for the coming season and has been let down over a planned new translation. The narrator steps into the breach, is commissioned to produce an alternative to both August Wilhelm von Schlegel and Erich Fried and, with the bargain ('ein System von Mißtrauen und Absicherungen'; p. 129) struck with Lärisch over the terms of the 'Bürgschaft' and Schlitzer's trip to Vienna, he settles to his task, taking over the designer's flat, car and typewriter, as well as sundry of his female companions.

The resolution of the tale comes a good deal more quickly than its preparation. For the narrator, the success of the experiment is not as immediately obvious as it is for Schlitzer, who enjoys an unqualified triumph in Vienna. Although the relationship with Lärisch blossoms, his Shakespeare translation for Knut Kallrath does not. His weeks in the 'Haupstadt der DDR' serve mainly to remind him how much a creature of the West he is. Schlitzer eventually returns to fulfil his part of the bargain, but not quite on time, and not before having precipitated the narrator into an act of brief, but fortunately, redeemable madness. In the last two pages of his tale, and as if we had not already been convinced of the fertile and imaginative new talent which has popped up here, Becker rounds off his story and the lives of his characters by providing us with a series of embryonic mini-plots involving the Canary Islands and South America, each of which would provide material for yarns no less ripping and far-fetched than the one he has just related.

III

What is one to make, overall, of Thorsten Becker's *Die Bürgschaft*? There may well be something in the reproach of Ebel and others that Becker, in his excursiveness, does not bear his erudition lightly, as is illustrated by a passage which we find on the second page of the tale:

> Der schlechteste Erzähler unterscheidet sich vom besten Romancier immer noch dadurch, daß er die Geschichte nicht in seinem Kopf gebaut hat, bevor er sie erzählt. Marx' Beispiel von der Biene und dem Baumeister vom Anfang des 5. Kapitels des 1. Bandes des 'Kapitals' hat, wie es bei philosophischen Beispielen der Fall zu sein pflegt, zu vielen Mißverständnissen geführt. (Aus den Korinthenbriefen zitiere ich nicht, man weiß also gleich, welche Musik hier gespielt wird.) Was gilt, ist: der kluge Mann baut vor, der schlaue läßt vorbauen. (p. 6)

One may well feel here that an element of self-irony, coupled as it is elsewhere with the self-deflating abruptness with which he is able to descend from an elevated level of discourse down to the earthy and everyday, is not always sufficient to dispel the notion that this is a young man well pleased with himself and the intellectual baggage he has managed to assemble in his twenty-eight years. Despite, however, a certain occasional reserve on points such as this, one is nonetheless appreciative of iconoclastic critical vignettes such as his dissection of the shortcomings of an Ariane Mnouchkine production of *Richard II* in the Deutschlandhalle in West Berlin. This is above all an account of the disappointment he had felt, when recalling the hypnotic, euphoric effect of a performance of *1789* at the Cartoucherie de Vincennes, of later watching Mnouchkine's 'japanische Version der in französischer Sprache dargebotenen elisabethanischen Erinnerung an das englische Spätmittel-alter', a production, as he sees it, of misconceived genius, and one, furthermore, which had the potential to reproduce the raw, folk vitality of the Cartoucherie, but only succeeded in crushing it, 'als hätte die

Deutschlandhalle sich aus der fetten Volksnutte in eine spröde Jungfer verwandelt, die das Ereignis mit verschlossenen Poren über sich ergehen läßt' (p. 108).

But where Becker is, of course, at his most beguiling is in pinpointing what is different about the GDR. This is not just a matter of scenery, of a particularly precise evocation of the mood of this or that cafe — of the jealously guarded charms of 'Die Möwe' for instance, the favourite hangout for East Berlin's artists and intellectuals: 'ein großer Salon im Stil des fin de siecle, der es mit den besten Restaurants von Paris aufnehmen konnte' (p. 112), or the Bismarck Hotel, choice relic of yesteryear, miraculously preserved in its advancing state of shabby decay. Although in moments of incipient panic (when it seems, as in Schiller, that his friend Schlitzer might not redeem the pledge) he is made conscious of his West German roots and West German identity, the sense of belonging back in the other half of Germany only rarely tempts him to the game of odious (and otiose) comparisons. Shakespeare and the King's 'prison monologue' in Act 5, Scene 3 of *Richard II* ('I have been studying how I may compare/ This prison where I live unto the world;/ And, for because the world is populous/ And here is not a creature but myself,/ I cannot do it') come to his rescue here. They remind him that 'Vergleiche auf der Stelle treten' (p. 145), that he is not in East Berlin as a one-day, 'Zwangsumtausch', gawking tourist. He is there, we feel, to experience at first hand Peter Schneider's proposition that forty years of division not only produced two German states, but also 'Zwei Lebenskulturen';[18] he is there not only to register these differences but, more crucially, to live them 'als arbeitender Mensch' (p. 117).

It is this aspect of the tale (and no amount of intellectual narcissism on Becker's part can detract from the overall effect) which leaves the reader, for all the hocus pocus of the plot, with the impression of having read a profoundly realistic fiction, of having come much closer to an understanding of the relationship between two quite separate Germanys, which now, from our present perspective, find themselves in a process of troubled and problematic fusion. This establishment of the separateness was an aspect of the book which impressed even sceptical reviewers when it was first published. Wolfram Schütte, writing in the *Frankfurter Rundschau*, praised the work for having captured 'feinste Schwebstoffe der bundesrepublikanischen und deutschdemokratischen Realität'; he talked of 'der neugierig-aufmerksame Blick auf das

Eigenartige und Gegensätzliche der Lebensweisen' as being 'das wirklich Aufregende, der erstaunliche Zugewinn an sinnlicher Erfahrung und Reflexion von Thorsten Becker's erster Prosaarbeit'.[19] This is all very well, but Schütte is infuriatingly vague about precisely what it is that Becker has managed to pin down in such exciting fashion.

One might attempt here one's own tentative compilation. Certainly, as has already been indicated, he has caught the ambience of certain locales, buildings which are anachronistic, strangely unreal hangovers from the past — pubs, clubs and the aforementioned Hotel Bismarck, for instance: 'Schon beim Eintreten war der so endlos beschriebene und zur Phrase kaputtzitierte Geist des Berlins der zwanziger Jahre zu spüren. Aber eben nur der Geist, der in Muff und Staub, nicht aber in Fleisch und Blut lebt' (p. 77). He is perceptive too about irritating aspects of day-to-day life in the GDR — the fact that 'Dienst am Kunden aber ist verpönt' and the customer 'wie eine unausrottbare Landplage behandelt wird' (p. 78), as well as about the relaxed modesty of manner which he regards as the characteristic posture of the GDR citizens, and which was embodied so charismatically in Knuth Kallrath: talent plus self-effacement. It is a devastating combination, which is thin on the ground in the Federal Republic but which, so Becker would have us believe, is the order of the day in the GDR.

But what, one wants to ask, looking back on this book several years after its publication, and at a point where the historical situation of the two Germanys has changed in a fashion beyond all conceivable expectation and anticipation, does all of this amount to? How is one to evaluate what now comes to resemble an almost nostalgic depiction of the values and life style of a society which (as developments since November 1989 have so graphically revealed) was, in its ethos and economic structures, hopelessly out of tune with the harsh requirements of the modern world? The expectations which Becker's narrator brings to his experience of the GDR have a resonance and repercussions beyond the pages of this particular fiction. To put the argument rather bluntly, they might seem to be further testament to that paucity of haul when the West German writer has looked eastwards and to socialism in search of Utopian vision. The affection, for instance, for what amounts to a certain quality of fecklessness in everyday GDR life, his admiration for an endearing reluctance to function along the lines of the streamlined heartlessness of Western capitalism and, above all, the proposal implicit in his view of East German society that there may be something of substance and worth preserving about the GDR might possibly be seen as moving Becker in the direction of that fuzzy self-delusion amongst certain sections of West Germany's intelligentsia which Peter Schneider caught with such wicked eloquence in the figure of the political activist in *Der Mauerspringer* who, we recall, draws all her strength for the struggle against capitalism in the West by creating a totally erroneous picture of the virtues of socialism in the East: 'Im Osten, so scheint es, kann sie sich von den Strapazen des Kampfes im Westen erholen, hier endlich findet sie teilnehmende Zuhörer, hier kann sie Atem schöpfen. Der empfindliche Ausgleich funktioniert aber nur, solange sie in dem Gefühl, aus der schlimmsten aller denkbaren Welten zu kommen, nicht durch östliche Leidensgeschichten beeinträchtigt ist' (p. 66). It is on this score that Becker is saved by the wit, scurrilous jollity and sheer exuberance of his text. It is these qualities which rescue *Die Bürgschaft*, in its view of what the GDR might have to offer, from being merely a kind of authentically decked-out mirage, a wish-dream born of the psychological need to conjure into being, regardless of their tenuous point of contact with reality, comforting alternatives to the perceived or imagined malaises of the West.

There is, in conclusion, one further vital point to be made. In 1981, Konrad Franke concluded an article on GDR literature of the 1970s with the words: 'Eine der Eigenschaften von Kunst, von Literatur, ist, daß sie Künftiges vorher weiß.'[20] We are reminded of this in the general preposterousness of *Die Bürgschaft*. When, after the deal has been struck which will enable Schlitzer to go off to Vienna and the narrator to remain in East Berlin, Lärisch observes 'das sind so die Momente, wo ich am Sozialismus zweifele' (p. 131), he is saying far more than he could ever have realized. This bargain, along with the jocular extravagance with which Becker rounds off his tale, are, in their proposal of the unthinkable, uncannily prophetic. 'Wahnsinn' the readers of *Die Bürgschaft* might well have murmured in 1986, unaware that this would also be the response to events in November 1989 which would outstrip, in the extent of their unimaginableness, even the wildest extremes of Thorsten Becker's fantasy.

NOTES

1   Bertolt Brecht: 'Bemerkungen' in *Der aufhaltsame Aufstieg des Arturo Ui*, 8th edn, Frankfurt/Main, 1975, p.132.
2   Hermann Kant: *Die Aula*, Berlin (GDR), 1965, p. 115.
3   Ibid, p. 224.
4   Peter Schneider: *Der Mauerspringer*, Darmstadt, 1982.
5   Werner Herzog: 'Absurde Anfälle der Ordnung', *Der Spiegel*, 24 May 1982, p. 210.
6   Stefan Heym: 'Mein Richard' in Heym: *Die richtige Einstellung und andere Erzählungen*, Munich, 1976, pp. 146—65. For a discussion of the relationship between Heym's story and Schneider's see Gordon Burgess: '"Was da ist, das ist [nicht] mein": The Case of Peter Schneider' in Arthur Williams, Stuart Parkes and Roland Smith (eds): *Literature on the Threshold. The German Novel in the 1980s*, Oxford, 1990, pp. 107—22, esp. pp. 110—4.
7   Peter Schneider: *Deutsche Ängste. Sieben Essays*, Darmstadt, 1988.
8   Schneider: *Der Mauerspringer*, p. 117. Stuart Parkes refers to the same passage (p. 199 above). It is interesting also in this context to consider the contributions to this volume by Andrea Reiter (pp. 321—36 above) and Katrin Kohl (pp. 339—56 above), both of which investigate aspects of language and pose the question about similarities and differences between East and West German usage.
9   '"Ich war ein Aktivist der DDR". Der ostdeutsche Schriftsteller Hermann Kant über seine Rolle und den Stellenwert der Literatur im SED-Regime', *Der Spiegel*, 6 August 1990, p. 158.
10 Thorsten Becker: *Die Bürgschaft*, Zurich, 1985. All page references in the text are to this edition.
11 Thorsten Becker: *Die Nase*, Darmstadt, 1987.
12 Letter to Schiller of 5 September 1798, in Emil Staiger (ed.): *Der Briefwechsel zwischen Schiller und Goethe*, Frankfurt/Main, 1966, p. 675.
13 In Julius Petersen and Friedrich Beißner (eds): *Schillers Werke. Nationalausgabe. Erster Band. Gedichte in der Reihenfolge ihres Erscheinens 1776—1799*, Weimar, 1943, p. 425.
14 HO — 'Handelsorganisation', the state-controlled retailing organization.
15 Becker's otherwise keen eye for detail deserts him here. There was no such rank in the *Stasi*.
16 Marcel Reich-Ranicki: 'Eine deutsch-deutsche Geschichte. Thorsten Becker, ein junger Autor aus West-Berlin', *FAZ*, 9 November 1985. It should be noted that Reich-Ranicki's enthusiasm for Becker ('Ich glaube an das Talent von Thorsten Becker') did not extend to his second work. It was left to Franz Josef Görtz to deliver a scathing judgement of *Die Nase* (*FAZ*, 6 October 1987).
17 Martin Ebel: 'Die Launen des Verspielten', *Badische Zeitung*, 18/19 January 1986.
18 Schneider: *Der Mauerspringer*, p. 14.
19 Wolfram Schütte: 'Gemütlichkeit mit Poltergeist. Thorsten Beckers deutsch-deutsche Erzählung *Die Bürgschaft*', *FR*, 15 February 1986.
20 Konrad Franke: '"Wer zurückschaut erkennt, daß das Gemeinsame wächst." Zur DDR-Literatur in den 70er Jahren', *Die Horen*, vol. 26, no. 4, Winter 1981, p. 6. Franke is, of course, quoting Heinrich Mann: 'Was eine Gesellschaft oder ein Jahrhundert werden, weiß die Literatur im voraus — oder niemand weiß es.' ('Die Macht des Wortes', *Die Neue Weltbühne*, vol. 4, no. 10, 7 March 1935, p. 285.)

DEUTSCHE ÖKOLYRIK:
COMPARATIVE OBSERVATIONS ON THE EMERGENCE AND EXPRESSION OF ENVIRONMENTAL CONSCIOUSNESS IN WEST AND EAST GERMAN POETRY

AXEL GOODBODY

I Ecology and Literature
I.i The Emergence of Public Debate on the Environment

Awareness of ecological problems is probably almost as old as man's detrimental influence on his environment.[1] The central principle of ecology, that of natural balance between the species, foreshadowed in the medieval conception of nature as the perfect ensemble of God's creation, led already in the eighteenth century to physico-theological concern for the protection of endangered plants and animals as indispensable parts of the divinely ordained whole. In 1868, Ernst Haeckel, the German popularizer of Darwin's theory of evolution, founded the discipline of *Oecologie*, defined as 'die Lehre vom Naturhaushalte', necessary for the understanding and control of change in the environment. Increasing industrialization was by then leading to scientific observation and chemical analysis of pollution, an early study of acid rain appearing as long ago as 1883.[2] Works of nineteenth-century literature reflecting nascent awareness of environmental problems include Thoreau's *Walden*,[3] Samuel Butler's *Erewhon*,[4] Ibsen's *An Enemy of the People*,[5] and Raabe's 'Pfisters Mühle'.[6]

However, ecological concern acquired a new dimension after the Second World War. The destruction of Hiroshima revealed man's ability to change the environment on a scale hitherto unimagined. The gap now also widened between the science of ecology, bent on optimal management of the environment, and broader public concern, associated with a desire to turn away from industrialization and militarism, and adopt a gentler, less exploitative relationship towards nature. The West German environmental 'movement' was a phenomenon of the 1970s, a national response to growing international recognition that postwar industrial expansion was leading to a serious disturbance of equilibrium between man and nature. Major theoretical contributions to the international debate on human ecology such as the works of Herbert Marcuse,[7] Lewis Mumford,[8] and Ernst Schumacher (*Small is Beautiful*)[9] were available in German translation, and the biologist Rachel Carson's pioneering study of the effects of DDT and other chemicals used as pesticides in agriculture, *Silent Spring*, became a German as well as an English bestseller.[10] The first economic recession in the Federal Republic in 1967 served as a warning of the dangers of reliance on economic growth. The MIT study *The Limits to Growth*, commissioned by the Club of Rome, which used computer simulation to assess the impact of variables on the future of mankind, and predicted a collapse of civilization if economic growth were to continue, stimulated intense debate in West Germany as elsewhere.[11] Finally, the oil crisis of 1973, when the OPEC countries raised prices and restricted output of crude oil, brought home to sceptics the practical limitations of Western economic strategy.

At the same time, signs of the impact of the economic miracle on the West German environment were becoming clearer: landscapes were being increasingly encroached on by road building and monotonous urbanization; rivers and lakes polluted by industrial waste, sewage and phosphates; certain species of plants and animals were discovered to be threatened with extinction; and in the 1980s ever increasing percentages of the German forests were diagnosed as dying from acid rain. In what seemed a relatively weak economic situation, with growing unemployment, West German governments hesitated to introduce stricter environmental legislation which might overburden industry. The threat to the environment was registered by local and national groups[12] and attracted increasing attention in the media.[13] The gradual emergence of a popular Green ideology led to the founding of the Green Party, which won its first electoral successes in 1979. Though new environmental laws were passed in 1980, and ecological issues were displaced by the Peace Movement at the forefront of public consciousness, nuclear energy remained a sphere of public conflict for some years, and environmental concerns have been kept in the public eye by both both local and international crises and campaigns. From the start the environmental movement of the 1970s embraced different groups, each with their own distinct political motivation and interests — managers and bureaucrats who established a profit-seeking eco-industrial lobby on the one extreme, and eco-freaks, either aspiring to complete self-sufficiency, or motivated by escapism and anarchistic delight in the collapse of the establishment on the other. In the wake of the student movement many with left-wing views played an active part: the environmental situation was interpreted as symptomic of a general political and socio-cultural crisis. Environmentalism became an ideology seeking to replace crude materialist utilitarianism with the sometimes anarchic, sometimes irrational, but nonetheless genuine search for an alternative way of life based on a reconciliation between man and nature.[14]

I.ii Environmental Literature and Ökolyrik

This environmental movement was reflected in West German literature, and, perhaps more surprisingly, particularly in poetry. Hans Christoph Buch writes in the introduction to a special number of the Berlin journal *Tintenfisch* entitled *Thema: Natur. Oder Warum ein Gespräch über Bäume heute kein Verbrechen mehr ist* of the rediscovery of nature by his generation: 'Die Wiederentdeckung der Natur, bis vor kurzem noch synonym mit Ausflippen und großer Verweigerung, ist zum Schlüsselwort für die späten 70er Jahre geworden, so wie der Aufbruch in die Gesellschaft für die späten 60er.'[15] By 'rediscovery' Buch means recognition of the value of the natural environment in the wake of the antinuclear demonstrations in Wyhl and Brokdorf, and the expression of this in verse and prose. Together with essays and short prose, he presents poems by some fifteen German writers, ranging from the hermetic Peter Huchel to the protest singer Walter Moßmann. The revival of public interest in nature poetry in the late 1970s that this heralded was largely a response to the new perception of the vulnerability of our environment. This is shown by a number of subsequent anthologies: Edgar Marsch's collection of twentieth-century German nature poems *Moderne deutsche Naturlyrik*[16] contains a substantial afterword in which the importance of the ecological *Warngedicht*[17] is stressed. Alexander von Bormann's thematically arranged cross-section of six centuries of nature poetry *Die Erde will ein freies Geleit*[18] has, again, an afterword 'Vom Realismus der Naturlyrik', stressing the environmental dimension already present in the title. Von Bormann argues that the central role of nature poetry since the late eighteenth century has been to counter instrumental reason, and show how freedom can be achieved only through renunciation of our domination over nature and our fellow men. Finally, there is the specialist anthology of environmental poetry *Im Gewitter der Geraden*, published by the professor of political science, expert on environmental legislation, writer on the politics of citizens' action groups and amateur poet and Germanist Peter Cornelius Mayer-Tasch.[19]

Despite the weakness of many well-meant environmental poems (including some in the Mayer-Tasch anthology), which lack argumentative conviction and appreciation of the wider issues raised as well as linguistic and poetic subtlety, despite the resulting scorn of critics for the genre[20] and a general reluctance by serious writers to have their work classified as *Umweltlyrik* or *Ökolyrik*,[21] environmental literature and poetry in the broader sense are by no means necessarily trivial, and they are of particular interest to those concerned with the interface of contemporary politics and culture. *Ökolyrik*, defined by Maren-Grisebach as 'Beschreibung, Erlebnis und Innenschau von Natur [...] aber aufgehoben in einer die Naturzerstörung beklagenden oder anklagenden, kritischen Haltung',[22] has indeed gradually become respectable subject matter for Germanists.[23] In addition to on-the-whole brief but informative and insightful articles by Mayer-Tasch,[24] the journalist Hubertus Knabe,[25] the poet Hans-Jürgen Heise[26] and the Germanist Susanne Mittag,[27] German environmental poetry is also discussed in the introduction and two contributions to Norbert Mecklenburg's *Naturlyrik und Gesellschaft*,[28] in papers devoted to West and East German poetry given at an American symposium and published in Reinhold Grimm's *Natur und Natürlichkeit*,[29] and in the final chapter of Jürgen Haupt's comprehensive book *Natur und Lyrik*.[30]

Environmental poetry is more than a mere document of social and political culture. It goes beyond the narrowly mimetic depiction of landscapes, polemic triteness and subservience of art to political interest. Its roots lie in the poetry of physico-theology (Brockes, for instance), in nature poems implicitly or explicitly rejecting exploitation and subjugation of nature (for instance much Romantic verse), and in poems of all ages warning against war, violence and human hubris. Some of the best poems of the 1970s are *Ökolyrik* in this sense, blending description and protest with historical reflection and analysis, and fusing these with personal emotion, grappling with significant conflicts of interest and expressing them with precision and originality.

I.iii Two German Literatures?

It has generally been held that GDR writers lagged behind their West German counterparts in recognizing and criticizing environmental damage, and that this blindness towards environmental dangers, reflecting of course the political values and priorities of not only the SED, but also the majority of the population, constituted a significant difference between West and East German literatures. In a scathing commentary on Volker Braun's poem 'Durchgearbeitete Landschaft' written in 1971, Peter Rühmkorf wrote in 1975 that the first half of the poem reveals 'einen beinahe brutalistisch-conquistadorischen Impetus' unthinkable in the West:

> So etwas ist neu für unsere Ohren und Augen und es will uns auch nur schwer in den Kopf. Wo wir für die Erhaltung arkadischer Naturzustände gern auf die Barrikaden gehen, entzündet sich der Enthusiasmus eines DDR-Kollegen gerade an so gewaltsamen Eingriffen, die ein lieblich-ungebildetes Idyll aus seiner Unschuld reißen. Wo Kolonisierung und Kultivation für uns fast wesensgleich geworden sind mit einer Verlustwirtschaft, die auf Deubelkomm-raus und Mensch-hau-ab drauflos dräniert, kriegen wir es hier mit einer Pioniermentalität zu tun, die über ein hübsches Pastorale wegschreitet als wäre es nur unwegsamer Dreck.[31]

The reasons for the persistence of such a mentality in the GDR while the environmental movement in the Federal Republic was in full swing have been seen as slower industrial development, in turn responsible for priority remaining with economic growth, the attempts of bureaucratic socialism to use satisfaction of the material needs of the population as a source of legitimation for the system, ideologically founded faith in technological advance, and ignorance of the economic costs of pollution. As Hans Magnus Enzensberger wrote in a critical article on political ecology in 1973, despite his acknowledgement of Marx's vision of a reconciliation of man and nature in the early *Economic and Philosophical Manuscripts*: 'Marxism [today] as a defensive mechanism, as a talisman against the demands of reality, as a collection of exorcisms — these are tendencies which we all have reasons to take note of and combat. The issue of ecology offers but one example.'[32]

Awareness of ecological problems in the GDR was discouraged. Statistics were withheld, and if public distrust of nuclear power came late, it was partly because protests against nuclear power stations in the West had been consistently played down in the GDR media. But was there really such a great difference between the treatment of environmental issues in East and West German creative writing as this would suggest, either in the 1970s, or before and since? Have the 'two literatures' here been significantly out of step? On the basis of examples from poetry anthologies published in the 1970s and 1980s,[33] I shall first examine the origins of ecological consciousness in West Germany, and sketch out subsequent trends. By then looking at parallels in East German poems over the past thirty years (taking into consideration the question to what extent ecological issues were publicly debated in the GDR, and commenting on the greater role poetry played in this process than in the West), it should be possible to draw conclusions as to the existence of an underlying identity of concern for the environment which may be characteristic of German culture in both East and West.

II West German Environmental Poetry
II.i Environmental Issues in the Poems of the 1950s and 1960s

Although specific social and political issues are rarely treated in the poetry of the 1950s, poets such as Günter Eich and Ingeborg Bachmann express their sense of unease with social developments and their scepticism regarding the future in powerful apocalyptic images. Concern at the development of technology and the impact of industrialization on our lives blends here with misgivings over conventional rearmament, man's potential for self-destruction through nuclear weapons, suppression of the past and the giving away of chances to reform society. Eich's forebodings and sense of personal guilt find expression in poems from the volume *Botschaften des Regens* such as 'Im Sonnenlicht', in which he suggests that we shall be called to account for our actions, including the squandering of resources — a phrase which can be interpreted in ecological terms:

> [...]
> Was üppig sie [die Sonne] gab,
> was wir genommen ohne Besinnen,
> das unverlangte Geschenk, —
> eines bestürzenden Tages
> wird es zurückverlangt.
> (*Die Erde will*, p. 416)

A similarly ominous poem expressing reservations about the bureaucratic management and commercial exploitation of nature, written also in the late 1940s or early 1950s, is 'Wald, Bestand an Bäumen, zählbar':

Wald, Bestand an Bäumen, zählbar,
Schonungen, Abholzung, Holz- und
       Papierindustrie,
Mischwald ist am rentabelsten
[...]
Zivilisationslandschaft

Zauberwald Merlins
Einhorn (das Tier, das es nicht gibt)
   das uns bevorsteht,
   das wir nicht wollten
   die vergessene Zukunft
      (*Im Gewitter*, p. 78,
      also *Die Erde will*, p. 323)

Nature's revenge on man for his abuse, implicit in the threat of the closing lines here, is a recurring theme in Eich's poems and radio plays in
the 1950s. It reflects less any irrational belief in nature's actual ability to
strike back, than man's ultimate vulnerability because of his dependence
on nature for life.

Ingeborg Bachmann's comparable misgivings over the reckless exploitation of natural resources and the release of destructive energies by
science and technology are expressed in 'Freies Geleit (Aria II)':

Die Erde will keinen Rauchpilz tragen,
kein Geschöpf ausspeien vorm Himmel,
mit Regen und Zornesblitzen abschaffen
die unerhörten Stimmen des Verderbens.
[...]
Die Erde will ein freies Geleit ins All
jeden Tag aus der Nacht haben,
daß noch tausend und ein Morgen wird
von der alten Schönheit jungen Gnaden.
(*Die Erde will*, p. 417)

Von Bormann points to the pertinence of the phrase 'freies Geleit': like a
prisoner who can dictate terms to his captors, nature holds our lives in
its hands, and is in a position to demand safe conduct. This poem was
written in 1957 — a year of atomic bomb tests which evoked a response
in the GDR too.[34] In March 1958, the year of the 'Kampf dem Atomtod'
campaign, motivated by dread of atomic destruction and fear of a resurgence of German militarism, Bachmann was one of the signatories, together with Eich, Wolfgang Weyrauch,[35] Hans Magnus Enzensberger,
Peter Rühmkorf and others, of a statement in the Munich journal *Die
Kultur* protesting against Adenauer's atomic policy. The straightforward
but nonetheless moving poems of the less well-known Dagmar Nick

'Aufruf', 'Apokalypse' and 'Wir' (*Im Gewitter*, pp. 202, 228, 230), constitute a similarly impassioned plea for a change of direction:

> [...]
> Aus den verwaisten Atommeilern
> wird sich Verwesung ergießen
> über die Erde,
> und die verkrüppelten Rosen
> werden die Schöpfung verneinen.
> Unüberwindliche Stille wird sein
> auf dem Schlachtfeld Europa.
> (*Im Gewitter*, p. 228)

However, the truly outstanding figure in German environmental poetry in the late 1950s and 1960s is Hans Magnus Enzensberger. Already before pioneering the politicization of literature in the later 1960s, he was at the forefront in Germany in ecological concern. Indeed, environmental issues are indissolubly linked with his interest in the Third World and global political problems. Few were so well informed and so perspicacious on the one hand, and so lucid and eloquent on the other. Enzensberger's poem 'fremder garten', published in *verteidigung der wölfe* in 1957, was ahead of its time in discussing chemicals in vegetables, oil slicks at sea, atmospheric pollution and the sinister silence of a poisoned environment:

> es ist heiß, das gift kocht in den tomaten.
> hinter den gärten rollen versäumte züge vorbei,
> das verbotene schiff heult hinter den türmen.
> [...]
> die signale verdorren. das schiff speit öl in den hafen
> und wendet. ruß, ein fettes, rieselndes tuch
> deckt den garten. mittag, und keine grille.
> (*Im Gewitter*, p. 66,
> also *Die Erde will*, pp. 295f.)

Another poem in the same volume, 'aussicht auf amortisation',[36] is a vehement satire on progress: 'Fortschritt' is identified with frenzied demolition and reconstruction in cities, computers and cybernetics, atmospheric pollution and superfluous affluence, and its logical conclusion is exposed as preparation for another war. Enzensberger's scorn for progress is taken up again in the later poem 'weiterung' (1964, *Im Gewitter*, pp. 219f.), a deeply pessimistic statement on the future of humanity. Quite a number of poems in Enzensberger's second volume, *landessprache* (1960) are concerned with the environment. 'das ende der eulen' and 'ich, der präsident und die biber' (*Im Gewitter*, pp. 221f., 225) are an indictment of man's domination of nature, his quest for short-term profit at the expense of allowing whole species of animals and plants to become extinct, in a world of polar warming, in which everything is monitored by radar, surrounded by safety barriers and military manoeuvres, and man is oblivious to the dangers of nuclear weapons. 'isotop' and 'an alle fernsprechteilnehmer' (*Im Gewitter*, pp. 117, 171f.) prophesy a creeping death as a result of the 'dürre flut' of nuclear contamination, radiation serving at the same time as a metaphor for man's complacent self-indulgence regarding material goods and blind faith in technology. It is interesting to note the Romantic roots of such seemingly rational criticism. The poems of Enzensberger's first two volumes reveal earth mysticism and a regressive tendency reminiscent of Gottfried Benn. His criticism of modern society and man's alienation in it is essentially individualist, and contains elements of escapism, anticivilizatory irrationalism and élitist scorn for the masses. The impetus behind such poems as 'spur der zukunft' (*Im Gewitter*, p. 221) and 'nänie auf den apfel' (*Im Gewitter*, p. 220), castigating man's destruction of the earth, and rejecting his plans for the future ('ich will es nicht leiden,/ was wir langsam, langsam, langsam begehen'), reflects no belief in socialism offering a practicable alternative to capitalist exploitation, but rather a stance of aestheticized vitalism. This was to change for a period in the late 1960s and early 1970s: in his 'Critique of Political Ecology' in 1973 Enzensberger regards the achievement of ecological balance as a prerequisite for 'the rule of freedom' with which true socialism is identical.[37]

II.ii The Revival of Interest in Nature in the Late 1960s, Agitatory Verse and Resignation in the 1970s

Leaving aside Enzensberger, remarkably little West German poetry in the 1960s was concerned with ecological problems. Only towards the end of the decade came recognition that a conversation about trees was not necessarily a crime, to use Brecht's celebrated phrase.[38] Erich Fried, who emerged as one of the most important political poets in the decade, came to domestic environmental issues via Vietnam. His poem 'Gespräch über Bäume', published in 1967, was one of the first in a series of texts making the point that nature as a topic no longer distracted from political issues, but rather led to the heart of them. It presents the trauma of the 1960s, the brutal subjugation of an impoverished people by a wealthy imperial power in the name of freedom and democracy, involving destruction of nature on a massive scale through napalm and blanket bombing. In the first of three verses relativizing the domestic concerns of everyday life by contrasting them with the situation in Vietnam, the curling up of leaves on Fried's pear tree leads the poet to reflect on the chemical defoliation practised by the Americans in Vietnam:

> Seit der Gärtner die Zweige gestutzt hat
> sind meine Äpfel größer
> Aber die Blätter des Birnbaums
> sind krank. Sie rollen sich ein
>
> In Vietnam sind die Bäume entlaubt
> [...]
> (*Moderne deutsche Naturlyrik*, p. 180)

Fried's much anthologized, nonetheless ambivalent poem 'Neue Naturdichtung' (*Moderne deutsche Naturlyrik*, p. 179; *Im Gewitter*, p. 58; *Die Erde will*, pp. 455f.), published in 1972, demands of the modern nature poet a revelation of the contradictions in society (here exposure of the exploitation and destruction of landscapes by speculators) and reveals the inappropriateness as the subject of poetry of private aesthetic experience of nature. However at the same time Fried is here ironically critical of the self-satisfaction of *poésie engagée*, and appears to suggest the importance of remaining open to new sensual experiences. A number of established nature poets began to adopt an ecologically critical stance by the early 1970s: Karl Krolow published 'Es wird immer windiger' in 1975 (*Im Gewitter*, p. 130), and the aging Marieluise Kaschnitz revolted against man's destruction of himself and the environment in 'Die Gärten', and against 'Notwendigkeiten/ der EWG' in 'Notwendigkeiten' (*Im Gewitter*, pp. 48, 62f., also *Die Erde will*, p. 402).

A wave of politically engaged writing in the early 1970s continued the impetus of the student movement in the ecological sphere. On the one hand there were the polemical aphorisms of Arnfrid Astel (e.g. 'Umweltverschmutzung', 'Blendend weiße Zähne', *Im Gewitter*, p. 73) or Rolf Haufs, indictments of the inequity of ownership of land and power in poems such as 'Kein schöner Land' and 'Besitzverhältnisse' (*Im Gewitter*, pp. 174f., 196f.) by the DKP member and co-founder of 'Hamburg linksliterarisch' and the 'Hamburger Gruppe schreibender Arbeiter' Peter Schütt, and the *Alltagslyrik* of Ludwig Fels (e.g. 'Natur', 'Konsumterror' and 'Müll-Ode', *Im Gewitter*, pp. 52, 150f., 153f.) or Bodo Morshäuser. On the other hand, the tradition of protest songs was taken up by environmental campaigners and proved particularly effective when linked with the revival of dialect poetry. Walter Moßmann's 'In Mueders Stübele',[39] written in Allemanic dialect, was accessible to both Germans and French living in the area near the proposed site of the nuclear power station at Wyhl in Baden-Württemberg. His 'Ballade von Seveso' (*Thema: Natur*, pp. 123—5), which draws parallels between the disaster following an Italian chemical explosion and acid rain in the Federal Republic, and the felling of trees for airport runways, motorways and building programmes, also provided a rallying point in the environmental movement.[40]

Alongside such agitatory poetry integrated in the ecological movement, what has been called 'Lyrik der beschädigten Welt'[41] emerged after the political and cultural *Tendenzwende* of 1974. The anger and protest of the student movement yielded to disillusionment, resignation and irony in a political climate of repression. The public was better informed about general political issues, and German and international ecological developments than ever before, but seemingly unable to bring about significant change in either field. The threat to and exploitation of the environment reflect the helplessness and fears of the individual. The waste land of Rolf-Dieter Brinkmann's poems in *Westwärts 1 & 2* (published posthumously in 1975), a disturbed landscape of neglect and individual isolation, a no-man's-land between city and country, featuring hoardings and empty parking lots, abandoned cars and polluted rivers, eerily lit by blinking neon signs, were to exercise a powerful influence in the later 1970s. In 'Gedicht' (*Im Gewitter*, p. 106) Brinkmann responds to a 'zerstörte Landschaft mit/ Konservendosen', 'und Staub,/ zerstückelte Pavane, aus totem// Neon, Zeitungen und Schienen', with thoughts of death ('was krieg ich jetzt,/ einen Tag älter, tiefer und tot?') and withdrawal from reality ('Wer hat gesagt, daß sowas Leben/ ist? Ich gehe in ein/ anderes Blau').

Jürgen Theobaldy's 'Ohne Blumen' (*Thema: Natur*, p. 13, also *Im Gewitter*, pp. 165f.) revokes Utopian ideals ('Die Utopien sind zurück/ in die Schubladen gepackt worden') and describes a demonstration at Brokdorf, on the lower Elbe, in 1977, in a tone of utter despondency:

> die Leute gehen in schmalen Schlangen
> über die Felder. Ein Graben,
> dahinter Rollen aus Stacheldraht,
> schmutzige Polizisten, die Gesichter
> abwesend hingehalten in die Teleobjektive.
> [...]

> Auf welcher Seite geht die Geschichte
> vorwärts? Wörter, ausgefallen wie Zähne,
> es sieht schlimm aus, sagt einer
> und verweigert den Schluß, der ermuntern
> soll.
> [...]
> Deine Angst hat
> im Februar Geburtstag, lese ich bei dir,
> meine im März. Schwarzes Orakel, wir
> können die letzten sein, die letzten,
> mit erstickten Gitarren gelehnt irgendwohin,
> für das es nie mehr einen Namen geben
> wird, kein Lied, keinen Rhythmus, nichts.

Nicolas Born's important elegy 'Entsorgt' (*Im Gewitter*, pp. 115f.) argues that man has become 'entsorgt [...] von sich selbst', or relieved of his responsibility and individuality, in a world in which fear of the danger nuclear reactors constitute has worn off as part of everyday life, a life 'am Tropf/ der Systeme', in which he is 'gefangen in verruchter Vernunft', with 'kein Schritt mehr frei, kein Atem/ kein Wasser unerfaßt'. Born's speech on the award of the *Bremer Literaturpreis* in 1977 reveals a strange mixture of impassioned plea for an end to the madness of Germany's nuclear energy programme and the planned destruction of natural resources through economic growth, with passivity: 'Ich habe weder zu warnen noch zu mahnen, denn ich bin nicht, weil Schriftsteller, auch ein Moralist' (*Thema: Natur*, p. 115). This stance exemplifies the condition he diagnoses in his generation: 'Unsere Sinne und unser Bewußtsein sind schon weitgehend anästhesiert.'

Jürgen Becker, perhaps the foremost contemporary West German landscape poet, similarly records an environment formed and deformed by man in poems such as 'Privatbereich' (*Moderne deutsche Naturlyrik*, p. 239; *Im Gewitter*, p. 55) from the volume *Das Ende der Landschaftsmalerei* (1974), precisely observing the impact of industrialization, deforestation, tourism, road construction, air traffic and suburban gardeners. However the critical impulse is again blunted by the passivity of the observer, by the incidental and casual nature of his record of abuse of the environment. His 'Natur-Gedicht', inspired by the 'Kahlschlag, Kieshügel, Krater' of a construction site, ends in an ambivalent blend of melancholy acceptance and critical irony:

> nichts Neues; kaputte Natur,
> aber ich vergesse das gern,
> solange ein Strauch steht
> (*Moderne deutsche Naturlyrik*, pp. 239f.,
> also *Im Gewitter*, p. 54)

Günter Kunert's poetry is here more radical: the volumes he has published since moving to the Federal Republic in 1979 reveal a vivid consciousness of threatening ecological catastrophe and apocalyptic vision, expressed in a tone of angry melancholy. 'Unterwegs nach Utopia II' (*Moderne deutsche Naturlyrik*, pp. 216f., also *Im Gewitter*, pp. 224f.) relates how flight from a landscape of concrete 'grau und gründlich' ends only in an artificial paradise of green-coloured glass. 'Irgendetwas' (*Im Gewitter*, pp. 178f.), reminiscent of Enzensberger's 'an alle fernsprechteilnehmer', uses the insidious contamination of radiation as an image for our corruption by modern civilization. The poems 'Lagebericht' (*Im Gewitter*, p. 173), 'Predigt' (*Im Gewitter*, p. 229), 'Erinnerung an Babylon' (*Im Gewitter*, p. 90f.) and 'Mutation' (*Die Erde will*, pp. 424f.) exemplify Kunert's ever increasing pessimism:

> Nur noch Natur
> ist uns geblieben oder was
> von ihr geblieben ist
> [...]
>   Wir sitzen
> im schwarzen Licht
> essen Gift trinken Säure
> wir denken wir leben
> und verschieben die Folgen
> auf Morgen
>   (*Im Gewitter*, p. 173)
>
>
> [...]
> Unaufgeräumte Spätzeit
> kurz vor dem Dunkelwerden erfüllt
> von Blech aus Fabriken
> Rädern und Gedränge
> von Worten die jeden überfahren
> geregelt
> ist alles längst
> wenig noch zu ordnen
> ein paar Einzelne einzuschwören
> auf den Tod mit dem
> klangvollen Namen
>
> Nacht heißt die letzte Zuflucht
> Finsternis und freiwillige Abwesenheit
> Starr auf dem Rücken liegen bleiben
> Die Flügel gefaltet
> im Gebet um Vergessensein.
>   (*Im Gewitter*, p. 229)

III Environmental Issues in East German Literature
III.i First Doubts Concerning Technology and Progress in the GDR in the 1960s

The West German anthologies from which texts have been quoted contain texts by a dozen poets writing in the GDR. At least two anthologies, Edgar Marsch's *Moderne deutsche Naturlyrik* and Mayer-Tasch's *Im Gewitter der Geraden* would have included more had their editors been granted permission by the authors or copyright-holding GDR publishers.[42] To round off the picture I have therefore also consulted *Die eigene Stimme*, a representative survey of forty years of GDR poetry edited by the East German expert on nature poetry Ursula Heukenkamp together with the poets Heinz Kahlau and Wulf Kirsten in 1988.[43] The following picture emerges: Protest against the testing of atomic bombs in the 1950s comparable to Weyrauch's, Eich's or Bachmann's is to be found in Stephan Hermlin's 'Die Vögel und der Test' (1957, *Die Erde will*, pp. 418f., also *Die eigene Stimme*, p. 89), which describes birds being forced to change their migration route by an atomic explosion, concluding: 'Laßt diese Änderung euer Herz erschüttern...', and Armin Müller's 'Ich habe den Thunfisch gegessen' (also 1957, in *Die eigene Stimme*, pp. 178-81). Poems from Peter Huchel's volume *Chausseen Chausseen* (1963) such as 'Das Zeichen' (*Die Erde will*, pp. 22f.) are close to the apocalyptically prophetic tone and metaphysical imagery of Eich and Bachmann.[44] 'Die Rückkehr', a poem from Huchel's last volume *Die neunte Stunde*, written after he had moved to the West, shows the poet's consistent stance of uncompromising pessimism:

> Die stumme Gesellschaft,
> in Kähnen kam sie hierher,
> noch einmal
> den ungebrochenen Glanz des Wassers zu sehen,
> die Gewißheit des Sommers,
> die Hibiscusblüte in der Farbe der Mitra.
> [...]
> Die Kähne versanken
> im wäßrigen Schatten der Erlen.
>> (*Thema: Natur*, p. 118;
>> *Im Gewitter*, p. 226,
>> and *Die Erde will*, p. 423)

More significant for the politico-cultural discourse in the GDR in the 1960s were the views expressed in the heated debate on poetry in the youth magazine *Forum* in 1966. In response to an editorial enquiry as to the consequences of the technological revolution for the content and structure of poetry, Günter Kunert called official premises and assumptions in question by stressing the destructive potential of modern technology and distinguishing between advances in technology and social and humanitarian progress: 'Mir scheint als bedeutendste technische Revolution [...] die Massenvernichtung von Menschen, das möglich gewordene Ende allen Lebens. Am Anfang des technischen Zeitalters steht Auschwitz, steht Hiroshima, die ich nur in bezug auf gesellschaftlich organisiert verwendete Technik hier in einem Atemzug nenne.'[45] Kunert's mother was Jewish, so it is not surprising that he here mentions Auschwitz and submitted the poem 'Notizen in Kreide'[46] with its reminder of the fate of six million Jews together with his response. In fact his fundamental scepticism regarding technology had already been expressed in poems such as 'Laika' (*Moderne deutsche Naturlyrik*, p. 215, also *Im Gewitter*, p. 235) from the volume *Erinnerung an einen Planeten* in 1963, and his opposition to nuclear weapons in 'Botschaft' (reminiscent of Eich) and 'Der Schatten' (*Die eigene Stimme*, pp. 163—6) from *Der ungebetene Gast* (1965), the volume marking his transition from enlightenment optimism to sceptical individualism. Warning of the fatal consequences of a technological progress with which man's moral and ethical development cannot keep pace is a constant theme in Kunert's *Warngedichte* in the 1960s and 1970s, which treat damage to the environment, bureaucracy, industrialization and social alienation besides the atomic threat. As with Enzensberger, some of Kunert's early poems, such as 'Der Herbst spielt' (*Moderne deutsche Naturlyrik*, p. 215), indicate his basic stance as they reveal how he derives comfort from the idea of nature's permanence; he also shares the West German poet's tendency towards sweeping rejection of modern civilization.[47]

Accused of an 'intellektuell hilflose spätbürgerliche Gesamthaltung' by the editor of *Forum*, Rudolph Bahro (who was to withdraw his support for the Party in 1968, and publish his analysis of GDR political and ecological problems *Die Alternative* in 1977), Kunert was supported by a small number of younger poets including Rainer Kirsch, Sarah Kirsch and Karl Mickel. In 1965 Rainer and Sarah Kirsch had questioned faith in technology in their poetry volume *Gespräch mit dem Saurier*.[48] Their environmental awareness is revealed in anthologized texts from the 1970s — Sarah Kirsch's characteristic landscape poem 'Im Sommer', which expresses the tension between longing for withdrawal into idyllic scenes and consciousness of their deceptive nature when news comes from outside ('Noch fliegt die Graugans, spaziert der Storch/ Durch unvergiftete Wiesen [...] Wenn man hier keine Zeitung hält/ Ist die Welt in Ordnung'),[49] (*Thema: Natur*, p. 63; *Moderne deutsche Naturlyrik*, p. 251; *Die Erde will*, p. 124), and Rainer Kirsch's more prosaic 'Protokoll':

> [...]
> In lila Bächen
> Fahren die Laugen in die Flüsse, eisern
> Stehn die Politiker. Ich geh am Abend
> Durch Sägewerke, die schwarz stehn gleich Wäldern
> Und zu Papiermühlen hinführn, welche Rollen
> Herstellen für Plakate, die man klebt
> Mit Texten SCHÜTZT DEN WALD; noch wächst das Gras
> Ich hörs nicht aber riech es, das ist Hoffnung.
> (*Thema: Natur*, p. 100,
> and *Im Gewitter*, p. 210)

After the building of the Berlin Wall the cultural and political authorities were for a time prepared to accept franker recognition of the shortcomings of everyday reality in the GDR — passages in Christa Wolf's novel *Der geteilte Himmel* and Erik Neutsch's *Spur der Steine* acknowledge smog and the pollution of rivers in the industrialized south of the Republic.[50] Erwin Strittmatter's shorter prose reveals a gradual revision of the anthropocentric world view of the 1960s, and his growing unease about the environment, though his diaries in which this development is most clearly expressed were not published until 1981.[51] Nature poetry was arguably at a relative disadvantage, because of official expectations of harmony. Poets such as Georg Maurer, Johannes R. Becher and Louis Fürnberg had depicted landscapes whose beauty stood for social harmony and a harmonious relationship between man and nature. Pollution and disturbance of environmental balance were regarded as regrettable but isolated and temporary phenomena. Nonetheless, traces of environmental concern are discernible in a number of poems written in the 1960s. Kito Lorenc writes bilingually in Sorbian and German about his native Lausitz, which was at this time bearing the brunt of industrial expansion in the GDR through exploitation of the brown coal beneath its woods, fields and villages. While supporting industrial progress as the source of man's material well-being, he is not silent regarding the losses incurred in the process. The elegiac poem 'Struga' (1966, *Die eigene Stimme*, pp. 271f.) relates how the river has been rerouted and channelled, 'übelriechend', 'ein Abwasser, trüb', 'wässernde Strieme/ im räudigen Fell der Landschaft'. Reiner Kunze uses commercial afforestation as the source of powerful images for social oppression of the individual in 'Sensible Wege' and 'Der Hochwald erzieht seine Bäume' (1969, *Die Erde will*, pp. 406f.). In a striking poem entitled 'Das Flachland vor Leipzig' (*Die eigene Stimme*, p. 279), published in 1966, Elke Erb reviews the flat, bare, dusty landscape around Leipzig and finds herself called by the primeval stare of a goose to reflect on man's potential for self-destruction and destruction of the planet. Less challenging are Jens Gerlach's satirical verses 'kriegserklärung', 'zeitenwandel' and 'weekend-report', from the volume *Der See*, exposing man's impact as tourist on the countryside (*Im Gewitter*, pp. 51, 92f., 138—42).

The generation of poets who emerged in the 1960s, who have been regarded in the West as exemplifying 'pioneering mentality' (Volker Braun, Heinz Czechowski, Wulf Kirsten, Karl Mickel and others), reveal already, on closer examination of their work in the late 1960s, tensions between enthusiasm for the state industrialization programme and consciousness of the ecological dangers involved. The Dresden and Leipzig poet Heinz Czechowski's 'Wasserfahrt' (1967, *Im Gewitter*, pp. 216f.), in which the flow of river water serves as central image for the inevitability of progress, ends on a note of caution, asking the price of technological development:

> [...]
> Es muß doch da etwas sein,
> Was den Fortschritt befiehlt, dieses
> Gleiten auf sanften Gewässern,
> Auf Schienen, Elektronengehirnen, Systemen,
> Kalkulierbaren: Rückkoppelung
> Auf die Erscheinung des Menschen.
>
> Aber wenn da etwas verlorenging
> Vom Liebesgeflüster, von
> Der Fahrt auf dem Fluß, vom Grün
> Und der Wölbung des Bergs, was
> Blieb?[52]

Volker Braun has, of course, been seen as the principal protagonist of the pioneering or 'Promethean' approach, terms used by Western critics to imply naive anachronism, and it would indeed be foolish to suggest that poems such as 'Von Martschuks Leuten', 'Das weite Feld' or 'Messe'[53] did not reflect supreme confidence in man's ability to control and shape his environment. However others, while retaining their optimistic impetus, are not necessarily silent on the hardships industrialization inflicted on GDR workers or the violence done to the landscape.[54] Many texts from the volume *Gegen die symmetrische Welt*, written between 1969 and 1973, integrate elements of melancholic scepticism, irritation, and suppressed consciousness of loss. Braun fuses pride and optimism over a landscape which documents human intelligence and achievement with traces of anger and sorrow over the violence done to the human environment. The title of the poem 'Landwüst' (*Moderne deutsche Naturlyrik*, pp. 253f., *Die Erde will*, pp. 426f.) refers to a village in Braun's native Vogtland. However, it seems reasonable to associate it also with the historical violence related in the poem, and the provocative ruthlessness which speaks from the lines 'Natürlich bleibt nichts./ Nichts bleibt natürlich'. Similarly, the cumulative impact of the past participles describing brown coal mining in the much anthologized poem 'Durchgearbeitete Landschaft' (*Moderne deutsche Naturlyrik*, pp. 254f.; *Im Gewitter*, p. 42; *Die Erde will*, p. 428) — 'verendet', 'durchlöchert', 'ausgepumpt, umzingelt', 'aufgerissen', 'weggeschnitten', 'überfahren', 'abgeteuft', 'ausgelöffelt', 'zerhackt, verschüttet,/ zersiebt', 'durchgewalkt und entseelt und zerklüftet' — and adjectives such as 'mitleidlos' must relativize the harmony of the 'newborn' landscape at the end, and leave us conscious of the ambivalence of the phrase describing the lake: 'der Erde/ Aufgeschlagenes Auge'. It is interesting to compare Karl Mickel's thematically related poem 'Der See' (*Die eigene Stimme*, p. 202). This was written in 1963, and was at the centre of the debate on poetry in *Forum* in 1966. Fiercely criticized by the establishment arbiter Hans Koch, it appears at first reading to share the anarcho-vitalist ruthlessness of the young Volker Braun, but ultimately exposes the shortcomings of state-approved activism through its violent images and the allusion to rotting vegetation and refuse. In the early 1970s Mickel wrote poems attacking pollution ('Mottek sagt 1', *Die eigene Stimme*, pp. 203f.), and inhuman working practices ('Bier. Für Leising', *Die eigene Stimme*, p. 205).

III.ii The Environmental Debate in the 1970s

The 1970s witnessed gradual official willingness to face up to the existence of environmental problems in the GDR and considerable unofficial ecological concern, opening up a public debate in which literature, including poetry, has played a part. By 1977, Harald Hartung was writing 'Inzwischen verfängt der Hinweis auf die Rückständigkeit der DDR-Entwicklung nicht mehr.'[55] Some seventy percent of the GDR's energy has been derived from burning lignite, or brown coal, which produces quantities of dust and ash in mining and combustion.[56] The first environmental legislation in the GDR was introduced in 1970, and in 1973 a budget was set aside for an environmental investment programme. There was some genuine improvement in the early 1970s, however increasing economic pressures and the sharp rise in oil prices then necessitated a return to expansion of coal production, and even exploitation of new deposits with a particularly high sulphur content. Open-cast mining has meant whole villages disappearing in the relatively densely populated Halle-Leipzig area, and the associated lowering of the water table has affected the agriculture of the region. Few major industries could afford to install and use effective filters for smoke and effluents. At the same time inefficient and environmentally damaging farming techniques actually became more widespread in agricultural cooperatives, where dubious amelioration of soils was carried out and heavy machinery necessitated insensitive standardization; fertilizers and pesticides were used to excess, and the reorganization of labour along industrial lines meant the loss of a sense of individual responsibility on the part of the worker for the animals or fields he or she worked.

Perception of such deterioration and recognition that environmental policies had not been successful led to the founding of the *Gesellschaft für Natur und Umwelt* in 1980, an organization mediating between official state bodies and unofficial environmental groups. Its members were in the main professionally involved with environmental issues: botanists, foresters, commercial growers, ornithologists, meteorologists and architects. In addition to practical initiatives they formed the first eco-lobby in the GDR, which, modest though it was, exercised some influence over administrative decisions. Within the church ecological issues had been debated since the early 1970s. Environmental groups were formed, local campaigns carried through, circulars published, and an environmental library established to disseminate information and encourage research. Though the limitations of natural resources were discussed in official journals, and practical methods of environmental protection welcomed where they were not too costly, the Club of Rome report was officially dismissed as an attempt to stabilize capitalism, and radical proposals for a socialist alternative to growth such as Wolfgang Harich's *Kommunismus ohne Wachstum? Babeuf und der Club of Rome* (Reinbek, 1975) and Rudolph Bahro's *Die Alternative. Zur Kritik des real existierenden Sozialismus* (Cologne, 1977) remained anathema. It would thus be wrong to suggest a linear or uniform development of ecological concern.

Literary contributions to a more open-minded public dialogue on the environment throughout the 1970s included doubts as to aspects of scientific progress expressed periodically by Christa Wolf, from her story 'Neue Lebensansichten eines Katers' (1970) onwards, Plenzdorf's challenge to progress and achievement as social ideals in *Die neuen Leiden des jungen W.* (1972),[57] and publications in journals by Erwin Strittmatter, Jurij Brezan and Joseph Pischel.[58] In 1979 Kunert was able to publish a letter to the editor of *Sinn und Form*, explaining why he had spoken of a 'symmetry' of environmental problems facing socialist and capitalist countries, together with a critique of industrialization, alienation, loss of individuality and economic growth.[59] Hanns Cibulka's novel *Swantow*, which describes the genesis of the powerful environmental poem 'Lagebericht', was written in 1980, and published in extract form in *Sinn und Form* in 1981, appearing in book form in 1982. Cibulka questions the security of nuclear reactors in the GDR, as well as calling for a more general change in values. His book was at the centre of a broad public debate 1982—1984, and has been described by Anita Mallinckrodt as exercising 'a significant influence on changing political culture values in the GDR'.[60] Other prose works reflecting the growth of public concern for the environment in the early 1980s have included Benno Pludra's novel for children *Insel der Schwäne* (1980), of which a controversial film was made in 1983, Jurij Brezan's *Krabat oder die Verwandlung der Welt* (1980), Monika Maron's *Flugasche* (1981), Gabriele Eckart's documentary 'Havelobst' (1984) and stories by Joachim Nowotny and others, followed by Christa Wolf's warnings of depersonalization as the price of progress in her Frankfurt lectures in 1983 (*Kassandra*), and *Störfall* on the Chernobyl disaster in 1986.[61]

Whereas literature in general has provided a forum for the discussion of topics largely excluded from the media in the GDR, up to the late 1970s poets were freer than prose writers to treat ecological issues, perhaps because they have traditionally championed the non-utilitarian, or even the irrational, perhaps also because their audience and possible impact were limited. (Poetry readings, often held in churches, have however been a feature of the environmental movement in the GDR.) Older writers such as Hanns Cibulka and Walter Werner, the 'middle generation' (Kirsten, Czechowski, Mickel and Braun), also Ulrich Berkes,

Jürgen Rennert, Axel Schulze and Richard Pietraß, and the younger poets Thomas Rosenlöcher, Gabriele Eckart, Steffen Mensching and Ralph Grüneberger published poems containing outright criticism in the 1970s, often however, as in the West, fused with resignation.[62] This qualitative change, dating from around 1970, was registered and welcomed in a series of articles by GDR Germanists at the end of the decade. Wulf Kirsten's anthology *Veränderte Landschaft* (1979) was the first GDR collection of nature poetry with an appreciable ecological dimension. Ursula Heukenkamp wrote in her review in 1980:

> Das bejahende Verhältnis zur Industrielandschaft wandelt sich schnell. Die Beispiele ließen sich ergänzen. Beton, Rauch und Öl verunstalten die Landschaften in der Lyrik der 70er Jahre. Und der Rauch kann nicht mehr als tröstliches Zeichen der Anwesenheit vom Menschen in der Natur verstanden werden. Ebenso wie Öl und Beton zeigt er vielmehr den Zwiespalt zwischen den unmittelbaren Bedürfnissen des Individuums und dem gegebenen Stand der gesellschaftlichen Nutzung der Natur als Rohstoff an.[63]

In an article entitled 'Abschied von der schönen Natur', she writes in 1981 of the poets' new sense of the preservation of nature as a 'moral imperative', and of their 'Abfallandschaften' both as 'Appell an die ökologische Vernunft' and social metaphor: 'So ist der Wildwuchs der Landschaft unbewältigte Widersprüchlichkeit der Gesellschaft.'[64] Finally, Klaus Schuhmann reviews the ecological poetry of the early 1980s in an article entitled 'Lageberichte zur ökologischen Situation' in 1986, beginning: 'Die Zeit der heiter-beschaulichen dichterischen Ausflüge ins Naturrefugium ist ebenso vorbei wie die der stürmisch-prometheischen Natureroberungen, von denen die Lyrik der DDR lange Zeit nicht schlecht lebte.'[65]

Among the examples of such poetry to be found in the anthologies examined are Volker Braun's 'Die Mummelfälle' (*Im Gewitter*, pp. 99f.), describing the deterioration of a historic beauty spot through water pollution, litter from tourists, and damage to trees from acid rain, written 1980 and published 1983,[66] and a number of poems published by Heinz Czechowski in the 1970s, including 'Flußfahrt' (1973, *Die eigene Stimme*, pp. 223—5), with its castigation of the spewing of lead from petrol fumes,[67] and 'Landschaftsschutzgebiet' (1978, *Im Gewitter*, pp. 43f.), a bitter, polemic record of hypocrisy and seemingly arbitrary destruction: 'Der Baggerzahn ist der Zahn unserer Zeit, hoch türmt er/ die ach so verletzliche Haut des Planeten.' Axel Schulze, one of the first GDR poets to describe pollution in landscape poetry, and author of critical texts in the 1970s such as 'Menzer Forst' (1973, *Die eigene Stimme*, p. 320), has not emerged as an authoritative voice on the environment. His depiction of the industrialized landscape in Sachsen-Anhalt assumes all too readily nature's ability to regenerate, and is relativized by the idyllic scenes in much of his verse. Wulf Kirsten's poems are here more consistent, tracing the destruction of villages through unrestricted building, atmospheric pollution and acid rain, and the undignified demise of the rural way of life ('dorf' (1974), 'der bleibaum'(1975), 'schiefergebirge' (1976), 'lebensspuren' (1979—1981), in *Die eigene Stimme*, pp. 266—70). Jürgen Rennert is represented by 'An den Caputher Gärten' (1974), describing with melancholy the monotony of the vast fruit orchards west of Berlin, testifying to bureaucratic incompetence and hypocrisy:

> [...]
> Gerümpel. Stahlbetonverliese:
> Die Regenwasserauffangbecken
> Der braunen Obstbaumparadiese.
> Es stirbt das Land an seinen Zwecken.
> (*Die eigene Stimme*, pp. 328f.)

Finally, Richard Pietraß presents a tree fighting for its life in the city in 'Der Ringende'(1979, *Die Erde will*, p. 324, and *Die eigene Stimme*, p. 333), and predicts nature's revenge in Eich-like terms in 'Die Schattenalge' (1981, *Die eigene Stimme*, pp. 333f.) through the image of a seaweed which thrives on man's destruction of the environment.

IV Conclusion
Environmental Concern as a Factor Unifying East and West German Culture

If it is true that the shift in political-culture values in the GDR towards ecological considerations took place about a decade later than in the West, this pattern is only partially mirrored in the sphere of literature. The position in the GDR in the 1960s was less single-mindedly Promethean than has sometimes been stated, and we have seen that if one disregards Enzensberger, environmental concern in the West was at this time practically limited to the nuclear issue, *Ökolyrik* only emerging at the end of the decade. By no means all impulses are then directed from West to East either: we observe a roughly parallel development, in which essentially conservative concern for the preservation of nature, with roots in Romanticism, acquires a progressive or emancipatory dimension. In both West and East German poetry this process is linked with a revival of regionalism (the Sorbs Jurij Brezan, Jurij Koch and Kito Lorenc playing a significant part in the GDR), and a revaluation of the concept of *Heimat*.[68] Shared environmental experience and shared apprehensions led in the 1970s to disillusionment and resignation, in a political climate showing certain similarities in the two German states. The intrinsic differences betwen the two literatures were then partially bridged in the 1970s — in poetry perhaps more so than in narrative fiction. Jürgen Becker in the West, Heinz Czechowski in the GDR, to take but two examples, draw constant parallels between the threat of self-destruction through environmental damage and the arms race, the one becoming a paradigm of the other. German environmental literature in East and West has provided a documentation and a warning. At its weakest, it consists in the West of abstract dogmatic statement of Green ideology, ignoring other social problems, or passive acceptance of the subject as victim of an inhuman society, and in the East indulges in hypocrisy or escapism. At its best, it has successfully fused analysis of individual experience and feeling with social concern, and formulated with honesty the tension between the social necessities of technological advance and respect for nature.

GDR literature has been less isolated than sometimes suggested: Wulf Kirsten for instance has dated his ecological concern as beginning in 1969 or 1970, when he read Rachel Carson's *Silent Spring*.[69] Western and Eastern poets alike have taken Brecht's 'An die Nachgeborenen' and other nature poems as a starting point, and if Eich, Bachmann and Enzensberger have influenced younger GDR poets, Huchel's imagery is also perceptible in some of the eschatological poems of the later 1970s and 1980s in the West. Indeed, of the writers moving from East to West, at least Kunert and Sarah Kirsch have not found themselves out of step. GDR writers facing up to the consequences and implications of man's short-sighted exploitation of nature in the 1970s and 1980s had to come to terms with their own earlier views and *Aufbauoptimismus*, and the results have been at times a more reflected and significant contribution to ecological poetry than glib political statement or *Fortschrittspessimismus* in the West.[70] The integration almost unnoticed of East German texts in all the West German anthologies examined is a final indication of how ecology has served as a focus for broad consciousness of social and political problems in both Germanys over the last twenty years, and reflected concern for the future of humanity going beyond any individual state.[71]

NOTES

1 Miscellaneous information on the history of ecology and the ecological movement in Germany is to be found in *Börsenblatt für den deutschen Buchhandel*, 28 April 1987 (Schwerpunkt-Nr. 'Ökologie'), pp. 1269—364, which also contains Susanne Mittag's brief but stimulating article on environmental poetry: 'Aber der Herr sprach Es werde Mensch Und die Erde ward wüst und leer', pp. 1344—7. See further Rolf Peter Sieferle (ed.): *Fortschritte der Naturzerstörung*, Frankfurt/Main, 1988; Ludwig Trepl: *Geschichte der Ökologie. Vom 17. Jahrhundert bis zur Gegenwart. 10 Vorlesungen*, Frankfurt/Main, 1987; Ulrich Linse: *Ökopax und Anarchie. Eine Geschichte der ökologischen Bewegungen in Deutschland*, Munich, 1986; Klaus-Georg Wey: *Umweltpolitik in Deutschland. Kurze Geschichte des Umweltschutzes in Deutschland seit 1900*, Opladen, 1982.

2 Julius von Schröder and Carl Reuss (eds): *Die Beschädigung der Vegetation durch Rauch und die Oberharzer Hüttenrauchschäden*, Berlin, 1883 (Hildesheim, 1986).

3 Henry David Thoreau: *Walden. The Duty of Civil Disobedience*, ed. by M. Meyer, Harmondsworth, 1983 (1st edn: *Walden, or Life in the Woods*, Boston, 1854).

4 Samuel Butler: *Erewhon*, ed. by Peter Modford, Harmondsworth, 1970 (1st edn: *Erewhon, or Over the Range*, Edinburgh, 1872).

5 Henrik Ibsen: *An Enemy of the People. The Wild Duck. Rosmerholm*, Oxford, 1988 (1st edn: *En Folkefiende*, Copenhagen, 1882).

6 Wilhelm Raabe: *Sämtliche Werke*, ed. by K. Hoppe et al., Göttingen, 1960ff., XVI (1st edn: Leipzig, 1884). For an informative and perceptive, though polemically anti-ecological introduction, see Jeffrey L. Sammons: *Raabe. Pfisters Mühle*, London, 1988.

7 For instance *One-dimensional Man. Studies in the Ideology of Advanced Industrial Society*, New York, 1964 (= *Der eindimensionale Mensch*, Darmstadt, 1967).

8 In particular *The Myth of the Machine*, New York, 1967—70 (= *Mythos der Maschine*, Vienna, 1974, and in the Fischer Alternativreihe, Frankfurt/Main, 1977).

9 E. F. Schumacher: *Small is Beautiful. A Study of Economics as if People Mattered*, New York, 1973 (= *Die Rückkehr zum menschlichen Maß. Alternativen für Wirtschaft und Technik*, Reinbek, 1977).

10 Rachel Louise Carson: *Silent Spring*, New York, 1962 (= *Der stumme Frühling*, Munich, 1963, and in dtv, 1968).

11 Dennis Meadows et al.: *The Limits to Growth. A Report for the Club of Rome's Project on the Predicament of Mankind*, New York, 1972 (= *Die Grenzen des Wachstums*, Stuttgart, 1972).

12 For example, the Bundesverband Bürgerinitiativen Umweltschutz (founded in 1972) and the Bund für Umwelt und Naturschutz Deutschland (founded in 1975).

13 In 1975 the conservative politician Herbert Gruhl published his widely read book *Ein Planet wird geplündert*, and the enormous success of the 'Fischer Alternativ-Reihe', of which this was the opening number, is indicative of the new interest in ecological issues outside the fringe Left or Right.

14 The idea of nature as a subject with which man must be reconciled was adapted by the young Karl Marx from Schelling, and has been expanded on by Adorno, Bloch (who speaks of the necessity of an 'alliance' between man and nature), Marcuse and Habermas. See Jürgen Haupt: '"Gespräch über Bäume". Zum Natur- und Entfremdungsproblem in sozialistischer Lyrik der Gegenwart', *Die Horen*, vol. 88, 1972, pp. 8—23; Silvia Volckmann: *Zeit der Kirschen? Das Naturbild in der deutschen Gegenwartslyrik: Jürgen Becker, Sarah Kirsch, Wolf Biermann, Hans Magnus Enzensberger*, Königstein/

Ts., 1982, pp. 17—33; Jürgen Haupt: *Natur und Lyrik. Naturbeziehungen im 20. Jahrhundert*, Stuttgart, 1983, pp. 207—27 ('Theorie: Gesellschafts-Philosophie und Naturutopie').

15 *Tintenfisch 12. Thema: Natur. Oder: Warum ein Gespräch über Bäume heute kein Verbrechen mehr ist*, ed. by Hans Christoph Buch, Berlin 1977, p. 7.

16 Edgar Marsch (ed.): *Moderne deutsche Naturlyrik*, Stuttgart, 1980.

17 The term 'Warngedicht' has been in use in both West and East Germany since the 1960s, referring to contemporary political poems seeking to provoke the reader through the presentation of negative examples. See Erich Fried's volume *Warngedichte*, Munich, 1964, and Marieluise de Waijer-Wilke: 'The *Warngedicht* in the work of Günter Kunert: its reception as political poetry', *GDR Monitor*, vol. 14, Winter 1985/6, pp. 14—27.

18 Alexander von Bormann (ed.): *Die Erde will ein freies Geleit. Deutsche Naturlyrik aus sechs Jahrhunderten*, Frankfurt/Main, 1984.

19 Peter Cornelius Mayer-Tasch (ed.): *Im Gewitter der Geraden. Deutsche Ökolyrik 1950—1980*, Munich, 1981.

20 See Manon Maren-Grisebach: 'Was heißt hier Ökolyrik? Beitrag zu einer zeitgemäßen Literaturkritik', in Lothar Jordan, Axel Marquardt, Winfried Woesler (eds): *Lyrik — Erlebnis und Kritik. Gedichte und Aufsätze des dritten und vierten Lyrikertreffens in Münster*, Frankfurt/Main, 1988, pp. 264—70; also Hiltrud Gnüg: 'Die Aufhebung des Naturgedichts in der Lyrik der Gegenwart', in Lothar Jordan, Axel Marquardt, Winfried Woesler (eds): *Lyrik — von allen Seiten. Gedichte und Aufsätze des ersten Lyrikertreffens in Münster*, Frankfurt/Main, 1981, p. 282.

21 See for instance the East German Heinz Czechowski, who writes of his friend Wulf Kirsten's poem 'Lebensspuren': 'Es ist kein "grünes" Gedicht und vermeidet streng das Vokabular des auch bei uns üppig aus dem Boden schießenden "Umweltlyrik"' ('Gegen den Strich', *ndl*, vol. 32, no.12, 1984, p. 88).

22 Maren-Grisebach, 'Was heißt hier Ökolyrik?', p. 266. Her use of the term is consciously provocative: 'Ich lasse es provokativ bei dem disparaten und anstößigen Kompositum', p. 264. Mayer-Tasch, one of the first to use the term, is equally conscious of its humorous connotations. His intention, as an outsider in the West German *Kulturbetrieb*, is both ironic and polemical (see his 'Einführung: Ökologische Lyrik als Dokument der Politischen Kultur' to *Im Gewitter der Geraden*, p. 11).

23 Since 1982 'Ökolyrik' has been listed almost annually in the keyword index of Hanns W. Eppelsheimer, Clemens Köttelwesch, Bernhard Koßmann (eds): *Bibliographie der deutschen Sprach- und Literaturwissenschaft*, Frankfurt/Main, 1957ff., together with 'Umwelt', 'Umweltschutz' and 'Umweltzerstörung'. Corresponding entries in Winfried Bauer et al. (eds): *Germanistik. Internationales Referatenorgen mit bibliographischen Hinweisen*, Tübingen, 1960ff., have been less frequent.

24 See Mayer-Tasch: 'Einführung: Ökologische Lyrik...', pp. 9—26; also the articles 'Ökolyrik. Trauerarbeit im Versmaß', *Natur. Horst Sterns Umweltmagazin*, no. 6, June 1982, pp. 88—92; and 'In schwarzen Spiegeln Regenbögen. Die ökologische Krise in der Prosa', *Universitas*, no.9, 1987, pp. 932—46.

25 Hubertus Knabe: 'Zweifel an der Industriegesellschaft. Ökologische Kritik in der erzählenden DDR-Literatur' in Redaktion Deutschland Archiv (ed.): *Umweltprobleme und Umweltbewußtsein in der DDR*, Köln, 1985, pp. 201—50.

26 Hans-Jürgen Heise: 'Grün, wie ich dich liebe, Grün. Vom Naturgedicht zur Ökolyrik' in *Einen Galgen für den Dichter. Stichworte zur Lyrik*, Weingarten, 1986, pp. 74—88.

27 Mittag: 'Aber der Herr sprach...' (see note 1).

28 Norbert Mecklenburg: 'Naturlyrik und Gesellschaft. Stichworte zu Theorie, Geschichte und Kritik eines poetischen Genres'; Harald Hartung: 'Neuere Naturlyrik in der DDR'; and Thomas Rothschildt: 'Durchgearbeitete Landschaft. Die Auseinandersetzung mit dem Naturgedicht in einer Gegenwart der zerstörten Natur' in Norbert Mecklenburg (ed.): *Naturlyrik und Gesellschaft*, Stuttgart, 1977, pp. 7—32, 179—97, 198—214.

29 David Bathrick: 'Die Zerstörung oder der Anfang der Vernunft? Lyrik und Naturbeherrschung in der DDR' and Ralph Buechler et al.: 'Grauer Alltagsschmutz und grüne Lyrik. Zur Naturlyrik in der BRD' in Reinhold Grimm and Jost Hermand (eds): *Natur und Natürlichkeit. Stationen des Grünen in der deutschen Literatur*, Königstein/Ts., 1981, pp. 150—67, 168—95.

30 Haupt: *Natur und Lyrik,* (see note 14), chapter 4: 'Sozialistische Naturlyrik in Ost und West: Versuche', pp. 135—227.

31 Peter Rühmkorf: 'Ein Poet mit viel Puste' in *Strömungslehre 1. Poesie,* Reinbek, 1978, p. 94.

32 Hans Magnus Enzensberger: 'A Critique of Political Ecology' in *Dreamers of the Absolute. Essays on Politics, Crime and Culture,* London, 1988, p. 276 (= 'Ökologie und Politik oder Die Zukunft der Industrialisierung', *Kursbuch,* no. 33, October 1973, pp. 1—42).

33 Sources for texts from the anthologies in notes 15, 16, 18 and 19 above will be quoted as *Thema: Natur, Moderne deutsche Naturlyrik, Die Erde will,* and *Im Gewitter.*

34 See reference to poems by Stephan Hermlin and Armin Müller on p. 386.

35 Wolfgang Weyrauch is another poet whose work reflects these events. Poems such as 'Gesang um nicht zu sterben' and the curious 'Atom und Aloe', which presents apocalyptic destruction ending in idyllic scenes for the survivors (see Wolfgang Weyrauch: *Atom und Aloe. Gesammelte Gedichte,* ed. by Hans Bender, Frankfurt/Main, 1987, pp. 49f., 68f.), and the moving radio play *Die japanischen Fischer* were written in the mid-1950s.

36 Hans Magnus Enzensberger: *verteidigung der wölfe,* Frankfurt/Main, 1957, pp. 88f.

37 Enzensberger: 'A Critique of Political Ecology', p. 295.

38 Literary responses to the famous lines: 'Was sind das für Zeiten, wo/ Ein Gespräch über Bäume fast ein Verbrechen ist/ Weil es ein Schweigen über so viele Untaten einschließt!' (Bertolt Brecht: *Gesammelte Werke in 20 Bänden,* Frankfurt/Main, vol. IX, p. 723) already included Peter Huchel: 'Der Garten des Theophrast' (1963), Günter Eich: 'Vorsicht' (1966), Erich Fried: 'Gespräch über Bäume' (1967), Paul Celan: 'Ein Blatt' (1971), and Hans Magnus Enzensberger: 'Zwei Fehler' (1971), before ecological concern led writers to make the point with monotonous regularity that 'ein Gespräch über Bäume' now necessarily touched on environmental 'Untaten', and allusion to Brecht's lines became an irritating cliché. See for example Peter Schütt: 'Bundesrepublik' (1971), W.H. Fritz: 'Bäume' (1976), the subtitle of Hans Christoph Buch's collection of environmental texts: *Thema Natur* (1977) and Gregor Laschen: 'Naturgedicht 7' (1979).

39 See Walter Moßmann and Peter Schleuning: *Alte und neue politische Lieder. Entstehung und Gebrauch, Texte und Noten,* Reinbek, 1978, p. 98.

40 A further dialect poet with significant environmental involvement was the Low German writer Oswald Andrae, who treats the energy crisis, unemployment and damage to the environment in the provinces through attempts to dispose of chemical and nuclear waste in his 'Brokdorp-Song' and 'Umweltsüük'. See Buechler et al.: 'Grauer Alltagsschmutz und grüne Lyrik', pp. 189—91.

41 The phrase echoes Adorno ('das beschädigte Leben', from *Minima Moralia*), and has been used by, among others, Ralf Schnell: *Die Literatur der Bundesrepublik Deutschland. Autoren, Geschichte, Literaturbetrieb,* Stuttgart, 1986, p. 314.

42 See *Moderne deutsche Naturlyrik,* p. 307, and *Im Gewitter,* p. 20.

43 Ursula Heukenkamp, Heinz Kahlau, Wulf Kirsten (eds): *Die eigene Stimme. Lyrik der DDR,* Berlin (GDR), 1988. Though Wulf Kirsten's earlier anthology of GDR nature poetry *Veränderte Landschaft* (Leipzig, 1979) contains a number of environmental poems, East German *Umweltlyrik* is better represented in the later volume. I understand the East Berlin poet Richard Pietraß has been preparing a new anthology of GDR environmental poetry: one hopes this will not fall victim to changing political circumstances. The recent special number of *ndl* on the environment (vol. 37, no.11, 1989), which includes poems by Peter Gosse, Thomas Rosenlöcher, Rolf Richter, Erhard Scherner, Reimar Gilsenbach and Wolfgang Brockel together with essays and prose contributions by Jurij Brezan, Joachim Nowotny, Matthias Körner, Heinz Kahlau, Jurij Koch and others, seems likely to mark the culmination of GDR-specific literary treatment of environmental issues.

44 Two powerful poems from the same volume curiously passed over in anthologies are 'An taube Ohren der Geschlechter', which relates the devastation of North Africa after the fall of Carthage, and man's inability to learn from such destruction, and 'Psalm', with which the volume ends, which must surely refer to man's self-destruction through nuclear war: 'Daß aus dem Samen des Menschen/ Kein Mensch/ Und aus dem Samen des Ölbaums/ Kein Ölbaum/ Werde,/ Es ist zu messen/ Mit der Elle des Todes.// Die da wohnen/ Unter der Erde/ In einer Kugel aus Zement,/ Ihre Stärke gleicht/ Dem Halm/ Im

peitschenden Schnee.// Die Öde wird Geschichte./ Termiten schreiben sie/ Mit ihren Zangen/ In den Sand.// Und nicht erforscht wird werden/ Ein Geschlecht,/ Eifrig bemüht,/ Sich zu vernichten.' (*Chausseen Chausseen*, Frankfurt, 1963, pp. 77 and 84)

45 *Forum*, vol. 20, no. 10, 1966, p. 23. Quoted in Bathrick: 'Die Zerstörung oder...', p. 150.

46 See Günter Kunert: *Verkündigung des Wetters*, München, 1966, pp. 7f.

47 See Haupt: *Natur und Lyrik*, pp. 201f., 217. Kunert's views on the future of society are closer to Adorno and Horkheimer's argument that the enlightenment has come to counter emancipation (in *Dialektik der Aufklärung* (1947)) than to Bloch's or Marcuse's optimism regarding a reconciliation of man and nature through a benevolent technology.

48 Poems from this volume (Berlin, 1965) such as Sarah Kirsch's 'Der Saurier', in which the fate of the dinosaur serves as a warning example for man, and Rainer Kirsch's 'Gespräch mit dem Saurier', which calls on man to turn away from 'Erfindungen, Technik, Verbrauch,/ Atomstrahlung, Mutation', also 'Bootsfahrt' or 'Marktgang', which refer to the problems of pollution and destruction of the landscape, albeit ending on an optimistic note, have not, to my knowledge, since been reprinted.

49 Subsequent environmental poems by Sarah Kirsch include 'Beginn der Zerstörung', 'Die Ebene', 'Ende des Jahres', 'Sommerabend' and 'Valet', from the volume *Erdreich*, Stuttgart, 1982.

50 See Knabe: 'Zweifel an der Industriegesellschaft', p. 204. Relevant passages in *Der geteilte Himmel* include 'dieses verfluchte Wasser, das nach Chemie stank, seit sie denken konnten' on the opening page, 'Jedes Kind konnte hier die Richtung des Windes nach dem vorherrschenden Geruch bestimmen: Chemie oder Malzkaffee oder Braunkohle. Über allem diese Dunstglocke, Industrieabgase, die sich schwer atmen', 'das zerstreute, durch Dreck und Ruß gefilterte Licht', 'der [Fluß] war [...] nützlicher und unfreundlicher geworden: er führte watteweißen Schaum mit sich, der übel roch und vom Chemiewerk bis weit hinter die Stadt den Fisch vergiftete', and 'Teppiche muß man hier jeden Tag absaugen, sie verstauben unglaublich' (Munich, 16th edn, 1983, pp. 7, 27f., 78).

51 See Knabe: 'Zweifel an der Industriegesellschaft', p. 205.

52 Czechowski's consciousness of the ambivalent potential of science, esp. nuclear technology, leads him to a position of active engagement, presumably against their abuse, in 'Reisen', from the same volume: 'Die Wolke. Der Regen. Die Fruchtbarkeit./ Die fruchtbare Wissenschaft./ Die Wolke. Der Regen. Die Furchtbarkeit./ Die furchtbare Wissenschaft.// Die Natur unterm Grauen der Mutationen. [...] Im Netz der Bilder/ Entsteht der Gedanke./ Klärt sich und formt sich./ Tätig sein.' (*Wasserfahrt*, Halle/Saale, 1967, pp. 122f.) See Ian Hilton, pp. 401—11 below, for an analysis of Czechowski's nature poetry.

53 See Volker Braun: *Wir und nicht sie*, Frankfurt/Main, 1970, pp. 9f., 14, 15.

54 For instance Volker Braun: 'Das Vogtland' or 'Die Industrie', in *Wir und nicht sie*, pp. 12f., and *Gegen die symmetrische Welt*, Frankfurt/Main, 1974, pp. 23—5.

55 Hartung: 'Neuere Naturlyrik in der DDR', (see note 28), p. 196. Hartung is admittedly discussing GDR poetry, and Günter Kunert in particular.

56 My information on GDR environmental problems and the public debate on them is based on articles by Cord Schwartau, Andreas Kurjo, Werner Gruhn, Gerhard Timm, Peter Wensierski and Hubertus Knabe in Redaktion Deutschland Archiv: *Umweltprobleme und Umweltbewußtsein in der DDR*, (see note 25), and on Anita Mallinckrodt: *The Environmental Dialogue in the GDR. Literature, Church, Party and Interest Groups in Their Socio-Political Context. A Research Concept and Case Study*, Lanham, Maryland, 1987.

57 See Mallinckrodt: *The Environmental Dialogue in the GDR*, p. 32.

58 Erwin Strittmatter mentioned pollution in an interview with Heinz Plavius ('Produktivkraft Poesie') in *ndl*, vol. 21, no. 5, 1973, p. 6; in the same year Brezan spoke at a German-Soviet writers' colloquium of man's impoverishment through technology ('Geschichten von Menschen in der Menschenwelt', *ndl*, vol. 22, no. 4, 1974, pp. 20f.), and the Rostock professor of German Literature Joseph Pischel included reference to ecological dangers and alienation in a cautious but balanced paper: 'Das Verhältnis Mensch-Natur in der Selbstverständigung von Schriftstellern der DDR', (*Weimarer Beiträge*, 1976, no.1, pp. 74—99), quoting Brezan extensively and referring to Strittmatter and a speech by Franz Fühmann at the seventh Writers' Union Congress in 1973.

59 Günter Kunert: 'Anläßlich Ritsos: Ein Briefwechsel zwischen Günter Kunert und Wilhelm Girnus', *Sinn und Form*, vol. 31, no. 4, 1979, pp. 850—3. This was however followed by a sharp rebuff by Girnus in the same issue.

60 Anita Mallinckrodt: 'Environmental Dialogue in the GDR. The Literary Challenge to the Sanctity of "Progress"', *GDR Monitor*, vol. 16, Winter 1986/87, pp. 1—26; here p. 20. See also the chapter 'Case Study: Hanns Cibulka's *Swantow*' in Mallinckrodt: *The Environmental Dialogue in the GDR*.

61 For bibliographical details and more detailed discussion of the treatment of environmental issues in GDR prose again see Knabe: 'Zweifel an der Industriegesellschaft', esp. pp. 216—8, and Mallinckrodt: *The Environmental Dialogue in the GDR*, p. 90.

62 See Wolfgang Ertl: 'Sintflut und Apokalypse: Überlegungen zur Umweltlyrik in der DDR und BRD' in Ingrid K.J. Williams (ed.): *GDR: Individual and Society. Conference Proceedings of the International Conference on the GDR*, Ealing College of Higher Education, 1987, pp. 79—90; also his 'Ökolyrik in der DDR: Eine Beispielreihe', in Margy Gerber et al. (eds): *Studies in GDR Culture and Society* 5, Lanham, 1985, pp. 221—35.

63 Ursula Heuenkamp: 'Landschaften. Anmerkungen zu einer Lyrik-Anthologie', *Zeitschrift für Germanistik*, no. 3, 1980, p. 339.

64 Ursula Heuenkamp: 'Der Abschied von der schönen Natur. Natur in der DDR-Lyrik und ihre Veränderung' in Hans Kaufmann (ed.): *Tendenzen und Beispiele. Zur DDR-Literatur in den siebziger Jahren*, Leipzig, 1981, pp. 221—60; here pp. 256, 249, 255.

65 Klaus Schuhmann: 'Lageberichte zur ökologischen Situation — Beobachtungen zur Lyrik der 80er Jahre' in *DDR-Literatur '85 im Gespräch*, Berlin(GDR), p. 23.

66 Katrin Kohl, pp. 345—6 above, also discusses this poem.

67 See Ian Hilton, pp. 404 and 406 below, for further comment on this poem.

66 See also pp. 382—3, 388 and 392 above. For information on the dramatist and prose writer Jurij Koch see Peter Barker: 'Interview with Jurij Koch', *GDR Monitor*, vol. 21, Summer 1989, pp. 49—58. See also Helfried W. Seliger (ed.): *Der Begriff 'Heimat' in der deutschen Gegenwartsliteratur*, Munich, 1987. Ian Hilton, p. 401 below, describes Heinz Czechowski as a *Heimatdichter*.

68 Presumably in the dtv paperback edition (see note 10). See Wulf Kirsten: 'Selbstauskunft. Interview mit Peter Hamm', in Bernhard Rübenach (ed.): *Peter-Huchel-Preis. Ein Jahrbuch: 1987. Wulf Kirsten. Texte. Dokumente. Materialien*, Moos, 1987, p. 48: 'Ich war sehr, sehr lange blauäugig, habe eine heile Welt in mir herumgetragen, habe überall nur heile Welt gesehen. Erst 1969/70 wurde ich auf das Buch *Der stumme Frühling* von Rachel Carson hingewiesen, das ich mir besorgt und mit glühenden Ohren gelesen habe. Da erst habe ich angefangen, mich um diese Dinge zu kümmern [...] Das Umdenken begann ziemlich rapid, ich habe mein Bewußtsein geschärft, habe die Welt mit anderen Augen gesehen, habe sie dann daraufhin auch beobachtet.'

69 *Aufbauoptimismus*: faith in technology, in the historical context of the postwar socialist reconstruction period in the GDR (1950s and early 1960s). *Fortschrittspessimismus*: disbelief in (technical and social) progress, or historical pessimism, common in the mid 1970s. On the relative merits of FRG and GDR environmental poetry see Hiltrud Gnüg: 'Die Aufhebung des Naturgedichts in der Lyrik der Gegenwart' in Jordan, Marquardt, Woesler: *Lyrik — von allen Seiten...*, (see note 20), pp. 264—83, and the final chapter in Volckmann: *Zeit der Kirschen?...*, (see note 14), pp. 227—48.

70 Reinhard Opitz speaks of 'eine Dominanz von Fragestellungen menschheitsgeschichtlichen Ausmaßes' in contemporary GDR writing and the moral search for a future perspective for man in general, including environmental questions and the destructive potential of arms and new technologies as well as individual alienation through social and economic pressures, *Zeitschrift für deutsche Philosophie*, no. 9, 1985, p. 840. See Eckart Förtsch: 'Fragen menschheitsgeschichtlichen Ausmaßes. Wissenschaft, Technik, Umwelt', in Gisela Helwig (ed.): *Die DDR-Gesellschaft im Spiegel ihrer Literatur*, Köln, 1986, pp. 85—112.

HEINZ CZECHOWSKI:
THE DARKENED FACE OF NATURE

IAN HILTON

In meinen Gedichten
Gibts neben Helle noch Dunkelheit
('Einst')

Among the eleven volumes of poetry to have appeared since 1962 in
East and West Germany from the pen of Heinz Czechowski,[1] the title of
a selection of verse published by the Neue Bremer Presse in 1989 catches
the eye: *Sanft gehen wie Tiere die Berge neben dem Fluß*. Afficionados of
Czechowski's writings immediately recognize the words as constituting
the core of one of his earliest poems, 'An der Elbe'. Indeed the first three
poems in the afore-mentioned selection — 'An der Elbe', 'Sächsischer
Nachmittag', 'Auf eine im Feuer versunkene Stadt' — spearhead the
abiding source of poetic inspiration for Czechowski: namely Saxony
(*Böhmisch, Preußisch, Anhaltinisch*), but particularly the Elbe valley and its
villages, and the urban landscape of his home town of Dresden.[2]

At the time of writing his first verses in his early twenties ('An der
Elbe', for instance, was written in 1957), Czechowski was open to the
poetic influences of Storm, Brecht and Huchel.[3] The impact of the last-
named was particularly strong:

> Wesentlich aber — Huchels Gedichte ließen mich eine Wahlverwandtschaft
> spüren, weil ich durch sie die Landschaft meiner Kindheit, zu der ich mein
> Verhältnis bis dahin nicht artikulieren konnte, sehen und fassen lernte: Mor-
> tizburg, die Teiche, Gräben, Gewässer, das Schilf und die Reusen [...] Die
> aufgeschriebene Wahrnehmung dieser Landschaft ist also nicht durch das
> traditionelle romantische Naturgedicht gegangen, sie fand sich präzise be-
> nannt bei Huchel.[4]

In one sense therefore Czechowski can be considered a *Heimatdichter* in
the way that Huchel's verse, redolent of the Havel and Brandenburg,
makes *him* a regional poet.

At first sight, lines like 'Sanft gehen wie Tiere die Berge neben dem
Fluß' ('An der Elbe', *IB*, p. 5) or 'Hier möcht ich bleiben, wo/ An den
Hängen ewiges Grün' ('Wasserfahrt', *IB*, p. 32) smack of an idyllic vision.

And how otherwise should we react to the rhetorical question posed in 'Stadtgang':

> [...] Was
> Soll ich bedichten? Die Bäume,
> Die an den Hängen stehn,
> Die milde Landschaft,
> Die sanften Hügel? — Hier
> Bliebe ich gern!
> (*IB*, p. 67)

Who indeed would not gladly tarry? And we may similarly allow ourselves to be misled by these lines from another poem:

> O schönes Land, zwischen die Berge und den Strom gebreitet:
> Durch deine Haine, Fluren arglos ziehn —
> (*IB*, p. 6)

But it is the dash at the end of the second line that provides the clue. Czechowski is really at pains to dissuade us from this (or any other) phantasy. It is the darkened face of nature, 'die *un*heile Welt', that he here seeks to portray. For the third line, after the dash of the above-quoted example, runs: 'Wer könnte es, wenn er ein Deutscher ist?' All notion of an idyll becomes totally misplaced in the context of the poem in question and Czechowski rightly brings the reader down to earth with a bump: for the lines come from Czechowski's own poetic memorial to the concentration camp of Terezin, 'Theresienstadt'. Similarly, in the earlier mentioned example from the poem 'Stadtgang', those quoted lines are juxtaposed with an expressed awareness of the presence of death imposed on nature.[5] In such gentle surrounds the memories of war linger on:

> [...]
> Den Toten ein Kreuz, oben
> Hinter den Wäldern über der Stadt,
> Den Namenlosen.

The recapturing of the past, the drumming up of childhood memories does not conjure up for Czechowski the pure sense of innocence; the evocation of nature does not act as a bulwark against the horrors of war. For him, being ten years of age meant witnessing the bombing of Dresden on 13 February 1945: 'Das Eindringen von Bombenflugzeugen in einen Kindheitsraum [...] war natürlich im Maurerschen Sinne eine Welterfahrung. Erfahrung größerer Welt, eine tragische, eine vom Tod betroffene.'[6] Rather then, and understandably so, Nature's face is hostile and bleak. The poem 'Dresdner Vorstadt 1945' (with its echoes of Huchel's 'Der Rückzug'?) illustrates the point:

> Dem Weiß, das alle Mühsal deckt,
> Entsteigt kein Laut.
> Schwarz aufgefahren, Gleis auf Gleis,
> Waggons —
> Kriegswinter — ohne Haut,
> Die längst Gerippe um Gerippe ließ.
> Wind schwirrt.
> Draht schneidet tief.
> Nicht eine Krähe, die sich hier verirrt.
>   (*IB*, p. 7)

The bombing of Dresden remains to this day the central experience for Czechowski. The incidence of words denoting decay, destruction (*verfallen, zerstören, zerfallen, zerbrechen*) is striking in his vocabulary; illustrations, in imagery drawn from nature, proliferate in his verse — even in his recent volume *Mein Venedig* (Berlin, 1989) (and how is *that* for a symbolic title?) — of the physical void: 'leichter/ Dunst über den Gärten, gegen/ Über verfallne Fassaden, die Lücke, die/ Der letzte Krieg hinterließ' ('Abgeschlossene Landschaft', *MV*, p. 23); and sometimes accompanied by an imprecise air of threat, as in 'Jagdzeit'(*S*, p. 57): 'Umstellt sind die Gärten, entlaubt'. And no less lasting are the emotional, the spiritual scars. The short prose passage 'Landschaft bei Machern' (*MV*, p. 83) describes an old man still reminiscing, in his search for a meaning to life, on the fate of people back in the 'SA-Zeit' — these past memories juxtaposed with the present activities of the grandchildren who, seeking to bring order into their gardens through the process of cutting hedges, needlessly destroy the nests of innocent and hapless birds. Whilst, against the urban setting of Dresden again, the poem 'Damals' (this time so dissimilar in tone to Huchel's poem of the same title) attempts to map the shifting ground of innocence in time of war:

> Damals,
> Als ich noch nichts
> Von Gedichten wußte und gar nichts
> von Mädchen und Frauen
> und kaum etwas von Gott
> Und nicht viel
> von Stalin, doch vielleicht etwas mehr
> von Hitler, Goebbels und Göring,
> Damals
> War alles anders als heute und lange noch

> Stand der zerschossene Bus vor der Drogerie Bochnig,
> Und lange noch
> lag das Wrack der ME 109
> Im Wald gleich hinter der Mauer,
> die zur SS-Kaserne gehörte, und die —
> das sah ich mit eigenen Augen —
> von Häftlingen in gestreiftem Drillich errichtet wurde.
> [...]
>
> (*MV*, p. 10)

Czechowski's poems therefore are landscapes, external: based essentially, as indicated, on his Saxon *Heimatland*, 'eine Landschaft aus Schönheit und Wehmut' ('Sächsischer Nachmittag', *S*, p. 8); and internal: as in reflective and ironic manner, tinged with melancholy, he expresses his awareness of the presence of the past. The idyll is then really far removed from his thoughts as he exhorts his beloved land to reveal truths:

> Jetzt sprich deine Sprache, Land,
> Verschweig nichts
> Mit postkartenreifen Idyllen
> [...]
>
> ('Flußfahrt', *IB*, p. 59)

His attitude to fascism is clearly defined in his verse. And communism? For someone whose later education at least took place during the birth pangs of the new East German state, there is not much evidence of any political idyll, either, in Czechowski's work of the 1960s and 1970s. The poem 'Wasserfahrt' indeed points up the 'Fahren/Erfahren', 'Leben/Erleben' syndrome discussed by Walfried Hartinger.[7] Granted: the last stanza of 'Reisen' *is* a positive declaration: 'Im Netz der Bilder/ Entsteht der Gedanke./ Klärt sich und formt sich:/ Tätig sein' (*IB*, p. 13). And progress is in evidence in 'Peripherie': 'Rostiges Eisen/ Gräbt sich durchs Brachfeld,/ Bagger zerbrechen/ Zerfallende Hütten' (*S*, p. 24). We are familiar with the concluding line of the poem 'Brief' (*IB*, p. 36), which provided, we remember, the title of a well-known anthology: *In diesem besseren Land*.[8] These signs we do not ignore, but it is more lipservice than belief on Czechowski's part. The pioneering spirit, praise of the work ethic that we find expressed (and provocatively so) by Volker Braun (in, for example, 'Jugendobjekt') is essentially absent in Czechowski's work. Indeed the note of query and qualification is evident already in the title poem of that 1967 volume, *Wasserfahrt*:

> [...]
> Aber was greifen wir denn
> mit dem Gedanken? —

Kommunismus? Eine Vision, Durchgangsstufe
Der Menschheit, zu welchen
Erreichbaren Fernen?
[...]
Aber
Es muß doch da etwas sein,
Das den Fortschritt befiehlt,
Dieses Gleiten auf sanften Gewässern,
Auf Schienen, Elektronengehirnen, Systemen,
Kalkulierbaren: Rückkopplung
auf die Erscheinung des Menschen.

Aber wenn da etwas verlorenging
Vom Liebesgeflüster, von
Der Fahrt auf dem Fluß, vom Grün
Und der Wölbung des Bergs, was
Blieb?
(*IB*, p. 32)

And as disillusionment increasingly sets in, so Czechowski's scepticism, his resolve to 'speak the truth', strikes home — not least in the recent volumes *Kein näheres Zeichen* (Halle/Saale, 1987) and *Mein Venedig* (1989), as he takes his fellow poets to task. Thus he addresses Volker Braun in the poem 'An meinen Freund V.B.': 'und erlaube mir, zu fragen,/ Wie's um die Wahrheit steht bei uns im Osten [...] Ja, es ist Zeit, zu reden' (*MV*, p. 34).[9] Similarly, critical allusion to another Volker Braun poem, this time 'Landwüst', occurs in 'Im Allgemeinen': 'So/ Schließt sich um uns/ Brauns grüne Schlinge/ Mit Fußangeln und/ Selbstschüssen'(*MV*, p. 84). And the ironic note is struck in 'Industrieviertel P', where the workers are portrayed as the 'Werktätigen [...] alles/ Idealische Typen, fast/ Wie in Mickels Gedichten' (*MV*, p. 86).

The title of this last mentioned poem incidentally serves as a reminder to us that it would be all too easy to discover in Czechowski's verse ample illustration of the darkened face of nature (and human nature) portrayed in the context of environmental pollution. Czechowski's work, from early volumes to late, displays signs of the *Ökolyrik* trend,[10] as he too boards the lead-free wagon. The ironic thrust immediately manifests itself in 'Ich bin pausenlos auf Achse gewesen':

[...]
Ja, du mein gutes sauberes Ländchen: hinter den Wäldern
Stehn die Fabriken, Rauchsäulen
Stützen den Himmel und Flüsse durchziehn dich,
Von Ölen und Abfällen schwarz
[...]
(*Wmb*, p. 33)

We note the juxtaposing of the greenery in Thuringia and the smoke-laden air over Leuna in 'Thüringen grün' (*IB*, p. 74). The Elbe valley too suffers from man's motorized assault:

> [...]
> Zu beiden Seiten des Flusses
> Nehmen Autokolonnen
> Mit tödlichem Blei
> Das Grün unter Beschuß
> [...]
>
> ('Flußfahrt', *IB*, p. 60)

The river itself does not escape: 'In der von Abwässern jeglicher Art/ Vergifteten Elbe', run the opening lines of 'Diät' (*Wmb*, p. 75). The poisoning of the water and the air, the destruction of the earth and the forest occasion his poetic protest no less in the 1980s. Thus in 'Noch ein Gedicht':

> [...]
> Der Regen kommt uns sauer an,
> Das süße Leben wird gepriesen,
> Die neuen Autos halten dann
> Auf grünlackierten toten Wiesen.
> [...]
>
> (*MV*, p. 56)

In 'Kritisches Bewußtsein' a journey by train provides the stimulus:

> [...]
> Von Bitterfeld bis Schönefeld:
> Bauplatz und Schrottplatz
> Kaum zu unterscheiden.
> [...]
> Es scheint, das Land besteht aus Müllabladeplätzen.
> Die grauen Reiher, diese schönen Tiere,
> Stehn, scheint es, ratlos im Verfall.
> Die Wälder wie verfilzte Gräser, Sperrgebiete.
> [...]
>
> (*KnZ*, p. 58)

The innocuous-sounding 'Spaziergang', redolent of many an eighteenth- or nineteenth-century poetic walk, actually leads us from thoughts of the sublime to the figurative pits:

> Als ich durchs Rosental ging,
> Standen die Bäume Parade.
> Die Erde, ein freundlicher Stern,
> War das, was ich suchte.
> Doch die vertriebenen Paradiese
> Blühen jetzt anderswo

[...]
Doch als ich näher kam,
Erkannt ich den schwarzen
Stinkenden Tümpel, ein Wind
Von der Kläranlage ergänzte
Vortrefflich die Szene. Dort,
Wo die Kleingärtner hausen,
Zwischen Kürbis und Sellerie, Rettich und Aster,
Brach keuchend aus Buschwerk hervor
Eine Rüsselmaske im Tarnanzug
[...]

(*IF*, p. 80)

Similarly, the poem 'Wir' (*KnZ*, p. 135) shows (formalistically too, incidentally, in the progressive reduction of length of line and stanza) the remorseless diminution of values through man's apparent resolve to destroy nature and ultimately himself. The title indicates our corporate responsibility for this whittling away process.

Everything then has its price, progress too, we read in 'Abendblatt' — not only in the countryside:

[...]
Ein paar Silos darin, Betonungeheuer,
Ähnlich dem Mischfutterwerk,
Das die Aussicht auf Querfurt verstellt
[...]

but also in the urban landscape:

[...] Mein Gott, und der Beton
Frißt sich weiter und weiter
In die Altstadt hinein:
Ins Abrißviertel der Leute
Die von der gestundeten Zeit reden,
Um zu vertauschen Außenabort und Rattenplage
Gegen Dusche mit Innenklosett
[...]
Der altehrwürdige Dom
Zerfällt sowieso, und die Türme
Von St. Marien werden vielleicht eines Tages
Nur noch auf einem Bild
Von Feininger konserviert sein.
(*Wmb*, p. 14)

Here, incidentally, as frequently elsewhere in his verse, Czechowski deftly juxtaposes images of material, technological advances and their concommitant destructive factor, and those images symbolic of past cultural and civilizing values. Perhaps one should read Mörike, unless it be already too late, Czechowski recommends in 'Im Allgemeinen': 'Denn

wo nicht/ Die Industrie uns unserer Sinne/ Benimmt, tut es/ Die Gülle'
(*MV*, p. 84). Reactors and Hölderlin are conflicting, irreconcilable oppo-
sites in 'Besuch' (*KnZ*, p. 167). Huchel, the Arnims and Lessing are set
against the 'Müllabladeplätze' in 'Kritisches Bewußtsein' (*KnZ*, p. 58).
This last poem well depicts the poet's bemoaning of the loss of the 'heile
Welt' not merely in the narrower confines of current ecological issues,
but in the wider context of the historical process itself:

> [...]
> In der Dichter Land
> Wird die Vergangenheit bewältigt.
> Der Arnims Gräber, Huchels Wilhelmshorst —
> O Land, o Lessing-Land,
> In dem sich so viel Traurigkeit versammelt.
> Ein Volk von Jägern und Gejagten
> Beginnt, in die Geschichte einzugehen.
> [...]

Wolfgang Hildesheimer's ecological cry 'Was ist das alles, wenn die
Natur stirbt'[11] is here effectively subsumed in Czechowski's putative
lament 'Was ist das alles, wenn das Land stirbt'.[12]

Events of the past, then, continue to stick in the memory ('Nur die
Ereignisse/ Sind im Gedächtnis geblieben' ('Frieden', *KnZ*, p. 23)), giving
the poet cause for mistrust. 'Ich/ mißtraue dem ganzheitlichen Weltbild,/ das manche, glaubte man ihnen,/ noch immer besitzen', we read
in the opening poem 'Weltbild' of the volume *Mein Venedig* (p. 9). Similarly, in the poem 'Bilanz' (from the volume *Mein Venedig* — not the
poem of the same title to be found in *Kein näheres Zeichen*):

> [...]
> Geblieben
> Sind letzten Endes
> Nur Gräber und Grüfte, Namen,
> Die den meisten
> Schon nichts mehr bedeuten.
>
> Um weiterzukommen
> Hilft letzten Endes
> Nur das Mißtrauen
> Gegenüber den guten Ratschlägen und
> Vor allem sich selbst.
> [...]
>
> (*MV*, p. 40)

There remains no place nor time for idylls, for deceits, those

> [...]
> Kartengrüße lügender Fotografen:
> Heile Dächer,
> Heile Welten,
> Gleich
> Der Sortenreinheit
> Polierter Früchte
> Auf Bilderbuch-Märkten
> [...]
> ('Im Allgemeinen', *MV*, p. 84))

Rather do we hear the critical, resigned voice of the poet in advancing middle years who has witnessed it all before. Man, he feels, has learnt nothing from the experiences of history:

> [...]
> Nein, Deutsche,
> Ihr habt nicht gelernt,
> Da Unsagbare sagbar zu machen:
> Euer Auschwitz,
> Euer Theresienstadt,
> Eure Himmlers und Heydrichs
> Und eure Jugend,
> Die sich selbst auf den Arm nimmt —
>
> Nein, es geht weiter,
> Sancta Simplicitas, alles
> Ein einziger Kommentar
> Zu dem Kontinuum,
> Aus dem
> Nichts gelernt worden ist
> In aller Stille.
> ('In aller Stille', *KnZ*, p. 138)

Saxony has traditionally occupied a key geographical and political position in central Europe ('In zwei Stunden durch Sachsen,/ Die Achse entlang,/ Um die sich Europa einst drehte' ('Missingsch', *S*, p. 37)); and Czechowski's close identification with the regional landscape enables the poet therefore to contemplate the course of European history (and, by extension, world events) in this heartland from earliest times, 'wo einst das karolingische Großreich/ Endete, so wie/ Alle Träume einst enden'. The old 'Meißnische' region has provided many a striking example in the past. It continues so to do no less now, the poet powerfully portrays, in a poem which looks to the post-October events of 1989, 'Historische Reminiszenz':

Was hat man uns nicht
Alles eingeredet: daß
Uns Monokulturen bekömmlicher sein sollen
Als Vielfalt, und daß die Versteppung des Landes
Erst dessen wahre
Schönheit uns offenbare... Heute, so scheint es,
Ist wieder ein Tag,
An dem man uns einreden will: Nun
Wird alles gut!
Wenn ich die Augen schließe,
Hör ich die Rufe der Masse
Wie Brandung. Auf diesem Platz,
Der einmal eine der schönsten
Europas war,
Gedenk ich der Toten, die
Auf diesem Pflaster verbrannten. Wie Pollen
Treiben die Wörter des Kanzlers
Über die Köpfe. Versprochen wird jetzt:
Den Skeptischen Mut,
Den Trauernden Freude und selbst
Noch dem Folterknecht
Auskömmliche Rente. Versprochen wird auch:
Die Schnellbahnstraße,
Ein dichteres Telefonnetz, mehr Fernsehkanäle,
Umweltfreundliche
Krokodile, Tränen,
Die glücklich machen wie Drogen, die Liebe —
Kostspielig und doch
Erreichbar für jedermann. Selbst der Tod
Wird einbezogen in dieses Fest der Versöhnung:
Die Dresdener Bank,
Dank sei dem Eisernen Kanzler! —
Zieht jetzt Bilanz in der dreimal
Zerstörten Stadt an der Elbe, während das Volk
Sich zu zerstreiten beginnt, um seinen Anteil
An einer Ordnung, von der niemand weiß,
Wer *nun* den Kopf hinhalten wird
Für die Vergangenheit des
Immerwährenden
Historischen Augenblicks. Demokratischer Aufbruch
Ins Niemandsland
Zwischen gestern
Und morgen...

Dresden, 19.12.1989
(*Planet*, no. 80, p. 72)[13]

The dating of the poem marks the occasion of the visit by Chancellor Kohl to Dresden; the event stirs Czechowski to survey past glories and disasters associated with that city of the Elbe (and hence of Germany) from the late nineteenth century through to the present day, via two World Wars and four decades of communism. If the younger generation can at the outset display on occasion a certain pessimism at the turn of events,[14] what then of the attitude of the middle generation? We should hardly be surprised at Czechowski's less than optimistic assessment. Hopes, realities, illusions? History will show. 'Die Zukunft ist schon Geschichte' ('Im Allgemeinen', *MV*, p. 85). But composing *Warngedichte*, be it in Wuischke in the gentle rain or in Leipzig (or Bergen-Enkheim), remains his self-appointed task, recording the future that is already history:

> Es wird nichts verziehen.
> Die Geschichte braucht keine Gedichte. Um mich herum
> Sehe ich Schlachtfelder, nicht
> Eingebildete: wirkliche,
> [...]
>
> Morgen stehe ich auf
> Und beginne von vorn:
> Es wird nichts verziehen.
> Ich schreibe.
> ('Augenmaß', *S*, p. 56)

NOTES

1   Heinz Czechowski was born in Dresden where, as a boy, he witnessed the bombing and destruction of the city. That experience has remained a central image for him as a writer. He initially trained as a graphic artist, but went to the Johannes R. Becher Literaturinstitut in Leipzig where Georg Maurer proved influential for him. Czechowski then worked as *Lektor* at the Mitteldeutscher Verlag, Halle/Saale (1961—1965). He continued to live in Leipzig, though in recent years he has travelled widely throughout Europe (including Britain) and in 1990 was appointed *Stadtschreiber* in Bergen-Enkheim near Frankfurt/Oder. His published volumes of verse include (the abbreviations indicated are used in references in the text): *Nachmittag eines Liebespaares*, Halle/Saale, 1962; *Wasserfahrt*, Halle/Saale, 1967; *Schafe und Sterne*, Halle/Saale, 1975; *Was mich betrifft* (*Wmb*), Halle/Saale, 1981; *Ich, beispielsweise* (*IB*), Leipzig, 1982; *An Freund und Feind*, Munich, 1983; *Kein näheres Zeichen* (*KnZ*), Halle/Saale, 1987; *Ich und die Folgen* (*IF*), Reinbek, 1987; *Mein Venedig* (*MV*), Berlin, 1989; *Sanft gehen wie Tiere die Berge neben dem Fluß* (*S*), Bremen, 1989; *Auf eine im Feuer versunkene Stadt*, Halle-Leipzig, 1990.

2   See Czechowski in conversation with Christel and Walfried Hartinger (*IB*, p. 118). Poems on the Elbe would include 'Das Elbtal', 'Wasserfahrt', 'Flußfahrt'. Saxony comes alive for Czechowski in so many poems: 'Da/ ist die Welt gegenwärtig/ In sächsisch-böhmischen Dörfern' ('Flußfahrt'); in 'Missingsch', 'Lessing in Meißen', 'Hubertusberg', 'Alt-Kaditz', etc. There is frequent mention of real places, small towns and villages, in the Saxon landscape: Meißen, Strehla, Radeburg, Batzdorf, Scharfenberg, Wurzen, Oschatz. Dresden has been at the centre of his experience from childhood on, to a degree that he has now published a collection of poems and pieces on that subject under the title *Auf eine im Feuer versunkene Stadt*.

3   *IB*, pp. 122f.

4   *IB*, p. 122. Derivative touches of Huchel can be found in some of Czechowski's early poems (for example, 'Cleviner Herbst', *IB*, p. 5; 'Dresdner Vorstadt 1945', *IB*, p. 7). The poem 'Winterreise (Radistschew)', *IB*, p. 54, is dedicated to the older poet. References

to Huchel can be found in 'Kritisches Bewußtsein', *KnZ*, p. 58, and 'Als die Wörter verboten waren', *Planet*, 80, April/May 1990, p. 74.

5   Anthony Williams, pp. 255—67 above, explores similar themes in relation to Bobrowski, Grass and Siegfried Lenz.

6   *IB*, p. 118. His indebtedness to Georg Maurer may be gauged in some measure by Czechowski's words (*IB*, pp. 123—6); in the dedication of the poem 'In diesem Sommer' (*IB*, p. 54) to him, and, on the fourth anniversary of his death, of the poem 'Georg Maurer' (*IB*, p. 82); and in his editing of a selection of Maurer's essays, speeches and letters under the title *Georg Maurer. Was vermag Lyrik*, Leipzig, 1982.

7   Walfried Hartinger: 'Gedichte im Gespräch. Zur Produktion, Vermittlung und Rezeption der DDR-Lyrik' in J. Flood (ed.): *Ein Moment des erfahrenen Lebens. Zur Lyrik der DDR*, Amsterdam, 1987, pp. 6—21; here p. 13.

8   Karl Mickel and Adolf Endler (eds): *In diesem besseren Land*, Berlin (GDR), 1966.

9   Czechowski specifically picks up here the viewpoint expressed by Braun in his poem 'Das Leben' (*Langsam knirschender Morgen*, Frankfurt/Main, 1987).

10   See also Axel Goodbody's major article on 'Deutsche Ökolyrik' in this volume (pp. 373—96 above, esp. pp. 389 and 395 in relation to Czechowski).

11   See Wolfgang Hildesheimer and Marc Guetg: 'Nein, es ist zu Ende, und das Ende ist absehbar' in V. Jehle (ed.): *Wolfgang Hildesheimer*, Frankfurt/Main, 1989, pp. 363—70; here p. 367.

12   In conversation with the present writer, 8 February 1990.

13   I am grateful to Heinz Czechowski for permission to quote this poem.

14   Thus, for example, Steffen Mensching (b.1958), in his poem 'Öde an einem klemmenden Buchstaben und Heinz C.' (*ndl*, vol. 38, no. 3, p. 50). Czechowski has expressed his reservations too in 'Euphorie und Katzenjammer', an essay contained in Michael Naumann (ed.): *Die Geschichte ist offen*, Reinbek, 1990, pp. 31—43. Karen Leeder also refers to Mensching's peom, p. 424 below.

'POESIE IST EINE GEGENSPRACHE':
YOUNG GDR POETS IN SEARCH OF A POLITICAL IDENTITY

KAREN J LEEDER

In his 'Rede über Lyrik und Gesellschaft', Adorno identified the poetic voice as one articulating different concerns from the dominant, ideologically determined discourse: 'Kunstwerke jedoch haben ihre Größe einzig daran, daß sie sprechen lassen, was die Ideologie verbirgt.'[1] Poetry was often understood in the GDR as a voice of 'opposition', as an arena in which they could articulate political and personal aspirations which would otherwise have remained unvoiced in the highly regulated public sphere.[2] Volker Braun gave powerful expression to this understanding in his essay 'Rimbaud. Ein Psalm der Aktualität', where he spoke of poetry as an antidote to the 'Betriebsblindheit der Ideologie', whose essential 'contra-diction' existed in both its project and its structure.[3] He summed it up perhaps most cogently: 'Poesie ist eine Gegensprache' (p. 982). Rainer Schedlinski, one of the youngest generation of poets in the GDR, has warned, in terms which echo Braun's, that it is exactly this form of 'speaking against' ('jene Sprache *gegen* die öffentliche Sprache') which will disappear in the new German state. For, he claims, in the open society of the West neither the particular voice of the unofficial GDR poet, nor indeed the marginalized alternative voice per se, will survive without compromise. They will simply be re-institutionalized, swallowed in the throng of pluralism.[4]

The unification of the two Germanys propelled literature into the centre of the political debate. In particular commentators have been concerned with the role writers from the GDR will play in the atomized and market-controlled literary environment of the West.[5] Speaking in March 1989 Christa Wolf cited Heine's ironic response to his freedom from German censorship: 'Ich fühle mich sehr ratlos'. She, however, endorsed the experience of GDR writers who had lived their lives under censorship and insisted that their function and strategies would not necessarily change all that much, 'bloß weil die Mächtigen wechseln, mit denen wir uns auseinandersetzen müssen'.[6] Heiner Müller, on the other hand, has identified the changes as a radical form of release for GDR literature. He draws a parallel between the differing functions of photography and painting on the one hand, and those of the free press and literature on the other. With the introduction of de-centralized media, literature will be relieved of its responsibility to act as a substitute for documentary 'truth'. Instead, it will be able to reclaim an essential autonomy which it had been forced to relinquish to the socialist ideology: 'Durch diesen Prozeß wird Literatur wieder frei, sich ihrer eigentlichen Aufgabe zu widmen: die Wirklichkeit so wie sie ist unmöglich zu machen.'[7]

Both Wolf and Müller were born in 1929 and lived through the antifascist struggle and the Utopianism of the *Aufbau* years. Both belong to the small percentage of GDR writers who have found international success in East and West. Critical attention has focused recently, however, on the differences between writers like these and the youngest generation of writers in the GDR, those who were 'born into' the established socialist state.[8] It is interesting to note that for many of them the recent changes have provoked feelings of 'große Lähmung', a response curiously akin to that of Heine: 'Wir sind selber ratlos'.[9] Their disorientation, like that of the authors who left the GDR in the wake of the 'Biermann affair', is the result, among other things, of a radical challenge to their understanding of the premise and function of their writing. It is this 'understanding' that I want to explore now, by attempting to define the nature of the relationship between the dominant discourse and the voice articulated against it ('Machtwort' and 'Gegenwort') in the work of some of these young writers.[10] Such a discussion must assess whether the relationship between the two is one of confrontation or simple negation, or whether it is instead a form of parallel culture, existing alongside the official one and possibly seeking a dialogue with it.

When the work of the young generation was first given official recognition in 1979, it was immediately clear that many of the writers were breaking fundamentally with the orthodox traditions of socialist literature.[11] They expressly dissociated themselves from the so-called 'DDR-Messianismus' of the *Aufbau* years: 'Kein früher Braun heute', claimed Uwe Kolbe.[12] The feeling that Braun's (and his generation's) understanding of literature is outmoded, irrelevant, even antagonistic to the realities of the present day, is given forceful expression by three different authors in the anthology of new GDR literature published in 1985, *Berührung ist nur eine Randerscheinung*.[13] Their dispute with Braun centres on his early conviction that he and his work, whatever criticisms he might articulate in it, would necessarily be integrated into the development of the socialist state. Today, the young authors born into the GDR feel that they have been born too late, and that the slow progress of socialism continues impervious to their individual designs and aspirations. For them literature has taken on a very different meaning. They use it as a means to express their sense of marginalization and political inarticulacy: some of them, along notoriously radical lines. 'Die Literatur ist eine Art Opposition [...] Ein bestimmtes Bewußtsein von einem Ungenügen braucht Literatur als Gegenwehr gegen ihre Umwelt, auch gegen politische Konzeption und meinetwegen auch gegen die Philosophie, sagen wir gegen kollektive Vereinnahmung.'[14]

The notion of the writer as one half of an antagonistic opposition was taken up by Günter Kunert, writing in 1988 about the dilemma of young authors coming from East to West. The political and poetic language he discerns in the East is one determined by the confrontation of 'Systemsprache' and 'individuelle Sprache'. He concludes: 'Aus dieser Konfrontation erwächst naturnotwendig Gegnerschaft'. The writer is forced into a static role as 'Gegenbild des Funktionärs'. His/her political understanding becomes conditioned by the need for intractable resistance: 'Ihr ganzes Selbstverständnis möglicherweise auch ihre Intention resultieren aus nichts anderem als dem inneren Widerstand gegen das sie und alle unterdrückende System.'[15] A poetry which defines its identity only in opposition to the restraints which regulate its existence will be left floundering if those restraints are removed. It has denied itself the possibility of advocating a prior position, except through the refractions of negation.[16]

However, many observers have claimed to perceive a quite different impetus within the work of the young poets. Using Kolbe's perhaps infamous 'Hände im Schoß' attitude as a starting point, critics in East and West have discerned a growing 'Desorientierung und Ziellosigkeit'.[17] This is best expressed in the *Aussteiger* mentality symbolized in the alternative Prenzlauer Berg scene.[18] In her introduction to the anthology *Berührung ist nur eine Randerscheinung*, Elke Erb contends that this literature moves *beyond* 'folgenlose Kritik' and 'konfrontative Positionen' and that this is: 'die Konsequenz des *Austritts* aus dem autoritären System, der *Entlassung* aus der Vormundschaft eines übergeordneten Sinns' (*Berührung ist nur...*, p. 15; my italics — KJL). In effect, she also pre-empts the argument that these poets are using their marginalized position as a vantage point from which to criticize the existing order. For her it represents a release into a different zone. Although Anneli Hartmann rejects descriptions of this zone simply as a form of refuge, she too identifies a lack of revolutionary impetus in the work and defines the goal of the poetry not as direct opposition: 'nicht unmittelbar gegen das Bestehende gerichtet', but rather as an attempt, 'jenseits von diesem anzusiedeln'.[19]

In his 'Rimbaud' essay Volker Braun also takes up the theme of an alternative reality posited and inhabited by literature: 'die **Freiheit** beginnt jenseits' (p. 989). What is more, he passes an initial, and critical, judgement on the 'vermeintliche[n] Neutöner' (p. 990) of the literary scene. His piece however is much more than the, perhaps inevitable, carping between literary generations. On one level, it represents an exploration of Braun's affinity with the poet Rimbaud, whom he claims as a long-standing 'Gewährsmann meiner Erfahrungen'(p. 978). This affinity is based largely on a political reading of Rimbaud, which highlights Rimbaud's revolutionary interest and translates his radical gesture of departure into a revolutionary act.[20] On another level, the piece champions the legacy of the 'avant-garde'. This is understood as an impetus rather than a historical phenomenon; Braun includes Surrealism, Modernism and the work of the Beat Generation, for example. His aim is to reclaim its potential for the literary canon of GDR, but, in so doing, he also sets out a response to the work of Heiner Müller and Elke Erb. Most important as the subtitle: 'Ein Psalm der Aktualität' (from the second of Rimbaud's letters known as the 'lettres du Voyant'; to Paul Demeny, 15 May 1871) suggests, it is an essay into the very premise of poetry and its function in the GDR.[21]

At the centre is the opposition of stagnation: 'Geschichte auf dem Abstellgleis. Status quo' (p. 982), and revolutionary movement: 'Entgrenzung aller Sinne' (p. 984). This is translated into a concrete and political topography in which 'Provinz' represents the ossified regimentation of the GDR and 'Revolution' the vagabond expedition 'ins innerste Afrika' (p. 995). Rimbaud's incursions into that Unknown, his 'illuminations' are also translated by Braun into more concrete political visions. Rimbaud's elusive goal, 'le lieu et le formel' becomes in Braun's essay 'die Formel für ein menschliches Leben, den Ort der Poesie' and is linked explicitly to a revolutionary socialist future (p. 983).[22] In doing this, Braun claims Rimbaud firmly for the tradition of political poet-seer. This tradition has been widely cultivated in the GDR, particularly in the spirit of Becher, and is a theme explored by Braun with reference to Hölderlin, whom he recalls here also (p. 983).[23] Braun also sets Rimbaud in opposition to the impervious and destructive force of history, as demonstrated in Müller's *Hamletmaschine*: 'Die Küste Europas, unter unsern Füßen Plastikmüll, gedunsene Fische, der Schrott der Kriege. Die fetten Leiber gegen das Gemurmel des Meeres gebreitet, Windflüchter, von den Sendern besudelt. In unserem Rücken die Megamaschine, die langsam vorwärts drängt in den Schlick' (p. 984). In a conflation of fragments from *Hamletmaschine* and *Medea-Material*, Braun demonstrates the ruins of Europe, and endorses Rimbaud's search for alternative ambitions.[24]

Rimbaud's quest for a future 'langage universel' with which to articulate his vision is taken up by Braun, significantly and polemically, in the central idea of a 'Gegensprache'.[25] It is here that he expressly rejects 'poesie pure' (p. 996), which he sees as the domain endorsed by Elke Erb's poetological statements. He scorns the hygenic naivety of poetry which refuses to engage itself (pp. 986, 990). Instead, he takes up Rimbaud's 'impure' poetry, which has been distilled from extremities of experience; and, by a sleight of hand, Braun then slips into the 'impurity' of revolutionary poetry. Elke Erb's poetic model does not, he claims, engage on behalf of change: 'Literarische Befreiungeffekte, nicht die Befreiung der Literatur; das Ordnungsmodell und der Harmoniezwang werden bei dieser Erb-Sache umgangen, aber nicht zerbrochen' (p. 996). When he claims 'Die Gegensprache, sie wird auch Fürsprache sein' (p. 985), it is clear that the language he is seeking is not in any way an abdication, nor simple opposition, but the enactment of a Utopian alternative in the here and now: 'die Wirklichkeit öffnen' (p. 990).[26]

It is for lack of such positive 'engagement' that he criticizes the young writers — primarily the 'experimental' language poets to be featured in the Anderson—Erb anthology a year later. He takes up a quotation from Sascha Anderson himself and uses it to question the premise of the new poetry: 'ihre "monologe gehen fremd"'.[27] He accuses the young poets of abdicating their responsibility to their society: 'Fluchten wieder, aber auf Hasenpfoten', and (recalling Hölderlin) to the tradition of revolutionary poetry: 'Gesang, ihr unfreundlich Asyl, nur ein privates Eigentum'(p. 983). In physical terms he reiterates his own allegiances: 'Keine Ausflüchte' (p. 994). And in poetic terms he rejects writing which has degenerated into self-fulfilling monologue, or the 'geistloser Hand-betrieb der Avantgarde' (p. 990). Despite some praise (p. 990), the judgement is generally negative.

The sort of commitment and revolutionary anticipation which Braun claims is exceptional in their work in fact underlies far more of the poetry of the young generation than he suggests. Elke Erb defines it negatively, claiming that the young poets will no longer allow themselves to become dependent on official panaceas (*Berührung ist nur...*, p. 16). The poetry itself, however, seems to articulate a more differentiated view. Leonard Lorek writes about the ballast of failed Utopias which have been jettisoned underway and significantly equates them with the 'großen abgenutzten worte' (*Berührung ist nur...*, p. 122). Sascha Anderson is cautious about 'das utopische/ st/ ichwort'.[28] It is clearly in the very diction, the language, that these Utopias have forfeited their validity. Even in a society like the GDR, where abdication can be immediately understood as an expression of political militancy, it is a mistake to see this reticence even primarily as a form of resignation or withdrawal. Remarkable indeed is the hunger with which poets seek to colonize and articulate a sphere of experience marginalized by the dominant ideology, not by abandoning it but by uncovering and redressing what has been suppressed within it. The formulas have proved bankrupt and so have been replaced with new aspirations. Those aspirations are smaller, more human, more profane: the Utopia is to be found *within* the authentic experience of the individual and expressed in a language, born of it.[29]

There seem to be two generally identifiable and quite separate approaches to this new language amongst the young poets. The first, as one might expect from the imagery of Braun's essay, is eminently visual. Poems like those of Steffen Mensching, Hans-Eckardt Wenzel, Kerstin Hensel or Kathrin Schmidt, different as they are, are governed by pictures of a sensual and concrete reality. This is not to say that they simply reproduce reality in the manner of a photograph. Theirs is 'eine Art utopischer Realismus'.[30] They seek to see through to suppressed levels of existence and to rehabilitate what Hensel has called 'unsere vielfach verratenen Zonen des Lebens'.[31] Sometimes what has been denied up to now is painfully fundamental: everyday reality, folk mythology, nature, erotic and individual love. The second attempt to formulate a new language is based instead on linguistic strategy, in some ways reminiscent of Rimbaud's own 'alchimie du verbe'. It is championed by a group of 'experimental' poets who have only recently come to prominence, although they have been distributing poetry privately in the GDR for many years. The work, among others, of Bert Papenfuß-Gorek, Stefan Döring and Rainer Schedlinski is calculated experiment — to borrow a phrase from Anderson, 'vers aus der retorte'.[32] Of course the boundaries between these two tendencies are not absolute, but they provide a useful framework for discussing the prevailing trends.

For the poets who adhere to the visual presentation of this *Grenz-überschreitung*, the gesture of 'seeing though' is fundamental. 'Durch-blick' is a term which Braun uses repeatedly in his Rimbaud essay, and it is found frequently in many of the younger poets' work. Steffen Mensching's 'Erinnerung an eine Milchglasscheibe' is perhaps programmatic:

> Der Januar war schneeig.
> Ich hatte eine Scheibe.
> Ich wußte, wenn ich reibe,
> Verwelkt der blinde Frost.
> Ich drückte mit der Stirne
> Und küßte lang das weiße Glas.
> Einer fragte, siehst du was.
> Durch sagte ich seh ich. [33]

This sort of metaphor, drawn from the everyday but with resonances far beyond, is very common in the work of these poets. Their poems are full of images of barriers, boundaries and barbed-wire — the stifling limitations set to their world in physical, but also in ideological and personal terms. These are limitations which were set before they were born and which have become so established that at times they seem impenetrable. Yet they are countered by a 'weltoffene Haut' and a militant 'Sehn-sucht'.[34] Heiner Müller points out the radical possibilities of longing: 'Das Einzige, was ein Kunstwerk kann, ist Sehnsucht wecken nach einem anderen Zustand der Welt. Und dieser Sehnsucht ist revolutio-när.'[35] This longing enacts the revolutionary breaking of boundaries. It is translated into the glimpses of sky and sea and the open road beyond. One is reminded of the exotic promise of Goethe's 'Mignon', quoted in the Rimbaud essay, and Braun's own 'Das Meer, das dagegen ist' from the poem 'Das innerste Afrika'.[36] It would be wrong to equate this impetus with a simple desire to escape, to turn to the West for example. The goal is a Utopian reformulation of the here and now.

Another very forceful physical correlative of the Utopian ideal is given in Mensching's 'Auf einem Bein, nachts nackt'.

> Auf einem Bein, nachts, nackt
> In der Küche stehend, schöpfte ich wieder
> Seltsamen Mut, als du mir Ungelenkem,
> Tropfnassem, das Handtuch, wortlos, gabst,
> An das ich nicht ranlangen konnte [37]

In concrete terms this is a very unremarkable gesture between loved ones. The resonance of the extraordinary 'seltsamen Mut' which that gesture engenders, however, is an intimation of a world 'wo der Mensch dem Menschen ein Helfer ist'.[38] A similar gesture is presented in more explicitly political terms in the poem 'Ist dir aufgefallen...' of 1986. A nervous smile exchanged between the poetic subject and an American soldier in a children's bookshop transcends barriers of hostile prejudice and reveals:

> [...] daß dieser Augenblick
> eine Sekunde oder zwei
> sehr seltsam war, so verzweifelt, utopisch blödsinnig
> hoffnungsvoll zeitlos kurz entwaffnend [39]

The single breath of the poem culminates in a string of adjectives suspended unpunctuated at the end. The familiar formula 'sehr seltsam' is answered in the final adjective 'entwaffnend' which acts as a bridge between the personal and political levels of the poem.

Although the diction of the various poets varies greatly from the blunt, sometimes coarse colloquialism of Wenzel to the compelling alchemy of fairy-tale and domesticity of Hensel, there is a committed core to their work.

This is also the case with many of the 'experimental' language poets included in *Berührung ist nur eine Randerscheinung*, or, more recently, in the equally contentious *Sprache und Antwort*.[40] They represent the other quite different approach to formulating a new, alternative language. Once again the key concept of 'Sehnsucht' as a revolutionary force is taken up, this time by Leonhard Lorek. He dissects it and draws out the meanings of 'sucht' and 'suche': 'sucht: sehnsucht: sucht. nur haftet sehnsucht im üblichen sprachbenutz was passives an. leben: die möglichkeit der sucht nachzukommen. und die möglichkeit immer neue zu schaffen' (*Berührung ist nur...*, p. 121). For these poets the new can only be apprehended within the mechanisms of language. In the poem 'mit den worten sterben die bilder' for example, Stefan Döring expresses the modulation from 'spruch' through 'anspruch' and 'einspruch' to 'ausspruch'. This poem also demonstrates that, for these poets at least, the 'movement' at the heart of their work is not to be presented in images but quite literally in the movement of language made visible: 'alle bilder werden wörtlich genommen' (*Sprache und Antwort*, p. 89).

Bert Papenfuß-Gorek demonstrates this most effectively in his 'wortflug':

> meine umwelt gebrichts
> an geschlechtlichkeit
> & noch solchen wortschaetzen
> so ich schaetz aller leute
> noch solcher wortschaetze
> gegen ferfestigungen
> ferfestigter zungen
> & bekwehmlichkeiten
> trott zu beschreiten
> dergestalt gleichgeschalt
> ist selbst in blutgeflut
> strammstand noch der anstand
> so wortschritt um schritt
> flugs ich wortflog
> eingesehens
>   unfersehens
>   schrifttriftig
> m e i n e haupttracht
> der sinntracht trachtet
> spiel ich sinntrachtwegen
> wortspare durch blosses
> auslassen ein, also :
> liegen worte
> wenn ihr ruhe wollt
>   brach
> sitzen worte
> wenn ihr daran wollt
>   bereit
> stehen worte
> wenn ihr gedicht wollt
>   dikk da
> gehen worte
> wenn ihr weiter wollt
>   noch weiter
> laufen worte
> wenn ihr dorthin wollt
>   wort —
> flugs um bestimmten
> forkommnissen zuforzukommen
> for ort beim wort
>   dass kommunismus
>   kommen muss [41]

In this literal pursuit of language the poet responds to the 'gestanzte Festtagskunst' (Braun, p. 990) of officialdom. Words are dislocated, forced out of their habitual contexts and meanings in order to discover a new autonomy. Movement is a central theme for several of the language poets. It is, however, Papenfuß-Gorek who articulates that most radically and links it most firmly with the theme of 'Grenzüberschreitung'. In his 'SOndern' this is expressed in very visual terms:

> 3 schrei gegen die wand
> schreib es an die wand
> schreite durch die wand [42]

It will be clear from just these examples that the language of these poets has not been reduced to merely a material function as in the concrete poetry of the West in the 1960s. Instead they call on a tradition of the 'Avantgarde', focusing especially on Chlebnikov and the Russian Futurists.[43] The forms are used very precisely in order to uncover and to subvert the mechanisms of language, but also of thought. Various strategies are engaged in order to challenge the dominant discourse. Most obvious is the break with orthographical conventions, which is often implemented so as to throw up alternative meanings concealed within words. Words are fractured, so that prefixes and suffixes are liberated and can be read in connection with the words preceding or following them. The use of '&' serves to highlight the severance and repetition. Also, Papenfuß-Gorek and Döring in particular often introduce neologisms, words of *Rotwelsch*, or manipulate words so as to allow a second, alternative layer of meaning to emerge from beneath the surface of the first.[44] Alexander von Bormann has exposed an alternative reading of Stefan Döring's 'wortfege', which is based on the interchangeability of the letters 'f' and 'w'.

> weinsinnig im daseinsfrack
> feilt an windungen seiner selbst
> wahrlässig er allzu windig
>
> im gewühl fühlt er herum
> und windet sich nochmal heraus
> fund, kaum geborgen, bloss wort
>
> [...]

Bormann suggests that the 'subtext' can be understood as the authentic version, and equated with the author's own position. He bases this presumably on the emotive content.[45] The poet's life is thus seen as a wreckage ('daseinswrack'), and he is seeking means of escape ('fortwege'). However, I believe the tension created between the levels of meaning should not be dismissed so lightly. The very opposition of 'wrack' and 'frack' highlights the discrepancy between official appearances and the inner state of the individual. This opposition is sustained in the many references to what is hidden from view and what is revealed. Indeed, the poem is a self-conscious exercise in balancing these. The constant tandem of 'wortfege' with 'fortwege', and 'bloss wort' with 'bloss fort' for example indicates that Döring is not simply shedding a layer of language. Although never moving beyond a rather unsophisticated statement of the multireferentiality of language, the poem is in many ways a practical demonstration of Sascha Anderson's contention: 'ich habe ausser meiner sprache keine/ mittel meine sprache zu verlassen'.[46]

Such strategies demand a very active form of reading. The reader must slow down and test his reactions and associations. This correlates directly with the writer's task. Although he/she is seeking primarily to combat what Kolbe calls the 'Metasprache': 'die Sprache der Sprachreglung, die Kollektivlüge der herrschenden Sprache', it is not simply a question of formulating a negative version with which to oppose it. Kolbe concludes: 'Ich zitiere Versatzstücke, um zu sehen, wie sie in der veränderten Grammatik meines Denkens reagieren (*Berührung ist nur...*, p. 41). The poets must dismantle the monolithic formulas of public rhetoric and test the single parts against experience. Anneli Hartmann suggests the effect is eine 'Dokumentation der Sinnleere', which, she adds, might suggest the possibility of an alternative.[47] It seems, on the contrary, to be at once a search for meaning, and, importantly, a response to the meaninglessness of a ritualized and formulaic ideological rhetoric, which suppresses the language of experience. Rainer Schedlinski stresses the 'sinnstiftende Pflicht' of the poet and Kolbe too speaks of 'der heilose Versuch Sinn zu pumpen'.[48]

In the new Germany both the experience of the poets and the language in which it can move will be radically different. The audience too, bombarded by the verbiage of the market, will not perhaps be attuned to the finely wrought mechanisms of a poetry developed under censorship. More important, its status as language will have changed. Without the 'Klandestinität' which it suffered and enjoyed in the GDR its purchase on reality will be very different.[49] Just as the historical Avant-garde were reabsorbed by the institution of 'Art', and the impetus they represented was translated into a commodity, so this alternative language may lose the distinctive identity it has claimed in the open discourse of the West.[50] Of course it can be argued that this has already taken place to some extent. The once apparently coherent impetus of the Prenzlauer Berg collective has long since dissolved and reformulated in often antagonistic groupings. Equally, the recent publications of several of the younger authors in Gerhard Wolf's 'Außer der Reihe' series with the Aufbau-Verlag indicates that the divisions between official and unofficial are not as watertight as they might once have seemed. Rainer Schedlinski, for example, blames the accessibility of the Western media for having pre-empted the possibility of an authentic language of opposition in the GDR.[51] He claims that the aspirations of many in East Germany and the 'alternative' language they found to articulate them have become synonymous with the bankrupt formulations of capitalism. Recent publications by Braun, Mensching and many others, however, suggest that neither their language(s) nor the impetus of their poetry will be lost in the transition. In a selection of poems entitled 'Unvollendeter Tag', published in March 1990, Mensching expresses the paradoxical 'Gegensprache' of one caught up in a form of breaking barriers which he might not have wished for. In 'Öde an einem klemmenden Buchstaben und Heinz C.', a malfunctioning typewriter key turns the poet's would-be odes into wastelands of lost possibilities. Equally the 'o' of open-mouthed adoration absents itself in the face of the future.

> [...] Gejubelt
> wird schön genug und wenn ich
> Anstatt des wunderbar uffenen Lauts
> Lauter Nullen einsetze, fällt das hier
> Siewiesau
> Keinem mehr auf.[52]

His 'lauter Nullen' represents a bitter protest that nothing has been won, that socialism has sold out. His poetry has not. If these young GDR poets are to bring their understanding of poetry into the new Germany, as the ultimate anticommodity, a self-conscious and constant voice agitating for a better world — this most literal 'speaking against' seems a good place to start.

NOTES

1   Theodor Adorno: 'Rede über Lyrik und Gesellschaft' in *Gesammelte Schriften*, ed. by Ralf Tiedemann, Frankfurt/Main, 1974, vol. XI, pp. 49-68; here p. 51.

2   Václav Havel examines the problematic readings of the word 'opposition' in his essay 'The Power of the Powerless', translated by P. Wilson, in Jan Vladistlav (ed.): *Václav Havel; or, Living in Truth*, London, 1986, pp. 72—80.

3   Volker Braun: 'Rimbaud. Ein Psalm der Aktualität'. This was originally presented in Mainz in 1984 and was subsequently printed as an essay in *Sinn und Form*, vol. 37, no. 5, 1985, 978—98; here p. 986. References in the text are to this source. See also Katrin Kohl's analysis of language in poetry, esp. pp. 342—50 above. The discussion of language is also an important aspect of Thomas Beckermann's analysis of recent GDR prose works, pp. 97—115 above.

4   Rainer Schedlinski: 'Zwischen Nostalgie und Utopie. Ein Postscriptum' in Michael Naumann (ed.): *Die Geschichte ist offen*, Reinbek, 1990, pp. 183—6; here p. 185. See also the discussion of Botho Strauß's view of the poet and the German language by Arthur Williams, esp. pp. 462—65 below.

5   See for example Naumann: *Die Geschichte ist offen*, Heiner Müller: *Zur Lage der Nation* (Berlin, 1990), and also *Oktober 1989: Wider den Schlaf der Vernunft* (Neues Leben/Temperamente, Berlin (GDR), and Elefantenpress, Berlin/West, 1989). The analyses of the situation in late 1989 and early 1990 by Theo Buck (pp. 21—44 above) and Helmut Peitsch (pp. 155—82 above) provide ample evidence of the role of literature and writers in the process of unification.

6   Christa Wolf: '"Heine, die Zensur und Wir". Rede auf dem Außerordentlichen Schriftsteller Kongreß der DDR, 3.3.1990', quoted in Wolf: *Im Dialog. Aktuelle Texte*, Frankfurt/Main, 1990, pp. 163—8; here p. 168.

7   Müller: *Zur Lage der Nation*, pp. 21, 23.

8   See for example Anneli Hartmann: 'Der Generationswechsel — ein ästhetischer Wechsel? Schreibweisen und Traditionsbezüge in der jüngsten DDR-Lyrik', in Paul Gerhard Klussmann and Heinrich Mohr (eds): *Jahrbuch zur Literatur in der DDR*, no. 4, Bonn, 1985, pp. 109—34. See also, in particular, the contribution to this volume by Joseph Pischel, pp. 117—26 above.

9   Peter Warwerzinek, Bert Papenfuß-Gorek, Rainer Schedlinski and Kerstin Hensel at a reading in Frankfurt, *Volkszeitung*, 2 February 1990, p. 16.

10 This is set up as a premise in Alexander von Bormann: 'Rede-Wendungen. Zur Rhetorik des gegenwärtigen Gedichts in der DDR' in Christine Cosentino, Wolfgang Ertl and Gerd Labroisse (eds): *DDR-Lyrik im Kontext*, Amsterdam, 1988 (= *Amsterdamer Beiträge zur neueren Germanistik*, vol. 28), pp. 89—143; here p. 97. Although he credits poetry with 'eine oppositionelle, eine subversive Kraft', he does not define the precise relationship between the poetic language and that which it is subverting.

11 Cf. Siegfried Rönisch: 'Notizen über eine neue Autorengeneration', *Weimarer Beiträge*, vol. 25, no. 7, 1979, pp. 5—10.

12 '"Ohne den Leser geht es nicht". Ursula Heukenkamp im Gespräch mit Gerd Adloff, Gabriele Eckart, Uwe Kolbe, Bernd Wagner', *Weimarer Beiträge*, vol. 25, no. 7, 1979, pp. 41—52; here p. 46.

13 Sascha Anderson and Elke Erb (eds): *Berührung ist nur eine Randerscheinung. Neue Literatur aus der DDR*, Cologne, 1985. The authors are: Uwe Kolbe (pp. 40—1), Leonhard Lorek (pp. 123—4) and Fritz-Hendrick Melle (p. 147). Further references will be given after quotations in the text.

14 Stephan Ernst in '"Vorbild-Leitbild". Joachim Nowotny im Gespräch mit Wolfgang Berger, Stephan Ernst, Ingrid Hildebrandt, Rainer Hohberg, Annerose Kirchner, Christine Lindner, Thomas Rosenlöcher', *Weimarer Beiträge*, vol. 25, no. 7, 1979, pp. 11—23; here p. 17.

15 Günter Kunert: 'Deutsch-deutsches Exil' in Kunert (ed.): *Aus fremder Heimat. Zur Exilsituation heutiger Literatur*, Munich, 1988, pp. 100—10; here pp. 101, 107).

16 Kunert himself championed the use of the *Warngedicht* and likened it to a photographic negative upon which the positive image might be discernible, as a reversal of the exist-

ing. (See the *Forum-Debatte* or the discussion in Fritz J. Raddatz: *Traditionen und Tendenzen: Materialien zur Literatur der DDR*, Frankfurt/Main, 1972, p. 175.

17 Kolbe's self-consciously provocative statement of 1979: 'Meine Generation hat die Hände im Schoß, was engagiertes (!) Handeln betrifft' has been accorded an exaggerated degree of importance by critics in East and West. 'Ohne den Leser geht es nicht', p. 46. Also Christine Cosentino: '"ich habe ausser meiner sprache keine/ mittel meine sprache zu verlassen": Überlegungen zur Lyrik Sascha Andersons' in Cosentino et al: *DDR-Lyrik im Kontext*, pp. 195—222; here p. 216.

18 Cf.Gerhard Wolf: 'Befindlichkeit der Sprache, Befindlichkeit des Sprechenden: Zu einem Aspekt junger Lyrik der DDR', *Batería*, no. 7/8, 1988, pp. 4—13; here p. 7. This is a slightly extended version of the final essay of his *Wortlaut, Wortbruch, Wortlust: Dialog mit Dichtung*, Leipzig, 1988.

19 Anneli Hartmann: 'Schreiben in der Tradition der Avantgarde: Neue Lyrik in der DDR' in Cosentino et al: *DDR-Lyrik im Kontext*, pp. 1—37; here p. 12.

20 Cf. Ursula Heukenkamp: 'Metapher der Befreiung: Volker Braun, "Das innerste Afrika"' in Siegfried Rönisch (ed.): *DDR-Literatur 1987 im Gespräch*, Berlin (GDR), 1988, pp. 184—96.

21 Arthur Rimbaud: *Poésies*, ed. by Louis Forestier, 2nd rev. edn, Paris, 1984, p. 201.

22 Rimbaud: 'Vagabonds' from his *Illuminations*, in *Poésies*, p. 174.

23 See esp. Volker Braun: *Gegen die symmetrische Welt*, Halle/Saale, 1974. In his more recent *Training des aufrechten Gangs*, Halle-Leipzig, 1987, Hölderlin, Guevara and Braun are linked as poet-visionaries of revolution, pp. 55—8.

24 For a discussion of Müller's theatre see Axel Schalk's contribution to this volume, pp. 65—82 above, here esp. pp. 73—7. Joseph Pischel (p. 122 above) also refers to the mega-machines.

25 Rimbaud: *Poésies*, p. 203.

26 Of course this is in some ways a more visionary reformulation of his 1970 position 'Wir schreiben nicht mehr gegen die bestehende Gesellschaft sondern für sie, für ihre immanente Veränderung' in Volker Braun: *Es genügt nicht die einfache Wahrheit. Notate*, Leipzig, 1975, p. 75.

27 See also Anderson's response: 'Fixierung einer Metaphor — Antwort auf Volker Braun', *schaden*, 1 August 1985.

28 Sascha Anderson: *Jeder Satellit hat einen Killersatelliten: Gedichte*, Berlin/West, 1982, p. 109.

29 Cf. Braun: 'Rimbaud...', pp. 996f. This links with Rimbaud's emphasis on the human, even animal side of the Promethean poet 'voleur du feu' (*Poésies*, p. 203) which represents a reversal of the traditional GDR reading of the myth. Braun does not take the reference up explicitly, although it underpins much of what he does use.

30 Schedlinski: 'Zwischen Nostalgie und Utopie...', p. 183.

31 Kerstin Hensel: *Stilleben mit Zukunft*, Halle-Leipzig, 1988, p. 90.

32 Anderson: *Jeder Satellit...*, p. 72. Cf. Braun's imagery: 'Diese Poesie ist ja keine Zuflucht, sie ist ein Arbeitsraum, Laboratorium, wo nicht das Gold absoluter Wahrheit gesucht wird, sondern das akute Material der authentischen Erfahrung' ('Rimbaud...', p. 997).

33 Steffen Mensching: *Erinnerung an eine Milchglasscheibe*, Halle-Leipzig, 1984, p. 83. Poems by Steffen Mensching are quoted by kind permission of Mitteldeutscher Verlag (Halle-Leipzig).

34 Mensching: *Erinnerung...*, p. 9, and Hensel, *Stilleben...*, p. 81.

35 Heiner Müller: *Gesammelte Irrtümer*, Frankfurt/Main, 1986, p. 133.

36 First published in 1984 and included in Volker Braun: *Langsamer knirschender Morgen*, Halle-Leipzig, 1987, pp. 58—60.

37 Mensching: *Erinnerung...*, p. 88.

38 Bertolt Brecht: *Gesammelte Werke in 20 Bänden*, ed. by Suhrkamp Verlag in association with Elisabeth Hauptmann, Frankfurt/Main, 1967, vol. IX, p. 725.

39 Steffen Mensching: *Tuchfühlung*, Halle-Leipzig, 1986, p. 25.

40 Egmont Hesse (ed.): *Sprache und Antwort. Stimmen und Texte einer anderen Literatur aus der DDR*, Frankfurt/Main, 1988. References will be given after quotations in the text.

41 First published in Bert Papenfuß-Gorek: *dreizehntanz*, Berlin (GDR), 1988. Quoted from *SoJa*, Edition Galrev, Berlin, 1990, pp. 8—9, with kind permission of Bert Papenfuß-Gorek.
42 Papenfuß-Gorek: *SoJa*, p. 67.
43 Cf. Hartmann: 'Schreiben in der Tradition...', pp. 25—30.
44 For more detailed examples see Bormann: 'Rede-Wendungen. Zur Rhetorik...', pp. 89—143.
45 Hesse: *Sprache und Antwort*, p. 84. Cf. Bormann: 'Rede-Wendungen. Zur Rhetorik...', pp. 119f.
46 Anderson: *Jeder Satellit...*, p. 7.
47 Hartmann: 'Schreiben in der Tradition...', p. 10.
48 Schedlinski: 'Zwischen Nostalgie und Utopie...', p. 183, and Kolbe, *Berührung ist nur...*, p. 40.
49 Gert Neumann: 'Geheimsprache "Klandestinität"', based on a reading of Gilles Deleuze; *Sprache und Antwort*, pp. 129—44. See also Thomas Beckermann's discussion of Gert Neumann, pp. 108—14 above.
50 Cf. Peter Bürger: *Theorie der Avantgarde*, Frankfurt/Main, 1974.
51 Rainer Schedlinski: 'gibt es die ddr überhaupt?' in *Oktober 1989...*, pp. 4—9; here pp. 4f.
52 Mensching: 'Öde an einem klemmenden Buchstaben und Heinz C.', *ndl*, vol. 38, no. 3, 1990, pp. 50f.

THE CONCEPT OF IDENTITY
IN RECENT EAST AND WEST GERMAN WOMEN'S WRITING

RICARDA SCHMIDT

I

In the feminist research of the past fifteen years two different schools
have attempted to explain the reproduction of gendered identity: French
post-structuralism on the one hand, and Anglo-American object-relations theory on the other. The first is based on Lacan's rereading of
Freud and centres on the hypothesis that subjectivity is constituted
through the infant's entry into the symbolic order which functions according to the Law of the Father.[1] The second assumes that gendered
identity is reproduced in the concrete mother-child relationship in a nuclear family.[2] Both these schools have contributed to making gender a
major critical category in fields beyond psychoanalysis, affecting sociology, history, philosophy, literature and linguistics. Critical attention has
increasingly focused on pointing out that both theories are too complete,
too closed to account for the facts of historical change and of resistance
to the mechanisms of patriarchal enculturation.[3]

In this paper I want to investigate how the question of female
identity is treated in contemporary literature by East and West German
women writers. My aim is to relate theoretical analysis to literary genre,
style and mood, and to historical context, in order to explore literature's
specific contribution to the discussion of identity. I shall analyse two
texts by East German and two by West German writers: Monika Maron's
Die Überläuferin and Christa Wolf's *Sommerstück*, Helke Sander's *Die
Geschichten der drei Damen K.* and Uta Treder's *Luna Aelion*.[4] The four
texts can be grouped in various ways: two novels and two short stories;
two satirical texts and two serious ones; two fictional fantasies and two
reflections on everyday life; two texts which develop concrete positive
concepts of identity and two which imply a need for change only *ex
negativo*; two which tend to a heterogeneous concept of identity and two
which tend to a homogeneous one. However, the relationship between
these aspects defies a simple categorization into binary columns, as I
shall show in my interpretation.

II

In Maron's novel *Die Überläuferin*, the East Berlin historian Rosalind Polkowski finds herself in the fantastic situation of being completely cut off from the world, her legs paralysed, her mind free to search for her identity. The means of her search are her memories, her unconscious which materializes in surreal scenes, and four satirical intermezzos in which fantastic visitors to Rosalind's room conduct hilarious discussions. The characters of the intermezzos act on the 'stage' of Rosalind's fantasy — the intermezzos are written in the genre of a play, in dialogue. The nameless characters are identified by their attributes (e.g. 'Die Frau mit dem zarten Wesen'). They personify typical positions in GDR public opinion that Rosalind grew up with and to some extent internalized. Now she has gained enough distance from them to 'project' them in farcical form. Most prominent among them is 'Der Mann in der roten Uniform' who represents the official bureaucratic face of GDR socialism in statements like the following one:

> Sehr richtig, aber wer sagt es ihm. Hier stellt sich die Frage: wer wem. Und die Antwort lautet: ich. Ich sage es ihm, als Beauftragter meiner Behörde. Warum. Weil meine Behörde weiß, was für die Gesellschaft gut ist. Und wie bei Marx sehr richtig steht, ist, was für alle gut ist, für den einzelnen erst recht gut, womit wir dem Problem der Identität bedeutend nähergekommen sind. (p. 123)

Each intermezzo is devoted to the satirical discussion of one concept which all the characters seek to bring under social control in order to maintain the status quo: order and security, the family, identity and fantasy. Maron's text does not only switch to and fro between play and novel, but also between third-person narration with external focalization and Rosalind's first-person narration. These changes of the narrative voice do not follow a clear pattern, thus unsettling the reader's expectations of continuity and probability and preventing a neat separation between the levels of memory, fantasy and reflection.

Rosalind's fantastic freedom contrasts sharply with the 'real' life from which she has escaped: a life of 'lebenslange[r] Dienstverpflichtung' (p. 10), presenting her daily with a visual reminder of restrictions on the GDR citizen's movement, when she looks out of her tiny office on to the 'verbarrikadierte[n] Spree' (p. 11), and requiring of her all the virtues that capitalism demands of its alienated workforce: punctuality; thoroughness in routine work; toleration of banality, boredom, repetition, lack of meaning, lack of influence, lack of change and development;

an iron discipline keeping demands of body and soul under tight control.

In reviewing her life, Rosalind recalls how her friend Martha had critically described motherhood as the major social agency inculcating in children, by the exercise of a blend of power and love, the submission and obedience required by society:

> Der europäische Säugling lerne die Liebe als einen Akt der Unterwerfung kennen; das erste von ihm geliebte Wesen sei zugleich die Verkörperung der Macht: die Mutter. Sie könne verbieten, bestrafen, sie dürfe sogar schlagen, sie könne das Kind verhungern lassen oder es lieben. Je deutlicher der europäische Säugling seine Unterwerfung, seinen Gehorsam beweise, um so sicherer könne er ihrer Liebe sein. Die Liebe der Mutter sei der Lohn für den Gehorsam und die Unterwerfung die Bedingung für ihre Liebe, von der wiederum das Leben des Kindes abhänge. Demzufolge seien die Gefühle liebender Europäer ein nicht entwirrbares Chaos aus Zuneigung, sadistischer Herrschsucht, masochistischer Unterwürfigkeit, und es läge nahe, daß die so Liebenden sich zudem oft erpresserischer Methoden bedienten. (p. 71)[5]

But while motherhood is portrayed as the agency of law and order, producing sadomasochistic modes of feeling (in a European context, as the text stresses repeatedly, thus inserting the ethno-romantic ideal of other, happier, cultures into its fundamental criticism), its contribution to reproducing gendered identity is not examined, although patriarchal structures of adult life are touched upon.[6] Early childhood, however, is presented as a state which is to some extent pre-social, natural as it were. Thus Rosalind has memories of harmony between mind and body during childhood (p. 117). Childhood is also the time of naivety: as a child Rosalind believed in the aims of socialism and in the harmony between individual and society proclaimed in the socialist state (p. 64): but she has since experienced work, social conditions and her own internalization of social norms as so alienating and repressive that her body shows somatic reactions to her rational, socially well-adapted life. All this is a conventional enough problem, set in a historical context, and treated humorously, e.g. when Rosalind experiences the split between mind and body as the growing of a strange being inside her which does not leave room for her internal organs, so that the malfunctioning organs, 'die Mandeln, die Galle, am Ende sogar eine Niere' (pp. 9—10), have to be removed by surgery, providing her with a temporary feeling of oneness.

Rosalind's search for the unification of opposing parts — 'mit sich eins zu werden' (p. 120) — is, however, not endorsed by the movement of the novel. On the contrary, identity is satirically classed as 'Vokabular, das ihrem emanzipatorischen Rüstzeug entstammte' (p. 109) and

ridiculed as 'Paradiessucht' (p. 120) by Clairchen, a former friend of
Rosalind's brought to life again by Rosalind's surreal capacity for making the imaginary real.[7] Clairchen sees the wish for identity as the cause
of the experience of division:

> Wat solln dit sein: mit sich eins sein. Ick kannte mal eene, die rannte von Psy-
> chiater zu Psychiater und suchte bei denen ihre verlorene Identität, bis se
> rausjefunden hat, daß se durchschnittlich bejabt, durchschnittlich hübsch and
> durchschnittlich schlau is. Nu sitzt se inne Klapsmühle, gloobt, sie is Brigitte
> Bardot, ist jung, versteht sich, und fühlt sich janz mit sich identisch. (p. 121)

Against Rosalind's idealized view of her badly missed friend Martha's
closed identity, Clairchen maintains: 'Martha war fünf oder sechs oder
noch mehr, sagt Clairchen, jedenfalls is se nie auf die Idee jekommen,
eins sein zu wollen, was ihr erspart hat, sich wie zwei zu fühlen' (p. 121).

Moreover, identity is satirically unmasked in the third intermezzo
as a quality maintaining the status quo,[8] when the administrator of real
socialism, the man in red uniform, demands identity from everybody.
Lack of identity, in his opinion, leads to the undermining of law and order: 'Der unidentische Mensch denkt aufrührerisch und strebt Veränderungen an, was ihn zu einem gesellschaftsgefährdenden Subjekt, in
Einzelfällen sogar zum Kriminellen macht' (p. 125).

The aim he envisages for the citizens of his state is the brave new
world of 'identische Zufriedenheit unserer Menschen' (p. 126), based on
the right conviction, which is to be checked by his authority.

Rosalind rebels against such 'Friedhofsruhe' by literally pushing
her head through the wall. As she makes her way to the station, the
symbol of 'Aufbruch' associated with her lost friend Martha, the border-
lines between past, present and future, between reality and fantasy, are
blurred even more. Rosalind confronts her own potential for destruction
and rebellion as well as for cowardice and conformism, in various fantastic constellations of social politics — a bloody rebellion in the streets
of Berlin is among her fantasies (pp. 191—3)!

Among the surreal scenes of Rosalind's wandering, the effect of
patriarchal structures on women's identity is also wittily explored. Rosalind sees Martha almost being killed by a member of the 'Assoziation
dichtender Männer' (p. 155) for her bad writing. Seduction and persua-
sion are shown to be very nearly successful in convincing Martha (who
at times merges with the observing Rosalind, thus foreshadowing Rosalind's discovery of Martha as part of herself) that she has indeed committed an unpardonable crime by presuming to venture into the male

sphere of 'Dichtung'. Yet, while this fantastic vision humorously exposes the mechanisms of women's cultural exclusion, its presentation follows the same binary logic as the patriarchal thinking it criticizes in which femininity = nature is opposed to masculinity = mind. Here, only the evaluation is reversed, as the masculine priority, 'Sprache' (p. 155) or logos, connected with thanatos, is ridiculed as inferior to the feminine priority, 'Leben' (p. 155), connected with eros, the life-force.[9]

Rosalind's journey of self-discovery culminates in her finding her anarchic friend Martha in New York's Bowery, to which her fantastic walks through Berlin have mysteriously led her. Rosalind's discovery of herself, the repressed non-conformist part of herself, in Martha is depicted in dazzling shifts of pronouns (pp. 212f.).[10] However, the repressed aspect of the self does not simply embody the promise of happiness — Martha is down and out; its integration does not point towards a new whole, closed identity, but towards the consciousness of the multiplicity of identity. Rosalind registers 'die sehr verschiedenen Gefühle, von denen ich gleichzeitig befallen werde' (p. 218) which are epitomized in the statement 'Ich finde mich ekelhaft, so gefalle ich mir' (p. 219).

Yet, as with the scene that depicted the attempted execution by the 'Assoziation dichtender Männer', the fantasized scene of Roaslind's overcoming the limits of her old self is characterized by inherent contradictions that confirm old structures of thinking at the same time as criticizing them. When Rosalind learns to give in to the demands of her body, this liberation in the realm of fantasy from the dictates of her head occurs via the sexual mechanism of the missionary position (passed off as natural by being wrongly likened to the mating of animals), making her a passive object, moving to a man's rhythm, reducing her rational self to a mere shadow:

> Angelockt von meinen Schreien, kommt Billy. Wir wälzen uns auf dem harten Pflaster. Die mit den Blicken müssen über uns steigen oder um uns herum gehen. Ich habe die Augen geschlossen und bin begraben unter Billys Gestank. Billy stinkt nach Schnaps und dem Schweiß von sieben Nächten. Er drückt mir mit den Knien die Schenkel auseinander, und wir paaren uns wie das Vieh. Die Steine scheuern mir die Haut vom Fleisch, mein Kopf schlägt in Billys Rhythmus aufs Pflaster, durch meine Poren sickert Billys beißender Schweiß. Dann steht Billy auf und geht zurück zu den anderen. Ich bleibe liegen, ein in den Stein gebrannter Schatten. Mich gibt es nicht mehr, ich muß nichts mehr fürchten. (p. 219)

The fact that this fantasy displays less than liberating aspects: female submission and passivity, even masochism, as 'natural' expressions of Rosalind's freed sexuality on the one hand, the cliché of the animalistic virility of the black male on the other hand, is not reflected on in the text.[11] Thus the sadomasochistic form of loving the novel has named as the consequence of mothering is perpetuated in sadomasochistic sex that only apparently liberates the female subject from internalized social norms.

At the end of her fantastic visions Rosalind arrives back in her own room, at the starting point of her attempts to break away from established patterns of thinking. Yet her inner journey in the course of the novel has changed her view of things: 'Als würde sie vom falschen Ende durch ein Fernglas sehen, schrumpfte alles, was sie umgab, auf ein fernes unwirkliches Maß' (p. 221). She has grown out of the environment that used to confine her, by discovering many diverse aspects of herself instead of suppressing them, as she used to, in favour of a closed identity. The novel ends with an ambiguous reference to the ecstasy that Martha felt when she got soaked in a rainstorm and experienced a momentary vision of what a fulfilled life could be.[12] Martha had told Rosalind of it (in rather conventional, romantic terms) during their fantasized meeting: 'Ein unbekanntes Gefühl von Einverständnis klang in mir nach wie ein wunderbarer Akkord, als wäre ich selbst ein Instrument und etwas hätte alle Saiten in mir gleichzeitig so kunstvoll angeschlagen, daß nicht ein einziger Ton die berauschende Harmonie des Augenblicks störte' (p. 216).

It is the vision of a self in which no part is repressed and yet the different aspects of the self are not in conflict with each other.[13] However, this concept of identity has remained a momentary vision for Martha; it is not the achieved reality of her life. In 'real' life Martha searched for something 'mit aller Kraft' (p. 214), yet did not find it except in that one vision. She paid with her life to gain this one real experience (p. 213).

Rosalind might be on the verge of renouncing the dictatorship of her head over her body, to experience the same ecstasy, or she may be wistfully looking at such a possiblity that is still closed to her. Whether we interpret the ambiguous last sentence as the beginning of an individual revolt 'in reality', or as the heroine's resigned recognition of her inability for such a revolt, is ultimately not important, because a certain kind of life, of self, has been established as worthwhile, independent from the question of whether the heroine achieves it or not. In exploring the cost of gaining a 'real' experience in the protagonists Rosalind and Martha, Maron also humorously and imaginatively investigates patterns of thinking and feeling in the GDR, which both the heroine and her alter ego (who has been searching for the ideal father through most of the novel) have internalized in different ways. Crossing the borders between reality and fantasy, romanticism and satire, lyricism and caricature, between superego and the subconscious, first-person and third-person narration, the text portrays a heroine who deserts the firm ground of facts, reason and 'real' socialism for the discovery of a repressed psychic reality. Rosalind Polkowsky is an 'Überläuferin', a turncoat, whose act of desertion does not take place in the traditional realm of politics, but in patterns of thinking, feeling and living. The rejection of the concept of a closed identity as part of the status quo is a central part of her desertion. She learns to see the existence of a self that does not conform to established norms of identity as liberating both in a personal and a political context.

Yet, beside the intriguing features of irreverence, provocation, fantasy, humour, mixing of genres, moods, styles and perspectives, the decomposition of the old dream of identity in this novel also displays the influence of binary logic and an unquestioned acceptance of existing forms of sexual desire as a 'natural' rather than socially constructed aspect of subjectivity. Thus the text is as contradictory, ambiguous and without closure as the form of the multiple, heterogeneous self it suggests.[14]

III

Christa Wolf demonstrates an entirely different connection between subjectivity and GDR politics in *Sommerstück*. *Sommerstück* is a moving elegy on the lost hopes of a generation of socialists. It tries at the same time to hold on to the Utopian aspect of these hopes, performing *Erinnerungsarbeit* in the Blochian sense,[15] comprising both retrospective and prospective aspects. A group of friends, pushed to the edges of GDR society, have created an island for themselves by enjoying the intense though momentary feeling of fulfilled life which a summer in the country with like-minded people offered them. The narration of this memory is to demonstrate 'daß, wonach wir uns sehnen, als Möglichkeit in uns angelegt ist' (p. 160). That is, in face of the failing of the Utopian concept of socialism in the realm of politics, the Utopian idea itself is preserved by assessing fleeting moments in private life as proof of the potential of human beings for achieving harmony for the whole of society.

Although *Sommerstück* largely avoids first-person narration and tries to evoke the communal experience by shifting inner monologues and figural narration, alternating with first-person *plural* narration, some characters are more equal than others in this presentation. The figure Ellen, obviously the alter ego of the author, is developed as the most complex and positive, as well as the strongest, character. Ellen recognizes patriarchal structures as part of her oppression: 'die rechthaberischen kleinen Männer nahmen historische Dimension an, sie mußte ihnen entgegentreten und ihnen den Mund verbieten' (p. 78). But she classes her action in this sphere as 'Ersatzbefriedigung' (p. 78) for an opposition to state politics for which she does not see any opportunity.

Within Wolf's text only Ellen's subjectivity is related to language and to the historical development of the GDR, whereas other conflict-ridden characters are portrayed in a psychological, but not historical, causal nexus. Ellen overcomes the temporary destruction of her self-confidence by gaining self-knowledge and by freeing herself from the values of her society which she once shared:

> Daß sie sich nicht mehr wie ein von falschen Wörtern und Vorstellungen besetztes Land vorkam. Scham spricht nicht. Sonst müßte sie sagen: Ein mit eigener Zustimmung, aus eigenem freien Willen besetztes Land. Am allersichersten Ort hatte die fremde Macht, die Gewalt über sie gehabt hatte, sich vor ihr versteckt gehalten: in ihren Augen. So daß die fremde Macht mit meinen Augen sah, durch mich selbst, dachte Ellen. Und keiner des anderen, aber ich auch meiner selbst nicht gewahr werden konnte. Und daß ich denken mußte, den Femdkörper von mir abzutrennen, würde mich zerreißen. (p. 137)

By comparing the self to a country, and language and ideology to an occupying army, the assumption is made of an essential self that is separable from external influences. Once erroneously perceived as parts of the subject, the latter are now called 'fremde Macht' and 'Fremdkörper', thus echoing terminology of the Romantic period in which the other was first explored as a repressed aspect of the self.[16] However, as I have argued in more detail in another paper on *Sommerstück*,[17] the Romantic discovery is here reversed by a neat separation of the self from the foreign power, and thus the idea of a harmonious, noble, true self, modelled on classicism, is regained.

Wolf's *Sommerstück* and Maron's *Die Überläuferin* both depict an individual gaining insight into the cultural construction of her identity and overcoming its limitations, at least momentarily or on the level of fantasy. Thus they map out potentially liberated identity.

Both in Maron's and Wolf's texts, concepts of identity are developed against the demands of a corrupt political system for conformity in its citizens. But these concepts are positioned at opposite ends of the spectrum of possibilities.

Wolf develops through the protagonist Ellen what Lacan thought women were not capable of when he claimed 'LA femme n'existe pas'. She posits an imaginary identity towards which to strive. It is the closed, homogeneous, idealized identity which enlarges the subject and is the prerequisite for concepts like free will, sovereignty of the subject, and truth. Thus Wolf claims the idealist position of the transcendental subject for women, who have so far been excluded from that position.

Maron's novel subverts the demand for conformity by denouncing the concept of a closed identity itself as being part of the system of conformity. The text explores the liberating potential of the multi-facetedness of the female subject.

IV

While both Maron and Wolf portray the individual as potentially capable of becoming 'master' of her life, and develop positivized concepts of identity against the background of political oppression, the West German writers Helke Sander and Uta Treder examine female subjectivity primarily within the patriarchal structures of apparently ordinary everyday life, without creating concrete images of liberation. They both use the genre of the short story and emphasize those aspects of subjectivity that women have in common with other women. In film maker Helke Sander's literary debut, *Die Geschichten der drei Damen K.*, it is the fairly small group of West German feminist intellectuals of the late 1980s whose collective, yet not homogeneous, subjectivity is depicted. The text obviously alludes to Brecht's *Geschichten von Herrn Keuner*,[18] who is often just called Herr K. Brecht's stories teach a new morality in laconic parables. Herr K is cool, superior in intellect to those around him, surprising in his conclusions, wily — an abstraction rather than a rounded character, thus retaining an air of anonymity. He advocates a materialist view of the world, subverting idealist notions of truth, incorruptability, nobility, goodness, and uprightness.

Sander takes up the cool laconic tone of Brecht in most of her stories,[19] but otherwise makes decisive changes which are due to the fact
that 'K' here is female.

First of all, the unified male subject is replaced by three female
ones. Like Brecht, Sander uses third-person narration, but she places her
parables within a framework story which passes off the three Frau Ks as
the 'originators' of these stories. However, though each of Sander's three
Frau Ks has reached a high level of intellectual insight and professional
success, they are virtually indistinguishable from each other in the text.
They are not, and cannot be, truly original authors, for, both privately
and professionally, women are prevented from taking the position of a
unique subject. Their object position in patriarchal society makes their
experiences interchangeable, anonymous. Thus a collective female condition or identity precedes any individual 'identity' women may develop. In discussing their stories in the framework story the three Frau Ks
gain insight into this condition and into the different paradigms of moral
judgement in men and women which persist even after a generation of
feminism.[20]

Then, secondly, Sander's three Frau Ks are not serene spectators,
as Brecht's Herr K was. They suffer from a split between self-assurance
and vulnerability. Herr K's subject position is such an unquestioned prerequisite that it does not even have to be mentioned. Yet it presupposes
female submission, as becomes obvious in a story which, on the surface,
does not mention gender at all. Let me remind you what happens 'Wenn
Herr K. einen Menschen liebte':

> "Was tun Sie", wurde Herr K. gefragt, "wenn Sie einen Menschen lieben?" "Ich
> mache einen Entwurf von ihm", sagte Herr K., "und sorge, daß er ihm ähnlich
> wird." "Wer? Der Entwurf?" "Nein", sagte Herr K., "der Mensch."[21]

Of course we all know by now that this is not a brilliant revolutionary
idea of Brecht's, but exactly what men have always done to women:
made an image of them and by the 'gentle' pressures of patriarchal
society forced them to conform to the male image.

The fact that the implied gender positions of Herr K's parable are
not reversible is shown by the experiences of the three Frau Ks. Their
love for men does not result in men rising to women's ideas of partner-
ship and trust but, on the contrary, in men betraying women. This betrayal is narrated with sharp wit, emphasizing the insight gained from
men's behaviour rather than deploring the suffering of the victim. Thus,

for example, when Frau K, after having been left by her lover, reads through a life insurance policy he had negotiated for her, she discovers: 'Die Bedingungen waren so, daß der Freund im Falle ihres Todes die Prämie bekommen würde. Sollte sie aber leben, dann würde ihr das Geld im Alter von 85 Jahren ausbezahlt' (p. 20).

The three Frau Ks are survivors, there will be no 'Todesarten' for them.[22] But, lacking the Olympian serenity of Herr K, they get badly bruised. This is in spite of their intellectual insight into the power politics of gender, and, to a large extent, even because of their insight and self-assurance, which men find threatening, having been used for centuries to Herr K's model of loving.

Thirdly, the three Frau K's, even though they have developed a distance with regard to patriarchal structures of thought and behaviour, are by no means as free from these structures as Brecht's Herr K was from transcendental idealism. The Frau K with the life-insurance policy, for example, in spite of being a successful businesswoman, falls into the trap of traditional gender roles and thus co-operates in her own victimization when she lets her friend negotiate her policy for her:

> Dankbar saß sie zwischen den beiden Männern im Büro, die ihr das Gefühl gaben, das für sie Beste auszuhandeln [...] Breit gab sie sich dem Gefühl hin, wie herrlich es sei, diesen Mann zur Seite zu haben, der ihr das alles abnahm. Überwältigt lächelte sie ab und zu geradezu dämlich in beider Richtung. Sie war prallvoll mit Zuneigung und setzte ihn als Erben im Falle ihres Todes ein. (p. 19)

Sander refuses the idealization, aggrandizement, and perfection of Brecht's concept of Herr K. Her Frau Ks are not sages but women who have fought against the limitations of patriarchal femininity without gaining happiness, recognition, or even complete inner independence from patriarchal patterns. Their anonymity consists in their common vulnerability to patriarchy, not in the absence of vulnerability.

As readers we gain insight from Frau K's mistakes, not from her infallibility. But neither she nor the other Frau Ks are closed models of so-called false consciousness à la Mutter Courage. The Frau Ks do have a lot of insight, yet emotions and insight are wittily shown to be at odds. Why? What the Frau Ks discover in the discussion of their stories is the fourth dimension of Freudian psychoanalysis, the agency of an 'Über-Er' (p. 146) in them, which brings about the heterogeneity of their subjectivity.

Theoretically, an overcoming of patriarchy would lead to the abolition of the 'Über-Er', and thus heterogeneity could become homogeneity. But Sander's self-ironic and antiheroic style of writing does not allow one to deduce such a purist solution from her analysis of the status quo. Rather, its wry wit alerts the reader to incongruities and contradictions which are not readily dissolved in the simplicity of a homogeneous concept of self.

V

While Sander highlights the collective aspect of female subjectivity by depersonalizing her three protagonists, Uta Treder describes extremely idiosyncratic, often visionary or surreal, experiences, in her first collection of short stories, *Luna Aelion*. Yet by her subtle narrative technique she manages to illuminate collective aspects of female subjectivity in protagonists of very different cultural backgrounds, ranging from an old Greek Jewess under the Nazi occupation, to a heart surgeon, an Italian housewife and a Muslim teenager from a desert town. In all her stories Treder explores women's rebellion against the restrictions in their lives. The protagonists' deaths are often the only form of liberation that is open to their radical demands — deaths which are generally not described directly, but have to be inferred from the widening gap between the women's inner and outer lives and from the metaphors used to depict this development. I shall exemplify the complexity of Treder's treatment of female subjectivity by analysing one of her stories in some detail.

'Augen Blicke' begins with a female voice, speaking with vibrating immediacy about another woman's glance at her. Internal focalization gives us the impression of listening to thoughts being formulated at the moment of greatest emotional disturbance. The first-person narrator feels her identity dissolve under this glance.

Only by and by do we learn that this probing glance is that of a woman in a painting and that the setting of this eerie communication is that of the classical ghost story: a room in a castle by the seaside where the narrator spends one night as the guest of a countess. The narrator, who at times gains enough distance to summarize and analyse her life and her current persecution by the woman in the painting, identifies the latter as a 'Ritterfräulein' (a medieval noblewoman), who scrutinizes the modern woman's life for something that late medieval living conditions had denied her:

> Wen hat sie in ihrem Leben so angeblickt, wie sie mich anblickt? Wen hätte sie so ansehen wollen, wen hätte sie mit ihren Augen verfolgen wollen, wie sie mich verfolgt, wenn es der Sitte ihrer Zeit entsprochen hätte, die Augen auf das Objekt des Begehrens zu heften? [...] Mit der Schamlosigkeit ihres Krähenblicks nimmt sie sich mehr als dreihundert Jahre nach ihrem Tod, was ihr das Schicksal vorenthalten hat: An mir beginnt sie die Reinschrift ihres Lebens. (p. 33)

The term patriarchy is never used in this story, yet the 'fate' which had deprived the 'older' woman of the kind of life she desired doubtlessly refers to social restrictions on women. Her interest in the bathroom rituals of the 'younger' woman hints at the historical change (or lack of it) of female living conditions that is at issue here. But the contemporary woman's life, in spite of hygiene, travel and work, does not represent fulfilment either, as becomes clear from the *Ritterfräulein*'s scrutiny: 'Ihre Augen halten Gerichtstag in mir. [...] Nichts hält vor ihrem Blick stand' (pp. 33—4).

By projecting the narrator's own repressed expectations of life onto the glance of a painted *Ritterfräulein*, the story not only dramatizes a woman's split consciousness; it also provides female subjectivity with a historical depth and a relative standard for one to judge it by. If the narrator has to admit that she has realized as little of her desires as a *Ritterfräulein*, then her life falls out of the frame it seemed to be held in: 'Ich bin ganz haltlos, alles ist ganz haltlos' (p. 34).

The protagonist's desire to destroy the meaninglessness of her life is again projected onto the *Ritterfräulein*: 'Sie setzt mein Herz unter Wasser, es soll ertrinken, ersaufen wie Vieh [...] Sie will, daß ich verrecke unter ihrem begehrenden Blick, diese Totschlägerin' (p. 34). The outcome of this schizophrenic experience is to be inferred by the reader, to whom the prominent use of water metaphors foreshadows the implied consequences.

Appended to the protagonist's narration is the countess's sober report to the police about the disappearance of her guest, the publisher's editor Sybille Haffner, and about some errors of perception in Frau Haffner's notes on her experience. Thus the reader is given some hints as to the psychic reality which determined the protagonist's experience, without, however, being provided with a 'case history' that would completely explain the mysteries of the story. It is this openness which constitutes the fascination of Treder's style of writing: gaps that open up meaning instead of fixing it.

Following the tradition of Hoffmann and Poe, Treder in 'Augen Blicke' transposes their subject of a dissociation of identity to a woman. In this and her other stories, Treder concentrates on women's limited possibilities for living the life they want to live. She makes us aware of these limitations by showing, on a pre-discursive level, how they are inscribed in women's bodies. Her stories do not directly show a positivized concept of female identity, but rather explore different ways in which women experience and deal with restrictions. Yet the radical 'solution' of death, which her protagonists are not only forced into but also so often choose, seems to indicate a notion of purity and an ideal of homogeneity that are reminiscent of concepts of identity in eighteenth-century German classicism and in Wolf's *Kassandra*.[23] Death tragically confirms the impossibility for women of developing an identity for which there would be social space, and thus argues, *ex negativo*, for the need to develop such space.

VI

While Treder explores on a pre-rational level women's limited space for developing their identities, using indirect, fantastic, and poetic means, Sander presents sober, sharp and funny accounts of women's encounters with men, appealing to her readers' wit and reason. Neither of the two Western writers develops a concrete, positive image of female identity as do the two GDR writers, who set the question of identity primarily against the background of direct political oppression. Sander and Treder explore the complexities and problems of female subjectivity, the structural impossibility of female self-realization, in the much more diffuse context of 'ordinary' patriarchy, as it manifests itself in relations with lovers, husbands, employers, and in deeply entrenched patterns of behaviour, feeling and thinking. Readers will have to deduce for themselves what path to take to overcome the restrictions on female identity presented by the two writers. Yet the trajectory of their style of writing seems to point readers to search in opposite directions. The notion of tragedy and purity that is poetically expressed through the death of Treder's heroines, suggests, *ex negativo*, ideas of a closed, true, homogeneous self that women should one day be able to realize. Concentrating on women's encounters with patriarchy and their determination to survive within it in a laconic, wry style, Sander, on the other hand, implies a more down-to-earth view of identity: 'eine Vision von Autonomie' (p. 101) is dialectically linked to a keen awareness of women's heterogeneous modes of feeling, thus alerting the reader to the impossibility of ever achieving a 'simple' closed identity, yet pointing to the necessity of woman gaining both insight into her situation and more social space.

The different degrees of political oppression of the individual in the contexts of East and West seem to be directly related to the degree to which writers develop concrete, positive counter-ideals of identity (in the East) or suggest alternatives *ex negativo* (in the West).

The East German writers discussed here also differ from the West Germans in their attempts to set the genesis of their protagonists' identity crisis in a historical political context. For forty years of socialism, moving within a lifetime from its Utopian claim to create the new human being in a new society to its bureaucratic ossification, have provided the experience of rapid and radical changes in historical perspectives on society and the individual's role in it. This concrete historical approach to the question of identity adds insight which is not provided by the post-structuralist and object-relations theories mentioned at the beginning of my paper.

By contrast, the West German texts are characterized not only by a lack of concrete Utopian ideals, but also by a primarily synchronic rather than diachronic exploration. Even texts that cover a narrated time of several years do not show a concrete historical perspective comparable to that in the GDR texts. They explore aspects of female subjectivity in a sphere that is little affected by political change: the pre-discursive, subconscious, habitual sphere of everyday life. Lacking the belief in a Utopia, the West German writers tend to concentrate on exposing the continuity in the crippling conditions of female subjectivity beneath a veneer of superficial changes, and thus to suggest indirectly the need for more radical change. What they add to theoretical discussions of the reproduction of gendered identity is a refined awareness of the forms and conflicts of female identity in adult life. For specific literary ways of portraying reality (fantasy, satire, changes in perspective and time level, diffusion or depersonlization of identity etc.) achieve a more complex, suggestive and vivid view of contemporary female identity than theories do, in both East and West German texts.

Yet, beyond the Utopian outlook and the concrete historicity which differentiates East and West German writers, in another respect, contemporary problems of identity prove to be international, or at least transpolitical. Women writers in East and West are attracted by both heterogeneous and homogeneous concepts of identity. These concepts seem to be less connected with political reality than with a basic attitude to life, manifesting itself in styles of writing. The homogeneous concept of identity seems to stem from an idealist, purist point of view and to find expression in elegiac or lyrical prose, both in novel form and in short stories (Wolf and Treder). The heterogeneous concept tends to be connected with a more irreverent, sceptical attitude to life that is conveyed by satire and self-mockery (Maron and Sander).

In Wolf, the combination of homogeneity and positive Utopia leads to a revival of humanist concepts whose simplicity and purity are experienced by many as a less and less adequate view of the world to-day. Hence perhaps the increased attacks recently on Wolf's hitherto acclaimed Utopian vision and the growing interest in younger GDR writers like Maron who present a more heterogeneous world view (both in content and form).

Yet, as all the texts discussed in the paper testify, the desire for homogeneity does not simply disappear in a reality that is experienced as more and more fragmented. What distinguishes these texts from each other is the way they treat this desire and the function they attribute to it along a spectrum of possibilities reaching from that of an ideal to strive for at all costs, to that of a model that can no longer cope with the contradictions within the subject and the world.

However, even among texts that imply or state the conservative ideal of a homogeneous identity there may be great differences with regard to openness or closure. As Treder's fascinating stories prove, the implied concept of a homogeneous identity may nevertheless be combined with a narrative strategy that leaves plenty of room for conjecture, suggestion, imagination, contradiction, and showing rather than teaching, thus avoiding closure. Texts that argue for a heterogeneous concept of identity may, on the other hand, contain structures of binary opposition, i.e. closure (like Maron's novel). This should remind us that in literary analysis, too, we need to explore the existence of a heterogeneity of textual strategies, instead of evening out tensions and contradictions between them in order to subsume a text under a single explanatory model within a system of binary oppositions.

NOTES

I would like to thank Liselotte Glage, Chris Lyons, and Moray McGowan for comments on an earlier version of this paper. RS.

1 The best-known feminist representatives of this school are Hélène Cixous, Luce Irigaray and Julia Kristeva. See Cixous: 'Schreiben, Femininität, Veränderung', *Alternative*, nos 108/109, June/August 1976, pp. 134—47; Cixous: *Die unendliche Zirkulation des Begehrens*, Berlin, 1977; Cixous: *Weiblichkeit in der Schrift*, Berlin, 1980; Irigaray: *Das Geschlecht, das nicht eins ist*, Berlin, 1979; Irigaray: *Speculum. Spiegel des anderen Geschlechts*, Frankfurt/Main, 1980; Kristeva: *Die Revolution der poetischen Sprache*, Frankfurt/Main, 1978.

2 See Nancy Chodorow: *The Reproduction of Mothering. Psychoanalysis and the Sociology of Gender*, Berkeley, 1978; Carol Gilligan: *In a Different Voice. Psychological Theory and Women's Development*, Cambridge/Mass., 1982.

3 For criticisms of one or both schools, see Joan W. Scott: 'Gender: A Useful Category of Historical Analysis', *American Historical Review*, vol. 91, no. 5, 1986, pp. 1053—75; Rosalind Ann Jones: 'Writing the body: toward an understanding of *l'écriture féminine*' in Deborah Rosenfelt and Judith Newton (eds): *Feminist Criticism and Social Change*, London, 1985, pp. 86-101; Teresa de Lauretis: *Alice Doesn't. Feminism, Semiotics, Cinema*, Bloomington, 1984; Jill Conway, Susan C. Bourque, Joan W. Scott: 'Introduction: The Concept of Gender', *Daedalus*, vol. 116, no. 4, Fall 1987, pp. xxi—xxx; Janet Sayers: *Sexual Contradictions. Psychology, Psychanalysis, and Feminism*, London, 1986; Nancy K. Miller: 'Changing the Subject: Authorship, Writing and the Reader' in Teresa de Lauretis (ed.): *Feminist Studies/Critical Studies*, Bloomington, 1986, pp. 102—20; Regine Othmer-Vetter: '"Muttern" und das Erbe der Väter. Eine neuere Affäre zwischen Feminismus und Psychoanalyse?', *Feministische Studien*, vol. 7, no. 2, November 1989, pp. 99—106. For a general criticism of the post-structuralist 'abolition' of the subject in texts, see Andreas Huyssen: 'Postmoderne — eine amerikanische Internationale?' in Andreas Huyssen and Klaus R. Scherpe (eds): *Postmoderne. Zeichen eines kulturellen Wandels*, Reinbek, 1986, pp. 13—44, esp. p. 38; R. Radhakrishan: 'Feminist historiography and post-structuralist thought. Intersections and departures' in Elizabeth Meese and Alice Parker (eds): *The Difference Within. Feminism and Critical Theory*, Amsterdam, 1989, pp. 189—205.

4 References in the text are to Monika Maron: *Die Überläuferin*, Frankfurt/Main, 1988; Christa Wolf: *Sommerstück*, Frankfurt/Main, 1989; Helke Sander: *Die Geschichten der drei Damen K.*, Munich, 5th edn, 1988; Uta Treder: *Luna Aelion. Erzählungen*, Munich, 1989.

5 See also pp. 23, 30 and 48.

6 Cf. Martha saying, 'das sei ihr Privileg als Frau, eine Prostituierte werden' (p. 43). Rosalind blames her gender (and her class) for her feelings of inferiority to her husband Bruno. In this context gender is defined both in terms of culture ('das Gerede von Jugend' with regard to women, but not to men) and nature ('Hormone', p. 81). See also p. 112 on the exclusion of women from patriarchal culture for thousands of years.

7 Clairchen functions repeatedly as a supporter of resistance to social brainwashing when Rosalind feels prone to succumb to its pressures. See als pp. 177—80 when Rosalind begins to believe the accusations of the man in red uniform that her fantasies of violence show her desire to cause violence — rather than expressing her fear. Clairchen saves her from internalizing the guilt with which society tries to inculcate her, and thus functions as a reliable dissident voice.

8 See Ursula Mahrenholz: 'Der weiße Rabe fliegt. Zum Künstlerinnenroman im 20. Jahrhundert' in Gisela Brinker-Gabler (ed.): *Deutsche Literatur von Frauen*, 2 vols, Munich,

1988, vol. 2, pp. 445—59. Mahrenholz interprets *Die Überläuferin* as a simple search for a unified identity in which the protagonist overcomes the split in her identity by uniting the conformist, rational aspect of self (embodied in Rosalind) with the anarchic, fantastic, emotional one (embodied in her alter ego Martha). Mahrenholz neglects the fact that the concept of a closed identity is itself being questioned in the novel and shown as supporting the status quo.

9 An interesting point of comparison is offered in Gisela Shaw's disussion of Volker Braun's *Bodenloser Satz*, esp. pp. 89—90 above.

10 See also the preparation for this discovery in the breaking down of the separate identities of Rosalind and Martha through shifting pronouns on pp. 157—8, 160, 163.

11 It is not the sadomasochistic fantasies themselves which I view as problematic, but rather their structural position in the narrative. While other modes of feeling and behaviour are critically examined as socially constructed, the novel presents sadomasochistic modes of feeling simply as nature which needs to be freed from social constraints. Submission and masochism also appear as 'natural' aspects of female sexuality earlier in the novel, when Rosalind's rational control of her physical desire is portrayed. Her head suppresses 'das ergebene, zu masochistischen Empfindungen neigende Wesen des Körpers' and hardly ever allows her the 'Lust [...] der Unterwerfung' (p. 119). For a subtle analysis (in the framework of object-relations theory) of sadomasochistic fantasies as an aspect of the search for self, see Jessica Benjamin: 'Die Fesseln der Liebe: Zur Bedeutung der Unterwerfung in erotischen Beziehungen', *Feministische Studien*, vol. 4, no. 2, November 1985, pp. 10—33. In recent work on fantasy literature it has been posited that 'crossing the boundaries of gender as part of the act of reading and fantasizing' plays an important role (Cora Kaplan: '*The Thorn Birds*: fiction, fantasy, femininity' in Victor Burgin, James Donald, Cora Kaplan (eds): *Formations of Fantasy*, London, 1986, p. 151). Kaplan values this as liberating and argues that one should not assume a straightforward identification of the female reader with the often passive heroine. The observation that the female reader also identifies with male characters is certainly true and does not only apply to fantasy literature. Indeed, the implied reader in most literary texts is constructed as male, and a woman has to adopt a male position in order to appreciate the text. Women writers themselves have identified with the male position to such an extent that they have often used a male 'I' since a female 'I' did not seem to represent the human condition. I would argue, therefore, that crossing the boundaries of gender during the act of reading and fantasizing is not liberating in itself unless gender stereotypes are deconstructed. See also Judith Fetterley: *The Resisting Reader: A Feminist Approach to American Fiction*, Bloomington, 1978.

12 The novel's last sentence ('Den Mund weit öffnen und das Wasser in sich hineinlaufen lassen, naß werden, dachte sie, vom Regen naß werden, ja, das wäre schön.' p. 221) recalls Martha's experience of a rainstorm ('Ich öffnete den Mund, ließ das Wasser in mich hineinlaufen.' p. 215) which preceded her ecstatic vision of an unrepressed self.

13 The very conventionality of the metaphors, however, betrays the fact that a modern experience has not yet found adequate expression and that it still shows the traces of the old longing for a harmony between body and soul, i.e. wholeness, closed identity. Yet it is important to note that here the *momentary* aspect of the experience of harmony and the development of *all* aspects of identity are stressed. That is, the fulfilled self is envisaged, not as a stable identity, achieved by eliminating and overcoming aspects that do not fit into a homogenous concept, but as temporary ecstasy, due to an unfolding of all aspects, experienced as a rare sense of balance between heterogeneous facets of self.

14 An interesting comparison is offered by Thomas Beckermann's discussion of *Die Überläuferin*, pp. 99—101.

15 See Ernst Bloch: 'Entdeckung des Noch-Nicht-Bewußten oder der Dämmerung nach Vorwärts' in chapter 15 of his *Das Prinzip Hoffnung*, Gesamtausgabe, Frankfurt/Main, 1959, vol. V, pp. 129—203, esp. pp. 160f.: 'Das fortgeschrittenste Bewußtsein arbeitet derart auch in der Erinnerung und Vergessenheit nicht als in einem abgesunkenen und so geschlossenen Raum, sondern in einem offenen, im Raum des Prozesses und seiner Front. Dieser Raum aber ist ausschließlich mit Dämmerung nach vorwärts erfüllt, auch noch in seinen Exempeln aus fortbedeutender Vergangenheit; er ist mit bewußtseinsfähiger, gewußtseinsfähiger Lebendigkeit eines Noch-Nicht-Seins gefüllt.' See also the

discussion of Blochian thinking in Wolf's work in Andreas Huyssen: 'Auf den Spuren Ernst Blochs. Nachdenken über Christa Wolf' in Klaus Sauer (ed.): *Christa Wolf. Materialienbuch*, Darmstadt, 1979, pp. 81—97. Huyssen draws attention to the lack of mediation between individual self-actualization and social Utopia in both Bloch and Wolf. *Sommerstück* is discussed in relation to Sarah Kirsch's *Allerlei-Rauh* by Peter Graves (pp. 129—36 above) and is also mentioned by Joseph Pischel in his discussion of the 'loss of Utopia' (esp. pp. 119—22 above); Joseph Pischel points inter alia to Bloch's influence on Wolf.

16 See especially E. T. A. Hoffmann: 'Der Sandmann' in *Fantasie- und Nachtstücke*, Munich 1976, pp. 331—63.
17 Ricarda Schmidt: 'Die Dialektik zwischen Wort und Wirklichkeit, dem Selbst und dem Fremden in Christa Wolfs *Sommerstück*', a paper given at the Women in German Studies conference at the University of Salford, 11 November 1989. Accepted for publication in *German Life and Letters* (August 1991?).
18 Bertolt Brecht: *Geschichten von Herrn Keuner* in Suhrkamp Verlag and Elisabeth Hauptmann (eds): *Gesammelte Werke*, Frankfurt/Main, 1973, vol. XII, pp. 373—415.
19 There are some exceptions: 'Ausflug mit einem UFO' (pp. 51—87) and 'Ein Brief aus dem Urlaub' (pp. 91—101) are rather drawn out and overtly didactic.
20 See Coral Gilligan: *In a Different Voice...*
21 Brecht: *Geschichten von Herrn Keuner*, p. 386.
22 'Todesarten' is the title Ingeborg Bachmann gave to her planned novel cycle on women's victimization in patriarchy. Of this cycle, she published only *Malina* during her lifetime. The fragments *Der Fall Franza* and *Requiem für Fanny Goldmann* were published posthumously in Christine Koschel, Inge von Weidenbaum, Clemens Münster (eds): *Ingeborg Bachmann: Werke*, Munich, 2nd edn, 1982, vol. III: *Todesarten: Malina und unvollendete Romane*. See also the article by Elizabeth Boa in this volume, pp. 139—53 above.
23 Christa Wolf: *Kassandra*, Darmstadt, 1983.

BOTHO STRAUSS:
FROM IDENTITY CRISIS TO GERMAN *ENNUI*
— WHITHER THE POET?

ARTHUR WILLIAMS

I

It is an interesting and, perhaps, significant fact that none of the twenty-four contributions to this collection has so much as mentioned in passing the name of Botho Strauß; yet Strauß has been one of the most challenging of West German writers for almost two decades. For Volker Hage, Strauß is even 'der für die achtziger Jahre gewiß wichtigste Autor deutscher Sprache'.[1] While the lack of reference to Strauß in the present context might seem unsurprising to those who know only his plays or his earlier prose works, it is far from being the case that he has had nothing of relevance to say on the contemporary situation in Germany. The problems arising from the division of Germany for writers and German culture, the foreshortening and obscuring of cultural perspectives, the distortions and dangers arising from the continuing influence of the Nazi past, the escapist, unqualified espousal of commercial and, most insidiously, technological values which has placed in jeopardy a future in which new voices, new values and new language can flourish — all of this is central to Strauß's work from at least the end of the 1970s. No writer has undertaken a more thorough stock-taking of the German cultural household and, certainly, no writer anticipated more of the events of the past decade, in particular the *Historikerstreit* and the fall of the Berlin Wall, than Strauß.[2]

Strauß had, in fact, already consigned the Berlin Wall to archaeological time several months before the crucial events of 1989. At the same time he had also apparently reached a decision about his own future, namely that he would now be silent.[3] I refer to his small volume *Fragmente der Undeutlichkeit* (reviewed in *Die Zeit* on 6 October 1989),[4] the second of whose two short pieces is entitled 'Sigé' (Strauß offers the complex definition: 'Sigé ist das Schweigen der Ideen. Die Stätte. Der Schweigende, der Wächter') which ends with the poet indicating that his work has been a brief moment of time, his muse, it would appear, is leaving him and he himself preparing for silence: 'Dies aufrechte Gesicht steht blicklos und taub. Und was ich noch sage, bringt redlich die eigene Stille hervor.'[5] One could devoutly wish that some of Germany's foremost men of words, who are so concerned about the 'aufrechter Gang' of others and who provided so much raw material for the media over the period of change, might learn from their more troubled colleague.

It is worth pondering why such an obviously important figure has so completely escaped mention in this volume, particularly when not only does he seem to have anticipated crucial developments and events, but also when his work has much in common with that of writers given individual consideration here, above all, it seems to the present writer, representatives of GDR literature (particularly Volker Braun, Christoph Hein and Heiner Müller, but also Monika Maron and the younger poets). Firstly, Strauß seems to have made most of his work deliberately, not to say perversely, difficult at one level or another: his plays systematically challenge the director to scale new heights of technical virtuosity,[6] all but his earliest prose works require linguistic and reading skills that were more common in an earlier age,[7] and his poetry responds to nothing short of an exhausting and not always pleasurable dual application of tough exegesis and elastic imagination. Strauß is always fiercely and uncompromisingly intellectual, to the point where the abstruse tends to become opaque and the obvious all but obscure. Secondly, Strauß has never become involved in the game of journalistic tiddlywinks with such prefabricated counters as *Vaterland*, *Muttersprache*, and *Kulturnation*, and while much of his intellectual currency is of marked German provenance, he tends to search out cultural assets in a broad geographical and chronological framework.[8] Thirdly, Strauß rigorously eschews overt personal and autobiographical dimensions in his work and fundamentally abjures anything that could be even remotely construed as a contribution to the political debate.[9] While his poetic vision anticipated the *Historikerstreit* of the mid-1980s, his work was not part of it and made no direct contribution to it.[10] Similarly, nothing in his work will allow it to be bracketed with the *Literatenstreit* of the turn of the decade — except as a contrasting example of abstinence.

And yet, while the literary world that Strauß occupies is idiosyncratic, it relates fundamentally to life and events in contemporary Germany. Strauß gives the impression of someone fighting for his intellectual and creative life in a way that is reminiscent of Thomas Mann at the time of the First World War, although he is more detached (at least artistically) from current events than was Mann, whom Strauß once set out to research,[11] at the time of his *Betrachtungen eines Unpolitischen*,[12] and he does display a degree of awareness that Mann would, perhaps, have envied. Mann emerged from his bleak years of stock-taking and soul-searching with the strength (and knowledge) to face the even greater challenge of the worst period of German history — although he was unable later to face the greatest challenge of the invitation to return to the mutilated and mutated land of his birth. It remains to be seen whether the attachment of Strauß's birthplace (Naumburg/Saale) to the Germany he has grown up in will force him to revise his perspectives and help him to a new phase of creativity, just as it remains to be seen whether the next phase of German literature will belong to a generation of writers born in various parts of their now united fatherland but with common problems to face in relation to, for example, equality between the sexes,[13] the ecological challenge,[14] the reappraisal of the German and European cultural heritage (at last common again to East and West), the significance and sanctity of the individual,[15] the liberation of German literature and language from the dead weight of the recent and immediate past.[16] The question, for Strauß, is not whether the womb is still fertile in the Brechtian sense, whether the nightmares of Grass's Oskar, Müller's *Germania*, his own Grit and his 'Liebeslicht' are still seriously to be feared,[17] but rather whether the process of cultural cloning that characterizes contemporary West German life and the cultural lobotomy that threatens the thinking mind of the former GDR, which has proved itself much more resilient than many West German observers admit, will together render the dual union of the enlarged *Vaterland* and the relatively intact *Muttersprache* infertile, robbing literature and poetry of their potency for the foreseeable future. The question for Strauß, in his West German context, seems to be whether Sascha Anderson's 'retorte' (see p. 419 above) will itself turn out to be nothing better than an environmentally friendly disposable bottle.

II

Strauß's poetic silence, if one examines closely the image quoted above (p. 450), could be at least as much the product of the unseeing and unhearing public as of his own loss of speech, and at this level may be a sign of his despair at negative responses to his work. More fundamentally, it seems clear that his prolonged contemplation of the German condition, which started in the early 1970s as a problem of identity and seemed at times to reach moments of optimism, has brought him to a state of boredom, irritation and sterility. Writers who are the subject of much of this volume have been contributors, indeed major contributors to that German condition. These writers are part of Strauß's cultural heritage, his works reflect their literary world.[18] Strauß often uses literary allusion to bring his own work closer to reality, perhaps suggesting that the past lives on in the present in some measure by dint of its role in works of literature which are themselves constituents of present reality. The German Question is very much the problem of the generation before his; his dilemma is to establish how and where he and his generation fit in.[19] He drafts a position in a few lines in *Diese Erinnerung an einen, der nur einen Tag zu Gast war*:

> Jetzt erst entsteht uns —
> befreit uns von Scham die *eigene* Vergangenheit.
> Wir prüfen die Fotos, die Kleider, die Namen.
> Nichts war klein, keines entbehrlich.
> Nichts ist ruchlos vergangen,
> sondern wir wissen, fast plötzlich,
> daß es so gut war, das Unsere uns angemessen,
> weder dürftig noch blutig.[20]

Even so, his current position seems to suggest that he has failed to find his niche, that he sees his place and time as interim, without its own specific task, with no real identity of its own and with no voice unmistakably its own.[21] If he is at all representative (and his stock-taking, like that of Thomas Mann in *Betrachtungen eines Unpolitischen*, might fairly be regarded as at once personal and vicarious), then what Strauß has created is an image of an interim period, an interim generation: he speaks of a 'Zwischenzeit',[22] we might add the term 'Zwischengeneration', and we should perhaps not shy away either from recalling the term so often used in West Germany in recent decades of the 'verlorene Generation' — he is close to writers discussed above by Hella Ehlers (esp. pp. 233—8) and Julian Preece (esp. pp. 303—8).

It is tempting already to see the history of the GDR as a 'Zwischenzeit'; it will perhaps not be so long before harsh reality and, hopefully, a remnant of humane modesty will bring the former Federal

Republic to view itself as equally overtaken by history — only the unfortunate modus *operandi* of unification by invocation of Article 23 of the West German Basic Law,[23] its interim constitution, has prevented the examination of the more fundamental question of the modus *vivendi*.[24] Strauß had drawn his own conclusion about the interim state of the interim West German state certainly by the time of writing *Der junge Mann*, published in 1984, and his works of relevance since, the long poem *Diese Erinnerung an einen, der nur einen Tag zu Gast war* and the *Fragmente der Undeutlichkeit*, serve only to underline his conviction that the fixation about the recent past coupled with slavish worship of present wealth and luxury is little short of a stranglehold on Germany and German creative and intellectual life. While he undoubtedly pays tribute to his older contemporaries by mirroring their preoccupations in the motifs of his own works, the question he asks is how Germany is to break free of the grip of the past and find the life and energy to cope with the very real, but different problems of a future now becoming increasingly clear to us.

What is intriguing and significant about Strauß's view of his time is the perspective: all is at once keenly felt and yet is observed as from a great distance: 'Was war? Was in der Zwischenzeit? In der Zeit zwischen Zehe und Ferse [...] unser Leben — die Zwischenzeit — war ein Ereignis auf der untersten, unbestimmbarsten Szene der Materie. Ein Ich, ein Haus, ein Gast. Masselos und ungemessen.'[25] He could be speaking of the human race in the perspective of the universe. However, since the whole burden of his discourse in 'Sigé' concerns the role and voice of the poet[26] and the set of thoughts or fragments is triggered by some architectural ruins which include a wall and a town, 'wo in *zweien* Zertrümmertes und Vergessenes sich wieder ergänzen',[27] the whole piece lives and breathes the atmosphere of a divided land whose division has long been left behind by the march of time.[28]

A few lines later, working towards his second crucial insight, the different male and female perspectives, Strauß conjures up a somewhat bewildering image of a wall breached and the breach healed by people complementing each other, of silent stones speaking with a voice of power and magic. His vision, playing on the dual sense of the the word 'siren', melds harsh reality with myth and cherished dream: 'Die sich ergänzen, schließen die klaffende Lücke im Quaderverband der verfallenen Mauer. Das Schweigen der Steine gesundet. Stille wird zur betörendsten Sirene der Geschichte.' This is followed by what must now appear, particularly when liberated from its immediate context, almost a prophecy of events then soon to occur in his own divided city: 'Die Räume werden stürzen, diese Mauern auseinanderbrechen, gleich, jetzt, beim nächst höheren Herzschlag — wir erreichen die Grenze der Ergänzung, der Vereinbarkeit, da jedes Ding zu gewaltigem Stillstand erschüttert.' Balefully, almost, the man speaks (and one must assume that the attribution of the male role by Strauß, here as elsewhere, is de-liberate[29]): 'Wenn wir es wiederhergestellt haben, so werden wir allein entscheiden, was davon bleibt und was für immer zerstört werden muß.' The words uncannily prefigure so much of the debate now in progress about the future of aspects of GDR society and culture. Nor does Strauß's seer-like vision dissipate at this point, the next fragment contin-ues the thought even more chillingly: 'Ist die Inschrift entziffert, so wird sie für immer unkenntlich gemacht.'[30]

Strauß here acknowledges one of his sources as an Italian book on architecture and mythology,[31] the two realms he consistently links to-gether in his evocation of a timescale that allows a perspective on the German condition. Here, he has linked the idea of the walls through the connotation of silence with his title 'Sigé'. As we have seen, he also re-lates 'Sigé' to the figure of the 'Wächter', a figure that has been with him at least since his first novel, Rumor (1980),[32] and one he associates with watching (from ramparts) distant wars and keeping watch during the night, perhaps uttering a warning but never himself a participant in the events of history.[33] The figure of the 'watchman' evolves over the decade under discussion and becomes Strauß's metaphor for the poet in his time. Before he turns to this, Strauß develops briefly the motif of the differing perceptions of and approaches to history and time of men and women. The 'couple' at the beginning of 'Sigé' drift apart because the woman wants to fracture inexorable linear progression, 'der Weg des zweiten Mals ist der Weg der Genugtuung [...] Jedes Wiedersehen zerbricht einen Zeitpfeil'. Their differences are beginning to separate them, she is freeing herself from his embrace, their traditional roles potentially will be reversed. She says: 'Ich kenne dich nun lange genug, um zu erleben, daß dieses Kennen die fremdeste Macht ist, die je von mir Besitz ergriff'. He is no longer able to look her in the eye (a crucial idea in Der junge Mann, Strauß's novel about the situation of women) and feels that any future Odysseus must stay at home, while Penelope, now relying on his fidelity, 'draußen auf die Spuren ihrer Kindheit und der verlorenen Jugend reiste.'[34]

The problems of the divided homeland are closely interwoven with the problems of a divided human race, of which one half has so far been denied the freedom to develop because of the dominance of the values of the other. Strauß uses the idea of the wall in this context as well. A wall can offer a vantage point for the watchman, but renders him impotent to take direct action; it can also divide two parts that, to be complete and viable, need each other — and we should no forget the simple fact that both German states were republics, in German a feminine noun: it seems almost too obvious that Strauß should show a woman (or is it women?) divided by a wall and, having surmounted it, moving on in harmony. In fact, some of his most significant images of women show them either singing or as perfectly matched and harmonious pairs[35] while his men are either transfixed by history or, like the poet in the *Fragmente*, caught like naughty children on a wall they have scaled but cannot get down from: 'Aber mein Herz [...] saß wie das Kind auf der hohen Mauer, von der es allein nicht wieder herunterkam, die Kehle voll ungefälliger Töne.'[36]

III

One of the major problems which confronts the reader arises because Strauß writes constantly in fragmented forms within which he piles up multifaceted images and references. In *Paare Passanten*, that teeming source of pithy and intriguing phrases, he says: 'Jede Art von sondernder Beschreibung wirkt am Unheil der Zerstreuung und der Überinformation mit, durch das wir ohnehin schon bedroht genung sind',[37] and it is perhaps this fear of the isolated, incomplete and incoherent, the plague of our hypertechnologized world, that drives him to build up his layers of meaning not only thoughout individual works, but also through many different works. The fragmented form suggesting, in contrast to the neatly pre-packaged bytes of information supplied by the electronic media and to more linear narrative forms, that an active reader is expected to (re-)combine the open-ended pieces into associated groups and patterns. This means that the associations he reads into the idea of, for example, the wall are all, once he has created them, present all the time. Often he builds on ideas and metaphors used by others but which are now part of the intellectual currency of the time (in this he is, of course, close to many of his 'postmodern' contemporaries — one thinks perhaps primarily of Peter Handke and, possibly, Patrick Süskind, but also, in the context of this volume, of Thorsten Becker; see pp. 359—70 above). Strauß, it seems to me, is capable of developing such images to the point where they acquire new levels of significance; he is, in this sense, even in his theatre and prose, a poet of stature. In their multi-layered context, his images, provided one does not stifle them by too close an individual examination, are powerful, often overflowing with significance. He forces his reader to hold many fragments in memory in order to create perspective and orientation — even then final certainty and security remain elusive. Strauß, in this sense, is offering his literary works almost as a vaccine against the disease of fragmentation and isolation that threatens the life of contemporary culture and society. His is the eye of the fly, which of course not only perceives images in multiple facets but also facilitates a totally different sense of space and time to that of humans. He had used precisely this image to good effect in *Der junge Mann*.[38]

However, not all of Strauß's repertoire was available to him from the start and none of it has remained static. We can trace a number of developments of relevance to the present discussion if we pick up the individual threads at a sufficiently early point before he begins to weave them into their most complex patterns. It is also the case that Strauß himself was not able to control all of his threads simultaneously and, particularly in the mid-1980s, separated two main strands in order to subject them to adequate literary treatment. Much of the atmosphere and, indeed, the fundamental 'perception' in the plays *Der Park* (1983) and *Die Fremdenführerin* (1986) is closely related to important aspects of *Der junge Mann* and also of both *Diese Erinnerung an einen, der nur einen Tag zu Gast war* and *Fragmente der Undeutlichkeit*, although essentially the three latter occupy quite different territory from the plays and are directly germane to the discussion here, while the two plays are not. The two strands (roughly: the alienation of the the individual in contemporary society and the problem of the role of the poet/writer in the present day) were present together in *Paare Passanten* and were linked together, significantly, by specifically (West) German problems and preoccupations. The separation off, in the two plays, of the first strand to emerge, that treating the virtual impossibility of meaningful relations between the sexes (or simply individuals) in our contemporary 'pre-packaged' society, brought Strauß face to face increasingly not simply with the other major strand, his own role and significance as a poet, but also with the problem of his nationality and culture.[39]

The existential problem for the poet of German nationality is the way the burden of Germany's past forces itself upon him, invading and reducing his creative space. The poet is evicted from his cultural home, he is incapacitated and eventually silenced by the all-pervasive, all-consuming force of this 'German Dilemma': 'Das deutsche Entsetzen der deutsche Selbsthaß die deutsche Leere. Ich spürte Vergangenheit ansteigen wie Hochwasser in mir. Es verwüstete mein Wohnen und zwang mich, auf dem Dach meines Hauses zu biwakieren.'[40] And this from a writer who just four years earlier had placed at the centre of his long poem a passage in which, while he bewails Gemany's divided state, he still looks forward to a glorious 'Reunieren'. The lines are worth quoting in this context:

> Bin ich denn nicht geboren in meinem Vaterland?
>
> >Jena vor uns im lieblichen Tale< — sah ich's nicht früh
> und ging mit dem Vater am Ufer von Saale und Unstrut?
>
> Wann war das und wo?
>
> Kein Deutschland gekannt zeit meines Lebens.
> Zwei fremde Staaten nur, die mir verboten,
> je im Namen eines Volkes der Deutsche zu sein.
> Soviel Geschichte, um so zu enden?
>
> Man spüre einmal: das Herz eines Kleist und
> die Teilung des Lands. Man denke doch: welch ein Reunieren,
> wenn einer, in uns, die Bühne der Geschichte aufschlüg!
>
> Vielleicht, wer deutsch ist, lernt sich ergänzen.
> Und jedes Bruchstück Verständigung
> gleicht einer Zelle im nationellen Geweb,
> die immer den Bauplan des Ganzen enthält.[41]

In 1985 when the work appeared (it was completed in autumn 1984, very close in time and preoccupations to *Der junge Mann*) Strauß was savagely criticized for his choice of words.[42] I shall return to his approach to language below, my intention at this juncture is to emphasize the remarkable change of heart such a short time later and on the brink of the unification he here so fervently desires and almost predicts:

> Wie gut verstand ich: die Not, den Drang einer Zeit, eine Erneuerungs-, Verjüngungs-, Einigungsbewegung im ganzen Volk hervorzubringen [...] Wie gut

> aber verstand ich auch: daß ein solches Anrühren nur ein Fluchtversuch
> meiner bedrängten Ideen darstellte, eine lüsterne Frechheit des ermüdeten
> Geistes, der von seinem eigenen Durcheinander genug hatte, so wie er, falls
> sie je erreicht würde, auch von >Einigung< sehr bald genug hätte.[43]

Lines which perhaps should be taken together with the heart-rending sentence towards the end of 'Sigé': 'Und so könnte ich in jeder Minute vor Scham sterben darüber, was ich in der vorigen annahm zu sein.'[44] What is it that had occasioned this change? And, if he spoke in the early and mid-1980s with the voice of the seer, is it possible that his new mood also contains an element of prophetic truth from which the now united Germany might learn?

IV

It is interesting that Martin Walser (in a very recent article in *Die Zeit*,[45] but written, according to its carefully built in chronology, during spring 1990) has now turned his back on the *Literatenstreit* about Germany, the battle of 'Meinungen' that is the subject of several contributions to this volume,[46] in order to set about finding himself (again? at last?). He ends his article 'endlich [...] allein', with the sun warming his left cheek; the depiction is specific, implying perhaps a Biblical, or even a political allusion. To make his piece end on a rising cadence Walser refers, as evidence of a better literary world, to the two foremost exponents of the postmodern idiom, Peter Handke and Botho Strauß, comparing the latter's poetry (to its advantage) with the song of the blackbird in his garden. Handke, Walser believes, bears witness to the overcoming of 'Meinung'[47] in a book which 'seiner Schönheitsart nach auch vor hundert oder zweihundert Jahren hätte erscheinen können', while he feels that Strauß, at whose ideas this latter quotation at least hints, has broken free of the 'Meinungsstil' and generated 'nicht nur ein Geschichtsgefühl, sondern auch ein Geschichtsvertrauen.' The object of Walser's praise is *Diese Erinnerung an einen, der nur einen Tag zu Gast war*: 'Zum Glück gibt es dieses Gedicht [...] Wir wären arm dran, ohne dieses Gedicht aus dem Jahr 1984.' He cites the lines on Germany quoted above (p. 457).

Walser does not refer to any other work by Strauß, so the connection is not made between the long poem and the *Fragmente der Undeutlichkeit*, a book which is much closer to Walser's article both in time and in mood, for here we have, approximately twelve months apart, two German writers of different generations and with quite different public profiles, both at a loss about where they stand now as creative writers and, certainly in the case of Strauß, seriously doubting the viability of his poetic voice. It is of relevance here that Walser recognizes in Strauß a totally different voice from his own (possibly from that of his generation, for even where he and his peers are at odds they speak with the same voice); more particularly, it is relevant that Strauß has already out-stripped Walser in his reading of his day and age — as, indeed, he did both Heinrich Böll and Günter Grass, whose respective novels *Frauen vor Flußlandschaft* and *Die Rättin* appeared some time after *Der junge Mann*,[48] and the spirit of the *Historikerstreit*. Strauß should be, if these views of his work are at all correct, a figure to whom the new Germany could look for guidance and vitality as it moves into a new future in which old barriers have disappeared and old boundaries become permeable. Yet, if my reading of 'Sigé' holds good, he has already decided that he is not the one to assume the mantle of 'der Deutsche im Namen eines Volkes'. Strauß's present position in this respect is arguably close to that of Leon Pracht, the central figure of *Der junge Mann*, who fails at the beginning of the book to provide leadership when he most wants to play a leadership role and then, towards the end, by a despairing act of will, liberates the young Yossica from forces that have prevented her from realizing her true potential.[49] In this sense, the muse, who is clearly female, leaving the poet at the end of 'Sigé' might, in contrast to Heine's French mis-tress,[50] be construed as the next generation of poets striding away from the vicarious representative of a generation made impotent by its fixations and its consequent loss of awareness of fundamental issues.

Strauß's mood of resignation seems much more substantial than the passing cloud which might inspire a poem; his dilemma has existen-tial implications comparable with those facing some GDR writers at the present time.[51] Like them, Strauß despairs of his role; unlike them, it seems doubtful whether he was ever, even in the long poem, finally confident of his role. The two stories published in the mid-1970s in the little volume *Marlenes Schwester*[52] both address the problem of individual identity: the eponymous one is an eerie account of a self-sustaining circle of vampires, the other, 'Theorie der Drohung', narrates a period in the life of a writer from which he emerges as the woman he thought he had rescued from an asylum and with the certainty that everything he has written has already been written. 'Plagiat' is a term that would adequately describe the contemporary condition as here set out.[53]

The dependence of the individual on others for self-confirmation, confusing and confused twin figures (often of separate generations), barriers to communication, nervous and psychological breakdown are some of the trademarks of Strauß's work in the 1970s;[54] while some of these works (plays mainly, since his prose output at this time is less substantial) indicate German settings, the German situation as a factor in this condition only gradually becomes apparent. Strauß seems to have understood all the pain, isolation and confusion of postmodern man before he began to connect it (in his work) with the division of his native land and with the still murmuring nightmare voice of Germany's past.[55] His work in the 1970s does contain some painful echoes and images that recall that past, such as the poem in *Bekannte Gesichter, gemischte Gefühle* (1974) about ballroom dancers which suddenly alludes to Celan's *Todesfuge*: 'Ein deutsches Meisterpaar aus Königswinter',[56] and Moritz at the end of *Trilogie des Wiedersehens* (1976)[57] with a picture in a rejected style of art (reminiscent, among others, of George Grosz and called 'Karneval der Direktoren') hanging round his neck — these do produce a shudder of recognition, but the 'German dimension' is not crucial to the reality the works reflect. Indeed, *Trilogie des Wiedersehens* contains a great deal by way of ironic and amusing discussion of various kinds of reality and realism[58] and ends with a line which could almost serve as an epitaph for Strauß at this juncture: 'Und diese Abteilung nennt sich dann: >Einbildungen der Realität<. Dachten wir...'.[59] Even in *Kalldewey Farce* (1981), where a mysterious spook who embodies all the insidious attraction of a Hitler joins the characters at a party and eventually does not go away but disappears under the table, the past seems ultimately only gratuitously part of the present.[60]

Strauß's problem is how he can both confront this past, which is there but is so elusive, and, by doing so, overcome it. His methods are literary in every sense of the word. He brings the immediate past to life in the lives of his figures through a web of literary allusion (mainly to such writers as Walser, Grass, Böll and Borchert) enriched with potent images, giving it the power of onward transmission from generation to generation; thus it is shown to have the capacity to all but destroy the lives of those for whom it is not part of living memory.[61] He tackles this problem by using the qualities unique to art to create a new perspective which looks backwards, but only to provide orientation for forward movement.

He hints at the power of his medium in *Trilogie des Wiedersehens* when, in relation to the discussion of realism and reality, he has his writer figure, Peter, say: 'Wo ein Bild ist, hat die Wirklichkeit ein Loch. Wo ein Zeichen herrscht, hat das bezeichnete Ding nicht auch noch Platz.'[62] In *Paare Passanten* he expressed a similar idea, but with less confidence in the efficacy of art in the present: 'Das Kunstwerk bewahrte uns einst vor der totalen Diktatur der Gegenwart.'[63] In *Trilogie des Wiedersehens*, in close proximity in the text to the discussion of realism, there is also a discussion of dreams and myth — a reminder of the realms into which he often ventures in order to uncover a deeper truth about the human and, later, the German condition. The idea of making a hole in reality[64] brings to mind immediately one of his favourite motifs, the 'Riß', which seems to reflect Paul Valéry's perception of poetic insight and leads Strauß ultimately into the world of *Der junge Mann*, *Diese Erinnerung an einen, der nur einen Tag zu Gast war* and *Fragmente der Undeutlichkeit*. One point at which it is prefigured is when Moritz in *Trilogie des Wiedersehens*, who is plagued by dreams which warp his sense of time, describes vivid peripheral glimpses which seem to indicate a position balanced between hallucinatory insanity and poetic inspiration: 'Am laufenden Band, Einbildungen, Sinnestrug. Rechts und links an den Blickfeldrändern tauchen Figuren auf, die es in Wirklichkeit gar nicht gibt. Kommen und gehen und rufen mir zu. Ich bin geneigt, ihnen zu folgen, ich folge ihnen und gehe manchmal die seltsamsten Wege.'[65] We are close also to the Blochian motif discussed by Ricarda Schmidt in relation to Christa Wolf where the notion of a twilight region is used to overcome rigid boundaries and initiate forward movement.[66] It is precisely this that Strauß is attempting in the many dream-like sequences in *Der junge Mann* and the strange, geographically and chronologically transposed settings of this novel, the long poem and the fragments.

V

The present that Strauß is attempting to fracture is one which he perceives as petrified by the power of the recent past and the all-pervading, disabling, treacherous facility of postindustrial technologies. His is a problem of time, the 'Zeitpfeil' is probably as common an image in his work as the 'Riß'; his contemporaries' minds have been robbed of their sense of time and are thus caught in a strange state of limbo.[67] His task is to exorcise the ghost of the past. Here we must remember his plea for a past of his own, and perhaps contrast his approach with that suggested by the term *Trauerarbeit*.[68] It is not a past they have lived through that his figures have to recollect in order to gain relief and release from it. His is a past which, because of its overwhelming horror, defies all attempts to bring it into perspective; indeed, his generation does not have the means to bring it into perspective. This generation is biologically and, crucially, psychologically the product of a phenomenon which now inhabits the realms of the unconscious and of the imagination. At these levels it has a life of its own and is a potent and dangerous force. If the generation of Böll, Grass and Lenz needed the imaginative, creative dimension to make their presentation of a past that was literally theirs palatable to their peers and contemporaries, Strauß has to fight the burden of that past at the level at which it now operates, not as a known reality but as a reality transfigured through repressed memory and unhealthy imagination. He can bring the awful reality of this new state home to his readers by his evocation of a world of dreams and nightmares (reminiscent of both Grass and Müller) and by literary allusion, both of which afford common ground. He must also attempt to resolve the problem of time by creating a new sense of perspective, part and parcel of which is an attempt to write in a new way, in language which is proofed against association with the Nazi past and against contemporary preoccupations. This is the real malaise he brought to the surface in *Rumor*, to which Bekker, the 'rumorender Nachtwächter',[69] was unable to provide the antidote, for what was required, as expressed by his daughter, Grit, was 'jemanden mit Kräften, die ich gar nicht kenne. Jemanden, der mal eine ganz andere Sprache spricht.'[70] This, surely, is what Strauß was attempting in *Diese Erinnerung an einen, der nur einen Tag zu Gast war* — and, as noted, it was this that inflamed his critics.

It is helpful at this point to refer to an article by Botho Strauß which was published in the *Frankfurter Allgemeine Zeitung* on 23 May 1987.[71] In this long and erudite appreciation of Rudolph Borchardt, Strauß, who rarely uses the press as a vehicle for his ideas, particularly emphasizes Borchardt's ability to bridge time by translating texts into a language that is new, of which his translation of Dante is, for Strauß, the supreme example. The essay tells us a great deal that is immediately relevant to Strauß himself. Thus he says of Borchardt: 'Er will Ursprung

zu Ursprung fügen, über alles Vergängliche hinweg', an idea very similar to that associated with his 'Wächter'-poet.[72] The task that Strauß
seems to be attempting in his long poem could hardly be better circum-
scribed than in these words: 'Um das Erbe, das keiner mehr im Blut
trägt, schaffend zu erwerben, um große Literaturtraditionen des Abend-
lands, die verkannt oder verfälscht wurden, wiederzuentdecken und
fortzuführen, dazu bedarf es des wissensfrohen Dichters [...] mit herak-
leischer Stärke, der zu einen und nicht zu sondern gekommen ist, der's
zusammenfügen muß über die Jahrhunderte hin, der ganze Epochen
säubert, bis er auf den Kern ihrer Frühe stößt und ihn bloßlegt.' He
speaks of the 'mächtigen Propheten der Erinnerung' whose task it is 'die
Risse zu heilen, die Kontinuitäten zu gewährleisten' — he has moved on
somewhat from his Valérian view of the 'Riß' as the momentary glimpse
of the truth, although there is nothing to suggest that the poet's insight is
gained from a less oblique or ephemeral experience. The poet's particular strength as he faces this task is his knowledge of his mother tongue:
'Im Dichter bleibt der ganze Stammbaum seiner Muttersprache lebendig
und strebt auch an jenen Zweigen weiter, die in historischer Umgebung
ihr Wachstum längst beendet haben.' Strauß finds it amazing that Borchardt, who had fought so hard to overcome modernity, should be so
little known in a world striving for new concepts of 'Herkunft und
Überlieferung'. Borchardt had, he says, 'für die Entstehung von Vergangenheit nichts Geringeres geleistet als Musil für die Entstehung von
moderner Zeitgenossenschaft'; he goes on ultimately to set Borchardt
alongside Benjamin: 'Dennoch mag es — "im Spiel der geschichtlichen
Möglichkeiten" — erlaubt sein, sich vorzustellen, daß an der Pforte
unserer Demokratie nicht allein der Engel mit dem kritischen Schwert
gestanden hätte, der Wächter über Aufklärung und fortschrittliches Bewußtsein, sondern eben auch jener eines wissenden, schaffenden Be-
wahrens: daß also neben einem Benjamin auch ein Borchardt gestanden
hätte.'

Borchardt was not reconcilable, he goes on to say, with many of
the literary types we know today (he lists them, and reminds us of a
whole generation of both East and West German writers by naming in
first place the 'sozialverpflichteter Schriftsteller'), Borchardt was 'ein har-
ter Edler, kein Sonderling' and, recalling his references to Genet and
Baudelaire in Der junge Mann,[73] 'kein poète maudit, den die Moderne so
breitwillig in ihr Herz schloß'. Borchardt was of the 'Typus des Wieder-

bringers' for whom Strauß's contemporaries have no appreciation, but reading his work might, he hopes, 'mit diesem leidenschaftlichen Antipoden neue Spannungen in die deutsche Literatur der Moderne [...] tragen'.

Strauß himself delves into the realm of myth and dream, moving easily between a distant past and an equally distant future in *Der junge Mann* and *Diese Erinnerung an einen, der nur einen Tag zu Gast war*, seeing poetry as a defence against the arrow of time[74] and the poet-watch-keeper as capable of forming a bow that brings hitherto irreconcilable ends together.[75] This, one feels, is what Walser finds so positive. Certainly, it is possible to believe from the long poem that Strauß was hinting that he had at last found his spiritual home, which in *Paare Passanten* he had related to literature and language.[76] As I have noted, by the time he compiled his *Fragmente der Undeutlichkeit* he had again lost sight of and confidence in it (perhaps because much of his other work from about the time of the long poem had failed generally to gain public acclaim). In 'Sigé', Strauß is unable to find the new voice that he has drafted out as the antidote to the ills of the time, thus his task, as a poet, is to wait and watch, to restore some power of indeterminacy to words,[77] for his age is one in which words, like everything else, are readily available, disposable, consumer goods, in vogue one day, cast in the dust the next: 'Jetzt, da vielleicht Schwerwiegendes zu sagen wäre, stehen dafür die Münder von Unerfahrenen bereit, von Ungläubigen der Sprache, die es drängt, das Wichtigste endlich zu sagen, doch kommt es nur verkehrt, erschlafft, ausgespült heraus. Die Sprache, kaum verlautet, liegt auch schon wie ein leeres schrumpliges Glitzerkostüm im Arenastaub.'[78] People seem to want the poet to use his talent simply to depict the death throes of a dog run over on the road — or are they the death throes of the poet? The brutal pain evoked is strangely reminiscent of that inflicted upon Fritz Fühmann's Marsyas,[79] although here the poet is not unable to comprehend, only to communicate:

Viele waren da, die vom Dichter nichts als die letzten Zuckungen eines überfahrenen Hundes sehen wollten —
wenn der Herrenlose die Herrschaft verliert über das Rufen,
und der Riß, die Kluft, worin sein Schall noch irrte, macht sie trunken, begeisterte sie,
die Zuckung, der hochragende Abbruch, das arme Letzte mußte es sein: die Gesättigten kosteten nur noch Manie und Bruchstück. Ah! Dies verschleckte Schaudern![80]

Much of Strauß's despair in 'Sigé' is associated with his awareness of and sensitivity to the German condition as he lived it in the period immediately before the events of 1989 and 1990. He has, so far, not commented on these events in public,[81] but his position in the 1980s as revealed both in his earlier optimistic approach to his work and also in his more recent pessimism has not lost its validity, it has gained in relevance. The need has never been greater for German men of letters to search out healthy roots at deeper levels than the shallow, exhausted soil of the last decades, to investigate new perspectives on German history and culture. It is such points of orientation discovered in the past that will allow bearings to be taken for positive movement out of the current, stultified and stultifying view of things German into a new future. This latter must be a future in which a new language is found which will accommodate the common 'pattern in the living cells' of both former German states. Strauß may himself be too tied by and too exhausted from his struggle with the dual stranglehold of the German past and of contemporary consumer culture to provide the necessary new impulse, but others, as a number of articles in this collection have shown, are already pioneering such new ground.[82]

It is also the case that Strauß's work already exists as an important factor in the new common culture of the two Germanys; much of his wealth of ideas, of his declared heritage, is already reflected in the work of other authors discussed here. He may have little in common with Walser and his contemporaries in the West, and he will not be swayed, one feels, by belated compliments, but he does have much in common with Volker Braun, Christoph Hein and even Heiner Müller among several others. One wonders what chemistry might begin when the ends of this cultural arch are brought together, when these creative imaginations with their different experiences, views of the past and habits of language begin to interrelate more directly and openly than was possible hitherto. It would be a major loss to German literature and culture if Strauß has, in fact, decided to lay down his pen or to limit himself to writing for the theatre, particularly as the spectre of the German past could at last be on the point of at least initial exorcism, which will allow more immediate, existential problems of our contemporary world to take their proper place in the poets' consciousness and output. Even if the decision and the message I have here associated with 'Sigé' have been correctly interpreted and Strauß does indeed refrain from future comment of the themes of Germany, German culture and the role of the German poet, the 'rumorender Wächter' can retire satisfied that he has performed his rounds dutifully though the difficult twilight hours before dawn. Even if the full significance of his words was not immediately and fully understood by his still slumbering compatriots, the present silence is as much the product of their untuned ears as of his uncommon language. The new generation of writers, who are now making their own past, will perhaps recognize that his was the voice of the German poet at the moment when the glimpsed insight of a better future arising out of a better past fractured a reality that had for too long insisted on the rightness of its own fragmented view of history.

NOTES

1   Volker Hage: 'Zur deutschen Literatur 1989', introduction to Franz Josef Görtz, Volker Hage and Uwe Wittstock (eds): *Deutsche Literatur 1989. Jahresüberblick*, Stuttgart, 1990, pp. 5—41; here p. 40.
2   This is not to suggest that Strauß was in any way unique in this respect; it is, for example, interesting to compare aspects of Günter Grass's works: say, *Kopfgeburten oder die Deutschen sterben aus* (1980) along with his *Das Treffen in Telgte* (1979) and *Die Rättin* (1986), with the works by Strauß discussed in this essay. Others (Hans Magnus Enzensberger and Heiner Müller might be two quite different further examples) could also claim fairly to have explored related territory.
3   A new play by Strauß has just (as the final editing on this volume is in progress) been produced in Munich. The play, whose title *Schlußchor* is perhaps not without relevance in the present context, has as one of its themes the events of 9 November 1989. The review by Hellmuth Karasek ('Der deutsche Augenblick', *Der Spiegel*, no. 6, 11 February 1991, pp. 214—6) seems to suggest that the photographer's failure to snap the best pose of the night is Strauß's only 'schöner Einfall für ein deutsches Drama über einen historischen Augenblick'. Karasek indicates that the middle portion of the play is closer to themes associated in the present essay with Strauß's theatre; he makes the interesting remark: '"Deutsch" ist dieser Mittelteil nur sehr am Rande — obwohl er nirgends als in Deutschland spielen, nirgends als in Deutschland so geschrieben werden könnte.' Gerhard Stadelmaier writing in *FAZ* ('Ode an die Meute: Komödie der Deutschen', 4 February 1991) suggests the play might benefit from cutting, pointing at scenes which, from descriptions in various reviews, seem potentially to have something in common with the more horrific scenes of Heiner Müller; he quotes the words of one of the characters, Patrick: 'Mein Gott, wen interessiert das jetzt?', a sentiment which possibly echoes the quotation from *Fragmente der Undeutlichkeit* (p. 57) to the effect that the poet might very rapidly become bored with the idea of unity.
4   Botho Strauß: *Fragmente der Undeutlichkeit*, Munich, 1989.
5   Ibid, pp. 33—65 ('Sigé'), quotations pp. 44 and 65.
6   Of the very many possible examples: Strauß's first play, *Die Hypochonder* (1972), features a large aquarium which is eventually punctured by revolver bullets forcing one of the characters to plug the holes briefly with his fingers before the water squirts out, over several pages, onto the stage; one of his most recent plays, *Besucher* (1988), involves a female 'character' who is a loudspeaker on a pole which has one (female) hand — she is carried around by her lover and converses with him quite happily.

7   In his novel *Der junge Mann* (Munich 1984), Strauß used the term 'RomantischerRe-
     flexionsRoman' (p. 15) in a passage where he is pondering the problems of finding an
     appropriate narrative form in which to write when his contemporaries have lost all appre-
     ciation for literature. The dilemma is reflected in his prose and verse throughout the
     decade.
8   Strauß displays an enormous range of literary and philosophical sources, but he has a
     particular affinity with T. S. Eliot and Paul Valéry. It is interesting that several of his
     contemporaries, particularly Volker Braun, have discovered closer kinship with Arthur
     Rimbaud (see Gisela Shaw, Katrin Kohl, and Karen Leeder above pp. 86, 344, and
     416—9 and respectively).
9   Volker Hage's report of an interview with Strauß is perhaps the best source in terms of
     discovering Strauß's views on these matters: Volker Hage: 'Schreiben ist eine Séance.
     Der Künstler als nicht mehr junger Mann: Botho Strauß — ein Porträt', *Die Zeit*, 16 Jan-
     uary 1987, pp. 37—8 (also published together with an earlier interview as 'Schreiben ist
     eine Séance: Begegnung mit Botho Strauß' in Michael Radix (ed.): *Strauß lesen*,
     Munich, 1987, pp. 188—216).
10   I have discussed this and other aspects of Strauß's work of relevance to the present dis-
     cussion elsewhere, in 'Botho Strauß and the Land of his Fathers: From *Rumor* to *Der
     junge Mann*' in Arthur Williams, Stuart Parkes and Roland Smith (eds): *Literature on the
     Threshold. The German Novel in the 1980s*, Oxford, 1990, pp. 279—307; here particu-
     larly pp. 283f.
11   See Hage: 'Schreiben ist eine Séance... .
12   Thomas Mann: *Betrachtungen eines Unpolitischen*, on which he started work in 1915
     and which was first published in 1922. The first complete version was published only in
     1956 (after Mann's death) as part of the *Stockholmer Gesamtausgabe der Werke von
     Thomas Mann* (Fischer, Frankfurt/Main) ed. by Erika Mann.
13   See also Ricarda Schmidt (pp. 429—44 above) and Elizabeth Boa (pp. 139—53 above).
14   See also Ian Hilton (pp. 401—11 above) and esp. Axel Goodbody (pp. 373—96 above).
15   While this, ultimately is the theme which underpins all of the more specific topics in this
     volume, it is raised in an interesting context by Ian Huish (pp. 243—52 above).
16   The articles by Thomas Beckerman, Katrin Kohl and Karen Leeder (respectively pp.
     97—115, 339—56, and 413—24 above) indicate that answers are being sought, and
     perhaps found, to this fundamental problem.
17   There are references to the quotation from Brecht's *Der aufhaltsame Aufstieg des Arturo
     Ui* in the articles above by Dieter Stolz (p. 212) and Axel Schalk (p. 78), while Theo Buck
     reminds us of Goya's etching *The Sleep of Reason begets Monsters* (p. 22); Axel
     Schalk refers to the scene in *Germania. Tod in Berlin* where Hitler and Goebbels bring
     forth monsters (pp. 70—1 above); Anthony Willams (pp. 261—3) and Dieter Stolz (pp.
     209—15) remind us of the nightmares of Günter Grass and, particularly, of Oskar's
     hump (p. 262). It is possibly the latter that inspires Strauß's nightmare births in *Rumor*
     (Munich, 1980, pp. 189f.) and *Der junge Mann*, pp. 184f); see also my article: 'Botho
     Strauß and the Land of his Fathers...', pp. 284f. Grenouille in Patrick Süskind's *Das
     Parfum* (Zurich, 1985) might be regarded as a variation on this same theme.
18   See Arthur Williams: 'Botho Strauß and the Land of his Fathers...', pp. 285—7.
19   One of Strauß's preoccupations throughout the 1980s and earlier is the question of
     memory. He would certainly share some of the concerns of other writers as explored in
     this volume by, for example, Hella Ehlers (esp. pp. 225—8 above), although his own
     treatment of the theme is a great deal more complex and wide-ranging than that of
     perhaps any other author here considered. His stance does appear to change; in the
     immediate context here, the image of the old singer miming to a recording long forgotten
     comes to mind. This comes right at the end of *Die Widmung* (Munich, 1977), the final
     section of which (pp. 97—114) is headed 'Berlin ohne Ende': 'Der aus der Vergessenheit
     herbeigezerrte Künstler besaß weder die Übung noch, in diesen Minuten, das
     Gedächtnis, sein Lied einwandfrei lippensynchron vorzutäuschen. Einmal wagte die
     Kamera eine Großaufnahme, sprang aber sofort erschrocken zurück. Denn während die
     Erinnerung noch in großen Tönen sang, war der Mund des alten Mannes plötzlich
     zugefallen und zuckte textvergessen und murmelte Flüche' (p. 114). This image

contrasts so strongly with some of Strauß's female figures, particularly the girl at the end of *Paare Passanten* (Munich, 1981) who sings with a pure voice (p. 203).

20 Botho Strauß: *Diese Erinnerung an einen, der nur einen Tag zu Gast war*, Munich, 1985, p. 51. The italics here, as elsewhere, are by Strauß. Strauß often seems close to positions reflected in the *Vaterbücher* as discussed by Hella Ehlers (pp. 233—8 above).

21 This is a theme I have discussed in a paper (as yet unpublished) given at the University of Rostock colloquium on West German literature: 'Literatur und Zukunft — Zukunft der Literatur' (28—30 May 1990) which proceeds from a sentence found in *Rumor* (p. 78): 'Botho Strauß: "Bin ein Patriot, weiß aber nicht, an wen soll ich mich wenden."'

22 Strauß: *Fragmente der Undeutlichkeit*, p. 65.

23 Theo Buck, in particular, refers to this point (p. 25 above).

24 This has become a particularly relevant matter as the phenomenon of 'Abwicklung' has begun to mar the social development of the five east German *Länder* as fully sovereign constituent states of the extended West German democratic, social *Rechtsstaat*. See for example Dieter E. Zimmer writing in *Die Zeit*, 11 January 1991, p. 37: 'Abgewickelt. Der Schriftstellerverband der DDR löst sich auf: Sperrmüll am Ende eines Lebens'.

25 Strauß: *Fragmente der Undeutlichkeit*, p. 65. As indicated in note 2 above, Strauß is not the only writer to attempt this. See also Martin Lüdke: 'German Literature on the Threshold of the Twenty-First Century: A Critic's Perspective' in Williams, Parkes, Smith: *Literature on the Threshold...*, pp. 335—47.

26 Just a few paragraphs earlier he had made the point: 'Noch vor hundert Jahren war jede Stimme beheimatet.' Ibid, p. 61.

27 Ibid, p. 35.

28 This relates to powerful images in *Der junge Mann*, where Strauß is preoccupied with the importance of historical perspective, particularly to the section of the book headed 'Die Terrasse. (Belsazar. Fabeln am Morgen nach dem Fest)', pp. 177—82 and 294—305. Cf. Axel Schalk's remarks on Heiner Müller, esp. pp. 67 and 69—71 above.

29 I have discussed the way Strauß focuses on and manipulates gender in 'Botho Strauß and the Land of his Fathers...', particularly pp. 298f. See also Moray McGowan: '"Das Kapitel Mann ist beendet": "Female Texts" by Male Authors as Critiques of Patriarchy? Stefan Schütz and Botho Strauß' in Williams, Parkes, Smith: *Literature on the Threshold...*, pp. 263—78. Ricarda Schmidt refers to Monika Maron's use of a similar technique (p. 433 above).

30 The quotations are all from Strauß: *Fragmente der Undeutlichlichkeit*, pp. 36—7.

31 Strauß refers in a footnote to Anne e Patrick Poirier: *Architettura e mitologia*, Milan, 1984.

32 Strauß: *Rumor*, in particular pp. 197f.

33 Strauß: *Der junge Mann*, in particular pp. 42f. and p. 305, where Leon leaves his vantage point and begins to take direct action, and *Diese Erinnerung...*, in particular pp. 21, 28, 46. See also *Fragmente der Undeutlichkeit*, particularly pp. 44f.

34 Strauß: *Fragmente der Undeutlichkeit*, pp. 38f.

35 Apart from the singer at the end of *Paare Passanten* referred to in note 20 above, there are three (sets of) figures of particular relevance in *Der junge Mann*: the younger and elder Meros (pp. 237—41), the skaters, who are mother and daughter (p. 384) and Yossica, who has a beautiful voice (p. 293) and who suffers a disastrously split personality in a male dominated world from which she is ultimately rescued by Leon's act of will (p. 315f.). Cf. Elizabeth Boa's discussion os the 'incomplete' female persona, esp. 142—6 above.

36 Strauß: *Fragmente der Undeutlichkeit*, p. 55, and Der junge Mann, particularly p. 8.

37 Botho Strauß: *Paare Passanten*, p. 114.

38 Strauß: *Der junge Mann*, pp. 289f., where Almut, in the section 'Die Geschichte der Almut'(pp. 250-316), is confronted in a dream with a hopelessly fragmented reflection of herself in the eye of a cockchafer.

39 While *Paare Passanten* is essentially a collection of fragments, the book is divided into sections with headings and has a clear argument which traces the development suggested here.

40 Strauß: *Fragmente der Undeutlichkeit*, p. 54. This is, perhaps, the clearest statement of the theme that emerges in *Rumor* and is then pursued in the other works on the 1980s.

41 Strauß: *Diese Erinnerung...*, pp. 47f.
42 For example, Rolf Michaelis: 'Königsweg oder Holzweg', *Die Zeit*, 21 June 1985, p. 45.
43 Strauß: *Fragmente der Undeutlichkeit*, p. 56f.
44 Ibid, p. 61.
45 Martin Walser: 'Vormittag eines Schriftstellers: Über Deutschland reden — und die Folgen: Warum einer keine Lust mehr hat, am Streit der Meinungen teilzunehmen', *Die Zeit*, 14 December 1990, pp. 53f. I am grateful to Stuart Parkes for pointing out the reference to Strauß in an article I might otherwise have set aside.
46 See particularly Theo Buck (pp. 21—44), Axel Schalk (esp. pp. 80—1), Helmut Peitsch (pp. 155—82) and Stuart Parkes (pp. 187—203) above.
47 The book he refers to is Peter Handke: *Das Gewicht der Welt: ein Journal (November 1975 — März 1977)*, Salzburg, 1977. Walser manages, incidentally, to equate Utopian thinking with dogma and opinion — a view which might suggest that has has not left the 'Meinungsstreit' altogether behind and which challenges some of the use made of the concept of Utopia in these pages, particularly in the article by Joseph Pischel (pp. 117—26 above).
48 *Frauen vor Flußlandschaft. Roman in Dialogen und Selbstgesprächen* (Cologne, 1985), published posthumously, has been described as Böll's postmodern novel; it is certainly fragmentary, probably unfinished, and has been reworked for the theatre. Grass's *Die Rättin* was published in 1986 (Darmstadt).
49 These are aspects I have discusses in 'Botho Strauß and the Land of his Fathers...'. Yossica is, incidentally, one of two characters with a name (in a novel in which names are generally significant) which contains the element 'ossi', the other being Leon Pracht's mentor, Ossia. 'Ossi' and 'Wessi' have, of course, become increasingly significant terms over recent months.
50 Dieter Stolz draws our attention to the figure who brings relief to Heine in his tormented consideration of the German nightmare (p. 222 above).
51 Among these might be Christa Wolf, for whom Joseph Pischel holds out hope of a reorientation, and Heiner Müller, about whom Axel Schalk is perhaps less hopeful (respectively pp. 123—6 and 81 above).
52 Botho Strauß: *Marlenes Schwester. Zwei Erählungen*, Munich, 1975.
53 See, for example, Peter Bürger: 'Das Verschwinden der Bedeutung. Versuch einer postmodernen Lektüre von Michel Tournier, Botho Strauß und Peter Handke' in Peter Kemper (ed.): *'Postmoderne' oder Der Kampf um die Zukunft. Die Kontroverse in Wissenschaft, Kunst und Gesellschaft*, Frankfurt/Main, 1988, pp. 294—312; here p. 306.
54 In particular: the story *Die Widmung* (1977) and the plays *Die Hypochonder* (1972), *Bekannte Gesichter, gemischte Gefühle* (1974) and *Groß und klein* (1977).
55 The title of his novel *Rumor* declares its subject and the appearance of the theme in its own right.
56 Botho Strauß: *Die Hypochonder. Bekannte Gesichter, gemischte Gefühle. Zwei Theaterstücke*, Munich, 1979, p. 96.
57 Botho Strauß: *Trilogie des Wiedersehens. Groß und klein. Zwei Theaterstücke*, Munich, 1980, p. 123.
58 Ibid, pp. 9, 14, 24, 42, 53, 73, 77, 104f.
59 Ibid, p. 124.
60 Botho Strauß: *Kalldewey Farce*, Munich, 1981; the scene in question (pp. 41—56) is followed by dialogue that reveals the figure's lasting impact (pp. 57—66).
61 This seems to be a fundamental idea in both *Rumor* and *Der junge Mann*.
62 Strauß: *Trilogie des Wiedersehens...*, p. 42. Cf. Stefan Döring's 'mit den worten sterben die bilder', which is discussed by Karen Leeder, pp. 420—1 above.
63 Strauß: *Paare Passanten*, p. 111.
64 We are reminded by Strauß's use of the term 'Wirklichkeit' of the discussion of 'Wirklichkeit' and 'Realität' in Thomas Beckermann's article, esp. pp. 109—11 above.
65 Strauß: *Trilogie des Wiedersehens...*, p. 111.
66 See Ricarda Schmidt (note 13, p. 446 above) for the relevant quotation. Of the many references to 'Riß' in Strauß's work, perhaps the phrase 'die Einheit von Riß und Form' (*Paare Passanten*, p. 112) is the most tantalizing.
67 This again is one of the key themes of *Der junge Mann*.

68 Discussed above particularly by Hella Ehlers (pp. 225—40, esp. pp. 227—8 above).
69 Strauß: *Rumor*, p. 197.
70 Ibid, p. 53.
71 Botho Strauß: 'Die Distanz ertragen. Programm eines Wiederanfangs — Rudolf Borchardt und die Entstehung von Vergangenheit', *FAZ*, 23 May 1987. I am grateful to Wolfgang Emmerich for drawing my attention to this article and to Helmut Peitsch who provided the precise reference.
72 'Die Tour ist die eines Mannes, der die Enden/ zusammenfaßt, und packt das Bittere hier, das/ Feierliche dort wie ein Bieger; dem zustieß von allen/ das unverhoffteste Wort: Kelchschaft. Im Herzen Konvergenz' (*Diese Erinnerung...*, p. 28).
73 Strauß uses the term 'poète maudit' in *Der junge Mann* of Genet (p. 32) and combines the original 'poète maudit', Baudelaire with Hitler (pp. 184f.).
74 '[Der Erzähler] wird, wenn auch auf verlorenem Posten, bis zuletzt dem Zeit-Pfeil trotzen und den Schild der Poesie gegen ihn erheben' (*Der junge Mann*, p. 15). The position is close to that of Heiner Müller as set out by Axel Schalk (see esp. pp. 78—9 above).
75 See note 72 above.
76 'Man schreibt einzig im Auftrag der Literatur. Man schreibt unter Aufsicht alles bisher Geschriebenen. Man schreibt aber doch auch, um sich nach und nach eine geistige Heimat zu schaffen, wo man eine natürliche nicht mehr besitzt' and 'Es schafft ein tiefes Zuhaus und ein tiefes Exil, da in der Sprache zu sein' (*Paare Passanten*, pp. 103 and 101).
77 This is the burden of his argument in *Fragmente der Undeutlichkeit*, particularly pp. 46—50. His poet-watchman occupies an outpost from where he keeps watch for something different and new.
78 Strauß: *Fragmente der Undeutlichkeit*, p. 46.
79 The reference is to the article by Dennis Tate, pp. 285—96, esp. 285—6 above.
80 Strauß: *Fragmente der Undeutlichkeit*, p. 59.
81 But see note 3 above.
82 The articles in this volume by Thomas Beckermann (pp. 97—115), Katrin Kohl (pp. 339—56), Axel Goodbody (pp. 373—96), Karen Leeder (pp. 413—24) and Ricarda Schmidt (pp. 429—44) all address the matter of innovation in one way or another.

SELECT BIBLIOGRAPHY

PRIMARY TEXTS

Alfred Andersch: *Mein Verschwinden in Providence*, Zurich, 1971
Sascha Anderson: *Jeder Satellit hat einen Killersatelliten: Gedichte*, Berlin/West, 1982
Sascha Anderson and Elke Erb (eds): *Berührung ist nur eine Randerscheinung. Neue Literatur aus der DDR*, Cologne, 1985
Rudolf Augstein and Günter Grass: *DEUTSCHLAND, einig Vaterland? Ein Streitgespräch*, Göttingen, 1990
Ingeborg Bachmann: *Werke*, Vol. 3: *Todesarten: Malina und unvollendete Romane*, Munich, 1982
Jurek Becker: *Jakob der Lügner*, Berlin (GDR), 1969
Jurek Becker: *Die Irreführung der Behörden*, Rostock, 1973
Thorsten Becker: *Die Bürgschaft*, Zurich, 1985
—————: *Die Nase*, Darmstadt, 1987
Thomas Beckermann (ed.): *Reise durch die Gegenwart*, Frankfurt/Main, 1987
Johannes Bobrowski: *Gesammelte Werke*, ed. by Eberhard Haufe, 6 vols, Berlin (GDR), 1987
Heinrich Böll: *Gruppenbild mit Dame*, Cologne, 1971
—————: *Die verlorene Ehre der Katharina Blum*, Cologne, 1974
—————: *Fürsorgliche Belagerung*, Cologne, 1979
—————: *Was soll aus dem Jungen bloß werden*, Bornheim, 1981
—————: *Frauen vor Flußlandschaft. Roman in Dialogen und Selbstgesprächen*, Cologne, 1985
—————: *Ende der Bescheidenheit. Schriften und Reden 1969—1972*, ed. by Bernd Balzer, Munich, 1985
—————: *Es kann einem bange werden. Schriften und Reden 1976—1977*, ed. Bernd Balzer, Munich, 1985
Alexander von Bormann (ed.): *Die Erde will ein freies Geleit. Deutsche Naturlyrik aus sechs Jahrhunderten*, Frankfurt/Main, 1984
Volker Braun: *Wir und nicht sie*, Frankfurt/Main, 1970
—————: *Das ungezwungene Leben Kasts*, Frankfurt/Main, 1972 (rev. 1979)
—————: *Gegen die symmetrische Welt*, Frankfurt/Main, 1974
—————: *Es genügt nicht die einfache Wahrheit. Notate*, Leipzig, 1975
—————: *Stücke I*, Frankfurt/Main, 1975
—————: *Unvollendete Geschichte*, Frankfurt/Main, 1977
—————: *Training des aufrechten Gangs*, Halle/Saale, 1979
—————: *Hinze-Kunze-Roman*, Frankfurt/Main, 1985
—————: *Langsam knirschender Morgen. Gedichte*, Frankfurt/Main, 1987
—————: *Verheerende Folgen mangelnden Anscheins innerbetrieblicher Demokratie*, Frankfurt/Main, 1988
—————: *Stücke 2*, Berlin, 1989
—————: *Bodenloser Satz*, Frankfurt/Main, 1990
Bertolt Brecht: *Gesammelte Werke in 20 Bänden*, ed. by Suhrkamp Verlag in association with Elisabeth Hauptmann, Frankfurt/Main, 1967
—————: *Der aufhaltsame Aufstieg des Arturo Ui*, 8th edn, Frankfurt/Main, 1975
Günter de Bruyn: *Im Querschnitt. Prosa, Essay, Biographie*, Halle/Saale, 1979
Hans Christoph Buch (ed.): *Tintenfisch 12. Thema: Natur. Oder: Warum ein Gespräch über Bäume heute kein Verbrechen mehr ist*, Berlin, 1977
—————: *Tintenfisch 15. Thema: Deutschland*, Berlin, 1978
Peter O. Chotjewitz: *Saumlos*, Königstein/Ts., 1980
Heinz Czechowski: *Nachmittag eines Liebespaares*, Halle/Saale, 1962
—————: *Wasserfahrt*, Halle/Saale, 1967

——————: *Schafe und Sterne*, Halle/Saale, 1975
——————: *Was mich betrifft*, Halle/Saale, 1981
——————: *Ich, beispielsweise*, Leipzig, 1982
——————: *An Freund und Feind*, Munich, 1983
——————: *Kein näheres Zeichen*, Halle/Saale, 1987
——————: *Ich und die Folgen*, Reinbek, 1987
——————: *Mein Venedig*, Berlin, 1989
——————: *Sanft gehen wie Tiere die Berge neben dem Fluß*, Bremen, 1989
——————: *Auf eine im Feuer versunkene Stadt*, Halle/Saale, 1990
Eva Demski: *Hotel Hölle, Guten Tag*, Munich, 1987
Inge Deutschkorn: *Ich trage den gelben Stern*, Cologne, 1978
Deutschland, Deutschland. 47 Schriftsteller aus der BRD und der DDR schreiben über ihr Land, Salzburg, 1979
Tankred Dorst: *Die Reise nach Stettin*, Frankfurt/Main, 1984
Hans Magnus Enzensberger: *verteidigung der wölfe*, Frankfurt/Main, 1957
——————: *Deutschland, Deutschland unter anderem*, Frankfurt/Main, 1967
——————: *Palaver. Politische Überlegungen (1967—1973)*, Frankfurt/Main, 1974
Elke Erb: *Kastanienallee. Texte und Kommentare*, Salzburg, 1988
Fania Fenelon: *Mädchenorchester in Auschwitz*, Frankfurt/Main, 1980
Erich Fried: *Warngedichte*, Munich, 1964
Max Frisch: *Tagebuch 1966—1971*, Frankfurt/Main, 1972
Jürgen Fuchs: *Einmischung in eigene Angelegenheiten*, Reinbek, 1984
Franz Fühmann: *Die Nelke Nikos*, Berlin (GDR), 1953
——————: *Kameraden*, Berlin (GDR), 1955
——————: *Stürzende Schatten*, Berlin (GDR), 1959
——————: *Die Richtung der Märchen*, Berlin (GDR), 1962
——————: *Das Judenauto*, Berlin (GDR), 1962
——————: *König Ödipus: Gesammelte Erzählungen*, Berlin (GDR), 1966
——————: *Erzählungen 1955—1975*, Rostock, 1977
——————: *Gedichte und Nachdichtungen*, Rostock, 1978
——————: *Das Judenauto, Kabelkran und blauer Peter, Zweiundzwanzig Tage oder Die Hälfte des Lebens*, Rostock, 1979
——————: *Irrfahrt und Heimkehr des Odysseus, Prometheus, Der Geliebte der Morgenröte und andere Erzählungen*, Rostock, 1980
——————: *Essays, Gespräche, Aufsätze 1964—1981*, Rostock, 1983
——————: *Das Ohr des Dionysios: Nachgelassene Erzählungen*, Rostock, 1985
——————: *Simplicius Simplicissimus, Der Nibelunge Not und andere Arbeiten für den Film*, Rostock, 1987
——————: *Unter den Paranyas: Traum-Erzählungen und -Notate*, Rostock, 1988
Siegfrid Gauch: *Vaterspuren*, Königstein/Ts., 1979
Ralf Giordano: *Die Bertinis*, Frankfurt/Main, 1985
——————: *Die zweite Schuld oder Von der Last Deutscher zu sein*, Munich, 1990
Günter Grass: *Die Blechtrommel*, Darmstadt, 1959
——————: *Hundejahre*, Darmstadt, 1963
——————: *Über das Selbstverständliche. Reden, Aufsätze, Offene Briefe, Kommentare*, Darmstadt, 1968
——————: *Das Treffen in Telgte*, Darmstadt, 1979
——————: *Kopfgeburten oder die Deutschen sterben aus*, Darmstadt, 1980
——————: *Die Rättin*, Darmstadt, 1986
——————: *Werkausgabe in zehn Bänden*, ed. Volker Neuhaus, Darmstadt, 1987
——————: *Deutscher Lastenausgleich. Wider das dumpfe Einheitsgebot. Reden und Gespräche*, Frankfurt/Main, 1990
——————: *Ein Schnäppchen namens DDR*, Darmstadt, 1990
Günter Grass and Pavel Kohout: *Briefe über die Grenze. Versuch eines Ost-West Dialogs*, Hamburg, 1968
Peter Härtling: *Das Familienfest oder Das Ende der Geschichte*, Stuttgart, 1969
——————: *Das war der Hirbel*, Weinheim, 1973
——————: *Zwettl. Nachprüfung einer Erinnerung*, Darmstadt, 1973

—————: *Eine Frau*, Darmstadt, 1974
—————: *Oma*, Weinheim, 1975
—————: *Hölderlin*, Darmstadt, 1976
—————: *Theo haut ab*, Weinheim, 1977
—————: *Ben liebt Anna*, 1979
—————: *Nachgetragene Liebe*, Darmstadt, 1980
—————: *Alter John*, Weinheim, 1981
—————: *Die dreifache Maria*, Darmstadt, 1982
—————: *Jakob hinter der blauen Tür*, Weinheim, 1983
—————: *Felix Guttmann*, Darmstadt, 1985
—————: *Krücke. Roman für Kinder*, Weinheim, 1987
—————: *Waiblingers Augen*, Darmstadt, 1987
—————: *Der Wanderer*, Darmstadt, 1988
Wolfgang Hegewald: *Das Gegenteil der Fotografie* (1984)
—————: *Hoffmann, Ich und Teile der näheren Umgebung* (1985)
—————: *Jakob Oberlin oder Die Kunst der Heimat* (1987)
—————: *Verabredung in Rom*, 1988
Gert Heidenreich: *Die Gnade der späten Geburt. Sechs Erzählungen*, Munich, 1986
Christoph Hein: *Der fremde Freund*, Berlin (GDR), 1982
—————: *Öffentlich arbeiten. Essais und Gespräche*, Berlin (GDR), 1987
—————: *Der Tangospieler*, Berlin (GDR), 1989
Kerstin Hensel: *Stilleben mit Zukunft*, Halle, 1988
Egmont Hesse (ed.): *Sprache und Antwort. Stimmen und Texte einer anderen Literatur aus
    der DDR*, Frankfurt/Main, 1988
Ursula Heukenkamp, Heinz Kahlau, Wulf Kirsten (eds): *Die eigene Stimme. Lyrik der DDR*,
    Berlin (GDR), 1988
Stefan Heym: *Hostages*, New York, 1942 (= *Der Fall Glasenapp*, Leipzig, 1958; Munich,
    1976
—————: *Of Smiling Peace*, Boston, 1944
—————: *The Crusaders*, Boston, 1948 (= *Kreuzfahrer von heute*, Leipzig, 1950; *Der
    bittere Lorbeer*, Munich, 1950
—————: *The Eyes of Reason*, Boston, 1951 (= *Die Augen der Vernunft*, Leipzig, 1955;
    Munich, 1950
—————: *Goldsborough*, Leipzig, 1953; New York, 1954. Later published in German as
    Die Liebe der Miss Kennedy, Berlin (GDR), 1958, and as *Goldsborough*, Munich,
    1978
—————: *Die Schmähschrift oder Die Königin gegen Defoe*, Zurich, 1970; Leipzig, 1974
    (= *The Queen against Defoe and Other Stories*, New York, 1974)
—————: *Der König-David-Bericht*, Munich, 1972; Berlin (GDR), 1973 (= *The King David
    Report*, New York, 1973).
—————: *5 Tage im Juni*, Munich, 1974
—————: *Die richtige Einstellung und andere Erzählungen*, Munich, 1976
—————: *Collin*, Munich, 1979
—————: *Wege und Umwege. Streitbare Schriften aus fünf Jahrzehnten*, ed. by Peter
    Mallwitz, Munich, 1980
—————: *Ahasver*, Munich, 1981
—————: *Schwarzenberg*, Munich, 1984
—————: *Nachruf*, Munich, 1988
—————: *Einmischung*, ed. by Inge Heim and Heinfried Henniger, Gütersloh, 1990
Wolfgang Hilbig: *abwesenheit. gedichte*, Frankfurt/Main, 1979
—————: *Unterm Neomond. Erzählungen*, Frankfurt/Main, 1982
—————: *Stimme, Stimme. Gedichte und Prosa*, Leipzig, 1983
—————: *Der Brief. Drei Erzählungen*, Frankfurt/Main, 1985
—————: *die versprengung. gedichte*, Frankfurt/Main, 1986
—————: *Die Weiber*, Frankfurt/Main, 1986
—————: *Eine Übertragung. Roman*, Frankfurt/Main, 1989
Edgar Hilsenrath: *Nacht*, Cologne, 1978
Walter Höllerer: *Gedichte 1942—1982*, Frankfurt/Main, 1982

Gert Hofmann: *Die Denunziation*, Darmstadt, 1979
—————: *Unsere Eroberung*, Darmstadt, 1984
—————: *Veilchenfeld*, Darmstadt, 1986
—————: *Unsere Vergeßlichkeit*, Darmstadt, 1987
Peter Huchel: *Chausseen Chausseen*, Frankfurt, 1963
Bernd (Jayne-Ann) Igel: *Das Geschlecht der Häuser gebar mir fremde Orte* (1989)
Hans Henny Jahnn: *Werke und Tagebücher*, Hamburg, 1974
Ernst Jandl: *idyllen. gedichte*, Frankfurt/Main, 1989
Uwe Johnson: *Mutmaßungen über Jakob*, Frankfurt/Main, 1959
—————: *Das dritte Buch über Achim*, Frankfurt/Main, 1964
—————: *Zwei Ansichten*, Frankfurt/Main, 1965
—————: *Berliner Sachen. Aufsätze*, Frankfurt/Main, 1975
—————: *Jahrestage. Aus dem Leben von Gesine Cresspahl*, Frankfurt/Main, 4 vols,
    1970, 1971, 1973, 1983.
Hermann Kant: *Die Aula*, Berlin (GDR), 1965
—————: *Die Summe*, 3rd edn, Berlin, 1989
Rainer and Sarah Kirsch: *Gespräch mit dem Saurier*, Berlin, 1965
Sarah Kirsch: *Landaufenthalt*, Berlin (GDR), 1967 = *Gedichte*, Munich, 1969
—————: *Rückenwind*, Ebenhausen, 1977
—————: *Erklärung einiger Dinge*, Munich, 1978
—————: *Drachensteigen*, Ebenhausen, 1979
—————: *Erdreich*, Stuttgart, 1982
—————: *Allerlei-Rauh. Eine Chronik*, Stuttgart, 1988
Wulf Kirsten (ed.): *Veränderte Landschaft*, Leipzig, 1979
Hubertus Knabe (ed.): *Aufbruch in eine andere DDR*, Hamburg, 1990
Ilse Koehn: *Mischling zweiten Grades*, Reinbek, 1979
Helga Königsdorf: *1989 oder Ein Moment Schönheit*, Berlin, 1990
August Kühn: *Jahrgang 1922 oder Die Merkwürdigkeiten im Leben des Fritz Wachsmuth*,
    Munich, 1977
—————: *Wir kehren langsam zur Natur zurück*, Munich, 1984
Günter Kunert: *Verkündigung des Wetters*, München, 1966
————— (ed.): *Aus fremder Heimat. Zur Exilsituation heutiger Literatur*, Munich, 1988
Reiner Kunze: *Die wunderbaren Jahre. Prosa*, Frankfurt/Main, 1976
Roland Lang: *Die Mansarde*, Königstein/Ts., 1979
Katja Lange-Müller: *Wehleid — wie im Leben. Erzählungen* (1986)
—————: *Kasper Mauser — Die Feigheit vorm Freund* (1988)
Dieter Lattmann: *Die Brüder*, Frankfurt/Main, 1985
Siegfried Lenz: *Beziehungen. Ansichten und Bekenntnisse zur Literatur*, Munich, 1972
—————: *Heimatmuseum*, Hamburg, 1978
—————: *Elfenbeinturm und Barrikade. Erfahrungen am Schreibtisch*, Hamburg, 1983
—————: *Exerzierplatz*, Hamburg, 1985
Erich Loest: *Der Zorn des Schafes. Aus meinem Tageswerk*, Künzelsau, 1990
Kito Lorenc: *Wortland. Gedichte aus zwanzig Jahren*, Leipzig, 1984
Thomas Mann: *Betrachtungen eines Unpolitischen*, Frankfurt/Main, 1956
—————: *Leiden an Deutschland*, Frankfurt/Main, 1946
—————: *An die gesittete Welt. Politische Schriften und Reden im Exil*, Frankfurt/Main,
    1986
Monika Maron: *Flugasche. Roman*, Frankfurt/Main, 1981
—————: *Das Mißverständnis. Vier Erzählungen und ein Stück*, Frankfurt/Main, 1982
—————: *Die Überläuferin. Roman*, Frankfurt/Main, 1986
Monika Maron and Joseph von Westphalen: *Trotzdem herzliche Grüße. Ein deutsch-
    deutscher Briefwechsel*, Frankfurt/Main, 1988
Edgar Marsch (ed.): *Moderne deutsche Naturlyrik*, Stuttgart, 1980
Peter Cornelius Mayer-Tasch (ed.): *Im Gewitter der Geraden. Deutsche Ökolyrik
    1950—1980*, Munich, 1984
Christoph Meckel: *Suchbild. Über meinen Vater*, Düsseldorf, 1980
Steffen Mensching: *Erinnerung an eine Milchglasscheibe*, Halle, 1984
—————: *Tuchfühlung. Gedichte*, Cologne, 1987

Karl Mickel and Adolf Endler (eds): *In diesem besseren Land*, Berlin (GDR), 1966
Irmtraud Morgner: *Leben und Abenteuer der Trobadora Beatriz nach Zeugnissen ihrer Spielfrau Laura. Roman in 13 Büchern und sieben Intermezzos*, Berlin (GDR), 1974
Heiner Müller: *Geschichten aus der Produktion I. Stücke. Prosa. Gedichte. Protokolle*, Berlin, 1974
—————: *Stücke*, Berlin, 1975
—————: *Die Umsiedlerin oder Das Leben auf dem Lande*, Berlin, 1975 (contains *Die Schlacht. Szenen aus Deutschland*)
—————: *Germania Tod in Berlin*, Berlin, 1977
—————: *Mauser*, West Berlin, 1978 (contains *Die Hamletmaschine*)
—————: *Rotwelsch*, Berlin, 1982
—————: *Herzstück*, Berlin, 1983 (contains *Leben Gundlings Friedrich von Preußen Lessings Schlaf Traum Schrei. Ein Greuelmärchen*)
—————: *Gesammelte Irrtümer. Interviews und Gespräche*, Frankfurt/Main, 1986
—————: *Shakespeare Factory 1*, Berlin, 1985 (contains *Wolokolamsker Chaussee I: Russische Eröffnung*)
—————: *Shakespeare Factory 2*, Berlin, 1989 (contains *Wolokolamsker Chaussee II: Wald bei Moskau; Wolokolamsker Chaussee III: Das Duell; Wolokolamsker Chaussee IV: Kentauren; Wolokolamsker Chaussee V: Der Findling*)
—————: *Zur Lage der Nation. Heiner Müller im Interview mit Frank M. Raddatz*, Berlin, 1990
Michael Naumann (ed.): *Die Geschichte ist offen. DDR 1990: Hoffnung auf eine neue Republik. Schriftsteller aus der DDR über die Zukunftschancen ihres Landes*, Reinbek, 1990
Gert Neumann: *Die Schuld der Worte*, Frankfurt/Main, 1979 (Rostock, 1989)
—————: *Elf Uhr*, Frankfurt/Main, 1981
—————: 'Übungen jenseits der Möglichkeit', *Neue Rundschau*, vol. 97, no. 2/3, August 1986, pp. 49ff.
—————: 'Brief an Adam Michnik' in Thomas Beckermann (ed.): *Reise durch die Gegenwart*, Frankfurt/Main, 1987, pp. 343ff.
—————: *Die Stimme des Schweigens*, Leipzig, 1988
—————: *Die Klandestinität der Kesselreiniger. Ein Versuch des Sprechens*, Frankfurt/Main, 1989
Erik Neutsch: *Der Friede im Osten. Viertes Buch. Nahe der Grenze*, Halle/Saale, 1987
Dieter Noll: *Kippenberg*, Berlin (GDR), 1979
Oktober 1989. Wider den Schlaf der Vernunft, Verlag Neues Leben, Berlin (GDR), and Elefanten Press, West Berlin, 1989
Hanns Josef Ortheil: *Hecke*, Frankfurt/Main, 1983
Bert Pappenfuß-Gorek: *dreizehntanz*, Berlin (GDR), 1988
—————: *SoJa*, Edition Galrev, Berlin, 1990
Oskar Pastior: *Lesungen mit Tinnitus. Gedichte 1980-1985*, Munich, 1986
Ullrich Plenzdorf: *Die neuen Leiden des jungen W.*, Rostock, 1973
Ruth Rehmann: *Der Mann auf der Kanzel*, Munich, 1979
Hans Richter: *Werke und Wege: Kritiken, Aufsätze, Reden*, Halle/Saale, 1984
Helke Sander: *Die Geschichten der drei Damen K.*, Munich, 5th edn, 1988
Hans-Joachim Schädlich: *Versuchte Nähe*, Reinbek, 1977
Michael Schneider: *Die lange Wut zum langen Marsch. Aufsätze zur sozialistischen Politik und Literatur*, Reinbek, 1975
—————: *Den Kopf verkehrt aufgesetzt oder Die melancholische Linke. Aspekte des Kulturzerfalls in den siebziger Jahren*, Darmstadt, 1981
Peter Schneider: *Lenz. Eine Erzählung*, Berlin, 1973
—————: *...schon bist du ein Verfassungsfeind*, Berlin, 1975
—————: *Der Mauerspringer*, Darmstadt, 1982
—————: *Vati. Erzählung*, Darmstadt, 1987
—————: *Deutsche Ängste. Sieben Essays*, Darmstadt, 1988
Wolfdietrich Schnurre: *Ein Unglücksfall*, Munich, 1981
Georg Schwarz and Carl August Weber (eds): *Wir heißen Euch hoffen*, Munich, 1951
Valentin Senger: *Kaiserhofstr. 12*, Darmstadt, 1978

Klaus Stiller: *Weihnachten*, Munich, 1980
——————: *Zweite Berliner Begegnung. Den Frieden Erklären*, Darmstadt, 1983
Botho Strauß: *Marlenes Schwester. Zwei Erählungen*, Munich, 1975
——————: *Die Widmung*, Munich, 1977
——————: *Die Hypochonder. Bekannte Gesichter, gemischte Gefühle. Zwei Theaterstücke*, Munich, 1979
——————: *Trilogie des Wiedersehens. Groß und klein. Zwei Theaterstücke*, Munich, 1980
——————: *Rumor*, Munich, 1980
——————: *Paare Passanten*, Munich, 1981
——————: *Kalldewey Farce*, Munich, 1981
——————: *Der Park*, Munich, 1983
——————: *Der junge Mann*, Munich, 1984
——————: *Diese Erinnerung an einen, der nur einen Tag zu Gast war*, Munich, 1985
——————: *Die Fremdenführerin*, Munich, 1986
——————: *Besucher. Drei Stücke*, Munich, 1988
——————: *Fragmente der Undeutlichkeit*, Munich, 1989
Eva Strittmatter: *Heliotrop. Gedichte*, Berlin (GDR), 1983
Patrick Süskind: *Das Parfum*, Zurich, 1985
Jürgen Theobaldy: *Die Sommertour. Gedichte*, Reinbek, 1983
Uwe Timm: *Heißer Sommer*, Munich, 1974
Uta Treder: *Luna Aelion. Erzählungen*, Munich, 1989
Und sie bewegt sich doch... Texte wider die Resignation, published by the Fischer Taschenbuchverlag, Frankfurt/Main, no date
Bernward Vesper: *Die Reise. Romanessay. Ausgabe letzter Hand*, Frankfurt/Main, 1977
Klaus Wagenbach (ed.): *Das Atelier: Zeitgenössische deutsche Prosa*, Frankfurt/Main, 1962
——————: *Atlas, zusammengestellt von deutschen Autoren*, Berlin, 1965
——————: *Lesebuch: Deutsche Literatur der sechziger Jahre*, Berlin, 1968
Klaus Wagenbach, Winfried Stephan, Michael Krüger (eds): *Vaterland, Muttersprache. Deutsche Schriftsteller und ihr Staat von 1945 bis heute*, Berlin, 1979
Martin Walser: *Erfahrungen und Leseerfahrungen*, Frankfurt/Main, 1965
—————— (ed.): *Die Alternativen oder Brauchen wir eine neue Regierung?*, Reinbek, 1961
——————: *Wie und wovon handelt Literatur?*, Frankfurt/Main, 1973
——————: *Wer ist ein Schriftsteller?*, Frankfurt/Main, 1979
——————: *Geständnis auf Raten*, Frankfurt/Main, 1986
——————: *Dorle und Wolf*, Frankfurt/Main, 1987
——————: *Über Deutschland reden*, Frankfurt/Main, 1988
Fred Wander: *Der siebente Brunnen*, Berlin (GDR), 1970
Uwe Wandrey (ed.): *Kein schöner Land. Deutschsprachige Autoren zur Lage der Nation*, Reinbek, 1979
Peter Weiss: *Rapporte*, Frankfurt/Main, 1968
——————: *Notizbücher 1971—1980*, Frankfurt/Main, 1981
——————: *Die Ästhetik des Widerstands*, Frankfurt/Main, 3 vols, 1975, 1978, 1981
Joseph von Westphalen: *Warum ich trotzdem Seitensprünge mache. Fünfundzwanzig neue Entrüstungen*, Zürich, 1987
Wolfgang Weyrauch (ed.): *Ich lebe in der Bundesrepublik*, Munich, 1961
——————: *Atom und Aloe. Gesammelte Gedichte*, ed. by Hans Bender, Frankfurt/Main, 1987
Christa Wolf: *Der geteilte Himmel*, Halle/Saale, 1963
——————: *Nachdenken über Christa T.*, Halle/Saale, 1968
——————: *Aufsätze und Prosastücke*, Darmstadt, 1972
——————: *Kindheitsmuster*, Berlin (GDR), 1976
——————: *Lesen und Schreiben. Neue Sammlung*, 3rd edn, Darmstadt, 1982
——————: *Kassandra*, Darmstadt, 1983
——————: *Voraussetzungen einer Erzählung: Kassandra. Frankfurter Poetik-Vorlesungen*, Darmstadt, 1983
——————: *Störfall*, Berlin (GDR), 1986
——————: *Die Dimension des Autors. Essays und Aufsätze, Reden und Gespräche 1959—1985*, Darmstadt, 1987

——————: *Ansprachen*, Darmstadt, 1988
——————: *Sommerstück*, Frankfurt/Main, 1989
——————: *Was bleibt*, Frankfurt/Main, 1990
——————: *Im Dialog. Aktuelle Texte*, Frankfurt/Main, 1990
Gerhard Wolf: *Wortlaut, Wortbruch, Wortlust: Dialog mit Dichtung*, Leipzig, 1988
Peter Paul Zahl: *Die Glücklichen. Ein Schelmenroman*, Berlin, 1979
Jochen Ziem: *Der Junge*, Munich, 1980

SECONDARY TEXTS

Theodor W. Adorno: *Eingriffe. Neun kritische Modelle*, Frankfurt/Main, 1963
Heinz Ludwig Arnold (ed.): *Bestandsaufnahme Gegenwartsliteratur. Bundesrepublik
    Deutschland, Deutsche Demokratische Republik, Österreich, Schweiz*, Munich, 1988
Heinz Ludwig Arnold and Theo Buck (eds): *Positionen im deutschen Roman der sechziger
    Jahre*, Munich, 1974
Stefan Aust: *Der Baader-Meinhof-Komplex*, Hamburg, 1985
Autorenkollektiv (Leitung: Ernst Diehl): *Grundriß der deutschen Geschichte. Von den An-
    fängen der Geschichte des deutschen Volkes bis zur Gestaltung der entwickelten so-
    zialistischen Gesellschaft in der Deutschen Demokratischen Republik. Klassenkampf
    — Tradition — Sozialismus*, 2nd edn, Berlin (GDR), 1979
Rudolf Bahro: *Die Alternative. Zur Kritik des real existierenden Sozialismus*, Cologne, 1977
Gabriele Bail: *Weibliche Indentität. Ingeborg Bachmanns "Malina"*, Göttingen, 1984
Winfried Bauer et al. (eds): *Germanistik. Internationales Referatenorgen mit biblio-
    graphischen Hinweisen*, Tübingen, 1960ff.
Bericht der Bundesregierung und Materialien zur Lage der Nation 1971, published by the
    Bundesministerium für innerdeutsche Angelegenheiten, Bonn, 1971
Hans Joachim Bernhard: *Die Romane Heinrich Bölls: Gesellschaftskritik und Gesellschafts-
    utopie*, Berlin (GDR), 1970
——————: et al: *Geschichte der Literatur der Bundesrepublik Deutschland*, Berlin (GDR),
    1983
Ernst Bloch: *Das Prinzip Hoffnung*, vol. I, Berlin (GDR), 1954
——————: *Die Kunst, Schiller zu sprechen*, Frankfurt/Main, 1969
Harold Bloom: *The Anxiety of Influence. A Theory of Poetry*, Oxford, 1973
Wilfried von Bredow: *Deutschland — ein Provisorium*, Berlin, 1985
F. J. Breuer (ed.): *Das neue Soldaten-Liederbuch. Die bekanntesten und meistgesungenen
    Lieder unserer Wehrmacht*, Mainz, n.d.
Gisela Brinker-Gabler (ed.): *Deutsche Literatur von Frauen*, 2 vols, Munich, 1988
Hanspeter Brode: *Die Zeitgeschichte im erzählenden Werk von Günter Grass. Versuch einer
    Deutung der "Blechtrommel" und der "Danziger Trilogie"*, Frankfurt/Main, 1977
Georg Büchmann: *Geflügelte Worte. Der Zitatenschatz des deutschen Volkes*, 34th edn, ed.
    by Winfried Hofmann, Frankfurt/Main, 1981
Peter Bürger: *Theorie der Avantgarde*, Frankfurt/Main, 1974
Keith Bullivant (ed.): *After the 'Death' of Literature: West German Writing of the 1970s*,
    Oxford, 1989
Victor Burgin, James Donald, Cora Kaplan (eds): *Formations of Fantasy*, London, 1986
Rachel Louise Carson: *Silent Spring*, New York, 1962
Ulrich Chaussy: *Die drei Leben des Rudi Dutschke. Eine Biographie*, Darmstadt, 1983
Nancy Chodorow: *The Reproduction of Mothering. Psychoanalysis and the Sociology of
    Gender*, Berkeley, 1978
Hélène Cixous: *Die unendliche Zirkulation des Begehrens*, Berlin, 1977
——————: *Weiblichkeit in der Schrift*, Berlin, 1980
Christine Cosentino, Wolfgang Ertl and Gerd Labroisse (eds): *DDR-Lyrik im Kontext*,
    Amsterdamer Beiträge zur neueren Germanistik, vol. 26, 1988
Günter Cwojdrak: *Eine Prise Polemik. Sieben Essays zur westdeutschen Literatur*,
    Halle/Saale, 1965

Gerhard Dahne: *Zur Problematik des Geschichtsbewußtseins im Werk von Günter Grass*, Greifswald, 1970

Anne Diekmann and Willi Gohl (eds): *Das große Liederbuch*, Zurich, 1975

W. Eichhorn et al. (eds): *Das Menschenbild der marxistisch-leninistischen Philosophie*, Berlin (GDR), 1969

Wolfgang Emmerich: *Kleine Literaturgeschichte der DDR*, rev. ed., Frankfurt/Main, 1989

Hanns W. Eppelsheimer, Clemens Köttelwesch, Bernhard Koßmann (eds): *Bibliographie der deutschen Sprach- und Literaturwissenschaft*, Frankfurt/Main, 1957ff.

François Fejtö: *A History of the People's Democracies*, Harmondsworth, 1974

Judith Fetterley: *The Resisting Reader: A Feminist Approach to American Fiction*, Bloomington, 1978

Wolfgang Fleischer et al.: *Wortschatz der deutschen Sprache in der DDR*, Leipzig, 1987

John L. Flood (ed.): *'Ein Moment des erfahrenen Lebens': Zur Lyrik der DDR*, Amsterdam, 1987

Konrad Franke: *Die Literatur der Deutschen Demokratischen Republik*, Munich, 1971

Günter Gaus: *Wo Deutschland liegt. Eine Ortsbestimmung*, Hamburg, 1983

Hans-Jürgen Geerdts (ed.): *Literatur der Deutschen Demokratischen Republik in Einzel-darstellungen*, Berlin (GDR), vol. 1, 1976; vol. 2, 1979

Hans-Joachim Gelberg (ed.): *Peter Härtling für Kinder*, Weinheim, 1989

Margy Gerber et al. (eds): *Studies in GDR Culture and Society* 5, Lanham, 1985

———— (ed.): *Studies in GDR Culture and Society* 10, Lanham, 1990

Sandra M. Gilbert and Susan Gubar: *The Madwoman in the Attic. The Woman Writer and the Nineteenth-Century Literary Imagination*, New Haven, 1984

Carol Gilligan: *In a Different Voice. Psychological Theory and Women's Development*, Cambridge/Mass., 1982

Franz Josef Görtz, Volker Hage and Uwe Wittstock (eds): *Deutsche Literatur 1989. Jahresüberblick*, Stuttgart, 1990

Karl-Heinz Götze and Klaus R. Scherpe (eds): *"Ästhetik des Widerstands" lesen*, Berlin, 1981

Hermann L. Gremliza: *Krautland einig Vaterland*, Hamburg, 1990

Reinhold Grimm and Jost Hermand (eds): *Natur und Natürlichkeit. Stationen des Grünen in der deutschen Literatur*, Königstein/Ts., 1981

Max von der Grün: *Wie war das eigentlich? Kindheit und Jugend im Dritten Reich*, Darmstadt, 1979

Frank Grützbach (ed.): *Freies Geleit für Ulrike Meinhof: Ein Artikel und seine Folgen*, Cologne, 1972.

Herbert Gruhl: *Ein Planet wird geplündert*, Frankfurt/Main, 1975

Jürgen Habermas: *Strukturwandel der Öffentlichkeit*, Darmstadt, 1962

———— (ed.): *Stichworte zur "Geistigen Situation der Zeit"*, Frankfurt/Main, 1979

————: *Die neue Unübersichtlichkeit*, Frankfurt/Main, 1985

————: *Die nachholende Revolution*, Frankfurt/Main, 1990

Jens Hacker and Horst Rögner-Francke (eds): *Die DDR und die Tradition*, Gesellschaft für Deutschlandforschung, Jahrbuch 1981, Heidelberg, 1981

Volker Hage and Adolf Fink (eds): *Deutsche Literatur 1981. Ein Jahresüberblick*, Stuttgart, 1982

Gerhard Hahn (ed.): *Die deutschen geistlichen Lieder*, Tübingen, 1967

Michael Hamburger: *From Prophecy to Exorcism*, London, 1965

Wolfgang Harich: *Kommunismus ohne Wachstum? Babeuf und der Club of Rome*, Reinbek, 1975

Jürgen Haupt: *Natur und Lyrik. Naturbeziehungen im 20. Jahrhundert*, Stuttgart, 1983

Robert Havemann: *Die Stimme des Gewissens. Texte eines deutschen Antistalinisten*, Reinbek, 1990

Ronald Hayman: *Günter Grass*, London, 1985

Hans-Jürgen Heise: *Einen Galgen für den Dichter. Stichworte zur Lyrik*, Weingarten, 1986

Gisela Helwig (ed.): *Die DDR-Gesellschaft im Spiegel ihrer Literatur*, Köln, 1986

Egmont Hesse (ed.): *Sprache & Antwort. Stimmen und Texte einer anderen Literatur aus der DDR*, Frankfurt/Main, 1988

Erhard Hexelschneider and Erhard John: *Kultur als einigendes Band? Eine Auseinander-*
setzung mit der These von der "einheitlichen deutschen Kulturnation", Berlin, 1984
Historikerstreit. Die Dokumentation der Kontroverse um die Einzigartigkeit der national-
sozialistischen Judenvernichtung, Munich, 1987
Arno Hochmuth (ed.): *Literatur im Blickpunkt. Zum Menschenbild in der Literatur der beiden*
deutschen Staaten, Berlin (GDR), 1965
Frank Hörnigk (ed.): *Heiner Müller. Material, Texte und Kommentare*, West Berlin, 1989
Therese Hörnigk: *Christa Wolf*, Göttingen, 1989
Hilmar Hoffmann (ed.): *Gegen den Versuch, Vergangenheit zu verbiegen*, Frankfurt/Main,
1987
Peter Uwe Hohendahl and Patricia Herminghouse (eds): *Literatur in der DDR in den sieb-*
ziger Jahren, Frankfurt/Main, 1983
Peter Uwe Hohendahl and Egon Schwarz (eds): *Exil und Innere Emigration. II. Internationale*
Tagung in St. Louis, Frankfurt/Main, 1973
Bernd Hüppauf (ed.): *'Die Mühen der Ebenen.' Kontinuität und Wandel in der deutschen*
Literatur und Gesellschaft 1945—1949, Heidelberg, 1981
Andreas Huyssen and Klaus R. Scherpe (eds): *Postmoderne. Zeichen eines kulturellen*
Wandels, Reinbek, 1986
Luce Irigaray: *Das Geschlecht, das nicht eins ist*, Berlin, 1979
————: *Speculum. Spiegel des anderen Geschlechts*, Frankfurt/Main, 1980
Manfred Jäger: *Sozialliteraten. Funktion und Selbstverständnis der Schriftsteller in der DDR*,
Düsseldorf, 1973
————: *Kultur und Politik in der DDR*, Cologne, 1982
Klaus Jarmatz (ed.): *Kritik in der Zeit: Der Sozialismus, seine Literatur, ihre Entwicklung*,
Halle/Saale, 1970
Klaus Jarmatz et al. (eds): *Weggenossen: Fünfzehn Schriftsteller der DDR*, Leipzig, 1975
V. Jehle (ed.): *Wolfgang Hildesheimer*, Frankfurt/Main, 1989
Lothar Jordan, Axel Marquardt, Winfried Woesler (eds): *Lyrik — von allen Seiten. Gedichte*
und Aufsätze des ersten Lyrikertreffens in Münster, Frankfurt/Main, 1981
————: *Lyrik — Erlebnis und Kritik. Gedichte und Aufsätze des dritten und vierten*
Lyrikertreffens in Münster, Frankfurt/Main, 1988
Georg Just: *Darstellung und Appell in der "Blechtrommel" von Günter Grass*, Frankfurt/Main,
1972
Hans Kaufmann (ed.): *Tendenzen und Beispiele. Zur DDR-Literatur in den siebziger Jahren*,
Leipzig, 1981
Peter Kemper (ed.): *'Postmoderne' oder Der Kampf um die Zukunft. Die Kontroverse in*
Wissenschaft, Kunst und Gesellschaft, Frankfurt/Main, 1988
Paul Gerhard Klussmann and Heinrich Mohr (eds): *Jahrbuch zur Literatur in der DDR*, no. 4,
Bonn, 1985
Claus Koch: *Die Intelligenzblätter der Deutschen*, Berlin, 1989
Hans Christian Kosler (ed.): *Gert Hofmann: Auskunft für Leser*, Darmstadt, 1987
Helmut Kreuzer (ed.): *Pluralismus und Postmodernismus. Beiträge zur Literatur- und Kultur-*
geschichte der 80er Jahre, Frankfurt/Main, 1989
Julia Kristeva: *Die Revolution der poetischen Sprache*, Frankfurt/Main, 1978
Reinhard Kühnl: *Nation — Nationalismus — Nationale Frage. Was ist das und was soll das?*,
Cologne, 1986
———— (ed.): *Vergangenheit, die nicht vergeht*, Cologne, 1987
Anna K. Kuhn: *Christa Wolf's Utopian Vision, from Marxism to Feminism*, Cambridge, 1988
Wolfgang Kuttenkeuler (ed.): *Poesie und Politik*, Stuttgart, 1973
Teresa de Lauretis: *Alice Doesn't. Feminism, Semiotics, Cinema*, Bloomington, 1984
———— (ed.): *Feminist Studies/Critical Studies*, Bloomington, 1986
Reinhard Lettau (ed.): *Die Gruppe 47: Bericht, Kritik, Polemik. Ein Handbuch*, Darmstadt,
1967
Heiner Liechtenstein (ed.): *Die Fassbinder-Kontroverse oder Das Ende der Schonzeit*,
Königstein/Ts, 1986
Ulrich Linse: *Ökopax und Anarchie. Eine Geschichte der ökologischen Bewegungen in*
Deutschland, Munich, 1986
Erich Loest: *Bruder Franz: Drei Vorlesungen über Franz Fühmann*, Paderborn, 1986

Gert Loschütz (ed.): *Von Buch zu Buch — Günter Grass in der Kritik*, Neuwied, 1968
Anita Mallinckrodt: *The Environmental Dialogue in the GDR. Literature, Church, Party and Interest Groups in Their Socio-Political Context. A Research Concept and Case Study*, Lanham, Maryland, 1987
Eberhard Mannack: *Zwei Deutsche Literaturen?*, Kronberg, 1977
Herbert Marcuse: *One-dimensional Man. Studies in the Ideology of Advanced Industrial Society*, New York, 1964
Edgar Marsch (ed.): *Moderne deutsche Naturlyrik*, Stuttgart, 1980.
Hans Mayer: *Deutsche Literatur seit Thomas Mann*, Reinbek, 1967
Dennis Meadows et al.: *The Limits to Growth. A Report for the Club of Rome's Project on the Predicament of Mankind*, New York, 1972
Norbert Mecklenburg (ed.): *Naturlyrik und Gesellschaft*, Stuttgart, 1977
Elizabeth Meese and Alice Parker (eds): *The Difference Within. Feminism and Critical Theory*, Amsterdam, 1989
Wolfgang Michalka (ed.): *Die Deutsche Frage*, Wiesbaden, 1986
Alexander Mitscherlich: *Gesammelte Schriften IV. Sozialpsychologie 2* ed. by Klaus Menne, Frankfurt/Main, 1983
Walter Moßmann and Peter Schleuning: *Alte und neue politische Lieder. Entstehung und Gebrauch, Texte und Noten*, Reinbek, 1978
Helmut L. Müller: *Die literarische Republik. Westdeutsche Schriftsteller und die Politik*, Weinheim, 1982
Lewis Mumford: *The Myth of the Machine*, New York, 1967
Uwe Naumann (ed.): *Sammlung 4. Jahrbuch für antifaschistische Literatur und Kunst*, Frankfurt/Main, 1981
Volker Neuhaus: *Günter Grass*, Stuttgart, 1979
Niedersächsiche Landeszentrale für politische Bildung: *Die deutsche Frage*, 2nd ed., Hanover, 1982
K. Stuart Parkes: *Writers amd Politics in West Germany*, Beckenham, 1986
Helmut Peitsch and Rhys W. Williams (eds.): *Berlin seit dem Kriegsende*, Manchester, 1989
Heinz Plavius: *Zwischen Protest und Anpassung. Westdeutsche Literatur, Theorie, Funktion*, Halle/Saale, 1970
Wolfgang Pohrt: *Endstation. Über die Wiedergeburt der Nation*, Berlin, 1982
Fritz J. Raddatz: *Traditionen und Tendenzen: Materialien zur Literatur der DDR*, Frankfurt/Main, 1972
Michael Radix (ed.): *Strauß lesen*, Munich, 1987
Redaktion Deutschland Archiv (ed.): *Umweltprobleme und Umweltbewußtsein in der DDR*, Köln, 1985
John Reddick: *The 'Danzig Trilogy' of Günter Grass*, Oxford, 1975
Hans H. Reich: *Sprache und Politik. Untersuchungen zu Wortschatz und Wortwahl des offiziellen Sprachgebrauchs in der DDR*, Munich, 1968
Konrad Reich (ed.): *Trajekt 5: Franz Fühmann zum 50. Geburtstag*, Rostock, 1972
Marcel Reich-Ranicki: *Deutsche Literatur in Ost und West*, Munich, 1963
————: *Literatur der kleinen Schritte: Deutsche Schriftsteller heute*, Frankfurt/Main, 1971
J. H. Reid: *Literature without Taboos. The New East German Literature*, Oxford, 1990
Ursula Reinhold: *Antihumanismus in der westdeutschen Literatur*, Berlin (GDR), 1971
————: *Literatur und Klassenkampf*, Berlin (GDR), 1976 (= *Herausforderung Literatur*, Munich, 1976)
Frank-Raymund Richter: *Die zerschlagene Wirklichkeit. Überlegungen zur Form der Danziger-Trilogie von Günter Grass*, Bonn, 1977
————: *Günter Grass. Die Vergangenheitsbewältigung in der Danziger—Trilogie*, Bonn, 1979
Hans Richter: *Werke und Wege: Kritiken, Aufsätze, Reden*, Halle/Saale, 1984
Siegfried Rönisch (ed.): *DDR-Literatur '83 [etc] im Gespräch*, Berlin (GDR), 1984 [etc]
Deborah Rosenfelt and Judith Newton (eds): *Feminist Criticism and Social Change*, London, 1985
Gerhard Rostin, Eberhard Haufe and Bernd Leistner (eds): *Johannes Bobrowski. Selbstzeugnisse und neue Beiträge über sein Werk*, Berlin (GDR), 1975

Ekkehart Rudolph (ed.): *Protokoll zur Person. Autoren über sich und ihr Werk*, Munich, 1971
————: *Aussage zur Person. Zwölf deutsche Schriftsteller im Gespräch mit Ekkehart Rudolph*, Tübingen, 1977
Johanna Rudolph: *Lebendiges Erbe. Reden und Aufsätze zur Kunst und Literatur*, Leipzig, 1972
Bernhard Rübenach (ed.): *Peter-Huchel-Preis. Ein Jahrbuch: 1987. Wulf Kirsten. Texte. Dokumente. Materialien*, Moos, 1987
Jürgen Rühle: *Literatur und Revolution. Die Schriftsteller und der Kommunismus in der Epoche Lenins und Stalins*, Frankfurt/Main, 1987
Peter Rühmkorf: *Strömungslehre: I Poesie*, Reinbek, 1978
Günther Rüther (ed.): *Kulturbetrieb und Literatur in der DDR*, Cologne, 2nd ed., 1988
Jeffrey L. Sammons: *Raabe. Pfisters Mühle*, London, 1988
Klaus Sauer (ed.): *Christa Wolf. Materialienbuch*, Darmstadt, 1979
Janet Sayers: *Sexual Contradictions. Psychology, Psychanalysis, and Feminism*, London, 1986
Helmut Schelsky: *Die skeptische Generation*, Düsseldorf, 1957
————: *Die Arbeit tun die anderen*, Munich, 1977
Irmela Schneider: *Kritische Rezeption. "Die Blechtrommel" als Modell*, Frankfurt/Main, 1975
Michael Schneider: *Die lange Wut zum langen Marsch. Aufsätze zur sozialistischen Politik und Literatur*, Reinbek, 1975
————: *Der Kopf verkehrt aufgesetzt oder Die melancholische Linke. Aspekte des Kulturzerfalls in den siebziger Jahren*, Darmstadt, 1981
Ralf Schnell: *Die Literatur der Bundesrepublik Deutschland. Autoren, Geschichte, Literaturbetrieb*, Stuttgart, 1986
Charles Schüddekopf (ed.): *Wir sind das Volk. Flugschriften, Aufrufe und Texte einer deutschen Revolution*, Reinbek, 1990
Hans Jürgen Schultz (ed.): *Der Friede und die Unruhestifter. Herausforderungen deutschsprachiger Schriftsteller im 20. Jahrhundert*, Frankfurt/Main, 1973
Genia Schulz: *Heiner Müller*, Stuttgart, 1980
E. F. Schumacher: *Small is Beautiful. A Study of Economics as if People Mattered*, New York, 1973
Hans Schwab-Felisch (ed.): *"Der Ruf". Eine deutsche Nachkriegszeitschrift*, Munich, 1962
Helfried W. Seliger (ed.): *Der Begriff 'Heimat' in der deutschen Gegenwartsliteratur*, Munich, 1987
Richard Sheppard (ed.): *New Ways in Germanistik*, Oxford, 1990
Rolf Peter Sieferle (ed.): *Fortschritte der Naturzerstörung*, Frankfurt/Main, 1988
Peter Sloterdijk: *Versprechen auf Deutsch. Rede über das eigene Land*, Frankfurt/Main, 1990
Kurt Sontheimer: *Das Elend unserer Intellektuellen*, Hamburg, 1976
Inge Stephan and Sigrid Weigel: *Die verborgene Frau*, Argument-Sonderband, AS 96, Berlin, 1983
Wolfgang Storch (ed.): *Explosion of a memory Heiner Müller DDR. Ein Arbeitsbuch*, West Berlin, 1988
Irene Charlotte Streul: *Westdeutsche Literatur in der DDR*, Stuttgart, 1988
Tony Tanner: *Adultery in the Novel. Contract and Transgression*, Baltimore, 1979
Noel Thomas: *The narrative works of Günter Grass. A critical interpretation*, Amsterdam, 1982
Ludwig Trepl: *Geschichte der Ökologie. Vom 17. Jahrhundert bis zur Gegenwart. 10 Vorlesungen*, Frankfurt/Main, 1987
Gudrun Uhlig (ed.): *Autor, Werk und Kritik. Inhaltsangaben, Kritiken und Textproben für den Literaturunterricht*, 3 vols, Munich, 1969—1972
Jan Vladistlav (ed.): *Václav Havel; or, Living in Truth*, London, 1986
Silvia Volckmann: *Zeit der Kirschen? Das Naturbild in der deutschen Gegenwartslyrik: Jürgen Becker, Sarah Kirsch, Wolf Biermann, Hans Magnus Enzensberger*, Königstein/Ts., 1982
Heinrich Vormweg: *Günter Grass*, Reinbek, 1986
Hermann Weber: *Geschichte der DDR*, Munich, 1985

Hilde Weise-Standfest (ed.): *Schriftsteller der Deutschen Demokratischen Republik und ihre Werke*, Leipzig, 1956

Klaus-Georg Wey: *Umweltpolitik in Deutschland. Kurze Geschichte des Umweltschutzes in Deutschland seit 1900*

Alois Wierlacher (ed.): *Das Fremde und das Eigene. Prolegomena zu einer interkulturellen Germanistik*, Munich, 1985

Benno von Wiese: *Zwischen Utopie und Wirklichkeit. Studien zur deutschen Literatur*, Düsseldorf, 1963

Arthur Williams, Stuart Parkes and Roland Smith (eds): *Literature on the Threshold. The German Novel in the 1980s*, Oxford, 1990

Ingrid K.J. Williams (ed.): *GDR: Individual and Society. Conference Proceedings of the International Conference on the GDR*, Ealing College of Higher Education, 1987

Dorothee Wilms: *Beiträge zur Deutschlandpolitik*, Bonn, no date (1988)

Wolfgang Wippermann (ed.): *Der konsequente Wahn. Ideologie und Politik Adolf Hitlers*, Munich, 1989

Uwe Wittstock: *Franz Fühmann*, Munich, 1988

—————: *Von der Stalinallee zum Prenzlauer Berg. Wege der DDR-Literatur 1949—1989*, Munich, 1989

Jürgen Wolf (ed.): *Materialien. Ulrich Plenzdorf: 'Die neuen Leiden des jungen W.'*, Stuttgart, 1980

Reinhold Zachau: *Stefan Heym*, Munich, 1982

Peter Paul Zahl: *Ergreifende oder ergriffene Literatur. Zur Rezeption "moderner Klassik"*, Frankfurt/Main, 1978

INDEX

The categories in this index are intended to be broad. Thus, for example, 'Unity' includes both 'unification' and 're-unification' as well as the equivalent German terms.

NOTES ON CONTRIBUTORS

Thomas Beckermann: Studied German, Sociology and Philosophy at the University of Hamburg. His thesis for his Dr. phil. (also at Hamburg) was written on Martin Walser. He taught for a short time at the University of Tokyo as a Visiting Lecturer. He is noted for his work with some of Germany's best publishing houses. He was Lektor with the Suhrkamp Verlag and then, for a long and successful period, editor of the *Collection S. Fischer* and of the *Neue Rundschau*. In addition to his many articles on Contemporary German Literature, he has published books on Max Frisch, Martin Walser and Hubert Fichte. He teaches at the J. W. Goethe-Universität, Frankfurt, and in 1990 became the Director of the Literaturhaus, Frankfurt.

Elizabeth Boa: Graduated at the University of Glasgow before completing her Ph.D. at the University of Nottingham, where she is now Senior Lecturer in German. Her extensive list of publications includes articles on Musil, Grass, Wieland, Rilke, Brecht, Lessing, Kroetz, Dürrenmatt, Büchner, Wedekind and Kafka. She specializes in Feminist Criticism, as in her articles 'Feminist Approaches to Kafka's *The Castle*' and 'Women Writing about Women Writing and Ingeborg Bachmann's *Malina*' in *New Ways in Germanistik* (ed. by Richard Sheppard, 1990). In 1987 she published *The Sexual Circus: Wedekind's Theatre of Subversion*.

Theo Buck: Professor for Neuere Deutsche Literaturgeschichte at the Rheinisch-Westfälische Technische Hochschule, Aachen. His impressive list of publications includes articles on German Literature from the eighteenth century to the present: Goethe, Büchner, Fontane, Raabe, the Literature of the Weimar Republic, Brecht, Celan, Johnson and Heiner Müller are just a few of his subjects. He has edited a number of important volumes in the series *Literaturhistorische Untersuchungen* and *Literaturwissenschaft — Gesellschaftswissenschaft* (co-editor). While some of his most recent work has been on Georg Büchner (Büchner Studien, 1990), earlier titles include: *Positionen im deutschen Roman der sechziger Jahre* (1974), *Interpretationen zu Bertolt Brecht: Parabel und episches Theater* (1979), *Tendenzen der deutschen Literatur zwischen 1918 und 1945* (1985) and *Grammatik einer neuen Liebe. Anmerkungen zu Georg Büchners Marion-Figur* (1986).

Hella Ehlers: Studied German and Slavonic Languages at the University of Rostock, where she became an *Assistent* while writing a thesis for her Dr. phil. on the 'Werkkreis Literatur der Arbeitswelt'. This was followed by several years in the GDR Kulturzentrum in Stockholm, after which she returned to Rostock to take up a post as *Oberassistent* in the Institut für Germanistik with special responsibilities for German Literature in the Twentieth Century. Her particular field is West German Literature, above all the reflection of and on fascism in the work of younger writers.

Axel Goodbody: Studied German and French at Trinity College, Dublin, before teaching English and German at the University of Kiel, where he gained both his M.A. and his Dr. phil. He is now Lecturer in German at the University of Bath with specialisms in Twentieth Century German Literature and History. He has published widely in his main research fields of Contemporary German Poetry, Comparative Aspects of East and West German Literature, and Environmental Literature. His major publication in these fields came in 1984: *Natursprache. Ein dichtungstheoretisches Konzept der Romantik und seine Wiederaufnahme in der modernen Naturlyrik (Novalis — Eichendorff — Lehmann — Eich)*.

Peter Graves: A graduate of King's College, University of London, and of Brown University, USA, he is now Lecturer in German at the University of Leicester. His special field is Contemporary German Literature with particular reference to GDR Literature. He has written on a wide variety of authors from the Romantics to younger GDR writers. He has published several articles on Christa Wolf and his conversations with Reiner Kunze and Sarah Kirsch. He is a frequent contributor to the *Times Literary Supplement* on contemporary German literature and politics. In 1985 he published *Three Contemporary German Poets: Wolf Biermann, Sarah Kirsch, Reiner Kunze.*

Ian Hilton: Studied at the Unversity of Southampton, where he also gained his Ph.D. He is now Senior Lecturer in German at the University of Wales, (Coleg Prifysgol Gogledd Cymru — University College of North Wales, Bangor). He has taught in Canada, at the universities of Calgary and British Columbia, Vancouver. He is a former editor of *Modern Languages* and has an impressive list of publications, mainly on poets and poetry but also including aspects of translation, musical settings, and German-Welsh literary connections. His books include: *Peter Weiss. A Search for Affinities* (1970), *Peter Huchel. Plough a Lonely Furrow* (1986) and *Peter Weiss: Marat/Sade* (1990).

Ian Huish: Teaches German part-time at Westminster School and also works as a psychotherapist in Oxford. He has an impressive list of publications since the mid-1970s. He has specialized in particular on the work of Ödön von Horváth, publishing many of his works with notes and introductions. His *Horváth: A Study* (1980) is best known in the paperback version: *A Student's Guide to Horváth.* His translation of Horváth's *Figaro läßt sich scheiden* (*Figaro gets Divorced*) was premiered at the Gate Theatre in March 1990 and is about to be published (March 1991) by the Absolute Press, Bath. He has also written on Thomas Mann, Jura Soyfer and Carl Zuckmayer.

Martin Kane: Studied at the University of Leeds and then went on to complete his Ph.D. at the University of Birmingham. He is now Senior Lecturer in German and European Studies at the University of Kent at Canterbury. In 1987 he published *Weimar Germany and the Limits of Political Art. A Study of the Work of George Grosz and Ernst Toller.* His long list of articles and contributions to books is doubly impressive when his range of subjects is noted. He has written on Thomas Mann and Visconti, Hubert Fichte, Walter Kempowski, Brecht, Lukács, Christa Wolf, Wallraff, the West German lyric, Piscator, comparative aspects of East and West German literature, Dieter Eue, Paul Celan, Peter Weiss, and many more.

Katrin Kohl: Studied at at the University of London, where she also gained both her M.A. and her Ph.D. She is now Tutorial Fellow in German at Jesus College, Oxford. She is an editor of the journal of the *Association for Modern German Studies* and is noted for her highly successful work with the BBC. Her special fields extend from Klopstock to Contemporary German Poetry and aspects of Phonetics.

Karen J Leeder: Studied at Oxford University and is now Fellow and Lecturer in German at Emmanuel College, Cambridge. She is currently completing a doctoral thesis on the work of the youngest generation of poets in the GDR, including their transition into a united Germany. She is also preparing a bilingual anthology of recent poetry by young German writers.

Stuart Parkes: Graduated at Oxford University before completing his Ph.D. at Bradford University. He is now Senior Lecturer in German at Sheffield City Polytechnic. He has published a number of articles on Contemporary German Literature and Society, particularly on GDR Literature and the interrelationship between literature and politics. Among his subjects have been: Erik Neutsch, Christa Wolf, Ödön von Horváth and particularly Martin Walser. His book on *Writers and Politics in West Germany* was published in 1986. He is co-editor (with Arthur Williams and Roland Smith) of *Literature on the Threshold. The German Novel in the 1980s* (1990).

Helmut Peitsch: Studied in Berlin, where he also gained his Dr. phil. (habil.). He is now Lecturer in German at the University of Wales (University College of Swansea). It is virtually impossible to summarize adequately the range of his publications, thus in 1982 and 1984 he was co-author (with J. Hermand and K. R. Scherpe) of two volumes on *Nachkriegsliteratur in Westdeutschland 1945—49* and in 1989 he published *'Deutschlands Gedächtnis an seine dunkelste Zeit'. Zur Funktion der Autobiographik in den Westzonen Deutschlands und den Westsektoren von Berlin 1945 bis 1949*, but his articles examine Lessing, the student movement, Brecht, Plivier, Weyrauch, Prussian aspects of German fascism, tradition and cultural heritage, Peter Weiss, the *Gruppe 47*, Therese Huber, *Musikpolitik*, Klaus Stiller, Karin Reschke, Monica Streit, Hans Henny Jahnn, GDR Literature, and many aspects of the presentation of fascism in German literature.

Joseph Pischel: Professor in the Institut für Germanistik of the Universität Rostock, where he became responsible for German Literature in the Twentieth Century in 1979. He has publications of note on Christa Wolf, aspects of criticism, *Exilliteratur* and Lion Feuchtwanger. Feuchtwanger was the subject of his first thesis, the second addressed the *Ästhetisch-poetologische Selbstverständigung der DDR-Schriftsteller in den siebziger und achtziger Jahren.*

Julian Preece: A graduate of the University of Oxford, where he is now a Junior Fellow at The Queen's College. He is currently completing his Ph.D. thesis on the treatment of history in the novels of Günter Grass.

Andrea Reiter: Studied at the University of Salzburg, where she also completed her Dr. phil. She has carried out research and taught at the University of Southampton and at St. Patrick's College in Ireland. She has published a book on the computer analysis of a contemporary right-wing Austrian journal and articles on Franz Kafka, the musical quality of Thomas Bernhard's prose style, on the use of computing in literary analysis and on the prose and poetry of a group of right-wing writers in Austria. She is currently completing a monograph on concentration-camp memoirs.

Axel Schalk: Studied German and History together with Philosophy, Education and Theatre in Hamburg and Berlin before completing his doctorate at the Technische Universität, Berlin, on *'Geschichtsmaschinen'. Über den Umgang mit der Historie in der Dramatik des technischen Zeitalters*, which was published by Carl Winter Verlag, Heidelberg, in 1989. He has worked at the Deutsches Schauspielhaus in Hamburg and is a fully qualified teacher. Currently a freelance writer specializing in contemporary literature, particularly theatre.

Ricarda Schmidt: Studied at the universities of Hanover and Hull, and gained her Dr. phil. at the University of Hanover. She has taught English and German at universities in Germany, Britain and France. She is now Lecturer in German at the University of Sheffield. She has published widely on Critical Theory and on German and Anglo-American women's writing, including a book on *Westdeutsche Frauenliteratur in den 70er Jahren* (1982; 2nd edn 1990) and articles on Christa Wolf, Jutta Heinrich, Angela Carter, Mrs Humphry Ward, Jean Rhys, on fantasies of women and nature, and on myth in contemporary writing, as well as on the alleged existence of *écriture féminine* in E.T.A. Hoffmann.

Gisela Shaw: Studied English and Philosophy at the universities of Mainz and Bonn. She gained her Dr. phil. at Bonn with a thesis on the reception of Kantian philosophy in Great Britain (published 1969). She has a B.A. from the Northwestern University of Missouri, where she was a Fulbright Student of American literature and history, and an M.Phil. from Bath University for a thesis on GDR Literature. She is now Senior Lecturer in German at Bristol Polytechnic. She has published widely on philosophy and contemporary German literature, especially of the GDR) and is currently working on two projects soon to be published: on the legal professions in Germany and, as a contributor, on aspects of German for Business.

Roland Smith: Studied at the University of London, carried out research for both his M.A. and his Ph.D. at the University of Bradford where he is now Lecturer in German. His special field is GDR Studies and he has published particularly on the role of the Church in the GDR. He is co-editor (with Arthur Williams and Stuart Parkes) of *Literature on the Threshold. The German Novel in the 1980s* (1990).

Dieter Stolz: Studied at the University of Münster and both the Freie Universität and the Technische Universität in Berlin. He is currently working towards his Dr. phil. at the TU on the strictly literary dimension of Günter Grass's *oeuvre*. He has published on Grass's early writing and aspects of the absurd. He is a freelance writer, mainly for the cultural columns of a variety of newspapers.

Dennis Tate: Studied at the universities of Dublin, McMaster and Warwick, gaining his Ph.D. at the latter. He is Senior Lecturer in German Studies at the University of Bath and has specialisms in Twentieth Century German Literature and Society, with particular reference to GDR Literature. He has published widely in these fields, most notably: *The East German Novel: Identity, Community, Continuity* (1984), *European Socialist Realism* (co-editor, 1988), and *Günter de Bruyn: Märkische Forschungen* (1990).

Anthony Williams: Studied at both undergraduate and postgraduate level at the University of Newcastle upon Tyne. He is now Lecturer in German at The Queen's University of Belfast. His field extends over German Literature, Society and History from the Eighteenth Century to the Present. He has published on such varied figures as Friedrich Schiller, Heinrich Heine and Johannes Bobrowski.

Arthur Williams: Studied at the University of Keele both as an undergraduate and postgraduate. He is now Senior Lecturer in German Studies at the University of Bradford. His particular fields are the Contemporary Society of Germany and Contemporary German Literature (West German). He has published on Thomas Mann, GDR education, West German social policy and the media in West Germany, particularly the governance of broadcasting (*Broadcasting and Democracy in West Germany*, 1976). Since 1985 he has returned to literature and has developed interests in the novel and the work of Botho Strauß. He is co-editor (with Stuart Parkes and Roland Smith) of *Literature on the Theshold. The German Novel in the 1980s* (1990).

Jochen Wittmann: A graduate of the University of Münster who is writing his Dr. phil. thesis on Günter Grass, with particular reference to *Die Blechtrommel*. He has recently taken up a post as a journalist with *PRINZ*, one of Berlin's major illustrateds. Apart from the literature columns, for which he is responsible, he particularly enjoys his work for his two other briefs, 'Theater' and 'Essen und Trinken'.

Sarah Brickwood: Studied at the University of Cambridge before completing her M.A. in Interpreting and Translating at the University of Bradford. She is currently working as a translator and interpreter in Paris. She is carrying out preliminary studies for a research project into aspects of GDR Literature.